Investment in Human Capital

Investment in Human Capital
Edited by B. F. KIKER

University of South Carolina Pres
Columbia, South Carolina

LIBRARY OF CONGRESS CATALOG CARD DATA:

Kiker, B   F   comp.
Investment in human capital, edited by B. F. Kiker.
[1st ed.] Columbia, University of South Carolina Press
[1971]

xii, 608 p. illus. 24 cm.
Includes bibliographical references.
1. Human capital—Addresses, essays, lectures. I. Title.

HB501.5.K54   331   70–120581
ISBN 0–87249–189–7   MARC

TO JANE AND TODD

Contents

Contents

Contents

Preface

In recent years economists have devoted a great deal of effort toward developing and quantifying the concept of "human capital" and toward applying it, through the concept of investment in the formation of human capital, to such activities as education and training, human migration, and medical care. These economists assert that expenditures on man which lead to increases in future productivity are investment in capital and that it is useful to treat them in both theory and practice as capital formation. The quantity of the literature on the concept of human capital has been large and is growing. All the major economic journals are devoting space to articles on the concept. Many of them, for example, *The Journal of Political Economy* (Supplement, October, 1962), have published supplements on the "notion," and at least one new journal, *The Journal of Human Resources,* devoted exclusively to human resources, has been instituted. Certainly, many of the authors who have contributed these articles are among the most distinguished economists in the world.

Contributions to the theory of human capital have appeared almost exclusively in journals (a notable exception, however, is Gary S. Becker's landmark, *Human Capital*); hence, in many cases, they are not easily accessible to students or professors who find it convenient to have research materials at hand. The objective of this book is to provide a partial remedy for this situation.

This volume is a summary of a substantial segment of current research on the human capital concept. Part I deals with the nature and measurement of the concept of human capital. It consists of three sections: The Concept of Human Capital, Theory of Human Investment, and Human Capital: In Retrospect. Contributors to Part I are T. W. Schultz, H. G. Schaffer, Gary S. Becker, and B. F. Kiker. Part II presents arguments for the importance of human capital as a factor in national economic growth and is divided into two sections — The Growth Residual and the Human Factor, and Revamping the Social Accounts. Articles included in this section are by Odd Aukrust, Robert Solow, and John W. Kendrick. Part III deals with the application of the theory of human capital investment to education. Far more intensive work has been done on education as an investment than on any of the other components of human capital. The four sections in Part

III are Education and Earnings, Benefit-Cost Analysis, Education in Production, and Human Capital and Occupational Choice. The authors are Yoram Ben-Porath, Herman P. Miller, H. S. Houthakker, Giora Hanoch, Jacob Mincer, Burton A. Weisbrod, W. Lee Hansen, Bruce W. Wilkinson, Finis Welch, Maurice Benewitz, Albert Zucker, Corindo Cipriani, and Arnie R. Melnik. Part IV deals with health care as an investment and includes contributions by Selma J. Mushkin, Francis d'A. Collings, Herbert E. Klarman, and Jack Wiseman. Part V describes the types of research being conducted on human migration and the theory of human capital. The articles were written by Larry A. Sjaastad, Herbert Grubel, Anthony Scott, Mary Jean Bowman, Robert G. Myers, and Hans-Joachim Bodenhöfer. Part VI treats the problem of regional income differences within the human capital theoretical framework and considers the tax treatment of human capital. Contributors are Finis Welch, Richard Goode, and A. G. Holtmann.

While I would have liked to include all of the significant contributions to the human capital literature since the "re-birth" of the concept in the late 1950's, a budgetary constraint and the necessity of keeping the book within a manageable length required that choices be somewhat personal. Hence, article length and reprint fees were factors that ultimately influenced my decision to eliminate several articles. In a few cases, I was unable to secure permission to reprint articles which I had hoped to include, primarily because they are part of books that are still in print.

I am, of course, indebted to the authors and publishers for their permission to reprint the articles appearing herein. For helpful suggestions on the contents of the volume, I wish to thank T. W. Schultz, Marshall R. Colberg, A. G. Holtmann, Adger B. Carroll, William L. Miller, and Simon Rottenberg. However, the usual disclaimers hold.

B. F. KIKER
University of South Carolina

PART I Nature and Measurement

Introduction

The "re-birth" of the concept of human capital can be precisely dated from T. W. Schultz's presidential address at the 1960 meeting of the American Economic Association. In this pioneering address, which is the lead article in this volume, Schultz suggests why economists have been reluctant to undertake a systematic analysis of human capital. He then sketches some paradoxes and puzzles about the United States economy which might be resolved once human capital is considered. His major effort, however, is directed toward the scope and substance of human capital. Professor Schultz's address resulted in what M. Blaug has called "a sudden acceleration of research . . . and . . . proliferation of publications"[1] in the area of human capital.

One difficulty in treating expenditures for the "improvement of man" as capital is that the capital investment features of these expenditures cannot be fully separated from their "consumption" features. Several critics of the human capital concept have said that the inseparability of consumption and investment makes the entire analysis of human capital dubious. H. G. Shaffer, in a comment (Reading 2) on Schultz's address, suggests reasons to support this view: Expenditures for "improvement of man" may be undertaken for reason other than the expectations of a financial gain; they have no traceable effects on future output; and even if such expenditures were undertaken with a view to profit and had a traceable effect on output, the expenditure decision may not be rational in the sense that the human capital project is compared with alternative investment projects before undertaking.

Although the available data are inadequate to refute Shaffer's views, Professor Schultz in reply (Reading 3) correctly points out that, although the consumption-investment dichotomy presents serious conceptual and computational difficulties, the economic logic for treating human investments within the capital theoretical framework is clear.

Schultz's reply is followed by the introduction of a lecture given recently by Gary S. Becker at the University of Michigan (Reading

---

[1] M. Blaug (ed.), *Economics of Education*, 1 (Baltimore: Penguin Books, Inc., 1968), p. 11.

4). This excerpt sets out the basic theoretical framework within which investments in human capital embodied in a "typical" person and in society can be analyzed. In essence, Becker applies, with some modifications, conventional capital (or investment) theory to investment in human beings.

Although Schultz's work was the impetus for current research and publications in the area of human capital, the concept of human capital by no means began with Schultz. I have chosen to conclude Part I of the volume with my own essay (Reading 5) in which I attempt to show that the concept of human capital was somewhat prominent in economic thinking from the time of Sir William Petty until Alfred Marshall disregarded the notion as "unrealistic."

A. The Concept of Human Capital

1. Investment in Human Capital*
THEODORE W. SCHULTZ
University of Chicago

Although it is obvious that people acquire useful skills and knowledge, it is not obvious that these skills and knowledge are a form of capital, that this capital is in substantial part a product of deliberate investment, that it has grown in Western societies at a much faster rate than conventional (nonhuman) capital, and that its growth may well be the most distinctive feature of the economic system. It has been widely observed that increases in national output have been large compared with the increases of land, man-hours, and physical reproducible capital. Investment in human capital is probably the major explanation for this difference.

Much of what we call consumption constitutes investment in human capital. Direct expenditures on education, health, and internal migration to take advantage of better job opportunities are clear examples. Earnings foregone by mature students attending school and by workers acquiring on-the-job training are equally clear examples. Yet nowhere do these enter into our national accounts. The use of leisure time to improve skills and knowledge is widespread and it too is unrecorded. In these and similar ways the *quality* of human effort can be greatly improved and its productivity enhanced. I shall contend that such investment in human capital accounts for most of the impressive rise in the real earnings per worker.

I shall comment, first, on the reasons why economists have shied away from the explicit analysis of investment in human capital, and then, on the capacity of such investment to explain many a puzzle about economic growth. Mainly, however, I shall concentrate on the scope and substance of human capital and its formation. In closing I shall consider some social and policy implications.

*Reprinted from "Investment in Human Capital," *American Economic Review* 51 (March, 1961): 1–17.

Economists have long known that people are an important part of the wealth of nations. Measured by what labor contributes to output, the productive capacity of human beings is now vastly larger than all other forms of wealth taken together. What economists have not stressed is the simple truth that people invest in themselves and that these investments are very large. Although economists are seldom timid in entering on abstract analysis and are often proud of being impractical, they have not been bold in coming to grips with this form of investment. Whenever they come even close, they proceed gingerly as if they were stepping into deep water. No doubt there are reasons for being wary. Deep-seated moral and philosophical issues are ever present. Free men are first and foremost the end to be served by economic endeavor; they are not property or marketable assets. And not least, it has been all too convenient in marginal productivity analysis to treat labor as if it were a unique bundle of innate abilities that are wholly free of capital.

The mere thought of investment in human beings is offensive to some among us.[1] Our values and beliefs inhibit us from looking upon human beings as capital goods, except in slavery, and this we abhor. We are not unaffected by the long struggle to rid society of indentured service and to evolve political and legal institutions to keep men free from bondage. These are achievements that we prize highly. Hence, to treat human beings as wealth that can be augmented by investment runs counter to deeply held values. It seems to reduce man once again to a mere material component, to something akin to property. And for man to look upon himself as a capital good, even if it did not impair his freedom, may seem to debase him. No less a person than J. S. Mill at one time insisted that the people of a country should not be looked upon as wealth because wealth existed only for the sake of people [15]. But surely Mill was wrong; there is nothing in the concept of human wealth contrary to his idea that it exists only for the advantage of people. By investing in themselves, people can enlarge the range of choice available to them. It is one way free men can enhance their welfare.

Among the few who have looked upon human beings as capital, there are three distinguished names. The philosopher-economist

---

[1] This paragraph draws on the introduction to my Teller Lecture [16].

Adam Smith boldly included all of the acquired and useful abilities of all of the inhabitants of a country as a part of capital. So did H. von Thünen, who then went on to argue that the concept of capital applied to man did not degrade him or impair his freedom and dignity, but on the contrary that the failure to apply the concept was especially pernicious in wars; ". . . for here . . . one will sacrifice in a battle a hundred human beings in the prime of their lives without a thought in order to save one gun." The reason is that ". . . the purchase of a cannon causes an outlay of public funds, whereas human beings are to be had for nothing by means of a mere conscription decree" [20]. Irving Fisher also clearly and cogently presented an all-inclusive concept of capital [6]. Yet the main stream of thought has held that it is neither appropriate nor practical to apply the concept of capital to human beings. Marshall [11], whose great prestige goes far to explain why this view was accepted, held that while human beings are incontestably capital from an abstract and mathematical point of view, it would be out of touch with the market place to treat them as capital in practical analyses. Investment in human beings has accordingly seldom been incorporated in the formal core of economics, even though many economists, including Marshall, have seen its relevance at one point or another in what they have written.

The failure to treat human resources explicitly as a form of capital, as a produced means of production, as the product of investment, has fostered the retention of the classical notion of labor as a capacity to do manual work requiring little knowledge and skill, a capacity with which, according to this notion, laborers are endowed about equally. This notion of labor was wrong in the classical period and it is patently wrong now. Counting individuals who can and want to work and treating such a count as a measure of the quantity of an economic factor is no more meaningful than it would be to count the number of all manner of machines to determine their economic importance either as a stock of capital or as a flow of productive services.

Laborers have become capitalists not from a diffusion of the ownership of corporation stocks, as folklore would have it, but from the acquisition of knowledge and skill that have economic value [9]. This knowledge and skill are in great part the product of investment and, combined with other human investment, predominantly account for the productive superiority of the technically advanced countries. To omit them in studying economic growth is like trying to explain Soviet ideology without Marx.

Nature and Measurement

Many paradoxes and puzzles about our dynamic, growing economy can be resolved once human investment is taken into account. Let me begin by sketching some that are minor though not trivial.

When farm people take nonfarm jobs they earn substantially less than industrial workers of the same race, age, and sex. Similarly nonwhite urban males earn much less than white males even after allowance is made for the effects of differences in unemployment, age, city size and region [21]. Because these differentials in earnings correspond closely to corresponding differentials in education, they strongly suggest that the one is a consequence of the other. Negroes who operate farms, whether as tenants or as owners, earn much less than whites on comparable farms.[2] Fortunately, crops and livestock are not vulnerable to the blight of discrimination. The large differences in earnings seem rather to reflect mainly the differences in health and education. Workers in the South on the average earn appreciably less than in the North or West and they also have on the average less education. Most migratory farm workers earn very little indeed by comparison with other workers. Many of them have virtually no schooling, are in poor health, are unskilled, and have little ability to do useful work. To urge that the differences in the amount of human investment may explain these differences in earnings seems elementary. Of more recent vintage are observations showing younger workers at a competitive advantage; for example, young men entering the labor force are said to have an advantage over unemployed older workers in obtaining satisfactory jobs. Most of these young people possess twelve years of school, most of the older workers six years or less. The observed advantage of these younger workers may therefore result not from inflexibilities in social security or in retirement programs, or from sociological preference of employers, but from real differences in productivity connected with one form of human investment, i.e., education. And yet another example, the curve relating income to age tends to be steeper for skilled than for unskilled persons. Investment in on-the-job training seems a likely explanation, as I shall note later.

Economic growth requires much internal migration of workers to adjust to changing job opportunities [10]. Young men and women

[2]Based on unpublished preliminary results obtained by Joseph Willett in his Ph.D. research at the University of Chicago.

6

move more readily than older workers. Surely this makes economic sense when one recognizes that the costs of such migration are a form of human investment. Young people have more years ahead of them than older workers during which they can realize on such an investment. Hence it takes less of a wage differential to make it economically advantageous for them to move, or, to put it differently, young people can expect a higher return on their investment in migration than older people. This differential may explain selective migration without requiring an appeal to sociological differences between young and old people.

The examples so far given are for investment in human beings that yield a return over a long period. This is true equally of investment in education, training, and migration of young people. Not all investments in human beings are of this kind; some are more nearly akin to current inputs as for example expenditures on food and shelter in some countries where work is mainly the application of brute human force, calling for energy and stamina, and where the intake of food is far from enough to do a full day's work. On the "hungry" steppes and in the teeming valleys of Asia, millions of adult males have so meager a diet that they cannot do more than a few hours of hard work. To call them underemployed does not seem pertinent. Under such circumstances it is certainly meaningful to treat food partly as consumption and partly as a current "producer good," as some Indian economists have done. Let us not forget that Western economists during the early decades of industrialization and even in the time of Marshall and Pigou often connected additional food for workers with increases in labor productivity.

Let me now pass on to three major perplexing questions closely connected with the riddle of economic growth. First, consider the long-period behavior of the capital-income ratio. We were taught that a country which amassed more reproducible capital relative to its land and labor would employ such capital in greater "depth" because of its growing abundance and cheapness. But apparently this is not what happens. On the contrary, the estimates now available show that less of such capital tends to be employed relative to income as economic growth proceeds. Are we to infer that the ratio of capital to income has no relevance in explaining either poverty or opulence? Or that a rise of this ratio is not a prerequisite to economic growth? These questions raise fundamental issues bearing on motives and preferences for holding wealth as well as on the motives for particular investments and the stock of capital thereby accumulated. For my purpose all that needs to be said is that these estimates of capital-income ratios refer to only a part of all capital. They exclude in particular, and most unfortunately, any human capital. Yet human capital has surely been increasing at a rate substantially greater than reproducible (nonhuman) capital. We cannot, therefore, infer from these estimates that the stock of *all* capital has been decreasing relative to income. On the contrary, if we accept the not implausible assumption that the motives and preferences of people, the technical opportunities open to them, and the uncertainty associated with economic growth during particular periods were leading people to maintain roughly a constant ratio between *all* capital and income, the decline in the estimated capital-income ratio[3] is simply a signal that human capital has been increasing relatively not only to conventional capital but also to income.

The bumper crop of estimates that show national income increasing faster than national resources raises a second and not unrelated puzzle. The income of the United States has been increasing at a much higher rate than the combined amount of land, man-hours worked and the stock of reproducible capital used to produce the income. Moreover, the discrepancy between the two rates has become larger from one business cycle to the next during recent decades [5]. To call this discrepancy a measure of "resource productivity" gives a name to our ignorance but does not dispel it. If we accept these estimates, the connections between national resources and national income have become loose and tenuous over time. Unless this discrepancy can be resolved, received theory of production applied to inputs and outputs as currently measured is a toy and not a tool for studying economic growth.

Two sets of forces probably account for the discrepancy, if we neglect entirely the index number and aggregation problems that bedevil all estimates of such global aggregates as total output and total input. One is returns to scale; the second, the large improvements in the quality of inputs that have occured but have been omitted from the input estimates. Our economy has undoubtedly been ex-

---

[3] I leave aside here the difficulties inherent in identifying and measuring both the nonhuman capital and the income entering into estimates of this ratio. There are index number and aggregation problems aplenty, and not all improvements in the quality of this capital have been accounted for, as I shall note later.

periencing increasing returns to scale at some points offset by decreasing returns at others. If we can succeed in identifying and measuring the net gains, they may turn out to have been substantial. The improvements in the quality of inputs that have not been adequately allowed for are no doubt partly in material (nonhuman) capital. My own conception, however, is that both this defect and the omission of economies of scale are minor sources of discrepancy between the rates of growth of inputs and outputs compared to the improvements in human capacity that have been omitted.

A small step takes us from these two puzzles raised by existing estimates to a third which brings us to the heart of the matter, namely the essentially unexplained large increase in real earnings of workers. Can this be a windfall? Or a quasi rent pending the adjustment in the supply of labor? Or, a pure rent reflecting the fixed amount of labor? It seems far more reasonable that it represents rather a return to the investment that has been made in human beings. The observed growth in productivity per unit of labor is simply a consequence of holding the unit of labor constant over time although in fact this unit of labor has been increasing as a result of a steadily growing amount of human capital per worker. As I read our record, the human capital component has become very large as a consequence of human investment.

Another aspect of the same basic question, which admits of the same resolution, is the rapid postwar recovery of countries that had suffered severe destruction of plant and equipment during the war. The toll from bombing was all too visible in the factories laid flat, the railroad yards, bridges, and harbors wrecked, and the cities in ruin. Structures, equipment and inventories were all heaps of rubble. Not so visible, yet large, was the toll from the wartime depletion of the physical plant that escaped destruction by bombs. Economists were called upon to assess the implications of these wartime losses for recovery. In retrospect, it is clear that they overestimated the prospective retarding effects of these losses. Having had a small hand in this effort, I have had a special reason for looking back and wondering why the judgments that we formed soon after the war proved to be so far from the mark. The explanation that now is clear is that we gave altogether too much weight to nonhuman capital in making these assessments. We fell into this error, I am convinced, because we did not have a concept of *all* capital and, therefore, failed to take account of human capital and the important part that it plays in production in a modern economy.

Nature and Measurement

Let me close this section with a comment on poor countries, for which there are virtually no solid estimates. I have been impressed by repeatedly expressed judgments, especially by those who have a responsibility in making capital available to poor countries, about the low rate at which these countries can absorb additional capital. New capital from outside can be put to good use, it is said, only when it is added "slowly and gradually." But this experience is at variance with the widely held impression that countries are poor fundamentally because they are starved for capital and that additional capital is truly the key to their more rapid economic growth. The reconciliation is again, I believe, to be found in emphasis on particular forms of capital. The new capital available to these countries from outside as a rule goes into the formation of structures, equipment and sometimes also into inventories. But it is generally not available for additional investment in man. Consequently, human capabilities do not stay abreast of physical capital, and they do become limiting factors in economic growth. It should come as no surprise, therefore, that the absorption rate of capital to augment only particular nonhuman resources is necessarily low. The Horvat [8] formulation of the optimum rate of investment which treats knowledge and skill as a critical investment variable in determining the rate of economic growth is both relevant and important.

III. SCOPE AND SUBSTANCE OF THESE INVESTMENTS

What are human investments? Can they be distinguished from consumption? Is it at all feasible to identify and measure them? What do they contribute to income? Granted that they seem amorphous compared to brick and mortar, and hard to get at compared to the investment accounts of corporations, they assuredly are not a fragment; they are rather like the contents of Pandora's box, full of difficulties and hope.

Human resources obviously have both quantitative and qualitative dimensions. The number of people, the proportion who enter upon useful work, and hours worked are essentially quantitative characteristics. To make my task tolerably manageable, I shall neglect these and consider only such quality components as skill, knowledge, and similar attributes that affect particular human capabilities to do productive work. In so far as expenditures to enhance such capabilities also increase the value productivity of human effort (labor), they will yield a positive rate of return.[4]

How can we estimate the magnitude of human investment? The practice followed in connection with physical capital goods is to estimate the magnitude of capital formation by expenditures made to produce the capital goods. This practice would suffice also for the formation of human capital. However, for human capital there is an additional problem that is less pressing for physical capital goods: how to distinguish between expenditures for consumption and for investment. This distinction bristles with both conceptual and practical difficulties. We can think of three classes of expenditures: expenditures that satisfy consumer preferences and in no way enhance the capabilities under discussion—these represent pure consumption; expenditures that enhance capabilities and do not satisfy any preferences underlying consumption—these represent pure investment; and expenditures that have both effects. Most relevant activities clearly are in the third class, partly consumption and partly investment, which is why the task of identifying each component is so formidable and why the measurement of capital formation by expenditures is less useful for human investment than for investment in physical goods. In principle there is an alternative method for estimating human investment, namely by its yield rather than by its cost. While any capability produced by human investment becomes a part of the human agent and hence cannot be sold; it is nevertheless "in touch with the market place" by affecting the wages and salaries the human agent can earn. The resulting increase in earnings is the yield on the investment.[5]

Despite the difficulty of exact measurement at this stage of our understanding of human investment, many insights can be gained by examining some of the more important activities that improve human capabilities. I shall concentrate on five major categories: (1) health facilities and services, broadly conceived to include all expenditures that affect the life expectancy, strength and stamina, and the vigor

---

[4]Even so, our *observed* return can be either negative, zero or positive because our observations are drawn from a world where there is uncertainty and imperfect knowledge and where there are windfall gains and losses and mistakes aplenty.

[5]In principle, the value of the investment can be determined by discounting the additional future earnings it yields just as the value of a physical capital good can be determined by discounting its income stream.

and vitality of a people; (2) on-the-job training, including old-style apprenticeship organized by firms; (3) formally organized education at the elementary, secondary, and higher levels; (4) study programs for adults that are not organized by firms, including extension programs notably in agriculture; (5) migration of individuals and families to adjust to changing job opportunities. Except for education, not much is known about these activities that is germane here. I shall refrain from commenting on study programs for adults, although in agriculture the extension services of the several states play an important role in transmitting new knowledge and in developing skills of farmers [17]. Nor shall I elaborate further on internal migration related to economic growth.

Health activities have both quantity and quality implications. Such speculations as economists have engaged in about the effects of improvements in health[6] have been predominantly in connection with population growth, which is to say with quantity. But surely health measures also enhance the quality of human resources. So also may additional food and better shelter, especially in underdeveloped countries.

The change in the role of food as people become richer sheds light on one of the conceptual problems already referred to. I have pointed out that extra food in some poor countries has the attribute of a "producer good." This attribute of food, however, diminishes as the consumption of food rises, and there comes a point at which any further increase in food becomes pure consumption.[7] Clothing, housing and perhaps medical services may be similar.

My comment about on-the-job training will consist of a conjecture on the amount of such training, a note on the decline of apprenticeship, and then a useful economic theorem on who bears the costs of such training. Surprisingly little is known about on-the-job training in modern industry. About all that can be said is that the expansion of education has not eliminated it. It seems likely, however, that some

[6]Health economics is in its infancy; there are two medical journals with "economics" in their titles, two bureaus for economic research in private associations (one in the American Medical and the other in the American Dental Association), and not a few studies and papers by outside scholars. Selma Mushkin's survey is very useful with its pertinent economic insights, though she may have underestimated somewhat the influence of the economic behavior of people in striving for health [14].

[7]For instance, the income elasticity of the demand for food continues to be positive even after the point is reached where additional food no longer has the attribute of a "producer good."

of the training formerly undertaken by firms has been discontinued and other training programs have been instituted to adjust both to the rise in the education of workers and to changes in the demands for new skills. The amount invested annually in such training can only be a guess. H. F. Clark places it near to equal to the amount spent on formal education.[8] Even if it were only one-half as large, it would represent currently an annual gross investment of about $15 billion. Elsewhere, too, it is thought to be important. For example, some observers have been impressed by the amount of such training under way in plants in the Soviet Union.[9] Meanwhile, apprenticeship has all but disappeared, partly because it is now inefficient and partly because schools now perform many of its functions. Its disappearance has been hastened no doubt by the difficulty of enforcing apprenticeship agreements. Legally they have come to smack of indentured service. The underlying economic factors and behavior are clear enough. The apprentice is prepared to serve during the initial period when his productivity is less than the cost of his keep and of his training. Later, however, unless he is legally restrained, he will seek other employment when his productivity begins to exceed the cost of keep and training, which is the period during which a master would expect to recoup on his earlier outlay.

To study on-the-job training Gary Becker [1] advances the theorem that in competitive markets employees pay all the costs of their training and none of these costs are ultimately borne by the firm. Becker points out several implications. The notion that expenditures on training by a firm generate external economies for other firms is not consistent with this theorem. The theorem also indicates one force favoring the transfer from on-the-job training to attending school. Since on-the-job training reduces the net earnings of workers at the beginning and raises them later on, this theorem also provides an explanation for the "steeper slope of the curve relating income to age," for skilled than unskilled workers, referred to earlier.[10] What all

---

[8]Based on comments made by Harold F. Clark at the Merrill Center for Economics, summer 1959; also, see [4].

[9]Based on observations made by a team of U.S. economists of which I was a member; see *Saturday Rev.*, Jan. 21, 1961.

[10]Becker has also noted still another implication arising out of the fact that the income and capital investment aspects of on-the-job training are tied together, which gives rise to "permanent" and "transitory" income effects that may have substantial explanatory value.

this adds up to is that the stage is set to undertake meaningful economic studies of on-the-job training.

Happily we reach firmer ground in regard to education. Investment in education has risen at a rapid rate and by itself may well account for a substantial part of the otherwise unexplained rise in earnings. I shall do no more than summarize some preliminary results about the total costs of education including income foregone by students, the apparent relation of these costs to consumer income and to alternative investments, the rise of the stock of education in the labor force, returns to education, and the contribution that the increase in the stock of education may have made to earnings and to national income.

It is not difficult to estimate the conventional costs of education consisting of the costs of the services of teachers, librarians, administrators, of maintaining and operating the educational plant, and interest on the capital embodied in the educational plant. It is far more difficult to estimate another component of total cost, the income foregone by students. Yet this component should be included and it is far from negligible. In the United States, for example, well over half of the costs of higher education consists of income foregone by students. As early as 1900, this income foregone accounted for about one-fourth of the total costs of elementary, secondary and higher education. By 1956, it represented over two-fifths of all costs. The rising significance of foregone income has been a major factor in the marked upward trend in the total real costs of education which, measured in current prices, increased from $400 million in 1900 to $28.7 billion in 1956 [18]. The percentage rise in educational costs was about three and a half times as large as in consumer income, which would imply a high income elasticity of the demand for education, if education were regarded as pure consumption.[11] Educational costs also rose about three and a half times as rapidly as did the gross formation of physical capital in dollars. If we were to treat education as pure investment this result would suggest that the returns to education were relatively more attractive than those to nonhuman capital.[12]

---

[11] Had other things stayed constant this suggests an income elasticity of 3.5. Among the things that did change, the prices of educational services rose relative to other consumer prices, perhaps offset in part by improvements in the quality of educational services.

[12] This of course assumes among other things that the relationship between gross and net have not changed or have changed in the same proportion. Estimates are from my essay, "Education and Economic Growth" [19].

Much schooling is acquired by persons who are not treated as income earners in most economic analysis, particularly, of course, women. To analyze the effect of growth in schooling on earnings, it is therefore necessary to distinguish between the stock of education in the population and the amount in the labor force. Years of school completed are far from satisfactory as a measure because of the marked increases that have taken place in the number of days of school attendance of enrolled students and because much more of the education of workers consists of high school and higher education than formerly. My preliminary estimates suggest that the stock of education in the labor force rose about eight and a half times between 1900 and 1956, whereas the stock of reproducible capital rose four and a half times, both in 1956 prices. These estimates are, of course, subject to many qualifications.[13] Nevertheless, both the magnitude and the rate of increase of this form of human capital have been such that they could be an important key to the riddle of economic growth.[14]

The exciting work under way is on the return to education. In spite of the flood of high school and college graduates, the return has not become trivial. Even the lower limits of the estimates show that the return to such education has been in the neighborhood of the return to nonhuman capital. This is what most of these estimates show when they treat as costs all of the public and private expenditures on education and also the income foregone while attending school, and when they treat all of these costs as investment, allocating none to consumption.[15] But surely a part of these costs is consumption in

[13]From [19, Sec. 4]. These estimates of the stock of education are tentative and incomplete. They are incomplete in that they do not take into account fully the increases in the average life of this form of human capital arising out of the fact that relatively more of this education is held by younger people in the labor force than was true in earlier years; and, they are incomplete because no adjustment has been made for the improvements in education over time, increasing the quality of a year of school in ways other than those related to changes in the proportions represented by elementary, high school and higher education. Even so the stock of this form of human capital rose 8.5 times between 1900 and 1956 while the stock of reproducible nonhuman capital increased only 4.5 times, both in constant 1956 prices.

[14]In value terms this stock of education was only 22 percent as large as the stock of reproducible physical capital in 1900, whereas in 1956 it already had become 42 percent as large.

[15]Several comments are called for here. (1) The return to high school education appears to have declined substantially between the late 'thirties and early 'fifties and since then has leveled off, perhaps even risen somewhat, indicating a rate of return toward the end of the 'fifties about as high as that to higher education. (2) The return to college education seems to have risen somewhat since the late 'thirties in spite of the rapid

the sense that education creates a form of consumer capital[16] which has the attribute of improving the taste and the quality of consumption of students throughout the rest of their lives. If one were to allocate a substantial fraction of the total costs of this education to consumption, say one-half, this would, of course, double the observed rate of return to what would then become the investment component in education that enhances the productivity of man.

Fortunately, the problem of allocating the costs of education in the labor force between consumption and investment does not arise to plague us when we turn to the contribution that education makes to earnings and to national income because a change in allocation only alters the rate of return, not the total return. I noted at the outset that the unexplained increases in U. S. national income have been especially large in recent decades. On one set of assumptions, the unexplained part amounts to nearly three-fifths of the total increase between 1929 and 1956.[17] How much of this unexplained increase in

---

influx of college-trained individuals into the labor force. (3) Becker's estimates based on the difference in income between high school and college graduates based on urban males adjusted for ability, race, unemployment and mortality show a return of 9 percent to total college costs including both earnings foregone and conventional college costs, public and private and with none of these costs allocated to consumption (see his paper given at the American Economic Association meeting, December 1959 [2]). (4) The returns to this education in the case of nonwhite urban males, of rural males, and of females in the labor force may have been somewhat lower (see Becker [2]). (5) My own estimates, admittedly less complete than those of Becker and thus subject to additional qualifications, based mainly on lifetime income estimates of Herman P. Miller [12], lead to a return of about 11 percent to both high school and college education as of 1958. See [19, Sec. 5].

Whether the consumption component in education will ultimately dominate, in the sense that the investment component in education will diminish as these expenditures increase and a point will be reached where additional expenditures for education will be pure consumption (a zero return on however small a part one might treat as an investment), is an interesting speculation. This may come to pass, as it has in the case of food and shelter, but that eventuality appears very remote presently in view of the prevailing investment value of education and the new demands for knowledge and skill inherent in the nature of our technical and economic progress.

[16]The returns on this consumer capital will not appear in the wages and salaries that people earn.

[17]Real income doubled, rising from $150 to $302 billion in 1956 prices. Eighty-nine billions of the increase in real income is taken to be unexplained, or about 59 percent of the total increase. The stock of education in the labor force rose by $355 billion of which $69 billion is here allocated to the growth in the labor force to keep the per-worker stock of education constant, and $286 billion represents the increase in the level of this stock. See [19, Sec. 6] for an elaboration of the method and the relevant estimates.

income represents a return to education in the labor force? A lower limit suggests that about three-tenths of it, and an upper limit does not rule out that more than one-half of it came from this source.[18] These estimates also imply that between 36 and 70 per cent of the hitherto unexplained rise in the earnings of labor is explained by returns to the additional education of workers.

IV. A CONCLUDING NOTE ON POLICY

One proceeds at his own peril in discussing social implications and policy. The conventional hedge is to camouflage one's values and to wear the mantle of academic innocence. Let me proceed unprotected!

1. Our tax laws everywhere discriminate against human capital. Although the stock of such capital has become large and even though it is obvious that human capital, like other forms of reproducible capital, depreciates, becomes obsolete, and entails maintenance, our tax laws are all but blind on these matters.

2. Human capital deteriorates when it is idle because unemployment impairs the skills that workers have acquired. Losses in earnings can be cushioned by appropriate payments but these do not keep idleness from taking its toll from human capital.

3. There are many hindrances to the free choice of professions. Racial discrimination and religious discrimination are still widespread. Professional associations and governmental bodies also hinder entry, for example, into medicine. Such purposeful interference keeps the investment in this form of human capital substantially below its optimum [7].

4. It is indeed elementary to stress the greater imperfections of the capital market in providing funds for investment in human beings than for investment in physical goods. Much could be done to reduce these imperfections by reforms in tax and banking laws and by changes in banking practices. Long-term private and public loans to students are warranted.

5. Internal migration, notably the movement of farm people into industry, made necessary by the dynamics of our economic progress, requires substantial investments. In general, families in which the husbands and wives are already in the late thirties cannot afford to make these investments because the remaining payoff period for

[18] In percent, the lower estimate came out to 29 percent and the upper estimate to 56 percent.

17

them is too short. Yet society would gain if more of them would pull stakes and move because, in addition to the increase in productivity currently, the children of these families would be better located for employment when they were ready to enter the labor market. The case for making some of these investments on public account is by no means weak. Our farm programs have failed miserably these many years in not coming to grips with the costs and returns from off-farm migration.

6. The low earnings of particular people have long been a matter of public concern. Policy all too frequently concentrates only on the effects, ignoring the causes. No small part of the low earnings of many Negroes, Puerto Ricans, Mexican nationals, indigenous migratory farm workers, poor farm people and some of our older workers, reflects the failure to have invested in their health and education. Past mistakes are, of course, bygones, but for the sake of the next generation we can ill afford to continue making the same mistakes over again.

7. Is there a substantial underinvestment in human beings other than in these depressed groups? [2] This is an important question for economists. The evidence at hand is fragmentary. Nor will the answer be easily won. There undoubtedly have been overinvestments in some skills, for example, too many locomotive firemen and engineers, too many people trained to be farmers, and too many agricultural economists! Our schools are not free of loafers and some students lack the necessary talents. Nevertheless, underinvestment in knowledge and skill, relative to the amounts invested in nonhuman capital would appear to be the rule and not the exception for a number of reasons. The strong and increasing demands for this knowledge and skill in laborers are of fairly recent origin and it takes time to respond to them. In responding to these demands, we are heavily dependent upon cultural and political processes, and these are slow and the lags are long compared to the behavior of markets serving the formation of nonhuman capital. Where the capital market does serve human investments, it is subject to more imperfections than in financing physical capital. I have already stressed the fact that our tax laws discriminate in favor of nonhuman capital. Then, too, many individuals face serious uncertainty in assessing their innate talents when it comes to investing in themselves, especially through higher education. Nor is it easy either for public decisions or private behavior to untangle and properly assess the consumption and the investment components.

The fact that the return to high school and to higher education has been about as large as the return to conventional forms of capital when all of the costs of such education including income foregone by students are allocated to the investment component, creates a strong presumption that there has been underinvestment since, surely, much education is cultural and in that sense it is consumption. It is no wonder, in view of these circumstances, that there should be substantial underinvestment in human beings, even though we take pride, and properly so, in the support that we have given to education and to other activities that contribute to such investments.

8. Should the returns from public investment in human capital accrue to the individuals in whom it is made?[19] The policy issues implicit in this question run deep and they are full of perplexities pertaining both to resource allocation and to welfare. Physical capital that is formed by public investment is not transferred as a rule to particular individuals as a gift. It would greatly simplify the allocative process if public investment in human capital were placed on the same footing. What then is the logical basis for treating public investment in human capital differently? Presumably it turns on ideas about welfare. A strong welfare goal of our community is to reduce the unequal distribution of personal income among individuals and families. Our community has relied heavily on progressive income and inheritance taxation. Given public revenue from these sources, it may well be true that public investment in human capital, notably that entering into general education, is an effective and efficient set of expenditures for attaining this goal. Let me stress, however, that the state of knowledge about these issues is woefully meager.

9. My last policy comment is on assistance to underdeveloped countries to help them achieve economic growth. Here, even more than in domestic affairs, investment in human beings is likely to be underrated and neglected. It is inherent in the intellectual climate in which leaders and spokesmen of many of these countries find themselves. Our export of growth doctrines has contributed. These typically assign the stellar role to the formation of nonhuman capital, and take as an obvious fact the superabundance of human resources. Steel mills are the real symbol of industrialization. After all, the early

---

[19] I am indebted to Milton Friedman for bringing this issue to the fore in his comments on an early draft of this paper. See preface of [7] and also Jacob Mincer's pioneering paper [13].

industrialization of England did not depend on investments in the labor force. New funds and agencies are being authorized to transfer capital for physical goods to these countries. The World Bank and our Export-Import Bank have already had much experience. Then, too, measures have been taken to pave the way for the investment of more private (nonhuman) capital abroad. This one-sided effort is under way in spite of the fact that the knowledge and skills required to take on and use efficiently the superior techniques of production, the most valuable resource that we could make available to them, is in very short supply in these underdeveloped countries. Some growth of course can be had from the increase in more conventional capital even though the labor that is available is lacking both in skill and knowledge. But the rate of growth will be seriously limited. It simply is not possible to have the fruits of a modern agriculture and the abundance of modern industry without making large investments in human beings.

Truly, the most distinctive feature of our economic system is the growth in human capital. Without it there would be only hard, manual work and poverty except for those who have income from property. There is an early morning scene in Faulkner's *Intruder in the Dust*, of a poor, solitary cultivator at work in a field. Let me paraphrase that line, "The man without skills and knowledge leaning terrifically against nothing."

REFERENCES

1. G. S. Becker, preliminary draft of study undertaken for Nat. Bur. Econ. Research. New York 1960.
2. ———, "Underinvestment in College Education?," *Proc., Am. Econ. Rev.,* May 1960, *50*, 346–54.
3. P. R. Brahmanand and C. N. Vakil, *Planning for an Expanding Economy.* Bombay 1956.
4. H. F. Clark, "Potentialities of Educational Establishments Outside the Conventional Structure of Higher Education," *Financing Higher Education, 1960–70,* D. M. Keezer, ed. New York 1959.
5. Solomon Fabricant, *Basic Facts on Productivity Change,* Nat. Bur. Econ. Research, Occas. Paper 63. New York 1959. Table 5.
6. Irving Fisher, *The Nature of Capital and Income.* New York 1906.
7. Milton Friedman and Simon Kuznets, *Income from Independent Professional Practice,* Nat. Bur. Econ. Research. New York 1945.

8. B. Horvat, "The Optimum Rate of Investment," *Econ. Jour.*, Dec. 1958, *68*, 747–67.

9. H. G. Johnson, "The Political Economy of Opulence," *Can. Jour. Econ. and Pol. Sci.*, Nov. 1960, *26*, 552–64.

10. Simon Kuznets, *Income and Wealth in the United States*. Cambridge, England 1952. Sec. IV, Distribution by Industrial Origin.

11. Alfred Marshall, *Principles of Economics*, 8th ed. London 1930. App. E, pp. 787–88.

12. H. P. Miller, "Annual and Lifetime Income in Relation to Education: 1939–1959," *Am. Econ. Rev.*, Dec. 1960, *50*, 962–86.

13. Jacob Mincer, "Investment in Human Capital and Personal Income Distribution," *Jour. Pol. Econ.*, Aug. 1958, *66*, 281–302.

14. S. J. Mushkin, "Toward a Definition of Health Economics," *Public Health Reports*, U. S. Dept. of Health, Educ. and Welfare, Sept. 1958, *73*, 785–93.

15. J. S. Nicholson, "The Living Capital of the United Kingdom," *Econ. Jour.*, Mar. 1891, *1*, 95; see J. S. Mill, *Principles of Political Economy*, ed. W. J. Ashley, London 1909, p. 8.

16. T. W. Schultz, "Investment in Man: An Economist's View," *Soc. Serv. Rev.*, June 1959, *33*, 109–17.

17. ———, "Agriculture and the Application of Knowledge," *A Look to the Future*, W. K. Kellogg Foundation, Battle Creek, 1956, 54–78.

18. ———, "Capital Formation by Education," *Jour. Pol. Econ.*, Dec. 1960, *68*, Tables 3 through 7.

19. ———, "Education and Economic Growth," *Social Forces Influencing American Education*, H. G. Richey, ed. Chicago 1961.

20. H. von Thünen, *Der isolierte Staat*, 3rd ed., Vol. 2, Pt. 2, 1875, transl. by B. F. Hoselitz, reproduced by the Comp. Educ. Center, Univ. Chicago, pp. 140–52.

21. Morton Zeman, *A Quantitative Analysis of White-Nonwhite Income Differentials in the United States*. Unpublished doctoral dissertation, Univ. Chicago, 1955.

Investment in Human Capital: Comment*

HARRY G. SHAFFER

University of Kansas

The treatment of currently or potentially productive human beings as capital and/or wealth has a long history in economic literature.[1] But during the first half of the twentieth century, certainly, the overwhelming majority of economists, following Alfred Marshall [8, pp. 71–72], have shown a tendency to use the concept of capital as applicable only to that portion of the nonhuman, material, man-made stock of wealth which is utilized directly in further production.

In spite of "majority opinion" the application of the capital concept to man has not disappeared from economic literature[2] and the past few years especially have witnessed a revival of the idea in U.S. economic journals. In the forefront of scholarly efforts in this direction stands the work of Theodore W. Schultz [13]–[17].

I shall grant unequivocally that theoretical models, incontestable from an abstract or mathematical point of view, can be built on the basis of the application of the capital concept to man. Yet, I shall contend that it is generally inadvisable to treat man as human capital.

Schultz believes that the main reason for the opposition to the human capital concept is based on a somewhat irrational fear that to accept the concept would be morally wrong and degrading to free man [13, p. 572] [16, p. 2] [17, p. 110]. This, however, is not the reason for my opposition. It is my contention that, mainly for three reasons, economics has little to gain and much to lose by the universal application of the capital concept to man:

First, "investment in man" is essentially different from investment in non-human capital. The difference arises largely from the fact that,

---

*Reprinted from "Investment in Human Capital: Comment," *American Economic Review* (December, 1961): 1026–34.

[1]See for instance [11] [19, pp. 265–66] [5, p. 13] [4, p. 65].

[2]See [21, n., 255] for a short bibliography of articles in British, German, French, and Italian journals during the first three decades of the twentieth century.

as a general rule, at least a part of any one direct expenditure for the improvement of man is not investment as the term is usually used, i.e., it is undertaken for reasons other than the expectation of a monetary return, it has no traceable effects on future output and it satisfies wants directly. To the extent to which any part of such an expenditure is investment in this sense it is rarely if ever "rational" investment based on a careful comparison of alternate investment opportunities, with the anticipated monetary return and the degree of safety as guiding rods. Furthermore, any such part is inseparable from other parts which, not being classified as investment, are then conveniently referred to as consumption expenditure.

Secondly, were it possible to separate consumption expenditure from investment in man it would still remain a virtual impossibility to allocate a *specific* return to a *specific* investment in man (though aggregate expenditures for the improvement of man's skill, abilities, and productive capacities certainly have a positive influence of indeterminable magnitude on man's efficiency as a productive agent and, hence, on his output).

Finally, if consumption expenditure could be separated from investment in man, and if it were possible to compute the part of man's income that results from a given investment-in-man expenditure, it would in most instances still be ill-advised — from the point of view of social and economic welfare — to utilize the information thus obtained as the exclusive or even the primary basis for policy formation, public or private.[3]

I shall attempt to illustrate how these three arguments are applicable to expenditures on education. I shall then indicate briefly that the same arguments are applicable to direct expenditures on man for purposes other than his education.

I. EDUCATION: CONSUMPTION EXPENDITURE OR INVESTMENT?

Few U.S. social scientists today will argue with the basic spirit of Marshall's statement that: "There is no greater extravagance more

[3]Joan Robinson sees the main difference between investment in acquiring power and investment in income-yielding property in the fact that in a capitalist society the earning power is not a salable commodity in the sense which the income-yielding property is — a point not stressed in this paper. From this, she reaches the conclusion that "the present capital value of future personal earning has a metaphorical, not an actual financial meaning." While this seems a valid comment, her view that "From the point of view of the economy as a whole, the similarity is more important than the difference," is one contested in this paper [12, pp. 11–12].

prejudicial to the growth of national wealth than that wasteful negligence which allows genius that happens to be born of lowly parentage to expend itself in lowly work" [8, pp. 212]. But Marshall did not utilize this realization to treat expenditures for education as "investment in man," and neither should we.

Up to a certain age, public school attendance is compulsory and any private expenditures connected therewith (such as expenditures for notebooks, gym clothes, etc.) are taken out of the area of private decision-making (except for whatever influence the parent may have as a voter or vote-getter). Some parents decide to incur additional expenses, beyond those required by law, for their children's education. They may send their children to "better" private schools or to parochial schools, they may provide them with private dancing or piano lessons, they may employ the services of a French governess. But such expenditures, more often than not, are at least in part consumption expenditures as far as both the economic motivation of the investor and the economic effects on the individual and on society are concerned. Due to the inseparability of the consumption and the investment part of such expenditures (and for other reasons discussed below) the return on any incremental expenditure to either the individual or society is not computable.

When we turn from legally required minimum education to voluntary private expenditures for education at the high school and the college level it still seems quite impossible to explain human behavior in terms of capital investment (as we have been using the term). Many a parent who would not think of spending thousands of dollars to establish his son in business or who would at least require a partnership in such a business, does not hesitate to spend an equal amount on his son's education without expecting any monetary return for himself (and with higher anticipated life income for his son often at best one of several motivation factors). The young college student who finances his own education will probably enroll in many courses and read many books that would bear only a remote relation, if any, to future expected or realized income. Although some of these may be required for graduation and therefore may be of indirect economic value, it is in all probability still a fair evaluation of human motivation that "the prospects of achieving more subtle satisfactions from mastering a higher education are more compelling to many people than the prospects of greater financial success" [6. p. 308]. Any attempt to show that rational individuals tend to undertake expenditure on education up to the point where the marginal productivity of the human capital produced by the process of education equals the rate of interest—a point at which the marginal expenditure on education yields a return equal to the return on marginal expenditure for any other factor of production—would be a mockery of economic theory.

At best, we can go along with Schultz's contention that ". . . *some* individuals and families make decisions to invest in *some* kinds of education, either in themselves or in their children, with an eye to the earnings that they expect to see forthcoming from such expenditures on education."[4] And Schultz has to admit that in the case of expenditures on human beings, those for consumption and those for the purpose of increasing income are quite interwoven, "which is why the task of identifying each component is so formidable and why the measurement of capital formation by expenditures is less useful for human investment than for investment in physical goods" [16, p. 8]. He therefore proposes yield (measured in increased earnings) as an alternative method for estimating human investment.

II. EDUCATION AND INCOME

Studies showing a close correlation between schooling (measured in numbers of years of attendance and/or type of school attended) and success (measured in terms of social position and/or annual or life earnings) antedate the turn of the century.[5] Some recent studies attempt to measure the financial return to "investment" in education. The value of a college education in the late 1950's, for instance, has been estimated anywhere from $100,000 to almost $180,000 [2, p. 180] [7, p.28] [9, p. 981]. However, the present value of a lifetime income differential of nearly $106,000 between a high school and a college graduate amounts to a mere $3,305 when figured after taxes and when discounted at 8 percent [7, p. 28]—not an unreasonable rate of discount if one considers the risk involved in "investing" in a college education.

To obtain valid figures for lifetime incomes (on the basis of present actuarial tables), to correlate such figures with years of schooling, to compute the cost of such schooling in terms of private expenditures,

[4][13, pp. 572–73]. Emphasis mine.

[5]See [3] for a discussion of many of these early studies and a Bibliography of more than 125 books and journal articles on the subject published between 1898 and 1917.

public expenditures, and opportunity costs (*without* any attempt to segregate "consumption" from "investment in education" expenditures), to compute the rate of discount which will equate the expenditures with lifetime income differentials, and, finally, to compare this rate with the rate of return on investment in nonhuman capital — all these do not present insurmountable difficulties. But to establish a cause-effect relationship, to prove, in other words, that the income differential is the result of the additional education is quite a different matter. To do so, one would have to assume that the more educated individual does not differ from the less educated in any characteristic (other than education) that could explain part or all of the income differential. Such an assumption would be highly unrealistic as it is evident that there is a close correlation between intelligence and years of schooling (especially at the higher levels). There are also good indications of at least some correlation between the financial standing of parents and the years of schooling of their children. Finally, there is the possibility, if not the strong probability, that other factors such as connections, residence (urban vs. rural, North vs. South, etc.), occupational and cultural level of parents, health, etc, have some influence on years of school attendance. And surely all these factors have a direct bearing on income, independent of years of preparation.

In the early 'forties, Elbridge Sibley studied the case records of 2,158 Pennsylvania students and discovered that, at the below-college level, intelligence had a greater influence on years of education than parental status. However, as to the probability of spending at least one year in an institution of higher learning, "while the most intelligent boys have only a 4 to 1 advantage over the least intelligent, the sons of men in the highest occupational category enjoy an advantage of more than 10 to 1 over those from the lowest occupational level" [18, p. 330].[6] In his study of the relationship between income (annual and lifetime) and education for the years 1939–1959, Herman P. Miller noted that at least part of the higher income of those with more education could probably be accounted for by differences in intelligence, home environment, family connections, and other factors [9, p. 964] [6, p. 312]. D. S. Bridgman points to evidence that "unearned" (property) income of college graduates is higher than that

---

[6]Sibley's study was published in 1942. Since then (in the United States, at least) increased number of scholarships and public subsidization of education have certainly diminished the dependence of schooling upon parental status.

of noncollege-trained individuals and he expresses the view that factors such as ability and property income have been given insufficient recognition in the past as causal agents of higher income of the more educated [2].

In 1958, Jacob Mincer constructed a model to account for personal income distribution in terms of differential "investment" in education [10]. He started out with many admittedly oversimplified assumptions, one of which was the assumption of identical abilities. But when he relaxed this unrealistic assumption, the plausibility of a positive correlation between ability traits and amount of education (with the obvious effect on income distribution) became apparent [10, p. 286]. To this he added that "when incomes rather than earnings are considered, the positive association of property incomes with occupational level . . . magnifies income differences" (thus accentuating whatever effects the training factor per se might have) [10, p. 302]. Therefore, he could not and did not claim that a quantitative estimate of the effect of training on personal income distribution could be derived using his model.

J. R. Walsh, in his early (1935) study of the applicability of the capital concept to man, explained that in order to isolate the effect of education he would have to eliminate all other influences (such as ability, age, occupation, health, etc.) but that he had attempted no such elimination as he considered it impossible [21, p. 272]. Indeed, it is so completely impossible to eliminate all other influences[7] that one has to agree with Houthakker that ". . . we cannot even be sure that the apparent effect of education on income is not completely explicable in terms of intelligence and parents' income, so that the *specific* effect of education would be zero or even negative" [7, p. 28].

There is another factor that enhances the difficulty of determining the return on "investment in education." This factor I shall call "maintenance costs."

Certainly, whenever the financial return on any investment in nonhuman capital is computed, maintenance costs of the capital good are considered. But, to the best of my knowledge, such maintenance

---

[7]Theoretically it would not be necessary to eliminate all other influences, as partial (or multiple) correlation methods could be employed to allow for the effects of some other variables. However, amount of education is at least partly a matter of personal choice. As long as this is true, no matter how many factors have been considered, one can never be certain that there are not some unanalyzed variables influencing this choice which in themselves are responsible for the income differential attributed to education.

costs have been utterly neglected in the case of human capital by all economists who have advocated the application of the capital concept to man. These maintenance costs first arise during the investment period. The tuxedo, the evening dress, the more frequent haircuts may not be absolutely necessary for the increase in subsequent earning capacity but they are *de facto* expenses connected with higher education (and they might be indirectly necessary for the intended investment goals lest the anxiety and the loss of tranquility caused by their absence interfere with scholastic accomplishments). But maintenance costs by no means end with the completion of the investment period. A part of these continuous maintenance costs (such as the more expensive car, the more luxuriously dressed wife, and the more lavishly furnished home of the "organization man," or the more frequently washed shirt and the more frequently dry-cleaned suit of the white collar worker) are almost unavoidably connected with the retention of the position which yields the higher income to the more educated.

Another part of these maintenance costs, perhaps less compulsive but still widely prevalent, relates to increased qualitative (and to some extent also quantitative) consumption demands resulting from higher education, higher income, or both.[8] To the extent to which increased consumption expenditure results from increased income per se (which it will whenever the marginal propensity to consume is more than zero) it is independent of the cause of the increase in income. To the extent, however, to which increased consumption expenditure results from the educational development of greater cultural, aesthetic and discriminating tastes (which is not a separable part but rather a result of the aggregate education process), it reflects an increased expenditure directly and uniquely attributable to the specific type of investment (in education).[9] In time, these education-created expenditures will probably tend to become essential for the former student's efficient performance as a producer and, thus, part of the maintenance costs of the education-created human capital.[10]

[8]Other causes of increased consumption, if any, are disregarded as irrelevant to the main argument.

[9]That there is *some* education-created increase in consumption (and not just substitution of one kind of consumption for another) appears evident from observation.

[10]Schultz does not count such education-created consumption expenditures as maintenance costs. On the contrary, while acknowledging their existence, he suggests that the part of the cost of education that induces them be classified as consumption ex-

III. PUBLIC POLICY IN RELATION TO EXPENDITURE ON EDUCATION

At present, the investment-in-human-capital concept appears to be gaining in favor among "liberals" who apparently intend to utilize it as a rationalization of federal aid to education (and, secondarily, other governmental investment-in-man expenditures). Walter Heller, Chairman of the Council of Economic Advisers to the President, for instance, refers to the human mind as America's greatest resource and points to the "vast implications for public policy" embodied in the development of the investment-in-human-capital concept [20]. But nothing is more dangerous to the very position of the liberals, I fear, than to attempt to defend government expenditures for education as a type of collective business investment which will yield economic returns attractive to the investing society in terms of maximum increase in GNP over and above costs. To cite just one example of the untenable position to which such argumentation could lead: Schultz sees a direct correlation between the lower incomes of Negroes in the United States (as compared with whites) and their relatively lower productivity resulting from inadequate educational preparation [16, pp. 3–4][17, p. 109] and he considers an "investment" in their education as financially sound. But more specific studies clearly show that due to greater vocational opportunities, the income differential correlated with additional education is considerably higher for whites than for Negroes.[11] Were we to agree that the government should treat expenditures for education as investment, could not a good case be made for the decrease, if not the discontinuation, of governmental subsidization of nonwhite students and a consequently higher subsidization of the financially more remunerative white students?

By the same token, should society discourage advanced studies by women unless they can give some reasonable assurance that their "human capital" will be used even after they are married? Or should we – COULD WE??? – compute the indirect, long-range value of such women to society in terms of increased future productivity of their children whom they would perhaps rear more efficiently? The education of many young men and women who choose to prepare them-

---

penditure. By so decreasing the cost base for investment in education Schultz arrives at a higher rate of return on the investment than he would otherwise [16, pp. 12–13].

[11]In 1949, for instance, the difference in income between nonwhite males with one to three years in college (for the 45–54 year age group) was about $500 for the year while the corresponding differential for white males was about twice as great [6, p. 309].

selves for professions which they expect will yield them comparatively low monetary but comparatively high psychic incomes (such as teaching) might be of great value to society. But if we were to take return on investment as the guiding rod, how would we proceed? A teacher's *immediate, direct* contribution to GNP (equal to his gross income) would not be a true reflection of his value to society, and his *indirect, long-run* effect (expressed in terms of his influence on the income of others) is not measurable. Marshall proclaimed that: "All that is spent during many years in opening the means of higher education to the masses would be well paid for if it called out one more Newton or Darwin, Shakespeare or Beethoven" [8, p. 216]. Was Marshall wrong? I do not think he was. Yet, how would one obtain empirical evidence that such investment would be "well paid for"? How would one go about computing a significant rate of return on such an investment?

Indeed the advocate of more governmental aid to education who attempts to defend his proposal exclusively on an "it's sound investment policy" basis stands on shaky ground, for he would logically have to advise expenditures on education up to the point where the marginal productivity of the human capital created equaled the marginal productivity of other nonhuman capital, as well as the rate of interest. And what would this advocate of more government aid to education do if he were confronted with a study such as Becker's which reaches the conclusion that ". . . it would appear that direct returns alone cannot justify a large increase in expenditures on college education relative to expenditures on business capital" [1, p. 349]? He could find support in arguments such as Schultz's that Becker failed to take into consideration that a part of the expenditure on education is always for education as a pure consumer's good, that Becker therefore underestimated the return on investment in education, and that it is reasonable to assume that there has been underinvestment in education [16, p. 15]. But, on the other hand, our advocate of more government aid to education might also have to cope with the argument that Becker, perhaps, overestimated the return on investment in education, as no allowance was made in Becker's study for such parts of total returns as may have been attributable to factors other than education (as discussed in Part II above) or offset by increased "maintenance costs." And once the advocate of increased government aid to education reaches the conclusion that it is impossible to compute a scientifically unassailable rate of return for such investment, he loses even his theoretical basis for *any* government "investment" in education, forcing him once more to utilize arguments other than "it's sound investment policy" to defend his proposals.

IV. EXPENDITURES ON HUMAN BEINGS OTHER THAN FOR EDUCATION

For essentially the same reasons as presented in Parts I and II above, it seems for most purposes impractical, inconvenient, and of relatively little use to attempt the explanation of direct expenditures on man, other than for his education, in terms of the investment in human capital concept. And for essentially the same reasons as those presented in Part III above, it seems ill-advised to base governmental policy on such a concept.

Whether we deal with outlays on food, improved medical care, housing, recreational facilities, or other "investments in man," we once again are faced with the impossibility of separating consumption from investment in any of those areas and with the impossibility of computing scientifically valid marginal returns on any of these expenditures. And once again it might prove detrimental to the best interests of society (measured in terms other than aggregate economic returns on investment) to have governmental policy determined (or even substantially influenced) by an investor's point of view. Governmental programs, for instance, providing for medical care or financial assistance to individuals beyond the retirement age (individuals thus fully depreciated as human capital) would be difficult to defend from the point of view of profitable investment per se (except, perhaps, in terms of the greater tranquility and therefore productivity of those still serviceable as human capital); and slum clearance projects might be considered poor investments as compared with the improvement of golf courses that would aid in steadying the nerves of more productive human capital.

V. CONCLUSIONS

Whether productive human beings should be treated as capital and whether some direct expenditure intended for or resulting in an increase in their productive capacities should be treated as investment in human capital are not questions of principle. There is no "right" or "wrong" way, because what constitutes *capital* and what constitutes *investment* is a matter of definition. Should one decide to include under "investment in human capital" everything that tends to increase man's productivity, the overwhelming part of all expenditures

31

to which we usually refer as consumption expenditures would have to be considered investments. A substantial part of all expenditures for food, shelter, and clothing, many expenditures for recreation, entertainment, and travel, and even some expenditures for mere conveniences and luxuries would certainly need to be reclassified as investments to the extent to which they contribute, directly or indirectly, to the enhancement of a person's productivity.

While it is undeniable that the sum total of countless sensible expenditures on man (including expenditures for his education, health, proper nourishment, etc.) will tend, on the average, to have a beneficial impact upon his productivity, present and future, each of these expenditures individually and all of them in the aggregate consist of inseparable and indistinguishable parts of consumption and investment expenditures. The spender's motivation is essentially different from that of the investor in nonhuman capital. The return on the investment cannot be computed satisfactorily as both the amount of pure "investment" and the return to be allocated thereto are conjectural. And in society's allocation of productive resources for the advancement of economic and noneconomic welfare, the question of the financial wisdom of any direct expenditure on man must be reduced to one of secondary importance. We have come to accept as axioms that health is preferable to illness, knowledge preferable to ignorance, freedom (whatever the term may mean) preferable to slavery, peace preferable to war, etc. Governmental expenditures directed towards the realization of these preferences bear no necessary relation to their economic profitability as investments.

This paper's opposition to the application of the capital concept to man, then, is not based on any argument that such application is "wrong" but only that, more often than not, it would confuse more than elucidate, it would create more problems than it would solve, and—as a basis for public policy—it would be of questionable value.

REFERENCES

1. G. S. Becker, "Underinvestment in College Education," *Am. Econ. Rev.* Proc., May 1960, *50*, 346–54.
2. D. S. Bridgman, "Problems in Estimating the Monetary Value of College Education," *Rev. Econ. Stat.*, Aug. 1960 Suppl., *42*, 180–84.

3. A. Caswell Ellis, "The Money Value of Education," Dept. of the Interior, *Bureau of Education, Bull.*, 1917, No. 22, Washington 1917.
4. Irving Fisher, *The Nature of Capital and Income.* New York 1906.
5. ———, *The Theory of Interest.* New York 1930.
6. P. C. Glick and H. P. Miller, "Educational Level and Potential Income," *Am. Soc. Rev.*, June 1956, *21*, 307–12.
7. H. S. Houthakker, "Education and Income," *Rev. Econ. Stat.*, Feb. 1959, *41*, 24–28.
8. Alfred Marshall, *Principles of Economics*, 8th ed. London 1946.
9. H. P. Miller, "Annual and Lifetime Income in Relation to Education: 1939–1959," *Am. Econ. Rev.*, Dec. 1960, *50*, 962–86.
10. Jacob Mincer, "Investment in Human Capital and Personal Distribution of Income," *Jour. Pol. Econ.*, Aug. 1958, *66*, 281–302.
11. Sir William Petty, "Political Arithmetic" (first published in 1676), *The Economic Writings of Sir William Petty* (Charles Henry Hull, ed.), Cambridge, 1899, Vol. I, pp. 233–313.
12. Joan Robinson, *The Accumulation of Capital.* Homewood, Ill. 1956.
13. T. W. Schultz, "Capital Formation by Education," *Jour. Pol. Econ.*, Dec. 1960, *68*, 571–83.
14. ———, "Education and Economic Growth," in *Social Forces Influencing American Education*, H. G. Richey, ed., Chicago 1961.
15. ———, "Human Capital: A Growing Asset," *Sat. Rev.*, Jan. 21, 1961, 37–39.
16. ———, "Investment in Human Capital," *Am. Econ. Rev.*, March 1961, *51*, 1–17.
17. ———, "Investment in Man: An Economist's View," *Soc. Service Rev.*, June 1959, *33*, 109–17.
18. Elbridge Sibley, "Some Demographic Clues to Stratification," *Am. Soc. Rev.*, June 1942, 7, 322–30.
19. Adam Smith, *The Wealth of Nations*, Modern Lib. ed., New York 1937, 265–66.
20. *Time Magazine*, March 1961, p. 22.
21. J. R. Walsh, "Capital Concept Applied to Man," *Quart. Jour. Econ.*, Feb. 1935, *49*, 255–85.

Investment in Human Capital: Reply*

THEODORE W. SCHULTZ

University of Chigago

I am surprised and pleased that under the restraints of a presidential address to the American Economic Association, enough could be said to warrant so careful and valuable a comment. Harry G. Shaffer discusses some of the minor difficulties that arise in practice in distinguishing between consumption and investment expenditures in the formation of human capital and then examines in considerable detail, and in my judgment correctly, some major difficulties in identifying and measuring the earnings (return) that are associated with a particular investment in man. Shaffer does not object to the concepts of investment in man and human capital; on the contrary, he explicitly accepts the underlying theory. He is, also, careful to disassociate himself from those who believe that it is morally wrong to apply the concepts of investment and capital to people. However, if any new knowledge were attainable by the use of these concepts, despite the empirical difficulties, Shaffer appears to believe that such knowledge would be grossly misused—by implication, more so than other economic knowledge—in making policy decisions. This view of the relation between economic analysis and policy seems unreal and irrelevant.

Shaffer's first point is addressed to the question: When are educational expenditures consumption and when are they investment? This question deserves careful investigation because so much depends upon the correctness of the answer. To follow the conventional procedure of treating all such costs as serving only current consumption will not do. But to allocate all of these costs to investment in future earnings, is fully as extreme and unwarranted. Although the economic logic for allocating the costs of education is clear and compelling, no one has as yet developed a wholly satisfactory empirical procedure

*Reprinted from "Investment in Human Capital: Reply," *American Economic Review* 51 (December, 1961): 1035–39.

for identifying and measuring the particular resources that enter into each of these components. Faced with this difficulty, any allocation that one makes, based on such clues as seem relevant, must in all honesty be labeled "arbitrary." There is little intellectual comfort in the fact that a similar brand of arbitrariness characterizes other areas of analysis, for example, in the way expenditures for electricity and for automobiles used by farmers are divided and distributed between household and farm expenses, or the way a part of the costs of some private residences used for offices, libraries or studies are treated as business expenses.

In discussing the central question of allocating resources between consumption and investment, Shaffer emphasizes two facts, namely that most students attend public schools, and that up to a certain age school attendance is compulsory. But neither of these facts is relevant to a logical basis for distinguishing between consumption and investments. If education were altogether free, a person would presumably consume of it until he were satiated and "invest" in it until it would no longer increase his future earnings. If a part of the education expenditures were borne on public account, the direct private costs of education would of course be less than the total costs of education, and to the extent that such education increased the future earnings of the student, his private rate of return to what he spent on education would be higher than the rate of return to total educational expenditures entering into this part of his education. Thus, private incentives to consume and to invest in education are affected by public educational expenditures, but the fact that there are such public expenditures has no bearing on the question whether education is consumption or investment. The fact that some schooling is compulsory is also irrelevant to the question at hand. To argue that it applies is analogous to saying that a city ordinance which requires private owners of houses to install plumbing and sewage disposal facilities is a factor in determining whether such facilities are a consumer or producer durable. Clearly, the compulsory city ordinance does not provide a logical basis for distinguishing between these two types of durables.

Although Shaffer is clear in seeing the positive effects of education upon the future earnings of students, he believes that the economic motivations of students and parents to invest in education is weak or even nonexistent. They are, in Shaffer's view, strongly motivated as consumers of education but only weakly or not motivated at all as investors in education. Such a dichotomy with respect to economic motivations is far from convincing. It is undoubtedly true, as Shaffer points out, that some education is wholly for consumption, and obviously in that case there would be no investment opportunity, hence no bases for an investment motivation. But are there no economic motivations in the case of students who attend our medical schools, schools for dentists, lawyers and engineers to invest in each of these particular skills with an eye to increases in future earnings? I am sure that the prospects of larger future earnings play a strong motivating role in these situations. Let me observe again, however, that private incentives either to consume education or to invest in it are affected by the amount and the nature of public expenditures for education. It is of course true that any attempt to explain total behavior with regard to the allocation of all public and private resources entering into education, takes one beyond the scope of the conventional private economic calculus of people. In studying the responses of private individuals to whatever investment opportunities education affords, it should be borne in mind: (1) that where the capital market does serve human investment it is subject to more imperfections than in financing physical capital; (2) that most investment in people, notably in the case of education, is in a long-period capacity, for it has a relatively long life and it is thus subject to the additional uncertainties which this implies; (3) that many individuals face serious uncertainty in assessing their innate talents when it comes to investing in themselves; and (4) that our laws discriminate against human investments [3]. These factors affect the observed responses, and their adverse effects may be confused with the real economic response, other things equal, to a given rate of return which is then thought to be weak or nonexistent.

Let me do no more than restate the effects of education upon consumption and earnings. The consumption component of education is either for current consumption, satisfying consumer well-being in the present, like food, or for future consumption, like houses. Education can also improve the capabilities of people and thus enhance their future earnings. The investment formed by education is, therefore, of two parts: a future consumption component and a future earnings component.

In "Education and Economic Growth" [4], in examining education for consumption, I emphasized the current consumption component. It is now clear to me that most education that satisfies consumer preferences is for future consumption and that this component has substantial durability and it is, therefore, to the extent that it serves consumption, mainly an *enduring* consumer component, even more so than other consumer durables. As an enduring consumer component, it is the source of future utilities (and thus this component, also contributes to future real income) which in no way enters into *measured* national income.[1] This component accordingly is like investment in houses, automobiles, refrigerators and the like. Thus we have the following: (1) education for current consumption (which, it seems to me, is of minor importance); (2) education for long-period future consumption, making it an investment in an enduring consumer component, which is undoubtedly of considerable importance; and (3) education for skills and knowledge useful in economic endeavor and, thus, an investment in future earnings [5].

Shaffer's second point, which presents a number of the real difficulties that arise when one attempts to identify and measure the increase in earnings that are associated with education, is well founded. Differences in innate abilities, race, employment, mortality, and family connections all enter and must be faced. It should not distract from the merits of his presentation to observe that these several difficulties are very much in the forefront in the work of economists who to my knowledge are engaged in studying this set of problems. The forthcoming study by Becker [1] will be a landmark on this score as well as on other relevant theoretical and empirical issues. A major new study by Denison [2] is both bold and original in bringing aggregate analysis to bear on the *sources* of economic growth in the United States. He finds education to be one of the major sources of economic growth after adjusting for differences in innate abilities and associated characteristics that affect earnings independently of education. Shaffer introduces a concept which he calls "maintenance costs" which in terms of the studies available to him has been neglected. But Weisbrod [6] in his paper "The Valuation of Human Capital," builds on "the proposition that the value of a person to others is measured by any excess of his contribution to production over what he consumes from production — this difference being the amount by which everyone else benefits from his productivity." Weisbrod then proceeds to estimate the relevant consumption, or if you please,

---

[1]Immediately following my presidential address, "Investment in Human Capital," Abba Lerner pointed out to me in conversation the role of future utilities from education and that this part of education also represented an investment. His logical and precise mind helped to clarify my thinking on this point and I am much indebted to him.

"maintenance costs" thus conceived, and subtracts such costs from gross earnings to obtain net earnings to be capitalized.

I am reluctant to tread upon the boulders Shaffer has collected in his comments on policy. I suspect, however, from what he says about them that they are conglomerates of compressed sand and at best weak materials for his conclusions. To have started off by lecturing "liberals" on their rationalization of federal aid to education, is not conducive to a calm and reasoned discussion of the policy implications of expenditures for education. If the argument were that the knowledge now available about the increases in earnings from education is still too fragmentary to be of any use whatsoever in making policy decisions, it would deserve careful consideration. If the argument were that knowledge about the effects of education upon future earnings will be misused by people and therefore any efforts to acquire such knowledge should be very much discouraged, this conclusion from such an argument would be patently false.

The principal source of Shaffer's confusion in discussing policy arises from his belief that, if it were to become known that particular forms of education pay in terms of increases in future earnings, policy decisions which took this fact into account would necessarily no longer take into account any of the other important contributions of education. People, including those who make policy decisions, are simply not that monolithic in their evaluation of education. Shaffer's implied apprehension that society will proceed to deny advanced education to women merely because most of them do not enter the labor market is a pure illusion. If Shaffer only means that knowledge about economic returns accruing from investment in human capital, in terms of future earnings, *should not* be the exclusive basis for public policy decisions in making expenditures for education, we are in full agreement. My view on this issue can be stated very simply: It is altogether proper that people should prize highly the cultural contributions of education and they will continue to do exactly that; but it is very short-sighted of us not to see its economic contributions. Education has become a major source of economic growth [5] in winning the abundance that is to be had by developing a modern agriculture and industry. It simply would not be possible to have this abundance if our people were predominantly illiterate and unskilled. Education, therefore, in addition to having high cultural values, is presently also an investment in people to the extent that it improves their capabilities and thereby increases the future earnings of people.

Shaffer says that there are specific studies which "clearly show . . . the income differential correlated with additional education is considerably higher for whites than for Negroes," and suggests the inference that less rather than more should therefore be spent on education for Negroes, provided this were the sole criterion. The specific studies in this case are based on national averages, making no adjustments for the effects of city size, different rates of unemployment, regions, and the quality of education. Nor is any account taken of the differences in the cost of education, including income foregone by the students, which is fully half of the total cost of college education. Furthermore, should there still remain a differential, as is to be expected because of discrimination, the relevant figure is not this income differential but the absolute difference between the Negro who has, let us say, a college education and one who had only a high school education. The increase in earnings represented by this absolute difference is the reward to which one would turn in estimating the return on this investment. Zeman's [7] study, it seems to me, strongly supports the inference that differences in education are the major explanatory variable for the very large white-nonwhite income differentials in the United States.

Despite my serious misgivings about Shaffer's attempt to relate economic analysis and policy, I am, as I said at the outset, grateful to him for his most valuable comment.

REFERENCES

1. G. S. Becker, has a major study on Investment in Education virtually completed for the Nat. Bur. Econ. Research, New York.
2. E. F. Denison, *The Sources of Economic Growth in the United States and The Alternatives Before Us*, a study soon to be published by the Committee for Economic Development.
3. T. W. Schultz, "Investment in Human Capital," *Am. Econ. Rev.*, March 1961, *51*, 14–15.
4. ———, "Education and Economic Growth," *Social Forces Influencing American Education*, N. B. Henry, ed., Chicago 1961.
5. ———, "Education as a Source of Economic Growth," Paper No. 61–5, August 14, 1961, Dept. of Econ., University of Chicago.
6. B. A. Weisbrod, "The Valuation of Human Capital," *Jour. Pol. Econ.*, Oct. 1961, *69*, 425–36.
7. M. Zeman, *A Quantitative Analysis of White-Nonwhite Income Differentials in the United States*, unpublished doctoral dissertation, Univ. of Chicago, 1955.

B. Theory of Human Capital Investment

4. Optimal Investment in Human Capital*

GARY S. BECKER

*Columbia University and National Bureau
of Economic Research*

I have shown elsewhere that what I call the "net" earnings of a person at any age t (E_t) approximately equals the earnings he would have at t if no human capital had been invested in him (X_t) plus the total returns to him at t on investments made in him earlier (k_t) minus the cost to him of investments at t (C_t), as in

$$E_t = X_t + k_t - C_t. \tag{1}$$

Total returns depend on the amounts invested and their rates of return; for example, if returns on each investment were the same at all ages during the labor force period[1] total returns would be the sum of the products of the amounts invested and their rates of return, adjusted for the finiteness of the labor force period. Equation (1) could then be written as

$$E_t = X_t + \sum_{j=1}^{n} r_{t-j} f_{t-j} C_{t-j} - C_t, \tag{2}$$

where r_{t-j} is the rate of return on capital invested at $t-j$ and f_{t-j} is the finite life adjustment. I applied this analysis to various problems, including the shapes of age-earnings and age-wealth profiles, the relation between unemployment and on-the-job training, the so-called Leontief paradox and several others.[2]

*Excerpt from *Human Capital and the Personal Distribution of Income: An Analytical Approach* (Ann Arbor: Institute of Public Policy Studies and the Department of Economics, University of Michigan, 1967), pp. 2–12.

[1]This is the "one-hoss shay" assumption applied to human capital.

[2]See my *Human Capital* (Columbia University Press for the National Bureau of Economic Research, 1964), Chapters II–III.

I suggested that differences in the total amounts invested by different persons are related to differences in the rates of return obtainable, a suggestion that can explain why white urban males with high IQs acquire more education than others, or why the division of labor is limited by the extent of the market.[3] I did not, however, systematically develop a framework to explain why rates of return and investments differ so greatly among persons. This essay tries to develop such a framework. This not only provides a rigorous justification for these suggestions in *Human Capital*, but also begins to provide an explanation of the personal distribution of earnings.

The term X_t in equations (1) and (2) represents the earnings of a person that are unrelated to human capital invested in him, and are presumably, therefore, largely independent of his current choices. Particularly in developed economies but perhaps in most, there is sufficient investment in education, training, informal learning, health and just plain child rearing that the earnings unrelated to investment in human capital are a small part of the total. Indeed, in the developmental approaches to child rearing, all the earnings of a person are ultimately attributed to different kinds of investments made in him.[4] Consequently, there is considerable justification for the assumption that X_t is small and can be neglected, an assumption we make in this paper. In any case a significant X_t only slightly complicates the analysis and can be readily incorporated.

Another assumption made throughout most of the paper is that human capital is homogeneous in the sense that all units are perfect substitutes in production for each other and thus add the same amount of earnings. Of course, this assumption does not deny that some units may have been produced at considerably greater costs than others. The assumption of homogeneous human capital clearly differs in detail rather drastically from the usual emphasis on qualitative differences in education, training, and skills. I hope to demonstrate that these differences, while descriptively realistic and useful, are not required to understand the basic forces determining the distribution of earnings; indeed, they sometimes even distract attention from these determinants. Section 3g does, however, generalize the analysis to cover many kinds of human capital.

---

[3]See Ibid., pp. 52, 79–88, 90–104.

[4]See S. J. Mushkin, "Health as an Investment," *Journal of Political Economy*, LXX (Special Supplement, October 1962), pp. 149–51.

Figure 1 plots along the horizontal axis the amount invested in human capital measured for convenience by its cost rather than in physical units. Equal distances along the axis, therefore, do not necessarily measure equal numbers of physical units.

FIGURE 1

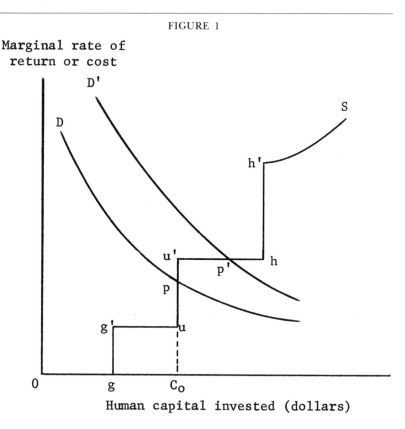

Marginal rate of return or cost

Human capital invested (dollars)

The curve D shows the marginal benefit, for simplicity measured by the rate of return, to a particular person on each additional dollar of investment, and is supposed to represent his demand curve for human capital. The curve S shows the effective marginal financing cost to him, measured for simplicity by the rate of interest, of each additional dollar invested, and represents in essence his supply curve of capital. If D exceeded S, the marginal rate of return would exceed the marginal rate of interest, and income would be increased by additional investment, while the opposite would be true if S exceeded D. Consequently, income is maximized by investing up to the point where $D = S$, given by p in the figure, and implying a total capital investment of OC_o.

The marginal rate of return depends on the time series of marginal returns and the marginal production cost of investment: if returns are constant for a long labor force period, it essentially equals the ratio of returns to these costs. Since all human capital is assumed to be homogeneous, even an extremely large percentage change in the capital invested by any one person would have a negligible effect on the total quantity of capital available. Consequently, in order to explain why the demand curves for human capital in Figure 1 are negatively inclined and not horizontal, other effects of capital accumulation must be analyzed.

The principal characteristic that distinguishes human from other kinds of capital is that, by definition, the former is imbedded or embodied in the person investing. This embodiment of human capital is the most important reason why marginal benefits decline as additional capital is accumulated. One obvious implication of embodiment is that since the memory capacity, physical size, etc. of each investor is limited, eventually diminishing returns set in from producing additional capital.[5] The result is increasing marginal costs of producing a dollar of returns.

Closely dependent on the embodiment of human capital is the importance of an investor's own time in the production of his own human capital.[6] Own time is so important that an increase in the amount invested in good part corresponds to an increase in the time spent investing:[7] in fact the only commonly used measures of schooling and training are years of schooling and training, measures entirely based on the input of own time. The cost of this time has been measured for several kinds of human capital, shown to be

[5] If $h = f(I, B)$, where h is the number of units of capital produced by a person per unit time, f is his production function, I is his capital investment in dollars per unit time, and B represents his physical and mental powers, then eventually $(\partial^2 h)/(\partial I^2) < 0$.

[6] The production function in the previous footnote can be expanded to $h = f(R,T,B)$, where R is the rate of input of other resources, and T is the rate of input of the investor's time per unit calendar time.

[7] If the horizontal axis in Figure 1 were replaced by one measuring investment time, the figure would be almost identical to those used in the "Austrian" theory of capital to explain optimal aging of trees or wine. Indeed, the main relevance of the Austrian approach in modern economies is to the study of investment in human capital!

generally important, and given the name "foregone earnings."[8]

If the elasticities of substitution between own time and teachers, books, and other inputs were infinite, the use of own time and the deferral of investments could be avoided, without cost, aside from the limitations imposed by B, by an accumulation of all the desired capital instantaneously through complete substitution of other inputs for own time. If substitution was significantly imperfect (which is the more likely situation), the elimination of own time would cause the marginal costs of producing human capital to be higher and rise faster as capital was accumulated than if it was combined optimally with other inputs. In the latter case, however, the accumulation of capital is necessarily spread out over a period of calendar time called the "investment period." Presumably there are optimal combinations of inputs over an optimal investment period that maximizes the present value of benefits from a given capital investment. The spreading out of capital accumulation forced by the importance of own time can, however, only reduce but not eliminate the decline in marginal benefits as more is accumulated.[9]

In the first place, with finite lifetimes, later investments cannot produce returns for as long as earlier ones and, therefore usually have smaller total benefits. This effect is important in societies with heavy adult mortality, but probably is not in the low mortality environment of modern Western societies. For unless fewer than approximately twenty years of working life remained, a reduction of say a year in the number of years remaining does not have much effect on the present value of benefits.[10] In the second place, later investments are less profitable than earlier ones because the present value of net benefits (or profits) are reduced merely by postponing them (and the reduction can be sizable, even for postponements of a few years).[11]

[8]See T. W. Schultz, "Capital Formation by Education," *Journal of Political Economy*, LXVIII (1960), pp. 571–83; or *Human Capital*, op. cit.

[9]The fact that a person's optimal stock of human capital is not immediately reached is often used in explaining the shape of his demand curve for human capital. On the problems in explaining why his optimal stock of nonhuman capital is not immediately reached, see D. W. Jorgenson, "The Theory of Investment Behavior" in *Determinants of Investment Behavior*, Universities-National Bureau Conference Series No. 18 (Columbia University Press for NBER, 1967).

[10]For a demonstration of this see *Human Capital*, op. cit.

[11]See ibid., p. 50.

A third consideration is probably of great importance, although one cannot yet measure its quantitative significance. Since nobody can use his time at any activity without taking with him all of his human capital, the latter enters as an input along with his time in the production of additional capital. Initially, at young ages, the value of the time is small and probably even negative because parents or other baby-sitting services have to be employed if he is not in school, or otherwise investing.[12] As he continues to invest, however, the capital accumulated becomes increasingly valuable, and so does his time.

Other things the same, an increase in the value of time raises the marginal cost of later investments compared to earlier ones since the former use more expensive time. For any given rate of increase in its value as he ages, the costs of later investments are relatively greater, the larger the share of foregone earnings in costs and the smaller the elasticity of substitution between own time and other inputs.[13] One other thing that may not remain the same is the productivity of time: just as a greater amount of human capital is more productive than a lesser amount of capital in the rest of the economy, so too it may be more productive when used to produce additional human capital itself.[14] Marginal costs of later investments would not be greater if the increased productivity of own time was at least as great as its increased value. Because own human capital is carried along with own time, more productive or not, I am inclined to believe that its effect on productivity would be less, at least eventually, than its effect on the cost of own time. If so, the accumulation of human capital would on balance eventually increase later investment costs,[15] and thus decrease the present value of later benefits.

[12] For an attempt to measure the value of such services provided by elementary schools, see B. Weisbrod, "Education and Investment in Human Capital," *Journal of Political Economy*, LXX (Special Supplement, October 1962), pp. 116–17.

[13] This elasticity is relevant because investors may try to economize on their more costly time by substituting other inputs for time. Rough evidence of such substitution in education is found in the tendency for more valuable resources to be used per hour of the time of more advanced than less advanced students. The elasticity probably does not exceed unity however, since the share of foregone earnings in total costs appears to rise with the level of education (see Schultz, op. cit.).

[14] If H measures the stock of human capital embodied in an investor, then the production function in footnote (6) can be expanded to include H, as in $h = f(R,T,H,B)$. The productivity of greater human capital means a positive sign to $\partial h/\partial H$.

[15] Even if the effect on productivity continued to exceed that on the cost of own time, diminishing returns would cause the decrease in investment costs to become smaller

To digress a moment, the presumption that the marginal costs of typical firms are rising[16] is usually rationalized in terms of a limited "entrepreneurial capacity," an input that can only be imperfectly replaced by managers and other hired inputs. "Entrepreneurial capacity" is a construct developed to reconcile competition, linear homogenous production functions and determinate firm sizes, and most writers agree that there are no obvious empirical counterparts.[17] Indeed, the extremely large size achieved by many firms suggests that, frequently at least, entrepreneurial capacity is not very limiting. Persons investing in human capital can be considered "firms" that combine such capital perhaps with other resources to produce earning power. Since "entrepreneurial" time is required to produce human capital, and since the latter is embodied in the entrepreneur, teachers, managers, and other hired resources can only imperfectly substitute for him. Therefore, in this case, "entrepreneurial capacity" is a definite concept, has a clear empirical counterpart, and, as has been indicated, can lead to significantly rising costs, which in turn limits the size of these "firms."

It is the sum of monetary benefits and the monetary equivalent of psychic benefits (which may be negative) from human capital, not just the former alone, that determines the demand curve for capital investment. If one makes the usual assumption of diminishing monetary equivalents, marginal psychic as well as monetary benefits would decline as capital is accumulated. The considerable uncertainty about future benefits also contributes to a negatively inclined demand curve if there is increasing marginal aversion to risk as more capital is accumulated.

SUPPLY CURVES

The supply curves in Figure 1 show the marginal cost of financing, as opposed to producing, an additional unit of capital. The marginal cost of financing can be measured, for simplicity, by the rate of

---

and smaller over time. (For an illustration of this in a model that is quite similar to, although more rigorously developed than, the one presented here, see Y. Ben-Porath, "The Production of Human Capital and the Life Cycle of Earnings" to be published in the *Journal of Political Economy*). On the other hand, the decrease in the present value of benefits that results from a decrease in the number of years remaining would become larger and larger over time.

[16]This presumption can be justified by the observation that usually only firms producing a limited share of the output of an industry manage to survive.

[17]See M. Friedman, *Price Theory* (Aldine Publishing Co., 1962).

interest that must be paid to finance an additional dollar of capital. If the annual repayment required on a "loan" was constant for the remaining period of labor force participation, the marginal rate of interest would simply equal the annual repayment on an additional dollar of funds, adjusted upward for the finiteness of the labor force period.

If the capital market were homogeneous, with no segmentation due to special subsidies or taxes, transaction costs, legal restrictions on lending or borrowing, etc., and if risk were constant, even a large change in the amount of capital used by any person would have a negligible effect on his marginal cost of funds since it would have a negligible effect on the funds available to others. In the actual world, however, the market for human capital is extremely segmented: there are local subsidies to public elementary and high schools, state and federal subsidies to certain undergraduate and graduate students, transaction costs that often make own funds considerably cheaper than borrowed funds, and significant legal limitations on the kind of borrowing that is permitted. The result is that, although certain sources of funds are cheaper than others, the amounts available to any person from the cheaper sources are usually rationed since the total demand for the funds tends to exceed their supply. This means that a person accumulating capital must shift from the cheapest, to the second cheapest, and on eventually to expensive sources. This shift from less to more expensive sources is primarily responsible for the positive inclination of the supply curve of funds even to one person. The rate of increase in each curve tends to be greater the greater the segmentation, since there is then greater diversity in the cost of different sources, and smaller amounts available from each.

The cheapest sources usually are gifts from parents, relatives, foundations and governments that can be used only for investment in human capital. Their cost to investors is nil, and is represented in Figure 1 by the Og segment of the supply curve S that lies along the horizontal axis.[18]

---

[18]Conceptual separation of production costs from financial conditions suggests that direct government and private subsidies to educational institutions and other "firms" producing human capital might be included in the Og segment. When so separated, demand curves incorporate all production costs, not only those borne by investors themselves, supply curves incorporate all subsidies, and the rates of return relate "private" returns to "social" costs (for definitions of "private" and "social" see *Human Capital*, op. cit., Chapter V).

Highly subsidized but not free loans from governments, universities, etc. that also can be used only for investment in human capital are somewhat more expensive: they are represented by the $g'u$ segment of S. Then come the resources of investors themselves, including inheritances and other outright gifts, that could be used elsewhere. Their cost is measured by the foregone opportunities represented by the $u'h$ segment of S. After these funds are exhausted, investors must turn either to commercial loans in the market place or to reductions in their own consumption during the investment period. These funds are usually available only at considerably higher, and somewhat rapidly rising costs: they are represented by the upward sloped segment $h'S$.

As emphasized earlier, the accumulation of human capital is not instantaneous, but is usually spread out over a lengthy investment period. The rate of increase in financing costs, like that in production costs, would generally be less, the more slowly capital is accumulated because, for example, the accumulation of own resources could reduce the need to rely on more expensive sources.[19] The rate of increase in each supply curve also depends, therefore, on the accumulation pattern that is chosen.

EQUILIBRIUM

Since both the stream of benefits and of financing costs depend on the path of capital accumulation, the latter cannot be chosen with respect to either alone. The rational decision is to select a path that maximizes the present value of "profits"; i.e., the present value of the difference between these benefits and costs. With a model as general as the one presented so far, the supply and demand curves shown in Figure 1 would not be uniquely determined nor independent of each other. In order to justify, therefore, uniqueness and independence and to permit a relatively simple analysis of income distribution, it is sufficient to assume that own time and hired inputs are used in fixed proportions to produce human capital, that a unit of hired inputs is available at a given price, and that a unit of own time is also available at a given price (foregone earnings)

[19]Superficially, there are many actual examples of the cost of funds depending on the period or stage of accumulation, such as the special subsidies to students of medicine or advanced physics. Many of these are best treated, however, as examples of a segmented capital market for different kinds of human capital, and are more appropriately discussed in section 3g, where the interaction among different kinds is analyzed.

up to a certain maximum amount, beyond which no time is available at any price. If the analysis of income distribution presented in this essay turns out to be useful, the implications of more general assumptions about the production of human capital should be explored.

With these assumptions, the value of benefits is given by the area under the unique demand curve shown in Figure 1, the value of financing costs by that under the unique supply curve,[20] and the maximum difference is found by investing up to their point of intersection. At that point, marginal benefits equal marginal financing costs, which can be taken to mean that the marginal rate of return equals the marginal rate of interest.

Corresponding to the optimal accumulation path is an optimal investment period. If both the returns on each dollar invested and the repayments on each dollar borrowed were constant for the remaining labor force period, the current value of total profits, which is the difference between total returns and total repayments, would rise throughout the optimal investment period. A peak would be reached at the end, remain constant at that level throughout the labor force period, and then drop to zero.

The earnings actually measured in national income accounts do not purport to represent the profits on human capital. For one thing, the costs of funds are not deducted from returns, regardless of whether they consist of direct interest payments, foregone income, or undesired reductions in consumption. During the investment period, moreover, some and often all the costs of producing human capital are implicitly deducted before reporting earnings.[21] Consequently, measured earnings after the investment period only represent total returns, while during the period it is a hybrid of returns and production costs. I discuss first and most extensively the factors determining the distribution of measured earnings after the investment period,

---

[20]For simplicity, the figures in this essay plot along the vertical axis marginal rates of return and interest on each additional dollar of investment rather than the present or current values of marginal benefits and financing costs. If returns and repayment costs were constant for indefinitely long periods, marginal rates of return and interest would exactly equal the current values of the flow of benefits and financing costs respectively on an additional dollar of investment.

[21]This intermingling of stocks and flows has many implications for age-earnings and age-wealth profiles that have been discussed elsewhere (see *Human Capital*, op. cit., Chapters II, III, and VII).

and only briefly consider the distribution of profits or of measured earnings during this period.

A major assumption of the remainder of this essay is that actual accumulation paths are always the same as optimal paths. Sufficient conditions for this assumption are that all persons are rational[22] and that neither uncertainty nor ignorance prevents them from achieving their aims. Of course, these are strong conditions, and a fuller model would make room for irrationality, uncertainty, discrepancies between actual and "desired" capital stocks, etc. Given, however, our rudimentary knowledge of the forces generating income distributions, it is instructive to determine how far even a simple model takes us. What impresses me about this model are the many insights it appears to provide into the forces generating inequality and skewness in the distribution of earnings and other income. In any case, it can be easily generalized to incorporate many of the considerations neglected, such as uncertainty, or discrepancies between actual and "desired" capital stocks.

[22]Since all persons are very young during much of their investment period, it may seem highly unrealistic to assume that their decisions are rational. Children have their decisions guided, however, as well as partly financed, by their parents, and as long as parents receive some monetary or psychic benefits from an increase in their children's economic well being, parents have an incentive to help children make wise decisions.

C. Human Capital: In Retrospect

5. The Historical Roots of the Concept of Human Capital*

B. F. KIKER

University of South Carolina

In recent years, economists have devoted a great deal of effort to developing and quantifying the concept of "human capital" and to applying it, through the concept of investment in the formation of human capital, to such activities as education, whether academic study or on-the-job training, migration, and medical care.[1] The concept of human capital, however, is by no means new. The object of this paper is to review some of the past literature, in order primarily to determine which authors treated human beings as capital, their motives for doing so, and their procedures for valuing man as capital. Although this essay is not exhaustive, it will be shown, in essence, that the concept of human capital was somewhat prominent in economic thinking until Marshall discarded the notion as "unrealistic."

Economists who considered human beings or their skills as capital include such well-known names in the history of economic thought as Petty, Smith, Say, Senior, List, von Thünen, Roscher, Bagehot, Ernst Engel, Sidgwick, Walras, and Fisher. Basically, two methods have been used to estimate the value of human beings: the cost-of-production and the capitalized-earnings procedures. The former procedure consists of estimating the real costs (usually net of maintenance) incurred in "producing" a human being; the latter consists of estimating the present value of an individual's future income stream (either net or gross of maintenance). Several motives for treating human beings as capital and valuing them in money terms have been found: (1) to demonstrate the power of a nation; (2) to determine the economic

*Reprinted from "The Historical Roots of the Concept of Human Capital," *Journal of Political Economy*, LXXIV (October, 1966). Copyright by The University of Chicago Press.

[1] See, for example: Schultz (1959, 1961a, 1961b, 1962); Weisbrod (1961); Machlup (1962); Mushkin (1962); Becker (1964).

effects of education, health investment, and migration; (3) to propose tax schemes believed to be more equitable than existing ones; (4) to determine the total cost of war; (5) to awaken the public to the need for life and health conservation and the significance of the economic life of an individual to his family and country; and (6) to aid courts and compensation boards in making fair decisions in cases dealing with compensation for personal injury and death.

I

Statisticians and actuaries have developed relatively scientific procedures for estimating the money (or capital) values of either a human being as such or the population of a nation. Their methods, which are essentially a cost-of-production approach or some form of a capitalized-earnings approach, are examined in this section, as are variations in the approaches.

One of the first attempts to estimate the money value of a human being was made around 1691 by Sir William Petty. Labor to him was the "father of wealth." It must therefore be included in any estimate of national wealth. This led Petty to place a money value on laborers. Petty's interest in the monetary evaluation of human beings developed out of his interest in public finance (Hull, 1899, I, 589–95). Soon, however, he used the notion of human capital in attempts to demonstrate the power of England (Hull, 1899, I, 505–13; II, 192), the economic effects of migration (Hull, 1899, I, 192), the money value of human life destroyed in war (Hull, 1899, I, 152), and the monetary loss to a nation resulting from deaths (Hull, 1899, I, 108–10). Petty estimated the value of the stock of human capital by capitalizing the wage bill to perpetuity, at the market interest rate; the wage bill he determined by deducting property income from national income (Hull, 1899, I, 108).[2]

Petty's method makes no allowance for the cost of maintenance of workers before capitalization.[3] In spite of this limitation, his proce-

[2]Petty's evaluation of human beings in money terms was bitterly satirized by Dean Swift in his "A Modest Proposal for Preventing the Children of Poor People from Being a Burden to Their Parents or the Country."

[3]Perhaps, however, no great error is committed if maintenance costs are not considered when this approach is taken. Almost three hundred years later Mushkin and Weisbrod (1963, p. 595) assert: "Maintenance of physical capital prolongs its life, and thereby reduces annual depreciation. The result is that the reported stock of physical capital net of depreciation is larger than it would be if maintenance expenditures were lower. If depreciation were reduced by the exact amount of maintenance expenditures this

dure gives a close approximation for determining the capital value of a nation. It is wholly inadequate, however, when used for purposes where human-capital values by age, sex, and economic status are needed, as in several of the cases mentioned above.

The first truly scientific procedure and the one followed today by many economists and others for finding the capital or money value of a human being was devised in 1853 by William Farr. Like Petty's, Farr's interest in the evaluation of human capital developed out of his interest in public finance. He advocated the substitution for the existing English income tax system of a property tax that would include property consisting of the capitalized value of earning capacity. His procedure for estimating the latter was to calculate the present value of an individual's net future earnings (future earnings minus personal living expenses), allowance being made for deaths in accordance with a life table (Farr, 1853). Farr's work suggests a way in which "human capital" can be a misleading analogy. He suggested that since human beings are productive they should be regarded and taxed as capital. Since this would oblige people to pay tax on wealth that they do not have in hand, it could lead to absurd results.[4] Farr's method was almost identical with the method utilized some eighty years later by Louis Dublin and Alfred Lotka (1930). Their procedure is discussed below.

Ernst Engel, writing around 1883, preferred a cost-of-production procedure for estimating the monetary value of human beings. Although he discussed Petty's approach and modified it somewhat to allow for the limited number of years a man is employed, he felt that the yield value of certain human beings (for example, a Goethe, Newton or Benjamin Franklin) could not be determined. Since, however, their rearing was a cost to their parents, it might be estimated and taken as a measure of their monetary value to society. This monetary value at age x may be determined from a formula:

$$C_x = c_0\{1 + x + k[x(x+1)/2]\},$$

where C_x is the total cost of producing a human being (neglecting interest, depreciation, and maintenance) through age x, c_0 denotes

---

would be equivalent to counting the maintenance as investment. Thus the treatment of maintenance of human and non-human capital may be reasonably consistent after all."

[4] Imagine a tax structure in which Elizabeth Taylor's tax bill at age sixteen is the same function of her capitalized expected earnings as a landlord's tax bill is of his capitalized expected earnings.

costs incurred up to the point of birth, and k is the annual percentage increase in cost. The constant, c_0, was empirically found by Engel to be 100, 200, and 300 marks for the lower, middle, and upper German social classes, respectively. He observed k to be 0.1. This formula applies, however, only when $x \leqq 26$. After age twenty-six the individual was assumed by Engel to be "fully produced" (Engel, 1883, pp. 15–20, 58–78; Sencini, 1908, pp. 481–86).[5]

There is, however, no simple and necessary relationship between the cost of producing an item and its economic value. This is especially true for human beings, whose cost of production is not undertaken primarily with a view to economic gain. Although I see very little use for the cost-of-production procedure in evaluating human beings as such, a modification of Engel's approach is useful in determining the components, such as education and health-service capital, of a human-capital value. This is so simply because it is less difficult to estimate the direct (and opportunity, if appropriate) cost incurred in forming a particular component of human-capital value than to attribute future earning differentials to specific items such as education and health services.

Theodor Wittstein in 1867 defined human beings as capital goods and employed a variation of both Farr's capitalized-earnings and Engel's cost-of-production approaches to value human capital. Wittstein's interest in the concept of human capital arose from a desire to determine a guide to be used as a basis for claims for compensation from loss of life. Since he assumed that an individual's lifetime earnings are equal to his lifetime maintenance cost plus education, the approaches yield the same estimates—which inevitably come out to be zero at birth. His procedure may be summarized in the following formulas:

$$C_{(n)} = aR_{(0)}\frac{L_{(0)}}{L_{(n)}}r^n - aR_{(n)},$$

$$C_{(n)} = XR_{(N)}\frac{L_{(N)}}{L_{(n)}}p^{N-n} - aR_{(n)},$$

where a is annual consumption expenditures including education for

---

[5] A French economist of the early eighteenth century, Richard Cantillon, discussed the cost of rearing a child (both free and slave) to working age. He estimated this cost to be equal to twice the value of the land needed to sustain an adult male. This formula applied to both slaves and freemen, since "free peasants . . . will probably maintain them[selves] upon a better foot than slaves according to the custom of the place he lives in" and will require, therefore, more land (Cantillon, 1959, p. 35).

an average German male in a particular occupation, $r = (1 + i)$, where i is the market interest rate; $p = 1/r$; $L_{(n)}$ is the number of men living at age n in a life table; $R_{(n)}$ is the value at age n of a 1-thaler annuity (for a given r and purchased at birth); X is the value of the future output of an average man in a particular occupation; N is the age at which this man enters the labor force (Wittstein, 1867).

Wittstein (1867, p. 50) assumed for simplicity that a and X are constant over the life of an individual. He asserted, moreover, that the former equation (which is based on past values) for valuing a human being in money terms should be used when $N > n$ but that when $N < n$ the latter equation (which is based upon expected values) could be utilized more easily (Wittstein, 1867, p. 53). Although Wittstein's analysis is interesting, his basic postulate that lifetime earnings and lifetime maintenance cost are equal is unjustified. Moreover, any combination of the capitalized-earnings and cost-of-production methods is dangerous, owing to the possibility of duplication of values.

Dublin and Lotka were in the life-insurance business. They considered that calculations of human values could be useful in ascertaining how much life insurance a man should carry. Such calculations might also be useful in estimating the economic costs of preventable disease and premature death (Dublin and Lotka, 1930, Preface). The result of their calculations was a formula:

$$V_0 = \sum_{x=0}^{\infty} v^x P_x(y_x E_x - c_x),$$

where V_0 is the value of the individual at birth; $v^x = (1 + i)^{-x}$ is the present value of \$1.00 due x years later; P_x is the probability at birth of an individual living to age x; y_x is yearly earnings per individual from age x to $x + 1$; E_x is the proportion of individuals employed from age x to $x + 1$ (Farr had assumed full employment); c_x is the cost of living for an individual from age x to $x + 1$. To find the money value of an individual at a particular age, a, the formula may be modified (Dublin and Lotka, 1930, p. 167) to

$$V_a = \frac{P_0}{P_a}\left[\sum_{x=a}^{\infty} v^{x-a} P_x(y_x E_x - c_x)\right].$$

This method of capitalizing an individual's earnings, minus his consumption or maintenance, gives a useful estimate for some purposes. It estimates, for example, the economic value of the man to his family — which was Dublin and Lotka's purpose. If the wage earner is

55

killed, his family is impoverished by the amount of his contribution to them — which, presumably, is his income less his maintenance. There is considerable question, however, as to the validity of such an approach when the value of a human being to himself or in society is sought. To make estimates for these purposes, the capitalized-gross-earnings procedure (including living expenses) should be used.

The cost of producing (rearing) an individual, C, up to age a, according to Dublin and Lotka, is

$$C_a = \frac{1}{P_a}\left[\sum_{x=0}^{a-1} v^{x-a}P_x(c_x - y_xE_x)\right],$$

which may be simplified to

$$C_a = V_a - \frac{1}{P_a v^a}V_0.$$

Hence, the cost of producing an individual up to age a is equal to the difference between his value at age a and his value at birth, multiplied by $(1+i)^a/P_a$ (Dublin and Lotka, 1930, p. 168). This is, of course, a sophisticated version of Engel's approach.

Dublin, somewhat earlier, had estimated the capital value of the population of the United States in 1922 to be *five* times the stock of material wealth. The basis of this estimate is unknown and the estimate itself not entirely plausible, though it has been often quoted. His estimate of the size of this stock led him to advocate a more liberal expenditure policy for maintaining it (Dublin, 1928).

The works of Farr and Dublin and Lotka should be starting points for anyone interested in estimating either human-capital values or their components. Dublin and Lotka's discussion of the capitalized-earnings approach (either net or gross of living expenses) is clear, concise, and one of the best expositions available. Although there are obvious conceptual difficulties associated with this approach, it gives the most accurate results if the data necessary for measurement are available.

Allowances for depreciation are not taken into account when the cost-of-production approach to determine human-capital value is utilized. The capitalized-earnings approach, however, implicitly includes depreciation. Since a young man, *ceteris paribus*, is expected to be productive over a longer period than an older cohort, his capital value would be greater.

Maintenance costs were neglected by Petty and Engel. They were, however, considered to be equal to personal living expenses by Farr, Wittstein, and Dublin and Lotka. This was a dubious procedure then, particularly at the date Dublin and Lotka published, and would be wrong in developed countries today. Maintenance costs have been neglected by present-day economists who have advocated the human-capital concept. Some of these costs, however, are incurred during the investment period; a portion of them are continuous throughout the life of the human capital.[6]

II

From time to time throughout the history of economic thought, economists have included human beings, or their acquired abilities and skills, as a component of capital. Although some of them attempted to estimate the value of this capital—on both the microeconomic and the macroeconomic levels—and to employ these estimates for a specific purpose (for example, to estimate the total economic losses resulting from war), others have merely included human beings, or their acquired abilities and skills, in their definition of capital and recognized the importance of investment in human beings as a means of increasing their productivity. The latter group, generally, neither attempted an evaluation of human capital nor employed the concept for any specific purpose.[7] Most of these economists held that human beings should be included in the concept of capital for three reasons: (1) the cost of rearing and educating human beings is a real cost; (2) the product of their labor adds to the national wealth; (3) an expenditure on a human being that increases this product will, *ceteris paribus*, increase national wealth.

Although he did not specifically define the term "capital," Adam Smith included in his category of fixed capital the skills and useful abilities of human beings. The skill of a man, he said, may be regarded as a machine that has a genuine cost and returns a profit (Smith, 1937, pp. 101, 259–66). Jean Baptiste Say (1821, pp. 92–94) asserted likewise that since skills and abilities are acquired at a cost and tend to increase worker productivity they should be regarded as

[6]For other work similar to that discussed in this section see: Lüdtge (1873a, 1873b), Lindheim (1909), and Meyer (1930–32).

[7]There are, however, a few exceptions: List used the notion in demonstrating the importance of protectionism, and von Thünen advocated utilizing the notion as an aid in dealing out social justice. Marshall, moreover, offered some estimates of human-capital values.

capital. This was also the contention of John Stuart Mill (1909, p. 47), William Roscher (1878, p. 151), Walter Bagehot (1953, pp. 55–56), and, at the microeconomic level, Henry Sidgwick (1901, pp. 132–34). According to W. Stark, Jeremy Bentham's most interesting passage, from the point of view of economic theory, was one in which he stated that "labour is distinguished into mere physical exertion and the skill or mental power displayed in the exercise of the bodily act" (Stark, 1952, p. 53).

To Friedrich List, skills and acquired abilities of human beings, which are largely an inheritance from the past and the result of past labor and self-restraint, were the most important components of a nation's stock of capital. He asserted that, in both production and distribution, the contribution of this human capital to output must be considered (List, 1928, pp. 108–18).

These economists, who basically define capital as "produced means of production," do not explicitly include the human beings as capital. J. S. Mill (1909, p. 47) asserted: "The human being himself I do not class as wealth. He is the purpose for which wealth exists. But his acquired capacities, which exist only as a means, and have been called into existence by labor, fall rightly, as it seems to me, within that designation." Their reason for not explicitly including the man himself may be found in their interest in distribution and production. Sidgwick (1901, p. 134) pointed out: "We have to consider it [conventional capital] as a joint factor with labour in production, by the aid of which the labourers . . . are enabled to produce more than they would otherwise do; and in order to keep this view of it clear, we have to maintain the distinction between capital and labourers."

In contrast, J. R. McCulloch clearly defined the human being as such as capital: "Instead of understanding by capital all that portion of the produce of industry extrinsic to man, which may be made applicable to his support, and to the facilitating of production, there does not seem to be any good reason why man himself should not, and very many why he should be considered as forming a part of the national capital" (McCulloch, 1870, p. 66; see pp. 57, 67). He said, moreover, that there is a close analogy between conventional and human capital. An investment in a human being should yield a rate of return consistent with other investments, plus a normal rate of return determined by the market interest rate, during the probable lifetime of the individual (McCulloch, 1870, p. 66).

Nassau Senior suggested that human beings can usefully be treated as capital. In most of his discussion of the topic he referred to skills and acquired abilities and not to man himself (Senior, 1939, pp. 68–69, 204–6). On occasion, however, he treated the human being himself as capital with a maintenance cost – incurred with the expectation of obtaining a future yield (Senior, 1939, pp. 68–69). He asserted that there is little difference between talking about the value of a slave and about the value of a free man. The principal difference is that the free man sells himself for a certain period of time and only to a certain extent, whereas the slave is sold for his lifetime (Senior, 1939, p. 10).

Several current writers, dealing with investment in education, maintain that this investment is undertaken primarily for future return. It is interesting to compare this view to that of Senior (1939, pp. 205–6), who considered the higher education of a gentleman's son: "Neither the labour which the boy undergoes, nor the expense borne by his father, is incurred principally in order to obtain future profit. The boy works under the stimulus of immediate punishment. It never occurs to the father that . . . he is engaging in a speculation which is likely to be unprofitable. To witness a son's daily improvement is, with all well-disposed men . . . one of the sources of immediate gratification. The expense incurred for that purpose is as much repaid by immediate enjoyment as that which is incurred to obtain the most transitory pleasures. It is true that a further object may also be obtained but the immediate motive is ample."

Hence, not all education is undertaken with a view to future yields. It is, however, capital, and it is the "quantity and diffusion of this capital" that determine the wealth of a nation. Senior (1939, pp. 134–35) asserted, moreover, that the value of the stock of England's human capital exceeded the value of the stock of all Great Britain's "material capital."

Henry D. Macleod considered productive human beings as fixed capital. In his view, however, if they are not productive they do not enter economic analysis (Macleod, 1881, pp. 134, 205–6, 213). This view contrasted sharply with that of Léon Walras, who included all human beings in the concept of capital. And the value, or price, of these human beings, Walras (1954, pp. 40, 214–16, 271) said, is determined like that of any other capital good. He, moreover, was aware of the inner reluctance of economists to treat human beings as capital. He argued, however, that in pure theory "it is proper to abstract completely from considerations of justice and practical expediency" and to regard human beings "exclusively from the point of view of value in exchange" (Walras, 1954, p. 216).

Johann H. von Thünen also recognized this reluctance to evaluate human beings. But from this reluctance, he said, "stems lack of clarity and confusion of concepts on one of the most important points of political economy" (von Thünen, 1875, p. 5). "Moreover, it may be proved that freedom and dignity of man may be successfully preserved, even if he is subject to the laws of capital" (von Thünen, 1875, p. 5). Von Thünen asserted that many social injustices might be eliminated if expenditures that increase labor productivity were treated within the human-capital analytical framework. The capital value of these expenditures, moreover, should be included as a component of the aggregate capital stock (von Thünen, 1875, pp. 1–10). While many present-day writers attribute the absence of the notion of human capital from the mainstream of economic thought to sentimentalism (Schultz, 1959, p. 110), it is interesting to note that here (and in a number of other cases in the past) the presence of the idea was due to sentimentalism.

Although Alfred Marshall admitted that an estimate of the capital value of a man might be useful and discussed clearly the capitalized-net-earnings approach to human-capital evaluation (consumption being deducted from earnings before capitalizing), he disregarded the notion as "unrealistic," since human beings are not marketable (Marshall, 1959, pp. 469–70, 705–6).

Human beings are included in Irving Fisher's definition of capital. Capital, he asserted, is a "useful appropriated material object," and since human beings have these characteristics, consistency requires that they be included in the concept of capital (Fisher, 1897, pp. 201–2; 1927, pp. 5, 51–52, 68; 1965, pp. 12–13). Moreover, the skill of an individual is not capital in addition to the individual himself. It is, Fisher (1927, p. 9) said, the skilled individual who should be placed in the category of capital.

This brings up the interesting question: Are the value of skills and useful abilities and the value of an individual possessing them the same? Edward Denison (1964, p. 91) suggests that to speak of technological progress embodied in physical capital is simply to refer to changes in the quality of capital goods. An analogy may be made regarding human beings. Skills and acquired abilities are embodied in the human being and presumably increase his quality as a producing unit. Since these skills and abilities acquired by an individual are inalienable, it is questionable whether one should speak of them alone as capital; it is, if this view is taken, the skilled individual who is the capital. It has been suggested, however, that the answer to the question posed above depends upon the definition of value. If value is defined as "net benefit" to society where the excess of total output over total consumption determines net benefit, the addition of a skill or useful ability would increase output, whereas the addition of an individual increases not only output but also consumption. The value of a skill and a useful ability and the value of an individual, both measured by the amount of net benefit added, in this case might certainly be different (Dublin and Lotka, 1930, p. 4). Whether we call skills and acquired abilities only, or the acquirer of them, capital is relatively unimportant. The distinction, however, between skills and acquired abilities and the person is in any event important, for example, for purposes of taxation.

T. W. Schultz (1961*b*, p. 3) has pointed out that, "among the few [economists] who have looked upon human beings as capital, there are three distinguished names . . . Adam Smith . . . von Thünen . . . and Irving Fisher." Schultz (1959, p. 110) has asserted also that "the mainstream of modern economics has bypassed undertaking any systematic analysis of human wealth." It would be interesting to know the time period denoted by Schultz's use of the word "modern." Presumably, he means "current." If, however, another definition of "modern" were adopted (it has been said that modern economics began with Sir William Petty), his comment would be questionable.

III

As suggested above, the concept of human capital has been used to demonstrate the magnitude and economic importance of the stock of human resources. Estimates of the value of a nation's human wealth were thought to give some insight into the economic power of a nation.

While attempting to estimate the stock of human, or "living," capital in the United Kingdom in 1891, J. Shield Nicholson (1891) capitalized the portion of national income that he assumed to be derived from "living" capital.[8] To do so he attempted to find the capital value of such things as the wage bill, the earnings of management, the earn-

---

[8]This article appears as chapter v in Nicholson (1896). The central idea of these works (that is, recognizing human beings as capital and estimating their money value) is found also in Nicholson (1892).

ings of capitalists, the earnings of salaried government officials, and "domesticated humanity" (that is, the people of a nation "as 'things in themselves,' or rather superior domestic animals reared for their affectionate disposition and intellectual and moral activities") (Nicholson, 1896, pp. 112–14). He, unfortunately, included the latter category because it has a cost of maintenance, and he estimated its value by assuming that, since people spend 10 percent of their income on their own maintenance and 10 percent on rent, it is proper to value an individual as "a thing in itself" as equal in value to the house he occupies (Nicholson, 1896, p. 109). There is, of course, no simple relationship between the cost of production (or maintenance) of a good and its monetary value. Any attempt, moreover, to estimate in money terms the sentimental value of a human being "appears to be trifling with a serious subject."[9]

Nicholson capitalized the wage bill to determine the capital value of the "wage earner," and he added this to the other values he estimated, including the value of "domesticated humanity." Since the cost of production of wage earners appears in the estimate of the value of "domesticated humanity" and also in the estimate of the capitalized value of their earnings, there is a duplication of values, which seems to be historically characteristic of combinations of the cost-of-production and capitalized-earnings approaches. He concluded by asserting that the value of the stock of "living" capital of the United Kingdom was about *five* times the value of the stock of conventional capital (Nicholson, 1896, p. 114).

In his attempt to estimate the value of the stock of capital in France around 1900, Alfred de Foville asserted that any procedure for estimating the value of the stock of human capital by capitalizing the earnings before deducting consumption expenditures is incorrect. It is the error in this procedure, he averred, that has led writers to assert that the value of the stock of human capital is greater than the value of conventional capital. By deducting consumption expenditures (maintenance) from earnings and then applying Petty's method, he estimated the value of the stock of human capital in France. For some purposes, this approach is an improvement over Petty's, and it improves the analogy between the valuations of the aggregate stocks of human and conventional capital. He cautioned, however, that the

---

[9]This phrase was borrowed from Longfield (1931, pp. 201–2). He, however, was referring to estimating the cost of producing common laborers.

whole notion of human capital is dubious. How can the capital value of a Goethe, a Newton, or a Jeanne d'Arc be determined? he asked (De Foville, 1905).[10]

A French actuary, A. Barriol, in 1908 utilized Farr's capitalized-earnings procedure, although he did not deduct maintenance from earnings, to determine the "social value" of a man in France. He defined "social value" as the amount of his earnings that an individual restores to society. Since he implicitly assumed that lifetime consumption equals lifetime earnings, the "social value" of an individual depends upon his total earnings. He attempted to estimate this value by age groups by assuming certain earnings scales and capitalizing them, allowance being made for deaths in accordance with a mortality table (Barriol, 1910).

He used these values to attempt to estimate the total and per capita value of the stock of human capital in several countries. The French values were multiplied by the population in the various age groups of the particular country. These values were then summed and divided by the total population figure to obtain a weighted per capita average value of a citizen of the country in question. Since the countries he considered had different levels of economic development and therefore different levels of wages, he applied a coefficient of increase or reduction to his estimates to compensate for the difference. He recognized, moreover, that the values obtained were too high, since he had assumed the female to earn as much as the male. He adjusted for this by multiplying his estimates by a "reduction coefficient." Although his estimates of the capital (or social) value of a human being were not definitive, he concluded that they might offer some insight into the economic power of nations (Barriol, 1911).

Barriol's procedure for adjusting his figures is interesting but the results obviously dubious. His adjusted estimates, as will be pointed out subsequently, were used as a basis for computation by other writers.

Human capital, according to S. S. Huebner (1914), should receive the same scientific treatment that is given to conventional capital. This can be done, he said, by "capitalizing human life values with bonds to give them perpetuity as a working force and fluidity as a

[10]This, of course, is the same question asked by Engel. Engel's answer was that, although their cost of production could be estimated, it was impossible to determine their capitalized yield to society.

source of credit, of subjecting them to the principles of depreciation, and of using the sinking-fund method to assure realization of the contemplated object whenever man has a future business or family obligation to fulfill that involves the hazard of uncertainty of the duration of the working life" (Huebner, 1914, pp. 18–19). This scientific treatment of human values is justified, he said, because of their importance in economic affairs.

In general equilibrium theory, with short-term contracts postulated, entrepreneurs have little incentive to invest in the work force. Today, however, with long-run growth widely recognized as a dominant factor in business planning, Huebner's comment is particularly relevant. Entrepreneurs are becoming increasingly cognizant of the importance of investments that become an integral part of man, and such awareness is leading to deliberate investment in human beings (see Becker, 1962). Hence, a symmetrical treatment of the work force and conventional capital may be necessary.

Huebner (1914, pp. 18–19) estimated the value of the stock of human capital in the United States around 1914–capitalized at the market interest rate and allowing for deaths in accordance with a mortality table—to be *six* to *eight* times the value of the stock of the nation's conventional capital.

Edward A. Woods and Clarence B. Metzger employed five procedures to obtain five different estimates of the stock of human capital in the United States in 1920. They did this to show the very large monetary value and importance of the nation's population and "to awaken a sluggish public . . . by appealing to its material interest" to the needs of conserving human life (Woods and Metzger, 1927, p. 32).

Woods and Metzger's (1927, p. 101) first estimate of the value of the 1920 stock of human capital was based upon governmental suggestions of life insurance for workers. Their second method of valuing the stock of human capital was to base its value upon the value of property, that is, to approximate the former by applying a multiplier to the latter (Woods and Metzger, 1927, pp. 104–5). They applied several multipliers but concluded that "the multiple *five* seems to be the most accurate one to express life values to the national wealth" (Woods and Metzger, 1927, p. 106). Neither of these procedures, however, is scientifically valid.

Their third estimate employed the capitalized-national-income and the capitalized-wage-bill approaches. In the former case they capitalized the 1920 national income (Woods and Metzger, 1927, p. 108).

This estimate made the unrealistic assumption that all national income is the product of labor. In the latter case, following Petty, they capitalized the wage bill to obtain an estimate of the value of the human-capital stock (Woods and Metzger, 1927, pp. 110–11). The difficulty here is the separation of returns to conventional capital from those to labor. Moreover, they assumed that labor earnings were constant through time. Neither approach considers depreciation or maintenance. Both procedures imply that the "value of American society" goes on indefinitely (Woods and Metzger, 1927, p. 111).

The fourth estimate employed the familiar Farr-type capitalized-earnings approach. They estimated both gross and net values for the value of the 1920 stock of human capital. Unlike Farr, however, they assumed constant earnings and consumption expenditures in all age groups (Woods and Metzger, 1927, pp. 114–39).

Woods and Metzger realized that symmetry of treatment as between human and conventional capital is achieved only if depreciation, maintenance, and obsolescence are considered. Maintenance is accounted for when consumption expenditures are deducted from earnings and depreciation and obsolescence are allowed for by the manner in which average earnings are estimated: "This factor [depreciation and obsolescence] is taken into consideration in the make-up of the 'average yearly wage' for workers, which included the lower wages of old workers along with the higher ones of the more efficient producers. The former naturally receive less salary and wages than workers in the prime of life, health, and efficiency but the wages of the latter are diluted in the 'average' by the lower wages of the former group plus those of the very young, untrained workers" (Woods and Metzger, 1927, p. 122).

To make their fifth estimate of the value of the stock of human capital, Woods and Metzger (1927, p. 142) applied the per capita human-capital estimates of some Americans who had previously valued human beings to the 1920 population data. Several of these estimates, however, were limited to adult male values at specific ages for workers or were otherwise limited in scope.

They concluded that the monetary value of the population is a country's greatest asset, and that it is "important that public-spirited citizens and students of social welfare strongly support those movements conducive to the conservation of human life and the enjoyment of as perfect health as possible, so that the lives of productive individuals might be further lengthened and thereby add to the wealth of society" (Woods and Metzger, 1927, p. 162). This conclusion contrasts sharply with that of one present-day economist, who argues that the point has now been reached in developed countries where further increases in health expenditures will be "health-producing but not wealth-producing" and therefore, in an economic sense, unproductive (Lees, 1962). Although I view the latter argument as doubtful, definitive judgment cannot be reached until the quality of our information on this subject has improved. As will be pointed out below, many writers of the early twentieth century held Woods and Metzger's view.

IV

Economists and statisticians have utilized the human-capital concept to estimate the total economic losses to combatants resulting from war. The presumption is that a man's capitalized-earnings stream is capital and that his death or disability reduces the stock of wealth.

In attempting to estimate the total cost to the combatants of the Franco-German War, Sir Robert Giffen used what was essentially Petty's method of valuing in money terms the lives destroyed in the war. He emphasized, however, that his estimates were crude and imperfect and that the loss of human life was not amenable to monetary evaluation. Hence, he omitted it from his estimate of the total cost of the war (Giffen, 1880, pp. 29–31, 76).

Several writers utilized Barriol's estimates of the capital value of a man in an attempt to estimate the money value of human life destroyed as the result of World War I (Guyot, 1914; Crammond, 1915; Bogart, 1919, pp. 274–77). Man is capital, Yves Guyot (1914, pp. 1193–98) said, and society should be interested in loss of life not only for humanitarian but also for economic reasons. Although Ernest Bogart (1919, p. 274) asserted that an estimate of the monetary value of human lives destroyed in war is "a procedure of doubtful statistical propriety," he felt that only a monetary value could convey to the mind the enormous economic importance of these human lives destroyed.

These writers erred, however, in taking Barriol's adjusted estimates of the capital value of an average individual in the population to apply to the casualties of male combatants mainly of military age, particularly when the original unadjusted values were available. Bogart recognized the error. He said, however, that "it is evident from the fact that the estimates are low that the figures err on the side of underestimation rather than exaggeration, and that no grave error will be committed in using them" (Bogart, 1919, p. 275).

William S. Rossiter questioned the significance of including the capital value of life destroyed in estimates of the economic costs of war. The only case in which an estimate of human capital destroyed by war would have any significance, he said, would be that in which the value of the total stock of a nation's human capital had been computed and included in national wealth estimates. Then the loss resulting from war might be meaningfully compared with this estimate. With this in mind, he used Barriol's estimates to estimate the value of human life within the active male age group in the population of the nations at war in World War I (Rossiter, 1919).

Harold Boag (1916, p. 7) in 1916 considered the question of whether it is "correct to include in any estimates of the cost of war the diminution of capital due to loss of human life." He concluded that it is correct since there is a close analogy between "material and personal" capital (Boag, 1916, p. 9). Boag, moreover, enunciated several important points pertinent to human-capital evaluation: the method of evaluation should depend upon the purpose for which the estimates are to be used; care should be taken to avoid counting an item as both human and conventional capital; and the interdependence of the values of conventional and human capital should be kept in mind (Boag, 1916, p. 10).

Boag (1916, pp. 16–17) pointed out that the capitalized-earnings approach to human-capital evaluation is preferable since it attempts to value material things, while the cost-of-production approach may include expenditures on the individual apart from those that increase his earning power. And the "gross" concept is preferred when valuing monetary losses resulting from war: "In calculations of material loss, the loss of income is usually compared with the total national income and not with the national savings and, therefore, it is often better to arrive at a capitalized value of the diminution of gross income instead of the surplus income" (Boag, 1916, p. 14). Although Senior had previously suggested it, Boag was the first to point out explicitly one of the difficulties associated with the cost-of-production approach to human-capital evaluation: "It is impossible to determine how much of the cost of education, maintenance, etc., is strictly necessary to produce an income-earner, as distinct from those capacities for 'love, joy and admiration,' which may not be incidental to the production of material wealth" (Boag, 1916, p. 17). It has been suggested recently that the inseparability of consumption and investment makes the entire analysis of human (education) capital dubious (Shaffer, 1961, p. 1027). T. W. Schultz (1961c, p. 1035) correctly points out, however, that, although a wholly satisfactory empirical method for dealing with the consumption-investment dichotomy has not been found, the economic logic for allocating (education) expenditures between consumption and investment is clear.

J. M. Clark, in a discussion of the costs of World War I to the American people, included the monetary value of human life destroyed in the war and set forth a modified Farr-type capitalized-net-earnings procedure for computing the capital values. In order to determine the loss in human capital to dependents resulting from the war, Clark constructed an "imaginary army" which represented the characteristics (age and number of dependents) of the actual losses. He then multiplied human-capital values by age by the estimated corresponding numbers of losses so as to obtain the total value of human capital destroyed in the war (Clark, 1931).

V

The human-capital analytical framework has been employed in the past for some of the same purposes for which it is currently being used, namely, to demonstrate the economic profitability of human migration, health investment, premature-death prevention, and education.

An interesting discussion occurred around the end of the nineteenth century regarding the monetary value of immigration to the United States. There was general agreement that immigration was economically profitable to the United States and that the subject fitted properly within the human-capital analytical framework. There was, however, some question as to the degree of profitability and the procedure for calculating an immigrant's monetary value.

Friedrich Kapp utilized Engel's cost-of-production procedure which, it will be recalled, neglects depreciation and maintenance, to estimate the capital value of an immigrant arriving in the United States. He concluded that if the immigration trend continued the country would gain almost a million dollars a day in the value of its human capital (Kapp, 1870). Charles L. Brace criticized both Kapp's procedure for valuing immigrants and his estimates of their value.[11] He argued correctly that the capital value of an object is not determined solely by its cost of production but also by the demand for it. Hence, he said, each immigrant is worth to the country the capitalized difference between his contribution to output and his maintenance: "Each laborer's average cost to his employer is, say $20 per month and 'keep,' or about $400 per annum. It is believed that an ordinary profit on common labor upon a farm is from 15 to $18\frac{3}{4}$ percent. This would leave the gain to the country from $60 to $75 annually. This, at seven percent interest, would represent the capital value . . . about $1,000 or $1,100 for an average male laborer" (Kapp, 1870, p. 149).

Richmond Mayo-Smith, in 1895, followed Brace in criticizing Kapp's procedure for the monetary evaluation of immigrants. An immigrant who has ability and finds an opportunity to use it, Mayo-Smith said, has a monetary value to the country which he enters whatever the cost of his production. He furthermore considered the cost of rearing a child as a consumption expenditure. Although Mayo-Smith explicitly excluded human beings from the concept of capital—on the basis of the ownership criterion for defining capital—he clearly enunciated Farr's capitalized-net-earnings approach as the means for estimating their "economic" value. There is, however, a fallacy in this procedure, Mayo-Smith asserted, because the capitalized value of an immigrant's future earnings depends on his having an opportunity to earn them. Hence, he must secure employment upon his arrival. He must, moreover, secure it without displacing another worker. Otherwise, the stock of human wealth in the receiving country will not have increased (Mayo-Smith, 1901).[12]

In an article written in 1904, Miles M. Dawson proposed the use of actuarial principles for human-capital evaluation. He asserted correctly that the methods used by courts for determining compensation to others for the pecuniary injuries resulting from a death where another party is liable are unscientific. Actuarial science, utilizing the capitalized-net-earnings approach to human-capital evaluation, he said, furnishes the means of computing the monetary value of life

[11]The relevant part of Brace's criticism, which appeared in an article in the New York *Tribune,* is quoted by Kapp (1870, pp. 147–49).

[12]Similar discussions regarding the monetary, or capital, value of immigrants to other countries are now taking place. See, for example, Abraham-Frois (1964).

destroyed—given the age, net earnings, and general health of the decedent (Dawson, 1904). Although the human-capital concept is now being used on a small scale for such purposes, the concept should be exceedingly useful and likely to be more widely utilized.

Several works appeared in the first quarter of the twentieth century in which the authors utilized the human-capital analytical framework to attempt to ascertain monetary losses resulting from preventable illness and death (Fisher, 1908; Forsyth, 1914–15; Crum, 1919; Fisk, 1921). Their hypothesis was that illness and death involved a loss in human wealth and that a saving could be effected by preventing or postponing some of the preventable illnesses and deaths that occurred. To determine this saving, Irving Fisher suggested that Farr's capitalized-net-earnings approach be used to estimate the value of human beings. He estimated the money value of an average American by adjusting Farr's estimates to correct for the higher average earnings in the United States. He then used the age distribution of deaths and the "percentages of preventability" to estimate the average capital value of lives sacrificed by preventable deaths in 1907. The value of an average American multiplied by the 1907 U.S. population, Fisher said, gives a minimum estimate of the value of the stock of human capital existing in that year. This value, he asserted, greatly exceeded all other wealth (Fisher, 1908, pp. 739–41). There is, however, a serious error in Fisher's analysis. By substituting only average earnings of an American for average earnings of an Englishman in Farr's computations, Fisher implicitly assumed that maintenance costs were constant over time and equal in the two countries.[13]

Theoretically, since investments in health services increase the labor supply by reducing mortality, disability, and debility, it is necessary to assume that the existing population is below the optimum size (defined by a zero rate of return on the existing stock of conventional capital). Neither this assumption nor the assumption of full employment (when unaccounted for in the statistical procedure) was explicitly made by most past writers. General acceptance of the stationary-state notion and Say's Law accounts for this.

Turning now to education, J. R. Walsh (1935, p. 255) in 1935 pointed out: "Since the days of Sir William Petty, many economists have included man in the category of fixed capital, because like capital

---

[13]For a historical discussion of the relationship between health and the economic value of a man, see Sand (1952, pp. 583–87).

man costs an expense and serves to repay that expense with a profit. Their conclusions, however, have been carried on chiefly in general terms, reference being made to *all* men as capital, and to *all* kinds of expenses in rearing and training as their cost." Walsh then took up the subject now being treated by T. W. Schultz, Gary Becker, and others, of the economic importance of higher education. Walsh was particularly interested in whether expenditures incurred by persons for professional careers were a capital investment made in a profit-seeking, equalizing market, and in response to the same motives that lead to investments in conventional capital. He asserted that they were. To test his hypothesis he examined the earnings of men at various levels of education. Their present value was estimated, using the capitalized-gross-earnings approach, at the average age at which their education ended. The costs of the various levels of education were then estimated, and a comparison was made of these costs and capital values to determine if they were equal (Walsh, 1935, pp. 255–69).

Walsh found that the value of a general college education exceeded the cost of its acquisition. Hence, his hypothesis of a competitive equalizing market in education was rejected. When he calculated the capital values and costs of professional training, however, he found that cost exceeded value in the cases of M.A., Ph.D., and M.D. degree holders. The reason for this, Walsh said, was that only monetary returns were considered and individuals with these degrees receive special satisfactions and advantages such as travel, vacations, and service to man. A consideration of these factors would equate the value estimate to its cost. Value exceeded cost in the cases of engineers, B.B.A. degree holders, and lawyers. The reason for this, Walsh said, was because of a short-run excess demand for their services. More people would be trained in the occupations over time, and value would become equated to cost. Hence, he said, there is no evidence that the ordinary adjustment which is characteristic of a competitive market is prevented from taking place (Walsh, 1935, pp. 269–84).

Walsh's optimistic conclusion about the competitiveness of the market for education was, however, arrived at by questionable ad hoc arguments. In actual fact, he found that value of education differed from cost of training in every professional-training case he studied. When training costs exceeded the increment to capital value resulting from the training, he assumed a long-run market equilibrium and explained the disparity by bringing in additional value attributable to non-monetary remuneration; but when value exceeded cost he abandoned the assumption of long-run market equilibrium, and he explained the disparity by a short-run disequilibrium which he arbitrarily assumed would be eliminated by a long-run adjustment.

Walsh's work is open to two other criticisms. First, his inclusion of all the costs of room, board, and personal expenses in his estimates of the average cost of various levels of education (Walsh, 1935, pp. 267–69) is clearly wrong, because an individual would have to incur these costs whether he attended college or not. Second, he overlooked the possibility that earnings differentials may result from factors other than the level of education.

It should be pointed out that Walsh's work is quite similar to that currently being done on the economics of education. He applied the human-capital analytical framework to the topic and asked many of the questions being posed today.

VI

In summary, treating human beings within the capital analytical framework is by no means new. Many past economists, and non-economists, have considered human beings or their skills as capital. Although several motives for treating human beings as capital and valuing them in money terms are to be found in this literature, most of the well-known names in the history of economic thought neither attempted an evaluation of human capital nor employed the concept for any specific purpose. They did, however, include humans or their skills in their definition of capital and recognized the importance of investment in human beings as a factor increasing their productivity. Although some economists included man himself as capital, most of them included only human skill. The former view was taken by economists such as Walras and Fisher, whose theoretical approach did not necessitate their classifying the factors of production into the traditional trio of land, labor, and capital. The latter view, held particularly by the English Classical school, was adopted by economists interested in the distribution of income and the theory of production. Whether or not we define skills and/or the acquirer of them as capital is relatively unimportant. The distinction between skills and the person is important however. Economists, legislators, and private institutions when faced with concrete policy questions have fairly consistently recognized both that skills require prior effort and continuous maintenance and that to deny this analogy between humans and conventional capital in practice (for example, in tax laws and philanthropy) means a misuse of resources.

Since the human-capital concept was not fully explored by these economists, they did not calculate rates of return on investments in human beings. Recognition of the difficulty of resolving the investment-consumption dichotomy may have accounted for this failure.

Basically, two methods were used to estimate the value of human beings: the cost-of-production and the capitalized-earnings procedures. The former method is the less useful, since there is no simple and necessary relationship between the cost of producing an item and its economic value. The inseparability of consumption and investment and the difficulty of treating depreciation and maintenance make any cost-of-production value dubious. Economists engaged in research in this area will find little of value in past works in which this approach was adopted.

Farr's capitalized-earnings approach was the first truly scientific procedure and is the one followed today by the majority of economists for evaluating human beings. His work, and that of Dublin and Lotka, should be starting points for anyone interested in determining either human-capital values or their components. Use of this approach avoids the depreciation difficulty. Since a young man, *ceteris paribus*, is expected to be productive over a longer period than an older one, his capital value would be greater. Although maintenance costs were neglected by those who used the cost-of-production approach, they were considered by Farr and Dublin and Lotka to be equal to personal living expenses.

Current writers are employing the human-capital concept for many of the same purposes for which it was used in the past, namely, to demonstrate the economic profitability of human migration, health investment, premature-death prevention, and education. Since many of them fail to cite predecessors, it is hoped that this essay will be helpful as a reference source. The human-capital concept was also used by past writers to demonstrate the power of a nation, propose new tax schemes, determine the total cost of war, emphasize the economic significance of human life, and aid courts in making decisions in cases dealing with compensation for personal injury and death. These uses may suggest interesting additional problems to contemporary economists.

73

REFERENCES

Abraham-Frois, G. "Capital humain et migrations internationales," *Rev. d'écon. polit.*, LXXIV (March–April, 1964), 526–54.

Bagehot, Walter. *Economic Studies.* Stanford, Calif.: Academic Reprints, 1953.

Barriol, A. "La valeur sociale d'un individu," *Rev. écon. internat.* (December, 1910), pp. 552–55.

———. "Complément à la note sur la valeur sociale d'un individu," *ibid.* (May, 1911), pp. 356–61.

Becker, Gary S. "Investment in Human Capital: A Theoretical Analysis," *J.P.E.*, LXX, Suppl. (October, 1962), 9–49.

———. *Human Capital: A Theoretical and Empirical Analysis, with Special Reference to Education.* New York: National Bureau of Economic Research, 1964.

Boag, Harold. "Human Capital and the Cost of War," *Royal Statis. Soc.* (January, 1916), pp. 7–17.

Bogart, Ernest L. *Direct and Indirect Costs of the Great World War.* New York: Oxford Univ. Press, 1919.

Cantillon, Richard. *Essai sur la nature du commerce en général.* Translated by Henry Higgs. London: Frank Cass Co., 1959.

Clark, John M. *The Costs of World War to the American People.* New Haven, Conn.: Yale Univ. Press, 1931.

Crammond, Edgar. "The Cost of War," *J. Royal Statis. Soc.*, LXXVIII (May, 1915), 361–99.

Crum, Frederick S. "Public Accidents and Their Cost," *Proc. Nat. Safety Council* (8th Annual Safety Congress, 1919), pp. 1061–82.

Dawson, Miles H. "Valuation, in Actions for Damages for Negligence, of Human Life, Destroyed or Impaired," *Proc. Internat. Congress Actuaries*, I (1904), 929–39.

Denison, Edward F. "The Unimportance of the Embodied Question," *A.E.R.*, LIV (March, 1964), 90–93.

Dublin, Louis I. *Health and Wealth, a Survey of the Economics of World Health.* New York: Harper & Bros., 1928.

Dublin, Louis I., and Lotka, Alfred. *The Money Value of Man.* New York: Ronald Press Co., 1930.

Engel, Ernst. *Der Werth des Menschen.* Berlin: Verlag von Leonhard Simion, 1883.

Farr, William. "Equitable Taxation of Property," *J. Royal Statis. Soc.*, XVI (March, 1853), 1–45.

Fisher, Irving. "Senses of 'Capital,'" *Econ. J.*, VII (June, 1897), 199–213.

———. "Cost of Tuberculosis in the United States and Its Reduction." Read before the International Congress on Tuberculosis, Washington, 1908.

———. *The Nature of Capital and Income.* London: Macmillan & Co., 1927.

———. *The Theory of Interest.* New York: Augustus M. Kelly, 1965.

Fisk, Eugene L. "Health of Industrial Workers," *Waste in Industry.* Washington: Federated American Engineering Societies, 1921.

Forsyth, C. H. "Vital and Monetary Losses in the United States Due to Preventable Deaths," *American Statis. Assoc. Publication,* XIV (1914–15), 758–89.

Foville, A. de. "Ce que c'est la richesse d'un peuple," *Bull. Institut Internat. Statis.,* XIV (1905), 62–74.

Giffen, Robert. *Essays in Finance.* 1st ser. London: G. Bell & Sons, 1880.

Guyot, Yves M. "The Waste of War and the Trade of Tomorrow," *Nineteenth Century and After,* LXXVI (December, 1914), 1193–1206.

Huebner, S. S. "The Human Value in Business Compared with the Property Value," *Proc. Thirty-fifth Ann. Convention Nat. Assoc. Life Underwriters* (July, 1914), pp. 17–41.

Hull, Charles R. (ed.). *The Economic Writings of Sir William Petty.* 2 vols. Cambridge: Cambridge Univ. Press, 1899.

Kapp, Friedrich. *Immigration and the Commissioners of Emigration of the State of New York.* New York: E. Steigen & Co., 1870.

Lees, D. S. "An Economist Considers Other Alternatives," *Financing Medical Care,* ed. Helmut Shoeck. Caldwell, Idaho: Caxton Printers Ltd., 1962.

Lindheim, A. *Saluti Senectutis.* Leipzig und Wien: F. Deuticke, 1909.

List, Friedrich. *The National System of Political Economy.* Translated by Sampson S. Lloyd. New York: Longmans, Green & Co., 1928.

Longfield, Mountiford. *Lectures on Political Economy.* London: The London School of Economics and Political Science, 1931.

Lüdtge, R. "Über den Geldwert des Menschen," *Deutsche Versicherungszeitung,* No. 56 (1873). (*a*)

———. "Über den Versicherungswert des Menschen," *Deutsche Versicherungszeitung,* No. 62 (1873). (*b*)

McCulloch, J. R. *The Principles of Political Economy.* Alex. Murray & Son, 1870.

Machlup, Fritz. *The Production and Distribution of Knowledge in the United States.* Princeton, N.J.: Princeton Univ. Press, 1962.

Macleod, Henry D. *The Elements of Economics.* Vol. II. New York: D. Appleton & Co., 1881.

Marshall, Alfred. *Principles of Economics.* New York: Macmillan Co., 1959.

Mayo-Smith, Richmond. *Emigration and Immigration.* New York: Charles Scribner's Sons, 1901.

Meyer, Ida. "Der Geldwert des Menschenlebens und seine Beziehungen zur Versicherung," *Veroffentlichungen Deutschen Vereins Versicherungs-Wissenschaft,* XLVII (September, 1930 – May, 1932), 1–75.

Mill, John Stuart. *Principles of Political Economy.* New York: Longmans, Green & Co., 1909.

Mushkin, Selma J. (ed.). *Economics of Higher Education.* Washington: Government Printing Office, 1962.

Mushkin, Selma J., and Weisbrod, Burton A. "Investment in Health — Lifetime Health Expenditures on the 1960 Work Force," *Kyklos,* XVI (1963), 583–98.

Nicholson, J. Shield. "The Living Capital of the United Kingdom," *Econ. J.,* I (March, 1891), 95–107.

———. "Capital and Labour: Their Relative Strength," *ibid,* II (September, 1892), 478–90.

———. *Strikes and Social Problems.* London: Macmillan & Co., 1896.

Roscher, Wilhelm G. F. *Principles of Political Economy.* Translated by John J. Lalor. Chicago: Callaghan & Co., 1878.

Rossiter, William S. "The Statistical Side of the Economic Costs of War," *A.E.R.,* VI (March, 1919), 94–117.

Sand, René. *The Advance to Social Medicine.* London: Staples Press, 1952.

Say, Jean Baptiste. *A Treatise on Political Economy.* Vol. I. Translated by C. R. Prinsep. Boston: Wells & Lilly, 1821.

Schultz, T. W. "Investment in Man: An Economist's View," *Social Service Rev.,* XXXIII (June, 1959), 109–17.

———. "Education and Economic Growth," in H. G. Richey (ed.), *Social Forces Influencing American Education.* Chicago: Univ. of Chicago Press, 1961. (*a*)

———. "Investment in Human Capital," *A.E.R.,* LI (March, 1961), 1–17. (*b*)

———. "Investment in Human Capital: Reply," *ibid.,* LI (December, 1961), pp. 1035–59. (*c*).

——— (ed.). "Investment in Human Beings," *J.P.E.,* Vol. LXX, Suppl. (October, 1962).

Sencini, Guido. "Il metodo ordinario di calcodo del costo di produzione dell'umo," *Giornale degli Econ.,* XXXVI (1908), 481–96.

Senior, Nassau William. *An Outline of the Science of Political Economy.* New York: Farrar & Rinehart, 1939.

Sidgwick, Henry. *The Principles of Political Economy.* London: Macmillan & Co., 1901.

Smith, Adam. *The Wealth of Nations.* New York: Modern Library, 1937.

Stark, W. (ed.). *Jeremy Bentham's Economic Writing.* London: George Allen & Unwin, 1952.

Thünen, Johann Heinrich von. *Der isolierte Staat.* Vol. II, Part II. Translated by Bert F. Hoselitz. Chicago: Comparative Education Center, Univ. of Chicago; originally published 1875.

Walras, Léon. *Elements of Pure Economics.* Translated by William Jaffé. Homewood, Ill.: Richard D. Irwin, Inc., 1954.

Walsh, John R. "Capital Concept Applied to Man," *Q.J.E.,* XLIX (February, 1935), 255–85.

Weisbrod, Burton A. *Economics of Public Health.* Philadelphia: Univ. of Pennsylvania Press, 1961.

Wittstein, Theodor. *Mathematische Statistik und deren Anwendung auf National-Ökonomie und Versicherung-wissenschaft.* Hanover: Hahn'sche Hofbuchlandlung, 1867.

Woods, Edward A., and Metzger, Clarence B. *America's Human Wealth: Money Value of Human Life.* New York: F. S. Crofts & Co., 1927.

PART II Human Capital and Economic Growth

Introduction

During recent years in developed countries, increases in national income have been more than proportional to increases in the traditional factors of production—land, labor, and physical reproducible capital. Many economists maintain that part of the explanation for the divergence between inputs and outputs is that the improvement which has occurred in the quality of the labor force often has been neglected as an input. Moses Abramovitz asserts that:

On the side of the capital, there is a chronic underestimate of investment and accumulated stock because, for purposes of measurement, we identify capital formation with the net increase of land, structures, durable equipment, commodity stocks, and foreign claims. But underlying this conventional definition of investment is a more fundamental concept which is broader; namely, any use of resources which helps increase our output in future periods. And if we attempt to broaden the operational definition, then a number of additional categories of expenditures would have to be included, principally those for health, education, and research.[1]

Several empirical studies have been done which attempt to explain the "residual" of unexplained growth in national income. Perhaps the best known is an article by Odd Aukrust, the first reading (Reading 6) in this part of the volume. Aukrust, employing the conventional Cobb-Douglas assumptions, suggests that the rate of growth in an industrial economy is not strongly influenced by the rate of conventional capital formation. He finds that in the 1948–1955 period in Norway, the growth in national income of 3.4 percent was found to be composed of 0.46 percent from increased employment, 1.2 percent from increased conventional capital, and 1.81 percent from the "human factors" (defined vaguely as organization, professional skills, and technical knowledge). Aukrust mentions a similar study by Robert Solow of the United States private nonfarm sector for the year 1900–1949 that produced very similar results.

The second reading (Reading 7) in this section is a comment on Aukrust's article by Robert Solow. Professor Solow theorizes that the

[1]Moses Abramovitz, "Resources and Output Trends in the United States since 1870," *American Economic Review*, XLVI (May, 1956), pp. 12–13.

residual (Aukrust's "human factor") is complementary as a factor of production with conventional capital and can contribute to output only if it is embodied in capital. Hence, he believes that conventional investment is substantially more important in production than Aukrust suggests.

John Kendrick, in a 1956 Occasional Paper for the National Bureau of Economic Research, reports that increased factor productivity accounted for over 50 percent of the 3.3 percent average annual rate of growth in real output in the United States between 1899 and 1953 and that increased use of conventional inputs accounted for less than half of this increase. He says that by measuring inputs in terms of that base year period, economists are neglecting changes per factor unit in the services of human capital accumulated in order to increase the efficiency of resources in future periods. Since this study for the NBER, Professor Kendrick has exerted a great deal of effort toward defining clearly and quantifying the flows and stock of human capital. The final reading (Reading 8) in this part is an account of his research efforts.

A. The Growth Residual and the Human Factor

6. Investment and Economic Growth*
ODD AUKRUST

I. INTRODUCTION

This paper is a mixture of theory, empirical facts, and speculations of an economic and political nature: these last in order to provoke a lively discussion.

My starting-point is a thesis which occurs in most popular theories of economic growth, and which also seems to be becoming generally accepted as a guide for economic and political thinking. I believe this thesis can be formulated as follows: *Experience shows that the national product of a country will increase at about the same rate as the country's real capital.* From this it follows that the rate of growth in national product must depend directly on how fast real capital increases. If it is possible to increase investments, it follows that the rate of economic growth can be increased in the same proportion.

Such consideration has led policy makers aiming at economic growth to concentrate on actions designed to increase investments. The results of such policies have, however, not always been up to expectations. The high rates of investments in Norway and Sweden have not led to a correspondingly high rate of increase in national products. What is the explanation? Is the explanation to be sought in the composition of investments? Have there been many bad investments? Has this economic policy been a failure?

In my opinion, the answer must be sought in quite a different field. In the following I will try to show that the relationships between investments and increase in production are far more complicated than generally assumed. I shall try to show that *"the human factor"* (*organization, professional skills and technical knowledge*) is at least as important to the rate of economic growth as the volume of physical capital.

*Reprinted from "Investment and Economic Growth," *Productivity Measurement Review*, XVI (February, 1959), 35–50.

If this is correct, it will have obvious implications for economic policy. I will return to this point in the last part of the paper.

II. THE THEORY OF A CONSTANT CAPITAL OUTPUT COEFFICIENT

1. SIMPLE THEORIES OF ECONOMIC GROWTH

One of the economists who first took up problems connected with economic growth was Gustav Cassel. In his textbook there is a special chapter discussing "the society of continuous steady progress." One of the problems he discusses is the rate of growth in a modern industrial economy.

Cassel's basic hypothesis is what today is generally referred to as "the assumption of a constant capital output coefficient." He assumes that the ratio, real capital/national product, is a given, technologically determined number. From this it follows that production can be increased only through investment (savings) and that the rate of increase will be directly proportional with the rate of saving (rate of investment). However, the rate of saving alone is not decisive. The magnitude of the capital output ratio is also important. The more capital one requires to produce one unit, the smaller will be the increase in production resulting from a certain saving. One can show that the rate of growth in the national product will be inversely proportional to the marginal capital output ratio, so that we have:

$$\text{Rate of growth (in percent)} = 100 \times \frac{\text{Rate of saving}}{\text{Capital output ratio}}$$

By the help of this formula, one can calculate the rate of progress resulting from different values of the rate of saving and the capital output ratio. (See Table 1.)

Cassel who did not have the wealth of national income statistics which we have today, estimated the rate of saving in a modern economy to be about 0.2 and the capital output ratio to be about 6. From these estimates he concluded that the "normal rate of growth" for an economy should be about 3 percent. This conclusion is probably the origin of the idea which seems to have taken such a firm hold on the minds of economists: namely, that a rate of growth of 3 percent per year can be considered as "normal" for a modern industrial economy. (The annex shows that the long-term rate of growth in most industrial economies has been considerably lower.)

TABLE 1

Rate of growth when the rate of saving and
the capital output are given

Rate of growth in national products (p.c. per year)

Capital Output Ratio	Rate of Saving				
	0.05	0.10	0.17	0.20	0.25
2	2.5	5.0	7.7	10.0	12.5
3	1.7	3.3	5.9	6.7	8.3
4	1.3	2.5	3.3	5.0	6.3
5	1.0	2.0	3.9	4.0	5.0
6	0.8	1.7	2.7	3.3	4.2

The idea of a constant marginal capital output ratio has recently turned up again in several theories of economic growth. The idea is found in the well-known growth models of Evsey D. Domar and Roy Harrod. From the literature on economic theory, the idea seems to have penetrated and gradually become accepted in the economic and political debate.

2. EMPIRICAL DATA CONCERNING INPUT AND OUTPUT RATES

It is not possible here to describe in detail the many attempts which have been made to estimate marginal capital output ratios statistically. Such measurements present many problems. To eliminate the effects of business cycles and other fluctuations, one needs statistics of national product (in constant prices) for a very long period. This leads to a number of difficult problems of deflation. The statistical uncertainty becomes considerable and there are only a few countries which have sufficiently good statistics for such calculations to be made with a fair amount of confidence. Most studies have given estimates of the capital output ratios between 3.0 and 4.0, i.e. considerably less than 6.0 as estimated by Cassel. Table 2, which is taken from a study by Leibenstein, illustrates this point.

For the Soviet Union, a recent estimate gives a capital output ratio of 3.0, or possibly somewhat lower, for the period 1928–1937.[1]

The graph shows estimates of real capital and net national products for Norway. The curve has a number of irregular fluctuations. If,

[1] Alexander Eckstein and Peter Gutman, "Capital and Output in the Soviet Union 1928–1937," Rev. Ec. Stats., 1956, pp. 436–444.

TABLE 2

Country	Period	Marginal Capital Output Ratio
Mexico	1940–1950	2.1
United States	1879–1929	3.0
Sweden	1896–1929	3.3
British Guinea	1943–1951	3.5
Australia	1913–1938	3.9
Ceylon	1953–1959	4.0
Canada	1911–1939	4.2
Great Britain	1865–1919	5.9
Japan	1913–1939	6.1
The Netherlands	1913–1939	7.4
France	–	7.4

however, we consider only the boom years in 1900, 1916, 1930 and 1937, we find that these years lie on a straight line which corresponds to a marginal capital output ratio of 3.0.

For the post-war years, the marginal capital output ratio has been considerably higher and it seems to have a tendency to increase further. A glance at the figure shows that a curve including only the post-war years would be considerably steeper than a curve for the pre-war years. For the years 1947–1951, the marginal capital output ratio is 4.4 and for the years 1951–1956 it is 5.5.

In general, it seems that the following conclusions can be drawn from the various studies which have been made in this field:

 i) In most countries there has been a surprisingly constant relationship between increases in capital and national product, i.e., over a longer period the capital output ratio has remained very stable.

 ii) For shorter periods, such as business cycles or the war years, we find exactly the opposite. Over such periods the marginal capital output ratio can show large fluctuations.

 iii) The capital output ratios, both the average and the marginal, vary from one country to another. In general, the ratio seems to increase with prosperity. Adler who has studied the question maintains that marginal capital output ratios of about 2.0 or slightly more are normal for countries like India.[2] For Latin

[2]John H. Adler, "World Economic Growth—Retrospect and Prospect," Rev. Ec. Stats., 1956, pp. 273–285.

Real Capital and Net National Product in Norway
1900–1939 and 1946–1956 at 1938 Prices

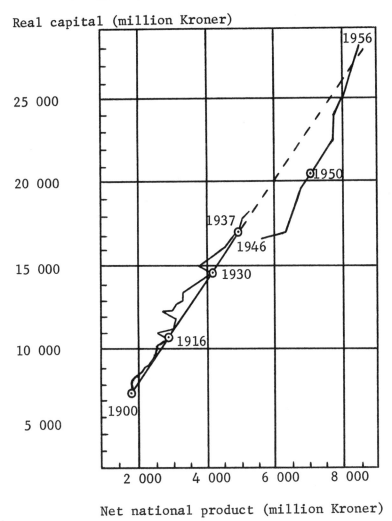

Net national product (million Kroner)

America, he considers the normal to be about 3.0, and for most
countries in Western Europe and for the U.S. and Canada,
about 4.0. There is, however, a large number of exceptions to
these "normal" rates.

Human Capital and Economic Growth

The available statistics do not lead us to expect an absolutely constant ratio between the rate of investment and the rate of growth. This in itself is not really surprising.

3. The Assumption that the Capital Output Ratio is Constant

The idea that the production function of the economy should have a shape which leads to a constant capital output ratio is obviously open to criticism. The most evident weakness of the hypothesis is that it neglects factors of production other than plant and equipment, such as, for instance, the level of technical knowledge of managers and workers, i.e., the "human factor." The idea that the capital output ratio should be constant does in fact contradict almost everything we have learned about economic laws of production. This is so obvious that no further comments are required. We shall, however, return to the question, in Section IV. Here, we will take up another question, namely, the influence the composition of the investments may have on the capital output ratio.

A certain investment, for instance the construction of a new factory, will generally affect the economy's productive capacity in three ways:

i) When the factory starts operating it will show a net value added, which will be the factory's contribution to the national product. This contribution can be called the *direct* or *internal* capacity effect of the investment. Normally it will be positive, but it can vary a great deal according to how profitable the factory turns out to be and also according to how labor intensive it is. In addition to this direct capacity effect, the investment can have *external* capacity effects which can take two forms.

ii) The workers of the new factory must come from other already operating firms (assuming full employment). As a result, the contribution to the national product from these firms will be reduced, i.e., the *substitution effect* of the investment under consideration will be negative. This is probably normal, although the opposite could happen by investment in labor-saving devices.

iii) The new investment will also affect production in other industries in other ways, so that output in these industries will change (Marshall's "External Economics"). The normal is presumably that net output in these other industries will increase, so that the *complementary effect* of the investment will be positive. One would expect this effect to be particularly important in the case of certain public investments, such as roads, railways, schools, lighthouses, etc. The effect can, however, also be negative. In many cities we are certainly beyond a point where more automobiles will *reduce* transport capacity, where each individual firm must use more and more trucks to get its own goods delivered. The result is that when all firms do this, traffic will constantly become slower and slower.

The total *capacity* effect of a certain investment, or what we might call its *social capacity* effect, will be the sum of the three effects mentioned. It follows that this total effect can be quite different from the direct capacity effect. It can be larger as well as smaller.

Attempts to measure total capacity effects of various forms of investment have as far as I know not been undertaken in any country. We have here a very tempting research subject, and a problem, the solution of which could have great practical importance for investment policy.[3] Industry should, however, have considerable experience of how this problem presents itself in practice and it will be interesting if this experience could be made available to the public.

As far as I can see, there is no mechanism which will ensure automatically that the investments with highest social capacity effect are carried out. We must, therefore, assume that the effect of a certain amount of investment can vary a great deal according to the form the investment takes. This immediately leads us on to the question of how the capital output ratio is influenced by the composition of the investments. It will be particularly interesting if one can find out how far such variations can explain the differences in the capital output ratio which we find between countries and between different periods within one country.

---

[3] A study of this question could, for instance, throw light on the rather doubtful distinction between productive and unproductive investments. When one uses these expressions one is usually thinking only of the direct capacity effect of the investments. I suspect that the difference between the various forms of investment will appear less marked if one also takes into consideration the substitution effect and the complementary effect. In general, one could expect that in cases where the direct capacity effect is smaller, the other effects will be positive and probably very large. (Residential buildings and new roads can often have a considerable complementary effect and at the same time they will not take away labor from other production, as a new factory would do.)

III. THE COMPOSITION OF THE INVESTMENTS

As mentioned earlier, no country has statistics showing the total capacity effect of the various forms of investment. The available figures are capital output ratios (average or marginal) for different sectors, i.e., figures which in general only reflect changes in the direct capacity effect. However, such figures also have a certain interest.

Table 3, which in columns 1, 2 and 3 gives capital output ratios for Norway during the post-war years, clearly shows that certain sectors are using more capital than others per unit produced. The lowest

TABLE 3

Average and Marginal Capital Output Ratios

Industry	Average Ratios 1948 (1)	Average Ratios 1955 (2)	Marginal Ratios 1946–55 (3)	Percentage of Total Investments Average 1935–39 (4)	Percentage of Total Investments Average 1949–53 (5)
1. Agriculture, forestry and fishing	3.7	4.9	7.5	13.7	8.5
2. Mining, manufacturing and construction	1.1	1.4	1.9	17.8	20.0
3. Power supply	6.1	7.4	15.6	3.4	6.9
4. Residential building	16.4	17.6	16.8	21.3	18.8
5. Shipping and whaling	2.8	3.2	2.9	16.9	23.2
6. Land transportation*	6.7	7.9	9.6	16.0	12.0
7. Services	1.1	1.5	3.3	10.9	10.6
	2.9	3.3	4.0	100.0	100.0

*Public consumption capital such as roads and harbors are included in sector 6. Administrative public buildings, schools, hospitals, etc., are included in sector 7.

capital output ratios are found in mining, manufacturing, construction and certain service sectors. Agriculture, forestry, fishing, shipping and whaling occupy an intermediary position. (Shipping uses much capital per person employed but not per unit produced.) Power supply and land transportation have capital output ratios which are considerably higher. The highest of all ratios is found in residential building.

For Western Germany corresponding figures are available in a study by Ferdinand Grünig.[4] However, Grünig uses a concept *gross*

[4] Ferdinand Grünig, *Versuch einer Volksvermögensrechnung der Deutschen Bundesrepublik.* (*Deutsches Institut für Wirtschaftsforschung: Sonderhefte, Neue Folge*, No. 41).

capital output ratio defined as the ratio between original cost of the capital equipment (without depreciation) and output. He finds that this ratio is from 12.5 for residential buildings (28.5 if controlled rents are taken as basis), about 10 for power supply and transport, and between 1.1 and 1.4 for manufacturing industries. For distribution and certain service activities, the ratio may be smaller than 1.0. The wide dispersion indicated by both the German and Norwegian figures is confirmed by American[5] and English[6] studies. The English figures show that just within the manufacturing industry the ratio varies from 1.4–9.2, with an average of 2.8.

This dispersion of capital output ratios leads one to expect that a ratio calculated as an average of all sectors will depend on how investments are distributed among the sectors. Can, for instance, the high marginal capital output ratio for Norway during the post-war years be explained in this way? The answer is "no." Table 3, column 3, shows that the marginal ratios have been above the averages for practically all sectors. This indicates that the exceptionally high ratios of the post-war years have been a feature common to all parts of the economy. A glance at the distribution of investments before and after the war (columns 4 and 5) makes it quite clear that the changes which have taken place cannot explain why the marginal capital output ratio has increased. Sectors with high ratios (power supply, housing, land transport, etc.) have had a smaller share of total investments in the years 1949–1953 than in 1935–1939.

IV. PHYSICAL CAPITAL AND THE HUMAN FACTOR

1. THE PROBLEM

Our analysis so far has shown that the assumption of a constant marginal capital output ratio is unlikely to lead us to a realistic production function for the economy as a whole. This assumption does not seem very plausible on the basis of theoretical considerations concerning laws of production. It has also little support in the empirical material available. To a Norwegian, it is, for instance, natural to point out that the assumption is unable to explain the rather peculiar development in Norway during the last years, where, in fact, invest-

[5]R. A. Gordon: "Population Growth, Housing and the Capital Coefficient," Am. Ec. Rev., June, 1956.

[6]T. Barna, "The Replacement Cost of Fixed Assets in British Manufacturing Industry in 1955," in Journ. Royal Stat. Society, Series A, Vol. 120, Part 1, 1957.

ments at a record level have led to a relatively modest rate of growth in national product.

If the assumption of a constant marginal capital output ratio is rejected, what shall we then put in its place? What relationships can we then assume to exist between investments and national product?

Economic theory has traditionally considered three or four main groups of factors of production: capital, including land, labor and what we could call "organization" or, if preferred, the "human factor." Why not base our thinking on this?

If, however, we try to formulate a production function where capital, labor and organization enter as variables, we will soon run into two difficulties. One is that the factor "organization" is not measurable (it can be difficult enough to measure inputs of capital and labor). The factor "organization" includes a conglomerate of factors: the technical and commercial knowledge of managers, employees and workers, their qualities as leaders, their will and ability to work, the whole social setting and the international situation in which production takes place. In other words, the factor "organization" will have to include all elements which, together with input of capital and labor, determine what the results of the productive activity will be. To compute an index for all this is not possible.

The second difficulty is that the shape of a production function including these three variables is unknown, i.e., we do not know exactly *how* a change in the factor combination will influence the result. We can fall back on general considerations from the theory of production but this is not enough to enable us to decide on a particular shape of the function.

Both these problems cause difficulties if we try to determine the production function of a production economy empirically. We can only overcome these problems by making assumptions.

2. An empirical study for Norway

In the study which I will now describe, the difficulties have been overcome in the following way:

i) It was assumed that input of the factor "organization" has increased at a constant rate during the whole period of investigation. Under this assumption, the factor "organization" can be brought into the production function in the form of an exponential trend. We have no possibility of deciding how realistic this assumption is.

ii) It is assumed that the relation between output and input of capital, labor and organization can be represented by a Cobb-Douglas function. This production function implies that national product increases when input of capital, labor or organization increases, and that increased input of only one factor will lead to decreasing marginal productivity for this factor.

The problem is by these assumptions brought into a form which makes it possible to determine empirically how changes in real capital, employment and organization influence the national product.[7]

Space does not permit us going into technical details of the computations. It is sufficient to say that the calculations are based on data for the period 1900–1955 (with the exception of the years of World War II) and that the main results can be summarized as follows:

i) An increase of 1 percent in the amount of real capital will, if there is no change in employment and organization, lead to an increase of 0.2 percent in national product.

ii) An increase of 1 percent in employment will, if capital and organization remain constant, lead to an increase of 0.7 percent in national product.

iii) If capital and employment remain constant, national product will increase by 1.8 percent per year as a result of the human factor, i.e., as a result of gradual improvement in organization and technique.

One must obviously use some caution when interpreting these figures. It is probably most "correct" to interpret them as valid for factor variations not deviating too much from the "normal."

We can get a clearer picture of what these results imply by split-

---

[7]Under the two assumptions mentioned, the production function can be written:

$$R_t = aK_t^\alpha N_t^\beta (e^{ht})^\lambda$$

Where: R_t = National product
K_t = Real capital (at depreciated replacement cost)
N_t = Employment (in man-years)
e^{ht} = Index of organization (assumed to increase by a constant rate h)

a, α, β, h and λ are constants. It is convenient to put $h\lambda = \gamma$, since it is the product which is of interest in the following.

The constants were determined from the data for 1900–1939 and 1946–1955 as follows:

$a = 2.262$	$\alpha = 0.203$	$\beta = 0.763$	$\gamma = 0.0181$
	(0.101)	(0.192)	(0.0029)

The standard errors are given in brackets.

ting up the growth in national product for the period 1948–1955, according to causes. During this period employment increased by an average of 0.6 percent a year whilst capital increased by 5.6 percent. We then find:

Growth caused by:

Increased employment...	$0.76 \times 0.6 = 0.46$ percent per year
Increased capital...........	$0.20 \times 5.6 = 1.12$ percent per year
Better organization	$= 1.81$ percent per year
Total growth rate	$= 3.39$ percent per year

Actual growth in the period under consideration was on the average 3.4 percent a year.

One should, however, add that it is not only for these years that the formula seems to give a good fit. A comparison shows that for 32 out of the 50 years the formula gives estimates which differ by less than 3 percent from the actual national product. Only in five years is this difference greater than 7 percent.[8]

The fact that the formula seems to fit the data very well is, of course, no guarantee that our model is a realistic one. The results of econometric studies should, in general, be received with a good deal of scepticism. (The results are, however, never worse than the theoretical considerations and the statistical data on which they are based. Some of the ultra-sceptics seem to believe this.) In our particular case, the Norwegian results do, however, receive a surprising amount of support from two similar studies which have recently been carried out in other countries.

3. An American and a Finnish study

The first of these two studies is from the U.S.A. It was made by Robert Solow and is based on statistics of "private non-farm activity" for the years 1900–1949.[9] His method is slightly different from the one used in the Norwegian study, but the problems he studies are

[8]The large deviations occur particularly in years with high unemployment, i.e., in years when capital equipment was not fully utilized. This is just what we could expect. Since we have in all calculations considered the real capital in actual existence, we obviously get too high an estimate of national product when a part of this capital is not being utilized. If, for instance, 20 percent of the capital is idle this will, with our estimated values of the parameters, give a reduction of 4 percent in national product.

[9]Robert Solow, "Technical Change and the Aggregate Production Function", Rev. Ec. Stats., August, 1951.

the same. Solow assumes that total output is determined by capital, employment and organization (which he calls "technique"), and seeks to determine the shape of the production function.

He assumes that the production function is of the Cobb-Douglas type and that a pari-passu law is fulfilled. He finds that an increase in real capital of 1 percent will give an increase in output of 0.35 percent (the Norwegian study gave 0.20 percent), and further that an increase in employment of 1 percent leads to an increase of 0.65 percent in output (for Norway, 0.76 percent). The effect of the gradual improvement in organization is estimated by Solow to be 1.5 percent a year (for Norway, 1.8 percent).

The other study concerns Finland and was recently published by Olavi Niitamo.[10] It is different from the other two studies in the sense that it only covers the manufacturing industry and not the whole economy. Niitamo had no statistics of capital employed, so instead he worked on the assumption that consumption of electricity by industry is a measure of real capital employed. This assumption obviously reduces the significance of his calculations and it may possibly be rash to quote his studies as support for the assumptions made for Norway. One of the models studied by Niitamo is, however, a Cobb-Douglas function with an exponential trend term (Model 4). This model is practically identical with the model used in the Norwegian study. Niitamo finds from this model that an increase in real capital (electricity consumption) of 1 percent gives an increase in output of 0.26 percent, a similar increase in employment gives 0.74 percent increase in output. The trend term is estimated to 1.2 percent a year. The models used both by Solow and Niitamo give a very high degree of agreement between the estimated and the actual output figures.

4. COMMENTS ON THE FINDINGS

There are several reasons which call for criticism when one comments on the results of such studies. The purpose of this paper is, however, to discuss economic growth and not econometric methodology. I shall, therefore, not discuss in any detail the objections which can be made to the studies, but I will briefly refer to the reservations made by the authors themselves in their presentation of the results.

[10] Olavi Niitamo, "Development of Productivity in Finnish Industry 1925–1952," Prod. Maes. Rev., No. 15, November, 1958.

It is, however, necessary to deal with one general objection because it has direct implications for the interpretation of the results. We have tacitly assumed that "organization" and "real capital" enter independently into the production function. This means that national product can be increased by increased input of capital even if this capital increase is not accompanied by better organization and vice versa. The latter is a particularly doubtful assumption. It is, therefore, possible that calculations of this type can give an exaggerated impression of the increase in output which can be reached through better organization alone, i.e., improved organization without *simultaneous* increase in the real capital. There is, however, no doubt that a considerable increase in production could take place even if net investments were zero over a period of several years, if for instance worn-out machinery is replaced by more efficient machines which do not cost more. One could also imagine that certain phases of production are re-organized so that less capital is required.

However, even if we exercise a large amount of scepticism it is difficult to avoid being stricken by the amazing agreement between the three studies, in spite of the differences in method. This appears most clearly when we bring together the three sets of estimates as is done in Table 4.

When we see how these three production functions each fit the data in an excellent manner, we are forced, as far as I can see, to accept that these very simple models represent something essential of the production structure in a modern industrial economy. There is also reason to believe, at least until the contrary is proved, that the order of magnitude of the different coefficients is correctly determined.

If we examine the figures more closely, we will find most surprising

TABLE 4

Country	Percent Increase in Output (by 1 % increase in capital input)	Percent Increase in Output (by 1 % increase in labor input)	Percent Annual Increase in Output (resulting from better organization)
Norway (1900–1955) (whole economy)	0.20	0.76	1.8
U.S.A. (1909–1949) (private non-farm activity)	0.35	0.65	1.5
Finland (1925–1952) (Manufacturing)	0.26	0.74	1.2

that increases in real capital have such small effects on the volume of production. At the same time, we get a very high value in the trend factor which we have interpreted as the effect of the human factor, i.e., of better organization and technique.

But, is there any reason to be surprised at this? Haven't we got an abundance of facts which show that, in spite of all, the human factor — man's increasing understanding of his environment and his better utilization of the possibilities open to him — is the decisive factor determining how rapidly humanity shall progress?

There are, for instance, many people who maintain that the high rate of growth in the Soviet Union essentially is the result of the breadth of the Soviet system of education. It is also relevant that the number of engineers, scientists and mathematicians in the U.S.A. today may constitute more than 1 percent of the total labor force, and that the number of American engineers, chemists and mathematicians since 1870 has increased seventeen times more rapidly than the total labor force.

The importance of the factor "organization" is also confirmed by information available from individual firms. According to a newspaper report, the Volvo factories found, in a particular case, that one worker could be saved by the investing of 61,000 kroner in machines. The same saving could also be achieved by purchasing new tools for 30,000 kroner. "Investments" of only 7,000 kroner in work study were, however, sufficient to save one worker. It should be easy to find other examples of this kind.

Personally, I have no difficulty in accepting the results of these three studies. If, however, we accept these results, we also have to accept the conclusions which I will discuss in the following chapter.

V. SOME ECONOMIC AND POLITICAL IMPLICATIONS

Conclusion 1. The marginal capital output ratio is not constant. The ratios will increase when investments increase. This will be normal when increase in capital is not the *only* factor which determines the size of output.[11]

---

[11] We can derive the following expression for the marginal capital output ratio:

$$\frac{dK_t}{dR_t} = \frac{1}{\frac{R_t}{dK_t}\left\{0.76\frac{dN_t}{N_t} + 0.0181d_t\right\} + 0.20\frac{R_t}{K_t}}$$

where the symbols are the same as these in the footnote No. 7. This will vanish with dK_t, and will increase with the increased dK_t. Applied to the Norwegian data for 1948–1955, this formula gives a capital output ratio of 5.1, which is the same as the value found by direct observations for this period.

97

We have thus found a reasonable explanation of the high values of marginal capital output ratios observed in Norway after the war. This does not necessarily mean that the investments have not been unproductive. Neither does it mean that the composition of investments has changed. (We showed above that this was not the case.) On the other hand, we can conclude that the present high marginal capital output ratio in Norway is likely to decline in the future if investment is reduced to a more normal level. On this point I am inclined to be more optimistic with regard to the future than I was a couple of years ago, before the study I have described had been completed.

Conclusion 2. Growth models assuming a constant marginal capital output ratio, such as the models of Cassel, Domar and Harrod, are not very realistic. These models are, therefore, bad instruments for analyzing what will happen if there should be any substantial changes in the level of investment. We must, for instance, assume that Table 1 is directly misleading.

Conclusion 3. The possibilities of accelerating economic growth by increased investments are considerably smaller than we have been used to assume so far. [12]

In Table 5, I have indicated the growth rates which it seems reasonable to expect under alternative assumptions concerning the rate of net investment and the annual increase in employment. For these calculations I have used an average of the coefficients which have been found in the Norwegian, American and Finnish studies. I have assumed that an increase of 1 percent in real capital will increase national product by 0.25 percent and that an increase of 1 percent in employment will give an increase in production of 0.75 percent, and that the factor "organization" can lead to an annual increase in production of 1.5 percent. I have, therefore, assumed that the average capital output ratio is 3.5 which corresponds to the present situation in Norway.

The table shows that the rate of growth is not strongly influenced by the level of investment. If we, for instance, assume an increase in employment of 0.5 percent a year, it will be necessary to maintain a rate of investment as high as 15 percent in order to increase national

---

[12] This follows from the fact that the rate of growth in national product increases more slowly than investments. The mathematical proof of this proposition is very simple.

TABLE 5

Probable annual growth in national product under
alternative hypotheses about investment and employment

Rate of Investment (net investment in percent of national product)	Growth Rate of National Product with Increase* in Employment			
	0	0.5	1.0	1.5
0	1.5	1.8	2.2	2.5
5	1.9	2.2	2.6	2.9
10	2.3	2.6	3.0	3.3
15	2.8	3.1	3.5	3.8
20	3.2	3.5	3.9	4.2
25	3.6	3.9	4.3	4.6

*Percent per year.

product by 3.1 percent a year. In order to increase the rate of growth to 4 percent, net investments will have to be more than 25 percent of the national product.

It seems that the rate of growth which can be attained in a modern industrial economy is not strongly influenced by the investment policy which is applied. Whether investments are high or low, within reasonable limits, national product will increase by 2–3 percent a year, if the volume of employment remains constant. This is mainly because the human factor alone is sufficient to ensure a growth of 1.5 percent. The growth can be accelerated to slightly above 3 percent if the level of investment is maintained exceptionally high, but the possibilities are not very great.

Conclusion 4. The normal rate of growth for countries such as those in Western Europe can be assumed to be about 2 percent *per inhabitant*. In these countries, net investments during the last couple of generations have been about 10 percent of national product. This should, according to the table, give an increase in production per capita between 2.3 percent in countries with a constant level of employment and 1.8 percent in countries where employment increases 1.5 percent a year.

Conclusion 5. The "human factor" as the driving force in the process of economic growth deserves much greater attention than it has received so far. It is not unlikely that economic growth can be considerably increased if we make new efforts in the fields of education and scientific research.

I want to stress that in formulating this last conclusion I deliberately step outside what is rigorously proved by the study above. What I have been able to show is that at best there seems to be a trend factor which together with increases in capital and employment can explain the large increase in production which has taken place during the recent decades. I have shown further that the effect of this trend factor seems to be important compared to the effect of increases in real capital.

I have not given any proof that it really is the "human factor" which is the cause of this trend. That it is so is at the moment only a statement which is supported by some evidence from considerations of a theoretical nature and from what we know about the importance of individual efforts. Personally, I have during the last few years become more and more convinced that the good technician, scientist or manager may be the most important asset of the firm in which he works.

If it is correct that a trend factor with considerable effect exists, and reflects the influence of the "human factor," it is natural to believe that the rate of progress can be increased not only by increasing real capital, but also by a conscious effort to improve man himself.

If this paper has any practical implication at all, it is that we should, as an outcome of purely economic considerations, concentrate our attention on man as a factor of production. So far, our economic policy, aiming at rapid economic growth, has concentrated on investment. We have tried to increase the rate of progress by keeping the level of investment high. We ought to reconsider our plans and policies, and look into the possibilities of achieving greater gains by increasing our efforts in the fields of research and education.

7. Investment and Economic Growth: Some Comments*

ROBERT M. SOLOW
Massachusetts Institute of Technology

I. INTRODUCTION

These notes are intended as a contribution to the discussion of Aukrust's provocative paper.[1] They are more conversation than controversy; I think Aukrust will agree with what I say, in general if not in detail. But if a lively discussion develops, as it ought, we are both probably in for some surprises. Gross empirical regularities in economics are rarely simple and straightforward. In this case particularly, I have the feeling that most of the results so far, including my own, rest on rather shaky foundations.

II. THE CAPITAL-OUTPUT RATIO

When I was a graduate student ten years ago, I don't remember ever hearing about the capital-output ratio. Today it sometimes seems as if students never hear about anything else. It's not clear that this is a step forward. Not many important questions about the allocation of resources turn on average productivities. Even when one turns to the marginal capital-output ratio the situation is not much improved. Changes in capital and output over very short periods tend to be dominated by business-cycle influences. Over longer periods the failure to hold "other things" constant makes the interpretation of the incremental ratio very vague. But if one could make allowances for changes in technology and in the inputs of labor and other factors one would simply be making some kind of approximation to the

*Reprinted from "Investment and Economic Growth: Some Comments," *Productivity Measurement Review*, XIX (November 1959), 62–68.

[1] Odd Aukrust, "Investment and Economic Growth," *Productivity Measurement Review*, XVI, February, 1959.

marginal productivity or marginal efficiency of capital. That would sound more like what I was taught. But then why all the fuss about capital-output ratios?

Leaving aside these purist's objections, one may still attach at least symptomatic importance to capital-output ratios. They do provide an *ex post* measure of the aggregate capital intensity of production. And if historically any strong empirical regularity turns up, it calls for explanation or at least for explaining away. Now it is often claimed that the regularity exists. If one imagines that the national product is a sort of composite commodity produced by labor, capital, and perhaps other primary inputs under the standard neo-classical laws of production, then since capital is the most rapidly increasing factor, the average productivity of capital should fall, i.e., the capital-output ratio should rise. But, for whatever they are worth, the data collected do not behave in this way. Some writers claim that the ratio is approximately constant; some time series show the ratio to be falling. In any case the theoretically expected rise is not often observed. What is the explanation? Aukrust provides one, and a very important one. I should like to stress that there are others, and that these are complementary, not competing, ways of accounting for the facts.

In the first place, there is pure technological progress, additions to our knowledge of processes, materials and nature. For the capital-output ratio to decline even in the face of rapid capital accumulation it is not necessary that technical progress be capital-saving. The more capital-saving it happens to be, other things equal, the less tendency there will be for the ratio to increase. But even if inventions tend to be capital-using, a sufficiently rapid rate of improvement of technique may still have the same effect.

Secondly, there is good reason to believe that in one sense the statistics grossly underestimate the volume of capital. I have in mind the fact that what we measure as "capital" consists exclusively of tangible capital goods. But most modern societies invest heavily in education (including, very importantly, primary and secondary education), in health, and in research. Some writers speak of this as intangible capital or human capital. The important thing is that from the economist's point of view it is capital and it is not represented in the numerator of the capital-output ratio. It is of great significance for the whole study of resource allocation in economic growth. And since this kind of capital formation has been growing much more rapidly than investment in physical assets, to omit it has the effect of biassing the *trend* in the capital-output ratio downward. Professor T. W. Schultz and his co-workers at the University of Chicago are now making a serious attack on this problem.[2] Some idea of the possible magnitude of this effect is given by Schultz's estimate that in the U.S. gross capital formation in the form of high school, college and university education was 4 percent of gross physical capital formation in 1900 and 28 percent in 1956.

A third possible explanation of the behavior of the capital-output ratio is that it reflects the existence of increasing returns to scale. The presumption that the average productivity of the most rapidly increasing factor must fall holds under constant returns to scale. It may fail if there are economies of scale either internal to particular industries or as a consequence of a finer division of labor as the economy grows. Then the greater relative abundance of capital may be offset by the scale effect.

It is true that the Cobb-Douglas function, when its elasticities are freely estimated by Aukrust, Niitamo or in my own paper, does not yield increasing returns, and in fact stays pretty close to constant returns to scale. But this result is not wholly convincing because of the strong intercorrelation between the time trend for technical progress and the effects of scale. Capital and labor tend to increase fairly steadily over time. Thus a multiple regression finds it difficult to impute more-than-proportional increases in output as between increases in scale and the mere passage of time. That the regressions seem to favor the trend term may be a consequence of its greater smoothness.

An example of the same phenomenon in a slightly different context occurs in Koyck's work on investment.[3] In analyzing the response of investment in certain industries to current and lagged output, Koyck allows both for a time trend and for something that corresponds to returns to scale. He finds that the strength of the time trend is very sensitive to whatever assumptions he makes about returns to scale.

This is a delicate empirical problem which would repay careful investigation.

[2]See, for instance, two papers by T. W. Schultz, "Gross Capital Formation Represented by High School, College and University Education in the United States, 1900–1956," Paper No. 5807, April 29, 1958; and "Investment in Man: An Economists's View," Paper No. 5905, February 19, 1959.

[3]L. M. Koyck, "Distributed Lags and Investment Analysis," North-Holland Publishing Company, 1954, Chapter IV.

Finally, a fourth possibility worth mentioning is that the aggregate capital-output ratio is an average over many sectors each of which has a different degree of capital intensity. In the course of long-period economic development the mix of sectors may change radically. It seems generally true, for instance, that the service industries have a low capital intensity. It also turns out that agriculture usually has an above-average capital-output ratio. To the extent that the composition of final output shifts over time away from agriculture and public utilities toward the products of light manufacturing and services, any tendency for the average productivity of capital to fall would be mitigated. It would even be possible for the capital-output ratio to rise in every sector at the same time as the aggregate capital-output ratio falls.

This change in the composition of output does not seem to account for the post-war Norwegian data given by Aukrust, but it may be of significance elsewhere and at other times.

One could no doubt think of still other ways of explaining the failure of capital-output ratios to rise.[4] But enough has been said to justify facetiously turning the question around to wonder why the ratio hasn't fallen faster. Note that all of the offsetting factors mentioned are essentially long-run, so that they leave open the possibility that short bursts of investment may run into diminishing returns. In any case, the considerations I have mentioned suggest many lines of research whose results, I suspect, would turn out to be more interesting than the answer to the original questions.

III. INVESTMENT AND "ORGANIZATION"

The most challenging of Aukrust's conclusions is that "the possibilities of accelerating economic growth by increased investments are considerably smaller than we have been used to assume so far." This corresponds to the estimate made by Fabricant, Kendrick, and others that something over 75 percent of the increase in output per man-hour since 1900 is attributable to technical progress rather than to the formation of capital.[5] One is reminded of Ricardo and Mill talking

[4]For instance, it is widely believed that time series underestimate the "true" rate of increase of output by failing to give proper weight to quality improvements. This effect may cancel out between capital and output, but it is not inconceivable that the underestimate is greater in the case of capital.

[5]See, for instance, S. Fabricant, "Basic Facts on Productivity Change," New York: National Bureau of Economic Research, 1959.

about diminishing returns and the stationary state at the very moment when the industrial revolution was radically changing the basis of human subsistence. Has economics been barking up the wrong tree ever since?

Aukrust carefully qualifies his results by noting (page 96) that it may be unrealistic to imagine that "organization" and real capital (or technical progress and investment) enter the production functions independently. Thus the model he uses may "give an exaggerated impression of the increase in output which can be reached through better organization alone . . . without *simultaneous* increase in the real capital." In my own terminology, technical progress may need to be embodied in appropriate capital goods before it can have an effect on output. So an interaction arises between the effective rate of technical progress and the rate of gross capital formation. I have experimented with a model in which this is the case.[6]

In this alternative model, the stock of capital goods is assumed to consist of layers or "vintages" according to the instant of time at which the capital goods were constructed. Technical progress is assumed to be neutral and exponential in time; capital goods of each vintage embody the very newest technique at their time of construction, but are not affected by any subsequent improvements. Thus old machines have to compete with newer machines. This is reflected in second-hand values and in the conclusion that older machines will be used less labor-intensively than newer machines. With an optimal (competitive allocation of labor to different vintages of machines, a modified production function can be deduced which relates output to the input of labor and to a weighted sum of the whole past history of gross investments.

A lot of assumptions go into this model, and even so it is not as simple to apply as the one described by Aukrust. I have made a rough and tentative application to data for the U. S. between 1919 and 1953, with results which I should like briefly to summarize.

The "pure" rate of technical progress is estimated to be larger than in the earlier models, closer to 2.5 percent per year rather than 1.5 percent. This is to be expected, since the weight of the old capital stock creates a drag on the increase of output per head. But at the

---

[6]Full details are given in a paper, "Investment and Technical Progress" read at the First Stanford Symposium on Mathematical Methods in the Social Sciences, in June, 1959. It will be published by the Stanford University Press in 1960 as part of the Proceedings of the Symposium.

same time the alternative model makes increases in output rather more sensitive to increases in capital formation than it is under the earlier assumptions. Let me illustrate this by a numerical example comparing the two models. Imagine an economy which has been going along forever with a constant rate of gross investment. The rate of improvement of technique $\lambda = .015$. The elasticities of output with respect to labor and capital are .7 and .3 respectively. The average length of life of capital goods is 20 years. The labor force is stationary, for simplicity. Now suddenly the rate of gross investment is doubled and remains at the higher level for ten years. At the end of that period, by how much will GNP have increased? According to the model used by Aukrust, Niitamo and my earlier paper, output will increase by 28 percent. According to the alternative model the increase would be 35 percent. In both cases, if the doubling of gross investment had not taken place, the 10-year increase in output would have been 16 percent. Thus the first model imputes an extra 12 percent increase in output to the burst of capital formation; the second model imputes 19 percent.

Actually a more significant comparison would be one using $\lambda = .015$ for the first model and $\lambda = .030$ for the second, since the two models seem to imply different values of this parameter. In this case, the first model behaves as above. But the second model predicts a 61 percent increase in output as against a 35 percent increase without the added burst of gross investment. Thus the earlier model attributes an extra 12 percent increase in output to the investment program, the newer model makes that figure 26 percent.

Of course, a doubling of gross capital formation is a rather sensational change. But I have chosen the figures simply in order to make the comparison stand out. I am not interested in the exact magnitudes but merely in the conclusion that allowance for the interaction between real capital and "organization" does restore the rate of investment to a position of some importance as a factor in economic growth. But quite clearly it must share that position with the factor of organization or technical change or whatever one chooses to call it. Aukrust is surely right in suggesting that the latter deserves more attention than economists have given it so far.

Two other consequences of the alternative model deserve mention here. One is that the alternative model reduces to the earlier model with the capital stock measured by its value in terms of consumer goods *when durable assets are valued with perfect foresight.* This involves not only correct prediction of future technical change and obsolescence but also of future gross capital formation. Thus it is hardly an attainable ideal. The second consequence is that under opposite assumptions, when all durable assets are expected always to retain what value they happen to have at present, the capital-output ratio will be constant. But this requires that the public hold to naive expectations even though the expectations are continually being falsified. So it is equally as unlikely a state of affairs as its opposite.

In the old days we used to think about the level of this and the size of that. Then Harrod and Domar taught us the salutary habit of thinking in terms of rates of growth. May I suggest that this habit can be carried too far? In the first place, equal rates of growth preserve relative differences. If your bank and mine both pay 3 percent but your account is twice as large as mine at the start, it will always be twice as large as mine, and the absolute dollar difference between us gets larger and larger. Secondly, the full effect of small differences in growth rates may be felt only after a long time.

Let me call attention to Aukrust's Table 5 (page 99) which gives the growth rate of national product for various rates of increase in employment and various values of the net investment/national product ratio, and for fixed values of the other parameters (capital and labor elasticities of .25 and .75, $\lambda = .015$, capital-output ratio = 3.5). The point it makes is valid for the initial period of time but may perhaps be wrongly interpreted. For one thing, in the nature of the model once all the other parameters are specified, the capital-output ratio is no longer open to choice; it will change as governed by the production function, λ, at the savings ratio. But for the initial stretch of time one may take it as approximately constant. Secondly, in the long run, the rate of growth of output is *independent* of the savings ratio, depending only on λ, the rate of growth of employment, and the production function. But this is an example of how deceptive it can be to talk only in terms of growth rates. For if two otherwise identical economies have different savings ratios, even if they eventually come to grow at the same rate, the national income of the one with the higher savings ratio will be higher by a constant factor, and by an ever-widening difference. Thirdly, this effect is present even for short periods in which from arbitrary initial conditions the rate of growth is not constant. That is why I chose to frame my numerical examples in the preceding section in terms of increments over a stated interval of time.

A final example of the apparent paradoxes which may stem from exclusive attention to gross rates comes from comparing the two models described in the preceding section. They are clearly different and describe different kinds of idealized economic systems. In general they contain quite different implications about the course of events. Yet if one imagines two economies, one described by each model, with the same parameters, but which have both always experienced constant growth rates of employment and of gross investment, then both economies will have gross products growing *at the same rate.* The greater optimism of the earlier model shows itself only in that it predicts a national product higher by a constant factor which is larger the larger is λ.

V. CONCLUSION

I hope to have won a little territory back for the effectiveness of investment. How much is hard to say. We could use much more scouting in the directions suggested by Dr. Aukrust's important paper.

B. Revamping the Social Accounts

8. Total Investment, Capital and Economic Growth*

JOHN W. KENDRICK

The George Washington University

This paper is a progress report on the research I have under way on total investment, capital, and economic growth.[1] The theoretical basis of the study is simple, yet fundamental. It relates to the definition of investment as the use of resources released from current consumption through saving for the purpose of preserving and increasing output- and income-producing capacity for the future. Part of gross saving and investment is required to offset the decline in value of stocks of capital as they age (as estimated through depreciation or "capital consumption" allowances), or to replace capital items as they are retired. The excess of gross investment over (a) depreciation and (b) retirements represents the increment to the (a) net stock, and (b) the gross stock of capital, respectively. The notion of "maintaining capital intact" in the first sense relates to preservation of the real net income-producing ability of capital through sufficient new investment to offset depreciation; in the second sense, gross investment must offset retirements in order to preserve the output-producing capacity of the stock (given adequate current maintenance expenditures). Thus, real net investment in the first sense augments real net capital stock and thus real net income-producing capacity; in the second sense, we might better refer to real "incremental" investment as

*Reprinted from "Total Investment, Capital and Economic Growth," *Proceedings of the Business and Economic Statistics Section of the American Statistical Association, 1967*, pp. 268–75.

[1]The research is supported by a grant from the National Science Foundation, and is part of a larger set of studies in the national income accounts I am conducting for the National Bureau of Economic Research. (See the forty-seventh *Annual* Report of N.B.E.R., Part II, pp. 9–15.) I am indebted for valuable assistance on this project to Jennifer Rowley, Lenore Wagner, Yvonne Lethem, and Calvin Shelton. This version of the paper has been revised to take account of later estimates.

augmenting real gross capital stock and thus real output-producing capacity.

Since capital may be viewed as productive capacity, it is clear that the study of investment and capital increase should form a central part of the study of economic growth, which is usually defined in terms of the growth of real income and product. If investment and capital are defined comprehensively then the growth of real total stock of capital should largely "explain" the growth of real income. In fact, real income may be viewed as the return to capital (human and nonhuman) employed in the productive process. If the rate of return were constant (implying also a steady rate of utilization), the trends of real income and real capital stock would parallel each other, and their growth rates would be equal. Actually, given imperfections of knowledge, foresight, competition, and economic rationality, and changes in the degrees of imperfection, the rates of return on various types of capital, and thus on total capital, would tend to vary through time.

But since this paper is not intended to be primarily theoretical, we shall not pursue these paths further here. We shall now move to describe the total gross investment estimates — briefly, since this work has been written up elsewhere.[2] Then, we shall describe the methods used to obtain the real gross stock estimates, and summarize our preliminary findings on the growth and changes in composition of total gross stocks, and the relationship of our stock estimates to the corresponding gross income and product estimates. We have not yet reached the stage of estimating depreciation and net stocks for all categories of capital, so the discussions are confined to gross investment and stock.

GROSS INVESTMENT

As indicated in Table 2, we have greatly expanded the concept and measures of investment used in the official Commerce Department estimates of gross national product, which is largely based on the Keynesian framework. The department includes business purchases of durable structures and equipment, net business inventory accumulation, and net foreign investment. We cover all current outlays, tangible and intangible by all sectors, business and non-business, which expand future income and output-producing capacity. This

[2] *Ibid.*

major expansion was undertaken, as indicated above, to make possible a more complete analysis of the anatomy of economic growth. It has also involved some adjustments to the G.N.P. concept and estimates, which will also be described briefly.

Under the heading of tangible investment, in addition to business capital outlays, we include purchases of structures, durable goods, and additions to inventories by governments and households. The Commerce Department already includes new residential construction for owner-occupancy as well as for rentals, and imputes a rental value to owner-occupied dwelling units, recognizing that otherwise G.N.P. and the investment component will be distorted by ownership-shifts. The same reasoning can be applied to all durable goods and inventories since shifts in sector of ownership can, and do, take place. This is particularly the case in the increasing opportunities for house-holds, and governments, to lease equipment as well as structures from business enterprises, or to purchase the services, as an alternative to owning the capital goods themselves.[3]

The chief forms of intangible investments are shown in Table 2 — education and training, research and development, medical and health, and mobility costs. We have discussed that rationale of in-cluding these items as investment elsewhere.[4] To summarize here, it is clear that all the outlays, regardless of the sector financing, contrib-ute to future income-producing capacity, particularly if psychic income flowing from better education, and better health, is included. Some indeterminate portion of education (small) and of health out-lays (probably larger) represents current consumption; but not know-ing how to segregate this portion, we have included all of the outlays for education and half of health outlays. Insofar as some of the in-tangible investment (especially research and development) is charged by business as a current expense, an upward adjustment of the official G.N.P. estimates was required for the sake of consistency. We also added to G.N.P. the imputed compensation for schoolwork, the opportunity cost of students, which is the largest part of educational expense.

The final category we add to the official investment estimates is one on which less work has been done by others — the costs of rearing

[3] See Thomas Juster, *Household Capital Formation and Financing,* 1897–1962.

[4] John W. Kendrick, "Restructuring the National Economic accounts for Investment and Growth Analysis," *Statistisk Tidskrift,* Stockholm, 1966:5.

children to working age. This is tangible human investment, based on the cumulative average expenditures per child at various ages up to 14. At age 14, some boys and girls start work; for those who remain in school we estimate opportunity costs, which are not very different from subsistence costs at that age. The logic of estimating rearing costs as investment is that these outlays compete with other forms of investment for scarce funds. Further, it makes it possible to place all human investment and capital on a monetary basis, consistent with nonhuman investment and capital.

SUMMARY OF GROSS INVESTMENT TRENDS

Total gross investment can be compared with G.N.P. adjusted for consistency as indicated above. Note that when we add business investments charged to current expense, imputed compensation of students, and imputed rentals on non-business capital goods, G.N.P. so adjusted rises from 122 percent of official G.N.P. in 1929 to around 130 percent in 1966 (see Table 1). As shown in Table 2, the grand total of investment rose from 44.3 percent of adjusted G.N.P. in 1929 to about 51.1 percent in 1966. Gross tangible nonhuman investment showed only a slight relative increase, however, offset by a relative decline in the rearing costs ratio. The relative increase in the total investment ratio can be entirely traced to the intangibles. The largest proportionate increases came in the research and development category; the largest absolute increases came in education and training, followed by medical and health outlays. Mobility costs was the type of intangible investment which increased no faster than real G.N.P.

When we look at investment by sector (Table 3), it can be seen that most of the investment increase came in the government sector, total public gross investment rising from about 5 percent of adjusted G.N.P. in 1929 to 11 percent in 1966. This rise was due chiefly to an approximate doubling in the net receipts of governments relative to adjusted G.N.P., but there was also a modest rise in the proportion of net receipts devoted to investment. In the case of the personal sector, the ratio of gross disposable personal income to adjusted G.N.P. dropped significantly, but this was more than offset by an increase in the proportion of the income devoted to investment. In the business sector, there was no pronounced trend either in the ratio of gross retained income to G.N.P., nor in the ratio of gross investment to gross retained income.

TABLE 1

Adjustments of Commerce Department Estimates of Gross National Product
Required for Consistency with Total Investment Estimates

(Billions of dollars)

	1929	1940	1948	1957	1966[p]
GNP Commerce concept	103.1	99.7	257.6	441.1	747.6
Plus:					
Households and institutions					
Imputed student compensation	5.7	7.6	18.0	32.8	70.5
Imputed rentals on durables (ex. maint.) and inventories	10.6	8.7	20.3	46.5	75.9
Imputed rentals on institutional plant over Commerce institutional depreciation	.2	.2	.6	1.6	3.5
Business:					
Tangible investment charged to current account	.5	.6	1.8	3.1	4.0
Intangible investment charged to current account	2.2	2.1	7.0	12.4	27.0
Government:					
Imputed rentals on land, durables (ex. maint.) and inventories	3.5	4.2	20.9	32.7	49.2
Equals: G.N.P. Adjusted	125.9	123.0	326.1	570.2	977.8
Ratio: Adjusted to Commerce G.N.P.	1.22	1.23	1.27	1.29	1.31

Detail may not add to totals due to rounding.
p = preliminary

TABLE 2
Total Tangible and Intangible Investments in Relation to Adjusted U.S. Gross National Product
(Billions of dollars and percentages)

	1929 Billions of dollars	1929 Percent of G.N.P.	1948 Billions of dollars	1948 Percent of G.N.P.	1966ᵖ Billions of dollars	1966ᵖ Percent of G.N.P.
Gross tangible domestic investment	29.6	23.5	77.6	23.8	244.7	25.0
Structures	11.5	9.1	27.8	8.5	78.1	8.0
Business		4.9		3.4		3.2
Durable equipment	15.7	12.4	44.7	13.7	145.6	14.9
Business		4.6		6.0		5.7
Change in inventories	2.4	1.9	5.1	1.6	21.1	2.2
Business		1.4		1.4		1.5
Net foreign investment	0.8	0.6	1.9	0.6	2.2	0.2
Intangible investment	15.7	12.5	45.0	13.8	198.2	20.3
Education and training	11.0	8.7	30.8	9.4	136.7	14.0
Business		1.3		1.5		1.8
Medical and health	1.9	1.5	5.2	1.6	21.5	2.2
Business		0.1		0.1		0.1
Research and Development	0.2	0.2	2.4	0.7	22.8	2.3
Business		0.1		0.3		0.7
Mobility costs	2.5	2.0	6.6	2.0	17.3	1.8
Business		0.2		0.3		0.2
Rearing Costs (households)	9.8	7.8	18.3	5.6	54.6	5.6
Total investment	55.8	44.3	142.8	43.8	499.8	51.1
Adjusted G.N.P.	125.9	100.0	326.1	100.0	977.8	100.0

Detail may not add to totals due to rounding.
p = preliminary

TABLE 3

Disposable Receipts and Expenditures, Current and Capital, by Sector of the U.S. Economy

(Billions of dollars and percentages)

	1929			1948			1966ᵖ		
	Billions of dollars	Percent of adjusted G.N.P.	Percent of sector revenue	Billions of dollars	Percent of adjusted G.N.P.	Percent of sector revenue	Billions of dollars	Percent of adjusted G.N.P.	Percent of sector revenue
Gross disposable personal income*	98.9	78.6	100.0	228.4	70.0	100.0	657.8	67.3	100.0
Current consumption expenditures	63.6		64.3	143.7		62.9	377.9		57.5
Total investment	33.2	26.4	33.6	81.3	24.9	35.6	260.7	26.7	39.6
Net financial investment	2.1		2.1	3.4		1.5	19.2		2.9
Gross business retained income*	12.9	10.2	100.0	34.2	10.5	100.0	113.2	11.6	100.0
Total investment	15.9	12.6	123.4	42.2	13.0	123.5	128.6	13.2	113.6
Net financial investment	-3.0		-23.4	-8.0		-23.5	-15.4		-13.6
Gross government receipts*	13.0	10.3	100.0	61.0	18.7	100.0	207.2	21.2	100.0
Current purchases	6.1		47.2	35.1		57.5	97.2		46.9
Total investment	5.9	4.7	45.3	17.3	5.3	28.4	108.2	11.1	52.3
Net financial investment	1.0		7.5	8.6		14.0	1.8		0.8
Net foreign transfers	0.4	0.3		4.5	1.4		2.9	0.3	
Net exports	1.1	0.9		6.4	2.0		5.1	0.5	
Net foreign claims	-0.8	-0.6		-1.9	-0.6		-2.2	-0.2	
Total income	125.2	99.4		328.1	100.6		981.1	100.3	
Statistical discrepancy	0.7	0.6		-2.0	-0.6		-3.3	-0.3	
Total G.N.P., adjusted	125.9	100.0		326.1	100.0		977.8	100.0	

*Gross of capital consumption, but net of transfers to other sectors.

Detail may not add to totals due to rounding.

p = preliminary

These summary numbers indicate clearly that the total investment and saving concepts will require considerable rethinking of macroeconomic relationships, particularly the aggregate and personal saving functions. Instead of a relatively constant fraction of national product going into saving and investment, as indicated by the narrower, official concepts, it is clear that as real per-capita income and product have grown, a rising proportion has been channeled into forward-looking outlays. Likewise, personal saving (total investment plus net financial investment in Table 3) has risen significantly in relation to disposable personal income (gross), in contrast to the saving- and consumption-functions based on the official concepts and estimates, which indicate a relatively constant proportionate allocation between present satisfactions and provision for the future.

In the business sector, the inclusion of capital outlays charged to current expense (particularly the intangibles) indicates a stronger upward investment trend than that based on tangibles charged to capital account. And the fact that government has been responsible for most of the relative increase in total investment requires some reappraisal of the role of governments in promoting economic growth.

TOTAL CAPITAL STOCK

What has been the result of the strong upward relative trend of intangible and total investment, in terms of the total gross capital stock? Since there have been no previous attempts to estimate stocks resulting from all the major types of intangible investment, and to combine these with estimates of tangible capital stocks, I shall first describe briefly our methodology with particular reference to the intangibles. As a general proposition, it should be noted that the stock estimates are based on the costs of the capital goods and services. Assuming rational behavior, the original investment cost equals the present (discounted) value of the expected future income stream. But in the gross stock estimates, no allowance is made for depreciation as the stocks age; further, in the case of human investments, it would be unrealistic to assume any very precise calculus, particularly in the decision to have and to rear children. Thus, the gross stocks represent replacement costs as of the current or base year, and not the "value" of the capital.

The estimates of tangible reproducible (nonhuman) capital were made by the familiar perpetual inventory method using constant (1958) dollar outlays. Annual real gross outlays, by types of structures and durable equipment, were retired from stock over periods centered on the estimated average lifetimes. It is well known that the stock estimates vary somewhat depending on the assumed average lifetimes, mortality curves, and the degree of detail employed, etc. We plan in the final report to perform some sensitivity analyses, to see how much difference is made by variations of methodology within a reasonable range. The estimates presented here represent our "best" assumptions. The estimates of business inventories, net foreign assets, and land are based on those of Raymond Goldsmith.[5]

For rearing costs, we estimated the cumulative average cost per child up to age 14, year by year (beginning 95 years prior to the beginning of the number of persons in each annual cohort). This method takes very precise account of the annual "retirements" (death) of individuals from the human capital stock each year. Our Variant A takes account of the gradual rise in planes of living with respect to actual rearing costs. The "A" estimates thus reflect both changes in population and in average actual rearing expenses. Variant B holds rearing costs at the average per person in stock as of 1929. Thus, the "B" estimates, in real terms, reflect only the changes in population and its age composition.

The education, general training, and medical and health outlays are handled in a similar manner. That is, we estimate the average annual expenditures by single age brackets, cumulate for each cohort, and multiply by the numbers of persons in each age bracket each year. The extensive calculations required for the stock estimates were made by electronic computer.

Since rearing costs, education and general training, and health costs were estimated for the population as a whole, it was necessary to isolate that portion of total stock embodied in the active (employed) labor force. To do this, we first divided the stock into that embodied in persons under 14 years of age, and 14 and over. To the latter stock, we applied employment/population ratios to stocks by age groupings. Then, to estimate the portion of productive human capital employed in the private domestic business sector, we applied ratios

---

[5]See *The National Wealth of the United States in the Postwar Period* (Princeton University Press for the National Bureau of Economic Research, 1962).

of persons engaged in that sector to total persons engaged (Commerce Department estimates, adjusted upward to include unpaid family workers).

For specific training and the job search, hiring, and frictional unemployment portions of mobility costs, we estimated the average periods of employment in one job and kept the related investments in stock for these periods. For the migration portion of mobility costs, we cumulated costs using the average number of years workers remain in a given locality as the average lifetime of the investment.

In the case of basic research (about 10 percent of total R&D), we cumulated real costs without allowance for retirements on the grounds that all advances in basic knowledge contribute to further advance. The estimates of stock resulting from applied research and development involved several pieces of information: (a) the portion of each year's AR&D representing completed projects; (b) the average time lag between completion of AR&D and incorporation in new products and processes; (c) the average lives of products and processes; and (d) a distribution of retirements around the average lives. Since this information was not available from secondary sources, a questionnaire was sent to a sample of industrial laboratories, and our numbers were based on approximately 40 replies. The survey results will be described in a separate paper.

TOTAL PRODUCTIVE CAPITAL – TRENDS AND COMPOSITION

Summing all types of productive capital, tangible and intangible, in constant prices, we find that the aggregate (Variant A) approximately tripled between 1929 and 1966 – an average annual rate of growth of 3 percent (see Table 4a). Intangible capital grew far more than the tangible, increasing 426 percent over the period, compared with an increase of 160 percent in the tangible nonhuman capital. Tangible human capital increased by 167 percent by Variant A, which takes account of rising real rearing costs; whereas by Variant B the increase was 65 percent, which approximates the growth of total employment.

As a result of these relative trends, the stock of tangible nonhuman capital fell from 69 percent of the total in 1929 to 61 percent in 1966. Intangible capital rose sharply from 20 to 29 percent. Tangible human capital fell from 11 to 10 percent by Variant A – more if calculated on the basis of Variant B.

TABLE 4a

Employed Gross National Wealth – U.S. Economy[1]

(Billions of 1958 dollars and percentages)

	1929 $ billions	1929 Percent distrib.	1948 $ billions	1948 Percent distrib.	1948 Index (1929 = 100)	1966ᵖ $ billions	1966ᵖ Percent distrib.	1966ᵖ Index (1929 = 100)
Tangible, nonhuman								
Structures	643	34.3	885	29.7	137.6	1,547	28.2	240.7
Durable equipment	285	15.2	563	18.9	197.7	1,110	20.2	389.3
Inventories	107	5.7	144	4.8	134.6	278	5.1	260.3
Monetary metals & net foreign assets	32	1.7	42	1.4	132.7	62	1.1	195.2
Land	227	12.1	265	8.9	116.7	366	6.7	161.1
Sub-total	1,293	69.1	1,898	63.8	146.8	3,362	61.2	260.0
Tangible, human								
Variant A[2]	208	11.1	345	11.6	165.9	555	10.1	266.7
Variant B[3]	208		285		137.0	343		164.9
Intangible								
Basic Research	1	0.1	5	0.2	392.3	26	0.5	1,992.3
Applied rsch. & dev.	6	0.3	26	0.9	474.5	136	2.5	2,469.1
Education & training	299	16.0	603	20.3	201.4	1,229	22.4	410.7
Medical & health	33	1.7	61	2.0	185.6	133	2.4	406.1
Mobility costs	32	1.7	38	1.3	116.1	55	1.0	171.2
Sub-total	371	19.8	732	24.6	197.3	1,579	28.7	425.5
Total productive capital								
Variant A	1,872	100.0	2,976	100.0	158.9	5,496	100.0	293.6
Variant B	1,872		2,916		155.8	5,284		282.3

[1] Detail figures may not add precisely to totals because of rounding. Estimates are subject to revision.
[2] Cumulated rearing costs, reflecting rising planes of living.
[3] Cumulated rearing costs, based on average rearing costs per capita as of 1929.
p = preliminary

119

Within the tangible sub-total, land showed a relative decline, structures fell to a smaller relative extent, while durable equipment showed a significant relative growth. Within the intangible sub-total, the stocks resulting from research and development increased about twenty-fold, education and training rose to 411 percent of the 1929 base, and medical and health stocks rose to 406. Cumulative mobility costs rose by little more than the active labor force.

In the private domestic business economy alone (Table 4b), the total capital stock grew at a somewhat slower pace, reflecting the increasing relative importance of the government sector. Tangible nonhuman assets play a smaller relative role in the business sector, and fell from 58 to 44 percent of the total. The role of the intangibles is greater, and the relative increase from 1929 to 1966 was almost as great as in the total economy.

RELATION OF TOTAL CAPITAL TO G.N.P.

Of particular interest is the relationship of total productive capital to gross national product. It will be recalled that the broad hypothesis behind the present research project is that the secular movements of real gross national wealth should largely explain those of real gross national product. How well do the new total wealth estimates support the hypothesis?

Between 1929 and 1966, real G.N.P. (adjusted) rose by 241 percent, or at an average annual rate of 3.4 percent; real gross national wealth rose by 197 percent, an average annual rate of 3.0 percent. The ratio of the two variables (G.N.P./G.N.W., or average "total productivity") increased from 12.5 to 14.5 percent—an increase of 16 percent, or 0.4 percent a year, on average. Thus, the growth of total real gross productive wealth statistically "explains" almost 90 percent of the growth in real G.N.P., as adjusted (see Table 5).

A serious drawback to using the estimates for the total economy is that the real G.N.P. originating in the sectors other than private domestic business (general governments, households and nonprofit institutions, and rest-of-world) is estimated in terms of the real labor and capital compensation originating. Since real factor compensation is estimated in such a way as to move closely with the real factor stocks, the ratios of real G.N.P. to real G.N.W. in the non-business sectors do not have independent significance. For this reason, in Table 5 we also show the ratios for the private domestic business

TABLE 4b

Employed Gross National Wealth – Private Domestic Business Sector[1]

(Billions of 1958 dollars and percentages)

	1929 $ billions	1929 Percent distrib.	1948 $ billions	1948 Percent distrib.	1948 Index (1929 = 100)	1966ᵖ $ billions	1966ᵖ Percent distrib.	1966ᵖ Index (1929 = 100)
Tangible, nonhuman								
Structures	319	26.7	295	18.4	92.5	486	17.0	152.4
Durable equipment	132	11.0	161	10.0	122.5	382	13.4	289.6
Inventories	74	6.2	95	5.9	128.6	169	5.9	228.3
Land	173	14.5	176	10.9	101.3	212	7.4	122.7
Sub-total	698	58.4	728	45.3	104.2	1,250	43.8	179.0
Tangible, human								
Variant A[2]	179	15.0	285	17.8	159.5	416	14.6	232.6
Variant B[3]	179		234		130.7	258		144.1
Intangible								
Basic research	1	0.1	5	0.3	392.3	26	0.9	1,992.3
Applied rsch. & dev.	5	0.4	22	1.3	421.6	107	3.8	2,100.0
Education & training	256	21.4	484	30.1	189.0	910	31.9	355.5
Medical & health	28	2.4	51	3.2	180.2	102	3.6	361.1
Mobility costs	28	2.4	32	2.0	113.9	43	1.5	154.4
Sub-total	319	26.7	593	36.9	186.2	1,188	41.6	372.9
Total productive capital								
Variant A	1,196	100.0	1,606	100.0	134.3	2,854	100.0	238.7
Variant B	1,196		1,555		130.0	2,696		225.4

[1] Detail figures may not add precisely to totals because of rounding. Estimates are subject to revision.

[2] Cumulated rearing costs, reflecting rising planes of living.

[3] Cumulated rearing costs, based on average rearing costs per capita as of 1929.

p = preliminary

121

TABLE 5

Employed Real Gross National Wealth—Product Relationships
Total Economy and Private Domestic Business Sector
(Billions of 1958 dollars and index numbers, 1929 = 100)

		1929	1940	1948	1957	1966
Total economy						
G.N.W.	(billions)	1,872	2,153	2,976	4,098	5,496
	(index)	100.0	115.0	158.9	218.9	293.6
G.N.P.[1], adjusted	(billions)	234	263	391	550	799
	(index)	100.0	112.3	166.9	234.8	341.2
G.N.P.[1]/G.N.W.	(percent)	12.5	12.2	13.1	13.4	14.5
	(index)	100.0	97.6	105.0	107.3	116.2
Private domestic business						
G.N.W.	(billions)	1,196	1,302	1,606	2,135	2,854
	(index)	100.0	108.8	134.3	178.5	238.7
G.N.P., adjusted	(billions)	176	192	279	381	562
	(index)	100.0	109.0	158.9	216.8	319.9
G.N.P./G.N.W.	(percent)	14.7	14.7	17.4	17.8	19.7
	(index)	100.0	100.1	118.3	121.4	134.0

[1] Excluding imputed student compensation.
Detail may not add to totals due to rounding.
p = preliminary. All estimates are subject to revision.

sector alone, since in this major portion of the economy, the real G.N.P. estimates are independent of the real G.N.W. estimates.

Here, real product rose by 3.2 percent a year on average, real wealth by 2.4 percent, and total productivity by 0.8 percent. Thus, the growth of real wealth "explains" a somewhat smaller portion − 75 percent − of the growth of real product in the private domestic business sector than in the economy as a whole.

One would not expect a perfect correlation between movements in G.N.W. and G.N.P., of course. In the first place, since investments, particularly the human investments, are not made on a purely rational basis, each major type may have different average and marginal rates of return. Thus, changes in the mix of the capital stock could affect income and product. Further, the rate of return on total investment and stock, even assuming an optimum mix, could change over time.

Second, there are variables other than the volume of total capital that affect the movements of output. Among the most important are: (a) changes in the rates of utilization of both the human and non-human stocks of productive capital; (b) economies of scale − although I personally think that such potential economies generally require investment for realization; (c) changes in the degree of economic efficiency in allocation and use of resources; and (d) speed of adjustment of resources to dynamic change.

Finally, the underlying data are imperfect, and estimating methodology is not unambiguous. Alternative stock estimates are in preparation, for purposes of sensitivity analysis.

We plan next to experiment with statistical production function analysis, in order to arrive at exponents for the several major types of capital, and to evaluate the relative importance of the several additional variables that influence stock-flow relationships. But I believe that pending the results of further analysis, the material presented here strongly supports the thesis that analysis of economic growth and projections into the future will be significantly strengthened by taking into account all types of productive wealth.

PART III Investment in Education

Introduction

The concept of human capital is being widely used by economists as a means of emphasizing the importance of education, both formal and on the job, in developing human resources. Efforts are being made to determine, from both the microeconomic and macroeconomic points of view, the amount of human capital investment attributable to education and its yield. Much emphasis is being placed on this factor as a source of ecomomic growth.

The first reading (Reading 9) in Part III is a theoretical article by Yoram Ben-Porath. Professor Ben-Porath relates the share of individual's earning profiles to properties of the production function of human capital. He then assesses the implications of these relations.

Basic to human capital evaluation procedures are age-income profiles by level of education. Accordingly, the second reading (Reading 10) in this part is a well-known article by Herman Miller. Dr. Miller calculates lifetime income values by level of education. He, however, does not discount the income streams back to the time when the decision to acquire the education was made, which is necessary to acquire estimates of human capital values. Since a present dollar is clearly more valuable than a future one, discounting obviously is desirable.

H. S. Houthakker, in the third reading (Reading 11) in this part, estimates, using alternative interest rates, the capital value of income streams associated with various levels of education. Although Professor Houthakker does not discuss the basis for choosing a discount rate, the result of any present-value calculation obviously depends heavily upon the discount rate chosen. There is no simple answer to the question of what is the appropriate discount rate. In calculating an educational project where public funds are to be used, the correct interest rate should be the rate of return that could have been earned in the private sector of the economy when the decision is made to commit funds to the public project. William Baumol suggests that this rate should be twice the average rate of return (after taxes, assuming a tax rate of 50 percent) on corporate investments.[1] If the students themselves (or their parents) are contemplating investing in

---

[1]W. J. Baumol, "On the Social Rate of Discount," *American Economic Review*, LVIII (September, 1968), pp. 788–802.

education, perhaps the average rate of return on corporate investments would be the appropriate interest rate. It may be necessary, however, to adjust for risk and uncertainty. Certainly risk and uncertainty reduce the value of any stream of future earnings, and it is possible to account in part for this by employing a discount rate that includes a risk factor. The difficulty of choosing a "correct" discount rate is recognized by all the contributors to this volume.

The final reading (Reading 12) in Section A of Part III is by Giora Hanoch. In the first section of his paper, Hanoch estimates male expected earnings in the United States in 1959 by age and education, after standardizing for such factors as expected secular growth, mortality, expected improvements in the quality of education, cyclical variations in earnings, changes in market conditions for various skills, and progressive taxation of earnings. The second section of Hanoch's paper deals with deriving internal rates of return on education. Hence, the second part of Hanoch's paper looks ahead to the next section of Part III of the volume which deals with benefit-cost analysis.

Section B of Part III develops what has come to be known as the "benefit-cost" approach to assessing an investment project. One of the reasons for estimating the human capital value attributable to education is to compare this value with the cost incurred to produce it in order to see if education is a "profitable" investment. Another way of looking at the same question is to compute the internal rate of return obtained on the cost of education and compare it with rates obtained on alternative investments.

W. Lee Hansen, in the first reading (Reading 13) in this section, estimates internal rates of return on both social (total) and private expenditures on education. Although he fails to adjust for ability and other differences, his estimates are supported by those of Hanoch.

Most analyses of private rates of return fail to evaluate the "financial option"—that is, the value of the opportunity to get further education—associated with a given level of education. Since further education usually leads to an increase in earnings, the "option" to continue education has a value. The "financial option" as well as other indirect returns to, or external benefits of, education is investigated in the second contribution to this section by Burton A. Weisbrod (Reading 14).

The rate-of-return approach to assessing an educational project has received severe criticism. A major difficulty with this approach is that the earnings differential stream may change sign more than once. Hence there can be as many rates of return as there are changes in sign. This difficulty led Bruce Wilkinson to discard this approach in favor of the present-value approach. His analysis is presented as the third reading (Reading 15) in this section.

Since any expenditure on an individual which increases his productivity may be thought of as an investment in human capital, on-the-job training can usefully be treated within the human capital analytical framework. Although a vast amount of literature is available on the investment aspect of formal education, very little has appeared on this aspect of on-the-job training. A few writers, however, have included on-the-job training in their theoretical analysis of formal education, and there has been one excellent article by Jacob Mincer which deals specifically with the investment aspect of on-the-job training. Professor Mincer's method of estimating on-the-job training investment, as defined and measured in terms of its cost in foregone earnings, captures the cost of learning from experience in his estimation procedure. He, unfortunately, fails to include direct on-the-job training costs in his calculations. Mincer's article is the fourth reading (Reading 16) in this section.

In considering the question of why the incentive has been maintained for a relative expansion in the supply of skilled labor in the United States, Finis Welch, in Section C of Part III (Reading 17), develops a new and interesting approach to education as an input in the production process.

In the lead article (Reading 18) in Section D of Part III, Maurice C. Benewitz and Albert Zucker employ Irving Fisher's "marginal rate of time preference" as a determinant of investments in human capital that are associated with occupational choice.

A worker's acquired skill may be rendered obsolete by a change in the state of the arts or tastes. An interesting question is: can a worker profitably hedge against the risk of skill obsolescence through the acquisition of a second skill which is maintained in reserve. This question is investigated by C. J. Cipriani in the second article (Reading 19) in Section D. Arie R. Melnik, in a comment (Reading 20) on Cipriani's article, extends Cipriani's analysis.

A. Education and Earnings

9. Production of Human Capital and the Life Cycle of Earnings*

YORAM BEN-PORATH
University of Chicago

The application of capital theory to decisions on individual improvement, and in particular improvement of earning capacity, has provided a framework for the understanding of many aspects of observed behavior regarding education, health, occupational choice, mobility, etc., as rational investment of present resources for the purpose of enjoying future returns. The formulation by Friedman and Kuznets (1945) and the significant development of the theory by Becker (1962, 1964) and Mincer (1958, 1962) provided a novel view of the life cycle of earnings by linking it to the time profile of investment in human capital: People make most of their investments in themselves when they are young, and to a large extent by foregoing current earnings. Observed earnings are therefore relatively low at early years, and they rise as investment declines and as returns on past investments are realized. The main reason why investment is undertaken mostly by the young is that they have a longer period over which they can receive returns on their investment. The purpose of this paper is to combine that part of the argument concerning the demand for human capital with a more explicit treatment of the supply, or cost conditions, facing the individual.

It is hard to think of forms of human capital that the individual can acquire as final goods—he has to participate in the creation of his human capital. His own abilities, innate or acquired, the quality of co-operating inputs, the constraints and opportunities offered by the institutional setup—all determine the "technology," or the production function.[1] Together with the relevant factor prices, the properties of

*Reprinted from "The Production of Human Capital and the Life Cycle of Earnings," *Journal of Political Economy*, LXXV (August, 1967), 352–365. Copyright by The University of Chicago Press.

[1] Such a production [function] has been recently introduced also by Becker (1966).

the production function determine the optimal way in which any quantity of human capital is to be produced and determine the cost of production. I shall show how the production function (through supply or cost conditions) enters into the determination of the optimal path of investment, analyze some of the implications for the individual's allocation of time, and demonstrate how the life cycle of earnings can be affected by various properties of the production function.

The basic model generates some of the qualitative characteristics of the observed life cycle of earnings—typically, an initial period of no earnings followed by a period in which earnings rise at a declining rate and, eventually, decline. Actual, or observed, earnings turn out to be always lower, to change faster, and to peak at a later age than the attainable maximum, the earning capacity of the individual. The reverse is true of the relation between observed earnings and earnings net of all investment costs: the former are always higher, change slower, and peak at an earlier date than the latter. The model thus specifies the nature of the bias that may exist when earnings are used, as they often have been, to infer changes in productive capacity with age.

I. THE MODEL

In addition to the assumptions incorporated in the production function, to be discussed later, I assume:

1. Individual utility is not a function of activities involving time as an input.

2. There is a fixed amount of time to be allocated every period to activities that produce earnings and additions to the stock of human capital.

3. The stock of human capital, K, of which every individual has some initial endowment, is homogeneous and subject to an exogenously given rate of deterioration, δ.

4. The stock of human capital is not an argument in the individual's utility function.

5. Unlimited borrowing and lending take place at a constant rate of interest, r.

The first two assumptions express the fact that leisure is ignored in this analysis. In conjunction with the other assumptions they allow the partition of the individual's decision-making into two stages:

Investment in Education

a) The individual allocates the given periods of time between earning and producing human capital and finds the corresponding outlays on investment that maximize the discounted value of any time t of disposable earnings (defined below) from t to T, where T is assumed with certainty to be the end of life.

b) Given the optimal time path of disposable earnings, the individual decides on the timing of the consumption. This is the point of departure of the life-cycle theories of consumption, which take the stream of earnings as given and explain consumption as dependent upon it.

The stock of human capital is defined as a concept analogous to "machines" in the case of tangible capital. There is a market in which the services of human capital are traded, and a rental, a_0, is determined for the services of a unit of human capital, K, per unit of time. The sum of the services offered in the market by various individuals is an input into the production of other goods and services. It may well have a diminishing marginal productivity, which will cause a downward-sloping aggregate demand curve for the services of human capital. Each individual is assumed, however, to possess only a small fraction of the total homogeneous stock of human capital in the economy and is regarded as a perfect competitor facing a given rental a_0, which is independent of the volume of services that he offers in the market. Earning capacity at time t, Y_t, is therefore the maximum services of human capital the individual can offer in the market valued by the rental a_0.

$$Y_t = a_0 K_t. \tag{1}$$

Let E_t be disposable earnings in period t—the portion of current earnings disposable for purposes of consumption or the purchase of non-human assets. It may be smaller than earning capacity if the individual engages in production of human capital; other uses for time are excluded by assumption. The difference $(Y_t - E_t)$ is the cost of investment I_t; it depends on the production function and on input prices.

Let (2) be the production function of human capital:

$$Q_t = \beta_0 (s_t K_t)^{\beta_1} D_t^{\beta_2}, \tag{2}$$

where $\beta_1, \beta_2 > 0$ and $\beta_1 + \beta_2 < 1$; Q is the flow of human capital produced. D is the quantity of purchased inputs, the price of which is denoted by P_d; s_t is the fraction of the available stock of human capital allocated to the production of human capital, so that $s_t K_t$ is the quantity of human capital allocated for the purpose. If activities are not "mixed," that is, if there is no joint production of earnings and of human capital, then s_t is also the proportion of time devoted to the production of human capital. The fraction s_t is constrained by the condition

$$0 \leq s_t \leq 1. \tag{3}$$

(The properties of the production function including the assumption of decreasing returns to scale are discussed in a subsequent section.) The rate of change of the capital stock is given by (4):

$$\dot{K}_t = Q_t - \delta K_t \tag{4}$$

(a dot above any variable indicates a derivative with respect to time), where δ is the rate by which the stock of human capital deteriorates. Equations (1) and (4) imply that a unit of capital can be used from the moment that it is produced.

Investment costs have two components:

$$I_t = a_0 s_t K_t + P_d D_t, \tag{5}$$

that is, (a) opportunity costs, or "foregone earnings" (the value of the productive services withdrawn from the market), and (b) the direct costs of purchased goods and services. Minimizing I_t with respect to s_t and D_t, subject to (2) and ignoring (3), we get (6) as a condition for a minimum of (5):

$$\frac{a_0 s_t K_t}{P_d D_t} = \frac{\beta_1}{\beta_2}. \tag{6}$$

From (2) and (6) substituted into (5) we get investment costs as function of output:

$$I_t = \frac{\beta_1 + \beta_2}{\beta_1} a_0 \left(\frac{\beta_1 P_d}{\beta_2 a_0}\right)^{\beta_2/(\beta_1+\beta_2)} \times \left(\frac{Q_t}{\beta_0}\right)^{[1/(\beta_1+\beta_2)]} \tag{7}$$

The objective of the individual at any time t is to maximize the present value of his disposable earnings:

$$W_t = \int_t^T e^{-rv} [a_0 K(v) - I(v)] dv. \tag{8}$$

The objective expressed by (8) is treated as applicable to an individual from birth; up to a given age actual decisions are made by his parents, and if they were to take into account the full future life of their child, (8) still expresses the relevant maximand under the assumptions of the model. If the parents do not take into account the full economic life of their child, or in the extreme case where only the period of attachment to the present household is considered, less investment would be undertaken, and the age of entry into the labor force would be lower.

The problem posed here is suitable for treatment by the techniques of optimal control. Three phases are suggested by the constraints on s, the fraction of human capital, or time, allocated to the production of human capital: (i) The available stock of human capital K_t, even when fully allocated to produce human capital, is not large enough to provide the flow of services demanded given the relevant prices. The upper bound on s is thus an effective constraint. (ii) The available stock is large enough to supply the services demanded and more, so that $0 < s < 1$ and the services of human capital are truly a variable factor. (iii) The stock of capital is too big so that the optimal policy requires more disinvestment than is feasible through deterioration, that is, to produce negative quantities of human capital. Here s_t is constrained by its lower bound.[2]

The first phase is by definition a period in which no human capital is allocated to the market so that no earnings are realized. Using conventional tools, we shall first analyze the later phases in which $s < 1$ and then shall return to discuss the first.

---

[2] In terms of the techniques developed by Pontryagin et al., the maximization of (8) subject to (2), (3), and (4) involves the maximization of the Hamiltonian

$$H : e^{-rt}[(1 - s)a_0 K - P_d D] + q(Q - \delta K),$$ (1′)

where q is the discounted shadow price of investment in human capital

$$\dot{q} = -\frac{\partial H}{\partial K} = -e^{-rt}(1 - s)a_0 - q\left(\beta_1 \frac{Q}{K} - \delta\right).$$

In terms of current prices $\psi = q e^{rt}$

$$\dot{\psi} = -(1 - s)a_0 - \psi\left[\beta_1 \frac{Q}{K} - (\delta + r)\right];$$ (2′)

Transversality condition:

$$\psi(T)K(T) = 0.$$ (3′)

First-order conditions for the maximization of (1′):

$$\frac{\partial H}{\partial s} = -a_0 K e^{-rt} + \psi e^{-rt}\frac{Q}{s}\beta_1 \geqslant 0.$$ (4′)

$$\frac{\partial H}{\partial D} = -P_d e^{-rt} + \psi e^{-rt}\frac{Q}{D}\beta_2 = 0.$$ (5′)

A systematic analysis of a variant of this problem, using the techniques of optimal control, is pursued in an unpublished note by Eytan Sheshinski.

Differentiating (7) with respect to Q we get (9), the marginal cost of producing human capital; it is a rising function of the quantity produced starting from the origin and is independent of the size of the existing stock of capital of the individual.

$$MC_t = \frac{a_0}{\beta_0\beta_1}\left(\frac{\beta_1 P_d}{\beta_2 a_0}\right)^{\beta_2/(\beta_1+\beta_2)} \times \left(\frac{Q_t}{\beta_0}\right)^{[1/(\beta_1+\beta_2)]-1} \tag{9}$$

The value at time t of acquiring an additional unit of human capital is the discounted value to that time of the additions to earnings that the undepreciated part of this unit will bring about. This is the "demand price" of human capital, given by (10). This price is

$$P_t = a_0\int_t^T e^{-(r+\delta)v}dv = \frac{a_0}{r+\delta}\left[1 - e^{-(r+\delta)(T-t)}\right], \tag{10}$$

independent of the number of units added or the existing stock. It is a declining function of time because of the presence of the finite horizon.[3] The optimal production of human capital is determined by equating the marginal cost to the price. Equating (9) and (10) we can solve for Q as shown in equation (11).

$$Q_t = \beta_0\left(\frac{\beta_0\beta_1}{r+\delta}\right)^{(\beta_1+\beta_2)/(1-\beta_1-\beta_2)}\left(\frac{\beta_2 a_0}{\beta_1 P_d}\right)^{\beta_2/(1-\beta_1-\beta_2)}\left[1 - e^{-(r+\delta)(T-t)}\right]^{(\beta_1+\beta_2)/(1-\beta_1-\beta_2)}$$

$$= N[1 - e^{-(r+\delta)(T-t)}]^{(\beta_1+\beta_2)/(1-\beta_1-\beta_2)} \geq 0. \tag{11}$$

The production of human capital, Q, the gross additions to the stock, are always positive except when $t=T$. At the date of compulsory retirement, T, the human capital loses its value, $P(T)=0$ (see eq. [10]). No production is undertaken at period T, and the stock of human capital is reduced by sK (see eq. [3]). The point $t=T$ lies in the third phase. The reason why only this point lies in this phase is that for any earlier age, $t < T$, the demand price of human capital is positive, and the fact that the marginal cost curve starts from the origin insures that some positive quantity will always be produced. This would be true of any production function homogeneous of a degree less than 1 in these inputs.

The market prices that enter into the determination of the optimal production of human capital Q are: r, the rate of interest; a_0, the ren-

[3]In terms of the framework of n.2 we are operating in the phase where (4′) holds exactly as equality. Substituting (4′), (5′), and (2) into (2′), and given (3′), we get a differential equation to which (10) is a solution.

tal on human capital; and P_d, the price of purchased inputs. Differentiating (11) with respect to these shows that Q varies inversely with the rate of interest and with the price of purchased inputs and directly with the rental on human capital. It is, however, only the *ratio* between the last two that is important. The elasticity of Q with respect to the relative price a_0/P_a is $\beta_2/(1 - \beta_1 - \beta_2)$. When $\beta_2 = 0$, that is, when purchased inputs do not enter into the production of human capital, changes in a_0, the price of the services of human capital, do not affect the quantity produced. The obvious reason is that in this case, when the services of human capital are the only input, a rise in a_0 raises marginal cost by exactly the same amount that it raises the value of a unit of human capital. Needless to say, all this discussion refers to alternative stationary price levels when the current prices are expected to prevail throughout the individual's lifetime. Q_t is larger the larger the parameters of the production function β_0, β_1, β_2; the greater the length of economic life T; and the lower the rate of deterioration, which has exactly the same effect as the rate of interest.

As t rises, the flow of Q produced declines, as indicated by (12), the derivative of Q with respect to t:

$$\dot{Q} = \frac{\beta_1 + \beta_2}{1 - \beta_1 - \beta_2} N[1 - e^{-(r+\delta)(T-t)}]^{[(\beta_1-\beta_2)/(1-\beta_1-\beta_2)]-1}$$

$$\times e^{(r+\delta)(T-t)}[-(r+\delta)] \leq 0. \tag{12}$$

What we have here is a marginal cost curve as a function of Q starting from the origin and remaining stationary through time, and a perfectly elastic demand curve which slides down with time, thus creating a pattern of positive but declining optimal quantities of Q to be produced (Fig. 1). If the horizon were infinite, the demand curve would not slide down, and there would be at this phase one stationary rate of production of human capital (given by N in eq. [11]). Note that we are saying something about the *gross* additions to stock of human capital but not about the *net* additions, which depend also on the rate of depreciation and the size of the existing stock. If the initial stock is very high, net additions may be negative from an early age. If we think of the normal case as one where the capital stock does rise over a period, eventually as gross additions become very small and the stock becomes large this must be reversed, and toward the end of life, T, the stock will decline, if there is any deterioration.

What are the implications of this pattern of investment for the life cycle of earnings? Disposable earnings were defined as the difference

FIGURE 1

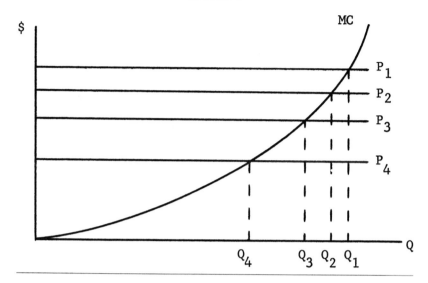

between earning capacity and investment outlays; their rate of change over time is given by (13).

$$\dot{E}_t = a_0 \dot{K}_t - \dot{I}_t. \tag{13}$$

Let us define "observed earnings" $\hat{E}$ to be actual earnings realized in the labor market (14).

$$\hat{E}_t = a_0 K_t - \frac{\beta_1}{\beta_1 + \beta_2} I_t. \tag{14}$$

They are larger than disposable earnings by the direct costs $P_d D$ and smaller than earning capacity by foregone earnings. Their rate of change over time is given by (15).

$$\dot{\hat{E}} = a_0 \dot{K}_t - \frac{\beta_1}{\beta_1 + \beta_2} \dot{I}_t = a_o \dot{Q}_t - \frac{\beta_1}{\beta_1 + \beta_2} (MC_t) \dot{Q}_t - a_0 \delta K_t. \tag{15}$$

$\dot{I}$ is always negative (except when $t = T$), so that the change in observed earnings is always algebraically larger than the change in earning capacity and smaller than the change in disposable earnings

$$\left(\frac{\beta_1}{\beta_1 + \beta_2} < 1 \right).$$

Thus, the curve of observed earnings exaggerates the rate of increase of earning capacity when the latter increases and understates its decline when it declines. In particular, when we observe an individual at the peak of his earnings he is already past the peak of his productive capacity. The existence of a downturn in observed earnings is here only a consequence of depreciation (recall that interactions with "leisure" are excluded by assumption). If depreciation is zero, there is always, except at T, an increase in the three types of earnings, and at each point in time their rank by rate of change will be the reverse of their rank by level.

From the second derivative of observed earnings with respect to time (16), we learn more about the shape of the life cycle of earnings:

$$\ddot{E} = Q_t \left\{ a_0 - \frac{(r+\delta)MC_t}{1 - e^{-(r+\delta)(T-t)}} \frac{\beta_1}{\beta_1+\beta_2} \times \left[1 - \frac{1}{1 - \beta_1 - \beta_2} e^{-(r+\delta)(T+t)} \right] \right\} \qquad (16)$$

$$- a_0 \delta Q_t + a_0 \delta^2 K_t.$$

If there is no deterioration, that is, $\delta = 0$, the ever rising curve of observed earnings is always concave from below. This is also true of the rising portion of the curve when $\delta > 0$. If $\beta_1 + \beta_2 > \frac{1}{2}$, there will be a certain range in the vicinity of $t = T$ where the curve is convex from below.[4] All these qualitative results hold for any production function homogeneous of a degree smaller than 1 in sK and in D.

The preceding discussion relates to the phase where the optimal s, the fraction of human capital or time allocated to the production of human capital, is smaller than 1. As indicated before, the maximization of (8) may, however, require that there will be a phase of complete specialization in the production of human capital in which $s = 1$ and the size of the stock is an effective constraint.

[4] Q is negative, and the term in braces is positive: from the equality between (11) and (12)

$$a_0 = \frac{r+\delta}{1 - e^{-(r+\delta)(T-t)}} MC.$$

The right-hand side of this equality is here multiplied by a term always smaller than $+1$ and deducted from the left side so that the difference is positive and the first term is negative. If $\delta = 0$ and there is no deterioration, the other two terms vanish, and the curve of observed earnings is always concave from below. This is also true of the curve of disposable earnings with 1 substituted for $\beta_1/(\beta_1 + \beta_2)$. When $\delta > 0$, concavity is assured for the range where $\dot{K} = Q - \delta K > 0$. If $\beta_1 + \beta_2 > \frac{1}{2}$, the first term tends to zero as $t \to T$; in the vicinity of $t = T$, $\dot{K} < 0$, so in this case the earnings curve will have there a shape that is convex from below.

Movement along the marginal cost curve (7) by increasing Q implies an increase in the required sK. Once $s = 1$ is reached, larger rates of production can be achieved only by combining more purchased inputs with a fixed flow of services of human capital, thereby increasing costs at à higher rate than is implied by (7). The marginal cost curve described by (7) is a long-run envelope from which steeper marginal cost curves rise up, corresponding to alternative levels of the available stock of human capital. When people are young the value of a unit of human capital is only negligibly affected by the finite horizon T, so demand for human capital is relatively high. On the other hand, the available stock is still small; therefore the marginal cost curve rises up from the long-run curve, (7), at relatively small output, so that at a young age production is likely to occur at outputs where $s = 1$.

Note that the demand price given by (10) is now only the lower limit of the true shadow price of human capital. An increase in the stock of human capital implies a reduction in future costs of production of human capital. The precise value of this depends on the future quantities of Q that will be produced between t and t^*, the date of transfer from the first to the second phase. While in phase (ii), where $0 < s < 1$, we were able to determine the optimal Q_t by the intersection of demand and supply schedules independent of the future levels of Q, here only a complete, dynamic program in which the effects of present actions on future condition are explicitly taken into account will generate an optimal path of investment.

Phase (i) is identified by the absence of earnings. Another distinguishing characteristic of this phase is that the relaxation of the constraint K_t which lowers the marginal cost curve may induce a pattern of increasing investment with age, both through the allocation of the services of a growing stock of human capital for the purpose and through higher direct expenditure on D, justified by the higher marginal productivity of D that the increased K brings about. A phase of increasing direct costs in the early period when no earnings are realized is certainly not inconsistent with the real world.[5]

The age t^* when the individual enters the second phase and leaves the first is of great importance, because this is the date at which positive earnings begin to be realized. From the preceding discussion it

[5] An explicit solution of our problem for the case in which $\beta_2 = 0$ is simple but not interesting. The interesting aspects of the problem derive from the possibility of using purchased inputs.

should be clear that $K(t^*)$ is a declining function of t^*.[6] K_0 is the initial endowment of human capital, which, following the definition of K, is proportional to the maximum earnings the individual can realize when he "starts." All other parameters given, the larger this initial endowment, the earlier will be the date t^* at which specialization stops, noting that K_0 is an initial endowment only in terms of the capacity to earn, while we hold constant the capacity to increase human capital thus defined, which is reflected in the β's of the production function.

II. THE PRODUCTION FUNCTION ROLE AND IMPLICATIONS

The technology which the individual faces when he makes decisions about investing in himself is a complicated system of technical and institutional relationships covering a wide spectrum of activities including formal education, acquisition of skills on the job, child care, nutrition, health, etc. By writing down a simple production function of the sort used here we are attempting, not to reproduce this system, but only to provide a framework within which some of the possible characteristics of the technology can be considered and their implications studied.

A. PURCHASED INPUTS, TIME, AND THE SERVICES OF HUMAN CAPITAL

Both the theory and the measurement of investment in human capital (see Schultz, 1963) emphasize the importance of foregone earnings alongside direct cost. A composite surrogate for direct cost here is D, the index of purchased inputs which stands for anything from tuition to vitamin pills. The presence of opportunities for some substitution between purchased and own inputs has a "smoothing" effect on behavior and helps the individual overcome the constraints of his limited time and sometimes modify the effects of its increasing cost.

The nature of and the role played by own inputs require some further discussion. In the production function so far considered, own inputs are represented by the product sK. K is the total stock of human capital; s is described as a fraction that can take any value between 0 and 1. We shall first regard s as a measure of the allocation of time

[6]This can be verified by substituting $s - 1$ into (4'), letting it hold as an equality, and substituting into it also the value of Q and ψ using (2), (5'), and the solution of (2') referred to in n.3.

to the production of human capital, although this interpretation is not necessary.[7]

At any time t the stock of capital K_t is given. If we were to assume that any activity the individual engages in produces either human capital or earnings but not both, then the allocation of time between these two types of activities is also the allocation of the services of the existing stock of human capital. The larger the stock of human capital, the larger the earnings per unit of time that the individual could get in the market and therefore the higher the foregone earnings from diverting a unit of time away from the market (see Becker, 1965). Whether this should or should not affect the relative attractiveness of non-market activities hinges on whether the change that made an hour in the market more rewarding also made more productive an hour outside the market, in our case an hour of producing human capital.

The question is whether the real production relation involved is stable in terms of time or in terms of some other variable. The way we *defined* human capital was to make the production of earnings stable in terms of its services, rather than in terms of time as such. By making (sK) the relevant input in the production function of human capital we are also *asserting* that this other process is stable in terms of the services of human capital rather than in terms of time as such. The main implication of this formulation in terms of the allocation of time is that, when K is higher, the higher costs of an hour diverted away from the market (because of the higher foregone earnings) are exactly matched by the greater productivity of time in the production of human capital, so that the marginal cost curve of producing the latter is independent of the stock of human capital in the range where the constraint on s is not effective.

By arguing that in the production of human capital the services of human capital rather than time as such are relevant we gain some analytical simplicity, because beyond the period of complete specialization in the production of human capital the benefits associated with acquiring a unit of human capital, the addition to future dispos-

---

[7]Note that time enters in two completely different ways—t, which moves the individual along his life cycle and which is being treated as continuous, and s_t, which is a measure of the allocation of time at any point in t. If we were to treat t as an index of discrete periods, and if s were understood as referring to the allocation of each such period, this dual meaning probably would have posed no problem.

able earnings, do not depend on the future allocation between the market and the production of human capital. This is the reason why the dynamic programing problem that was referred to in relation to phase (i) degenerated into a much simpler decision problem in phase (ii). Analytical convenience is, however, no substitute for relevance. In a general production function both time as such and human capital would appear as inputs, and if we consider again the Cobb-Douglas case, s and K may appear with different coefficients. Thus, consider (17):

$$Q = \beta_0 s^{\gamma_1} K^{\gamma_2} D^{\beta_2} = \beta_0 s^{\gamma_1 - \gamma_2}(sK)^{\gamma_2} D^{\beta_2}; \; 0 < \gamma_1, \gamma_2, \beta_2 < 1. \tag{17}$$

The corresponding marginal cost curve is (18):

$$MC_t = \frac{a_0}{\beta_0 \gamma_1} \left(\frac{\gamma_1}{\beta_2} \frac{P_d}{a_0}\right)^{\beta_2/(\gamma_1 + \beta_2)} \times \left(\frac{Q_t}{\beta_0}\right)^{[1/(\gamma_1 + \beta_2)] - 1} K_t^{(\gamma_1 - \gamma_2)/(\gamma_1 + \beta_2)}. \tag{18}$$

If $\gamma_1 = \gamma_2$, we get an expression identical to (2), with γ_1 replacing β_1. If $\gamma_1 > \gamma_2$, the marginal cost curve is shifting upward as K increases. This can be viewed as a case where time plays an independent part in the production of human capital or, more directly, as a case where the larger productivity of time in the market indicated by an increase in K is not completely matched by a larger productivity in the production of human capital, so that the cost of the latter in terms of the former rises. The case where $\gamma_1 = \gamma_2$ implies, for example, that the more highly educated person is also better equipped for learning, so that his higher opportunity cost is matched by the greater amount of skills that he can acquire per hour. If this is not so, then the situation that we are describing now is relevant. A limiting case would be one in which human capital does not at all affect the ability to produce more human capital, $\gamma_2 = 0$.

In the basic model considered before, the decline over time in investment beyond the period of complete specialization is brought about by the downward drift, due to the approaching horizon T of the demand function, along a stationary, upward-sloping marginal cost curve. In the situation now described, as K increases the cost curve shifts upward. In young age, when $T - t$ is large, the quantitative effect of changes in t on the demand price is small, and the shifts in the cost function may be more important for changes in investment than in the downward drift of the demand curve. The role of purchased inputs here is also clear — the larger the β_2, the smaller the effect of K on the marginal cost.

The other case, in which $\gamma_2 > \gamma_1$, also cannot be ruled out. Here capital accumulation reduces the cost of producing human capital, and it is possible even in phase (ii) to have a stretch of time over which investment rises rather than declines (the downward shift in the costs being more important than the declines in demand). The corresponding life cycle may then have an early convex portion. Eventually the declining marginal productivity of K (due to $\gamma_2 < 1$) and the growing effect of the approaching horizon T will turn the rise in investment into a decline, and the life cycle will have the familiar S-shape.

B. THE ROLE OF RISING COSTS

With a homogeneous stock of human capital, the services of which are sold at a fixed price in a competitive market, both the determination of a finite desired stock and the speed in which the available stock is adjusted to the desired level depend on the cost of acquiring human capital. If human capital could be acquired at a fixed (or declining) cost without limitation, that is, if the supply schedule were perfectly elastic or declining, the desired stock would be either zero or infinite, and the optimal adjustment would be instantaneous. In the case of the demand for tangible capital, costs of adjustment are sometimes introduced to explain investment as a function of the interest rate. In the case of the aggregate economy, it is the rising cost of investment goods in terms of consumption goods that provides the negative slope of the aggregate demand function of investment (the marginal efficiency of investment curve) and a finite rate of investment.

The nature of human capital, the fact that it has to be produced by the individual, makes for some similarity in the considerations involved and provides a natural basis for dealing with the question of what makes the rate of investment and the attained stock of human capital finite. One form in which constraint on the rate of investment could come about is from individual capacity limitations solely. Thus, consider the case in which (2) $\beta_1 + \beta_2 = 1$, $\beta_1 > 0$, and $\beta_2 \geq 0$. In every period the available stock of human capital K_1 is given. Costs would be constant up to that level of output which implies $s = 1$, that is,

$$Q = \beta_0 K \left(\frac{a_0}{P_d} \frac{\beta_1}{\beta_1} \right)^{\beta_2}.$$

For larger outputs marginal costs would rise (if $\beta_2 > 0$) or become infinite (if $\beta_2 = 0$). In either case, given the nature of the demand for human capital, the optimum rate of investment would always imply a value of 1 or 0 for $s > n$, the allocation of all the services of the available stock of human capital either to the production of human capital or to the labor market, but not to both. Because of the declining demand over time for human capital, a period of complete specialization in the production of human capital (phase [i]), if it comes, must precede the period of complete specialization in market work (phase [iii]). The resulting life cycle of (observed) earnings would therefore have a portion of zero earnings and then a jump to some positive level, which would be stationary in the absence of depreciation and declining in its presence.

Neither this implied life cycle of earnings nor the behavior to which it is related is supported by what we know of the real world. The basic model allows for an initial period of complete specialization in the production of human capital and, correspondingly, a period of zero observed earnings. But if we assume that the sum of the production elasticities of the variable inputs is smaller than 1 ($\beta_1 + \beta_2$ in eq. [2] and $\gamma_1 + \beta_2$ in eq. [17], the more general formulation), marginal cost rises continuously even before the capacity constraint is reached. This is the source of the existence of a phase (ii), a period in which $0 < s < 1$, when the individual engages simultaneously, or alternately, in work in the market and in the production of his human capital. (A more complicated functional form could have allowed increasing returns to scale at small outputs and eventually decreasing returns. This may be more plausible and still would provide the eventual check on the rate of investment.)

In this framework, where there is not "automatic" growth in earnings, increase in earning can come only from the allocation of more services of human capital to the market. This can be either because of a reduction in what is allocated to investment (s_t) or because of an increase in the total stock available (K). In order for some positive earnings to be observed there must be some work in the market; in order for earnings to decline there must be some investment that either increases from period to period the total available stock or, by itself declining, raises the fraction allocated to the market. The closer the sum of the production elasticities of the variable factors to 1, that is, the closer we get to constant returns to scale in terms of the variable factors, the more concave is the life cycle of earnings; the case of constant marginal cost in which the life cycle of earnings is a one-step function is the limiting case.

Throughout the preceding discussions s_t has been interpreted as a parameter of the allocation of time. If there are, however, activities in which earnings and human capital can be jointly produced, then s_t loses this meaning. We have many examples of learning on the job in which the time spent on the job cannot be allocated in any meaningful sense between pure work and pure learning; jointness is too prevalent to be excluded. We can still think of the individual as being faced with a production frontier indicating the possible combination of flows of earnings and of human capital that he can produce. Movements along this frontier, however, would not necessarily represent shifts between pure activities but, rather, represent movement between activities, each offering a different mix of earnings and additions to productive capacity. Shifts along this frontier are represented by the control s_t, and they may involve a change in occupations, of jobs within the occupation, or of function with the job. The less numerous and close together are these alternative combinations, the smaller is the justification for the continuous differentiable frontier implied by our formulation. Discontinuities and kinks in this production frontier are translated into kinks and jumps in the life cycle of earnings. In either case, it is clear that s_t becomes an empty concept once it has lost its link with the observable phenomenon of the allocation of time.

III. THE MODEL AND AGGREGATE EARNING PROFILES

The preceding section clarifies the role played in this framework by increasing costs in the explanation of a gradually rising portion in the *individual* life cycle of earnings. The purpose of the present section is to show that even within this framework an explanation of cohort life cycles of earnings, or of the cross-section profile of earnings, can be provided without the assumption of rising costs. Thus, assume for simplicity that $\beta_2 = \delta = 0$ and $\beta_1 = 1$. By the argument presented in the preceding section, the individual life cycle will be a stepwise function.

The marginal (and average) cost of producing human capital is (a_0/β_0), β_0 differing among people. The higher is β_0, the later comes the date t^* when the downward-drifting demand price crosses it from above—which is the date when people jump from observed earnings of zero to their earning capacity. By equating a_0/β_0 with P (10) we get (19):

$$t^* = T + \frac{1}{r} \ln \left(1 - \frac{r}{\beta_0} \right).$$

(19)

The time path of the stock of human capital is given by

$$K_t = K_0 e^{\beta_0 t} \quad \text{for} \quad 0 \le t \le t^*; \tag{20}$$

$$K_t = K_0 e^{\beta_0 t^*} \quad \text{for} \quad t^* \le t \le T.$$

Observed earnings are zero for $0 < t < t^*$ and are equal to earning capacity afterward.

$$E_t = a_0 K_0 e^{\beta_0 t} = a_0 K_0 e^{\beta_0 \{T + (1/r) \ \ln[1 - (r/\beta_0)]\}}. \tag{21}$$

Using (21) we can see that, given $a_0 K_0$, earnings on the time of "emergence," t^*, and beyond it, are an increasing convex function of t^*. If in a given cohort K_0 and β_0 are not negatively correlated, we can expect to observe a rising curve as we follow the earnings history of the cohort through time (or as we examine the cross-section profile of earnings of a completely static population, with stationary distributions by β_0 and K_0, in a static economy). The exact form of the curve depends on the distribution of the cohort by β_0; reasonable distributions by β_0 can generate a curve with the familiar S-shape.

SUMMARY AND SOME OPEN QUESTIONS

To the theory of investment in man we have added here a production function of human capital and explored some of the implications of its properties for the optimal path of accumulation of human capital and the life cycle of earnings. The concepts and parameters introduced raise again some familiar problems and are used to focus attention on some others. In lieu of a summary we shall now refer to a few of these.

1. The particular definition of human capital K used is a measure of a quantity of a source of productive services. It is the stock that produces labor services in "standard units" and is thus the analogue of "machines" in the case of tangible capital. This should be sharply distinguished from W_t (defined in [8]), which is the *value* of the individual as a productive factor. It is affected by a broader view of the individual's productivity, by his durability, and by the rate of interest, and it can be misleading as a quantity measure of an input in any given point in time. Being a part of the individual's net worth (and the price that he could get for himself in a competitive slave market), it is probably better described as "human wealth."

2. The speed of adjustment, the rate at which the individual increases the stock of human capital, determines the ultimate size of this

stock. The considerations affecting the speed of adjustment and the path of investment with age merit an explicit analysis. The mechanism provided here relies on the introduction of dependence between the marginal cost of producing human capital and the rate of production (a justification for this can come from the "learning curve" considerations). Beyond a certain point the saving in costs from postponing investment to the next period compensates for the loss of the returns that would have come from getting the unit of capital a period earlier.

Rising costs result here from a certain specification of the technology. The properties of the production function and the parameters introduced draw attention to certain distinctions that have to be made when the conglomerate of abilities and external conditions is considered and the implications of its properties are explored.

3. In discussing the "initial endowment" of individuals a different role is played by the initial endowment in terms of the ability to earn in the market (K_0) and the abilities to produce additions to earning capacity. These consist of the ability to make efficient use of inputs purchasable in the market, D (expressed by β_0 and β_2), and of one's own time $(\beta_0, \beta_1,$ or γ_1 in [17]). A related issue is to what extent the individual, as he increases his human capital, K, also raises his efficiency in the production of K (in eq. [17]; this is expressed by the distinction between γ_1 and γ_2). This question is related to the homogeneity of human capital.

4. The possibility of producing human capital in addition to earnings means that the "real output" of the individual consists of earnings plus the value of human capital produced, when the latter is evaluated by its shadow price. This will be a measure of by how much total inactivity at a given period would affect W.

5. Not much has been said of δ, the rate of deterioration. Consideration ought to be given to cases where δ is negative rather than positive as assumed here and also to the dependence of deterioration on the allocation of human capital to different activities.

6. The horizon T is treated here as exogenous. Opening the analysis to include leisure will, of course, make retirement endogenous, but even if T is the date of death there can be types of investments that will affect that date.

7. The three market prices—the rate of interest r, the rental on human capital a_0, and the price of purchased inputs P_d—affect behavior in the expected way. These are the parameters of the models that public policy can most directly attack. The framework presented

here may prove convenient for mapping possible effects of public policy and their interaction with ability factors.

8. Various problems of measurement are implied but not directly discussed. One of these is the relation between the integral of investment costs, (7), over stretches of time and the integral of $\dot{K}$, or of Q. The problem of measurement in this model hinges on the measurability of s_t, which is a question about the prevalence of activities in which human capital and earnings are jointly produced. When s_t is an observable phenomenon of the allocation of time, the model becomes operational, but, without it, much is lost.

9. We have abstracted here from uncertainty and from capital rationing two important considerations in investment in human capital which should be incorporated in a complete analysis.

10. A natural extension of the two-way choice analyzed here between activities producing current earnings and investment in human capital would be to deal with the three-way choice involving also the allocation of time for activities of a consumptive nature, following the approach of Becker (1965).

The reader probably does not have to be told how simplifying many of the assumptions are and how many additional aspects of investment in human capital and of the determination of the life cycle of earnings are relevant. The main purpose of this paper was to raise some more questions rather than provide definite answers.

REFERENCES

Becker, G. S. "Investment in Human Capital: A Theoretic Analysis," *J.P.E.*, LXX, No. 5, Part 2 (October, 1962), 9–49.

——. *Human Capital.* New York: Columbia Univ. Press (for the National Bureau of Economic Research), 1964.

——. "A Theory of the Allocation of Time," *Econ. J.*, Vol. LXXV (September, 1965).

——. "Human Capital and the Personal Distribution of Income: An Analytical Approach." New York: National Bureau of Economic Research, October, 1966 (mimeographed).

Friedman, M., and Kuznets, S. *Income from Independent Professions.* New York: National Bureau of Economic Research, 1945.

Mincer, J. "Investment in Human Capital and Personal Income Distribution," *J.P.E.*, LXVI, No. 4 (August, 1958), 281–302.

——. "On-the-Job Training: Costs, Returns, and Some Implications," *ibid.*, LXX, No. 5, Part 2 (October, 1962), 50–79.

Schultz, T. W. *The Economic Value of Education.* New York: Columbia Univ. Press, 1963.

10. Annual and Lifetime Income in Relation to Education: 1939–1959*

HERMAN P. MILLER
Bureau of the Census

Nearly one-quarter of a century has elapsed since Harold F. Clark and his colleagues produced their pioneer study on life earnings in selected occupations [5]. Clark expressed the hope that his rough procedures would be improved upon with time and that the figures would be recalculated at least annually. Aside from a relatively few attempts, however, the challenge has not been taken up by contemporary economists or statisticians despite an increased need for such information. In part, this neglect must be attributed to a lack of data. Although a vast amount of data can be found on hourly, daily, or weekly wages for many skilled trades, information on annual earnings, which are used as a basis for computing lifetime earnings, is still quite scarce. The picture has changed somewhat as a result of the past two decennial censuses and the annual income surveys conducted by the Bureau of the Census since 1945. It is the purpose of this study to examine the relationship between income and education as revealed in these data. The first two sections consider the findings with regard to annual income and the third section presents some newly developed data on lifetime income for men with different amounts of schooling.

Although the material gains of an education have been selected for study, the intent has not been to slur the more subtle satisfactions that come with greater educational attainment. The cultural and social advantages associated with more schooling may well be worth their cost in time, money, and effort, even if the economic advantages should cease to exist. The only justification for focusing on the eco-

*Reprinted from "Annual and Lifetime Income in Relation to Education," *American Economic Review*, L (December, 1960), 962–986.

nomic advantages is that at present they are the only ones capable of even approximate measurement.

Since the present study makes no allowance for the individual and social costs incurred in the completion of additional schooling, the income gains associated with greater educational attainment, as shown in this report, are overstated. Even if allowance were made for these costs, however, the evidence available from recent studies suggests that an investment in schooling pays, on the average, a better return than most other investments.[1]

There is one further caution to be noted. Although the figures show that, on the average, there is a monetary return to the individual for an investment in education, there is no guarantee that such an investment will earn this rate of return in any given case. This fact seems obvious, but it is often ignored. In 1958, for example, about 2.7 million men with college degrees had incomes under $7,000 whereas 1.9 million high school graduates received more than this amount [21]. How can we explain the relatively low incomes of so many highly educated men and the higher incomes of so many men with relatively little education? The answer lies partly in response errors which abound in the reporting of income and education in household surveys and censuses;[2] but the differences cannot entirely be swept under the rug by attributing them to errors in the statistics. The major part of the explanation must be sought in differences in the quality of education, the abilities and efforts of individuals, and many other forces that impinge on the observed relationship between income and education. Many intelligent individuals never get as much schooling as they should, and too many individuals with relatively low intelligence get more schooling than they should. Training completed at inferior schools cannot be equated with equal amounts of time spent in training at excellent schools. For these and many other reasons it would be fallacious and perhaps even harmful to draw inferences about individual cases from the evidence presented here for the general population.

[1] This conclusion is based largely on [16]. See also [1] and [12].

[2] There is evidence that when a given set of questions on income or education is asked for an identical group of persons in surveys conducted several weeks apart, there are marked variations in the replies that are received. These variations contain overestimates as well as underestimates and they tend to cancel each other, leaving the resultant distributions unchanged. Although variability of response does not appear to create serious problems in one-dimensional distributions such as of income alone, it does tend to produce distortions when cross-classifications are considered.

151

Investment in Education

Numerous studies, conducted under varying economic conditions, have shown that persons with more schooling tend to earn more money. This relationship seems reasonable if it is assumed that the attainment of more schooling, particularly at the secondary school and college level, in some measure improves the productivity of the individual and thereby compensates for the investment of time, effort, and money. On the other hand, it is by no means inevitable that money invested in education will necessarily pay dividends or that the rate of return will be constant over time. There is always the possibility, indeed the probability, that the higher incomes of those with more years of schooling are due in part to differences in intelligence, home environment, family connections, and other factors which result from individual differences in ability and opportunity. Therefore, to some extent, the observed relationship between schooling and earnings may be a spurious one. It is, of course, difficult if at all possible to measure the extent to which these extraneous factors enter this relationship. There is, however, some evidence that "ability" as measured by scholastic achievement is highly correlated with earnings.[3]

Economists have also long argued that earnings differentials could be reduced by an increase in education. Von Thünen was one of the earliest proponents of the use of educational policy as a means of reducing income differentials. In 1826 he asked "why in a competitive organization the incomes of manual workers remained persistently so far below the incomes of manufacturers and farmers." His explanation was that "manual workers were lacking in the elements of school knowledge without which, in spite of any other qualifications, it was impossible to be an entrepreneur" [7, pp. 745–46]. In 1887, Marshall also saw in education the beneficent possibility for narrowing wage differentials.[4] More recently, Seymour Harris, noting the rapid rise in the extension of higher education, has expressed

---

[3]This conclusion is based on unpublished data underlying [3, pp. 175–97]. See also [4, pp. 1–19]. Preliminary findings from a current study in the Bell System tend to confirm the findings in [4].

[4]"The normal earnings of a carpenter and surveyor might be brought much nearer together than they are, by even so slight and easy an improvement on our present social arrangements as the extending to all persons of adequate natural ability the opportunity of receiving the training required for the higher ranks of industry." [15, p. 214].

152

concern about the possibility that the persistent increase in the supply of college-trained workers will so flood the market that "college students within the next twenty years are doomed to disappointment after graduation, as the number of coveted openings will be substantially less than the numbers seeking them." [11, p. 64]. The same concern has been expressed by several noted educators including James B. Conant [6, p. 198].

During a relatively short period, such as that considered in the present report, the tendency for education to result in a reduction of income differentials could be more than offset by an increase in the demand for the services of skilled workers due to technological changes in the economy. Since the supply of skilled workers, particularly those with college training, has increased considerably during the past generation, we shall attempt to determine to what extent the increase in the demand for their services has offset the tendency for their incomes to increase proportionately less than other workers.

Some of the basic statistics pertaining to the relationship between annual income and educational attainment are presented in Table 1, which shows the variations in average (mean) annual income over the past generation for men with different amounts of schooling.[5] The data are presented separately for each age group, as well as for all men 25 years old and over, in order to permit an examination of the figures without having to take account of changes in the age distribution of the population. Women have been excluded from the analysis; since a large proportion of them do not enter the labor market and many of those who do are employed on a part-time basis only, the relationship between their income and education may be distorted. In contrast, practically all adult men are full-time workers and it can therefore be assumed that any advantages which may accrue from more schooling are reflected in their incomes.

---

[5]For each year, the mean income was obtained as a summation of the product of the average income and the proportion of persons for each income level. For income levels below $10,000 in 1949, 1956, and 1958, below $6,000 for 1946, and below $5,000 for 1939, the midpoint of each class interval was assumed to be the average. For 1949, 1956, and 1958, $20,000 was used for the "$10,000 and over" interval; for 1946, $12,000 was used for the "$6,000 and over" interval; and for 1939, $9,000 was used for the "5,000 and over" interval. Medians corresponding to the means shown in Table 1 may be obtained from the author. Tax return data for recent years suggest a drop in the average for the open-end interval. An alternative calculation made for 1958, using a mean of $17,000 for the "tail", revealed no substantial changes in the relationships.

Investment in Education

Table 1 shows that in every year for which data are presented the completion of an additional level of schooling was associated with higher average incomes for men. This finding parallels that obtained in numerous other studies of the relationship between education and income dating back to the early part of this century [19, p. 115]. Although the income levels have changed considerably during the past 20 years, the basic relationship between the extent of schooling and income appears to have remained much the same. Contrary to the expectations of some analysts, the economic advantages accruing from the completion of additional years of schooling have not diminished in recent years.

Although income generally tends to increase with education, Table 1 shows that a year spent in completing a given level of schooling (e.g., the fourth year in high school) yields a greater return than any of the years leading up to graduation. This difference may reflect a selection in terms of ability between those who do and those who do not complete their schooling. Thus in 1958, men who started high school but did not graduate, received on the average an annual income of about $400 more per year of schooling than men who completed their schooling with graduation from elementary school. High school graduates, however, received about $500 more of annual income per year of schooling than men who started high school but never graduated. Similarly, men who attended college but did not graduate had, on the average, about $700 more per year of schooling than high school graduates. The comparable differential for college graduates was about $900 per year of schooling.[6]

The educational attainment of the population has grown considerably during the past generation. The proportion of college graduates has nearly doubled during the period and the proportion of high school graduates has also risen dramatically (Table 2). How has this change in the relative supply of more highly educated workers affected income differentials? Have the incomes of college graduates, relative to other groups in the population, been pushed down because of the relative increase in their numbers or has the demand for their services increased sufficiently to offset any tendency for their incomes to be lowered?

Although these questions cannot be answered categorically, there is some evidence that elementary school graduates have had smaller

[6]For similar findings based on earlier data see [10].

TABLE 1

Mean Income (or Earnings) for Males 25 Years of Age and Over, by
Years of School Completed and Age: 1939, 1946, 1949, 1956, and 1958

Years of School Completed and Age	1939[a]	1946[b]	1949[c]	1956[c]	1958[c]
Total: 25 Years Old and Over:					
Elementary: Total	$1,036	$2,041	$2,394	$3,107	$3,096
Less than 8 years[d]	— [e]	1,738	2,062	2,613	2,551
8 years	— [e]	2,327	2,829	3,732	3,769
High School: 1 to 3 years	1,379	2,449	3,226	4,480	4,618
4 years	1,661	2,939	3,784	5,439	5,567
College: 1 to 3 years	1,931	3,654	4,423	6,363	6,966
4 years or more	2,607	4,527	6,179	8,490	9,206
25 to 34 years:					
Elementary: Total	837	1,729	2,185	3,061	3,143
Less than 8 years[d]	— [e]	1,394	1,880	2,662	2,670
8 years	— [e]	2,011	2,540	3,685	3,663
High School: 1 to 3 years	1,150	2,062	2,837	4,407	4,341
4 years	1,335	2,335	3,246	4,813	4,909
College: 1 to 3 years	1,566	2,875	3,444	5,437	5,774
4 years or more	1,956	3,237	4,122	6,307	7,152
35 to 44 Years:					
Elementary: Total	1,110	2,095	2,610	3,694	3,686
Less than 8 years[d]	— [e]	1,730	2,244	3,169	3,023
8 years	— [e]	2,425	3,029	4,256	4,403
High School: 1 to 3 years	1,574	2,607	3,449	4,799	5,035
4 years	1,979	3,463	4,055	5,992	6,007
College: 1 to 3 years	2,270	4,069	5,014	7,131	8,015
4 years or more	3,141	5,054	7,085	9,790	10,106
45 to 54 Years:					
Elementary: Total	1,199	2,349	2,797	3,672	3,660
Less than 8 years[d]	— [e]	2,027	2,418	3,078	3,008
8 years	— [e]	2,629	3,247	4,289	4,337
High School: 1 to 3 years	1,732	2,959	3,725	4,876	4,864
4 years	2,256	3,744	4,689	6,104	6,295
College: 1 to 3 years	2,428	4,671	5,639	7,426	8,682
4 years or more	3,575	5,242	8,116	11,702	12,269
55 to 64 Years:					
Elementary: Total	1,057	2,082	2,577	3,462	3,436
Less than 8 years[d]	— [e]	1,814	2,278	2,922	2,956
8 years	— [e]	2,365	3,010	3,932	3,960

TABLE 1 *(continued)*

Mean Income (or Earnings) for Males 25 Years of Age and Over, by
Years of School Completed and Age: 1939, 1946, 1949, 1956, and 1958

Years of School Completed and Age	1939[a]	1946[b]	1949[c]	1956[c]	1958[c]
High School: 1 to 3 years	1,551	2,648	3,496	4,398	5,034
4 years	2,104	3,179	4,548	5,920	6,510
College: 1 to 3 years	2,065	3,888	5,162	6,677	6,992
4 years or more	3,247	5,461	7,655	9,595	10,966
65 Years Old and Over:					
Elementary: Total	—[e]	1,541	1,560	1,875	1,903
Less than 8 years[d]	—[e]	1,434	1,366	1,686	1,672
8 years	—[e]	1,670	1,898	2,247	2,337
High School: 1 to 3 years	—[e]	1,894	2,379	2,560	2,661
4 years	—[e]	2,601	3,115	3,314	3,036
College: 1 to 3 years	—[e]	2,720	3,435	4,269[f]	4,180
4 years or more	—[e]	3,902	5,421	5,835	6,091

[a]Restricted to persons reporting $1 or more of wage or salary income and less than $50 of other income for native white and Negro males 25 to 64 years old only.

[b]Total money earnings.

[c]Total money income.

[d]Includes persons reporting no years of school completed, not shown separately.

[e]Not available.

[f]Base is less than 100 sample cases.

Source: Data for 1939 derived from *1940 Census of Population, Education: Educational Attainment by Economic Characteristics and Marital Status,* Tables 29 and 31. Data for 1949 derived from *1950 Census of Population,* Ser. P-E, No. 5B, *Education,* Tables 12 and 13. Data for 1946, 1956, and 1958 derived from the consumer income supplements to the April 1947, March 1957, and March 1959 *Current Population Survey.*

Note regarding comparability of the figures: Neither the income concept nor the universe covered is directly comparable for all the years shown. Most of the differences, however, are relatively small and are not believed to seriously distort the relationships. Thus, for example, the figures for 1956 and 1958 are entirely comparable since they are based on the Current Population Survey and represent the total money income of the civilian noninstitutional male population 25 years old and over. The 1949 figures are based on the 1950 Census and also represent the total money income of all males 25 years old and over, including a relatively small number of institutional inmates. The 1946 figures are based on the Current Population Survey and represent the total money earnings (not total income) of the civilian noninstitutional male population 25 years old and over. Although the conceptual differences between income and earnings are substantial, the actual differences in the averages are quite small, primarily because the amount of nonearned income is small relative to the total and this type of income tends to be seriously underreported in household surveys of income. The figures for 1939 are based on the 1940 Census and are restricted to males 25–64 years of age with $1 or more of wage or salary income and less than $50 of nonwage income. For this group, of course,

TABLE 2

Percent Distribution by Years of School Completed
for Males 25 Years Old and Over

Years of School Completed		1940	1947	1950	1957	1959
Total		100	100	100	100	100
Elementary School: Total		62	51	49	42	39
	Less than 8 years[a]	34	_ [b]	28	23	22
	8 years	28	_ [b]	21	18	17
High School:	1 to 3 years	14	16	16	17	18
	4 years	12	18	18	22	23
College:	1 to 3 years	5	7	7	7	8
	4 years or more	5	6	7	9	10
Not reported		2	2	3	2	2

[a]Includes persons reporting no years of school completed, not shown separately.
[b]Not available.

Source: Data for 1940 derived from *1940 Census of Population:* Pt. 1, Vol. IV, *Characteristics by Age,* Table 18. Data for 1950 derived from *1950 Census of Population,* Ser. P-E, No. 5B, *Education,* Table 12. Data for 1947, 1957, and 1959 derived from the educational attainment supplements to the April 1947, March 1957, and March 1959 *Current Population Survey,* P-20, No. 15, Table 1; P-20, No. 77, Table 1; and P-20, No. 99, Table 1.

relative income gains than high school graduates, despite the reduction in their relative numbers. In contrast, the income differential between high school and college graduates has remained fairly constant over time and there is even some evidence that it has increased in favor of college graduates during the past few years (Table 3).

In the absence of 1939 income data for elementary school graduates, comparisons between the incomes of elementary and high school graduates must be restricted to the period since 1946. If attention is focused on these years, it is evident that the incomes of high school graduates have risen considerably more, in percentage terms, than those of elementary school graduates. In 1946, the differential between these two groups was only $600 or about 26 percent. By 1958, the differential rose to about $1,800 or 48 percent. This change is in

the averages represent total money income; however, the universe has been restricted, because of the way in which the data were collected, to those persons who received only wage or salary income. Only about three-fifths of all men 25–64 years old in 1940 were in this category. The effects of this restriction cannot be measured, but it is undoubtedly more important than restrictions cited for other years. It is also possible that this restriction affects college graduates more than persons with less schooling and for them tends to create an adverse selection since college graduates are more likely to have income other than earnings.

TABLE 3

Mean Income (or Earnings) by Level of School Completed,
for Males 25 Years Old and Over

	Elementary–High School Differential			High School–College Differential		
Year	Average Income			Average Income		
	Elementary School Graduate	High School Graduate	Percent Difference	High School Graduate	College Graduate	Percent Difference
1939	_ a	$1,661	_ a	$1,661	$2,607	57
1946	$2,327	2,939	26	2,939	4,527	54
1949	2,829	3,784	34	3,784	6,179	63
1956	3,732	5,439	46	5,439	8,490	56
1958	3,769	5,567	48	5,567	9,206	65

aNot available.
Source: Table 1.

part related to the fact that a large proportion of the elementary school graduates are employed in occupations such as farmers, farm laborers, and nonfarm laborers which tended to have lower relative income gains in recent years than most other occupations.[7] It is also possible, of course, that even for occupations such as operatives and craftsmen, in which a relatively large number of elementary school graduates are employed, high school graduates received relatively greater increases than persons who never attended high school. There is also a possibility that the reduction in the relative number of elementary school graduates reflects a constant transfer of the "cream" of that group to the high school group, so that the average elementary school graduate in 1958 may have been a less "able" person than in 1946; but there is no objective evidence on this point.

In contrast to the changing relationship between the incomes of elementary school and high school graduates, there has been relatively little change in the income differential between high school and college graduates. In 1939, the average income of college graduates was about $900, or 57 percent more than for high school graduates. In 1956, the absolute difference between the incomes of these two

---

[7][21, Table E] shows that median total money income of employed males increased between 1950 and 1958 by 3 percent for farm laborers, 51 percent for nonfarm laborers, and 27 percent for farmers. In contrast the median income during this period increased by 57 percent for professional workers, 54 percent for managers and officials, and 55 percent for craftsmen.

groups increased to $3,100, but the relative difference was unchanged. By 1958, the absolute difference rose to $3,600 and the relative difference also increased to 65 percent. The data suggest that during the recession years 1949 and 1958 the incomes of college graduates were less affected than other groups, reflecting, perhaps, a greater tendency for persons with lesser schooling to be subject to unemployment. There is also some possibility that the income gains for college graduates partly reflect a rise in the proportion of men in this group with graduate school training. The influence of this factor is probably quite small, however, since there is no evidence of a sharp rise in the proportion of college men with graduate training. Moreover, the income differential between all college graduates and those with graduate training is quite small, amounting to only about $200 in 1958 [21, p. 38].

Why has the relative income differential between high school and college graduates been maintained, and indeed recently increased, despite the large relative increase in the size of the college-trained population? One important part of the explanation must be that the demand for college graduates has kept pace with the supply. Due to our changing technology, the demand for trained workers has accelerated since the end of the second world war, and industry has absorbed the increased flow of graduates from our universities. The nature of this change can be seen most clearly by the sharp rise in the proportion of the labor force engaged in professional and managerial work, the two occupations in which the great majority of college graduates are employed. Table 4 shows that since 1940 there has been a relative increase of about 50 percent in the proportion of men employed in the two major occupation groups which serve as the major outlet for men with college training.

The conclusion based on Census Bureau data that the income differential between high school and college graduates has been maintained since 1939 presents a somewhat different picture from the one that might be obtained from other information. A study completed in 1957 by Blank and Stigler concludes that "the pronounced downward drift of earnings in all professions (except medicine) relative to earnings of the working population as a whole is well known. . . . This downward drift is known only since 1929, but one may plausibly conjecture that it began much earlier because the main force working in that direction — the rapid expansion in the number of trained professional workers — also began much

TABLE 4

Number and Percent of Males Employed in Professional
and Managerial Occupations

Major Occupation Group	Number (thousands)				Percent			
	1940	1950	1957	1959	1940	1950	1957	1959
Total employed males	33,750	40,519	43,273	42,842	100.0	100.0	100.0	100.0
Professional, technical and kindred workers	2,075	2,971	4,141	4,471	6.1	7.3	9.6	10.4
Managers, officials and proprietors, except farm	3,231	4,341	5,598	5,695	9.6	10.7	12.9	13.3

Source: Data for 1940 and 1950 from *U.S. Census of Population: 1950*, Vol. II, *Characteristics of the Population*, Pt. 1, Table 54. Data for 1957 and 1959 from Bureau of the Census, *Current Population Reports*, Ser. P-60, No. 27 and No. 33.

earlier" [2, p. 25]. There is no necessary inconsistency between this finding and the results based on census data described above since (a) Blank and Stigler measured trends since 1929 whereas the present study considers trends since 1939; and (b) college graduates are not all employed in professional jobs. In 1950, only about one-half of the male college graduates worked at professional jobs.[8] It is entirely possible that the differentials for college graduates as a whole have been maintained since 1950, but that the differential for the professional group has decreased. This could have happened if there was a substantial increase in the differential for college graduates employed in nonprofessional jobs.

Historical time series on income are not available for all, or even for many, professional occupations and much of the information that is available does not quite measure up to acceptable standards of reliability or comprehensiveness. The figures for engineers used by Blank and Stigler, for example, relate to median base monthly salary rates rather than annual earnings, and therefore cannot be readily compared with other estimates for the general population or for other professions. Moreover, the estimates for 1929, 1932, and 1934 are based on a mail survey in 1935 with a nonresponse rate of 67 percent

[8]Estimate derived from [23]. This source shows 1.6 million, or 55 percent, of all male college graduates classified as "professional, technical, and kindred workers." It is estimated that 1.5 million men were professional workers and that .1 million were technicians.

[2, p. 16]. The estimates for 1939, 1943, and 1946 are based on a mail survey in 1946 with a nonresponse rate of 47 percent [2, p. 111]. One might well question the credence that should be attached to an estimate of monthly income made five years after the income was earned, based on a survey in which about half or two-thirds of the population covered did not respond.

Blank and Stigler present indexes for 1929–1954 of the ratio of median monthly engineering salaries to average wage or salary or net income for full-time wage and salary employees, full-time manufacturing wage earners, lawyers, physicians, dentists, and college teachers. Incomes are shown for only five professional groups which in 1950 accounted for only about two-fifths of all male professional workers,[9] including engineers for whom the income data are of doubtful utility. The four professional occupations shown, excluding engineers, represented only about one-fifth of all male professional workers in 1950 [22].

Table 5 has been prepared to facilitate a closer examination of trends in professional incomes since 1939. This table contains the five series used by Blank and Stigler and a sixth, annual earnings of public school teachers. Excluding engineers, the relative figures for only two of the professions, college teachers and nonsalaried lawyers, show a distinct downward drift as compared with average earnings for all workers. The increase in income for doctors was somewhat better than, and for dentists about on a par with, that recorded by the average worker; and the increase for public school teachers was only slightly behind that recorded by the average full-time employee. On the basis of this limited evidence it cannot be concluded beyond a reasonable doubt that the income differential between professional and nonprofessional workers has been narrowed since 1939.[10]

[9] [22]. This source shows 3 million men classified as "professional, technical, or kindred workers." It is estimated that 2.5 million of these men were professional workers and that .5 million were technicians.

[10] Census Bureau data show that during 1939–1958 the median wage or salary income of professional workers rose 2.3 times as compared with gains ranging from 2.7–2.9 times for craftsmen, operatives, service workers and nonfarm laborers [21, p. 6]. These data tend to support the view that professional workers made smaller relative income gains than the general working population during this period. The data, however, are subject to the limitation of being restricted to persons with wage or salary income and therefore exclude independent professionals. Moreover, the data also show that it was only during the first half of the period that professional workers made the lower relative gains. Since 1950, the relative gains in wages and salaries and total income have been greater for professional workers than for the general working population.

TABLE 5

Earnings of Full-Time Employees in All Industries, and of Selected Professional and Nonprofessional Occupations

Year	Average Annual Earnings per Full-Time Employee, all Industries	Average Annual Salary		Average Annual Net Income			Median Base Monthly Salary Rate Engineers[b]
		Public School Teachers[a]	College Teachers	Non-Salaried Lawyers	Non-Salaried Physicians	Non-Salaried Dentists	
Dollar Values							
1939	$1,264	–	–	$ 4,391	$ 4,229	$3,096	$277
1940	1,300	$1,441	$2,906	4,507	4,441	3,314	–
1941	1,443	–	–	4,794	5,047	3,782	–
1942	1,709	1,507	2,914	5,527	6,735	4,625	334
1943	1,951	–	3,039	5,945	8,370	5,715	–
1944	2,108	1,728	3,331	6,504	9,802	6,649	–
1945	2,189	–	3,277	6,861	10,975	6,922	–
1946	2,356	1,995	3,465	6,951	10,202	6,381	409
1947	2,589	–	3,736	7,437	10,726	6,610	–
1948	2,795	2,639	4,123	8,003	11,327	7,039	–
1949	2,851	–	4,234	7,971	11,744	7,146	–
1950	3,008	3,010	4,354	8,349	12,324	7,436	–
1951	3,231	–	–	8,855	13,432	7,820	–
1952	3,414	3,450	5,106	9,021	–	–	–
1953	3,587	–	–	9,392	–	–	518
1954	3,670	3,825	–	10,258	–	–	–

Index:
1939 = 100[c]

Year							
1939	100	–	–	100	100	100	100
1940	103	100	100	103	105	107	–
1941	114	–	–	109	119	122	–
1942	135	105	100	126	159	149	–
1943	154	–	105	135	198	185	121
1944	167	120	115	148	232	215	–
1945	173	–	113	156	260	224	–
1946	186	138	119	158	241	206	148
1947	205	–	129	169	254	214	–
1948	221	183	142	182	268	227	–
1949	226	–	146	182	278	231	–
1950	238	209	150	190	291	240	–
1951	256	–	–	202	318	253	–
1952	270	239	176	205	–	–	–
1953	284	–	–	214	–	–	187
1954	290	265	–	234	–	–	–

[a]Public elementary and secondary school teachers, supervisors, and principals. Figures are for "school" years ending in the year indicated; for example, the figure shown for 1954 is for the school years 1953–1954.

[b]For 1953, graduate engineers only. All other figures are for graduates and nongraduates. The corresponding figure for graduate engineers for 1946 is $405.

[c]1940 was used as the base year for public school and college teachers.

Source: Bureau of the Census, *Historical Statistics of the United States-Colonial Times to 1957*, July 1960.

II. ANNUAL INCOME IN RELATION TO AGE AND EDUCATION: 1939–1958

Next to be considered is the impact of age on the relationship between educational attainment and earnings. As might be expected,
the advantages of additional years of schooling do not have a very
strong immediate impact on earnings. Inexperienced workers in most
occupations start at a relatively low level of earnings, but the latter
tend to increase as skill and experience are acquired. Therefore, the
financial benefits of additional schooling tend to accumulate over
time, and the greatest impact is felt during the period of peak earnings. These tendencies are clearly reflected in Table 6 which shows the
earnings at an average age of 30 (i.e., after about 10 years of work
experience) and 50 (i.e., about the age of peak earnings) for men with
different amounts of educational attainment. If data were available,
an average age of 22 might have provided a better basis for comparison, although at this age many persons undergoing professional
training have not yet completed their schooling. In each education
group (with the exception of the lowest one in 1958), the period of
maximum earnings is between 45 and 54 years of age.

In view of the limited range of earnings possible in most of the jobs
for which elementary school graduates can qualify, it is not surprising
that their annual earnings after a lifetime of work do not much exceed
their initial earnings. College graduates, on the other hand, tend to
work at jobs in which the possibilities of high earnings are much
greater and therefore have peak earnings which, on the average,
far exceed initial earnings.

Table 6 also shows that the differential between initial and peak
earnings has decreased progressively for elementary and high school
graduates, but has remained fairly constant for college graduates.
Evidently, among workers who have not attended college, the younger
groups have succeeded in making greater relative gains in earnings
than those with more experience. Between 1939 and 1949, these
gains were probably due in large measure to reduced unemployment
among the younger (and less skilled) groups. The further gains during the past decade may reflect the "across-the-board" increases in
union contracts during the postwar period which resulted in greater
relative gains for lower-paid workers and perhaps also the gradual
rise in the minimum wage required by law in many industries.

As previously noted in the discussion of the figures for all age
groups combined, there was no reduction in the income of college

TABLE 6

Mean Income (or Earnings) for Males 25 to 34 Years and 45 to 54 years
of Age, by Level of School Completed

Age and Level of School Completed	1939	1946	1949	1956	1958
Elementary school graduate:					
25 to 34 years	— ª	$2,011	$2,540	$3,685	$3,663
45 to 54 years	— ª	2,629	3,247	4,289	4,337
Percent increase	— ª	31	28	16	18
High school graduate:					
25 to 34 years	$1,335	2,335	3,246	4,813	4,909
45 to 54 years	2,256	3,744	4,689	6,104	6,295
Percent increase	69	60	44	27	28
College graduate:					
25 to 34 years	1,956	3,237	4,122	6,307	7,152
45 to 54 years	3,575	5,242	8,116	11,702	12,269
Percent increase	83	62	97	86	72

ªNot available.
Source: Table 1.

graduates relative to high school graduates despite the great rise in
the proportion of persons completing the requirements for a college
degree. Table 7 shows that among men 25 to 34 years old, the proportion of college graduates doubled between 1940 and 1959 whereas

TABLE 7

Percent Distribution by Years of School Completed for Males 25 to 34 Years Old

Years of School Completed		1940	1947	1950	1957	1959
Total		100	100	100	100	100
Elementary School:	Total	45	30	29	22	20
	Less than 8 yearsª	22	— ᵇ	16	12	11
	8 years	22	— ᵇ	13	10	9
High School:	1 to 3 years	21	23	21	22	20
	4 years	20	31	28	31	33
College:	1 to 3 years	7	9	10	10	11
	4 years or more	7	7	9	14	15
Not reported		1	1	3	1	1

ªIncludes persons reporting no years of school completed, not shown separately.
ᵇNot available.
Source: See source note for Table 2.

the proportion of men who terminated their schooling with elementary school graduation was reduced by two-thirds.

Table 8 shows that despite the relative decrease in the number of elementary school graduates 25 to 34 years old since 1946, their earnings have not risen as much as the earnings of high school graduates, and therefore the income differential between these two education groups has widened. Looked at another way, the earnings of elementary school graduates increased by about 82 percent between 1946 and 1958 as compared with an increase of about 110 percent for high school graduates and 121 percent for college graduates. This table also shows a comparative decline in the relative income position of younger college graduates, a tendency which appears to have been reversed in 1956–58.

TABLE 8

Mean Income, (or Earnings) by Level of School Completed for
Males 25 to 34 Years Old

Year	Elementary–High School Differential			High School–College Differential		
	Average Income		Percent Difference	Average Income		Percent Difference
	Elementary School Graduate	High School Graduate		High School Graduate	College Graduate	
1939	—[a]	$1,335	—[a]	$1,335	$1,956	47
1946	$2,011	2,335	16	2,335	3,237	39
1949	2,540	3,246	28	3,246	4,122	27
1956	3,685	4,813	31	4,813	6,307	31
1958	3,663	4,909	34	4,909	7,152	46

[a]Not available.
Source: Table 1.

The reduction in differentials between 1939 and 1956 in favor of the younger high school graduates could be in part the result of the large increase in the number of college graduates. It is significant, however, that the decrease in income differentials between high school and college graduates which took place between 1939 and 1946, was not accompanied by a relative increase in the number of college graduates. As Table 7 shows, only 7 percent of the men 25 to 34 years old in 1940 and 1947 were college graduates. It does appear, therefore, that other factors than the relative supply of college graduates must be responsible for the observed change in income differentials between these two groups. The greater relative gains for high school graduates between 1939–49 may in part be due to reductions in unemployment for this group; and the reversal in trend since that time is perhaps associated with a rising demand for college-trained personnel.

In evaluating income changes in relation to education for specific age groups, the experience of veterans and nonveterans during the past 12 years is worth considering. While the second world war was still in progress, the government instituted a program under the Servicemen's Readjustment Act of 1944 (the GI bill) designed to assist veterans in re-establishing themselves in civilian life. A most important part of this program was the provision of government-financed education intended to permanently improve the economic status of veterans. Nearly 8 million veterans of the second world war made use of the education and training benefits at a cost of $14.5 billion to the federal government. Over 2 million men received college and university training and an additional 3.5 million received free education below the college level at elementary and secondary schools, vocational and trade schools, technical institutions, and business schools [20, p. 28]—the largest program ever undertaken by the federal government in providing financial aid to individuals in completing their education and training.

The impact of the GI bill on the educational attainment of veterans is clearly shown in Table 9. In 1947, when most of the former servicemen were in the initial phase of their training under the GI bill, veterans were already a more highly educated group than nonveterans. This is, of course, to be expected since many men were rejected for military service because they were of low intelligence. There was no difference in the proportions of younger veterans and nonveterans who had completed college; but a larger proportion of the veterans had been exposed to some college training, even if they did not graduate. By 1952, this picture had changed considerably. The proportion of college graduates among younger veterans increased from 7 percent to 12 percent, as compared with an increase from 6 percent to 9 percent for nonveterans. At the lower educational levels, the gains for veterans were equally striking.

Since older veterans did not make as much use of the education and training provisions of the GI bill as the younger veterans, their educational attainment did not change as much. The most significant change for the older veterans was a sharp drop in the proportion who

TABLE 9

Percent Distribution by Years of School Completed for Male World War II
Veterans and Nonveterans by Age

Years of School Completed	World War II Veterans				Nonveterans			
	25 to 34 Years		35 to 44 Years		25 to 34 Years		35 to 44 Years	
	1947	1952	1947	1952	1947	1952	1947	1952
Number (thousands)	6,851	8,428	2,035	4,130	4,043	2,472	7,791	6,070
Total	100	100	100	100	100	100	100	100
Elementary: Total	24	20	37	27	40	43	48	41
Less than 5 years[a]	3	2	4	2	9	14	8	8
5 to 8 years	21	18	33	25	31	29	40	33
High School: Total	58	56	40	49	45	39	37	44
1 to 3 years	24	22	18	20	21	17	19	20
4 years	34	34	22	29	24	22	18	24
College: Total	17	23	20	23	13	16	14	15
1 to 3 years	10	11	8	11	7	7	7	8
4 or more years	7	12	12	12	6	9	7	7
Not reported	1	1	2	1	1	2	1	1

[a]Includes persons reporting no years of school completed, not shown separately
Source: Bureau of the Census, *Current Population Reports,* Ser. P–20, No 15, *Educational Attainment of the Civilian Population: April 1947,* Table 3; and Ser. P–20, No. 45, *School Enrollment, Educational Attainment and Illiteracy,* Oct. 1952, Table 16.

quit school upon completion of the eighth grade and an increase in
the proportion of high school graduates. Between 1947 and 1952
there was no change in the proportion of college graduates among
older veterans.

Are the shifting patterns of educational attainment for veterans and
nonveterans associated with corresponding income differences? Table
10 suggests an affirmative answer. Veterans in age groups which made
greatest use of the educational and training provisions of the Readjustment Act also made the greatest relative income gains during the post-
war period. In 1947, veterans 25 to 34 years old had somewhat lower
incomes than nonveterans despite their greater educational attainment. Thus, any selective factors which may have produced higher incomes for veterans were not operative immediately after the war. The
lower incomes of veterans were not operative immediately after the
war. The lower incomes of veterans at this time may have been due
to several factors including the greater work experience of the nonveterans as a result of their civilian employment during the war and
also the loss of civilian employment during 1947 by many veterans

TABLE 10

Comparison of Median Incomes of Male World War II
Veterans and Nonveterans, by Age and Extent of Employment

Year	Median Total Money Income				Ratio of Veterans' to Non-veterans' Income	
	25 to 34 Years		35 to 44 Years		25 to 34 Years	35 to 44 Years
	Veterans	Non-veterans	Veterans	Non-veterans		
Total						
1947	$2,401	$2,585	$2,689	$2,900	93	93
1948	2,734	2,692	3,045	3,046	102	100
1949	2,828	2,562	2,984	2,935	110	102
1950	3,058	2,626	3,291	3,234	116	102
1951	3,359	2,875	3,647	3,595	117	101
1952	3,631	3,065	3,834	3,602	118	106
1953	3,948	3,183	4,118	3,867	124	106
1954	3,978	3,073	4,227	3,818	129	111
1955	4,330	3,294	4,483	3,946	131	114
1956	4,675	3,712	4,853	4,220	126	115
1957	4,984	4,041	4,985	4,279	123	117
1958	5,010	4,171	5,225	4,306	120	121
Year-round full-time workers						
1955						
Percent	81	72	81	78	—	—
Median income	$4,630	$3,854	$4,679	$4,319	120	108
1956						
Percent	83	72	80	78	—	—
Median income	$4,944	$4,150	$5,122	$4,554	119	112
1957						
Percent	82	70	80	74	—	—
Median income	$5,321	$4,465	$5,321	$4,792	119	111
1958						
Percent	76	66	77	70	—	—
Median income	$5,453	$4,804	$5,609	$4,844	114	116

Source: Bureau of the Census, *Current Population Reports*, Ser. P–60, annual issues.

who went to school part time or who served in the armed forces during part of the year. By 1948, veterans and nonveterans had the same average incomes and in every year thereafter veterans received greater relative income gains, reaching a maximum differential of 30 percent in 1955. Because of the changing age composition of veterans in the 25 to 34 year age group during recent years, it is difficult to make meaningful comparisons between veterans and nonveterans in this age group since 1955.

A large proportion of the veterans who were 25 to 34 years old in 1947 have now moved into the 35 to 44 year age group. As a result, the income differential between veterans and nonveterans within this age group is now beginning to increase markedly. Until 1953, veterans who were 35 to 44 years old had only slightly higher incomes than nonveterans. By 1956, the differential increased to 15 percent and in 1958 it rose still further to 21 percent. These figures provide presumptive evidence that the educational training received by young veterans 12 years ago contributed in an important way to establishing for them a permanent advantage over nonveterans.

One small step toward bolstering this conclusion can be made by restricting the comparison to persons who are year-round full-time workers. In this way, account can be taken of the greater tendency for nonveterans to lose work, presumably because of ill health. Table 10 shows that the average income of veterans is about 20 percent higher than that of nonveterans even when account is taken of the differential effects of part-time employment.

III. LIFETIME INCOME IN RELATION TO EDUCATION: 1939–1958

Estimates of lifetime income provide summary measures of the financial returns associated with education which cannot be readily obtained from the annual data presented above.[11] The estimates of lifetime income presented here are derived figures — one might say synthetic figures — based on variations in the payments to individuals in different age and education groups at a given time, specifically the calendar years for which data are presented. The figures are, therefore, based on a cross-section of the population in 1939, 1946, 1949, 1956, and 1958, and not on life-cycle data which would trace a man's income from the time he starts to work until he retires. Actually there is some question whether life-cycle data would be more suitable for the present analysis; cross-section data have the advantage that "they are free from the influence of variants such as periods of industrial depression or unusual activity with their changes in opportunities for employment, in wage rates, and in the cost of living."[12]

[11]For additional information on the estimation of lifetime income see [5] [8] [9] [10] [13] [17].

[12][18, p. 9]. Also [14].

Standard life-table techniques were used in computing the figures shown in Table 11. First, an estimate was made of the number of 100,000 children born in 1939, 1946, 1949, 1956, and 1958 who would survive to each given year of age. These estimates were made from the appropriate life tables.[13] By way of illustration, it was estimated that out of 100,000 infants born alive in 1956, about 96,000 would survive to age 18, at which time they would enter the labor market. The basic problem consisted of estimating the life span of these 96,000 survivors and the amount of income they would receive during their lifetime. For this purpose, it was assumed that survival rates for men in each education group would be the same as for all white males in 1956. On this basis, it was estimated that these 96,000 men would live a total of nearly 5,000,000 man-years between age 18 and the time the last one died. It was further assumed that during each year of life, these men would receive an average income corresponding to that received by men in the same age group with the same amount of education. The averages used for this purpose are those shown above in Table 1 plus estimates for age groups under 25 based on published and unpublished data of the Census Bureau.[14] The averages (means) are based on persons reporting $1 or more of in-

[13]The following life tables were used: 1939, Life Table for White Males from *U.S. Life Tables and Actuarial Tables*, 1939–1941, Bureau of the Census, 1946; 1946, Abridged Life Table for White Males, 1946, *Vital Statistics of the United States*, 1946, Pt. I; 1949, Abridged Life Table for White Males, 1949, *Vital Statistics of the United States*, 1949, Pt. I; 1956, Abridged Life Table for White Males, 1956, *Vital Statistics — Special Reports,* Vol. 48, No. 6, June 19, 1958; 1958, Abridged Life Table for White Males, 1957, *Vital Statistics — Special Reports,* Vol. 50, No. 2, July 28, 1959. A more complete source could have been used for 1949, "United States Life Tables, 1949–51," *Vital Statistics — Special Reports,* Vol. 41, No. 1, November 23, 1954. It was not used, however, because of the desire to retain comparability with previous estimates for the same year shown in [10]. As noted below, however, there are other differences between the estimates shown here for 1949 and those contained in [10].

[14]Estimates of lifetime income based on medians rather than means may be obtained from the author. Some analysts contend that the median is a more useful basis than the mean for measuring lifetime income since it is less affected by extremes and more nearly shows what the "typical" individual may expect to receive. The more prevalent and more valid opinion (from a strictly mathematical viewpoint) is that the median should not be used for the computation of lifetime incomes. Thus, for example, Kuznets and Friedman advise that "the actuarial nature of the problem clearly requires arithmetic mean earnings, which are usually considerably higher than median earnings" [8, p. 87] and Houthakker states that "the median is clearly not the appropriate type of average for the present purpose" [13, p. 24].

TABLE 11

Lifetime Income (Earnings) Based on Arithmetic Means for Males in Selected Age Groups, by Years of School Completed

Years of School Completed and Age	1939[a]	1946[b]	1949[c]	1956[d]	1958[c]
Income from Age 18 to Death:					
Elementary: Total	—[e]	—[e]	$113,330	$154,593	$154,114
Less than 8 years[d]	—[e]	—[e]	98,222	132,736	129,764
8 years	—[e]	—[e]	132,683	180,857	181,695
High School: 1 to 3 years	—[e]	—[e]	152,068	205,277	211,193
4 years	—[e]	—[e]	185,279	253,631	257,557
College: 1 to 3 years	—[e]	—[e]	209,282	291,581	315,504
4 years or more	—[e]	—[e]	296,377	405,698	435,242
Income from Age 25 to Death:					
Elementary: Total	—[e]	$ 87,004	104,998	143,712	143,808
Less than 8 years[d]	—[e]	74,369	91,095	123,295	120,965
8 years	—[e]	98,702	122,787	168,004	169,976
High School: 1 to 3 years	—[e]	107,940	141,870	192,254	198,881
4 years	—[e]	135,852	174,740	237,776	241,844
College: 1 to 3 years	—[e]	161,699	201,938	281,553	305,395
4 years or more	—[e]	201,731	286,833	391,992	419,871

Income from Age 18 to 64:					
Elementary: Total	$ 40,005	—e	100,413	138,127	137,786
Less than 8 years^d	—e	—e	86,912	117,930	115,418
8 years	—e	—e	116,968	161,124	161,643
High School: 1 to 3 years	56,653	—e	132,371	182,795	188,362
4 years	71,453	—e	159,487	224,529	231,509
College: 1 to 3 years	77,775	—e	180,841	254,092	279,640
4 years or more	109,961	—e	251,493	354,457	382,982
Income from Age 25 to 64:					
Elementary: Total	37,172	74,071	91,932	127,047	127,286
Less than 8 years^d	—e	62,334	79,654	108,310	106,449
8 years	—e	84,687	106,889	148,033	149,687
High School: 1 to 3 years	53,011	92,044	121,943	169,501	175,779
4 years	67,383	114,023	148,649	208,322	215,487
College: 1 to 3 years	73,655	138,871	173,166	243,611	269,105
4 years or more	104,608	168,983	241,427	340,131	366,990

[a]Restricted to persons reporting $1 or more of wage or salary income and less than $50 of other income for native whites and Negroes.
[b]Total money earnings.
[c]Total money income.
[d]Includes persons reporting no years of school completed, not shown separately.
[e]Not available.

come, excluding the relatively small number of men in most age groups without income.[15]

There are several cautions that should be considered before discussing the figures in Table 11. First, the figures are not exactly comparable from year to year due to changes in the income concept. The data for 1939 are for wages and salaries, 1946 are for earnings, and 1949, 1956, and 1958 are for total income. These variations in concept may have some impact on changes over time. A more general consideration is the fact that the estimates reflect the economic conditions and other circumstances which existed in each of the years for which data are shown. Some of the differences from year to year may reflect changes in these circumstances. The increase, for example, in the value of a college education by about $140,000 between 1949 and 1958 reflects the increase in prices as well as changes in the underlying relationships. These factors demonstrate an important advantage of the cross-sectional approach used in preparing the estimates. Since the averages used for each year are based on the experience for that year, they implicitly provide estimates in dollars of constant purchasing power for persons in all age groups in that year.

A final caution relates to the possible intrusion of extraneous factors in the relationship between lifetime earnings and education. Family influence in the form of financial help while at college and assistance in obtaining relatively high-paying jobs cannot be ignored; but, at the same time, should not be exaggerated. In 1950, about one-third of the college students away from home came from families with less than average incomes.[16] Few of these students could expect much financial help from their families, or assistance in locating lucrative job opportunities.

In every year for which data are presented, additional schooling is associated with a very substantial increase in lifetime income. On the

[15]Comparable figures for 1949 in [10] and [13] are based on all persons reporting on income rather than just those reporting $1 or more. The method of computing the means in this report conforms to that generally used by the Bureau of the Census. In any event, the inclusion or exclusion of the zero income group would have little impact on the estimate of the mean for most age groups and on the estimate of lifetime income. A further difference between the figures for 1949 in the present report and in [10] and [13] relates to the ages covered by the estimates. In [10] the estimates cover incomes received between the ages of 22 and 74, and [13] the estimates cover incomes received from age 14 to death. In the present report estimates for various age groups are shown.

[16]Based on unpublished data in the Census Bureau's *Current Population Survey* for March 1950.

basis of conditions in 1958, an elementary school graduate could expect to receive during his lifetime about $52,000 (or two-fifths) more income, on the average, than the person who had no schooling or who terminated his formal education before completing the eighth grade. The difference between the expected lifetime income of the average elementary school and high school graduate was equally striking. In 1958, the average elementary school graduate could expect a lifetime income of about $182,000 as compared with about $258,000 for the average high school graduate. The expected income differential associated with the four years of high school education therefore amounted to about $76,000 or 42 percent.

Since a college degree is the "open sesame" to many, if not most, high-paying jobs, it should come as no surprise that the greatest income gains associated with additional schooling appear at the college level. On the basis of 1958 data, a college graduate could expect to receive about $435,000 income during his lifetime as compared with $258,000 for the average high school graduate. It can, therefore, be estimated that the approximately $4\frac{1}{2}$ years of schooling beyond the high school level were associated with an increase of about $177,000 in lifetime income or about $40,000 per year of schooling.

Due to the considerable decrease in the purchasing power of money during the past 20 years, meaningful comparisons over time in the absolute amount of lifetime income received by men with different amounts of schooling can be made only after some attempt has been made to adjust for price changes. However, some indication of the relative changes since 1939 in the lifetime incomes of elementary, high school, and college graduates can be made on the basis of the unadjusted data shown in Table 12. These data are restricted to the income received between the ages of 25 and 64 because this is the only age span for which data are available for each of the four years under consideration.

Since 1939 the more highly educated groups have clearly made the greater relative gains in expected lifetime income. Thus, for example, in 1946, high school graduates could expect to earn only 35 percent more between the ages of 25 and 64 than elementary school graduates. Twelve years later the differential in favor of the high school graduates increased to 44 percent, reflecting the fact that the expected income of high school graduates rose more rapidly during this period.

A comparison of the relative income gains expected by high school

TABLE 12

Income from Ages 25 to 64 for Males, by Level of School Completed

	Elementary–High School Differential			High School–College Differential		
Year	Elementary School Graduate	High School Graduate	Percent Difference	High School Graduate	College Graduate	Percent Difference
1939	— [a]	$ 67,383	— [a]	$ 67,383	$104,608	55
1946	$ 84,687	114,023	35	114,023	168,983	48
1949	106,889	148,649	39	148,649	241,427	62
1956	148,033	208,322	41	208,322	340,131	63
1958	149,687	215,487	44	215,487	366,990	70

[a] Not available.
Source: Table 11.

and college graduates reveals essentially the same pattern. Evidently, the differential in favor of college graduates dropped from 55 percent in 1939 to 48 percent immediately after the end of the second world war, probably because a larger proportion of the college graduates continued to serve in the armed forces during part of 1946. By 1958, however, the differential between high school and college graduates rose to 70 percent, reflecting a greater relative income gain for the college group. These figures support the conclusion presented earlier that the large increase in the number of college graduates during the postwar period has not adversely affected their income position.

A very crude attempt to adjust the data for price changes is presented in Table 13, where the current dollar estimates of lifetime income have been modified on the basis of the consumers price index, and the results are expressed in dollars of 1958 purchasing power. Here again the data are restricted to incomes received between the ages of 25 and 64 years in order to present estimates for each of the years under consideration. There are, of course, several important limitations to the adjustment that has been attempted. It is not clear, for example, that the consumers price index is equally applicable to each education group or that it can be applied to figures which include the farm population, since the index refers specifically to moderate-income urban wage-earner families. Moreover, since the figures under consideration refer to income expected to be received in the future, it is not clear that a price adjustment based on current data is applicable. For these and other reasons the estimates must be regarded as

TABLE 13

"Price-Adjusted" Income (Earnings) from Ages 25 to 64 for Males by Years of School Completed

(Dollars of 1958 purchasing power)

Years of School Completed		1939	1946	1949	1956	1958
Elementary:	Total	$ 77,281	$109,735	$111,568	$135,013	$127,286
	Less than 8 years[b]	—[a]	92,347	96,667	115,101	106,449
	8 years	—[a]	125,462	129,720	157,315	149,687
High School:	1 to 3 years	110,210	136,361	147,989	180,129	175,779
	4 years	140,089	168,923	180,399	221,384	215,487
College:	1 to 3 years	153,129	205,735	210,153	258,885	269,105
	4 years or more	217,480	250,345	292,994	361,457	366,990

[a]Not available.

[b]Includes persons reporting no years of school completed, not shown separately.

Source: Data in Table 11 adjusted by consumers price index.

only the roughest sort of approximations. Nevertheless, the figures do show that lifetime income, adjusted for price changes, has risen considerably since 1939 for all education groups. The rise amounted to about $75,000 (about 54 percent) for high school graduates and $150,000 (about 69 percent) for college graduates. A rise in "real" income was, of course, to be expected because of the general increase in productivity and incomes during this period.

IV. CONCLUSION

This study largely represents an attempt to ascertain if the marked increase in the number and proportion of high school and college graduates during the past generation has been associated with a reduction in income differentials for these groups. On theoretical grounds, such a reduction could be expected *in the long run*, assuming no changes in the demand for more highly educated workers. The period under consideration, however, is relatively short and is one in which there were changes in the demand for, as well as in the supply of, such workers. Therefore, no fundamental theoretical issues are involved in this paper. The problem is merely one of ascertaining what has taken place and why.

The figures show that despite large relative reductions in the supply of workers whose schooling did not extend beyond the eighth grade, this group had smaller relative income gains than high school graduates. On the other hand, the large relative increase in the supply of college-trained workers did not adversely affect their relative income position. On this basis it is concluded that the demand for more highly educated workers has kept pace with the increased supply of such workers and, as a result, their relative income position has not changed. The fact that the proportion of men employed in professional and managerial work—the two major outlets for college-trained men—increased by 50 percent during the past generation suggests that industry has absorbed the increased flow of graduates from our universities.

In this study an attempt has also been made to prepare estimates of lifetime income for persons with different amounts of educational attainment. These estimates, heretofore available only for 1949, have also been made for the years 1939, 1946, 1956 and 1958. The conclusions based on the lifetime data parallel, in most respects, those derived from the annual data.

REFERENCES

1. G. S. Becker, "Underinvestment in College Education," *Am. Econ. Rev., Proc.,* May 1960, *50,* 346–54.
2. D. M. Blank and G. J. Stigler, *The Demand and Supply of Scientific Personnel.* Princeton 1957.
3. D. S. Bridgman, "Earnings of Land Grant College Alumni and Former Students," *Jour. Engineering Education,* Nov. 1931, *22,* 175–97.
4. ———, "Success in College and Business," *Personnel Jour.* June 1930, *9,* 1–19.
5. H. F. Clark, *Life Earnings in Selected Occupations in the United States.* New York 1937.
6. J. B. Conant, *Education in a Divided World.* Cambridge, Mass. 1948.
7. A. G. B. Fisher, "Education and Relative Wage Rates," *Internat. Lab. Rev.,* June 1932, *25,* 742–64.
8. M. Friedman and S. Kuznets, *Income from Independent Professional Practice.* New York 1954.
9. P. C. Glick, "Educational Attainment and Occupational Advancement," *Transactions of the Second World Congress of Sociology,* Vol. II, London 1954, pp. 183–93.
10. P. C. Glick and H. P. Miller, "Educational Level and Potential Income," *Amer. Soc. Rev.* June 1956, 21, 307–12.
11. S. E. Harris, *The Market for College Graduates.* Cambridge, Mass. 1949.
12. E. V. Hollis, *Costs of Attending College.* Washington 1957.
13. H. S. Houthakker, "Education and Income," *Rev. Econ. Stat.,* Feb. 1959, *41,* 24–28.
14. W. I. King and D. Wiehl, "The Income Cycle in the Life of the Wage-Earner," *Public Health Reports,* Aug. 1924, *39,* 2133–40.
15. Alfred Marshall, "A Fair Rate of Wages," *Memorials of Alfred Marshall,* A. C. Pigou, ed., New York 1956, pp. 212–26.
16. T. W. Schultz, "Investment in Man: An Economist's View," *Soc. Service Rev.,* June 1959, *33,* 109–17.
17. J. R. Walsh, "Capital Concept Applied to Man," *Quart. Jour. Econ.,* Feb. 1935, *49,* 255–85.
18. W. S. Woytinsky, "Income Cycle in the Life of Families and Individuals," *Soc. Sec. Bull.,* June 1943, *6,* 8–17.
19. Educational Policies Commission, *Education and Economic Well-Being in American Democracy.* Nat. Education Assoc. and Am. Assoc. of School Admin., Washington, D. C., 1940.
20. President's Commission on Veterans' Pensions, *Readjustment Benefits: General Survey and Appraisal,* Staff Report No. IX, Pt. A, Washington, D. C., Sept. 1956.
21. U. S. Bureau of the Census, *Current Population Reports,* Ser. P–60, No. 33, Jan. 1960.

Investment in Education

22. *U. S. Census of Population: 1950,* Vol. II, *Characteristics of the Population,* Pt. 1, *United States Summary,* Table 124.
23. *U. S. Census of Population: 1950,* Vol. IV, *Special Reports,* Pt. 5, Ch. B, *Education,* Table 10.

11. Education and Income*

H. S. HOUTHAKKER
Massachusetts Institute of Technology

In the current debate on the financing of education, estimates of the money benefits which school attendance confers on ex-students are occasionally invoked. In an effort to shed some further light on this subject, this note presents some crude and limited calculations on the relation between education and income.

The approach to the estimation of life-time income chosen here is the so-called "cross-sectional" one, which involves the analysis of income received by people of different ages and educational histories during a single year. Relevant data are available from the 1950 Census of Population,[1] which tabulates total money incomes received in 1949 by a 3⅓ percent sample of the population aged 14 and over. Only males, irrespective of color, are considered in this paper.[1a]

The principal difficulty raised by this source of information[2] is that mean incomes are not stated; the table only gives the frequency

*Reprinted from "Education and Income," *Review of Economics and Statistics,* XLI (February, 1959), 24–28.

[1] U.S. Bureau of the Census, *U.S. Census of Population 1950,* Vol. IV, Special Reports, Part 5, Chapter B, "Education" (Washington, 1953).

[1a] This source has also been used by Paul C. Glick and Herman P. Miller of the U.S. Bureau of the Census. See Paul C. Glick, "Educational Attainment and Occupational Advancement," *Transactions of the Second World Congress of Sociology,* Vol. II (London, 1954), 183–93; and Paul C. Glick and Herman P. Miller, "Educational Level and Potential Income," *American Sociological Review,* XXI (1956), 307–12. Unfortunately I did not learn of the existence of these useful papers until the calculations here presented were completed, though I was familiar with Mr. Miller's Census Monograph, *Income of the American People* (New York, 1955), which surveys the basic data. In any case the duplication is not large, for Glick and Miller had a different starting age for lifetime income (22 rather than 14 years); they did not take income taxes into account, nor did they apply discount factors. Moreover they used a different procedure for estimating mean income (see below).

[2] Apart from questions of accuracy, for which see especially Miller, op. cit., I have made no attempt to correct numerically for any biases to which the data may be subject.

distribution and the median for each education-age group. The median is clearly not the appropriate type of average for the present purpose; since the distributions are all positively skew, it is uniformly less than the (estimated) mean. Moreover the ratio of mean to median is larger at higher levels of education, indicating that the distribution is more unequal there than at lower levels. Hence a calculation based on medians would not even give the right *proportions* between lifetime incomes for varying school attendance.

It was consequently necessary to estimate the mean incomes. For every income group (irrespective of age and education) a representative income was selected by inspection of the income distribution.[3] The figures used were as follows:

Income range	Representative income
$ 1– 499	$ 400
500– 999	900
1,000–1,499	1,400
1,500–1,999	1,800
2,000–2,499	2,300
2,500–2,999	2,800
3,000–3,999	3,500
4,000–4,999	4,400
5,000–5,999	5,400
6,000–6,999	6,300
7,000–9,999	8,000
10,000–over	22,000

The figure for the top group requires some explanation. It refers to an open-ended interval for which no information other than the *number* of incomes was collected. As is customary in these circumstances, it was assumed that the distribution of high incomes was of the Pareto type, an assumption for which the known points in the right-hand tail provided some support. The Pareto constant was estimated at about 1.9, from which the mean of $22,000 for incomes over $10,000 follows by a well-known formula.[4]

[3]Glick took the midpoint of each interval as its mean, a practice which leads to bias if the distribution is skew. It may be noted that the mean incomes for age-education groups as estimated by Glick are nearly all lower than in my Table I, though this is partly attributable to the difference discussed in the next footnote.

[4]Miller, op. cit., 153, notes that income tax returns of families and unrelated in-

By applying these representative incomes to the number of persons in each income-age-education group the mean income before tax for all age-education groups was estimated.[5] The results are given in Table 1. Some of the figures, particularly those in the top right hand corner, are based on so few observations that they should not be taken too literally. There were, for instance, only 85 college graduates for whom income was reported in the 18–19 years age bracket, and only 107 high school graduates in the 14–15 years bracket.

In order to provide some insight into the variablity of income within each cell, Table 1 also includes coefficients of variation (defined as the standard deviation divided by the estimated mean income). Actually the coefficient of variation is by no means an ideal measure for this purpose because the distribution within each cell has a rather unusual shape.[6] Thus in the younger and older age brackets the large number of zero incomes makes the distribution bimodal, resulting in a very large coefficient of variation. A better measure of variability is hard to find, however. It will be observed that the coefficient of variation for each education group falls off rather sharply with age, and then rises more slowly. The minimum appears to be reached at an earlier age in the lower education groups. Although the variability is relatively greater for high education groups at early ages, these groups show less variability in the highest age groups.

Table 2 shows income after tax. Only federal income taxes were taken into account. For each age-education-income group the representative income was multiplied by the tax rate, estimated as the ratio between "tax liability" and "adjusted gross income" in the appropriate bracket.[7] As in the case of income before tax, the figures were

---

dividuals for 1944 to 1949 with adjusted gross incomes over $10,000 had a mean of between $21,000 and $22,000, but that this figure would overstate the mean income of persons (to which the Census data refer). He therefore uses a mean of $20,000. I have nevertheless preferred a figure of $22,000 mostly because in the more highly educated groups, where relatively many incomes over $10,000 are to be found, the distribution is more unequal, so that a still larger mean would have been appropriate for those groups. In the groups where high incomes are few it makes less difference what mean is used.

[5] The not inconsiderable groups with "income not reported" and "school years not reported" had to be left out of account.

[6] It does not conform to any of the well-known distribution functions, such as the normal, the log-normal, or (except in the right-hand tail) the Pareto distribution.

[7] From U.S. Treasury Department, Internal Revenue Service, *Statistics of Income for 1949*, Part I (Washington, 1954); both taxable and non-taxable returns were considered.

TABLE 1

Mean Income Before Tax by Age and Years of School Completed[a]

(Coefficients of variation in parentheses)

| | Years of School Completed | | | | | | | |
| | Elementary | | | | High School | | College | |
Age	0	1–4	5–7	8	1–3	4	1–3	4 or more
14–15	$112	$127	$ 90	$121	$129	$809		
	(3.81)	(2.65)	(3.61)	(3.74)	(4.22)	(1.65)		
16–17	251	314	280	289	231	382	$361	
	(1.87)	(1.70)	(1.98)	(1.95)	(2.20)	(2.08)	(1.84)	
18–19	377	633	760	907	701	817	540	$887
	(1.39)	(1.07)	(1.08)	(1.12)	(1.20)	(1.02)	(1.36)	(1.07)
20–21	638	935	1147	1512	1543	1639	900	956
	(1.32)	(1.01)	(.84)	(.67)	(.78)	(.74)	(1.32)	(1.72)
22–24	809	1192	1511	1868	2136	2285	1653	1763
	(1.14)	(.81)	(.80)	(.69)	(.63)	(.64)	(.97)	(1.01)
25–29	1042	1474	1847	2292	2597	2934	2861	3135
	(1.34)	(.92)	(.72)	(.65)	(.58)	(.58)	(.81)	(.90)
30–34	1126	1667	2122	2646	2990	3465	4011	5042
	(.94)	(.87)	(.72)	(.69)	(.62)	(.66)	(.80)	(.88)
35–44	1450	1814	2405	2964	3385	3987	4972	7122
	(1.14)	(.93)	(.82)	(.77)	(.77)	(.84)	(.92)	(.89)
45–54	1671	2007	2534	3156	3640	4594	5609	8225
	(1.07)	(1.05)	(.95)	(.89)	(.96)	(.99)	(1.01)	(.89)
55–64	1780	1911	2336	2871	3349	4375	5070	7655
	(1.12)	(1.10)	(1.03)	(1.02)	(1.07)	(1.11)	(1.12)	(.97)
65–74	1095	1205	1555	1891	2348	3029	3514	5660
	(1.51)	(1.51)	(1.63)	(1.34)	(1.41)	(1.39)	(1.38)	(1.20)
75–	608	712	888	1078	1506	2021	2259	3531
	(2.08)	(1.84)	(1.99)	(1.96)	(1.91)	(1.96)	(1.81)	(1.64)

[a]Based on $3\frac{1}{2}$ percent sample from total U.S. male population. Income in 1949.

then weighted by the number of persons in each income group.

The after-tax incomes are plotted in Chart 1, from which it will be noticed that on the whole a longer school attendance is positively correlated with higher mean income, except for the age groups below 30. As discussed below, this cannot necessarily be interpreted as a causal relation. In all education groups annual income rises with age until a maximum is reached in the 45–54 age groups, though not until the 55–64 group for those who never attended school. After that the peak mean income falls off first slowly, then rather sharply.

These figures gain in interest when they are summed over all ages,

TABLE 2

Mean Income After Tax by Age and Years of School Completed[a]

				Years of School Completed				
	Elementary				High School		College	
Age	0	1–4	5–7	8	1–3	4	1–3	4 or more
14–15	$107	$125	$ 89	$119	$125	$769		
16–17	247	309	275	283	227	371	$352	
18–19	366	619	737	876	680	793	528	$855
20–21	619	904	1106	1452	1474	1564	860	904
22–24	782	1149	1445	1776	2024	2158	1567	1663
25–29	994	1406	1756	2164	2443	2745	2655	2878
30–34	1082	1585	2005	2478	2790	3202	3642	4461
35–44	1374	1714	2191	2750	3115	3614	4390	6044
45–54	1575	1878	2351	2899	3296	4062	4842	6835
55–64	1670	1789	2170	2633	3027	3844	4374	6360
65–74	1037	1137	1455	1751	2132	2692	3080	4757
75–	583	682	837	1004	1373	1784	1996	3001

[a] Based on $3\frac{1}{2}$ percent sample from total U.S. male population. Income and federal tax rate in 1949.

starting at the lowest age for which incomes are reported (14 years).[8] In order to give proper weights to the different ages, the chance of survival according to the mortality experience of 1949–51[9] was taken into account. Thus the weights refer to a hypothetical population whose age-composition was determined by the mortality after age 14 in those three years, whereas the actual composition of the 1949 population was of course the result of natality, mortality, and international migration during the preceding century.

Capitalization of a stream of income inevitably raises the question of discounting. I have no final opinion on this matter, and will confine myself to a statement of the arguments *pro* and *contra,* and a calculation based on some of the alternatives.

[8]Glick, op. cit., and Glick and Miller, op. cit., start at age 22, this being the age at which for nearly all people school attendance is completed. In doing so, however, they leave out of account the lack of earnings of the better-educated while at school, and consequently overstate the latter's advantage in lifetime income. Although perhaps more satisfactory in this respect, my procedure also fails to provide a complete picture, for it does not allow for income received while at school. On the other hand it does not consider tuition either, thereby introducing a wholly or partly compensating error.

[9]From U.S. Department of Health, Education, and Welfare, National Office of Vital Statistics, *United States Life Tables,* 1949–51, Special Reports, Vol. 41, No. I (Washington, 1954).

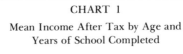

CHART 1

Mean Income After Tax by Age and
Years of School Completed

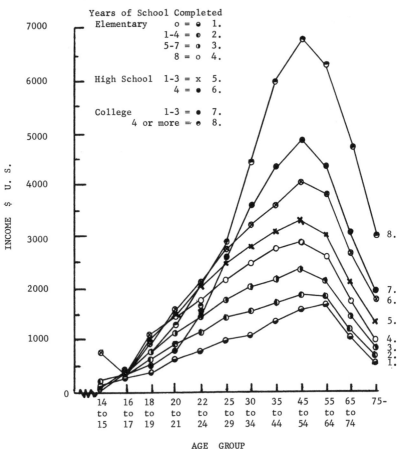

In favor of discounting are the obvious considerations that expenditure on education is an investment not fundamentally different from other investments, and that from a private point of view the cost of borrowing, and from a social point of view the return in alternative uses, should be taken into account. These considerations are not too helpful, however, in determining what rate of interest to use. The cost of borrowing for educational expenses is probably either very

186

low (for those with access to the more or less charitable funds established for that purpose) or very, even prohibitively, high (for those without such access and without suitable collateral). The rate of return in alternative uses is also far from uniform, depending as it does on the degree of riskiness and on imperfections of the capital market.

Arguments against using a discount rate are that some discounting is already implicit in the adjustment for survival, and that in a growing economy every individual may expect an upward trend in his own earnings superimposed on the cross-sectional pattern for a particular year. Perhaps neither of these two factors is sufficient in magnitude to make discounting unnecessary, but the reader who feels that they are has only to consult the first column of Table 3.

That table gives the capital value at age 14 of lifetime income, both before and after tax, for four different rates of interest. As one would expect, the capital values are very sensitive to the discount rate used, so that the figures in every column are much smaller than the corresponding figures in the column to the left. Moreover the proportionate reduction is the more considerable, the higher the level of education, in accordance with the previously noted fact that the income advantage of the better-educated does not apply to their early years. Taxes are also more important, absolutely and relatively, at higher levels of education.

Even so the capital values increase uniformly with level of schooling for all discount rates considered. In other words, the increment in capital value associated with each successive level of education is nearly always positive. The only exception is in the "College, 1–3 years" group, which at eight percent discount (and also, after tax, at six percent) has a lower capital value than the "High School, 4 years" group. Hence it may not be true, in the case of higher learning, that it is better to have loved and lost than never to have loved at all.

Many other conclusions may be drawn from Table 3, but they need not be spelled out here. Instead some remarks about the limitations of this type of analysis are in order. That the results are subject to the validity of the data and methods used hardly needs saying, though it may be worth repeating that the calculations are based entirely on 1949 patterns of income, school attendance, and mortality. What is perhaps more important is that Table 3, in particular, does not justify any immediate inferences concerning the money benefits attributable specifically to education as such, as distinct from the other factors that influence a man's income.

TABLE 3

Capital Value at Age 14 of Lifetime Income by Years of School Completed

Discount Rate (*percent*)	Before Tax				After Tax			
	0	3	6	8	0	3	6	8
Years of school completed:								
Elementary:								
0	$ 64,132	$ 26,220	$13,014	$ 8,896	$ 60,785	$24,944	$12,428	$ 8,515
1–4	79,386	33,939	17,492	12,179	75,021	32,189	16,638	11,730
5–7	100,430	42,758	21,834	15,098	93,571	40,006	20,537	14,252
8	124,105	52,923	27,037	18,700	115,277	49,425	25,380	17,592
High School:								
1–3	142,522	59,734	30,008	20,514	130,933	55,260	27,945	19,188
4	175,160	72,475	36,328	24,990	157,940	66,055	33,466	23,149
College:								
1–3	198,268	78,138	36,547	23,793	175,206	69,651	32,912	22,400
4 or more	280,989	106,269	47,546	30,085	238,761	91,335	41,432	26,454

This point (recognized also by Glick and Miller) may be illustrated from the figure of $100,000 often alleged to be the money value of a college education. This figure is presumably derived from Glick and Miller (*op. cit.*, 310) whose numerical results are similar to those in my Table 3, for zero discount rate, before tax. Granting even that interest and taxes may be ignored, it is still not true that an individual chosen at random could increase his lifetime income by $100,000 by completing 4 years of college plus a small amount of graduate work,[10] rather than stopping at high school. The reason is that those who had completed four or more years of college probably differ in at least two other respects from the population mean: they are likely to have a greater native or acquired intelligence (acquired, that is, prior to entering college), and come from families with higher incomes. Both these factors increase the chance of entering and completing college; both also increase the expected lifetime income in the absence of a college education. This is particularly true for the second factor, if only because a prosperous family background will normally lead to the inheritance of property income.

The implication is that the differences between successive rows in Table 3 systematically *overstate* the specific effects of education on income: the bias is all one-way. Indeed we cannot even be sure that the apparent effect of education on income is not completely explicable in terms of intelligence and parents' income, so that the *specific* effect of education would be zero or even negative. The evidence which could settle this point is not available; off-hand I would hardly expect the extreme possibility just mentioned to be realized. On the other hand the popular figure of $100,000 for the average value of a college education can only be regarded as an upper bound, from which little or nothing can be inferred concerning such questions as the proper level of college tuition.

---

[10] It is regrettable that the Census tabulations do not distinguish between those who completed four years of college and those with more than four years.

12. An Economic Analysis of Earnings and Schooling*

GIORA HANOCH

The Hebrew University

The flow of net earnings (y) that an individual expects to receive at a given time is assumed to be a function of his age (t), his schooling level (s), and various additional factors, lumped together throughout the following discussion in a vector of variables (Z). Thus, the earnings function $y(t, s; Z)$ embodies all the information concerning the lifetime earnings of an individual or a homogeneous group, with given characteristics (Z) for any acquired schooling level (s), apart from random fluctuations (the expected value of which is assumed to be zero).

The marginal effect of the s'th school year on earnings at age t can then be approximated by the difference: $D_t(s,Z) = y_t(s,Z) - y_t(s-1,Z)$, where the differences D_t are normally negative at first, during the schooling years, and later positive. The marginal internal rate of return (R) to the s'th school year is determined by

$$\sum_{t=0}^{N} (1 + R)^{-t} \cdot D_t(s, Z) = 0,$$

where the (constant) rate of discount (R) sets the present value of the sum of all the D_t equal to zero.

If the earnings function $y(t, s; Z)$ can be estimated within a group homogeneous with respect to the Z variables—in which there are nevertheless variations in the actual schooling (s) owing to varying tastes and supply conditions—then the schedule of internal rates of return $R(s)$ can be derived and can be identified as the demand of

*Reprinted from "An Economic Analysis of Earnings and Schoolings," *Journal of Human Resources*, II (Fall, 1967), 310–29 (Copyright 1967 by the Regents of the University of Wisconsin). This paper draws mainly from a Ph.D. dissertation: "Personal Earnings and Investment in Schooling," University of Chicago, 1965 (referred to as *Thesis*). Financial support was granted by the Ford Foundation, the National Science Foundation, and the University of Chicago.

the group for investment in education. A modest attempt to approximate this procedure empirically will be carried out and analyzed.

I. ESTIMATES OF INCOME-AGE PROFILES

The 1/1,000 sample of the 1960 Census, including more than 57,000 males over age 14, provides an unparalleled opportunity to simultaneously analyze the impact of a variety of factors on the earnings of a number of homogeneous subgroups, without being severely restricted by statistical considerations concerning sample fluctuations and unreliable estimates. Nevertheless, one should constantly keep in mind that statistical biases do not diminish with large sample size, and that large-scale data sources coupled with modern computer speed cannot be substitutes for caution, scrutiny, and judgment.

It is outside the scope of this presentation to review the various experiments which have been carried out or to describe in detail the considerations involved in choosing an appropriate functional form for the earnings function which incorporates a satisfactory set of variables.[1] However, some of the key methodological issues deserve mention. First, the selection of variables is important — i.e., whether to include as explanatory variables (in the set Z) of the earnings function variables which are themselves related to schooling and age. For example, given extensive mobility across occupation and industry lines, which depends in turn upon age and schooling, there is a real question as to the meaning of "holding constant" these variables in a regression analysis.[2]

[1] A more detailed discussion of the preparatory analyses and some of the considerations involved in this process are found in *Thesis*.

[2] If, on the one hand, occupation and industry are to be excluded from the analysis, the elements of ability, non-pecuniary returns, and motivations associated with these classifications will be lost. On the other hand, a high degree of mobility exists among occupations and among industries, and this mobility depends strongly on schooling and on age. Thus, "holding constant" the occupation or the industry allows only for intragroup differentials of earnings. It eliminates the effects of schooling and age on interoccupational or interindustry differentials. In other words, an individual who completed more years in school would expect to move upward in the occupational scale and perhaps to work in a better-paying industry. This is in fact the main channel by which he can realize returns on his additional investment in education. If he were to be restricted to the same occupation group or industry, he would have much less opportunity to increase his income. This could probably be more effectively resolved by use of a simultaneous-equations model to explain both earnings and occupational structure. However, it would require additional information on ability and on other factors which was not available. As a result, it was decided to exclude occupation and industry variables from the equations and thus avoid serious biases in the estimated coefficients of schooling which, after all, are the target estimates of this analysis.

Empirically, there is no variable which would strictly satisfy all the requirements imposed by theory. No variable (except race, perhaps) is truly exogeneous, is uncorrelated with the residuals of earnings, and is not subject to any degree of choice by the individual (implying some simultaneous-equations bias in a cross-section, resulting from dependence on the individual's earnings and schooling). Hence, one must weigh the benefits against the undesirable aspects of including each set of variables, experiment with the results, and finally make the arbitrary but unavoidable educated choice.

A similar problem concerning the form of the earnings function is the extent to which interactions among variables must be considered. This could be done either by explicitly defining some interaction variables (e.g., as a product of two variables), or by splitting the sample into subgroups, thus allowing for full interactions between the classifying factor and all the remaining explanatory variables.

And finally, additional questions arise with regard to the presentation of each variable which is quantitative in nature (e.g., earnings, age, schooling, size of place): should it appear in a continuous form (linear or logarithmic), or be represented by a group of characteristic or dummy variables, defined on intervals of its range. A qualitative factor can be represented only by a set of dummy variables, but the size and number of its subgroups are still open to arbitrary determination, which may affect the resulting estimates.

The final choices of subgroups and variables on which our estimates are based are described briefly below. The sample of individuals not attending school in 1959 was divided into 24 groups defined by race (white or nonwhite), region (South or non-South) and age (14–24, 25–34, 35–44, 45–54, 55–64, 65 and over). Table 1 summarizes the size and some characteristics of these groups.

Within each of the groups we estimated a separate linear regression equation of earnings (in dollars, including zero for persons with no earnings) on 23 explanatory variables, most of which were in dummy-variable form. These include (1) seven schooling-group variables (representing differences between eight school levels); (2) age (both a continuous variable for exact age and a dummy variable defined on the lower half of the group's age interval – e.g., a variable having the value 1 for age 25–29 and 0 for age 30–34 within a group of age 25–34);[3] (3) type of residence – size of place (in logs), and dummy var-

---

[3] The inclusion of both a continuous and a dummy form allows for two linear segments with a common slope but different intercepts.

iables for six groups defined as urban-rural-nonfarm-rural farm, inside or outside a metropolitan area; (4) origin (foreign-born parents, born in a different region); (5) mobility (length of time in a given place, change of residence since 1955, and also birth in a different

TABLE 1

Earnings and Schooling by Race/Region and Age: All Males
(Except Age 14–24 in School), 1959[a]

Race-region Age	No. persons	No. with No earnings	Mean earnings (dollars)[b]	Mean Schooling (years)
Total	50,211	7675	4242	10.0
Whites/North	33005	4745	4700	10.4
14–24	3719	393	2466	11.0
25–34	6345	232	5058	11.8
35–44	7179	282	6326	11.3
45–54	6232	326	6042	10.3
55–64	4519	535	5019	9.1
65–99	5011	2977	1620	7.6
Whites/South	12,186	1956	3838	9.6
14–24	1762	244	1885	10.2
25–34	2382	96	4306	11.0
35–44	2612	120	5373	10.4
45–54	2161	176	4949	9.5
55–64	1579	266	4099	8.5
65–99	1690	1054	1179	7.3
Nonwhites/North	2357	431	2941	8.4
14–24	326	77	1588	10.1
25–34	536	59	3216	10.3
35–44	557	46	3927	9.4
45–54	441	48	3390	7.7
55–64	260	59	2795	6.3
65–99	237	142	1185	5.4
Nonwhites/South	2663	543	1586	6.6
14–24	467	81	1087	8.4
25–34	511	54	2006	8.4
35–44	533	52	2130	7.0
45–54	478	48	1993	5.9
55–64	325	71	1493	4.7
65–99	349	237	338	3.7

[a]Source: *Thesis*, Table 2.
[b]Mean earnings for all persons, including persons with no earnings.

region), and some family attributes—(6) marital status, (7) size of family, (8) number of children.[4]

The next step in estimating the earnings function was to combine the fragmentary results of the separate regressions into a unified earnings-age profile for each school level, within each of the four major race-region groups. First the net earnings (y) are estimated within each age-schooling group, by choosing appropriate values for the other explanatory variables (Z) in each regression equation.

There are two types of Z-variables: (1) variables expected to vary with age, which should not be "held constant" among age groups (e.g., marital status, number of children); these were given their mean value in the specific age group considered; and (2) variables which may be correlated with age fortuitously in the given cross-sectional sample but which are not intrinsically associated with age (e.g., type of residence and origin variables). These were given the mean value of the total race-region group—i.e., of all age groups combined. It was decided not to hold constant any variable among race-regions, but to regard the race-regions as independent populations. Thus, Z is held constant among schooling groups in a given race-region, and sometimes among its various age groups; but comparisions are not made with another race-region by fixing a constant distribution of type of residence or family characteristics, e.g., in all race-regions.[5]

Using these methods and values, we estimated eight different earnings-age profiles, corresponding to the eight school levels, within each race-region. Each of these profiles, in turn, was constructed from disconnected linear segments, representing the relation between earnings and age for that school level, as estimated by the specific age-group regression. It does not seem reasonable to assume that such a collection of fragmentary segments may adequately represent the expected earnings function $y(s, t; Z)$. If it is desired to quantify and formalize an individual's vague expectations about his future earnings at given alternative school levels, or if the earnings function

---

[4] See *Thesis*, Table 3 and Appendix A, for detailed definitions of variables and some regression results.

[5] Such a procedure would, however, be appropriate for other purposes, such as the analysis of net regional or racial differentials in earnings. But for the estimation of internal rates of return it is more reasonable to assume that an individual who forms his expectations about earnings at future ages will base these expectations on conditions prevailing among people of his own race and region rather than among the total U.S. population.

were to represent the average behavior for a relatively large and stable homogeneous group, then smooth and well-behaved profiles could be expected. Because there is no reason to believe that the discontinuities and irregularities manifested by the estimated profiles represent any real and stable phenomenon, the profiles were transformed into smooth curves by using moving averages of the original estimated earnings at each single year of age. The form of the moving average was a simple mean of ten years, centered at the sixth year. This achieved reasonable smoothness, while preserving the general shape of the original profiles.

These estimated profiles, which serve as our best estimates of the earnings function of persons out of school, are summarized in Table 2, which shows, for each schooling level in a race-region, the smoothed

TABLE 2

Estimated Expected Earnings at Selected Ages by Schooling, in Race-Region: Persons Out of School, 1959[a]

(In dollars)

	Years of School Completed							
Age	0–4	5–7	8	9–11	12	13–15	16	17+
	Whites/North							
14	69	253						
18	670	1073	1174	1306				
22	1574	2131	2301	2519	2930			
27	2570	3160	3498	3924	4461	4558	5602	
37	3672	4397	4809	5398	6052	7019	8713	9578
47	3717	4466	4967	5478	6281	7745	10,109	12,138
57	3404	4092	4506	5292	6023	7393	9677	11,398
67	1840	2083	2382	3079	3897	4493	5969	8019
77	465	514	733	1213	1916	2151	3101	4931
	Whites/South							
14	46	332						
18	429	957	926	1151				
22	1020	1745	1828	2052	2454			
27	1767	2655	3022	3233	3847	4246	4965	
37	2860	3665	4004	4780	5520	6448	7992	9027
47	2775	3658	3950	4572	5802	7215	9109	11,146
57	2365	3060	3633	4008	5475	7018	8981	9665
67	1257	1595	2073	2258	3370	3611	4228	5905
77	230	415	727	820	1584	1332	1357	3258

TABLE 2 *(continued)*

Estimated Expected Earnings at Selected Ages by Schooling, in
Race-Region: Persons Out of School, 1959[a]

(In dollars)

Age	Years of School Completed							
	0–4	5–7	8	9–11	12	13–15	16	17+
			Nonwhites/North					
14	63	571						
18	510	1338	646	757				
22	1586	2175	1529	1736	2122			
27	3021	2711	2337	2705	3201	2866	3249	
37	2879	3310	3197	3618	3989	3876	5146	7834
47	2898	3362	3412	3608	4305	4183	4480	9129
57	2503	2763	3674	2984	3361	3551	2543	6561
67	1385	1409	1942	1917	1896	1983	1139	2241
77	697	625	824	1191	1100	1085	514	557
			Nonwhites/South					
14	91	340						
18	475	823	607	757				
22	960	1280	1146	1284	1420			
27	1459	1691	1775	1874	1976	1832	2169	
37	1924	1870	2159	2166	2597	2679	3986	3112
47	1785	1969	2197	2134	2868	2621	3260	3920
57	1495	1654	2128	2144	2091	2275	1827	4178
67	572	635	970	819	667	1725	575	2724
77	171	212	391	199	169	1178	171	1664

[a]Source: *Thesis*, Table 4. At spaces with no entry, persons of that age enrolled in school.

estimated profiles at selected ages. Figures 1 and 2 describe the complete profiles for whites, in the North and the South, respectively.

Earnings are given, on the average, only for ages above those when each school level is completed. To estimate the average postcompletion ages, the age distribution of persons enrolled in school was computed for each level completed. The integral age closest to the mean, plus one year, was selected as the age of entrance to the labor market. These ages are as follows:

Years of school completed:	0–4	5–7	8	9–11	12	13–15	16	17+
Age at first year out of school:	10	14	16	18	20	23	26	28

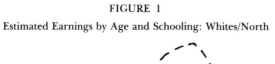

FIGURE 1

Estimated Earnings by Age and Schooling: Whites/North

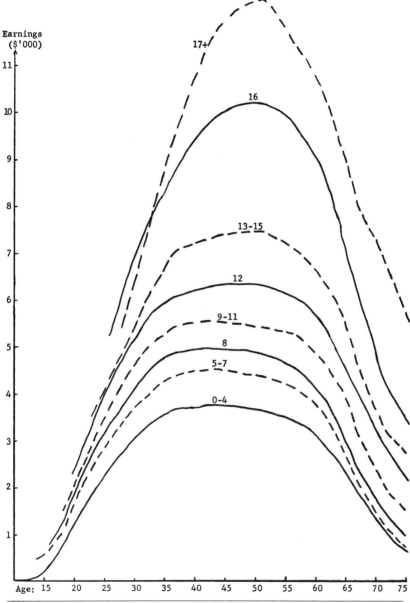

FIGURE 2

Estimated Earnings by Age and Schooling: Whites/South

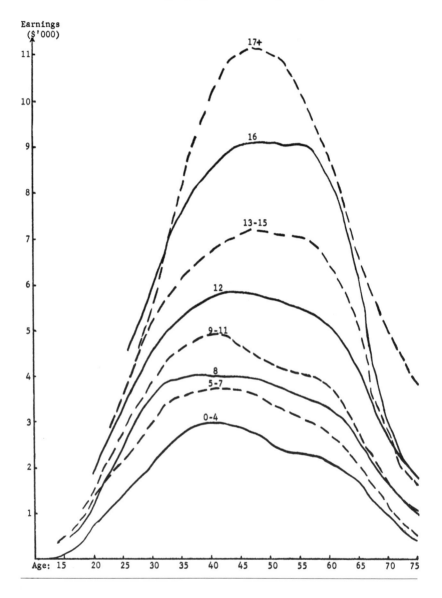

To complete this estimation of the earnings function, the earnings profiles should be supplemented with estimates of two types of earnings of persons attending school: the positive earnings of students who work during the school year or during vacations, and the negative, direct, private costs of education. In principle these estimates could be made separately and then combined to give average net earnings.

We did not have adequate data concerning the direct costs of education, classified by age, school level, race, and region, ordinarily required for this sort of analysis. In fact, even such detailed data would not be sufficient for our purposes, because such costs would have to be adjusted for other factors, as was done for earnings out of school. For example, it would be desirable to adjust the costs for differences in type and size of place of residence, for origin, or for mobility. Refined data of this nature might be derived from a special detailed survey of individual schooling expenditures or by the compilation of the required information in a future census. Making use of the crude data available today seems neither useful nor desirable, since it may only bias and blur our results. However, other studies based on more aggregative and crude data revealed that the average, direct, private costs of one year in school are nearly equal to the average yearly earnings of students, especially at the college level.[6] There is good reason to believe that these two magnitudes move in the same direction:

First, the higher the level of schooling, the higher the private costs and the higher the average student earnings. In elementary school, both costs (in public schools, which include a large majority of the elementary school students) and earnings are negligible. In high school, both increase — usually concomitantly with the class attended. In college, many students have sizable earnings, especially during the summer quarter; but costs are also high.[7]

---

[6] Gary S. Becker, *Human Capital*, Columbia University Press, 1964 (referred to as Becker), Chap. iv, p. 75, and Appendix A, sec. 2. The earnings of college students are estimated by Becker to amount to 25 percent of the earnings of high school graduates not attending school. The remaining 75 percent are "foregone earnings," which constitute 76 percent of total cost. Hence, total costs are about equal to total earnings out of school, and direct costs are about equal to earnings during school.

[7] In graduate school, however, earnings from all sources may exceed direct private costs, because many students receive fellowships and scholarships.

Second, student earnings and their average, direct, private costs tend to vary in the same direction among population groups. For example, non-whites usually spend less than whites on tuition and on other direct-cost items, and they enroll in higher proportions than do whites in the less expensive public schools; but their earnings are also lower, owing to lower wages and limited employment opportunities.

In view of the lack of detailed cost data and the apparent proximity of the two magnitudes, we assumed that earnings and direct costs cancel each other out in each of the student groups analyzed here at all levels of schooling. This implies that the net earnings during school are expected to equal zero in all cases, as indeed we assumed throughout the following analysis.[8]

It is not easy to evaluate the quality of the resulting estimates given in Table 2. The statistical process of their derivation is so complicated that appropriate confidence intervals could not be estimated by any direct method, although some extended simulation analysis would be useful in clarifying this aspect. However, statistical variability appears to be of a second order of importance, relative to more basic omissions and inadequacies of the data and of the estimation procedure. The most significant deficiencies of these estimates are discussed below, relative to the evaluation of rates of return to schooling derived from these estimates.

However, the limitations, reservations, and shortcomings (some of which seem unsurmountable in any empirical study), should not be over-emphasized to the point of discarding meaningful and valuable information in the name of purity. One can fill only a few gaps at a time, utilizing whatever information is available, while acknowledging its limitations and interpreting the results accordingly.

II. RATES OF RETURN AND THE DEMAND FOR SCHOOLING

The earnings-age profiles estimated above for various schooling levels are used to derive the internal rates of return in Table 3.

For each pair of schooling levels in a major race-region group, the rate indicated in the table is the average rate of return on the amount

---

[8] However, if better data about direct costs became available, it would be desirable to match them with data concerning students' earnings. For this purpose estimates of student earnings were carried out separately, but are not given here. Cf. *Thesis*, Table 5, and pp. 64–68.

TABLE 3

Estimates of Private Internal Rates of Return Among Schooling Levels, by Race and Region; Adjusted for Various Factors[a]

Higher Schooling Level in Each Comparison	Lower Schooling Level in Each Comparison						
	0–4	5–7	8	9–11	12	13–15	16
Whites/North							
5–7	[b]						
8	[b]	.218					
9–11	.474	.185	.163				
12	.331	.175	.161	.160			
13–15	.196	.125	.111	.097	.071		
16	.170	.124	.115	.107	.096	.122	
17+	.144	.110	.103	.096	.087	.095	.070
Whites/South							
5–7	[b]						
8	[b]	.144					
9–11	.662	.162	.182				
12	.441	.172	.186	.188			
13–15	.274	.139	.138	.127	.093		
16	.216	.131	.128	.120	.101	.110	
17+	.179	.118	.114	.107	.092	.091	.073
Nonwhites/North							
5–7	[b]						
8	.06	.01					
9–11	.13	.03	.23				
12	.18	.06	.23	.22			
13–15	.07	.03	.07	.04	[c]		
16	(.07)	(.03)	(.07)	(.04)	[d]	(.08)	
17+	(.12)	(.09)	(.13)	(.12)	(.10)	(.16)	(.23)
Nonwhites/South							
5–7	.89						
8	.27	.06					
9–11	.22	.06	.10				
12	.17	.08	.11	.12			
13–15	(.13)	(.08)	(.09)	(.09)	(.07)		
16	(.11)	(.07)	(.08)	(.08)	(.06)	(.07)	
17+	(.08)	(.06)	(.06)	(.06)	(.05)	(.06)	(.05)

[a] Source: *Thesis,* Table 6. Numbers in parentheses were based on too few observations to be reliable.

[b] Rate was above 1 (extremely high in most cases).

[c] Negative rate (−.05).

[d] Multiple solutions, with no rate between −0.1 and 1.0.

of schooling, which is the difference between the two levels. It is that rate of discount which equates the present values of the two corresponding earning streams at a given age. When related to adjacent schooling levels (e.g., eight and nine-to-eleven years of school), it could be regarded as a marginal rate of return, where the marginal unit is the difference in years between adjacent levels (two years, in most cases). Hence, the relation between the rates appearing on a diagonal in Table 3 and the amount of schooling in the corresponding row could be regarded as approximating the marginal efficiency of investment in schooling, when investment is measured in school years.[9] It is, therefore, the demand for schooling in that group.

Before the results of Table 3 are interpreted, some of the technical and conceptual shortcomings and deficiencies of these results should be examined.

A unique solution for an internal rate obtains only where the two profiles intersect just once. In some cases of multiple intersections, we chose arbitrarily the economically meaningful solution and discarded irrelevant solutions such as negative rates.[10]

Cases of multiple solutions are more common among groups of non-whites for two reasons. First, the higher sampling variability of the estimated profiles increases the probability of intersecting profiles. Second, smaller earning differences, which are associated with lower returns to schooling, decrease the stability of the solutions, increase their sensitivity to minor variations in the earnings profiles, and hence also increase the probability of multiple intersections. Any irregularity in the estimated earnings function is reflected and even emphasized by computing internal rates of return. The estimated profiles of nonwhites are less reliable statistically (owing to much smaller sample sizes, but apparently also to the lower quality of the data); but they also seem closer to one another, because of generally lower returns to schooling in these groups.

In general, we would be inclined to have more confidence in the

[9] The rates in each column can be interpreted as a schedule of average productivity. The quantitative relations between marginal and average rates are similar to the relations found in general between average and marginal magnitudes.

[10] These obtain whenever the earnings differences between the two schooling groups reverse their normal sign at old age, and these future "losses" are weighed more heavily than current or near-future "gains." In a money-economy with positive interest rates this is not acceptable, although such negative old-age differences are definitely possible—e.g., if persons with higher education retire earlier than less educated persons.

earnings profiles estimated above than in the numerical values of the internal rates discussed here. The values computed for internal rates seem to be highly sensitive to exactly those elements of the earnings profiles which are the least accurate and the most vulnerable to omissions and biases—i.e., mainly the measured net earnings at young ages, during the schooling period and shortly thereafter. In addition to the lack of data on schooling costs and the crude assumptions used here instead, reporting errors are more common among youngsters, whose employment and wages are less stable. Their reported earnings in the year of leaving the school are applicable in many cases to only a fraction of the year, or to a partial source of earnings. The computed rates are also sensitive to the exact length of the schooling period and the exact age of entry into the labor force—both determined here on the basis of crude estimates.[11] The general under-reporting of earnings may also bias the results, especially if associated with the level of schooling.

In addition to these statistical and technical reservations, many remaining conceptual and theoretical qualifications require clarification before these results can be used for economic analysis. It is not our intention to dwell at length on these qualifications, nor do we intend to use outside information and additional assumptions to modify the numerical results with various adjustments and corrections. Because of inadequate data, such adjustments cannot be complete; however, a partial adjustment may increase rather than decrease the over-all bias. Furthermore, adjustments and modifications may also mask the results of this particular sample, introducing a higher degree of arbitrariness, subjective judgment, and uncertainty concerning the source and reliability of these results.[12] For all these reasons, it seems preferable to list briefly the important biases, but to leave the numerical results intact.

The more important biases inherent in the estimated profiles and rates of return are those associated with ability. There is probably a

[11] This, however, seems to be less arbitrary than the procedure chosen in various studies, where it is assumed that one school year corresponds to one actual year of age, with no allowance for late-comers and older graduates. In fact, the difference in ages of completion may account for many of the differences in estimated rates of return between this and other studies. See Becker, p. 1962.

[12] However, the interested reader may estimate approximately the effect of each kind of adjustment on the resulting internal rates by inspecting its effect on the rates in another study in which such an adjustment was actually carried out.

significant positive correlation between ability to earn income—a combination of natural and acquired ability traits—and the level of schooling achieved. This obviously leads to a positive bias in the differentials between schooling levels and in rates of return to schooling.

Nonpecuniary returns (positive or negative), which are not measured as earnings, are another source of serious bias. Some of the variables used to estimate the earning function may have partially accounted for such factors (e.g., type of residence), but only to a limited extent. The consumption aspect of the schooling activity itself is also a form of nonpecuniary element. The over-all effect of all the various forms of nonpecuniary elements on the rates of return is unknown and difficult to evaluate, especially because many of these elements are not measurable or even quantifiable (such as status, satisfaction from learning, etc.).

Additional modifications of the rates of return are required in principle to adjust for mortality, for expected secular growth in incomes, for improvements over time in productivity and in the quality of schooling, for cyclical variations in earnings, for expected changes in relative supply and demand of various skills, for the progressive taxation of earnings, and for differences in the cost of living. These modifications, applied to the cross-sectional results, would accord with the theory that individuals and groups base their expectations about earnings not on conditions at a point in time among different age and schooling groups, but rather on the economic experience of cohorts over their lifetime.

Finally, it should be emphasized that the rates of return estimated and analyzed here are strictly private rates of return. Extensive modifications are required if one wishes to derive from them social rates of return, which take into account the considerable external effects of schooling.

Keeping in mind the drawbacks and limitations of these rates of return (Table 3), one may first examine the rates within the groups of whites. Although their order of magnitude is lower than usually claimed, it is considerably higher than rates of interest in the market and somewhat higher than average rates of return generally estimated for nonhuman capital.[13] The average rate for high school (relative

---

[13] See George S. Stigler, *Capital and Rates of Return in Manufacturing Industries* (Princeton: NBER, 1963).

to grade school or to high school dropouts: 12 against 8 or 9–11 years of school) is 16 percent for whites in the North and 19 percent in the South.[14]

College dropouts (13–15 vs. 12 years) showed relatively low marginal rates, as would be expected—7 and 9 percent in the North and South, respectively. The completion of college (16 vs. 13–15 years) shows return rates of 12 and 11 percent, respectively, although the average rate between college and high school (16 vs. 12) is only about 10 percent in both regions.[15]

The marginal rate of return to graduate school (dropouts and graduates, 17+ vs. 16 years) is surprisingly low: 7 percent in both regions. The assumption that direct costs equal student earnings may require more qualification in this case than at other levels, because many more students in graduate school get tuition scholarships and fellowships which are currently not reported as earnings. Nevertheless, it seems clear that the high earnings foregone by these students during school attendance reduce the attraction of graduate school as an economic investment, in spite of the large future returns.

Returns to the very low levels of education (5–7 and 8 vs. 0–4) are extremely high, mainly because of the negligible magnitude of both direct and indirect school costs at these levels. In fact, all levels of schooling, including graduate school, seem to bear very high returns relative to the level of virtually no education (0–4 years, the first column in the table). However, adjustment for differential ability might reduce these rates considerably.

In contrast, the last year of grade school bears significantly lower marginal returns than the fifth-to-seventh years, especially in the South. The marginal rates are 21.8 percent in the North, but only 14.4 in the South. The latter figure may reflect the fact that young boys dropping out of grade school before completion often stay

[14] Becker estimated rates of 16 percent for 1939 and 20 percent for 1949 cohorts of white males. The rates estimated by him for 1956, 1958, and 1959 were 25, 28, and 28 percent, respectively, for all males. The methods used were extremely crude, however, and based on survey rather than census data. The rate for 1959 was roughly estimated by inspection of earning differences between a survey in 1958 and summary tables of the 1960 Census (Becker, p. 128).

[15] Becker estimates this as 15 percent for all males. (Ibid.) However, besides all the other differences in detail, sources, and methods, the rates are not comparable owing to his inclusion of all graduate school entrants and graduates in the college-graduate group (Ibid., p. 74).

home or are unemployed in most of the country, but go to work in the South, thus increasing the foregone earnings component of costs and reducing the estimated rates of return.

Except for this last case, there seems to be a definite tendency for rates of return to whites to be higher in the South than in the North.[16] This probably reflects the relative shortage of skills in the South. Another explanation may be found in the lower costs per school year in the South, as explained below. However, the difference in the rates among regions is negligible at the university level (especially 17+ vs. 16 years).

The internal rates of return for nonwhites are generally low and relatively erratic, as was anticipated in view of the irregular nature of the estimated earnings profiles in these groups. Additional data and more extensive analysis might indicate whether these results merit any serious consideration.

The marginal rates appearing in the diagonals of Table 3, particularly the far more reliable rates estimated for whites, reveal a downward trend—i.e., the higher the amount of schooling, the lower the marginal internal rate. This seems to verify the conjecture that the marginal efficiency of investment in schooling is decreasing. Individuals would thus tend to increase their amount of schooling if the supply of investment funds shifted to the right, or if the marginal internal discount rate applicable to them were to decrease.

So far, the analysis has been restricted to the investment in education measured by a single dimension—namely, years of school. To convert the marginal efficiency schedule or the demand for schooling to conform with common economic usage, the estimated internal rates of return should be related to the amount invested in dollars.[17] This transformation could be effected by attributing to each level of schooling the total direct and indirect cost of completing that level— i.e., the total amount of money invested. This would give rise to a

---

[16]This is also a main finding in: Gary S. Becker and Barry R. Chiswick, "Education and the Distribution of Earnings," *American Economic Review*, (May 1966, pp. 358–69).

[17]Actual estimates of total costs for each level, as implied by the estimated earnings function, were not presented here—in view of the crude nature of the assumption about direct costs. They may be estimated on the basis of the earnings profiles given in Table 4. However, the numerical values of these costs are immaterial for the present general discussion.

An extensive discussion of the correct measurement of these costs is given by Becker, pp. 39–48.

different schedule, in which the investment-axis would be transformed from years into dollars. A schedule thus transformed should be cautiously interpreted, however. It is valid only for the "extensive" margin of investment in schooling and not for the "intensive" margin—i.e., it depicts the internal rate as a function of the money invested if variations in this amount occur by varying the number of school years completed. If, on the other hand, increases in the total amount invested by an individual occur through increases in the amount invested *per school year* (e.g., by a rise in tuitions or in the wages and employment opportunities of comparable persons outside the school—constituting a rise in foregone earnings—or by increase in the average distance traveled to school), then the rates of return applicable to these increasing investments may be totally different from the rates estimated here. This is because many additional restrictions are imposed on the one margin that are not imposed on the other. In most instances, changes in costs per year are not subject to a student's determination and choice; individuals may be forced out of an optimal position into one with larger deviations from the desired rate of return than those imposed in the other margin (of changing the number of school years). In some respects, however, individuals may be responsible for the "intensity" of costs per year (e.g., by transferring to a more expensive school or by hiring a private tutor), in which case they would probably equate the marginal rate in both margins.[18] In such situations the demand estimated above, expressed in dollars, would be applicable to intensive variations as well.

The discussion above was intended not as a digression from the main course of this analysis, but to clarify the comparison of demand schedules estimated for distinct groups. Attention is focused here on the differences between the four major race-region groups. One may assume for the sake of simplification that the following features obtain for the demand curves of the four race-region groups, abstracting from the necessary qualifications and modifications: (1) all these curves are downward-sloping; (2) in each region the schedule for whites is higher than for nonwhites; and (3) among whites, rates of return are higher in the South than in the North at low and medium school levels. It is also assumed that the intensive margin (of increasing

---

[18]That is, if we assume that individuals are in equilibrium on the extensive margin— e.g., that they have the desired number of school years.

costs per year of school) gives rise to the same schedules as the extensive margin (of increasing the number of years of school).

Given these assumptions and broad generalizations, one may inquire what factors cause the levels of marginal efficiency of investment to vary among different groups with the same number of school years invested? These may be classified into three major types of factors: quality of schooling, marginal market discrimination, and ability—in a broad sense.

The first factor—quality of schooling—implies differences among groups in the financial value of the units "years of school." These may represent differences in private investment per school year, differences in social investment accompanying them, or differences in the efficiency of these investments.[19]

The private investment for the same number of school years may be less for one group than for another. Hence, conversion of the schooling axis from units of years to dollars of private investment will shift to the *left*—or decrease—the demand schedule of the group with the lower costs per school year.[20] This might explain the higher rates of return estimated for whites in the South, compared with the North, since private costs per school year are probably lower in the South. Thus, rates corresponding to *equal investment in dollars* may be approximately equal in the two regions. Similarly, the discrepancy between whites and nonwhites in rates of return for equal investment is probably *greater* than that measured for equal schooling, because nonwhite students have, on the average, lower costs per year and thus get more school years per dollar privately invested. A conversion of the investment axis to dollars would cause a relative shift to the *left* of the lower nonwhite schedule, so that a larger difference between the rates of return would obtain at a given financial investment.

Presumably, social investment is positively correlated with private investment per school year, and perhaps also with the efficiency, or embodied quality, of these investments—all three factors being associated with "quality." Hence, standardizing the amount invested

[19]Efficiency may be defined here as real inputs applied in a school year, per unit of money spent on that year. It is not the marginal efficiency of investment as measured by its effect on incomes. A definition of quality of schooling based on the marginal returns from schooling would defeat its own purpose, of course.

[20]In addition to a shift in the level, this transformation would most probably change the slope and the shape of the schedules, because of a correlation between cost-differentials and schooling. This, however, will not affect the general conclusions drawn here.

by its conversion from units of school years to units of comparable quality (i.e., the comparable real amount of inputs to the school) will again shift to the left the demand for schooling of the lower-quality groups who have invested less per year (e.g., nonwhites). When the differences between the private rates of return to the two groups is evaluated at an equal amount of "standard schooling," it is *greater* than when evaluated at an equal number of years. Surprisingly, therefore, it appears that differences in the quality of schooling cannot "explain away" the fact that rates of return for whites are higher than for nonwhites.[21]

The second factor, market discrimination, depresses one group's private rates of return if the market price paid for services decreases, relative to the price paid for comparable services to the other group, as the level of education increases. It is important to note, however, that if discrimination affects all school levels equally, its existence per se ("average discrimination") may not affect the rates of return at all. Discrimination may even increase the marginal rate of return if foregone earnings are depressed by the same (absolute) amount as earnings at every age and school level. It is only an *increase in the degree of discrimination* with increased education, or a *marginal* discrimination, which can diminish the rate of return from schooling.[22] Thus, one may conclude that, if nonwhites' rates of return and demand for schooling are lower than those for whites because of discrimination in the labor market, this must be a *marginal* discrimination which is greater for persons with more education than for those with less. Whether such marginal discrimination exists is open to further study and requires additional information.

Ability, the third factor which causes differences between rates of return among race-region groups, comprises all the inherited and acquired traits which differ among groups and which are neither acquired in school nor eliminated by the schooling process—as far as these traits affect the efficient utilization of a real investment toward increasing earnings. Education and training outside the school,

---

[21] The conclusion in the text is valid only when the true marginal efficiency curve, correctly adjusted for biases and for dynamic elements, is indeed downward-sloping, both for the "extensive" margin and for the "intensive" one. If investment in social outlays per year of schooling is in a stage of rising marginal efficiency, this and similar results would not obtain. I am indebted to Professor T. W. Schultz for drawing my attention to this point.

[22] Cf. Becker, pp. 96–100.

motivation, innate ability, taste—in short, all social, psychological, and biological factors affecting a group's economic efficiency—should be included. If one is inclined to emphasize the environmental and social factors, then the disparity between rates of return to schooling in the two racial groups can be attributed entirely to some form of discrimination against nonwhites occurring in the schools, in the current labor market, or in the accumulated social burden.

III. CONCLUSIONS

In conclusion, it should be stressed that the above estimates and analysis refer to *private* rates of return and the private demand for schooling. The application of these to society requires modification of the estimated rates of return to take into account social costs and benefits, as well as the establishment of a criterion (such as a social rate of discount) for evaluating these social rates of return and for determining the desirability of additional schooling for a given group. However, any policy measures based on this evaluation must be made according to the determinants of private interest and return rates—so as to induce individuals to adapt their own behavior pattern to the socially desirable one. Hence, it is clear that the individual private rates and the associated private demand functions for schooling are essential data for the evaluation and determination of social decisions. The present study should thus be construed as a modest basis for a more complete analysis of income-determination and of decisions about education, from both the private and the social points of view.

B. Benefit-Cost Analysis

13. Total and Private Rates of Return to Investment in Schooling*

W. LEE HANSEN[1]
University of Wisconsin

The cost of schooling and the money returns resulting from investment in schooling are currently receiving more and more attention by economists, not only because of their possible implications for economic growth, but also because they may help individuals to determine how much they should invest in the development of their own human capital. This note provides some further evidence on these two topics; it presents estimates of internal rates of return based on both total and private resource costs for various amounts of schooling, from elementary school through college.

The fragmentary treatment of both the costs of schooling and the money returns to schooling found in much of the recent literature provided the stimulus for preparing these internal rate-of-return estimates. For example, Miller calculates life-time income values by level of schooling,[2] Houthakker estimates, on the basis of alternative discount rates, the present value of income streams associated with different levels of schooling,[3] Schultz provides estimates of total resource costs of education by broad level of schooling,[4] and Becker and Schultz calculate for several levels of education the expected

*Reprinted from "Total and Private Rates of Return to Investment in Schooling," *Journal of Political Economy*, LXXXI (April, 1963), 128–40. Copyright by The University of Chicago Press.

[1] This paper was completed while the author held a postdoctoral fellowship at the University of Chicago.

[2] Herman P. Miller, "Annual and Lifetime Income in Relation to Education: 1929–1959," *American Economic Review*, L (December, 1960), 962–86.

[3] H.S. Houthakker, "Education and Income," *Review of Economics and Statistics*, XLI (February, 1959), 24–28.

[4] Theodore W. Schultz, "Capital Formation by Education," *Journal of Political Economy*, LXVIII (December, 1960), 571–83.

rates of return, sometimes on a total resource cost basis and at other times on a private resource cost basis.[5] Given this diversity of treatment, it is difficult to obtain an over-all picture of the relationship among rates of return to different amounts of schooling or to see the nature of the differences between the rates of return as viewed by society and those viewed by individuals. Moreover, the relationship among the various methods of contrasting the economic gains from education—the lifetime income, the present value, and the rate of return comparisons—has been obscured.

It becomes important to understand what some of these relationships are when society and individuals allocate such a large portion of their resources to schooling. At the societal, level, for example, we might be interested in determining whether to allocate more funds to reduce the number of dropouts from high school or to stimulate an increased flow of college graduates. As individuals, we would more likely be concerned with deciding whether to continue or to terminate our schooling, on the basis of the relative costs that will be incurred and the benefits that will accrue. To this end, the comprehensive sets of internal rates of return developed here should be useful as a first approximation in seeking answers to questions of this kind.

At the outset, it should be made clear that the measured rates of return are money rates of return; any other costs and benefits associated with schooling are excluded from consideration. In addition, there are problems of measurement, many of which have not been resolved, that make the estimation of even direct money rates of return difficult. Some of these difficulties are discussed in Part I, which outlines the methods and data employed. Part II presents evidence on rates of return to total and to private resource investment in schooling. Part III contrasts three different methods of measuring the economic gains to schooling, while Part IV offers some concluding comments.

I. ESTIMATION PROCEDURES

To estimate internal rates of return to investments in schooling, we require data on costs—total resource costs and private resource

[5]Gary S. Becker, "Underinvestment in College Education?" *American Economic Review*, L (May, 1960), 346–54; and Theodore W. Schultz, "Education as a Source of Economic Growth" (Economics of Education Research Paper, August 15, 1961) (Mimeographed), and "Education and Economic Growth," *Social Forces Influencing American Education*, ed. H. G. Richey (Chicago, 1961). It should be noted that Schultz uses a short-cut method to derive his rate-of-return estimates.

costs—for various levels of schooling as well as data on age-income patterns by each level of schooling. From these, life-cycle cost-income streams can be established that show for each level of schooling the flows of costs incurred during schooling and the subsequent flows of additional income that can be attributed to that schooling, The internal rate of return is then estimated by finding that rate of discount that equates the present value of the cost outlays with the present value of the additional income flows.

The basic source of income data is the *1950 Census of Population*,[6] which provides distributions of income for males by age and level of schooling in 1949. From these, average income figures can be calculated for each age-schooling category, as shown in Table 1. Although Houthakker had previously presented such figures, his method of estimation produces a rather peculiar bias.[7] In addition, Houthakker's

TABLE 1

Average Income by Age and Years of School Completed,
Males, United States, 1949

Age	0	Elementary School			High School		College	
		1–4	5–7	8	1–3	4	1–3	4+
	$	$	$	$	$	$	$	$
14–15	610	350	365	406				
16–17	526	472	514	534	429			
18–19	684	713	885	1,069	941	955		
20–21	944	1,009	1,216	1,535	1,652	1,744	1,066	
22–24	1,093	1,227	1,562	1,931	2,191	2,363	1,784	1,926
25–34	1,337	1,603	2,027	2,540	2,837	3,246	3,444	4,122
35–44	1,605	1,842	2,457	3,029	3,449	4,055	5,014	7,085
45–54	1,812	2,073	2,650	3,247	3,725	4,689	5,639	8,116
55–64	2,000	2,045	2,478	3,010	3,496	4,548	5,162	7,655
65 or more	1,140	1,189	1,560	1,898	2,379	3,155	3,435	5,421

Source: See nn. 6 and 7.

[6]United States Bureau of the Census, *1950 Census of Population, Special Report*, P.E. No. 5B, *Education*, Table 12.

[7]The mean income figures used in this study were estimated by weighting the mid-values of each income size class by the numbers of income recipients in each size class, for each age-level-of-schooling category. A value of $20,000 was used for the mid-value of the open-ended class. Houthakker used a "representative" income in his weighting, in order to take account of the skewness. However, such a procedure superimposes the skewness of the entire distribution upon each age-level-of-schooling category; this leads to serious problems, particularly at the younger age levels, where the resulting mean income values will substantially overstate the "correct" values.

213

data show mean incomes of all males over age fourteen, whether they were receiving income or not. But to the extent that only income recipients are represented in the data shown here in Table 1, most of the males outside the labor force, either because of school attendance (younger males) or retirement (older males), are probably excluded. Exclusion of these groups seems likely to provide better estimates of the age-income profiles, particularly at their extremities.

In order to make the task of estimating the rates of return more manageable, the age-income profiles were assumed to commence at the "average" age of completion of each level of schooling.[8] For those with one to four years of schooling, the average amount of school completed was taken as two years; hence the age-income profile for this group was assumed to begin at age eight. For the next group, those with five to seven years of school, six years of schooling were assumed, so that its age-income profile begins at age twelve. The other level of education groups and the ages at which their age-income profiles were assumed to begin are as follows: eight years, age fourteen; one to three years of high school, age sixteen; four years of high school, age eighteen; one to three years of college, age twenty; and four years of college, age twenty two. In fact, however, for age groups under fourteen the age-income profiles take values of zero, because no income data are collected for these groups.[9]

Two major cost variants are used in the calculations—one for total resource costs and the other for private resource costs. The rationale and procedures for estimating total resource costs have been set forth by Schultz.[10] Total resource costs include (1) school costs incurred by society, that is, teacher's salaries, supplies, interest and depreciation on capital, (2) opportunity costs incurred by individuals, namely, income foregone during school attendance, and (3) incidental school-related costs incurred by individuals, for example, books and travel. Private resource costs include the same three components except that in (1) above, tuition and fees paid by individuals are substituted for society's costs which are normally defrayed through taxation.

[8]This is an oversimplification, but it did not seem worthwhile to deal with this in a more detailed fashion.

[9]It is unfortunate that such data are not collected since the earnings of male workers below age fourteen are assuredly not zero. Thus opportunity costs are understated to some extent.

[10]"Capital Formation by Education," op. cit.

In developing the cost figures used in these estimates, whether on a total or a private resource basis, the opportunity costs were taken directly from the age-income profiles of the alternative level of schooling being used in the calculations. For example, at age eighteen the opportunity cost for the person undertaking four years of college is the income that the high-school graduate would obtain from ages eighteen to twenty-one. This procedure made it unnecessary to rely upon indirectly estimated opportunity cost figures and yielded at the same time a more detailed set of opportunity costs by age and level of schooling.[11] In completing the estimates of per student total re-source cost, school costs paid by society and school-related expenditures incurred by individuals were derived from Schultz's results.[12] In completing the estimates of private resource costs, the amount of tuition and fees paid per student was obtained from already available estimates.[13] Again, the school-related costs from Schultz's work were used. While the latter costs have an arbitrary quality to them, they seem to be reasonable.[14] The cost figures, exclusive of opportunity costs, by age and grade are summarized in Table 2.

Lifetime cost-income streams were then constructed for each level of schooling with the help of the appropriate age-income profiles and the age-cost estimates. This was done by taking the difference between the cost-income profile for a given level of schooling and the income profile for the particular base level of schooling used in the comparison. For example, in the case of investment in four years of college, the income profile for the base group, high-school graduates, begins at age eighteen. The cost-income profile for the person who completes four years of college also begins at age eighteen; during the four years to age twenty-one it reflects both school and school-re-

---

[11] These opportunity cost figures tend to be slightly lower, on a per student basis, than those of Schultz, which average $583 for high school and $1,369 for college, on an annual basis.

[12] Ibid.

[13] Average college tuition and fees amounted to $245 in 1949 (see Ernest V. Hollis, "Trends in Tuition Charges and Fees," *Higher Education,* XII [June, 1956], 70). Actually, a figure of $245 was used; this figure was estimated from data on tuition and fees collected, reported for 1949–50 in *Biennial Survey of Education, 1955–56* (Washington; Government Printing Office, 1957), chap. iv. See sources to Table 2.

[14] Schultz simply assumed that these costs were 5 percent of income foregone at the high-school level and 10 percent of income foregone at the college level. The absolute figures derived from Schultz's work were used in these calculations even though the income foregone figures differed somewhat.

215

TABLE 2

Average Annual per Student Costs, Exclusive of Opportunity Costs,
by Age and Grade, United States, 1949*

Age	School Level (1)	Total Resource Costs			Private Resource Costs		
		School Costs (2)	Other Costs (3)	Total (4)	Tuition and Fees (5)	Other Costs (6)	Total (7)
		$	$	$	$	$	$
6–13	Elementary	201		201			
14–17	High School	354	31	385		31	31
18–21	College	801	142	943	245	142	387

*Though these cost data are indicated as being for 1950 in Schultz, "Capital Formation by Education," op. cit., they actually apply to the 1949–50 school year. Thus these data may overstate somewhat the costs of schooling relative to the income derived from that schooling.

Source: Col. (2) *elementary school:* Schultz, "Capital Formation by Education," op. cit., Table 3, col. (11), 1950, figure divided by number of elementary-school students in 1950, from *Statistical Abstract,* 1955, Table 152; *high school:* Schultz, "Capital Formation by Education," op. cit., Table 5, 1950, col. (4) divided by col. (1); *college;* ibid., Table 6, 6, 1950, col. (4) divided by col. (1). Col. (3), *elementary school:* assumed to be zero; *high school:* ibid., Table 5, 1950, col. (5) divided by col. (1); *college:* ibid., Table 6, 1950, col. (4) divided by col. (1). Col. (4), sum of cols. (2) and (3). Col. (5), *elementary school and high school:* assumed to be zero: *college:* based on average tuition and fee charges, derived from *Biennial Survey of Education, 1955–56,* chaps. i and iv, after adjusting veteran charges for non-tuition items (see n. 13). Col. (6), same as col. (3). Col. (7), sum of cols. (5) and (6).

lated costs and thereafter the somewhat higher income profile of the college graduate. The cost-income stream, the *difference* between these two profiles, reflects at ages eighteen to twenty-one both school and school-related costs as well as opportunity costs; at ages beyond twenty-one the difference reflects the net income stream resulting from four years of college. An additional adjustment is required to reflect the incidence of mortality; this involves adjusting the net cost-income stream downward to reflect the probabilities that at each age the costs or returns will not be incurred or received, respectively.[15] Finally, the internal rates of return must be estimated by finding that

[15]Calculated from United States Department of Health, Education and Welfare, National Office of Vital Statistics, *United States Life Tables, 1949–51* (Special Reports, Vol. XLI, No. 1 [Washington, 1954]). No attempt was made, however, to adjust for the incidence of unemployment, largely because of the difficulty of disentangling unemployment from non-labor-force status in the data, which show all males classified by the receipt or nonreceipt of income rather than by labor-force status.

rate of discount which sets the present value of the cost stream equal to the present value of the net return stream.

When considering private rates of return, it is important to show them on both a before- and after-tax basis. Not only will all rates of return be lower after tax, but also the relative declines in the rates will differ, given the progressivity of tax rates and the positive association between income and educational levels. The differences among the before-tax and after-tax rates could be of considerable importance to individuals in the determination of their own investment planning.

To estimate the after-tax incomes and rates of return, the original income data in Table 1 were adjusted for federal income tax payments; while it probably would have been desirable to adjust for all types of taxes, this could not be done in view of the paucity of data. Subsequently, the rates of return were calculated in the same way as described for the before-tax data. The actual after-tax income figures were obtained by multiplying each income figure by the appropriate ratio of after- to before-tax income, derived from Houthakker.[16] These ratios prove to be almost identical to those that would have resulted had the marginal tax rates been applied to the distributions of income recipients in calculating after-tax income.[17]

As in most empirical studies the available data prove to be somewhat unlike those that we require, and so the rate of return estimates do not provide a full picture of the profitability of schooling.[18] Therefore, several features of the data and the nature of their effects on age-income profiles, and hence on rates of return, deserve mention before the results are discussed. First, since only income rather than earnings data are available, the income profiles used reflect in part receipts from other assets. On the assumption that the relative income

[16]Houthakker, op. cit., calculated from Tables 1 and 2, pp. 25–26.

[17]Several of the education-age categories were adjusted for taxes by applying the average effective tax liability by size of income group to the midpoint of the size group to determine the mean tax paid. In general, the average effective tax rate derived for an education-age category was almost identical with that calculated by Houthakker.

Admittedly, the use of the average tax liability ignores the effects of age differences, family size, and so on, but it did not seem worthwhile to adjust for these factors, even to the limited extent that such adjustments could be attempted.

[18]The main criticisms of this whole approach have been expressed most fully and forcefully by Edward F. Renshaw, "Estimating the Returns to Education," *Review of Economics and Statistics,* XLII (August, 1960), 318–24.

from other assets is a positive function of the level of earnings itself, the impact of this would presumably be to raise the age-income profiles of the higher level of schooling groups. Second, certain problems of "mix" exist within the data. For example, among those with little schooling there may be heavy concentrations of certain minority groups, such as Negroes and Puerto Ricans. If they are effectively discriminated against, then the age-income profiles of the lower level of schooling groups would be depressed below their expected level. On the other hand, at higher levels of schooling the age-income profiles may be raised somewhat by reverse discrimination that favors sons, relatives, and others of higher social-economic status. Third, since those people who complete more schooling ordinarily possess greater intelligence, as measured by intelligence scores, some part of the differential income received might have accrued to them anyway. Although our present knowledge makes it difficult to separate the impact of intelligence and schooling, the observed income differences among the lower and higher levels of schooling undoubtedly overstate, and by increasing amounts, the differentials attributable to schooling.[19] Fourth, all cost elements were considered as investment even though some portions might better be regarded as consumption. To the extent that any of the cost is considered as consumption, the investment costs are overstated.[20] Fifth, all estimates rest on cross-section cost-income relationships and thereby ignore future shifts in the relationships of the cost-income streams. And finally, any number of other factors may impinge on the observed income differentials, in the form of education at home, on-the-job-training, and so forth.

While some would suggest that the presence of such problems seriously limits any conclusions concerning the empirical relationships between income and schooling, it nevertheless seems worthwhile to set forth the rate-of-return estimates in their crude form.[21] From them some preliminary conclusions about resource allocation can be drawn.

[19]Becker, op. cit., has made some adjustments for differences in ability, but his method of doing so is not yet available. Differences in intelligence at different levels of schooling are given in Dael Wolfe, *America's Resources of Specialized Talent* (New York: Harper and Bros., 1954), pp. 142–49.

[20]This point is discussed in T. W. Schultz, "Investment in Human Capital," *American Economic Review*, LI (March, 1961) 1–17.

[21]For another dissenting note see John Vaizey, *The Economics of Education* (London: Faber and Faber, 1962), chap. iii.

II. INTERNAL RATE-OF-RETURN ESTIMATES

A. THE RETURN TO TOTAL RESOURCE INVESTMENT

Internal rates of return to total resource investment in schooling appear in Table 3. The boxed figures in the diagonal to the right show the rates of return to each successive increment of schooling and can be interpreted as "marginal" rates of return. For example, the rate of return to the first two years of elementary school is 8.9 percent, to the next four years of elementary school 14.5 percent, and so on to the last two years of college 15.6 percent. Although the marginals provide all of the necessary information, average rates of return to successively more years of schooling can be derived from the marginals; since the average rates are of some interest, they are also shown in the columns. For example, in column (1) we see that at age six the expected rate of return to investment in two years of elementary schooling is 8.9 percent; the rate of return to investment in six years of elementary schooling (the weighted average of the two marginals) is 12.0 percent, and so on to the investment in sixteen years of schooling, which yields a 12.1 percent rate of return.

Several features of the configuration of rates of return deserve comment. First, the marginal rates rise over the first few years of schooling, reaching a peak with the completion of elementary school-

TABLE 3

Internal Rates of Return to Total Resource Investment in Schooling,
United States, Males, 1949*

To:	From: Age	Grade	(1) 6 1	(2) 8 3	(3) 12 7	(4) 14 9	(5) 16 11	(6) 18 13	(7) 20 15
(1)	7	2	8.9	. . . .	. . . .	. . . .	. . . .	. . . .	. . . .
(2)	11	6	12.0	14.5	. . . .	. . . .	. . . .	. . . .	. . . .
(3)	13	8	15.0	18.5	29.2	. . . .	. . . .	. . . .	. . . .
(4)	15	10	13.7	15.9	16.3	9.5	. . . .	. . . .	. . . .
(5)	17	12	13.6	15.4	15.3	11.4	13.7	. . . .	. . . .
(6)	19	14	11.3	12.1	11.1	8.2	8.2	5.4	. . . .
(7)	21	16	12.1	12.7	12.1	10.5	10.9	10.2	15.6

*All rate-of-return figures are subject to some error, since the estimation to one decimal place was made by interpolation between whole percentage figures.

ing. This clearly suggests that rapidly increasing returns to schooling prevail over the early years and that a small initial amount of schooling, the first two years, has relatively little impact on earning power. Second, the trend in the rates is downward thereafter, though it is not smooth by any means. While the rate of return to the first two years of high school drops dramatically, it rises somewhat with the completion of high school. The rate drops once again for the first two years of college, and it then displays a significant rise with the completion of four years of college. At this point one can only speculate as to the reasons underlying these declines.

Evidence such as this on the marginal or incremental rates of return is ordinarily used in discussing resource allocation. If on the basis of these rates of return a given amount of resources were to be spent on schooling, the ranking of the marginals from high to low is as follows: Grades 7–8, 15–16, 3–6, 11–12, 9–10, 0–2, and 13–14.[22] At an alternative rate of return to society of, say, 10 percent, investment in all grade levels except the last three would be justified. Were the alternative rate, say, 7 percent, only the last level would be excluded.

Viewing the matter in this fashion would be quite satisfactory if the rates of return declined steadily as we moved to successively higher increments of schooling, but because the marginal rates fluctuate some averaging is required. If we look at marginal rates for broader increments of schooling, for example, eight years of elementary school, four years of high school, and four years of college, then the rates of return to additional investment quite clearly decline, as shown by the respective figures: 15.0 percent (col. [1], row [3]), 11.4 percent (col. [4], row [5]), and 10.2 percent (col. [6], row [7]). At an alternative rate of return of 10 percent, investment in all levels of schooling becomes profitable. But were the original rates considered independently of each other and an alternative rate of return of 10 percent prevailed, it would not pay to permit any new enrolments, the schooling of those people in elementary school would be terminated at Grade 8, and of those people already in high school and college, only students in their last two years of each would be allowed to graduate. To allocate investment in schooling this way would obviously reflect a very short-run view of the implied economic opportunities.

However, it might be desirable to consider some longer time

---

[22] It is interesting to note that most states require compulsory school attendance at least to age fourteen (in effect, to the end of Grade 8).

horizon instead, particularly if the alternative rate of return were expected to remain reasonably constant over time. Given an alternative rate of return of, say, 10 percent, investment through the completion of college could easily be justified for each age group currently enrolled, since every rate of return figure in the bottom row (row [7]) of Table 3 exceeds 10 percent. Understandably, this result is no different than that obtained earlier.

On the basis of even longer-run considerations only the rate of return to investment in the schooling of new school entrants may be relevant, especially if schooling is thought of as a good to be purchased in large, indivisible quantities, for example, schooling from Grade 1 through college, or schooling from Grade 1 through high school. In this case the rates of return shown in column (1) indicate yields of 13.6 and 12.1 percent, respectively, and suggest the obvious advantages of seeing to it that everyone completes college or high school, as the case may be. In fact, this averaging of the marginal rates makes such investment attractive at an alternative rate as high as 12 percent.

B. The return to private resource investment

Internal rates of return to total resource costs of schooling are of undeniable importance in assessing the efficiency with which an economy's resources are allocated, but for individuals and/or their parents the relevant rates of return are those based upon private resource costs. These private rates of return both before and after tax are shown in Tables 4 and 5, respectively; the tables are to be read in the same fashion as Table 3.

For all levels of schooling under eight years, private rates of return have no real meaning (they are infinitely large) since opportunity costs are assumed to be zero, school-related costs are negligible, and tuition and fees are not charged. Above Grade 8, however, all private rates of return before tax are higher than the total rates of return shown in Table 3, with the greatest disparities appearing at the younger ages and lower levels of schooling, where individuals pay smaller proportions of total resource costs; private rates of return after tax are also higher than total rates of return with but two exceptions. Otherwise, the general configuration in both the columns and the diagonals appears to be about the same for both total and private rates, whether before or after tax, though the levels do differ.

When individuals and/or their parents plan an investment program

221

in schooling, the private rates of return justify securing more schooling than do the rates of return on total resource investment. For example, the marginal rates of return to elementary, high-school,

TABLE 4

Internal Rates of Return to Private Resource Investment in Schooling
before Tax, United States, Males, 1949*

To:	From: Age	Grade	(1) 6 1	(2) 8 3	(3) 12 7	(4) 14 9	(5) 16 11	(6) 18 13	(7) 20 15
(1)	7	2	†	....	....	....	....	....	....
(2)	11	6	†	†	....	....	....	....	....
(3)	13	8	†	†	†	....	....	....	....
(4)	15	10	28.3	34.6	25.9	12.7	....	....	....
(5)	17	12	25.6	29.4	23.3	15.3	18.6	....	....
(6)	19	14	18.1	18.7	14.8	10.4	9.5	6.2	....
(7)	21	16	18.2	18.7	16.2	12.9	13.0	11.6	18.7

*All rate-of-return figures are subject to some error, since the estimation to one decimal place had to be made by interpolation between whole percentage figures.
†This indicates an infinite rate-of-return, given the assumption that education is costless to the individual to the completion of eighth grade.

TABLE 5

Internal Rates of Return to Private Resource Investment in Schooling
after Tax, United States, Males, 1949*

To:	From: Age	Grade	(1) 6 1	(2) 8 3	(3) 12 7	(4) 14 9	(5) 16 11	(6) 18 13	(7) 20 15
(1)	7	2	†	....	....	....	....	....	....
(2)	11	6	†	†	....	....	....	....	....
(3)	13	8	†	†	†	....	....	....	....
(4)	15	10	27.9	33.0	24.8	12.3	....	....	....
(5)	17	12	25.2	28.2	22.2	14.5	17.5	....	....
(6)	19	14	17.2	17.5	13.7	9.4	8.5	5.1	....
(7)	21	16	17.2	17.3	14.4	11.5	11.4	10.1	16.7

*All rate-of-return figures are subject to some error, since the estimation to one decimal place had to be made by interpolation between whole percentage figures.
†This indicates an infinite rate-of-return, given the assumption of costless education to the individual through the completion of eighth grade.

and college schooling are infinite (col. [1], row [3]), 15.3 percent (col. [4], row [5]), and 11.6 percent (col. [6], row [7]), respectively. Thus, investment in schooling through college is still profitable even if the private alternative rate is as high as 11.5 percent. But, on an after-tax basis, the alternative rate of 10 percent just permits private investment at the college level (Table 5, col. [6], row [7]).

When schooling is viewed in large blocks, a somewhat different picture emerges. If the decision-making age is fourteen and the objective is to complete schooling through college, the alternative rate of return would have to exceed 12.9 percent (col. [4], row [7]) on a before-tax basis and 11.5 percent on an after-tax basis for the investment to be unprofitable. If the decision-making age is six and the objective is to complete schooling through college, the alternative rate would have to exceed 18.2 percent (col. [1], row [7]) on a before-tax basis and 17.2 percent on an after-tax basis, for the investment to be unprofitable.

A comparison of the total rates of return with the private rates of return after tax is of interest in suggesting the extent to which distortions in the private rates caused by federal income taxes are offset by the counter-distortion of subsidized schooling. An examination of the results in Tables 3 and 5 indicates that even though income taxes do substantially reduce the levels of private rates of return, public subsidization of schooling makes the private rates of return net of tax considerably more attractive than the rate of return earned on total resource investment. Only two exceptions appear (col. [6]); these suggest that the student pays more than his own way in securing schooling at the college level. This might indicate the need for a re-study of the assessment of the costs of college against the individual, unless the possible underinvestment in college training that would be produced is regarded as acceptable in some broader sense. But these exceptions aside, the fact that private rates of return after taxes exceed the total rates of return would, in the absence of restraints on sources of private financing, probably give rise to overinvestment in schooling by individuals. However, a fuller treatment of the effects of other forms of taxation and methods of financing schooling would be required before any definitive judgment could be reached.

III. ALTERNATIVE MEASURES OF PRIVATE ECONOMIC RETURNS FROM SCHOOLING

The economic returns to individuals from schooling can be observed from three different points of view: (1) the value of lifetime

223

income as set forth by Miller,[23] (2) the present value of lifetime income as set forth by Houthakker,[24] and (3) the rate of return on investment in schooling as set forth here. While the lifetime income and present value of lifetime income methods, particularly the former, are rather widely used, they are not relevant to ranking the direct economic returns to schooling when schooling is treated as a type of investment expenditure. Both of these methods completely ignore the costs of schooling, while the lifetime income approach suffers from the further defect of ignoring the time shape of the returns. Because the rankings of the economic returns differ so substantially, it seems desirable to present all three measures of the returns and to discuss them briefly. To make the comparisons more manageable, we shall deal only with the additional returns to different amounts of schooling as seen at age fourteen. The before- and after-tax results appear in the upper and lower halves, respectively, of Table 6.

The value of additional lifetime income associated with higher levels of schooling is frequently cited as a justification for investment in schooling by the individual. Clearly, the values of additional income resulting from successively greater amounts of schooling (col [1]), indicate that more schooling pays substantially larger dollar returns than less schooling.[25] But, since a portion of the costs of schooling is excluded from consideration,[26] the full extent to which these returns offset the costs of schooling is not at all clear. Even more important, the fact that the time flows of these returns also differ remains hidden in the calculation of the lifetime income values. By virtue of these omissions, the impression emerges that any and all amounts of schooling are worth obtaining.

Another method of measuring the economic returns to schooling involves comparing the present values of additional lifetime income, at various discount rates, to successively greater amounts of schooling. The values, at discount rates of 3, 6, 8, and 10 percent appear in col-

[23]Op. cit.

[24]Op. cit.

[25]The differences shown here differ somewhat from those that are derived from Miller and Houthakker because of differences in the assumed shapes and levels of the age-income profiles.

[26]Opportunity costs are reflected in the figures showing "additional" lifetime income inasmuch as the income of the person in school is set at zero while his income-earning counterpart receives a positive income; the difference appears in the cost-return stream and measures opportunity costs. However, the other private costs of schooling are omitted in this calculation.

TABLE 6

Alternative Methods of Comparing Value of Private Economic Returns to
Investment in Schooling, as Viewed at Age Fourteen, United States, Males, 1949

Schooling from Completion of Grade 8 to Completion of	Additional Lifetime Income (1)	Present Value of Additional Income at				Internal Rate of Return (Percent) (6)
		3 Percent (2)	6 Percent (3)	8 Percent (4)	10 Percent (5)	
		Before Tax				
	$	$	$	$	$	
2 years high school	16,802	7,756	2,301	1,190	545	12.7
4 years high school	46,038	18,156	6,488	3,601	1,949	15.3
2 years college	66,763	23,800	7,352	3,215	996	10.4
4 years college	141,468	49,429	17,252	8,722	4,135	12.9
		After Tax				
2 years high school	14,143	5,081	1,956	996	436	12.3
4 years high school	38,287	13.580	5,362	2,929	1,547	14.5
2 years college	52,485	17,000	5,364	2,084	336	9.4
4 years college	109,993	36,575	12,824	6,170	2,611	11.5

umns (2), (3), (4), and (5), respectively.[27] Again, schooling pays at any
or all of the discount rates used, though the rankings do shift about
as the discount rate is varied. For example, at 3 and 6 percent the
rankings coincide with those shown by the value of additional lifetime
income, but at an 8 percent discount rate schooling to the first two
years of college becomes absolutely less attractive financially than
schooling to high school, whether before or after tax. And at a 10 percent discount rate the after-tax return to schooling to the first two
years of college falls below that to the first two years of high school.
Even though the present-value figures are quite sensitive to the discount rate used, once again all schooling pays. But the basic flaw in
this method of calculation is the omission of some of the costs of
education from the calculation; specifically, the method fails to subtract the present value of the non-opportunity costs from the present
value of the additional income. Doing so would undoubtedly cause
some additional changes in the rankings, particularly at the higher
discount rates.

Finally, the rate-of-return approach remedies the defects inherent
in the other two methods. The relevant data on internal rates of

[27] The differences shown here differ somewhat from those derived from Houthakker
because of differences in the assumed shapes and levels of the age-income profiles.

225

return from Table 4 and 5 (see Table 6, col. [6]), reveal a much different ranking of the returns to schooling. On a before-tax basis, investment in schooling to completion of high school, with a 15.3 rate of return, yields by far the most attractive return, followed by schooling to college with 12.9 percent, and schooling to the first two years of high school with 12.7 percent; schooling to the first two years of college, with a 10.4 percent return, lags far behind.

When we shift to rates of return on an after-tax basis, the rankings of the return on schooling to the completion of college and to the completion of the first two years of high school change. Since the marginal tax rates are a function of the amount of the income differential, the effect of the tax on the college rate of return is decidedly greater than its effect on the rate of return to the first two years of high school, for example. Given the fact that the original rates of return were almost identical, the after-tax return to completion of college now drops considerably below that to completion of two years of high school.

In conclusion, it appears that ranking of the returns to investment in schooling by the rate-of-return method is clearly superior to the methods employed in the work of both Miller and Houthakker. Whether the more general rate-of-return rule is in fact superior to the present-value rule (when properly used) still remains an unsettled issue that will not be discussed here.[28]

IV. CONCLUSION

Estimates of the internal money rates of return to both total and private resource investment in schooling have been presented to provide a more complete picture of the costs of and returns to schooling. While the rates of return to private resource investment obviously exceed those to total resource investment, we find that the rates of return to the various increments of schooling also differ and have somewhat different implications for resource allocation at both the societal and individual level. Basically, the marginal rates of return rise with more schooling up to the completion of Grade 8 and then gradually fall off to the completion of college. We also find that private rates of return after tax almost invariably exceed the total rates of return, a situation that could presumably induce private overinvestment in

[28]For a fuller treatment of this point see J. Hirschleifer, "On the Theory of Optimal Investment Decision," *Journal of Political Economy*, LXVI (August, 1958), 329–52.

schooling. Finally, the rate of return provides a superior method of ranking the economic returns to investment in schooling than do the more conventional additional lifetime income or present value of additional lifetime income methods currently used.

Thus, one might conclude that the high rates of return to investment in schooling go a long way toward explaining, or justifying, this society's traditional faith in education, as well as the desire of individuals to take advantage of as much schooling as they can. But clearly we need to know much more about the relationship between income and ability, the importance of on-the-job training, the significance of education in the home, and so forth. My own suspicion is that full adjustment for these factors would have the effect of reducing the relative rates of return, especially at the higher levels of schooling.

In addition, we have barely begun to consider the possible disparity between the rate of return to total resource investment and the "social" rate of return to investment in schooling that takes additional account of those returns that are produced indirectly. Intuition as well as the little evidence available suggests that these returns may be considerable, but a full accounting of the economic value of schooling will have to await further work.[29]

[29] For an excellent analysis of some of the conceptual differences between private and social returns see Mary Jean Bowman, "Social Returns to Education," *International Social Sciences Review* (forthcoming), and Burton Weisbrod, "Education and Investment in Human Capital," *Journal of Political Economy: Supplement,* LXX (October, 1962), 106–23.

14. Education and Investment in Human Capital*

BURTON A. WEISBROD[1]

University of Wisconsin

I

As technological developments have altered production techniques, types of mechanical equipment, and varieties of outputs, society has begun to recognize that economic progress involves not only changes in machinery but also in men — not only expenditures on equipment but also on people. Investment in people makes it possible to take advantage of technical progress as well as to continue that progress. Improvements in health make investment in education more rewarding by extending life expectancy. Investment in education expands and extends knowledge, leading to advances which raise productivity and improve health. With investment in human capital and non-human capital both contributing to economic growth and welfare and in what is probably an interdependent manner, more attention should be paid to the adequacy of the level of expenditures on people.

The principal forms of direct investment in the productivity and well-being of people are: health, learning (both in school and on the job), and location (migration). Formal education and health constitute two large components of public and private spending in the United States. Private expenditures alone for hospital and physician services were over $18 billion in 1959, having risen from $8.6 billion in 1950.[2] Public education expenditures rose to $19.3 billion in 1960 from $7.3

*Reprinted from "Education and Investment in Human Capital," *Journal of Political Economy,* Supplement, LXX (October, 1962) 106–123. Copyright by The University of Chicago Press.

[1]The research reported herein was in part supported through the Cooperative Research Program of the Office of Education, United States Department of Health, Education, and Welfare.

[2]United States Department of Health, Education, and Welfare, *Health, Education and Welfare Trends, 1961* (Washington: Government Printing Office, 1961), p. 23.

billion at the turn of the decade.[3] Priced at cost, gross investment in education in the United States has risen from 9 percent of gross physical investment in 1900 to 34 percent in 1956.[4]

Investment in future productivity is occurring increasingly outside the private market and in intangible forms. Our traditional conception of investment as a private market phenomenon and only as tangible plant, machinery and equipment must give way to a broader concept which allows not only for government investment but also for intangible investment in the quality of human capital.

Most economic analysis of return from education has focused on the contribution of education to earning capacity (and, presumably, to production capacity). While this has been valuable, it is only part of the picture, and perhaps not even a large part. Even aside from market imperfections, which create inequalities between wage rates and marginal productivity, earnings are an incomplete measure of the productivity of education to the extent that production occurs outside the market. In addition, emphasis on incremental earnings attributable to education disregards external effects. Schooling benefits many persons other than the student. It benefits the student's future children, who will receive informal education in the home; and it benefits neighbors, who may be affected favorably by the social values developed in children by the schools and even by the quietness of the neighborhood while the schools are in session. Schooling benefits employers seeking a trained labor force; and it benefits the society at large by developing the basis for an informed electorate. Compulsory school attendance and public (rather than private) support for education in the United States both suggest that external economies from either the production or consumption of education are believed to be important.[5]

From the vantage point of one interested in Pareto optimal resource allocation, it is essential to consider all benefits from some action (as well as all costs). Whether the benefits (or costs) involve explicit financial payments, or whether they are internal to, or external from, a particular decision-maker is irrelevant.

In the private sector of the economy, private benefits from goods

[3]*Ibid.*, p. 53.

[4]T. W. Schultz, "Capital Formation by Education," *Journal of Political Economy*, December, 1960, p. 583.

[5]Similarly, but perhaps more clearly, compulsory smallpox vaccination together with public provision of vaccine reflects external economies of "consumption" of the vaccine.

and services are reflected in consumer demand; assuming economic rationality, competition, and the absence of external effects, private producers will meet the demand in a socially optimum manner. But when goods and services either have significant external effects or are indivisible (in the sense that consumption by one person does not reduce consumption opportunities for others—as, for example, national defense), the private market is inadequate. If the public sector attempts to provide the service, and if consumer sovereignty is to reign, the extent of consumer demand must be judged. Thus arises the need for benefit-cost analysis.

Within the benefit-cost framework this paper focuses principal attention on the ways by which a society benefits from formal education, discussing much more briefly some of the ways by which it incurs costs in providing education. It is worth emphasizing that analyzing benefits (or costs) does not preclude specifying which people reap the returns (or incur the costs). We shall attempt to identify the benefits of education by recognizing the beneficiaries of the education process.

In the discussion which follows, a "benefit" of education will refer to anything that pushes outward the utility-possibility function for the society. Included would be (1) anything which increases production possibilities, such as increased labor productivity; (2) anything which reduces costs and thereby makes resources available for more productive uses, such as increased employment opportunities, which may release resources from law enforcement by cutting crime rates; and (3) anything which increases welfare possibilities directly, such as development of public-spiritedness or social consciousness of one's neighbor. Anything which merely alters relative prices without affecting total utility opportunities for the group under consideration will not be deemed a social benefit (or loss). For example, if expanded education reduces the number of household servants, so that the wage rates of those remaining rise, this rise would not constitute either a benefit or loss from education but rather a financial transfer. Without making interpersonal utility comparisons we cannot say more. Of course, the increased productivity of those with the additional education is a benefit of type 1.

In addition to an analysis of the forms of education benefits and the nature of the beneficiaries, I shall investigate opportunities for quantifying these returns and some implications of the benefits analysis for the financing of education.[6] In Section II, I shall consider benefits which the individual receives in the form of market opportunities — including additional earnings resulting from increased productivity and benefits which the individual receives in ways other than earnings. In Section III, I shall consider benefits which the individual does not capture but which accrue to other persons. Benefits from elementary, secondary, and higher education will receive attention.

II

In this section we examine those benefits of education (or returns from education) which are realized directly by the student. One form of such benefits is the "financial return" accompanying additional education. A second form is the "financial option" return. Previously unconsidered, this benefit involves the value of the opportunity to obtain still further education. Third are the non-monetary "opportunity options," involving the broadened individual employment choices which education permits; fourth are the opportunities for "hedging" against the vicissitudes of technological change. And fifth are the non-market benefits.

DIRECT FINANCIAL RETURN

Census Bureau data relating level of earnings to level of educational attainment show an unmistakable positive correlation. A number of investigators have estimated the percentage return from investment in education by attributing these observed earnings differentials to education.[7] Some have attempted to adjust for or, at least, to recog-

---

[6]While I shall refer throughout this paper to the research of others, I should like to mention particularly the excellent survey recently completed by Alice M. Rivlin; see her "Research in the Economics of Higher Education: Progress and Problems," in Selma J. Mushkin (ed.), *Economics of Higher Education* (hereinafter cited as "Higher Education") (Washington: United States Department of Health, Education, and Welfare forthcoming).

[7]On the relation between educational attainment and earnings see G. Becker, "Underinvestment in College Education?" *American Economic Review, Proceedings,* May, 1960, pp. 346–54; H. S. Houthakker, "Education and Income," *Review of Economics and Statistics,* February, 1959, pp. 24–28; H. P. Miller, "Annual and Lifetime Income in Relation to Education," *American Economic Review,* December, 1960, pp. 962–86; E. F. Renshaw, "Estimating the Returns to Education," *Review of Economics and Statistics,* August, 1960, pp. 318–24.

nize factors other than education which affect earnings and which are positively correlated with level of education. These include intelligence, ambition, informal education in the home, number of hours worked, family wealth, and social mobility. One factor which I believe has not been considered is that a positive correlation of educational attainment with family wealth suggests that those with more education may live longer and consequently tend to receive greater lifetime incomes, education aside, although it is true that longer life is not synonymous with longer working life. We are led to the presumption that, in general, persons who have obtained more education would have greater earnings than persons with less education, even without the additional schooling.[8] At the same time, at least one study has attempted to isolate some of the non-education variables affecting earnings, with the finding that median salaries rose with additional amounts of post-high-school education, even after adjustments were made for (1) level of high-school class rank, (2) intelligence-test scores, and (3) father's occupation.[9] Apparently at least part of the additional earnings of the more educated population are the results of their education.

Although earning differentials attributable to education may be of considerable significance to the recipients, the social significance depends upon the relationship between earnings and marginal productivities. However, we know that market imperfections may make earnings a poor measure of one's contribution to output and that in a growing economy cross-section age-earnings data will understate future earnings. Mary Jean Bowman has suggested that older workers may receive more than their marginal productivity because status and seniority rules may maintain income although their productivity is falling.[10] But even assuming that earnings equal current marginal productivity, estimation of lifetime productivity from cross-section earnings data tends to understate future productivity of today's young men; this is true because in a growing society each new cohort

---

[8]See D. S. Bridgman, "Problems in Estimating the Monetary Value of College Education," *Review of Economics and Statistics, Supplement,* August, 1960, p. 181.

[9]Dael Wolfle, "Economics and Educational Values," *Review of Economics and Statistics, Supplement,* August, 1960, pp. 178–179. See also his *America's Resources of Specialized Talent* (New York, Harper & Bros., 1954); and Wolfle and Joseph G. Smith, "The Occupational Value of Education for Superior High School Graduates," *Journal of Higher Education,* 1956, pp. 201–13.

[10]"Human Capital: Concepts and Measures," in Mushkin (ed.), *Higher Education.*

of people into the labor force comes with better education and knowledge. These two examples suggest that the observed current earnings of men are less than fully satisfactory as reflections of future marginal productivity. Much work remains before we can feel confident of our ability to measure adequately the productivity return to education. Perhaps more serious, because apparently it has not been recognized, is a methodological limitation to previous estimates of the financial return to education.

FINANCIAL OPTION RETURN

Given our interest in resource allocation, we should like to know what financial return from additional education a person can expect. I suggested above that earnings differentials associated with education-attainment differentials would have to be adjusted for differences in ability, ambition, and other variables before we could isolate the education effects; and that an adjustment for systematic differences between earnings and productivity would also be required. Let us assume that these adjustments have been made and that we have computed the present values of expected future earnings of an average person with J and with K years of education, *ceteris paribus;* it is my contention that this would be an erroneously low estimate of the gross return which may be expected from the additional education. The value of the additional education may be thought of as having two components: (*a*) the additional earnings resulting from completion of a given level of education (properly discounted to the present, of course) and (*b*) the value of the "option" to obtain still further education and the rewards accompanying it. It is (*b*) which I wish to elaborate upon here.

In formula (1) below, the first term represents the rate of return over cost for education unit j, as computed in the usual manner; it is the difference between the present value of expected future earnings of a person who has attained, but not exceeded, level j, and the present value of expected future earnings of a person without education j, as a percentage of the additional cost of obtaining j. This is the rate of return as computed heretofore.

Subsequent terms in the formula measure the option value of completing j and should be understood as follows: each of the R^* are rates of return on incremental education a, computed in the manner described in the paragraph above. $\bar{R}$ is the opportunity cost of expenditure on education in terms of the percentage return obtainable from the next best investment opportunity, so that $R_a^* - \bar{R}$ indicates any "super-normal" percentage return. $C_a =$ the marginal social cost of obtaining the incremental education a (where each cost ratio, C_a/C_j, is a weighting factor, permitting the percentage returns on the costs of various levels of education to be added), and P_a is the probability that a person who has attained level j will go on to various higher levels.

$$R_j = R_j^* + (R_k^* - \bar{R})\frac{C_k}{C_j} \cdot P_k + (R_l^* - \bar{R})\frac{C_l}{C_j} \cdot P_l + \cdots$$

$$+ (R_z^* - \bar{R})\frac{C_z}{C_j} \cdot P_z = R_j^* + \sum_{a=k}^{z} (R_a^* - \bar{R})\frac{C_a}{C_j} \cdot P_a. \tag{1}$$

Thus, for example, a decision to obtain a high-school education involves not only the likelihood of obtaining the additional earnings typically realized by a high-school graduate but also involves the value of the opportunity to pursue a college education.[11] The value of the option to obtain additional education will tend to be greater the more elementary the education. For the "highest" level of formal education, the value of the option is clearly zero,[12] except insofar as the education provides the option to pursue independent work.

The option-value approach attributes to investment in one level of schooling a portion of the additional return over cost which can be obtained from further education — specifically, that portion which is in excess of the opportunity cost rate of return. Although part of the return from college education is indeed attributed to high-school education, there is no double-counting involved. In fact, the procedure is the same as that involved in the valuation of any asset, where the decision to retain or discard it may be made at various times in the life of the asset. Consider the following case: a machine is offered for sale. The seller, anxious to make the sale, offers an

[11]Research by Jacob Mincer suggests that additional schooling also provides opportunities to obtain additional on-the-job training (see his "On-the-Job Training: Costs, Returns, and Some Implications," Table 1, in this Supplement). The value of this opportunity should be included in the financial option approach developed here.

[12]Thus, for estimating the return from college or graduate education, omission of the value of the option may not be quantitatively significant. At the same time, since the return from higher education as previously estimated seems to be close to the return on business investments, recognition of the value of the option might tip the balance.

inducement to the buyer in the form of a discount on the purchase of a replacement machine when the present one wears out. Analyzing the prospective buyer's current decision, we see that he is being offered a combination of (1) a machine now, and (2) a discount (or option) "ticket" for possible future use. Both may have value, and both should be considered by the prospective buyer.

Let us assume that the machine has been purchased and used, and the owner is now deciding whether he should buy a replacement. Needless to say, the rate of return expected from the prospective machine will be a function of its cost net of the discount. The profit-maximizing buyer will compare the rate of return on the net cost and compare it with the opportunity cost of capital. Thus, in a real sense, the discount ticket has entered into two decisions: to buy the original machine and to buy the replacement. But this is not equivalent to any erroneous double-counting.

The machine discount-ticket analogy also makes clear the point that the value of the option (or discount) cannot be negative. If a greater rate of return (or discount) is available elsewhere, the value of the option merely becomes zero, as long as it need not be used. Thus, as long as a high-school graduate need not go on to college the value of the option to go on cannot be negative. It is formally conceivable, however, that a positive option value of elementary-school education could consist of a negative value for the high-school component and a larger, positive value for the college component.

Formula (1) indicates that the value of the option to pursue additional schooling depends upon (1) the probability of its being exercised and (2) the expected value if exercised. Without further information, factor 1 may be estimated by the proportion of persons completing a particular level of education who go on to a higher level. The expected value of the option if exercised, factor 2, is any excess of the return on that increment of education over the return obtainable on the best comparable alternative investment, where the latter may be assumed to equal, say, 5 percent. Actually, the "excess" returns should be discounted back to the decision date from the time the higher education level would begin, but to illustrate the point simply I shall disregard this, at least to begin with.

According to some recent estimates reported elsewhere, the return to the individual on total high-school costs (including foregone earnings) for white urban males in 1939[13] was approximately 14 percent and the return on college costs for those who graduated was estimated at 9 percent.[14] We might assume the return to be somewhat lower—say, 8 percent—for those who did not complete their college training.[15] Then with approximately 44 percent of high-school male graduates beginning college and 24 percent graduating,[16] the a priori expected return on a social investment in high-school education in 1939 was, substituting in equation (1) above, 17.4 percent, as shown in equation (2):

High-School Graduates	College Graduates	Some College (Assumed = 2 years)	
14	$+ \quad (9-5)(2.70)(.24)$	$+ (8-5)(1.35)(.20)$	(2)

$$= 14 + 2.6 + 0.8 = 17.4 \text{ percent.}$$

To reiterate, the first term, 14, is the estimated percentage return to high-school education. In subsequent terms, the first element is an estimate of the return in excess of alternatives, obtainable on additional education; the second element is the total cost of the additional education as a proportion of the cost of high-school education;[17] the third element is the proportion of high-school graduates who obtain the additional education. If the returns to college education were discounted back four years to the date at which high-school education was initiated, at a 5 percent discount rate the expected return to high-school education would drop to $14 + 2.1 + 0.7 = 16.8$, instead of 17.4 percent.

[13]T. W. Schultz, "Education and Economic Growth," *Social Forces Influencing American Education* (hereinafter cited as "Economic Growth") (Chicago: National Society for the Study of Education, 1961), chap. iii, referring to G. S. Becker's work. H. H. Villard has seriously disagreed with these estimates. See his "Discussion" of Becker's "Underinvestment in College Education?" in *American Economic Review, Proceedings,* May, 1960, pp. 375–78. See also W. L. Hansen, "Rate of Return on Human versus Non-human Investment" (draft paper, October, 1960).

[14]Schultz, "Economic Growth," p. 78.

[15]While this paper deals with education benefits, quantitative comparison of benefits with costs are made to help assess the relative magnitudes of benefits. In doing this I do not intend to imply complete satisfaction with the cost estimates. The appendix of this paper presents some of the issues involved in defining and measuring social costs.

[16]Computed from 1960 data for males of ages 25–29, in United States Bureau of the Census, *Current Population Reports: Population Characteristics, Projections of Educational Attainments in the United States, 1960–1980* (hereinafter cited as *Educational Attainments*) (Series P–20, No. 91, [January 12, 1959, p. 8, Table 2]).

[17]Computed from data in Schultz, "Economic Growth," p. 79.

In the example above it was assumed that a decision to complete high school would be realized with certainty. Other assumptions could be fitted easily into the framework. And if knowledge existed regarding the prospective high-school student's college plans, then *average* probabilities of his continuation should not be used.

If the option value of education has been overlooked by parents as it has been by economists there would be a tendency toward underinvestment in education. If time horizons are short so that, for example, a prospective high-school student and his parents sometimes fail to consider that a few years later the child may wish he could be going on to college, there will be a systematic downward bias to the valuation of education by individuals. Even disregarding graduate education, the option value of high-school education increased the rate of return on high-school costs from 14 to 17 percent, considering only the "monetary" returns. For grade-school education, recognition of the value of the option to obtain additional education increases the expected 1939 return even more substantially above the previous estimate of 35 percent,[18] as shown in equation (3):

Grade-School Graduates	High-School Graduates	College Graduates	Some College (Assumed = 2 years)
35 $+$	$(14-5)(2.3)(.67)$ +	$(9-5)(6.3)(.16)$ +	$(8-5)(3.1)(.13)$

$$(3)$$

$$= 35 + 13.9 + 3.8 + 1.2 = 53.9 \text{ percent.}$$

The option turns out the be quite valuable indeed, increasing the return on elementary education from 35 to 54 percent. It could be argued in this case that whether the return is 35 percent or 54 percent[19] is relatively immaterial for policy purposes, both being con-

[18]Again disregarding the discounting. The 35 percent estimate is from Schultz, "Economic Growth," p. 81. Relative costs were estimated from the same source (p. 79), except that Schultz's elementary-school cost figure was doubled, since it applied to only four years of school. The proportions of children continuing on to higher education were estimated from *Educational Attainments*, p. 8.

In this paper I do not discuss any option value for college education; however, there may be a positive option value related to opportunities for graduate study and additional on-the-job training.

[19]Previous estimates of rates of returns represented a discounting of costs and returns back to the beginning of that particular level of schooling; since our time bench mark is the beginning of grade school, the values of the high-school and college options should be discounted back to the beginning of grade school. Doing so, at a discount rate of 5 percent, reduces the 54 percent return to $35 + 9.5 + 2.1 + 0.7 = 47.3$. The return would almost certainly be larger if persons obtaining only some high-school education were considered.

siderably greater than available alternatives. However, given the state of our confidence in the previously computed rates of return, it is comforting to see the estimates moved further from the decision-making margin. Of course, in addition to these returns, assuming they are attributable solely to education, are the non-market returns to education, including the direct consumption value of learning and the opportunity to lead the "full life."

The words "option" and "opportunity" have appeared in the discussion above a number of times. Indeed, it seems that in many respects the value of education is a function of the additional options which became available to a person having it—job options, income-leisure-security options, additional-schooling options, on-the-job learning options, way-of-life options.

Recognizing the existence of such options suggests a possible means of estimating the monetary equivalent value of non-monetary returns from education. Thus, the college graduate who chooses to go to graduate school and then enter academic life may be assumed to obtain a total (not merely monetary) return on his graduate education costs at least equal to what he could have obtained from a comparable alternative investment. In general, added education permits widened job choices, and to some extent people with more education will choose employment which provides non-monetary rewards (for example, greater security) at the expense of monetary rewards. To the extent that this is correct and that knowledge of alternatives exists, previous estimates of the individual returns to education, utilizing incremental earnings figures for people with two different levels of education, have had a downward bias. If monetary returns from, say, graduate education turn out to be less than comparable alternative returns, the difference would be a minimum measure of non-monetary returns, though not necessarily of the employment-associated return alone.

"HEDGING" OPTION

There is another respect in which education provides a person with options: the increased ability to adjust to changing job opportunities. With a rapid pace of technological change, adaptability (which may be a noteworthy output of additional education) becomes important.

238

Education may be viewed as a type of private (and social) hedge against technological displacement of skills. New technology often requires new skills and knowledge;[20] and those persons having more education are likely to be in a position to adjust more easily than those with less education, and to reap the returns from education which the new technology has made possible. This line of reasoning suggests that a more general academic curriculum is desirable since it permits greater flexibility than a curriculum which requires earlier specialization.

Insofar as the return resulting from greater flexibility is realized in the form of earnings, it will be reflected directly in the estimated monetary value of education. The hedging option has additional value, however, to the extent that people have a preference for greater security and stability of earnings.

The hypothesis that added schooling develops added labor-force flexibility and thereby facilitates adjustments to changing skill requirements suggests the following implication: the greater the level of an individual's formal education attainment, the more he can benefit from additional on-the-job training, and, therefore, the more on-the-job training he will obtain. Jacob Mincer's data support this view;[21] through time, investment in learning on the job is increasingly being concentrated on persons with education beyond elementary school. He estimates that in all three years, 1939, 1949, and 1958, on-the-job training costs per person were positively correlated with the level of education. Moreover, a trend is observable—in 1939, on-the-job training costs per person with elementary education were 38 percent of costs per college-educated person; in 1949 they were 30 percent; and by 1958, 28 percent. Over the twenty-year period, training costs per capita for elementary-educated persons actually declined (in constant dollars), while they climbed 13 percent for college-trained persons.

[20]This view seems to be shared by H. Coombs, who states that "there will be many unpredictable shifts in the proportions needed of specific categories of . . . manpower. Thus, it will be important . . . to enlarge the total supply of high ability manpower available for all purposes" ("Some Economic Aspects of Educational Development," in International Association of Universities, *Some Economic Aspects of Educational Development in Europe*, Paris: International Universities Bureau, 1961, p. 78).

[21]*Op. cit.*, Tables 1 and 2. But E. F. Renshaw predicts that the principal educational requirements of the 1960's, with respect to the labor force, will be directed toward trade schools and apprenticeship programs ("Investment in Human Capital" [unpublished manuscript, 1960] p. 13).

So far we have discussed the return to education which is realized by the individual in terms of his employment conditions. But some of the value of education to the individual accrues in other forms. For example, the fruits of literacy—an output of elementary education—include, in addition to consumption aspects, the implicit value of its non-market use. To illustrate: when a person prepares his own income tax return he performs a service made possible by his literacy. Were this service provided through the market, it would be priced and included in national income.[22]

Assume that roughly fifty million of the sixty million personal income-tax returns filed per year are prepared by the taxpayer himself. At a value of $5.00 per return, a low estimate of an average charge by an accountant for preparing a not-too-complex return, we arrive at an annual market value of the tax-return services performed by taxpayers for themselves of $250 million. Relative to Schultz's estimate of total elementary-school costs of $7.8 billion in 1956,[23] this suggests a current-year return of 3.2 percent of the current investment in literacy! And this is only one, obviously minor, form of return from literacy which the individual enjoys.

This attempt to place a value on a particular use of literacy is subject to at least the following criticism: were it not for the widespread

[22]It could be argued that the service (like many others in national income and product) is not a final output, but a cost item (cost of tax collection), and thus should not be included in estimates of production; but since it is often difficult to distinguish clearly outputs from inputs in our national accounts, and since our national income and product accounts principally measure effort expended, it would be interesting to make some estimate of the market-value equivalent of the services performed by a person in preparing his own income-tax return.

Inclusion of the value of this non-market production as an educational benefit presupposes that this represents a net increase in the value of the individual's total non-market activities and that the opportunity cost of performing additional non-market production is essentially zero.

Richard Goode has suggested that, although the failure to consider non-market production leads to understatement of the return to education, "nevertheless, there seems to be little danger that this omission will lead to an undervaluation of educational benefits in comparing time periods, countries, and population groups with different amounts of formal education." He presents "the hypothesis that the greater the amount of formal education the greater the proportion of goods and services acquired through the market. If this is true, estimates based on money earnings or national income statistics may exaggerate the contribution of education to real income differentials or growth."

[23]"Economic Growth," p. 64, Table 5.

literacy in this country we would probably not have the present type of income-tax system operating, and, therefore, we would adjust to illiteracy in a less costly way than having others (say, accountants) prepare tens of millions of returns. The adjustment might involve government tax assessments or a resort to another type of tax such as one on expenditures. This suggests that the literacy value estimate above is on the high side, in terms of the alternative tax collection cost in the absence of literacy.

I have attempted a very rough estimate of the alternative cost of collecting an alternative form of tax—a sales tax— which would not require such a literate population, in order to compare it with the collection cost of the income tax.[24] The assumption is that a principal reason for the relative tax-collection efficiency of the income tax is the work performed by the taxpayer in preparing his own return. For the year 1940, the all-states average cost of collecting state personal income taxes was $1.50 per $100 collected, while the comparable figure for the general sales taxes of states was $2.00 per $100 collected. In the same year, collection costs per $100 of federal personal income tax were estimated at $1.68,[25] while there was, of course, no federal sales tax.[26]

In the absence of a superior alternative I have assumed that, as was true for the state tax-collection costs presented above, a federal sales tax would cost one-third more to collect than the federal personal income tax. Assuming the 1960 Internal Revenue Service estimate of collection costs, of approximately forty cents per $100, to apply to the personal income tax, then a one-third increase in the cost of collecting $50 billion (1959 individual income-tax receipts) would involve an additional $66 million—approximately 0.8 percent of elementary-school costs.[27]

---

[24]This disregards the different distributive effects of the two forms of tax.

[25]James W. Martain, "Costs of Tax Administration: Statistics of Public Expenses," *Bulletin of the National Tax Association,* February, 1944, pp. 132–47, as cited in Charles A. Benson, *The Economics of Public Education* (Boston, Houghton-Mifflin Co., 1961), p. 145.

[26]Estimation of collection costs is subject to the common difficulty of the allocation of joint costs; furthermore, we really know little about scale economies in tax collection, or about the difference in degree of enforcement of state and federal taxes, so that it is dangerous to apply state cost figures to the federal level.

[27]Actually we should note that a number of years of education is required to develop "literate" people but also that, once developed, they presumably retain the knowledge. Were we to take into account the number of tax returns an average person may be expected to file during his lifetime, a higher rate of return would appear.

III

In this section we consider the benefits of education which are external to the student. If all the benefits of education accrued to the student, then, assuming utility-maximizing behavior and access to capital markets, there would be little reason for public concern about the adequacy of education expenditures — unless publicly supported education were an efficient way of altering the personal distribution of income in a desired way.

Income redistribution effects aside, it seems clear that access to the capital market is imperfect and also that a child, even at high-school or college age, is in a poor position to make sensible long-run decisions regarding the amount or type of education, though advice from teachers, counselors, and parents may improve the decision. But these imperfections hardly appear to justify the massive public expenditures in support of education — more than $19 billion in 1960, including capital outlays.[28] We are led to the position that, to understand why education is of public concern as well as to project demand for education and determine whether expanded education is warranted on allocative efficiency grounds, we should pay more attention to identifying and quantifying external benefits of education.[29] This section of the paper suggests a framework for analyzing these benefits and considers opportunities for measurement.

As economists, our interest in external benefits is typically related to the question of whether all benefits (as well as costs) of some action are taken into account by the decision-maker. The issue is whether the benefits are or are not captured by the decision-maker, since the assumption of profit maximization has the implication that benefits will be recognized by the decision-maker if, but only if, he is able to obtain them. Insofar as parents and children make joint decisions on purchases of education, with none of them being a very expert, experienced buyer, those benefits which are less apparent and indirect are likely to be overlooked. Parents thinking of their children may even neglect the less direct benefits to themselves, discussed below. Moreover, benefits to non-family members are probably not considered at all.

In principle, the recipients of external benefits from some activity

[28]*Health, Education and Welfare Trends*, 1961, *op. cit.*, pp. 52, 53.

[29]It is true, however, that economies of scale (with respect to the number of students) would also be a sufficient explanation for the public interest in education.

(for example, education) should be willing to subsidize the activity and, indeed, should seek to subsidize it. The voting mechanism and taxation provide the means for subsidization. Analysis of voting behavior may shed some light on the question whether external benefits are recognized and have an effect on decisions. But regardless whether or not subsidies are actually paid by "outsiders," we need to identify and measure the magnitudes of external benefits to determine the rate of return on resources devoted to education.

Persons receiving external benefits from a student's education may be divided into three broad groups, though the same people may be in more than one: (1) residence-related beneficiaries—those who benefit by virtue of some relationship between their place of residence and that of the subject; (2) employment-related beneficiaries—those who benefit by virtue of some employment relationship with the subject; (3) society in general.

RESIDENCE-RELATED BENEFICIARIES

Current family of the subject.—While the purpose of schooling is obviously education, the manner in which it is provided may result in incidental, and even accidental, by-products; in the case of elementary education, such a by-product is child care. Schools make it possible for mothers who would otherwise be supervising their youngsters to do other things. For those mothers who choose to work, we have an estimate of the productivity of the child-care services—their earnings. This rests on the assumption that the mothers would not work if a sitter had to be hired but do work when the child is in school. If mothers would make other child-care arrangements in the absence of schools, then a better measure of value than earnings obtained would be the cost of hiring a baby sitter or making some alternative custodial arrangement.

In March, 1956, there were 3.5 million working mothers in the United States with children six to eleven years of age.[30] Assuming that as few as one million of these mothers would not work except for the schools (the others being willing to let their children stay with hired persons or simply care for themselves), and assuming $2,000 as the earnings of each mother during the school year, the value of the child-care services of elementary school may be estimated as

[30]United States Bureau of the Census, *Marital and Family Status of Workers: 1956* (Series P–50, No. 73 [April, 1957]), p. 11, Table 3.

roughly \$2 billion per year.[31] Estimating total resource costs (excluding capital outlays but including implicit interest and depreciation) of public and private elementary schools in 1956 at \$7.8 billion,[32] we reach the startling conclusion that elementary-school support provided a return of 25 percent of cost in the by-product form of child-care services, alone.[33] This disregards the value of these services to mothers who do not choose to work; since the value is certainly greater than zero, the total value of the child care is even more than 25 percent of cost.

The increased production from working mothers tends to offset the foregone production from students in school. Various writers have emphasized students' foregone earnings as a cost of education, and have debated its magnitude,[34] but have not considered the fact that some mothers' earnings are made possible by the fact that children forego earnings to remain in school.

Future family of the subject.—When the student reaches adulthood and becomes a parent, the children will benefit from his or her education by virtue of the informal education which the children receive in the home. The presence and relevance of such education is recognized, but to my knowledge no attempts to estimate its value have been made. If scores on achievement tests could be related to educational attainments of parents, adjusting for variation in students' ability, we might obtain some information about the extent of education in the home. This might be translated into equivalent years in school, to which a value, perhaps average cost, could be attributed.

If we think of the investment-consumption distinction as involving whether or not benefits accrue in the "present" (consumption) or in the "future" (investment), then education has an investment component in the form of these intergeneration benefits.[35] If we gen-

[31]For those mothers who would be willing to hire baby sitters, obtainable for, perhaps, \$1,000 per year, the value of the school child-care services is this alternative cost of \$1,000, instead of \$2,000. Of the 3.5 million working mothers with children six to eleven years old, approximately 1.5 million also had children twelve to seventeen. Some of the older children could conceivably care for the younger ones; but even considering the remaining 2 million, the assumption that one-half would not work except for the care provided by schools seems plausible and even conservative.

[32]Schultz, "Economic Growth," p. 85.

[33]If working mothers employ housekeepers as substitutes and if they incur other additional costs in working (for example, transportation and additional clothes), these added costs should be deducted from the gross returns.

[34]See Appendix below.

[35]Schultz has also recognized this point: "The education of women . . . reduces the subsequent effective costs of education because of the critical role that mothers play in

eralize the conception of investment to include not only intertemporal benefits,[36] but also interpersonal benefits, then the child-care role of schools, discussed above, represents an investment in the productivity of mothers. Similarly, other interpersonal benefits examined below will constitute investment aspects of educational expenditures.

Neighbors.—As we consider more extended groups, beginning with the individual receiving the education and then his family (present and future), we come to his neighbors. Education affects them at least in the following ways: by inculcating acceptable social values and behavior norms in the community children and by providing children with alternatives to unsupervised activities which may have antisocial consequences. The second is essentially of short-period significance—during the time the child is of school age. The first effect is clearly of long-period consequence, following the student as he grows, and as he moves. As the student achieves adulthood, and as he migrates, the social values developed in part through his education continue to affect his "neighbors."[37]

The hypothesis that education does affect neighbors might be tested by studying voting behavior on school issues among non-parents. We might expect that their voting would be influenced by the extent to which students emigrate after completion of school, so that any potential external benefits or costs to neighbors would be realized by persons in other communities. Perhaps some notion of the magnitude of external, neighborhood benefits—at least to the extent they are recognized—could be obtained in this manner.

Taxpayers.—Related to the effects of education on neighbors are the effects on those who pay (directly or indirectly) for the consequences of the lack of education. For example, insofar as lack of education leads to employment difficulties and crime, law enforcement costs will tend to be high. Thus may education provide social

---

motivating their children to obtain an education and to perform well while they are attending school. Thus, if we could get at the factors underlying the perpetuation of education, it is likely that we would discover that the education of many persons not in the labor force contributes heavily to the effective perpetuation of the stock of education. To the extent that this is true, some part of the education not in the labor force contributes to this investment process" ("Economic Growth," pp. 74–75).

[36]Tax implications of the existence of intertemporal education returns have been discussed by R. Goode, "Educational Expenditures and Income Tax," in Mushkin (ed.), *Higher Education.*

[37]One writer points out: "Education has effects on the caliber of voluntary community activities: choral groups, drama, clubs, local art shows, etc." (Benson, *op. cit.,* p. 349).

benefits by reducing the need for incurring these "avoidance costs," to the advantage of taxpayers.

Education also benefits taxpayers in other communities. The migration of poorly educated persons having behavioral patterns and educational attainments differing from those prevailing in the new areas may necessitate additional effort and expense to permit the in-migrant children to adjust to the new school conditions.[38] Thus, people in areas of in-migration have a stake in the education of children in the areas of out-migration. People who are or may be in the same fiscal unit with an individual have a financial stake in his education.

EMPLOYMENT-RELATED BENEFICIARIES

The education of one worker may have favorable external effects on the productivity of others. Where production involves the cooperative effort of workers, flexibility and adaptability of one worker will redound to the advantage of others. Productivity of each member of the group influences the productivity of each other member. In such a case, each worker has a financial interest in the education of his fellow workers. Again, the relevance of this interdependence for the present context rests on the assumption that education develops the properties of flexibility and adaptability. Further analysis is required to determine the extent to which the assumption is valid, and if it is, to estimate its significance.

Employers may also have a financial interest in the schooling and training of their employees. Much of education improves the quality of the labor force and thereby bestows some benefits to employers of the workers insofar as market imperfections or the "specific"[39] nature of the education result in failure of the employer to pay the marginal revenue product of a worker.

[38]See, for example, C. F. Schmid, V. A. Miller, and B. Abu-Laban, "Impact of Recent Negro Migration on Seattle Schools," *International Population Conference Papers* (Vienna: *Union International pour l'Etude Scientifique de la Population*, 1959), pp. 674–83.

[39]As the term is used by Gary S. Becker "specific" training is that which raises the marginal productivity of the worker in one firm more than it raises his productivity in other firms. By contrast, "general" training raises marginal productivity equally in many firms. Since, under competitive conditions, wage rates are determined by workers' marginal productivities in other firms, a worker with "specific" training would be expected to receive a wage less than his actual marginal revenue productivity but more than his alternative productivity (see the paper by Becker in this Supplement).

246

Society in General

Some of the benefits from education are enjoyed by individuals and groups that are reasonably identifiable, as we have seen. But some of the benefits are distributed broadly either spatially or temporally, so that the nature of individual beneficiaries is obscure. These shall be considered under the heading, "Society in General," which thus becomes somewhat of a residual category of benefits.

Literacy is not only of value to the individual possessing it and to employers but also is of value to others. Without widespread literacy the significance of books, newspapers, and similar media for the transmission of information would dwindle; and it seems fair to say that the communication of information is of vital importance to the maintenance of competition and, indeed, to the existence of a market economy, as well as to the maintenance of political democracy.

Along the same lines it should be noted that the substantial role played by checking deposits in our economy requires, among other things, generalized literacy and competence with arithmetic operations. It is not necessary to argue the issue of cause versus effect, but only to recognize the essentiality of literacy — a principal output of elementary education — to the present state of our economic development. Nor does saying this deny the possibility that other factors were also indispensable to growth.

Equality of opportunity seems to be a frequently expressed social goal. Education plays a prominent role in discussions of this goal, since the financial and other obstacles to education confronted by some people are important barriers to its achievement.[40] If equality of opportunity is a social goal, then education pays social returns over and above the private returns to the recipients of the education.

Although the long-term effect of education on future earnings is surely the most powerful income distribution consequence of education,[41] there are also some short-term effects. These occur through

[40]Even if it were true that educating everyone would widen the personal distribution of earnings compared with what it would be with less education, it would not follow that additional education for some people would worsen their relative or absolute economic position.

[41]The relation between education and income distribution has been studied by J. Mincer ("Investment in Human Capital and Personal Income Distribution," *Journal of Political Economy*, August, 1958, pp. 281–302) and L. Soltow ("The Distribution of Income Related to Changes in the Distributions of Education, Age and Occupation," *Review of Economics and Statistics*, November, 1960, pp. 450–53).

the provision by schools of things traditionally considered to be private consumer goods and services—including subsidized lunch programs, musical instrument lessons, and driver-training courses.

Earlier we distinguished between the output of education in the form of the student's training and the output of the system or means by which the training was accomplished—the latter being illustrated by custodial or child-care services. The same distinction may be made with respect to higher education, the point being that the training of students is not the only output of schools; a joint product is the research activity of college and university faculties, from which society reaps benefits. It is undoubtedly true that were it not for the higher-education system the volume of basic research would be smaller. A question exists regarding the extent to which the value of the research is reflected in salaries and, thereby, in private returns. The relation of education to research and of research to social returns deserves more attention from economists.[42]

Training of persons in particular kinds of skills may result in important external benefits if there are bottlenecks to economic development. In the context of underdeveloped economies, one writer, while particularly noting the political significance of primary and higher education, and the prestige significance of the latter, argues: "Secondary education is essential to the training of 'medium' personnel (elementary teachers, monitors, officials, middle classes). The shortage of such people is today a real obstacle to economic development."[43] But without perfect capital markets and appropriate subsidization programs, these socially valuable people may be unable to capture for themselves the full value of their contribution. Therefore, their earnings would understate the full benefits of their education.

IV

In the preceding pages I have asked: "Who receive the benefits from education?" In addition, I have considered some of the limited possibilities for quantifying certain of the benefits. As plans are developed for future research I urge that more attention be directed to the spatial and temporal dimensions of these benefits.

[42]For an interesting study of returns from research see Z. Griliches, "Research Costs and Social Returns: Hybrid Corn and Related Innovations," *Journal of Political Economy*, October, 1958, pp. 419–31.

[43]Micheal Debeauvals, "Economic Problems of Education in the Underdeveloped Countries," in International Association of Universities, *op. cit.*, pp. 116–17.

While much work remains, we might summarize our findings. We have noted that some of the benefits of education are realized at the time the education is being received (that is, in the "short" run); others, after the formal education has been completed (that is, in the "long" run). Benefits to mothers, in terms of the child-care role of schools, and benefits to neighbors, in keeping children "off the streets" are realized while the education is being obtained. Any benefits associated with subsequent employment of the student as well as benefits to the student's future children are realized later.

We have found, further, that benefits from education occur not only at various times but also in various places. The benefits of education do not necessarily accrue to people in the area or in the school district which financed the child's education. In particular, some of the benefits depend upon the individual's place of residence, which may change. Location of many residence-related benefits as well as employment-related benefits will be determined partly by population migration, though this is not generally true of benefits to family members and to society as a whole. While it is not necessarily true that total benefits will depend upon one's location, the point is that the particular beneficiaries will be a function of the location of the individual. Thus, the process of migration is a process of spatial shifting of some of the external effects of education.

Some interesting questions are raised simply by the recognition that external benefits of education exist, and that they are not all in broad, amorphous form; that is, that to some extent these benefits accrue to particular, rather well-defined, groups. Thus, to the extent that the education system at the elementary level is producing child-care services as an output, benefit-principle taxation would suggest that families of the children might pay for these benefits.[44] In general, a desire to use this taxation principle would imply attempts to identify various groups of education beneficiaries and to assess taxes in recognition of the distribution of benefits.[45]

It seems to me that there is a legitimate question concerning the justice of requiring broad, public support for education insofar as the benefits are narrow and private, except as an income-redistributive device. For example, to the extent that there is really no educational sacrifice involved in having children attend split-shift classes,

[44]This point came out in a discussion with Julius Margolis.

[45]This is not to argue that the benefit principle, in contrast to the ability-to-pay or some other principle, should necessarily prevail.

so that the real motive for the abolition of split-shifts is to make life more comfortable for mothers who have all of their children in school at the same time, then a question of equity arises: should non-parents be expected to share the costs associated with the provision of these child-care services for parents? The answer may not be an unequivocal "no," but the question deserves further consideration. Except for lack of information, or a disavowal of benefit-principle taxation, there is little rationale for failure of our education-tax system to recognize the existence of particular groups of beneficiaries.

There is another strong reason in addition to the alleged justice of benefit-principle taxation for identifying benefits and beneficiaries. To the extent that the distribution of tax burdens for the support of education differs substantially from the distribution of education benefits, it is likely that education will be either undersupported or oversupported from an allocative-efficiency standpoint, given the existing preference structure and distribution of income and wealth.[46]

Both with respect to equity and to efficiency in education finance, the increasing phenomenon of migration needs to be recognized. Insofar as some of the benefits of education depend upon the location of the individual and insofar as this location is a variable over his lifetime, some of the benefits from education accrue to people who have played no part at all in the financing of this particular person's education. This would seem to be especially pertinent with respect to areas of substantial net in- or out-migration. Areas experiencing net in-migration might be expected, on benefit-principle grounds, to subsidize areas of net out-migration, particularly if highly productive people are involved. Subsidy in the opposite direction might be justified insofar as the in-migrants to an area are relatively unproductive compared to its out-migrants. Needless to say, there are good and powerful arguments in favor of keeping all the financing of education at a local level. However, a thorough analysis of the issue would seem to require recognition of the points raised here.

The analytic approach to benefit identification employed in this paper is one of many alternatives; it does appear to have the advantage of focusing on the time and the location of education benefits, and these are relevant to the study both of efficiency in the allocation of resources between education and other ends and of equity in the financing of education.

[46]However, an objective of education may be to change the distribution.

It is clear that even with much additional effort we shall be unable to measure all the relevant benefits of education. At the same time the following four points are worth noting, and they summarize the views expressed in this paper: (1) identification of benefits is the logical step prior to measurement and, therefore, recognizing the forms of benefits represents some progress; (2) determination of what it is we are trying to measure will make it easier to develop useful quantification methods; (3) some reasonable measures of some education benefits are possible; (4) even partial measurement may disclose benefits sufficiently sizable to indicate a profitable investment, so that consideration of the non-measured benefits would, a fortiori, support the expenditure decision.

In any event, and however difficult the measurement task is, it remains true that education expenditure decisions will be made, and they will be made on the basis of whatever information is available.

APPENDIX: COSTS OF EDUCATION

The objective here is to consider briefly, at the conceptual level, some of the issues involved in estimating costs of education. There is no doubt that a complete picture of the cost of education would include all foregone opportunities, whether or not reflected by actual expenditures. Thus, the attempt to measure foregone production by looking at foregone earnings of students in school is fully appropriate. There is, of course, the difficult question of how to estimate the foregone earnings—in particular, whether they may be estimated by looking at the earnings of people of comparable age and sex who were not in school.

One of the issues is whether those in school are not, in general, more able and ambitious, so that their opportunity cost of schooling exceeds the earnings by their "drop-out" counterparts. Another involves the effect on earnings (actually, on the value of marginal productivity) of a large influx to the labor market, such as would occur if all college, or all high-school, students entered the labor force.

But it seems to me that this latter issue is beside the point. Studies involving cost and benefits of education are surely not directed to the question whether there should or should not be education. Rather the issue is the profitability or productivity of reasonably small increments or decrements to education. The issue is whether fewer or more people should be encouraged to go further in school. Only marginal changes are being contemplated.

Still on the subject of estimating foregone production among students by estimating foregone earnings, there is the additional question of the validity of using earnings of employed people when there is a question whether resources released from the schools would or would not find employment. Thus, the view is not uncommon that measuring foregone earnings of students by the earnings of presently employed people is satisfactory only if there is little unemployment.[47] This question arises frequently, especially when public investment is being considered. Thus, it inevitably arises when the economic efficiency of public health expenditures is being discussed; would the additional labor resources made available by an improvement in public health be able to find employment? And with regard to education, would labor resources released from schools be able to find employment?

It seems to me to be analytically unwise to mix study of the allocative efficiency of additional expenditures on education with study of the efficiency of monetary and fiscal policy in maintaining full employment. I would like to urge that in looking at the question of whether to invest more in education, we consider what students could earn and produce, not what they might actually earn or produce, as affected by unemployment. The efficiency of educational expenditures in dealing with unemployment is a quite different question from the efficiency of education as an allocation problem. Although there might be short-run transitional unemployment associated with some movement of students into the labor force, the basic issue of investment in people through education is of the long run.[48]

The alternative production foregone because of education also involves the government services used by educational institutions. Since many of these services are rendered without charge to the

---

[47]See, for example, Rivlin, *op. cit.*, p. 12.

[48]Mary Jean Bowman shares this view: "Such validity, if any, as may attach to it (the view that marginal social opportunity costs of education are zero when unemployment is serious) is in any case limited to short term marginal valuations, whereas we are interested in long-term averages and aggregates. When long-term aggregate human capital formation is the focus, social opportunity costs are not zero even with chronic unemployment" ("Human Capital: Concepts and Measures," in Mushkin (ed.), *Higher Education*).

schools, they are generally, and mistakenly, omitted from discussion of costs. Recognition by R. C. Blitz of the relevance of these services to estimation of education costs is a valid and important point.[49] However, estimating the social cost of these services as equal to the value of the property and sales taxes which the schools would have paid had they not been exempt is conceptually inappropriate (albeit perhaps pragmatically reasonable). To the extent that the services rendered to schools by governments are "pure public services," the actual marginal cost of providing these services to the school is zero. The essence of "pure" public services is that everyone may enjoy them in common, and the consumption by one person does not subtract from the amount available to others. For example, it is not at all clear how much additional police or fire services will be required in a community by virtue of the fact that there is a school within its limits.

At the same time, services performed by governments are never entirely of a "pure public service" nature — particularly in the long run (for example, public libraries, which are frequently used by students) — so the marginal cost of providing them to a school will, in general, exceed zero. But the marginal cost is likely to be below average cost and, therefore, to be below the estimated foregone property and sales taxes, which are related to average costs of providing public services.

Since social costs represent alternatives foregone, it is certainly not correct to include among the costs of education costs which would have been incurred anyway; therefore, all the food, shelter, and clothing costs of students while they are at school should not be considered a cost of education.[50] At the same time, if any of these maintenance costs are higher for students than they would be were the children not in school, then these additional costs are justifiably charged against the education process. If additional clothing, laundry, and transportation costs are incurred by virtue of a person being a student, these incremental costs are quite relevant to the issue of the productivity of investment in education. Such cost may be particularly high for college students living away from home, though they may not equal zero for college students living at home, or for elementary or high-school students.

---

[49]"The Nation's Education Outlay," in Mushkin (ed.), *Higher Education.*

[50]See discussion by Rivlin, *loc. cit.,* pp. 11–12, correctly criticizing the study by Harold F. Clark and Ruth E. Sobokov for including them.

15. Present Values of Lifetime Earnings for Different Occupations*

BRUCE W. WILKINSON

University of Western Ontario

In recent years there have been a number of attempts to use social rates-of-return to determine what has been the contribution of education to economic growth and what share of a nation's resources should in the future be devoted to education (see Schultz, 1963, and Hunt, 1964). The approach has been severely — and I believe correctly — criticized (Vaizey, 1958; Eckaus, 1964; and Wilkinson, 1965).

However, we should not be in haste to discard completely the use of rates-of-return or present discounted values in our analysis of economic-educational problems. *Private* rates-of-return or present discounted values as yet have not received the attention they deserve.[1] The purposes of this paper are, in fact, to examine discounted returns for several specific occupations and for various levels of educational attainment within these occupations and to review the meaning and significance of our observations.

Of particular interest is the suggestion that individuals may be responding to differences in expected net lifetime earnings, discounted at some common external rate, when selecting their occupations and when deciding upon the amount of education to acquire before entering an occupation. We find, for example, that discounted returns to various levels of education within jobs are roughly the same — which may mean that an equalization process has been occurring. We also find that the rising discounted returns to teachers rela-

---

*Reprinted from "Present Value of Lifetime Earnings for Different Occupations," *Journal of Political Economy*, LXXXIV (December, 1966), 556–572. Copyright 1966 by The University of Chicago Press.

[1] I do not claim originality for the suggestion that private present-value calculations may be important. Walsh (1935), Friedman and Kuznets (1954, pp. 84–87), and Blank and Stigler (1957, pp. 79–83) all employed such calculations in their analyses.

tive to engineers may be at least partly responsible for the increasing enrolments in colleges of education relative to engineering colleges.

Wide variations in returns to given amounts of education still exist, however. These variations suggest the importance of such factors as diversity in ability, on-the-job and off-the-job training, market imperfections such as the lack of knowledge of opportunities, and tradition-based wage-salary scales; but they do not necessarily refute the hypothesis that individuals may be implicitly considering disparities in present values of lifetime incomes when choosing among occupations or when selecting the amount of education to obtain prior to entering an occupation. These arguments as well as one or two other items of interest will be developed in the subsequent discussion.

In the following section I shall briefly indicate why I use present discounted values in my subsequent calculations rather than rates-of-return. In Section II, I review the nature of the earnings data employed in most of the subsequent discussion. Section III is devoted to an examination of net present values of lifetime earnings for broad levels of education and, more important, for particular occupations and levels of education within these occupations. The final section considers variations in the relation between expected discounted returns for the two occupations of teacher and engineer over time and the apparent effect of these variations on enrolments in the college courses prescribed for these vocations.

I. PRESENT VALUES

The superiority of the present-value rule over rates-of-return calculations has been demonstrated in other papers (see esp. Hirshliefer, 1958, and Feldstein and Flemming, 1964), so I need not enter into a detailed discussion of the reasons for my choice of this rule. It is worth mentioning, however, two or three advantages of the present-value approach that are of particular interest in this analysis.

First, if the rate-of-return approach is employed, then — where the *net* stream of revenues (after subtracting the one stream from the other) changes sign more than once — there can be as many rates-of-return as there are changes in sign of the revenue stream. The rate may also be imaginary under these circumstances. The possibility of more than one reversal in sign of the net revenues may be remote when one is dealing with two physical capital investments. But an examination of incomes of persons with varying amounts of education in different occupations indicates a number of cases where additional reversals do occur. The use of discounted values therefore precludes the complications that these changes may present.

Moreover, even if one and only one real solution were possible when there are a number of projects to be considered, it is much easier to calculate the present value of each project than it is to subtract one income stream from another and compute rates-of-return for *every* possible comparison of projects.[2]

Hansen (1963, pp. 137–40) apparently disregards these advantages of the present-value technique over the rate-of-return approach when he argues that the rate-of-return technique is superior. While he rightly criticizes Houthakker for not considering school and university costs of education when discounting, this is not a substantive criticism of the present-value technique itself. Only the mechanics of application are involved. Moreover, Hansen assumes that earnings foregone for persons with grade 8 or less are zero. Since there is normally no tuition charge for such schooling and incidental costs are negligible, his procedure implies that rates-of-return on these levels of schooling are infinitely large; hence, the results have little meaning. If present values are used, this difficulty does not arise.

II. THE DATA

The basic earnings data for *all* occupations in Canada are presented in Table 1. They include all males who either had a job or looked for work during the week prior to the 1961 Canadian Census, minus those who never worked and those self-employed or receiving no income, such as unpaid family workers. Certain aspects of these figures warrant discussion.

1. The exclusion of self-employed workers, particularly professionals, may cause returns to higher education to be underestimated.

2. The Census category "university degree" does not permit us to distinguish between persons with a three-year degree beyond Grade 12 and those with two degrees or graduate training entailing as much as twenty or more years of schooling. I have assumed sixteen years of schooling for this group—which probably *underestimates* average training time and thus *overstates* returns to a university degree. Such overstatement may offset to a large extent, if not completely, any

---

[2]Moreover, if, as in the present study, several discount rates are employed, *crude* rates-of-return can easily be imputed from the present-value calculations if desired. I do this at one or two junctures in the subsequent analysis.

TABLE 1

Average Annual Wage and Salary Earnings, Age and Years
of Schooling Completed, Males, Canada, 1961

Age	Years of Schooling Completed				
	Grade 5 to the End of Elementary	High School One to Two	High School Four	Some University	University Degree
15–19	$1,135	$1,193	$1,205	$ 722	. . . . . .
20–24	2,195	2,654	2,943	2,007	$3,008
25–34	3,125	3,781	4,454	4,750	5,923
35–44	3,436	4,165	5,188	5,968	7,927
45–54	3,452	4,205	5,395	6,075	8,336
55–64	3,352	4,058	5,096	5,686	8,066
65–over	2,489	2,972	3,710	4,128	5,981

Source: Canada, Dominion Bureau of Statistics, 1963.

tendency for returns to university people to be understated because of neglecting self-employed professional people.

3. In the first, second, and fourth education categories shown, the earnings data refer to averages of more than one year's schooling. For the grouping "Grade 5 to the end of elementary school," Grade 8 is assumed; for "high school, one to two years," Grade 10; and for "some university," two years beyond Grade 12. The effect of my assumptions will be to underestimate the returns from Grade 8 and Grade 10 education (or, conversely, cause a relative overestimate of the returns to higher education), because the figures used include earnings of individuals with less education. The assumption that "some university" equals fourteen years of schooling should not, however, be far amiss. It implies that students drop out after their first or second year in a university depending upon whether they live in the provinces that require thirteen or only twelve years of schooling, respectively, before they may enter a university.[3]

4. The wage-salary figures cover earnings during the previous twelve months of all those who either possessed a job or looked for work during the week prior to the Census. The figures, therefore, already reflect unemployment rates without a special adjustment

[3]About one-half of the ten provinces require thirteen years schooling prior to university entrance. No detailed dropout data is available, but the Dominion Bureau of Statistics estimates that most students who leave university do so during or after their first two years.

257

being required. That is, the earnings of many of those who worked only a part of the year will be included in the average figures, thus lowering them. Only people who have dropped out of the labor force entirely because of repeated failure to obtain work are omitted. Paucity of information on such people makes adjustment for it impossible.

5. Even if the figures for all educational levels reflect unemployment, the earnings may be too low for persons with some university in the fifteen to nineteen or twenty to twenty-four age cohorts. For example, annual average earnings of students *still attending university,* from summer and part-time employment during the academic year, were $725 (Canada, Dominion Bureau of Statistics, Education Division, 1963; Wilkinson, 1964, Appendix VI, Table A). This is a little *more* than the earnings for persons aged fifteen to nineteen with some university shown in Table 1. One might at first think the low Census earnings for these recent university dropouts compared to earnings of high school graduates in the same age cohorts, as well as to earnings of earlier university dropouts (who are now in the age twenty-five and over groups), may reflect some recent, basic worsening in society's attitude toward, and hence in the pay offered to, such persons. However, the same type of phenomenon can be observed in the calculations for the United States in 1949 by Hansen (1963, Table 1, p. 130), so I do not consider this a likely explanation. Nor would it be correct to suggest that unemployment is especially serious for such persons. Unpublished data from the Dominion Bureau of Statistics indicates that unemployment rates are considerably lower for this group than for similar-aged persons with less education. It is conceivable that part of the explanation is that university dropouts adopt careers involving much general on-the-job training, which would reduce their initial net earnings.

Also, there is some evidence, at least for the United States, that the average ability of college dropouts is the same as, or a little lower than, the ability of high school graduates with no college; in addition, the ability range, both up and down, is less for the college dropout than for the man with four years high school (see, for example, Becker, 1964, Table 4, p. 80). If these facts hold true for Canada, too, the low earnings of recent university dropouts aged fifteen to twenty-four relative to high school graduates in the same age groups may be partially traceable to the lower ability or to the greater range of ability among university dropouts. If one wishes to use this argument, however, one must also hypothesize that after age twenty-four, when the income of the college dropout begins to exceed that of the high school graduate, the extra education or on-the-job training of the college dropout is more than sufficient to compensate for any lack of ability he may have relative to the high school graduate.

The most plausible explanation relates to the fact that the university academic year terminates at the end of April, whereas the Census was conducted May 31. Consequently, in many cases the Census would have recorded the summer and part-time earnings during the previous twelve months of continuing students who were either working or looking for work in the week prior to enumeration and who had worked before—thus lowering the average yearly income figures for the relevant age-education cohorts as well as the estimated net returns from some university education.[4] An upward adjustment has thus been made for those with some university in the fifteen to nineteen and twenty to twenty-four age cohorts by considering their earnings as equal to the earnings of persons with four years of high school.[5]

6. The basic earnings data provide no indication of the extent to which the higher incomes of some of the people with additional education are due to their extra education or to such influences as parents' education, wealth, and positions; ability and motivation; and variations in the amounts of on-the-job and off-the-job training possessed by these people.

Since the above figures cover only wages and salaries and exclude other income such as interest or rents, a major portion (although not all) of the income that might result from family wealth and inheritance may already be eliminated.[6]

[4] Hansen (1963) ignores this fact in his analysis and concludes that the rate-of-return to some college education is extremely low. Yet, in the introduction to the data on which he bases his calculations, it states, "For men of college age, the relationship between income and education is less distinct than for men with other levels of education, possibly as a consequence of the fact that a large proportion of those in this age group who are enrolled in school have only part-time employment and therefore have relatively small earnings" (U.S. Department of Commerce, 1953, p. 11).

[5] The average earnings of those aged twenty to twenty-four with a university degree may also be understated to some extent because a number of these persons will have just graduated in May. Consequently, their income over the previous twelve months will include only earnings in May plus income from part-time work during the academic year or from employment the previous summer. I have not made any attempt to adjust for this possibility, but one should keep it in mind when interpreting the results.

[6] For an interesting study of the monetary value of parents' education for childrens' earnings, see Swift and Weisbrod (1965).

259

The significance of ability as a factor in determining whether a person finishes a particular level of schooling, and therefore the returns to different academic attainments, has been examined in several studies. Results have varied. Becker (1965, pp. 79–88 and 124–27) estimated that the rate-of-return on a college education for 1939 and 1949 in the United States would be reduced about 12 percent by adjustments for ability and that for a high school education the return would be lowered somewhat more. Employing some of the same data Becker used, Denison (1964, pp. 86–100) found support for his original assumption that about 60 percent of the crude percentage differential in earnings between levels of formal schooling was a result of education. Hunt (1964) considered a number of other factors in addition to ability, only to find returns to education *rising* or remaining roughly the same rather than *falling* as one would expect would occur when the effects of these other income determinants were excluded.

These results suggest that ability may have some importance but that the extent of its influence is still much in doubt. I shall make no fresh effort to isolate its effects. But I shall have more to say about its influence as well as the influence of several other factors when I come to discuss the implications of the observed similarities and differences in present discounted returns for different levels of education within and between occupations.

7. Finally, the data cover incomes at the Census date for persons of each age group at a given education level, not the actual lifetime earnings of these persons. I shall assume that these cross-section figures provide a reasonable approximation of the lifetime earnings that may be expected by an individual entering the labor force with a specified amount of education.[7]

The private costs of obtaining education consists of earnings foregone, tuition and incidental costs of schooling (dues, books, and transportation to school other than of a local nature), less summer and part-time earnings.

For university students, the average tuition in 1961 was $400, while incidental costs were about $150—making a total of $550. However, summer and part-time earnings averaged $725 (Canada, Do-

[7]Becker (1965, p. 73) adjusted his cross-section data for the secular growth in earnings per capita by assuming two annual rates of growth in the differential between college and high school earnings: 0.0125 and 0.02. Since these rates are, of necessity, largely speculative, there seemed little value in adopting this technique for the present study.

minion Bureau of Statistics, Education Division, 1963; Wilkinson, 1964, Appendix VI, Table A). Thus, on balance, these items yielded a *net return* to the university student.

Information is not available on incidental high school costs or summer and part-time earnings of high school students, so it will be assumed that they are equal. In any event, the sums involved would not be large and would be unlikely to affect materially the results which are rounded to the closest thousand dollars.

Earnings foregone need not be subtracted explicitly. Since I shall be discounting all earnings to age fourteen (the age when young people are presumed to have completed Grade 8), the opportunity costs of those remaining in school are already considered; their incomes from regular (not summer and part-time) employment are set at zero, while those persons of the same age already in the labor force are receiving positive income.[8]

Three discount rates are employed—5, 8, and 10 percent—to reflect three possible rates of time preference that individuals may have as well as different investment opportunities that may be open to them. For example, 5 percent is roughly the rate on long-term Government of Canada bonds; 8 percent is close to the estimated *average* rate-of-return (defined as the ratio of after-tax profits to capital) for U.S. manufacturing industries (Stigler, 1963, Table 10). Personal rates of time preference for some young people may be even higher than the 10 percent figure used. As the study by Ginzberg, Ginsburg, Axelrad, and Herma (1963, p. 134) has pointed out, "Money assumes so central a position in the scheme of values [of young people] as to overshadow education."[9] Thus, the rates employed can only be considered approximations.

In making the present-value calculations, both earnings and cost figures were reduced to account for mortality.[10] To arrive at net

---

[8]Space limitations prohibit a fuller discussion of the point; see Wilkinson (1964, pp. 238–40).

[9]If the interest rates charged on personal loans are any indication of what individuals' rates of time preference are, a much higher discount rate may be realistic in some cases; for example, studies by the U.S. Federal Reserve System (1957, pp. 50–60) show that the charges for personal loans range from 12 percent to 28 percent.

[10]The Canadian Life Table for 1965 was employed to compute the number of survivors at each age assuming there were 100,000 persons at age fourteen. Canada, Dominion Bureau of Statistics, Health and Welfare Division (1963, p. 228). To arrive at expected earnings for a person at a particular age, the observed income at that age was multiplied by the number of estimated survivors taken as a percentage of 100,000.

earnings *after* income tax, average tax payments in 1961 for each income group were subtracted from income adjusted for mortality.[11] Retirement age was assumed to be 65; even if it were a few years beyond this age, the lengthy discount period on earnings received after sixty-five would mean that the configuration of total present-value figures would be little affected.[12]

III. DISCOUNTED RETURNS FOR DIFFERENT LEVELS OF EDUCATION AND VARIOUS OCCUPATIONS

In Table 2, net present values of lifetime earnings for different levels of general education are presented.

TABLE 2

Private Net Present Values, After Income Tax, at Age
Fourteen, for Different Levels of Education,
all Occupations, Males, 1961

Level of Education	Present Discounted Values (thousands of dollars)		
	At 5 Percent	At 8 Percent	At 10 Percent
No high school	$42.7	$26.3	$20.2
Some high school (two years)	49.0	29.3	22.1
Four years high school	56.1	33.3	23.7
Some university (two years)	58.2	32.7	23.4
University degree (four years)	68.8	36.7	25.4

At a 5 percent discount rate, additional education yields greater present values in every case, although between four years high school and some university the difference is small relative to the disparity among other consecutive levels of education. At 8 and 10 percent, dollar variations in discounted net earnings among levels of schooling are, as one would expect, considerably smaller than at 5 percent,

[11]Average tax rates used were for 1960 (paid in 1961) as shown in Canada, Dominion Bureau of Statistics, Handbook and Library Division (1962, Table 17, p. 1040). As will be seen below, present values *before* income tax were also computed for a number of individual occupations.

[12]For example, the discounted returns at age fourteen of the difference between earnings of someone aged sixty-six with Grades 5–8 and someone of the same age with a university degree is only about $275 using a 5 percent discount rate, $64 at 8 percent, and less than $20 at 10 percent.

and from four years high school to some university there is even a slight decline.

Not only absolute dollar inequalities but also relative inequalities in discounted returns diminish as the interest rate rises. For example, the returns to a university degree are only 25.7 percent greater than the net returns to no high school when the 10 percent discount rate is employed, whereas they are 61.9 percent greater at the 5 percent rate.

It is evident, then, that if a sufficiently high discount rate were used, the discounted returns to a university education would be no greater than returns on an elementary school background. Knowing this, it is tempting to hypothesize that individuals who achieve only the lower levels of education have discount rates considerably higher than 10 percent (probably reflecting high marginal rates of time preference), so that for them the net present values of earnings from such education are equal to the present value of earnings from a university training.[13] There is no doubt an element of truth in this idea (particularly, as I shall indicate below, with respect to the implied conjecture that individuals are responding to divergences in present value of lifetime earnings, discounted at some specific external rate, in their choice of which level of schooling to obtain). But the grouping together of all occupations tends to exclude a number of other phenomena that warrant consideration and tends to oversimplify the problem of interpreting the observed variations in discounted returns to different levels of education.

Consider, then, net present values for various amounts of schooling within several specific occupational categories. The same source of data was used as for Table 2, and the qualifications offered earlier with respect to the data again apply. Table 3 shows net returns, at age fourteen, after income tax, for six occupations and for three levels of education within each occupation.[14]

[13]This statement contains the implicit assumption that *marginal* returns on education would be at least roughly similar to the average returns calculated from the Census figures. Obviously, the marginal returns govern, not the average.

[14]See Appendix Table A for returns to the same occupations and educational levels calculated *before* income tax deductions. When we consider the possibility of individuals responding to differences in discounted returns in choosing the amounts and types of education to obtain, there is some evidence to suggest that the return before income tax is the more relevant measure; see Grubel and Edwards (1964). These authors concluded from a survey of the reasons students have for entering particular occupations that income tax was not an important consideration. However, as a comparison of the

First, let us examine returns *within* occupations. At any one discount rate there exists a rough similarity of discounted net earnings for persons with varying amounts of education. In only two instances are inequalities in returns between any two levels of education, within one occupation, at a given rate of discount, greater than 10 percent. Both of these exceptions occur with respect to science and engineering technicians at the 10 percent external rate. In three other instances, differences in returns to varying education levels seem particularly small at all three discount rates: between laborers with some high school and four years high school, between carpenters with no high school and some high school, and between draftsmen with no high school and some high school.

These crude similarities in discounted returns within occupations at any one external rate may be accounted for in two ways.[15] First of all, we know that, if two income streams lie close together through most of their range, then, at discount rates such as those used in this study, the present values of the two streams, at any single rate, will be quite similar.[16] Second, if one or more of the external rates employed are very close to the internal rate-of-return (which equates to zero the differences in net revenue streams between two levels of schooling),

---

tables for returns before and after income tax will indicate, there is little difference between the two methods of computation in the resulting pattern of returns. (In fact, only for carpenters with four years high school at 8 percent discount rate, draftsmen with four years high school at 5 percent, and technicians with a university degree at 5 percent is there *any* variation in the pattern.) Consequently, our discussion would not be altered significantly regardless of which table we use.

It should also be noted that we are interested in considering only net private returns to people from various levels and types of education, not social returns. If social returns were our concern, earnings before tax would definitely have to be used, and we would then have to include all public expenditure for formal education and eliminate tuition fees to arrive at the unduplicated total of social costs of education.

[15] Several comments by Mary Jean Bowman were very helpful at this juncture.

[16] At lower external rates, the present values of the two streams being compared will show a considerably greater dollar discrepancy than any discrepancy we observe in Table 3. But even in these cases the *relative* divergence in the present values of the two streams will not be unlike the relative differences in Table 3. As an illustration, consider the divergence in net discounted lifetime earnings of laborers with some high school, when a zero external rate is used. The discrepancy in "discounted" returns (which in this case would equal the algebraic sum of the divergencies between the two streams through their range) is about $9,500. Although in absolute terms this amount perhaps seems large, in relative terms the figure is still slightly less than 10 percent of the total value of the lifetime earnings of laborers with no high school.

TABLE 3

Private Net Present Values, After Income
Tax, at Age Fourteen, for Different
Levels of Education, Selected Occupations,
Males, 1961

Occupation and Level of Education	Present Discounted Values (thousands of dollars)		
	At 5 Percent	At 8 Percent	At 10 Percent
Laborers:			
No high school	$33.3	$20.8	$16.1
Some high school	36.2	22.7	16.9
Four years high school	36.4	21.7	16.2
Carpenters:			
No high school	41.1	26.1	20.5
Some high school	42.7	26.4	20.3
Four years high school	44.3	25.1	19.9
Compositors and type-setters:			
No high school	57.6	35.4	27.2
Some high school	60.1	36.3	27.5
Four years high school	57.2	33.4	24.7
Draftsmen:			
No high school	59.3	36.5	28.2
Some high school	60.5	36.6	27.8
Four years high school	57.2	34.9	25.8
Science and engineering technicians:			
Four years high school	60.8	35.9	26.7
Some university	56.8	32.3	23.4
University degree	56.7	30.8	21.6
Engineers:			
Four years high school	72.5	41.6	30.6
Some university	71.8	40.1	28.7
University degree	76.5	40.8	28.3

then the discrepancies in the present-value figures at these external rates will be small.

Consider these two possible "explanations" for the case of laborers. The present value of four years high school is greater than some high school at 5 percent but less than some high school at 8 percent. Obviously, then, the internal rate between four years high school and some high school for laborers lies somewhere between these two external rates and is apparently much closer to the lower one. The similarity in present values between the two levels of schooling at 5 and 8 percent, especially at 5 percent, may therefore be attributed in part to these external rates not being far from the internal rate. Also, the original earnings data suggest that some of the correspondence in present values at these two rates may be attributed to the closeness of the income streams for persons with these two amounts of schooling. The rough agreement of returns at the 10 percent rate would have to be "explained" primarily by the closeness of income streams rather than because of this rate of discount being near the internal rate.

Similar discussions might be developed for comparisons between the other education levels in the laboring group and between education categories in other occupations as well, although varying degrees of emphasis would have to be placed on the two ways of accounting for the crude conformities of present values.[17]

Up to this juncture I have said nothing about the forces that may cause the income streams for varying amounts of schooling, within occupations, to be alike. This is not the place to enter into a detailed discussion of the many determinants of income similarities (or differ-

---

[17] In a like manner, we might "explain" the closeness of discounted returns to people of all occupations with four years high school and some university that was evident in Table 2. First, we may observe from Table 1 that the income streams for persons in these two educational levels are generally closer together than are the streams of any two other levels of schooling. (Remember, also, that before discounting I adjusted upward the income of those in the fifteen to nineteen and twenty to twenty-four age cohorts with some university to equal the incomes of those with four years high school in these age groups. Hence, the two streams would be even closer together than Table 1 indicates.) In addition, the 5 and 8 percent external rates are quite close to the internal rate on the investment in some university as compared to four years high school. This internal rate lies somewhere between 5 and 8 percent. (This is apparent from the fact that at the 5 percent discount rate some university has a higher present value than four years high school, whereas at the 8 percent rate four years high school gives the greatest discounted returns.) In contrast, the internal rate between any two other amounts of schooling lies somewhere above 10 percent.

entials) within occupations, but two broad statements might be made. First, it is clear that the similarities in returns to diverse amounts of schooling may be due in part to employers making only minor distinctions in the pay given to workers within occupations who have different amounts of education. Second, adjustments on the supply side by workers themselves may cause income streams for varying amounts of education to be close through their entire range.

Let me elaborate somewhat on this second statement. Suppose young people who are planning to become carpenters decide on the amount of education to obtain according to which level of schooling appears to offer the highest present value of lifetime earnings, discounted at some common rate such as 8 percent. If, then, the returns, discounted at 8 percent, to carpenters with some high school are greater than returns to carpenters with no high school, we should expect more of the young people entering carpentry to acquire some high school rather than entering the occupation with only public school education. That is, the supply curve of carpenters with some high school would shift to the right—thus competing down wages or salaries for this group and hence net returns.[18]

If 8 percent were the common external rate that all individuals were using in evaluating diverse investments in education, then, in general, the effect of this type of behavior by people (ignoring other complications for a moment) would be that returns at the margin, for different amounts of schooling, within occupations, would be equalized. Moreover, this process would tend to cause the income streams for the different levels of schooling within an occupation to be close to one another. Hence, at other rates of discount, such as the 5 and 10 percent rates used in Table 3, there would be crude similarities in discounted returns—as we in fact observe to be the case.[19]

[18] It is beyond my purpose in this paper to develop the detailed characteristics of the supply curve or the adjustment mechanism. It is sufficient to note that the supply curve would be a function of net lifetime earnings discounted at the 8 percent external rate, not of current income.

[19] Several assumptions are implicit in the above discussion. First, I have assumed that employers do pay different wages or salaries to workers according to the educational attainment of the workers. If employers made no distinction and paid all workers in an occupation the same amount regardless of their schooling, then automatically the individual with the least education in any one job would have the highest expected net present value of lifetime earnings—at whatever positive discount rate was chosen— simply because his costs of schooling would be less, yet his expected returns would be the same as for those with more education. In addition, under these circumstances, movements of persons within an occupation from one education category to another

There are, of course, a number of influences that would normally prevent perfect adjustment from occurring. Individuals may lack knowledge of opportunities for persons with varying amounts of education (see Stigler, 1962). In addition, because the decisions whether to leave school are highly individualistic, there will undoubtedly be some overshooting or undershooting in the numbers entering each education category. Moreover, the changing demands of the marketplace will lead to differences in returns at any point in time. In some cases, lack of funds may prevent persons from obtaining more education. Consequently, the observed discrepancies in the earnings from diverse amounts of education within occupations, discounted at 8 percent, could conceivably be attributed to these complicating factors.

It is perhaps worth emphasizing at this juncture that the foregoing analysis is highly speculative. One can say no more than that the observed results are not incompatible with the hypothesis that individuals may be choosing between more and less education before entering a particular job by a technique of implicitly discounting expected lifetime earnings at some common external rate, such as the 8 percent figure used above. Certainly, the data do not prove this hypothesis.[20]

(assuming no change in the total number of persons in that occupation) would have no effect upon discounted returns to a given amount of education. Second, I have assumed that employers' demand curves for each education level are less than perfectly elastic. If perfect elasticity prevailed, then of course changes in the supply of workers with a particular amount of education would have no effect upon the values of discounted earnings to different amounts of schooling. Third, I am again assuming that the marginal returns on education would be roughly comparable to the average returns presented in this paper.

Note also that the analysis has been phrased entirely in terms of the response of young people deciding whether to continue school or enter the labor force for the first time. A more complete discussion would entail consideration of the possible response of differences in returns, discounted at the assumed 8 percent interest rate, of older persons already in the labor force. Present values associated with diverse levels of education would differ from those shown in Table 3 depending upon the age of the worker and whether he resolves to obtain more education by enrolling in night classes or correspondence courses (in which case the major cost item—earnings foregone—would be zero) or by quitting work to do so. The response of older workers to differences in returns discounted at the 8 percent rate is likely, however, to be less complete simply because learning new material becomes more difficult as one grows older and because a man with family commitments may lack the time and/or financial resources to obtain additional education.

[20] There is one shred of evidence, however, that suggests that, if people are using some common rate of discount in choosing between education levels, this rate is proba-

Another interesting observation about returns to different amounts of education *within* occupations is that it is by no means always true that additional education, even for a single job, will result in higher discounted earnings, as Miller (1964, pp. 141–48) states is the case. For example, four years high school is not a worthwhile investment for either laborers or carpenters if their discount rates are either 8 or 10 percent. With respect to compositors and typesetters, four years high school is not profitable even at a 5 percent rate of discount. A similar pattern prevails for draftsmen, although even some high school is not profitable if the discount rate is 10 percent. For technicians, neither a university degree nor some university is a good investment; returns are highest at each discount rate for people with four years high school. For engineers, a university degree is clearly worthwhile if the discount rate is 5 percent, but not if it is 8 or 10 percent.

Of course, in some cases (engineers, for example) a certain level of general education is becoming almost a necessity — like a union card — so that individuals may have to achieve this level if they intend to enter that occupation. Moreover, the formal school system may be a much quicker way of achieving a particular level of skill than other methods of training. But still this does not deny that additional formal education may not yield higher discounted values from the individual's viewpoint.

---

bly less than 10 percent. Hence, the 8 percent figure I used in the above discussion may not be far wrong. Consider the following argument. If individuals were using some external rate *in excess of* 10 percent, then, if adjustment were complete and we applied a lower rate (such as 10 percent) to the stream of returns for each level of education within an occupation, we should expect to find discounted returns to persons with the most education within an occupation to be greater than the discounted returns to those with less education. (This should occur because the effect of using a rate lower than the one that equalizes present values at the margin is to assign a greater weight to the larger returns which the higher level of schooling yields once the individual finishes his education.) However, it does not occur in any occupation except for laborers with some high school compared with laborers having no high school, and compositors in the same two education categories. In contrast, if the common external rate that people are using is *less than* 10 percent, then, if adjustment were complete and we applied a 10 percent discount rate to the lifetime earnings of two education levels within an occupation, we should expect to find the lower level of schooling to have a higher discounted value than the higher amount of schooling — simply because the higher rate reduces the weight assigned to the higher incomes received by those with more schooling in their later working years. This is, in fact, what occurs between each consecutive pair of levels of education for four of the occupations (engineers, technicians, draftsmen, and carpenters), and in the other two occupations (laborers and compositors) between workers with some high school and workers with four years high school. I am indebted to Professor Harry Johnson for a comment which suggested this line of argument.

So far we have considered only returns to various amounts of education within occupations. When we compare discounted earnings for given levels of formal education for *different* occupations, we find significant variations in several cases. At each discount rate, for instance, discounted earnings from four years high school for an engineer are about double what a laborer with this education receives. Even carpenters receive several thousand dollars more than laborers with identical amounts of formal schooling.

These wide discrepancies existing among net present values in different occupations seem to suggest that, even if people are responding to discrepancies in expected future earnings for diverse amounts of education *within* occupations, discounted at some rate such as 8 percent, they certainly are not doing so in choosing between occupations. If they were, *and if no other influences were involved,* then there should have been movements of workers from the lower-paying occupations to the higher paying ones, raising wages (and hence discounted returns) in the former and competing down wages (and hence discounted returns) in the latter. However, there are a number of other influences involved, so that our static comparison of returns among occupations neither "proves" nor "disproves" the idea that individuals may be behaving as though they are looking at net anticipated earnings streams, discounted at 8 percent, when selecting their occupation. Let us examine a number of these factors.

The very nature of the occupations listed in Table 3 suggests that inequalities in the amounts of on-the-job training or off-the-job training such as may be obtained from technical schools, correspondence courses, evening courses, or private study may be important in accounting for the observed disparities in discounted returns. That is, the higher returns of carpenters, for example, compared to laborers with the same level of general schooling may reflect additional training that carpenters receive outside the formal school system. And the still greater returns of engineers with Grade 12 compared to carpenters with Grade 12 may reflect the greater amounts of on- and off-the-job training engineers obtain.

This seems to contradict the finding of Mincer (1962, p. 59) that the workers with more formal schooling are also the ones who obtain the most additional training. The amount of training appears to depend more upon the occupation one enters than on the level of education one achieves. However, Mincer's conclusion is broadly correct in that workers in the occupations with the higher discounted returns do, on the average, possess more formal schooling than do workers in the jobs with low discounted earnings.[21] Hence, if we look at just the *average* education levels in each occupation, it holds true that greater on- and off-the-job training is associated with greater amounts of formal schooling (assuming the amount of this training is accurately reflected by the differences in returns).

It is clear that something more must be introduced at this juncture if we are to explain why even those with less than the average amount of education in a particular occupation receive more training than persons with identical formal schooling in other occupations. The suggestion is that variations in ability are important. The 4 percent of all recorded engineers with only Grade 12 may have been more intelligent than laborers with Grade 12 and, hence, were able to learn more from twelve years in school than were those who are now laborers. Or their greater ability (which might well be interpreted broadly to include such traits as ambition and perseverance as well) may show itself by enabling them to absorb on-the-job or off-the-job training and providing the motivation for them to do so.

There is as yet no satisfactory way to separate the effect of ability from that of general education and training or to determine the extent to which ability differences control the amount of self-study or on-the-job training one undertakes.[22] We have to be content with the weak statement that ability inequalities may be largely responsible for the wide differences in returns to given levels of education either

---

[21] To illustrate, for both the engineering and laboring jobs those with Grade 12 comprised only 4 percent of the total men in each job. But 72 percent of the engineers had a university degree, whereas 51 percent of the laborers possessed only five to eight years schooling.

[22] See my earlier discussion of attempts to isolate the effects of ability. Becker (1962, pp. 30–37; 1964, pp. 37–48) has devised a method of estimating the total costs of on-the-job training, and Mincer (1962) used this approach to compute training costs in the United States for 1939, 1949, and 1958. But the technique requires the assumption that the rate-of-return on such training is the same as the rate on the additional formal schooling possessed by the individual involved. Consequently, although Mincer's attempt at estimating such costs is interesting, the assumption upon which it is based clearly leaves the results open to much question. Off-the-job-training costs would be even more difficult to estimate. However, if it is correct that the most important cost item for on-the-job training is earnings foregone, then off-the-job training (with no foregone earnings) would involve next to zero costs, and hence the returns to such training would likely be much higher than returns to training on the job.

directly or through their influence on the amount of training men receive after leaving school.[23]

Several other factors may account in part for the observed discrepancies in returns to given levels of education among occupations. First, when unemployment rates are high, as they were in 1960–61, it is well known that those in the lower-skill-cohorts generally experience unemployment rates much higher than the average rates. The lower net discounted returns in the lower-skill-groups, therefore, undoubtedly reflect to some extent the higher unemployment of these groups.[24]

Second, lack of knowledge regarding opportunities in those occupations with the higher discounted returns may have reduced the flow of young people into them and thereby prevented the wage-salary levels in these occupations from being competed down. Perhaps tradition-based wage-salary scales and variations in the bargaining power of the different occupational groups may also account for some inequalities of returns.

Some might also wish to argue that for the majority of the labor force there are non-pecuniary disadvantages associated with the higher-paying occupations that are compensated for by the additional earnings. This seems questionable—at least for the jobs under review here. Where the discounted returns are highest, working conditions on the whole are normally more agreeable. Moreover, there is some empirical evidence to suggest that even workers in occupations where net discounted returns are low would prefer those jobs where returns were higher.[25] The concept of "compensating differences"

[23] It should be noted, however, that if ability differences are important this does not mean that the higher returns in some jobs reflect a *shortage* of potentially able persons. Rather, it may suggest a lack of persons with their abilities fully developed. Studies by Dael Wolfe and others indicate that even in a society like the United States, where a higher proportion of young people attend university than anywhere else in the world, there still appears to be a significant reserve of potential intellectual talent that might be developed, given the appropriate environment; see Halsey (1961, esp. pp. 49–65 and 137–75).

[24] A related possibility, although one difficult to verify precisely, is that demand conditions may have been changing so rapidly in favor of the jobs requiring higher levels of skill that the supplies of such workers lagged behind. Hence, returns to such persons would rise.

[25] In a study by Canada, Department of Labour, workers from five occupations—electronic technicians, draftsmen, sheet-metal workers, tool- and die-makers, and floor-molders—were asked to rank these occupations as well as professional engineering, punch-press operation, and office work in terms of preference for themselves,

consequently does not appear to be an appropriate explanation of the variations in present values from a given level of education in the jobs in Table 3.

In summary, discounted values of earnings from diverse amounts of education within occupations appear to be relatively small at all three discount rates employed. The smallness of the differences indicates that one or more of these external rates are close to the internal rate-of-return and/or that the income streams are similar through their range. The similarity of income streams may be due in part to adjustments therein resulting from individuals employing some common rate of discount, such as 8 percent, and deciding upon the amount of education to obtain according to the present value of the income streams associated with the different amounts of education. The greater inequalities in returns among occupations suggest that variations in ability, on- and off-the-job training, knowledge regarding opportunities in the jobs with larger returns, unemployment rates for persons of different skill levels, and perhaps variations in bargaining power or tradition-based wage-salary scales are important in determining these returns. Also, the data indicate that additional education, even within occupations, does not always pay.

IV. CHANGES IN DISCOUNTED RETURNS TO TEACHERS AND ENGINEERS IN RELATION TO CHANGES IN COLLEGE ENROLMENTS

So far, in discussing the possibility that individuals may be considering present values of lifetime earnings, discounted at some common external rate, when selecting their occupation and education level, I have used only data for one point of time. A thorough test of the significance of this possibility would involve relating total changes in the numbers in various occupations, and education levels within occupations (excluding changes due to death and retirement), to changes over time in present values of earnings, discounted at the "appropriate" external rate, for these occupations and education levels. While the paucity of data makes a detailed study of this type impossible, there is some information available that permits rough

---

prestige, and occupation desired for their sons. The career of professional engineer almost invariably was ranked first on all three factors; electronic technicians followed, with drafting third. Sheet-metal work and tool- and die-making generally were next, while punch-press work, floor-molding, and office work were regarded as unattractive. Another more extensive study that produced similar results is that by Blishen (1958).

calculations to be made for two professions — teaching and engineering.

Thus, in Table 4, I show present values of lifetime incomes at 5, 8, and 10 percent rates of discount, for 1957 (the first year for which annual engineering earnings are available) and 1961, along with university enrolments in these two faculties for both years. The method of calculation is the same as for Tables 2 and 3, except that discounting has been done to age seventeen — when the decision on which faculty to enter at university must generally be made — rather than to age fourteen.

Accompanying the sizable increase in teachers' discounted earnings between 1957 and 1961 (17 percent at a 5 percent rate of discount and 19.7 percent at both the 8 and 10 percent discount rates — in constant 1957 dollars) was a 133 percent expansion of the enrolment in education. In contrast, there was a rise of only about 4 to 5 percent in discounted returns for engineers and a meager 3.8 percent increase in enrolment. An alternative way to make this comparison is to say that, while discounted returns to teachers rose from about 65 percent of engineers' earnings in 1957 to 72 percent in 1961, university enrolment in education rose from 24 percent to 54 percent of engineering enrolment.

Part of the increased enrolment in education may be due to the following: (1) the increasing numbers of women attending university frequently favor education, (2) teacher-training has been shifted from teachers' colleges to the university campus and such colleges have been incorporated in education faculties, and (3) the increasing numbers of students attending university may choose education because it is easier to finance than engineering: a person can take one or two years of training, then commence teaching and obtain the balance of his university education at summer school or by correspondence courses designed for this purpose.

But even if we assume that *three quarters* of the increased enrolment of students in education is a result of these influences, there would still be a 33 percent increase in enrolment in education associated with about a 19 percent real rise in net discounted lifetime earnings. The data suggest, in a crude way, that the net present value of lifetime income in diverse occupations, although undoubtedly calculated only roughly or implicitly (at some external rate people deem appropriate), may be important in persons' occupational selections.

It is not important whether present values of net earnings for dif-

TABLE 4

Present Discounted Values of Lifetime Incomes, at Age Seventeen, and University Enrolments, Teachers and Engineers, 1957 and 1961*

	Enrol-ment (N)	Thousands of Current Dollars			Thousands of Constant 1957 Dollars		
		At 5 Percent	At 8 Percent	At 10 Percent	At 5 Percent	At 8 Percent	At 10 Percent
		Teachers					
1957–58	3,406	$67.5	$40.7	$30.9	$67.5	$40.7	$30.9
1961–62	7,941	84.1	51.6	39.2	79.3	48.7	37.0
Increase	4,535	$16.6	$10.9	$ 8.3	$11.8	$ 8.0	$ 6.1
Percentage Increase	133.1	24.6	26.8	26.9	17.5	19.7	19.7
		Engineers					
1957–58	14,096	$106.5	$64.3	$48.3	$106.5	$64.3	$48.3
1961–62	14,611	117.6	71.1	53.6	110.9	67.1	50.6
Increase	535	$11.1	$ 6.8	$ 5.3	$4.4	$2.8	$2.3
Percentage Increase	3.8	10.4	10.6	10.9	4.1	4.3	4.7

*Since the cost-revenue statistics on teachers excluded Ontario and Quebec, the enrolment data have been adjusted to omit these two provinces as well. Enrolments for teachers are for the education faculty alone; no attempt has been made to estimate the numbers of arts and science students who also plan to enter the teaching profession.

Source: Wilkinson (1964, Appendix VI, Tables H–K).

ferent occupations (or even levels of education within occupations) are ever precisely equalized at some particular interest rate. Influences such as ability differences, on- and off-the-job training, market

APPENDIX TABLE A

Private Net Present Values, Before Income
Tax, at Age Fourteen, for Selected
Occupations, at Different Levels of
Education, Males, 1961

Occupation and Level of Education	Present Discounted Values (thousands of dollars)		
	At 5 Percent	At 8 Percent	At 10 Percent
Laborers:			
No high school	$35.0	$21.7	$16.8
Some high school	38.2	23.4	17.8
Four years high school	38.6	22.9	17.1
Carpenters:			
No high school	43.3	27.5	21.5
Some high school	45.3	27.9	21.4
Four years high school	47.2	28.2	21.1
Compositors and type-setters:			
No high school	62.6	37.7	28.9
Some high school	64.6	38.9	29.0
Four years high school	61.8	36.0	26.5
Draftsmen:			
No high school	63.4	39.0	30.0
Some high school	65.0	39.1	29.8
Four years high school	64.6	37.6	27.7
Science and engineering technicians:			
Four years high school	65.9	38.8	28.8
Some university	61.4	34.9	25.3
University degree	61.7	33.5	23.5
Engineers:			
Four years high school	79.5	45.6	33.3
Some university	79.2	44.1	31.5
University degree	85.6	45.5	31.4

imperfections, and rapid changes in demand for various types of workers would generally prevent complete equalization from occurring. Of much greater significance is the *tendency* for individuals to move into jobs or educational levels where, according to the discount rate they are using, the net present values of earnings are the largest.

Much more work must be done to either confirm or refute the conjectures outlined in the foregoing analysis. If they prove to be correct, a number of significant implications for labor market policy and educational policy will follow therefrom. But to discuss these here would be outside the scope of this paper.

REFERENCES

Becker, G. "Investment in Human Capital: A Theoretical Analysis," *J.P.E.*, LXX, Suppl. (October, 1962), 9–49.

———. *Human Capital. A Theoretical and Empirical Analysis with Special Reference to Education.* New York: National Bureau of Economic Research, 1964.

Blank, D. M., and Stigler, G. J. *The Demand and Supply of Scientific Personnel.* New York: National Bureau of Economic Research, 1957.

Blishen, B. H. "The Construction and Use of an Occupational Class Scale," *Canadian J. Econ. and Polit. Sci.*, XXIV (November, 1958), 519–531.

Canada, Department of Labour, Economics and Research Branch. *Acquisition of Skills.* Ottawa: Queen's Printer, 1960.

Canada, Dominion Bureau of Statistics, Census Division. Unpublished data from 1961 Census of Canada. Ottawa: Dominion Bureau of Statistics, 1963.

Canada, Dominion Bureau of Statistics, Education Division. *University Student Expenditure and Income in Canada, 1961–62*, Part II: *Canadian Undergraduate Students.* Ottawa: Queen's Printer, 1963.

Canada, Dominion Bureau of Statistics, Handbook and Library Division. *Canada Year Book 1962.* Ottawa: Queen's Printer, 1962.

Canada, Dominion Bureau of Statistics, Health and Welfare Division. *Vital Statistics, 1961.* Ottawa: Queen's Printer, 1963.

Denison, E. F. "Measuring the Contribution of Education (and the Residual) to Economic Growth: Appendix," *The Residual Factor and Economic Growth.* Paris: Organization for Economic Cooperation and Development, Study Group in the Economics of Education, 1964.

Eckaus, R. S. "Investment Criteria for Education and Training," *Rev. Econ. and Statis.*, XLVI (May, 1964), 181–90.

Feldstein, M. S., and Flemming, J. S. "The Problems of Time-Stream Evaluation: Present Value Versus Internal Rate of Return Values," *Bull. Econ. and Statis.*, XXVI (1964), 79–85.

Investment in Education

Friedman, M., and Kuznets, S. *Income from Independent Professional Practice.* New York: National Bureau of Economic Research, 1954.

Ginzberg, E., Ginsburg, S. W., Axelrad, S., and Herma, J. L. *Occupational Choice: An Approach to a General Theory.* New York: Columbia Univ. Press, 1963.

Grubel, H. G., and Edwards, D. R. "Personal Income Taxation and Choice of Professions," *Q.J.E.,* LXXVIII (February, 1964), 158–63.

Halsey, A. H. (ed.). *Ability and Educational Opportunity.* Paris: Organization for Economic Cooperation and Development, 1961.

Hansen, Lee. "Total and Private Returns to Investment in Schooling," *J.P.E.,* LXXI (April, 1963), 128–40.

Hirshleifer, J. "On the Theory of the Optimal Investment Decision," *J.P.E.,* LXVI (August, 1958), 329–52.

Hunt, S. J. *Income Determinants for College Graduates and the Return to Education Investment.* New Haven, Conn.: Yale Univ. Economic Growth Center, 1964.

Miller, Herman. *Rich Man, Poor Man.* New York: Thomas Y. Crowell Co., 1964.

Mincer, Jacob. "On-the-Job Training: Costs, Returns, and Some Implications," *J.P.E.,* LXX, Suppl. (October, 1962), 50–79.

Schultz, T. W. *The Economic Value of Education.* New York: Columbia Univ. Press, 1963.

Stigler, G. J. "Information in the Labor Market," *J.P.E.,* LXX, Suppl. (October, 1962), 94–105.

——. *Capital and Rates of Return in Manufacturing Industries.* Princeton, N.J.: National Bureau of Economic Research, 1963.

Swift, W. J., and Weisbrod, B. A. "On the Monetary Value of Education's Intergeneration Effects," *J.P.E.,* LXXIII (December, 1965), 643–49.

U.S. Department of Commerce, Bureau of the Census. *1950 United States Census of Population, Special Report.* "Education.") (P.E. No. 5–B.) Washington: Government Printing Office, 1953.

U.S. Federal Reserve System, Board of Governors. *Consumer Installment Credit,* Vol. I, Part I: "Growth and Import." Washington: Government Printing Office, 1957.

Vaizey, John. *The Economics of Education.* London: Allen & Unwin, 1958.

Walsh, J. R. "Capital Concept Applied to Man," *Q.J.E.,* XLIX (February, 1935), 255–85.

Wilkinson, B. W. "Some Economic Aspects of Education in Canada." Ph. D. dissertation, Mass. Inst. of Tech., 1964.

——. *Studies in the Economics of Education.* (Department of Labour, Economics and Research Branch, Occasional Paper No. 4.) Ottawa: Queen's Printer, 1965.

16. On-the-Job Training: Costs, Returns, and Some Implications*

JACOB MINCER[1]

Columbia University and National Bureau of Economic Research

INTRODUCTION

In the context of the economist's concern with education as a process of investment in manpower, it is important to be reminded that formal school instruction is neither an exclusive nor a sufficient method of training the labor force. Graduation from some level of schooling does not signify the completion of a training process. It is usually the end of a more general and preparatory stage, and the beginning of a more specialized and often prolonged process of acquisition of occupational skill, after entry into the labor force. This second stage, training on the job, ranges from formally organized activities such as apprenticeships and other training programs[2] to the informal processes of learning from experience. Indeed, historically, skills have been acquired mainly by experience on the job. The vast schooling system and the delayed entry into the labor force are distinctly modern phenomena.

*Reprinted from "On-The-Job Training: Costs, Returns, and Some Implications," *Journal of Political Economy*, Supplement, LXX (October, 1962), 50–79. Copyright by The University of Chicago Press.

[1] This work was stimulated and made possible by Gary Becker's fundamental theoretical analysis of investment in human capital. Financial support by the Carnegie Corporation of New York is gratefully acknowledged.

[2] A good sample of a growing literature on the subject includes P. H. Douglas, *American Apprenticeship and Industrial Education* (New York: Columbia University Press, 1921); United States Department of Labor, Bureau of Apprenticeship and Training, *Apprenticeships Past and Present* (Washington, 1955); *Apprentice Training* (Washington, 1956); and *Employee Training in New Jersey Industry* (Washington, 1960); National Manpower Council, *A Policy for Skilled Manpower* (New York: Columbia University Press, 1954) and *Improving the Work Skills of the Nation* (New York: Columbia University Press, 1955); H. F. Clark, and H. S. Sloan, *Classrooms in the Factories* (Rutherford, N.J.: Fairleigh Dickinson College, 1958); O. N. Serbein, *Educational Activities of Business* (Washington: American Council on Education, 1961).

279

As history suggests, it is useful to view the two broad classes of training not only as a sequence of stages but also as alternatives or substitutes. In many cases, the same degree of occupational skill can be achieved by "shortening" formal schooling and "lengthening" on-the-job training or by the reverse. The degree of substitutability between the two will, of course, vary among jobs and over time with changes in technology.

When training is viewed as a process of capital formation in people, three major empirical questions may be raised for economic analysis. (1) How large is the allocation of resources to the training process? (2) What is the rate of return on this form of investment? (3) How useful is knowledge about such investments in explaining particular features of labor-force behavior?

Recently flourishing research in these areas provides some tentative answers.[3] T. W. Schultz estimated the amount and growth of resources devoted by the economy to formal education. G. S. Becker estimated the rate of return to training at higher levels of education. In his National Bureau of Economic Research study, now in progress, Becker outlines the capital-theoretical approach to investment in people and shows it to be a tool of great analytical power and of extensive empirical relevance.

My first task in this paper is to estimate the amount of investment in on-the-job training. The estimates are indirect, and the concept of on-the-job training rather broad, but I am hopeful that results are at least suggestive of the orders of magnitude involved. The estimates and a discussion of their limitations are given in the first section of the paper. In the second section I attempt to estimate rates of return on some particular forms of on-the-job training, such as apprenticeships and medical specialization. The results are then compared with the rates of return on investment which includes both components: formal education and on-the-job training. In consequence, some tentative inferences are formulated about the separate components. In the final section of the paper I consider some preliminary empirical implications of my results. In particular, differentials in on-the-job training are related to income and employ-

---

[3]G. S. Becker, "Investment in People" (unpublished manuscript, National Bureau of Economic Research, 1961), and his "Underinvestment in College Education?" *American Economic Review, Papers and Proceedings*, May, 1960; T. W. Schultz, "Capital Formation in Education," *Journal of Political Economy*, December, 1960, and his "Investment in Human Capital," *American Economic Review*, March, 1961.

ment differentials among population subgroups, classified by levels of education, occupation, sex, and race. The observed behavior patterns seem largely consistent with the investment hypothesis underlying this study, though it was not possible in this preliminary empirical exploration to control for all other important factors at play.

I. ESTIMATES OF COSTS OF ON-THE-JOB TRAINING

For the purpose of this paper, the term "training" denotes investment in acquisition of skill or in improvement of worker productivity. The concept, therefore, includes schooling and training obtained on the job. The latter, under this definition, is a much broader concept than what is conveyed by the common usage of the word "on-the-job training." It includes formal and informal training programs in a job situation, as well as what is called "learning from experience."

The method of estimating the volume of investment in on-the-job training, which is described in this section, treats "learning from experience" as an investment in the same sense as are the more obvious forms of on-the-job training, such as, say, apprenticeship programs. Put in simple terms, an individual takes a job with an initially lower pay than he could otherwise get because he knows that he will benefit from the experience gained in the job taken.[4] In this sense, the opportunity to learn from experience involves an investment cost which is captured in the estimation method.

While data are much more scarce and the arithmetic is more arduous, calculation of on-the-job training costs is guided by the same theoretical principles[5] as the calculation of schooling costs. Costs of schooling consist of direct outlays (private tuition and public support), and of indirect, "invisible" opportunity costs, such as foregone earnings of students resulting from the necessary reduction of their labor-force activities while at school. Once the direct outlays are known, it is possible to infer the costs of an increment of schooling from comparative data on earnings of two sets of individuals: students,

[4]This proposition is sometimes questioned on the basis of casual observation. Greater learning from experience is characteristic of workers with greater motivation and ability, and their earnings at the early stages of the career may in some cases be as high or higher than those of other workers. But such finding that people with greater ability have higher productivity than others at any given stage of experience does not negate the existence of investment in on-the-job training, though it may bias the estimation of its magnitude.

[5]The conceptual and mathematical framework are developed and stated in Becker's "Investment in Human Capital: A Theoretical Analysis," in this Supplement.

and people similar to them with respect to previous educational attainment, age, sex, ability, except that they are "economically active" in the labor force and do not engage in additional schooling. In empirical work these conditions are approximated as well as data permit.

According to the available calculations,[6] foregone earnings constitute over half of total costs of schooling and about 75 percent of the costs borne by students. Foregone earnings bulk even more in the costs borne by trainees on the job. Indeed, nowadays it is difficult to think of any important direct payments by trainees, though in the past it was not uncommon for apprentices to pay their masters for the training. This does not mean, however, that no direct outlays are incurred in the training of workers on the job. Firms do spend sizable sums to finance apprenticeships and other training programs: equipment must be purchased and instructors paid. These sums presumably appear in accounts of firms as costs of training workers, though such data are rarely available.

Should all or a part of *firm outlays* be added to the sum of *foregone earnings of workers* to arrive at a total figure of costs of on-the-job training, indirect and direct? The answer is no, if *all* of the firm outlays are currently charged to the worker in the form of a reduction in wages. In this case the worker buys training services from the firm. The cost of the purchase is simply part of his foregone earnings — the other part being the difference between the actual marginal product of the trainee and the larger amount he could produce if he did not engage in training. Adding firm outlays in this case would constitute double counting.

It is likely, however, that some fraction of firm outlays is not charged currently to the workers but recouped by the firm at a later date.[7] The part of firm outlays which is not matched by current reductions in wages of trainees should be added to foregone earnings of workers. Unfortunately, it is impossible to estimate how large a fraction of firm outlays are costs borne by the firm. Worse yet, data

---

[6] See references in n 3.

[7] Under competitive conditions, all of the firm's costs will be charged to the worker if the training increases his future productivity in other firms just as much as in the firm in which he is training. Some fraction of costs will not be charged to the worker if the training contains elements of specificity, that is, if it increases the worker's future productivity in the firm more than in other firms. For a full exposition see Becker, "Investment in Human Capital . . . ," *op. cit.*

on costs of training (whether borne by firms or workers) are not only scarce but, in principle, highly unreliable. Such items as loss of production by experienced workers who are helping the trainees or wear and tear of equipment do not show up in any entry as direct costs of training. Rather, they are likely to be hidden in the wage and depreciation costs. Even if all costs of training were borne by firms, so that they would also pay all the foregone earnings of workers, only a fraction of costs would be revealed by accounting data. I conclude that an attempt to gauge costs of on-the-job training in the economy by accounting data of firms, even if they were made available, would lead to severe underestimates.

On the other hand, working with earnings data of workers to estimate their foregone earnings also leads to an underestimate, to the extent that some training costs are borne by firms. The calculation reported below is an estimate of foregone earnings of workers, using Census income data rather than firm accounting data. At least, in terms of population coverage, this is a complete calculation of what probably is the more important component of on-the-job training costs. The alternative procedure, of using firm data, is practically ruled out because of the meager supply of information, aside from the serious conceptual inadequacies. However, some attempt is made to supplement the estimates obtained from workers' income data with fragmentary estimates of firm costs.

A direct computation of foregone earnings of workers engaged in on-the-job training would be possible if data were available on their earnings during and after the period of training, and on earnings of a comparison group of workers who have the same amount of formal schooling and are otherwise similar to the trainees, but do not receive any on-the-job training. Presumably, the latter would have a flatter age-earnings profile than the former. That is, trainees would initially receive lower earnings than those not training, the difference representing costs of training. At a later age, earnings of trainees would rise above earnings of the untrained, the difference constituting a return on the investment. Unfortunately, it is impossible to classify workers empirically into such comparison groups.[8] Given the

[8]One interesting exception is the information obtained from an analysis of a sample of more than four hundred heads of households from the Consumer Union Panel, taken in 1959. The respondents were college-educated males who started on their first full-time job approximately twelve years before the survey date. The correlation between initial earnings of these individuals with their current earnings was used to

group, say, of all male college graduates, there is no readily available statistic which would provide information on differential amounts of on-the-job training received by subgroups, and no income data are provided by such subclassifications. Even the fragmentary information on apprenticeships does not satisfy these requirements.

Fortunately, an alternative procedure based on Becker's theoretical analysis of investment in people[9] permits utilization of the comprehensive income data available in the United States Censuses. The procedure consists of a comparison of two average income streams of workers differing by levels of schooling, such as male college graduates and high-school graduates.

Taking this comparison as an example, the procedure involves year-by-year estimation of training costs which a high-school graduate must incur in order to acquire a college education and the additional amount of training on the job which is, on the average, characteristic of college graduates. Such estimates are obtained on the assumption that the rate of return is the same on each year's investment whether at school or on the job.[10] In any given year j after high-school graduation, those who go on to, or have graduated from, college would have earnings (Y_j) which equal the earnings of high-school graduates (X_j) plus the income earned on differential investment in training made since graduation from high school, *provided no further investment in training was incurred by them during the year* j.

---

test the existence of investment in on-the-job training by the predicted effects on age-earnings profiles:

Consider Y_t, the earnings of any individual at time t, as consisting of four additive components: $\overline{Y}_t$, average earnings of the group; a_t, an ability component of the individual; c_t, the investment component (a cost if negative, return if positive); and u_t, a random component.

$$Y_t = \overline{Y}_t + a_t + c_t + u_t.$$

For simplicity assume that the components are not correlated with one another, and u is not correlated over time. Since $\overline{Y}_t$ is the same for all individuals in the group, the co-variance between earnings in the first and the twelfth year is:

$$\text{Cov}(Y_1, Y_{12}) = \text{Cov}(a + c + u_1, a_{12} + c_{12} + u_{12}) = \text{Cov}(a_1, a_{12}) + \text{Cov}(c_1, c_{12}).$$

The correlation was found to be very close to zero. Since the covariance of the ability factor is surely positive (and roughly equal to the variance of the ability component of earnings), the second covariance must be negative and equally sizable. That is, the larger (more negative) the initially foregone earnings (c_1), the larger (more positive) the return twelve years later (c_{12}).

[9]Becker, "Investment in Human Capital . . . ," *op. cit.*

[10]This assumption is later questioned. However, the fragmentary evidence in Sec. II below suggests that the assumption of equal rates is not unreasonable, when rates are computed on the sum of private and public costs of training.

Costs of (incremental) training in year j are, therefore, measured by the difference between Y_j and X_j augmented by the (foregone) return on the previous (incremental) costs.

The procedure and the basic data utilized in it are shown in detail in the Appendix. The first step in the procedure is to compute the rate of return (r) on the investment in training by which the two groups differ. This is done by equating the sum of discounted earnings differences to zero, after direct schooling outlays are netted out of earnings.

Once the rate of return is obtained, the comparison of net earnings streams Y_j and X_j permits the following step-by-step calculation of training costs: let $j = 1$ denote the first year of additional training. Then training costs in year 1 are $C_1 = X_1 - Y_1$, the observed income differential. In year 2 the costs are $C_2 = (X_2 + ra_1C_1) - Y_2$, the observed income differential, augmented by the (foregone) return on previous costs.[11] Proceeding sequentially, training costs in any year j are

$$C_j = X_j + \left(r \sum_{i=1}^{j-1} a_iC_i \right) - Y_j. \qquad ai = \frac{1}{1 - (1/1 + r)^{n-i}}, \qquad (1)$$

a is a correction factor for finite life,[12] n is the length of the working life.

Figures in Table 1 were computed in this fashion and cumulated over the working life. They constitute estimates of training costs: these are schooling costs before entry into the labor force and opportunity costs of on-the-job training afterward. The cumulation of annual costs over the working life stops at about fifteen to twenty years after entry into the labor force, since the computed training costs decline with age after labor-force entry and become negli-

---

[11] After a year of additional training, the income alternatives of the trainee are better than those indicated by the age profile X_j, which assumes no additional training.

[12] The correction factor a is not a sufficient correction for the effective length of the working life. Use of this factor alone assumes that all of a given cohort survive to a given age and have a 100 percent labor-force participation rate (after schooling) to this age. A complete correction should take into account mortality rates and the fraction of a cohort which is out of the labor force at each age. Adjustments for mortality and for labor-force participation were not incorporated in the estimating procedure. Neither have any significant effects on age-income profiles of males before the age of fifty. The effects on income *differentials* are small. According to Becker's work the mortality adjustment results in a small reduction of the rate of return, if the same mortality table is used for all education groups. The correction factor was used in the initial set of calculations, but discarded in the final revision, as it turned out to be negligible. Leaving out all these "survival" factors results in a small overstatement of costs, as is discussed later in the text.

TABLE 1

Lifetime Investment in Training Per Capita at School and On-the-Job, United States Males, 1939, 1949, 1958, by Level of Schooling

(In thousands)

Educational Level	Current Dollars						1954 Dollars*					
	Marginal Cost			Total Cost			Marginal Cost			Total Cost		
	School (1)	On-the-Job (2)	Sum (3)	School (4)	On-the-Job (5)	Sum (6)	School (1)	On-the-Job (2)	Sum (3)	School (4)	On-the-Job (5)	Sum (6)
1939:												
College	4.9	3.5	8.4	7.7	7.9	15.6	9.4	6.7	16.2	14.7	15.2	29.9
High school	2.0	2.4	4.4	2.8	4.4	7.2	3.9	4.6	8.5	5.2	8.5	13.7
Elementary school	.8	2.0	2.8	.8	2.0	2.8	1.3	3.9	5.2	1.3	3.9	5.2
1949:												
College	10.2	15.7	25.9	15.9	24.3	40.2	11.5	17.7	29.3	18.0	27.4	45.4
High school	4.1	4.7	8.8	5.7	8.6	14.2	4.6	5.3	9.9	6.4	9.7	16.0
Elementary school	1.6	3.9	5.5	1.6	3.9	5.5	1.8	4.4	6.2	1.8	4.4	6.2
1958:												
College	16.4	22.5	38.9	26.0	30.7	56.7	15.3	21.2	36.5	24.1	28.8	52.9
High school	7.1	2.9	10.0	9.5	8.2	17.7	6.6	2.7	9.3	8.8	7.6	16.4
Elementary school	2.4	5.3	7.7	2.4	5.3	7.7	2.2	4.9	7.1	2.2	4.9	7.1

*Deflated by the Bureau of Labor Statistics' Consumer Price Index.
Source: Appendix Tables A1–A7.

gible, fluctuating around zero, around age forty (see cols. [4], [5], and [6] in Appendix Tables A5–A7). The decline of training with age is consistent with a priori expectations about investment behavior: younger people have a greater incentive to invest in themselves than older ones, because they can collect the returns for a longer time.[13]

The age-earnings profiles which are the basic data used in deriving estimates of training costs are presented in Appendix Tables A1–A4. These are before-tax incomes of United States males (wage and salary in 1939, income in 1949 and in 1958), classified by age and education, and adjusted to approximate the relevant concepts. The adjustments involve netting out direct school costs and corrections for part-time employment of students during the period of school attendance. For these purposes, and in order to separate school and on-the-job training costs, the assumption was made that people with none up to eight years of schooling enter the labor force at age fourteen and have no foregone earnings while at school; high-school graduates enter the labor force at age eighteen and their foregone earnings during high-school attendance are obtainable by comparison with incomes of elementary-school graduates of the same age; college students graduate at ages twenty-two to twenty-three, and estimates of relevant income differentials are constructed in a similar way.

For each date and education group, year-by-year estimates of marginal costs of training were calculated by equation (1). An illustrative calculation is shown in Appendix Table A4. Detailed annual figures are shown in Tables A5–A7, columns (1), (2), and (3). The annual estimates of marginal costs are then cumulated horizontally in columns (4), (5), and (6) of Tables A5–A7, to obtain annual total costs of schooling and of on-the-job training. Summing the figures in each column yields, separately, lifetime total costs of schooling and of on-the-job training typical of groups with given levels of schooling per person. The results are presented in Table 1.

In reading this table it is important to distinguish between the "marginal" and "total" figures. The costs of attending high school, shown as marginal costs of high-school education, do not measure the total costs of schooling of the individual up to and including high school. For this purpose the costs of high-school attendance must be added to the costs of elementary-school attendance. Similarly, the costs of on-

---

[13] Becker, "Investment in Human Capital . . . ," *op. cit.*

the-job training of a high-school graduate as obtained by equation (1) are *additional* costs over and above the costs of on-the-job training incurred by elementary-school graduates. These marginal costs (col. [2] in Table 1) are first differences of the total costs of on-the-job training for graduates of any particular level of schooling, shown in column (5) of Table 1.

The estimates of on-the-job training costs in Table 1 are per capita magnitudes approximating the sum of resources the average male of a given educational level may be expected to invest in training on the job during his working life. Estimates of the aggregate investment by male workers in the economy during a given year are shown in Table 2. They are obtained by multiplying the year-by-year costs of training, as shown in Tables A5–A7 (cols. [4], [5], and [6]), by the number of workers[14] (student enrolment during the period of schooling) in the corresponding age and educational group (cols. [7], [8], and [9]). The cross-products are then summed to obtain aggregate costs corresponding to the total cost classifications in Table 1, columns (3), (4), and (5).

In contrast to Table 1, Table 2 represents actual opportunity costs in the economy, not expectations of individuals. The relative sizes of the two components of training costs, formal and on the job, are also different in the two tables. This is because the aggregative estimates in Table 2 depend on the age distribution of workers with given levels of educational attainment. Secular trends in population size and in educational attainments affect the relevant age distributions in a way which makes the aggregative on-the-job training costs somewhat smaller in relation to school costs than is true on the per capita basis.

Before proceeding to discussion and interpretation of the findings one must raise questions about their validity and reliability. A number of possible sources of bias are easily identified. First, the estimates of per capita training costs (Table 1) are based on cross-section income profiles. They, therefore, may approximate expectations of an average male of a given educational level, provided the differences between his earnings and earnings of males at the next lower educational level will change year after year in the future, precisely the way they do change in the cross-sectional comparison from one cohort to the next, one year older. If secular trends are expected to tilt both income

---

[14]To obtain estimates of investments by all workers, those with "some elementary schooling," "some high school," and "some college" have to be included in the calculation. It was assumed that their investment costs are halfway between investment costs of graduates at neighboring educational levels. See notes to Appendix Tables A5–A7.

TABLE 2

Aggregate Annual Investment in Training at School and On-the-Job,
United States Males, 1939, 1949, 1958, by Level of Schooling

(In $ billions)

Educational Level	1939			1949			1958		
	School	Job	Total	School	Job	Total	School	Job	Total
	Current Dollars								
College	1.1	1.0	2.1	3.8	4.3	8.1	8.7	8.7	17.4
High school	1.8	1.4	3.2	3.4	3.8	7.2	8.4	3.8	12.2
Elementary	.9	.6	1.5	2.1	.9	3.0	4.5	1.0	5.5
All levels	3.8	3.0	6.8	9.3	9.0	18.3	21.6	13.5	35.1
	1954 Dollars								
College	2.1	1.9	4.0	4.3	4.7	9.0	8.1	8.1	16.2
High school	3.5	2.7	6.2	3.8	4.2	8.0	7.8	3.5	11.3
Elementary	1.9	1.1	2.8	2.4	1.0	3.4	4.2	.9	5.1
All levels	7.3	5.7	13.0	10.5	9.9	20.4	20.1	12.5	32.6

Source: Appendix Tables A1–A7.

streams upward by the same percentage, the returns (income differentials at a later stage of life) are likely to increase somewhat, with
income differentials at an early stage largely unaffected. On this assumption, the procedure involves a small underestimate of the rate
of return since differentials later in life are heavily discounted. In
turn, this implies an understatement of costs, to the extent that costs
are, in part, a positive function of the discount rate (eq. [1]).

Another bias is introduced by using the cross-sectional patterns as
approximations for the true earnings streams. This is the misreport-
ing of years of schooling by Census respondents. According to Denison, the older the group in an education class, the larger the fraction
of persons reporting a level of education higher than the one they
reported at the previous Census.[15] This means that observed cross-
sectional age-income profiles are biased downward at older ages in
all educational groups except the lowest. The failure to tilt the income streams upward leads, as before, to an understatement of costs,
mainly at the upper levels of education.

For another reason, costs were underestimated also at the lower
levels of education. I compared the earnings stream of elementary-
school graduates with that of persons with one to four years of school-

[15]E. F. Denison, "A Note on Education, Economic Growth, and Gaps in Information," in this Supplement.

ing rather than with persons with zero schooling. The group with no schooling is small, and its composition so different from that of the other groups (it is heavily weighted with farm workers, single persons, and non-whites) that its age-earnings profile could not serve as a bench mark. To the extent that persons with zero to four years of schooling undergo some on-the-job training, which is undoubtedly true, the costs of such training have been omitted from my estimates.

An opposite bias is imparted by omission of the survival factors, as mentioned previously (n. 12). Lack of adjustment for mortality, for example, means that earnings differentials at later ages are overstated. Costs are therefore *overestimated*, because the rate of return is overestimated, though by a small amount.

The 1949 and 1958 income figures include property income in addition to labor income, and this too tends to widen differentials between profiles noticeably at later ages. This is because of a positive correlation of property income with age and with education. The result is a slight overestimate of costs by an overestimate of the rate of return.

A more serious question is posed by the assumption that differences in income streams of the groups compared are attributable to differences in training. Such an assumption disregards other factors which may affect shapes and levels of age profiles. Biases will arise if these other factors are not independent of the classificatory criteria: for example, the higher the years of schooling and the higher the age, the lower the fraction of males who are non-white. Farmers and farm laborers are disproportionately distributed in the low years of schooling and low age classes. Restriction of estimates to non-farm whites (as in 1939) avoids the distortions, but such data were not available for all the periods. It is clear, however, that, even in data which are quite homogeneous by Census criteria, certain selective or restrictive factors are not neutral with respect to the educational classification: people who undertake more training are likely to have higher intelligence quotients, higher parental income and education, more motivation and information.

The extent to which earnings of more trained persons exceed earnings of less trained persons is, therefore, an *overestimate* of the return on training. Part of the observed return is a return to these "ability" factors. But, for the same reasons, the observed data are likely to underestimate the costs incurred: if more capable high-school students enter college, their foregone earnings are probably underestimated by the observed earnings of the less capable high-school graduates who did not go on to college. It is difficult to say, a priori, how large such biases may be. But, if a correction for the "ability" factor involves a decrease in return and a simultaneous increase in cost via income differentials, it is clear that the relative decline in the rate of return must be larger than the relative increase in costs.[16] According to Becker an adjustment for class standing of high-school graduates brings the rate of return down by about 15 percent. If costs are underestimated, this figure measures the maximum amount of bias, when the dimension of ability which is measured by class standing is taken into account. Other factors may account for more.

Once again, the bias need not be in one direction. To the extent that the restrictive factors under discussion affect returns (earnings differentials after the training period) *without* affecting income differentials during the training period, the rate of return *and* costs are overestimated. This is because costs, as we computed them, are in part a positive function of the rate of return.

Possibly the largest source of downward bias in the estimation of costs was already mentioned: the omission of costs of training which are borne by firms. These costs do not show up in the income data at all. As a simple example, take the case of a firm which pays half the costs of training, the other half being paid by the worker. Later on, the firm captures half of the returns. Rates of return are not affected, and foregone earnings of workers are cut in half.

It is not possible to arrive at an overall notion of the direction of bias without knowing more about the magnitudes of each possible error. But, if there is some reason to believe that totals are underestimated, there are reasons to believe that the distortion is weaker when it comes to relative sizes of subtotals in the classifications of Tables 1 and 2. If ability factors bias costs in the comparison of college and high school, they have similar effects in the high school and elementary school.

The striking finding in Table 1 is that the opportunity costs of on-the-job training per male are almost without exception somewhat higher than costs of a comparable increment of schooling. But while per capita amounts of formal schooling (as measured by costs in

---

[16]The rate of return is a ratio of returns to costs, $r = k/c$. If only c were increased, with k left the same, the relative (percent) decrease in r would equal the relative increase in c. But, since k is decreased, the relative decrease in r is stronger than the relative increase in c.

constant dollars) grew between 1939 and 1958 at all levels, the corresponding quantities of on-the-job training per capita grew mainly at the higher educational levels.

On an aggregative basis (Table 2) on-the-job training costs were a little smaller than schooling costs in 1939 and grew at a slower rate than the former. Formal education expenditures grew rapidly at all levels during the 1939–58 period. On-the-job training expenditures grew just as fast as schooling at the highest educational level, increased before 1949 and decreased afterward at the high-school level, and continuously declined at the elementary-school level. The per capita figures (Table 1) indicate, however, that the decline in aggregate on-the-job training for the elementary-school class was not a result of a decline in costs per head but a decline in the number of heads. Similarly, the increase in on-the-job costs in the aggregate for the college class also consisted mainly in an increase in the number of heads rather than in training costs per head, particularly in the second decade.

One feature of the findings in Table 1 is worthy of closer attention: on-the-job training is a larger quantity the higher the level of education. This is not a truism as in the case of schooling, where the marginal quantities of schooling are positive by definition. There is nothing in the calculation of on-the-job training costs that would make the marginal quantities necessarily positive. In other words, the positive association between school training and on-the-job training is not definitional; it is an empirical inference from the observed income data. More training seems to involve more of both forms of training, though not in any fixed proportion. This is reasonable: school education is a prerequisite, a basis on which to build the further, more specialized training.

Some independent evidence on this positive association is provided by recent Department of Labor estimates of amounts of school and on-the-job training, both measured in school-grade equivalents, required for the acquisition of occupational skill in four thousand detailed occupations.[17] From the four thousand occupations listed in the publication, a sample of 158 occupations was selected on the basis of comparability with the 1950 Census occupational breakdown. The

[17]United States Department of Labor, Bureau of Employment Security, United States Employment Service, *Estimates of Worker Trait Requirements for 4,000 Jobs as Defined in the Dictionary of Occupational Titles* (Washington, 1956).

two measures of school and on-the-job training requirements given in rank form, were correlated with coefficient +.86.

The positive association between schooling and on-the-job training helps in understanding trends. It suggests that an expansion of education is likely to bring about an expansion of on-the-job training, a development indicated in Tables 1 and 2. To the extent that an expansion of education is induced by a decrease in its price relative to the price of on-the-job training, some substitution will take place, and education may grow at the expense of on-the-job training. Such factors, among others, may underlie the slower growth of on-the-job training than of schooling. More precisely, the data suggest slow or no growth of on-the-job training at the lower educational levels and pronounced growth at upper educational levels. This finding supports popular impressions about the changing levels of on-the-job training: a shift from apprenticeships to technicians, scientific personnel, and executive development programs. Such shifts may, in the aggregate, reflect the upward trend in supplies of labor with high levels of educational attainment and possibly some substitution phenomena at the lower levels. The questions about trends are very intriguing, but the data do not lend themselves to more than conjectures.

Turning to bodies of data other than the comprehensive income statistics, I tried to exploit them, though not very intensively, for two purposes: (1) to provide some empirical checks on the reliability of estimates based on foregone incomes of workers, (2) to form some guesses about firm costs or outlays.

1. On the basis of the BLS publication on skill requirements for 4,000 occupations, Eckaus estimated the average number of college-equivalent years of on-the-job training imbedded in the labor force (including females).[18] The estimate was 1.66 and 1.72 for 1939 and 1949, respectively. But these are average quantities for the whole age distribution, figures representing a stock. We are interested in the flow of current investment in on-the-job training, and this is incurred mainly by the younger age groups. These groups have higher education levels than the labor force as a whole and are, therefore, likely to invest more also in on-the-job training. In 1949 the age group

[18] R. S. Eckaus, "Education and Economic Growth," in Economics of Higher Education, ed. Selma J. Mushkin (Washington: United States Department of Health, Education, and Welfare [forthcoming]), Tables 1 and 2. College equivalence is implied in United States Department of Labor, Bureau of Employment Security, United States Employment Service, *op. cit.,* p. 111.

18–29 had a median schooling of 12 years compared to a labor force median of 10 years. The discrepancy between means was even greater. Since the investment in on-the-job training is higher at higher education levels, an upward adjustment is required. Using the ratio of medians to revise Eckaus' estimates upward, roughly in proportion, yields 1.99 and 2.06 years for 1939 and 1949 respectively.

In terms of equivalent college costs per year, 2.06 years of training would cost about $6,000 per member of the labor force in 1950, according to Table 1. The average female invests in on-the-job training about one-tenth as much as the average male,[19] and the number of females was slightly over a third of the total labor force in the age group 18–29. Hence, the implicit cost (C) of on-the-job training incurred per male in 1949 is:

$$\$5,200 = \tfrac{2}{3}C + \tfrac{1}{30}C$$

$$C = \$7,500.$$

This compares with our estimates of $8.600 costs of on-the-job training of male high-school graduates (Table 1, col. [5]), the modal group in the population. A similar calculation for 1939 yields about $3,600 to be compared with our estimate $4,400. Elements of subjectivity in the BLS-derived figures make the comparison difficult, but the fact that the two sets of estimates are not very far apart is encouraging.

Another piece of supplementary evidence is provided by data on the distribution of federal expenditures on the GI Bill for 1945–55. The expenditures and their distribution are given in Table 3. In columns (3) and (5) we compare the percentage distributions of expenditures: costs of college training of veterans during the ten-year period are compared with costs of college of all males in 1949; a similar comparison of veterans' costs is made with marginal costs of high school, and with total costs of on-the-job training of high-school graduates. The distributions (col. [3] and col. [5]) look reasonably comparable. The greater selectivity of veterans toward college and vocational training (trade schools and on the job) in comparison to all males is understandable in view of differences in age and in educational backgrounds already acquired.

2. Several recent surveys of training activites in firms have shown

[19] See Part III below.

TABLE 3

GI Bill Expenditures, by Level and Type of Training, 1945–55

Level of Training	No. of Veterans (Millions)	GI Bill Expenditures		All Males, Aggregates for 1949	
		$ Billions	Percent	$ Billions	Percent
	(1)	(2)	(3)	(4)	(5)
College	2.2	5.5	38.1	4.5	40.8
High school	1.4	2.2	15.3	3.3	30.0
Trade school	2.1	3.3	23.1		
On the job	2.1	3.5	24.5	3.2	29.2
Total	7.8	14.5	100.0	11.0	100.0

Source: Cols. (1) and (2), President's Commission on Veterans' Pensions, *Readjustment Benefits, Staff Report* (No. IX, Part B [Washington: Government Printing Office, September 12, 1956]), pp. 22–24, 30–32.

that such functions are carried by many firms.[20] Of course, only formally arranged programs are described in such surveys. Unfortunately, questions about costs are seldom raised in these surveys. Undoubtedly, it would be difficult to interpret the financial data, even if they were forthcoming. In only one of the recent studies were such questions asked, with these results:

Although questions were asked concerning total expenditures for in-company education, few firms replied — Perhaps the chief reason was that often the books of the firms were not kept in a manner that would make it easy to separate educational costs from other costs. Other reasons centered around questions of allocation and items to be considered as costs — The data reported are not comparable, since some of the figures include salaries and some exclude them. It is not certain that the figures reported include all in-company programs. In one case it was specifically stated that the figure reported was for one program.[21]

If the scant financial replies show in this survey are blown up to an aggregate, the result is an estimate below $1 billion for 1957, undoubtedly a severe underestimate of even those current firm outlays which are easily identifiable. Smaller case studies indicate that firm expenditures on formal training programs must be much larger:

[20] Clark and Sloan, *op. cit.*, Serbein, *op. cit.*, and the 1960 New Jersey Survey of the Bureau of Apprenticeships and Training.

[21] Serbein, *op. cit.*, pp. 9–10.

estimates range from $85 for an operative in training[22] to over $10,000 for an executive training program.[23] According to the recent comprehensive survey of New Jersey industries made by the Bureau of Apprenticeship and Training,[24] the proportion of workers participating in formal training programs in 1959 was about 5 percent. Of these 20 percent enrolled in management development programs, 10 percent in apprenticeships, 10 percent in technical (semiprofessional) training, 12 percent in sales training, and the rest in short programs of operative training, orientation, safety, etc. Applying almost any vaguely reasonable dollar figures—from $85 per operative to a conservative $2,000 per executive trainee per annum, and projecting to the aggregate labor force in recent years, yields an estimate of $2–$3 billion. But this, of course, misses all costs incurred in informal training, which is the typical situation: only 16.2 percent of firms in New Jersey had *formal* training programs.

One estimate which takes into account "invisible" costs of firms, including costs in informal training processes, can be obtained using figures shown in a recent study of California firms by the American Management Association.[25] In this study estimates were made of costs of labor turnover to the firm. The concept of replacement cost includes hiring costs such as advertising, recruitment, interviews, and separation costs; on-the-job training costs are defined more comprehensively as "the expense brought about by sub-standard production of new employees while learning their job assignments and becoming adjusted to their work environment; the dollar value of time spent by supervisors and other employees who assist in breaking in new employees on their job assignment, and costs of organized training programs."[26] These training costs per worker replacement were estimated at about $230. If hiring and separation costs are included the figure doubles. Multiplying these costs of a replacement by the total number of replacements in industry in 1958[27] yields an estimate of $7 billion. Inclusion of hiring and separation costs raises the estimate to

[22] "Training Manpower," *Fortune*, July, 1951.

[23] Clark and Sloan, *op. cit.*, p. 3.

[24] See references cited in n 2.

[25] Merchants and Manufacturers Association, *Labor Turnover: Causes, Costs and Methods of Control* (New York, February, 1959).

[26] *Ibid.*

[27] About thirty million, using the observed average monthly replacement rate of 4 percent.

$14 billion. The assumption that all of these costs are borne by the firms is, of course, highly questionable. How much is shifted back to the trainee in the form of a wage reduction is not known. At the same time, a large part of the opportunity cost of workers—the difference between what they did produce while in training and what they could produce if they did not train—is also missed in these figures.

All these heroic attempts to estimate firm costs add up to an uncomfortable range of uncertainty when it comes to answering the question: how much of firm costs should be added to the estimates of foregone incomes of workers? It is possible that billions of dollars are involved, but it is not clear how many.

Besides firm costs, two more items must be added to our estimates in Table 2 to get total costs of on-the-job training in the economy: training costs incurred by women and training expenditures in the Armed Forces. The latter are estimated at $1.6 billion[28] in 1959, and the former at $1.4 billion[29] in 1958. According to Table 2, aggregate opportunity costs of male workers were about $13.5 billion in 1958. Addition of the two items brings the figure up to $16.5 billion, more than half of the aggregate costs of schooling (males and females) in 1956.[30] The addition of possibly several billion dollars of costs borne by firms narrows the difference but may not close it. Since most of the on-the-job training costs are incurred by and spent on male workers, it is probably correct to say that, in the male half of the world on-the-job training—measured in dollar costs—is as important as formal schooling.

II. ESTIMATES OF RATES OF RETURN

An estimate of rates of return to on-the-job training is both desirable and difficult to obtain. The rate of return computed by equating the present values of net earnings of two education groups should not be interpreted as a rate of return on schooling costs. The computed rate is some average of rates of return to schooling and to on-the-job training. The hybrid rate depends on the weights (costs) of the two

[28] Includes military schools and training programs but excludes basic training and depreciation of equipment (estimated by R. C. Blitz in "The Nations Educational Outlay," in Mushkin (ed.), *Economics of Higher Education*.

[29] Based on 1949 estimates for female college graduates (see Part III, below).

[30] According to Schultz, the total cost of schooling was $28.7 billion in 1956 ("Investment in Human Capital," *op. cit.*).

training components and on the rates on each component.[31] If the rate on one component is known, the other can be approximated in a residual fashion. What is immediately important, the larger the difference between the rates of return on investment in schooling and in on-the-job training, the less accurate are the cost estimates in the preceding section, as well as the various recent estimates of rates of return on (school) education. If the rate of return on schooling exceeds the rate on on-the-job training, the estimates are on the low side.

It is not obvious, on a priori grounds, whether the money rate of return to on-the-job training is likely to be smaller or larger than the rate on formal education. It could be argued that non-pecuniary, "consumption" elements may be a more important part of the real return to formal education then to on-the-job training. If so, and if this were the only difference, the money rate of return on schooling would appear smaller than the rate to on-the-job training. Larger public subsidies to formal education would also have this effect, if returns are computed on total costs (private and public). These arguments are based on an assumption of equality of the real (pecuniary and non-pecuniary) private rate of return in both training sectors.

One could argue, however, that larger impediments to a flow of investment into formal education make for higher rates of return to schooling than to on-the-job training. Income constraints are less severe in the latter case as costs are more spread out over time. Perhaps more important is that this investment is undertaken at a later age and in the context of a concrete, existing work situation: there is much less uncertainty about future prospects, about one's own abilities and motivations, etc. These circumstances tend to produce a lower *real* rate of return to on-the-job training and may well reduce the *money* rate on it to a lower level than the money rate on formal education.

There are no comprehensive data comparable to the Census classifications by formal education level from which to compute rates to on-the-job training. The rates shown in Table 4 were estimated for a few selected skills for which tolerably good data are available. These refer to apprenticeship training in the several industries in which they are concentrated. All estimates are for 1949.

The rates of return on apprenticeship training were computed in

---

[31] It also depends on timing. The chronologically earlier component receives greater weight (see Becker, "Investment in Human Capital . . . ," *op. cit.*).

TABLE 4

Rates of Return on Apprenticeship Training, Selected Trades, 1949

| Trades | Assumptions about Alternative Income Streams | | |
	Operatives in Same Industries (1)	Operatives with Highest Schooling (2)	Assuming a 10 Percent Return on Additional Schooling (3)
Metal	16.4	10.4	9.5
Printing	16.0	12.6	9.0
Building	18.3	11.3	9.7

Source: Table A8.

three different ways providing a range of estimates, from the highest values in column (1) to the lowest in column (3) of Table 4. However, the lowest values (col. [3]) are conceptually the soundest. The computations involve equating to zero the present value of differentials between earnings of workers who served an apprenticeship and earnings of their assumed alternative occupational groups. During the period of training the apprentice receives an average wage W_a, after which he becomes a journeyman receiving an average wage W_m. A suitable alternative occupation,[32] where almost no training is involved, is the operative, and his average wage is W_o. The annual wage differential $d = W_a - W_o$ is negative during the training period and positive afterward, $k = W_m - W_o$ assumed constant for the rest of the working life. Under these assumptions, and disregarding a negligible correction for the finiteness of working life, the rate of return (r) is easily obtained from:[33]

$$(1 + r)^n = 1 + \frac{k}{d}, \tag{2}$$

[32] This occupation is more appropriate as an alternative, in terms of educational background, than laborers. Clerical work is an alternative, but it probably contains more on-the-job training than operative jobs, which involve at most a few months of training.

[33] Calculated from

$$d \cdot \sum_{i-1}^{n} \frac{1}{(1+r)^i} = k \cdot \sum_{j=n+1} \frac{1}{(1+r)^i}$$

The assumption of infinite life creates a negligible error.

where n is the number of years of training, or length of the apprenticeship.

Estimates in column (1) of Table 4 are based on comparisons of earnings of apprentices, journeymen, and operatives *in the same industries*. While operatives and corresponding craftsmen had the same median schooling, the apprentices had two to three more years of schooling than the other two groups in 1949. Thus k, the difference between earnings of journeymen and operatives, is computed correctly, holding formal schooling the same. But foregone earnings of apprentices are underestimated: having more schooling than the operatives with whom they are compared, the apprentices could earn more in alternative jobs. With returns correct and costs underestimated, figures in column (1) are too high.

In column (2) this defect is corrected to a large extent. In the calculation, k is the same as before, but d was computed from a comparison of wages of apprentices with wages of operatives whose schooling levels are closer to levels of apprentices, regardless of industry attachment. As Table A8 shows, however, median schooling of these operatives is still about a year less than of apprentices, so rates may still be overestimated.

In column (3) the same k is used again, but the opportunity cost is computed by adding to d (as computed in col. [1]) a return on additional years of (high-school) education[34] by which apprentices exceed the operatives with whom they are compared in column (1). This brings the rates down to the levels shown in column (3).

The estimates probably suffer from several biases. Operatives have some on-the-job training, but so do craftsmen after completion of apprenticeships. If the additional training of the latter exceeds that of the former, the rates of return on apprenticeships are overestimated. On the other hand, abstraction from secular rates of growth, as in the general case,[35] may have the opposite effect. It is also possible that union restrictions on entry to apprenticeships resulted in higher returns in the several fields selected in Table 4 than in other kinds of on-the-job training.[36]

---

[34] A 10 percent rate was used. Higher rates would lower the figures in col. (3) even more.

[35] See Part I, above.

[36] However, according to a recent study by H. G. Lewis, the impact of unionism on wage differentials was very small in the 1945–50 period ("Union Effects on Relative Wages," in *Aspects of Labor Economics* [National Bureau of Economic Research Conference, 1960 (New York, 1960)].

For a comparison with another high level of skill, I computed rates of return on medical specialization, comparing incomes of residents and specialists (after residency) with incomes of general practitioners. The computation utilizes age-income profiles of independent medical specialists, starting with an initial period of residency, with the income profile of independent general practitioners, starting with the first year in practice. Estimates of income in money and kind of residents were obtained from American Medical Association sources;[37] earnings from 1950 Census sources.[38] The calculation on before-tax incomes showed a return of 12.7 percent. A rough adjustment for taxes brought the rate down to 11.3 percent. It is difficult to judge whether this is high or low in comparison with apprenticeships.[39]

Table 5 compares estimated rates of return on apprenticeships and on training at the college level.

TABLE 5

Returns to "Education" and to On-the-Job Training, 1950

	Percent	
	College Level* (1)	On-the-Job Training† (2)
Total costs	11	9.0–12.7
Private costs before tax	14	
Private costs after tax	13	8.5–11.3

*Source: G. S. Becker, "Underinvestment in College Education?" *op. cit.*
†Range based on column 2 and 3 of Table 4, and on return to medical specialization.

[37] *Journal of the American Medical Association*, September 22, 1956, pp. 277 ff., and October 10, 1959, pp. 665 ff.

[38] "Income of Physicians," *Survey of Current Business*, July, 1951.

[39] The 1950 rate of return to medical specialization may have been above equilibrium. The proportion of specialists among physicians was less than half in 1950 and increased to about two-thirds by 1960 (according to *Medical Economics*, 1961). If this was a supply shift in response to a high level of demand, the rate of return on specialization should be less today than in 1950. Data from medical sources (*Physicians Earnings and Expenses*, published by *Medical Economics*, 1961) indicate that in 1959 the money income differential between specialists and general practitioners is no larger than it was in 1949, despite the fact that the average incomes of specialists rose over 60 percent during the period, residencies lengthened somewhat, and opportunity costs clearly increased. If the data are reliable, it would seem that rates of return today are a few percentage points lower than in 1949. Incidentally, estimates of rates of return on specialization in medicine have little bearing on the question of alleged monopoly returns in medicine. Whatever the barriers to entry into medicine, once a medical degree was obtained, institutional obstacles to specialization are weak.

Generalizing boldly, a comparison of columns (1) and (2) suggests that money rates of return (before tax) on *total costs* (public and private) are similar for school and on-the-job training. Figures in column 1 are weighted averages of returns on the two sectors; similarity of average and component means that rates on each component are alike. It does appear, however, that private rates of return are lower for the selected instances of on-the-job training than for total training at college levels. If the selected instances can be generalized, the rate of return on college education per se is somewhat underestimated by the figures in column (1). Apparently, the greater ease of investing in on-the-job training outweighs the possibly greater consumption elements in college education. Another intriguing implication is that the apparent, but not clearly documented, stability over time in the rates of return to training (both in school and on the job) may conceal a decline in the rate of return to formal education, given that investment in education seems to have grown faster than in on-the-job training, at least at the lower levels.

These conclusions are hazardous. The rates are not adjusted for ability factors. If there is a greater selectivity (based on ability) for admission into college, differences between adjusted rates in the two sectors may disappear, or reverse. But this is not at all obvious. More detailed data and intensive research are needed.

III. ON-THE-JOB TRAINING AS A FACTOR IN INCOME AND EMPLOYMENT BEHAVIOR

In the first section of this paper, the economic theory of investment in people was used to bring the very elusive process of on-the-job training under the measuring rod of money. In this section the theory will be used to produce additional measurements and to explain, in part, certain well-known but not well-understood patterns of income and employment in population subgroups. The empirical analyses sketched below are no more than preliminary, but perhaps they are sufficiently indicative.

A calculation of (marginal) on-the-job training costs per capita for female college graduates in 1949 provided two estimates: (*a*) $830, (*b*) $2,160. The comparable figure for males was $15,700 (Table 1, col. [2]). The calculation is the same as the one underlying Table 1. It is based on a comparison of net earnings of college and high-school graduates, given in Table A9. Estimate (*a*) is based on earnings data adjusted for (multiplied by) labor-force rates of women in the various age groups (Table A9, cols. [3] and [4]); estimate (*b*) is based on the unadjusted earnings (Table A9, cols. [1] and [2]). The adjustment for participation rates assumes that the return on investment in training of women (at college and on the job) is obtainable only in the labor market. If it is believed that this investment in training results also in the same amount of productivity increase in the·"home industry," earnings should not be adjusted by labor-force rates. This certainly cannot be assumed of investments on the job, but may be true of schooling. The estimate (*b*) based on unadjusted earnings is, of course, larger. Both assumptions are extreme, and, in principle, provide limits for a correct estimate.[40]

While formal education costs are not much smaller for females than for males, investments in on-the-job training are very small, about one-tenth (taking a middle figure between the two estimates) of the amounts invested by males. The figures may not be highly reliable, but their smallness is quite reasonable, in the light of investment theory: the average female expects to spend less than half her working life in the labor force. In particular, she has a high probability of dropping out of the work force for prolonged periods of child-rearing soon after, and possibly during, the training period. It is clear that returns on prolonged on-the-job training would be small. Hence pecuniary incentives to invest in on-the-job training leading to higher levels of skill are weak. And even when a girl plans on a career, that is, expects to be permanently attached to the labor force, the opportunity for investing in on-the-job training is likely to be limited. So long as there are some elements of specificity in any training programs or promotional schemes of the firm, the employer will prefer men to women trainees, even if the latter profess occupational ambitions. This also implies that to the extent that women do obtain specific training they bear a larger fraction of the total costs of such training than men and, therefore, that the difference between on-the-job training costs (including those borne by employees) for women and those for men is even larger than is suggested by our estimate.

Some direct evidence on scant female participation in on-the-job training is provided in a recent international survey.[41] In all countries

[40] Empirical evidence on labor-force behavior of married women is more consistent with the first than with the second assumption (see my "Labor Force Participation of Married Women," in *Aspects of Labor Economics, op. cit.*).

[41] "The Apprenticeships of Women and Girls," *International Labor Review*, October, 1955.

surveyed, apprenticeships are shorter for women than for men. They are half the length of male apprenticeships in the United States in bookbinding and in the garment industry, where women concentrate. In other industries, numbers of women apprentices are negligible, perhaps because of physical requirements but not because of any legal obstacles. It is interesting to find that, in contrast to other countries, applications for apprenticeships by women were quite numerous in the early postwar years in Germany and Austria. By 1949 in these countries, the number of skilled women in trades previously considered male was quite pronounced and increasing. Because of the war-caused imbalance in the sex ratio in the young age groups, unfavorable marriage prospects of young females clearly increased worker and employer expectations of their more permanent attachment to the labor force. Larger investment in on-the-job training became economical to both parties. Aside from patriotism, such motivations may play a role in the increased labor-force rates and job-training of women during wars in all countries. And the willingness of employers to train women as well as men is enhanced by governmental subsidies of the training function.

Returning to our estimates: the small amounts of investment in on-the-job training by females were derived from female age-income profiles. This procedure is, of course, equivalent to a hypothesis which emphasizes the lack of on-the-job training as the factor responsible for both the observed flatness of females' age-income profiles and the small differential between observed incomes of women of different levels of formal education.

A recent detailed study of income differentials between males and females shows that wage rates approach equality when the detailed job specification is identical for both sexes.[42] The rougher the occupational classification, the bigger the wage differentials at the higher skill levels. Lack of on-the-job training fits these phenomena quite well.

These same phenomena, however, are possibly attributable to differential market discrimination against women appearing at the more skilled job levels and increasing with levels of skill. The calculation based on Table A5 indeed revealed a somewhat lower rate (about two percentage points) of return on total training of women than of

---

[42] H. Sanborn, "Male-Female Income Differentials" (unpublished doctoral dissertation, University of Chicago, 1959).

men. The lower rate may reflect discrimination. Another explanation which is consistent with the investment hypothesis[43] is that, in view of the expected smaller rate of participation in the labor market, education of women is more strongly focused on the "consumption" sphere, and returns are in larger part non-pecuniary than for males. Hence the apparently smaller money rate of return.

In Table 6 a 1949 comparison of training costs of Negro and white males indicates much smaller investments in on-the-job training by

TABLE 6

Costs per Non-white Male of School and On-the-Job Training, 1949
(In $ thousands)

Educational Level	Marginal Costs		Total Costs		Total Costs of All United States Males	
	School	On the Job	School	On the Job	School	On the Job
College	8.05	3.98	13.20	7.87	15.9	24.3
High school	3.92	0.46	5.15	3.89	5.7	8.6
Elementary school	1.23	3.43	1.23	3.43	1.6	3.9
Source: Table A10 and Table 1.						

Negroes, though the investments are not negligible. The investment in on-the-job training is also smaller in relation to investment in formal schooling, suggesting a lesser access to on-the-job training than to formal education. Again, fragmentary direct evidence abounds on the small proportions of Negroes in apprenticeships and other training programs.

Conversely, the smaller amounts of on-the-job training received by Negroes than by whites is an interpretation of income differentials: the relative flatness of their age-income profiles and the smaller differentials in earnings by education (even when the latter are standardized in terms of cost). The lesser on-the-job training relative to school training of Negroes is an element in their occupational distribution. It creates an even lower skill concentration in the occupational distribution than would be predicted by the educational distribution.

[43] Yet another explanation, suggested by Becker ("Underinvestment in College Education?" *op. cit.*) is that the personal money returns shown above understate the money returns which actually accrue to women as family members. According to this argument family income differentials are the relevant measures.

As in the sex comparison this results in a statistical finding that the ratio of non-white to white incomes declines with increasing level of formal education.[44]

It has long been observed that at lower levels of skill and education workers are affected by a stronger incidence of unemployment than those at higher occupational and educational levels. The reasons for this phenomenon have never been clarified.

In his analysis of investment in people, Becker points out that, for a given demand situation, turnover and unemployment rates are likely to be milder under conditions of specific on-the-job training than elsewhere. Specific training is defined as an investment which increases the worker's marginal product in the firm in which he is trained more than elsewhere. According to this theory marginal products of specifically trained workers exceed their wages, but the latter are higher than in alternative employments.[45] Hence employers have more incentive to retain such workers, and these have more incentive to remain with the firm. The differential behavior is implicit both for cross-sectional observations and for cyclical changes. In a recent study, a similar hypothesis was elaborated and put to an empirical test by Walter Oi.[46] Oi related the severity of cyclical changes (1929–33) in employment to levels of wages in a particular industry and found an inverse correlation between the two. He also correlated average wages by industry with turnover rates for a number of industries at a given time. Here again the (partial) correlation was negative. Oi interprets his results as favorable evidence for the investment hypothesis, on the assumption that wage levels (by occupation and industry) are a proxy for amounts of specific training.

This is a bold assumption. Even if cross-sectional wage differentials (by occupation and industry) represented returns to training only, these conceptually reflect returns to two forms of training: school training which is "general," and on-the-job training which may be "general" or "specific." It is not easy to see why the total return should be particularly strongly correlated with what is probably the smallest component: that part of on-the-job training which is specific. Oi did not attempt to segregate the explanatory factors into "general" and

[44] See M. Zeman, "A Quantitative Analysis of White-Non-white Income Differentials in the United States" (unpublished doctoral dissertation, University of Chicago, 1955).

[45] Becker, "Investment in People," *op. cit.*

[46] "Labor as a Quasi-fixed Factor of Production" (unpublished doctoral dissertation, University of Chicago, 1961).

"specific" components of training because his data did not permit standardizations by education or by age. Without such standardizations the results are ambiguous. The wage rate reflects schooling as well as on-the-job training: a higher rate will prevail with very little on-the-job training but sufficiently more school training. This might obscure the relation which is tested. Conversely, the lack of control for age makes for a spurious correlation between the wage rate and turnover. Larger proportions of younger people in an industry, or occupation, mean both more turnover and lower wages.

In an attempt to get a stronger test of the investment hypothesis and more insight into factors affecting turnover and unemployment. I ran a multiple regression relating a hybrid unemployment and turnover variable to average full-time incomes in 1949 of males in eighty-seven detailed occupations, standardizing by educational level, age, and industrial distribution. The dependent variable (y) is the proportion of wage and salary workers who worked fifty to fifty-two weeks in 1949. This variable reflects both differential turnover and unemployment incidence among the groups, so it is well suited for the purpose.[47] The independent variables are full-time mean incomes in the occupations (X_1), median years of schooling (X_2), proportion of workers less than twenty-five years old (X_3), and (X_4) proportion of workers employed in durable-goods manufacturing and in construction.

The rationale for the choice of independent variables is as follows: according to the investment hypothesis, the turnover plus unemployment variable Y is a positive function of specific training costs, part of which are borne by workers, part by firms. Unfortunately, there are no data or readily available proxies for specific costs. I shall assume that such costs are positively related to the total of on-the-job training. This is a much weaker assumption than that of a positive correlation of specific training costs with wage rates.

Consider now the average wage X_1 in an occupation. This wage will tend to be higher, the higher is the average education X_2 and the greater the amount of on-the-job training in the occupation. For given values of X_2, larger X_1 will therefore tend to reflect more on-the-job training. Thus the sign of the partial regression coefficient of X_1

---

[47] The variable is also affected by seasonality. The obvious cases where seasonality is strong had fewer than 50 percent of workers employed year-round. To avoid arbitrariness, all occupations (more than twenty) with $y < 50$ percent were excluded from the analysis.

is expected to be positive. Conversely, for given occupational wage levels X_1, the higher the schooling X_2, the less on-the-job training in the occupation. Unless formal schooling itself has an effect on turnover and unemployment, the sign at X_2 should be negative. The two additional variables used in the regression, age, X_3 and industrial composition, X_4, standardize for factors other than training. Among persons less than twenty-five years of age there is more job and labor-force mobility than among older people, even when the other variables are held constant. X_4 crudely standardizes for effects of short-run demand fluctuations by industry.

Using these variables, the following regression was obtained (all variables are measured as deviations from their means; standard errors of regression coefficients are in parentheses):

$$y = 2.08X_1 + 1.86X_2 - 2.29X_3 - .74X_4$$
$$\quad\ (1.04) \qquad (.46) \qquad (.68) \qquad (.21)$$

$$R^2 = .65.$$

All variables are statistically significant. All signs, except that for X_2, conform to expectations. In particular, the positive effect of X_1 is consistent with the investment hypothesis.

Even if formal education per se had no effect on employment stability, the effects of on-the-job training (reflected in the coefficient at X_1) would explain the previously described systematic patterns of unemployment rates of workers classified by educational levels. As we have seen in Table 1, more on-the-job training is received by workers at higher educational levels.

However, in terms of the investment hypothesis, which emphasizes specific training in this context, the positive sign at X_2 is puzzling. Could it possibly reverse if the analysis were expanded to include such variables as urbanization, unionization, race, marital status? Such an expansion, if feasible, would be desirable. I experimented with inclusion of two easily accessible variables: X_5, percentage of males older than fifty-five, and X_6, percentage of non-whites in an occupation. Neither was statistically significant. Their inclusion did not increase the correlation coefficient, nor did it affect the coefficient of X_2. The inclusion of the racial variable X_6, however, lowered the coefficient of X_1 and weakened its reliability.

Is stability of employment affected by training, regardless of whether it is general or specific, acquired at school or on the job? One could argue, to be monistic, that educational levels are more strongly correlated with specific training than is on-the-job training. For example, the employer may be using information on educational attainment as an index of capability or suitability for selection to specific on-the-job training. If so, the coefficient of education (at X_2) "catches" more of the effects of specific training than does the coefficient at X_1. However, there may be good reasons for the behavior of X_2 other than the investment hypothesis, and it remains an open question for some significant exploration of unemployment phenomena.

Another way of discerning the effects of on-the-job training on employment stability is to compare population groups with the same amount of formal education but differing in on-the-job training. Comparisons by race and sex should serve the purpose. As we have seen (in this section and Table 1) the amounts invested in on-the-job training differ substantially among the groups compared within the same educational levels. It also appears that differences in amounts of on-the-job training increase with increasing educational level in both race and sex comparisons. If on-the-job training were a major factor in explaining differentials in employment stability, the investment hypothesis would predict higher unemployment rates for Negroes than for whites at each educational level and an increasing differential in rates the higher the educational level. A similar prediction would apply to the female-male comparison.

Data shown in Table 7 are differences between unemployment rates of Negro and white males classified by age and education in 1950. Negro unemployment rates are higher in almost all classifications; the difference is negligible at the lowest educational levels and, generally, increases with education. The differentials remain positive, but decrease at the highest educational level. Similar patterns have been observed by Harry Gilman for an occupational breakdown of the Negro and white male labor force, both for cross-sectional differences and cyclical changes.[48] In the occupational breakdown, the differentials increase with skill level in the "blue-collar" groups; differentials remain positive but the increase is halted in the "white-collar" groups. Additional factors, such as differential industrial attachments of "blue-collar" and "white-collar" groups are likely to be responsible for some of the deviations from the theoretical predictions. A multivariate anal-

[48]"Discrimination and the White-Non-white Unemployment Differentials" (doctoral dissertation, University of Chicago).

TABLE 7

Negro-White Unemployment Differentials,* by Age and Education,
United States Males, Civilian Labor Force, 1950

Years of Schooling	Age					Total
	25–29	30–34	35–44	45–54	55–64	
0	0.9	.8	−1.1	.3	.6	− .2
1–4	0.0	.2	.3	.3	.6	.3
5–7	.6	1.4	1.5	1.3	1.3	1.8
8	4.4	3.1	3.3	2.3	2.8	3.5
9–11	5.8	3.5	4.4	3.3	2.5	4.7
12	5.6	4.7	4.0	2.8	3.9	4.4
13–15	4.8	4.9	4.0	.4	3.8	3.8
16 or more	0.0	3.0	.9	.8	1.7	1.2

*Negro minus white unemployment rate.
Source: *U.S. Census of Population, 1950, Special Reports: Education,* Table 9.

ysis is clearly desirable. But, by and large, even the gross comparisons suggest that the investment hypothesis is relevant in explaining differences in the unemployment incidence of Negro and white labor.[49]

Comparison of unemployment rates of males and females, classified by education, show only small, apparently random, differences (Table 8). The levels are similar and decline with increasing education in

TABLE 8

Male-Female Unemployment Differentials,* by Age and Education,
Civilian Labor Force, 1950

Years of Schooling	Age				
	25–29	30–34	35–44	45–54	55–64
0	2.6	−1.4	.3	−.4	−1.5
1–4	2.5	2.2	1.4	.4	−1.4
5–7	.5	1.2	.3	.1	− .4
8	.3	1.0	.3	−.1	− .5
9–11	.8	.7	.5	.2	.3
12	−.1	.7	.1	−.3	− .6
13–15	−.6	.2	.1	−.4	− .6
16 or more	−.8	.7	.1	−.2	− .6

*Female minus male unemployment rate.
Source: *U.S. Census of Population, 1950, Special Reports, Education,* Table 9.

[49]The turnover regression analysis described before is also suggestive: once the levels of education and of on-the-job training were taken into account, the racial factor did not seem to have any discernible effects on turnover plus unemployment.

both groups. Does this mean that formal education affects unemployment rates and on-the-job training does not? This would be, prima facie, inconsistent with the other findings. A multivariate analysis is needed in which the net effect of the training factor could be isolated, in order to resolve this puzzle.[50]

SUMMARY

The empirical exploration described in this paper was designed to achieve several purposes: (1) to estimate the amount of resources invested in on-the-job training as distinguished from investments in the formal educational system, (2) to estimate rates of return on such investments, (3) to investigate the relevance of these investments to certain well-known but not well-understood patterns of income and employment behavior of population groups.

Since the research was exploratory rather than intensive, the conclusions reached are very tentative. Briefly stated: (1) Investment in on-the-job training is a very large component of total investment in education in the United States economy. Measured in terms of costs, it is as important as formal education for the male labor force and amounts to more than a half of total (male and female) expenditures on school education. Aggregate and per capita investments in on-the-job training have been increasing since 1939, though at a slower rate than investments in formal education. It seems, however, that on-the-job training has grown at a much faster rate at higher skill levels than at lower ones.

(2) The rate of return on selected investments in on-the-job training, such as apprenticeships and medical specialization, was not different from the rate of return on total costs of college education, both unadjusted for ability factors. However, the private return, that is, the return on private costs seems to be higher in formal education than in on-the-job training. These findings raise questions about possible downward biases in the calculated rates of return to education.

(3) The last section of the paper is a preliminary analysis of differential income and employment patterns of population groups, classified by education, occupation, sex, and race. The analyses are incomplete, but they suggest that new empirical knowledge about forms and amounts of investments in people can lead to a significant increase in

---

[50] The prevalence of women in cyclically insensitive jobs (clerical, government, teaching, and nursing) is an obviously plausible explanation.

our understanding of such major areas of economic behavior as income distribution, unemployment incidence, and labor mobility.

Empirical ventures into unexplored territory are hazardous. The margins of error are difficult to assess, and they are likely to be large. At least the findings should provoke further research. The need for more, better, and different data is evident. I hope that some guides for future research do emerge from this preliminary work.

Appendix

TABLE A1

Net Average Wage and Salary Incomes,* by Years of Schooling
and Age, White Urban Males, United States, 1939

(In dollars)

Age	Years of Schooling			
	16 or More	12	7–8	1–4
Less than 14†	−850	−850	−850	−340
14–15‡	−115	−115	281	258
16–17‡	−103	−103	352	315
18–19‡	−452	481	443	373
20–21‡	−400	755	579	431
22–24	1,028	947	750	503
25–29	1,661	1,244	959	648
30–34	2,395	1,606	1,179	802
35–44	3,147	2,073	1,434	916
45–54	3,483	2,286	1,570	1,018
55–64	3,147	2,105	1,439	950

*All income data are before tax.

†This now shows total rather than annual costs of elementary school per student.

‡Gross earnings of high-school and of college students were assumed to be one quarter of earnings of elementary-school graduates and of high-school graduates, respectively.

Source: Wage and Salary Incomes: Unpublished National Bureau of Economic Research materials of G. S. Becker, based on 1940 Population Census. Direct costs per student were derived from Tables 3, 5, and 6 in T. W. Schultz, "Capital Formation by Education," *Journal of Political Economy,* December, 1960, and from *Biennial Survey of Education in the United States, 1939–40.*

TABLE A2

Net Average Incomes,* by Years of Schooling and Age, United States Males, 1949

(In dollars)

Age	Years of Schooling			
	16+	12	8	1–3
Less than 14†	−1,576	−1,576	−1,576	−394
14–17‡	−205	−205	676	670
18–19‡	−910	1,071	1,079	720
20–21‡	−753	1,745	1,523	952
22–24	2,284	2,356	1,929	1,192
25–29	3,441	2,975	2,341	1,474
30–34	4,846	3,576	2,680	1,667
35–44	7,085	4,055	3,029	1,814
45–54	8,116	4,689	3,247	1,990
55–64	7,655	4,548	3,010	1,892

*See n. * in Table A1. Here income includes property income.
†See n. † in Table A1.
‡See n. ‡ in Table A1.
Source: Income data derived from *1950 Census of Population*, Ser. P-E, No. 5B, *Education*, Tables 12 and 13 (also H. P. Miller, "Income in Relation to Education," *American Economic Review*, December, 1960, Table 1. Direct costs per student derived from T. W. Schultz, *op. cit.*, and *Biennial Survey of Education, 1948–50*.

TABLE A3

Net Average Incomes,* by Years of Schooling and Age, United States Males, 1958

(In dollars)

Age	Years of Schooling			
	16+	12	8	0–4
Less than 14†	−2,400	−2,400	−2,400	−600
14–17‡	−224	−224	1,208	1,080
18–21‡	−682	2,800	1,910	1,532
22–24	3,663	3,537	2,520	1,931
25–29	5,723	4,381	3,223	2,387
30–34	7,889	5,182	3,848	2,757
35–44	10,106	6,007	4,403	3,023
45–54	11,214	6,295	4,337	3,008
55–64	10,966	6,110	3,960	2,956

Source: Income data derived from the March, 1959, *Current Population Survey*, and Miller, *op. cit.* Direct costs per student derived from *Statistical Abstract of the United States, 1960*.
*See n. * in Table A2.
†See n. † in Table A1.
‡See n. ‡ in Table A1.

Illustrative Calculation of Annual Incremental Costs of
Investment in Schooling and in On-the-Job Training
Male College Graduates, 1939

$(r = 11.0 \text{ Percent})*$

Age	Net Earnings of High School Graduates† (1)	Net Earnings of College Graduates† (2)	Differentials in Earnings ([1] − [2]) (3)	Returns on Last Year's Cost $(r \cdot C_{j-i})$ (4)	Return on All Previous Costs $(j-1$ $r \cdot \Sigma C_k$ $k = 18)$ (5)	Cost‡ at Age j ([3] + [5]) (6)
18	409	−468	877			877
19	563	−437	1,000	96	96	1,096
20	717	−407	1,124	121	217	1,341
21	793	−391	1,184	148	365	1,549
22	870	870	0	170	535	535
23	947	1,028	− 81	59	594	513
24	1,021	1,186	−165	56	650	485
25	1,095	1,344	−249	53	703	454
26	1,169	1,502	−333	50	753	420
27	1,244	1,661	−417	46	799	382
28	1,316	1,807	−491	42	841	350
29	1,388	1,954	−566	39	880	314
30	1,460	2,101	−641	35	915	274
31	1,533	2,248	−715	30	945	230
32	1,606	2,395	−789	25	970	181
33	1,668	2,495	−827	20	990	163
34	1,730	2,595	−865	18	1,008	143
35	1,792	2,695	−903	16	1,024	121
36	1,854	2,795	−941	13	1,037	96
37	1,916	2,895	−979	10	1,047	68
38	1,978	2,995	−1,017	7	1,054	37
39	2,041	3,096	−1,055	4	1,058	3

*Obtained by equating to zero the present value of col. (3) (continued to age 65).
†Age-earnings profiles from Table A1, interpolated within age groups.
‡School cost for ages 18–21; on-the-job training cost thereafter.

TABLE A5*

Estimated Cost of Schooling and of On-the-Job Training, by Age and Level of Education, United States Males, 1939

Age	Marginal Costs ($) Elementary School (r = 20.9) (1)	Marginal Costs ($) High School (r = 12.5) (2)	Marginal Costs ($) College (r = 11.0) (3)	Total Costs ($) Elementary School ([4] = [1]) (4)	Total Costs ($) High School ([1] + [2]) (5)	Total Costs ($) College ([1] + [2] + [3]) (6)	"Employment" (Thousands) Elementary School (7)	"Employment" (Thousands) High School (8)	"Employment" (Thousands) College (9)
14	510	0	0	510	510	510			
14	85	388	0	85	388	388	105.7		
15	98	455	0	98	455	455	105.7		
16	110	545	0	110	545	545	193.2		
17	125	643	0	125	643	643	193.2		
18	142	254	877	142	396	877	246.1	283.1	
19	133	200	1,096	133	333	1,096	246.1	283.1	
20	122	139	1,341	122	261	1,341	288.7	349.6	
21	108	148	1,549	108	256	1,549	288.7	349.6	
22	92	158	535	92	250	785	322.8	377.9	164.3
23	71	170	513	71	241	754	322.8	377.9	156.7
24	70	169	485	70	239	724	322.8	377.9	149.9
25	69	168	454	69	237	691	368.7	331.2	131.1
26	67	167	420	67	234	654	368.7	331.2	129.1
27	65	166	382	65	231	613	368.7	331.2	127.4
28	65	159	350	65	224	574	368.7	331.2	127.1
29	66	151	314	66	217	531	368.7	331.2	128.8
30	67	142	274	67	209	483	375.7	256.4	119.7
31	68	131	230	68	199	429	375.7	256.4	112.6

	(1)	(2)	(3)	(4)	(5)	(6)	(7)	(8)	(9)
32	118	69	181	69	187	368	375.7	256.4	108.6
33	105	64	163	64	169	332	375.7	256.4	104.7
34	90	58	143	58	148	291	375.7	256.4	101.2
35	73	51	121	51	124	245	360.4	167.1	90.0
36	54	42	96	42	96	192	360.4	167.1	67.2
37	37	31	68	31	67	135	360.4	167.1	67.2
38	18	18	37	18	32	69	360.4	167.1	67.2
39	4	4	3	4	4	7	360.4	167.1	67.2
Total cost of on-the-job training				2,000	4,400	7,900			

*Cols. (1), (2), (3) obtained by the method represented by eq. (1) in the text and illustrated in Table A4. Schooling costs are above the broken lines; on-the-job costs below it. r is the internal rate of return on the marginal costs. Columns terminate at ages when costs become zero. Thereafter they turn negative and positive for several runs; but they are small, and their sum is negligible.

Cols. (4), (5), (6) are horizontally cumulated costs for each year of training, separately for schooling (above the broken line), and for training on the job (below the broken line). Vertical sums (rounded) of training costs in col. (4), (5), (6) are shown in the bottom row. These are entered in col. (5) of text Table 1. Figures in col. (2) of text Table 1 are first differences of figures in col. (5), not vertical sums of col. (1, 2, 3) in Tables A5–A7.

Col. (7) includes male workers with eight years of education, plus half the workers with less than eight years and half the workers with more than eight and less than twelve years of schooling.

Col. (8) includes workers who have high-school education, plus half of the "some high-school" and of "some college" groups.

Col. (9) includes workers who have college education or more, plus half of the "some college" group.

In principle, the employment figures (cols. [7], [8], [9]) are supposed to represent numbers of workers of a given educational category by numbers of years elapsed since completion of schooling, and not by age. Clearly, all college students do not graduate at age twenty-two. Very few graduate at an earlier age, but large proportions do at later ages. The number of college graduates aged twenty-two, therefore, severely underestimates the number of persons who are in their first year after college graduation. The bias in numbers of workers, of course, reverses at later ages. However, since higher costs of on-the-job training decline with age, aggregate costs (Table 2) would be underestimated. This bias is roughly corrected at the college level (col. [9]) by the use of graduation rather than employment data. No such correction was made at the lower levels. Graduation at the lower levels cannot be equated with labor-force participation, and the problem of bias is less acute anyway: age dispersion at graduation and cost figures are much smaller.

Source: Cols. (7), (8), (9) 1940 Census of Population, Education, Tables 75, 76, 1950 Census of Population, G-E, No. 5B, Education, Table 9. Bureau of Labor Statistics, Special Labor Force Reports, No. 1, February, 1960, Table D; United States Department of Health, Education, and Welfare, Earned Degrees Conferred by Higher Educational Institutions, 1948–58; Biennial Survey of Education, before 1948.

TABLE A6*

Estimated Costs of Schooling and of On-the-Job Training, by Age and Level of Education, United States Males, 1949

Age	Marginal Costs ($)			Total Costs ($)			"Employment" (Thousands)		
	Elementary School (r = 22.2) (1)	High School (r = 11.8) (2)	College (r = 10.6) (3)	Elementary School (4)	High School (5)	College (6)	Elementary School (7)	High School (8)	College (9)
14	1,182	0	0	1,182	1,182	1,182			
14	375	777	0	375	777	777	98.3		
15	382	939	0	382	939	939	98.3		
16	377	1,121	0	377	1,121	1,121	184.1		
17	401	1,309	0	401	1,309	1,309	184.1		
18	316	544	1,881	316	860	1,881	233.1	425.5	
19	263	538	2,268	263	801	2,268	233.1	425.5	
20	231	441	2,778	231	672	2,778	244.7	415.7	
21	202	383	3,304	202	585	3,304	244.7	415.7	
22	157	363	1,143	157	520	1,663	285.1	443.7	342.0
23	125	329	1,273	125	454	1,727	285.1	443.7	266.7

24	130	315	1,329	130	445	1,774	285.1	443.7	204.7
25	129	307	1,335	129	436	1,771	303.5	476.8	118.3
26	123	293	1,311	123	416	1,727	303.5	476.8	114.6
27	108	268	1,294	108	376	1,670	303.5	476.8	112.0
28	114	264	1,267	114	378	1,640	303.5	476.8	138.6
29	104	255	1,260	104	359	1,619	303.5	476.8	169.7
30	102	225	1,252	102	327	1,579	329.5	442.1	169.2
31	94	196	1,218	94	290	1,508	329.5	442.1	173.1
32	76	148	1,150	76	224	1,374	329.5	442.1	164.2
33	45	161	1,075	45	206	1,281	329.5	442.1	157.8
34	30	154	1,008	30	184	1,192	329.5	442.1	150.1
35	16	167	884	16	183	1,067	379.3	387.5	139.5
36		151	763		151	914		387.5	125.8
37		143	599		143	742		387.5	125.8
38		149	432		149	581		387.5	125.8
39		156	228		156	384		387.5	125.8
40		129	47		129	176		267.5	115.8
41		89	17		89	106		267.5	115.8
42		65			65	65		267.5	115.8
43		17			17	17		267.5	115.8
Total cost of on-the-job training				3,902	8,600	24,300			

*See notes to Table A5.

319

TABLE A7*

Estimated Costs of Schooling and of On-the-Job Training, by Age and Level of Education, United States Males, 1958

Age	Marginal Costs ($)			Total Costs ($)			"Employment" (Thousands)		
	Elementary School ($r = 19.3$) (1)	High School ($r = 15.1$) (2)	College ($r = 11.5$) (3)	Elementary School (4)	High School (5)	College (6)	Elementary School (7)	High School (8)	College (9)
14	1,800	0	0	1,800	1,800	1,800			
14	296	1,266	0	296	1,266	1,266	65.8		
15	314	1,538	0	314	1,538	1,538	65.8		
16	303	1,917	0	303	1,917	1,917	73.8		
17	300	2,338	0	300	2,338	2,338	73.8		
18	297	225	3,246	297	522	3,246	191.5	361.4	
19	293	224	3,776	293	517	3,776	191.5	361.4	
20	289	223	4,368	289	512	4,368	182.4	432.3	
21	284	222	5,027	284	506	5,027	182.4	432.3	
22	278	220	2,090	278	498	2,588	182.4	432.3	385.7
23	271	217	2,001	271	488	2,489	182.4	432.3	360.0
24	262	214	1,902	262	476	2,378	182.4	432.3	335.3
25	251	211	1,891	251	462	2,353	254.5	502.1	285.4

26	237	208	1,880	237	445	2,325	254.5	502.1	289.0
27	221	204	1,660	221	425	2,085	254.5	502.1	304.4
28	202	200	1,528	202	402	1,930	254.5	502.1	332.7
29	180	195	1,367	180	375	1,752	254.5	502.1	387.3
30	161	189	1,197	161	350	1,547	254.5	502.1	392.2
31	153	183	1,149	153	336	1,485	254.5	502.1	359.5
32	144	175	1,096	144	319	1,415	254.5	502.1	264.2
33	133	165	1,037	133	298	1,335	254.5	502.1	192.2
34	120	154	971	120	274	1,245	254.5	502.1	125.9
35	104	141	898	104	245	1,143	323.5	501.6	117.1
36	85	126	815	85	211	1,026	323.5	501.6	114.0
37	63	109	719	63	172	991	323.5	501.6	140.6
38	37	89	616	37	126	742	323.5	501.6	171.7
39	6	67	501	6	73	574	323.5	501.6	175.6
40		43	423		43	466		501.6	165.0
41		16	339		16	355		501.6	165.0
42			245			246			165.0
43			144			144			165.0
44			27			27			165.0
Total cost of on-the-job training				5,300	8,200	30,700			

*See notes to Table A5.

TABLE A8

Average Wage and Salary Income and Median Years of Schooling of Apprentices, Operatives, and Journeymen in Three Industry Groups, 1949

	Metal Trades (4 Years)*		Printing and Publishing (5.5 Years)*		Construction (3.8 Years)*	
	Schooling	Wage	Schooling	Wage	Schooling	Wage
Apprentices	12.2	$2,480	12.2	$2,525	11.8	$2,576
Operatives (in same industry)	9.0	3,015	10.4	3,239	8.8	2,937
With more schooling†	11.3	3,286	11.3	3,500	11.3	3,208
Assuming a 10 percent return on schooling‡		3,415		3,540		3,340
Journeymen	9.5	3,534	10.9	4,138	8.9	3,216

*Average length of apprenticeship.
†In industries where they are found.
‡This return is added to the wage figure in second row. k = row 5 minus row 2; d_1 = row 2 minus row 1; d_2 = row 3 minus row 1; d_3 = row 4 minus row 1.

Source: *U.S. Census of Population, 1950: Special Reports, Occupational Characteristics*, Tables 10 and 23.

TABLE A9

Net Average Incomes of Females with and without Adjustment for
Labor-Force Participation Rates, by Level of Education and
Age, 1949

(In dollars)

Age	Unadjusted		Adjusted*	
	High School (1)	College (2)	High School (3)	College (4)
18–19	970	−786	970	−786
20–21	1,468	−706	1,468	−706
22–24	1,614	1,900	734	1,313
25–29	1,635	2,120	520	939
30–34	1,674	2,293	532	1,016
35–44	1,859	2,600	662	1,277
45–54	2,062	2,907	767	1,608
55–64	1,968	2,974	559	1,448

*Observed average incomes multiplied by labor-force rates after age twenty-two.
Rates from Gertrude Bancroft, *The American Labor Force* (New York: John Wiley & Son, 1958), Table D, p. 62.
Source: *U.S. Census of Population, 1950, Special Reports, Education,* Tables 10 and 12.

TABLE A10

Mean Incomes of Non-white Males, by Age and
Education Level, United States, 1950

(In dollars)

Age	No Schooling	Education		
		Elementary School	High School	College or More
18–19	570	809	809	
20–21	808	1,177	1,349	
22–24	997	1,520	1,783	1,555
25–29	1,109	1,747	2,137	2,121
30–34	1,187	1,916	2,374	2,950
35–44	1,300	2,008	2,453	3,437
45–54	1,254	2,068	2,419	3,639
55–64	1,108	1,921	2,238	3,246

Source: Computed from distributions given in *U.S. Census of Population, 1950,* Vol. IV, *Special Reports, Education,* Table 12.

C. Education in Production

17. Education in Production*

F. WELCH
Southern Methodist University and
National Bureau of Economic Research

There have been several studies of the demand for education as an investment good[1] which generally take input and product prices as given and concentrate on computing (internal) rates of return to investment in schooling. Although these estimates usually indicate returns that are high by most standards, there is considerable variation, both through time and space, which points to the need for a clearer understanding of the underlying factors affecting profitability of investment in people. For such an analysis, education must be viewed not only as an investment but also as a factor of production.

In this paper, I consider the question: Why has the incentive been maintained for a relative expansion in the supply of skilled labor in the United States? Three alternative explanations are considered, and one is pursued with an empirical analysis of factors determining relative wages among skill classes in agriculture. As we would expect for any factor of production, the evidence suggests that the return to education is affected by factor ratios, but ratios do not tell the whole story. In agriculture, much of the "leverage" distinguishing college graduates from less schooled persons has its roots in technical change as reflected in the level of research activity. Thus the incentive for acquiring a college education is based on dynamical considerations of changing technology; and if technology becomes stagnant, this incentive is reduced and may disappear.

*Reprinted from "Education in Production," *Journal of Political Economy*, LXXVIII (January 1970), 35–59. Copyright by The University of Chicago Press.

[1] See, for example, Gary S. Becker's estimates for college graduates (1960) and for high school graduates (1964).

Convincing evidence of the maintained incentive for acquiring schooling is found in Gary Becker's (1964) estimates of private rates of return which are reproduced in Table 1. When these rates of return are compared to the accompanying rise in average educational levels (Table 2), the paradox of education as a factor of production becomes clear: *With the phenomenal rise in average education, why have rates of return failed to decline?* As Table 2 shows, in 1940 about one adult in four had a high school education; by 1950, one in three had that much schooling; and the corresponding figure for 1960 is two in five. Thus, during two decades, the proportion of high school graduates increased by two-thirds, and the rate of return to a high school education increased by three-fourths (from 16 to 28 percent). During that same period, the proportion of college graduates also increased by two-thirds, and the rate of return to a college education failed to fall.

TABLE 1

Private Rates of Return from College and
High-School Education for Selected Years Since 1939
(percent)

Year of Cohort	College Graduate (1)	High-School Graduates (2)
1939	14.5	16
1949	13+	20
1956	12.4	25
1958	14.8	28
1959 1961	slightly higher than in 1958	

Source: Gary Becker, *Human Capital*, NBER, 1964, Table 14.

TABLE 2

Schooling of the Population, 25 Years
Old and Over. 1940–1960

Amount of Schooling	1940	1950	1960
A. Less than 8 years of school completed	31.8	26.7	22.1
B. 4 years of high school or more	24.1	33.4	40.1
C. Completed college	4.6	6.0	7.7

Source: U.S. Bureau of the Census, *Statistical Abstract of the United States: 1966.* (87th edition) Washington, D.C.: 1966. Table No. 154.

Investment in Education

It is obvious that changes have occurred to prevent the decline in returns to acquiring education that would normally accompany a rise in average educational levels. Presumably, these changes have resulted in growth in demand for the investment good, education, sufficient to absorb the increased supply with constant or rising returns. When the value of the services provided by education is determined in production, growth in demand for the investment good must be accompanied by growth in demand for the factor of production relative to supply cost.

The most creditable explanations of growth in the demand for education can be grouped as follows:

1. *Growth industries.* — The pattern of growth in the value of industrial output may have been such that the most rapidly expanding industries are the most skill intensive. The important considerations are the income and demand elasticities for the industries' products together with rates of income growth and differential rates of technical change.

If the impetus for expansion of an industry comes through expanding product demand, then income elasticities are important. As incomes rise, the composition of consumption changes; and if income elasticities of demand are positively related to the share of skilled labor among industries, the demand for skilled labor will rise relative to the demand for other forms of labor.

If the impetus for expansion comes from reduced costs of production, then demand elasticities are clearly relevant. Holding constant the level of technology in other industries, suppose that neutral technical change shifts the cost curves of all firms in an industry downward as a result of an equiproportionate increase in the marginal productivity of all factors. This change will result in an increased demand for factors used by the industry only if the resultant decline in product price is accompanied by a rise in total revenue, that is, if the demand for the industry's product is price elastic. Growth in total revenue is necessary for growth in the demand for factors used by an industry.[2] If growth rates in total revenue resulting from differential

[2]The rate of growth in total revenue resulting from neutral technical change is simply the rate of technical changes times the elasticity of total revenue with respect to technical change. Since a 1 percent increase in the marginal productivity of all factors results in (approximately) a 1 percent fall in product price, the elasticity of total revenue with respect to neutral technical change is the elasticity of total revenue with respect to product price (one plus the price elasticity of demand) with opposite sign. Com-

rates of neutral technical change are positively related among industries to the share of skilled labor, changing technology will increase the demand for skilled relative to unskilled labor.

The changing composition of industrial activity may have been an important source of growth in the demand for education, particularly in light of the expansion of the skill-intensive industries associated with government expenditures for defense, space exploration, research, and so forth.

2. *Non-neutrality in production.* — The changing composition of production may have increased the demand for education. There are two possibilities here:

a) Physical inputs other than labor may be relatively enhancing to the productivity of skilled labor. As the quantity and the quality of nonlabor inputs have increased through time, this growth may have tended to increase the productivity of more, relative to less, skilled labor.

b) Technical change may not be neutral between skill classes. It may be that increments in technology result in increments in the relative productivity of labor that are positively related to skill level.

Although the distinction between (a) and (b) disappears if we view the rise in the quality of nonlabor inputs as the embodiment of technical change, there is another sense in which technical change may be non-neutral between skills. Nelson and Phelps (1966) have argued that at any point in time the level of available technology differs from the level of embodied or used technology, the difference being the "technology gap." They also argue that one dimension of education is the ability to adjust to changing conditions and that another dimension may be the ability to innovate. As such, the productivity of education would be positively related to the rate of change in useful technology (the ability to change) and to the size of the technological gap (room for innovation). In this case, if the rate of utilization of technology is accelerating or if the technology gap is growing, the return to education will rise relative to that of other inputs.

---

bining the two "growth effects," the rate of change in an industry's total revenue (holding constant the quantity of factors used) is $\dot{I}\xi + \dot{r}(\mid \eta \mid -1)$, where $\dot{I}$ is the percentage growth rate in income; ξ, the income elasticity of demand; $\dot{r}$, the percentage rate of change in neutral factor productivity in this relative to the average of other industries; and η is the price elasticity of demand for the industry's product.

3. *Changing "quality" of schooling.*—Other things being equal, if the rate of skill assimilation (learning) per unit of resource commitment rises, the return to education will rise, relative to the cost.

From a social point of view, an increase in learning per unit of resource commitment corresponds to technical change in industries producing "learning."

From a private point of view, this change may refer to an increase in the commitment of resources whose costs are not borne privately relative to those that are. An increase in quality of schooling is an obvious example. In public schools, the most important private cost is the opportunity cost of school attendance. An increase in quality of schooling—either technical change in the production of schooling or an increase in the commitment of resources supplied by school systems—will result in increased learning per unit of student time in attendance and will increase the private return to school attendance.

While there may be numerous other explanations, I think that these represent the most fruitful avenues for research. The first refers to the changing composition of industrial activity and requires an analysis, industry by industry, of changes in skill requirements. The second refers to the physical production process and within it to the interrelationships between all productive factors including "technology" and is pursued in the final sections of this paper. Finally, there is quality of schooling. To date, we have been unable to say much about factors determining quality. Although we know something about factors determining test scores (production functions?), we have been unable to bridge the gap between test scores and the value of education.[3]

It should be noted that fully neutral technical growth which proceeds at the same rate in all industries is not included, although it is an explanation which has been put forward.[4] In his benchmark analysis, *Human Capital,* Becker (1964) indicated that fully neutral technical growth which is uniform in all industries, including those

---

[3]In particular see Thomas (1962) and Coleman (1966).

[4]See, in particular, Ruth Klinov-Malul (1966) where she states: "Suppose per capita income increases by K percent annually, in such a way that every earner gets an additional K percent of income each year. This in itself would make additional education more profitable, since absolute differentials will increase" (p. 7). This change is sufficient for an increased demand for education only if costs do not rise in proportion to returns, i.e., if there is technical change in producing education.

producing human capital, is capable of providing an incentive for expanding the relative supply of skilled labor. His argument is:

> If progress were uniform in all industries and neutral with respect to all factors, and if there were constant costs, initially all wages would rise by the same proportion and the prices of all goods including the output of industries supplying the investment in human capital would be unchanged. Since wage ratios would be unchanged, firms would have no incentive initially to alter their factor proportions. Wage differences, on the other hand, would rise at the same rate as wages and since investment costs would be unchanged, there would be an incentive to invest more in human capital and thus to increase the relative supply of skilled persons [p. 53].

There is no reason to doubt the validity of this argument. It is sufficient that *all* of Becker's "leverage" stems from the assumed technical growth in education-producing industries. Consider a situation in which neutral technical growth occurs in all industries *except* those producing education. In other industries, the return to all factors will rise as a result of the increased productivity. Thus, the return to education will have increased. Since the presumed growth is neutral, the increase in return will be proportional to that of other factors. But it is important that increased returns cannot be considered as providing an incentive to expand the supply of skilled labor unless it can be demonstrated that costs have not risen in proportion to returns. In this case, if education-producing industries are competitive purchasers of the inputs they use in the sense that the input supply functions facing the industry are perfectly elastic, costs will rise in proportion to returns, leaving the profitability of educational investments unaffected.[5] Education-producing industries will find that input prices will rise in response to improved alternatives in other industries, and, since productivity has not increased in the education industries, costs will rise in proportion to factor prices.

The primary purpose of this paper is to speculate about the nature of education when it is viewed as a factor of production. In doing so it seems natural to concentrate on factors determining marginal pro-

---

[5] "Profitability" refers to the rate of return on the investment. If there are capital market imperfections as is commonly asserted, since education is internally financed by the family, then this change could actually reduce the incentive to invest in schooling. This, because the cost of schooling would have increased. Of course, the family's earned income would also have increased.

ductivity or relative wages between schooling classes. Evidence provided by Zvi Griliches (1968) and reproduced in Table 3 shows that the time path of relative wages has been similar to Becker's estimates for the path of rates of return. For college graduates, relative wages have shown no downward tendency, and for high school graduates there is an apparent upward tendency, although it is less marked than seems true of rates of return.

TABLE 3

Ratios of Mean Incomes for U.S. Males
by Schooling Categories, 1939–1966

Selected Year	High School Graduates to Elementary School Graduates		College Graduates to High School Graduates	
1939	1.40[a]		1.57[c]	
1949	1.41	1.34[b]	1.63	
1958		1.48	1.65	
1959		1.30		1.51[d]
1963		1.49	1.45	
1966		1.56	1.52	

[a] Elementary: 7–8 years.
[b] Elementary: 8 years.
[c] College: 4+ years.
[d] College: 4 years.
Source: Zvi Griliches, "Notes on the Role of Education in Production Functions and Growth Accounting" (unpublished paper, Department of Economics, University of Chicago), May 1968.

In shifting the focus to relative wages we lose little information about factors affecting the profitability of educational investments since rates of return are likely to be dominated by relative wages, as is demonstrated in the agreement in their time paths. In fact, this association can easily be seen by simple manipulation of the internal rate formula.[6] For private rates of return, the most important factors

---

[6] Let

$$\sum_{t=1}^{L} R_t (1 + r)^{-t} = 0 \qquad (1)$$

define the internal rate of return, r, where R_t refers to net benefits in period t and L is the life of the investment. For an investment in schooling, net benefits correspond to cost incurred in school and afterwards to differences between the wage of schooled and unschooled labor.

are: (1) the relative wage, (2) the shape of the age-income profile, and (3) either quality of schooling or, what amounts to the same thing, the state of educational technology.

In the remainder of the paper, I concentrate on factors determining

---

Suppose that in order to acquire a given skill, it is necessary to attend school for e years; that without the skill, a laborer earns W_{ut} in period t; and, W_{st} with the skill. For this skill, the internal rate of return is given by

$$\sum_{t=1}^{e} W_{ut}(1 + r)^{-t} = \sum_{t=e+1}^{L} (W_{st} - W_{ut})(1 + r)^{-t}. \tag{2}$$

Notice that direct cost of schooling is ignored. When considering private rates of return to public elementary and secondary schooling, direct cost is often trivial in comparison to the student's opportunity cost and, even for college, private cost is dominated by opportunity cost. For example, Becker (1965, pp. 74–75) estimates that in 1939 about 74 percent of the private cost of college students was foregone income and the remaining 26 percent was direct cost. And in any case, I am concerned with partial effects of the variables in equation (2) on the internal rate of return and it is obvious that, *ceteris paribus*, an increase in direct cost will reduce the rate of return. There is an element of ambiguity here since skilled labor accounts for a fairly large share of direct cost. Thus, in considering the effects of an increase in the relative wage of skilled labor, this increase will cause both costs and returns to rise. Excluding direct cost from the analysis amounts to the assumption that the effect on the return to education of a change in the wage of skilled labor swamps the effect on cost.

In equation (2), factor W_{ut} to the left of each term and divide the equation by W'_u. We have then

$$\sum_{t=1}^{e} \frac{W_{ut}}{W'_u}(1 + r)^{-t} = \sum_{t=e+1}^{L} \frac{W_{ut}}{W'_u}\left(\frac{W_{st}}{W_{ut}} - 1\right)(1 + r)^{-t}. \tag{3}$$

Assume that

$$W'_u = \sum_{t=1}^{L} W_{ut},$$

i.e., W'_u is equal to the total undiscounted lifetime earnings of an unskilled laborer. Then $W_{ut}/W'_u = p_t$, is the proportion of the unskilled laborer's lifetime earnings realized in year t. The set of p's (p_t; $t = 1, \ldots, L$) can be considered as a distribution function which implies the shape of the lifetime age-earning profile for unskilled labor.

Since the first-order conditions for cost minimization require that marginal physical productivities of factors be proportionate to marginal factor costs, by assuming competitive markets in which factor prices are marginal factor costs and assuming cost minimization, we have the implication that W_{st}/W_{ut} is the marginal rate of substitution, MRS_t, of unskilled for skilled laborers in period t.

Substituting p_t and MRS_t into equation (3) gives

$$\sum_{t=1}^{e} p_t(1 + r)^{-t} = \sum_{t=e+1}^{L} p_t(MRS_t - 1)(1 + r)^{-t}. \tag{4}$$

Thus, the internal rate of return to schooling can be viewed as a function dominated by three classes of variables: first, the marginal rates of substitution (through time) between laborers with differing skills; second, the "shape" of the age-income profile; and third, the state of the "arts" in the production of skill. Restated, $r = r(MRS[t], p[t], e/L)$.

331

the productive value of education in a single industry. The changing composition of demand between industries and changes in the quality of schooling are left for another day.

Standard competitive theory, in its assumption of perfect information, rules out allocative ability as a source of the return to a factor. With complete information, there is no room for the concept of a superior alternative since in equilibrium all alternatives are equally good at the margin. That is, the perfect information assumption implies that the return to a factor is proportional to its marginal contribution to *physical* product. But, for education and some other intangibles, it is not clear that the direct contribution to physical production accounts for the total contribution to revenue. There have been attempts to modify the competitive model to allow for "entrepreneural capacity," but the return to this ability is almost always computed as a residual, total revenue less the cost of other things, which does not facilitate marginal analysis. Yet, firms clearly make marginal decisions vis-à-vis allocative abilities. They sometimes hire new "managers" and invest both in market and production information. As an alternative to computing marginal factor revenue as being proportional to marginal physical product in which all other things are held *constant,* I explore the implications of variations of an input (education) whose function, in part, is to *vary* the use of other inputs.

It seems plausible that the productive value of education has its roots in two distinct phenomena. Increased education simply may permit a worker to accomplish more with the resources at hand. This "worker effect" is the marginal product of education as marginal product is normally defined, that is, it is the increased output per unit change in education holding other factor quantities constant. On the other hand, increased education may enhance a worker's ability to acquire and decode information about costs and productive characteristics of other inputs. As such, a change in education results in a change in other inputs including, perhaps, the use of some "new" factors that otherwise would not be used. The return to education is therefore considered as consisting of two effects: a "worker effect" and an "allocative effect."

In recent years, we have stressed the importance of education as a factor of production and have included it, often as an adjustment for quality of labor, as a variable in estimates of production functions. Consider three "production functions" to distinguish the role of education in each: (1) the engineering production function of a single commodity; (2) a production function of gross sales; and (3) a production function of value added by some subset of factors supplied by the firm or industry, the other inputs being "purchased." As I show, when the marginal product of education is treated as a partial derivative, the composition of the bundle of "other things" held constant is crucial.

In each case, production is assumed to be technically efficient in the sense that for given inputs, physical output is maximized.

For the engineering function, we have

$$Q = q(X, E),$$

where Q, physical output, is a function of education, E, and other inputs, X. In this case, the marginal product of education is $\partial q / \partial E$ and refers only to the worker effect. As noted earlier, it refers to the ability to accomplish more (physical output), given the resources at hand. By including education or "knowledge" as an explicit factor of production, the concept of technical efficiency becomes something of a tautology. *Production is technically efficient if producers do not knowingly waste resources.* If they waste resources but are ignorant of doing so, the loss is attributed to a lack of knowledge. Presumably, the worker effect is related to the complexity of the physical production process. In the engineering function there is no room for allocative ability, since questions of allocation do not arise. In the remaining functions, education is excluded as an explicit factor. To include it would only reiterate the worker effect which is obvious in the engineering function.

Now consider gross sales for firms producing more than one product. With two commodities, we have,

$$Q = p_1 q_1(x_1) + p_2 q_2(x_2),$$

where p_1 and p_2 refer to the prices (assumed exogenous to the producer) of the respective commodities, q_1 and q_2. Both commodities are assumed to be functions of the input vector, X. The quantity of X used in producing q_1 is denoted by x_1 and similarly for x_2. In this case, assume that X is given, but that its allocation among competing uses x_1 and x_2 is not. Here, technical efficiency refers to being on the product transformation frontier, that is, of maximizing q_1, given q_2

Investment in Education

and X, and does not correspond to maximization of sales, Q, given X. To maximize Q, we have

$$\frac{\partial Q}{\partial x_1} = p_1\frac{\partial q_1}{\partial x_1} - p_2\frac{\partial q_2}{\partial x_2} = 0$$

as the first-order condition. Maximization of sales requires technical efficiency and that the marginal value product of X be equated between its competing uses. Suppose that productive capacities of some factors are not equally understood by all who use them so that Q, given X, is not necessarily maximized. Suppose further that the allocation of X among its alternatives is a function of education, that is, $x_1 = x_1(E)$. In this case, the marginal product of education,

$$\frac{\partial Q}{\partial E} = \left(p_1\frac{\partial q_1}{\partial x_1} - p_2\frac{\partial q_2}{\partial x_2}\right)\frac{dx_1}{dE}$$

is positive if education enhances allocative ability. Thus when education is treated as a factor in functions producing gross sales, if the allocation of inputs among alternatives is not an explicit part of the function, we have the inference that the marginal product of education includes gains in allocative efficiency as well as the worker effect.

In considering value added, assume that there is only one product. Nothing is gained by multiple products since the question of allocation between competing uses is obvious in the previous example. Value added is expressed as $Q = pq(X, Z) - p_xX$, where p refers to commodity price and q, physical product, is a function of purchased inputs, X, and inputs supplied by the firm or industry, Z. The price of X is p_x, and both p_x and p are assumed exogenous to the producer. Here, maximization of Q with respect to X gives $\partial Q/\partial X = p(\partial q/\partial x) - p_x = 0$, which is the marginal productivity theory, that is, in equilibrium the value of the marginal product of X should equal its price. When Q is maximized with respect to X, we have the inference that value added is a function of Z only. But, again assume that producers are not equally adept at assessing productivity and that the quantity of X purchased is a function of education. In this case, the marginal product of education,

$$\frac{\partial Q}{\partial E} = \left(p\frac{\partial q}{\partial x} - p_x\right)\frac{dX}{dE}.$$

Here, the question of the *ceteris paribus* bundle is obvious. If a produc-

334

tion function of value added is estimated and X is introduced as an explanatory variable, a positive marginal product denotes under-utilization (at the mean) and vice versa for a negative marginal product. Alternatively, X can be excluded as an explicit variable and education included, in which case the marginal product of education reflects comovement between X and E with any resulting allocative gains or losses. Thus, if a value-added function, based on multiple products, is estimated which specifies the quantity of supplied inputs, Z, but does not specify allocation among competing uses, and if purchased inputs are omitted, the marginal product of education will contain three elements. First is the worker effect, then there is the question of selecting the quantity of other inputs, and finally the allocation of these inputs among their alternatives.

These effects can be combined by considering a value-added production function in which there are two products produced, q_1 and q_2, and each is a function of three inputs: education, E; other inputs supplied by the firm, Z; and purchased inputs, X. The respective commodity prices are p_1 and p_2, and p_x is the price of X. We have value added by education and other supplied inputs,

$$Q = p_1 q_1(x_1, z_1, E_1) + p_2 q_2(x_2, z_2, E_2) - p_x X.$$

Where $E = E_1 + E_2$, $Z^0 = z_1 + z_2$, $X = x_1 + x_2$; and

$$1 = \frac{dE_1}{dE} + \frac{dE_2}{dE}, \qquad 0 = \frac{dz_1}{dE} + \frac{dz_2}{dE}, \quad \text{and} \quad \frac{dX}{dE} = \frac{dx_1}{dE} + \frac{dx_2}{dE}.$$

If value added is taken as a function of the total quantities of education and supplied inputs, $Q = f(E, Z^0)$, the marginal product of education,

$$\frac{\partial f}{\partial E} = p_2 \frac{\partial q_2}{\partial E} + \left(p_1 \frac{\partial q_1}{\partial E} - p_2 \frac{\partial q_2}{\partial E} \right) \frac{dE_1}{dE} + \left(p_1 \frac{\partial q_1}{\partial z} - p_2 \frac{\partial q_2}{\partial z} \right) \frac{dz_1}{dE}$$

$$+ \left(p_1 \frac{\partial q_1}{\partial x} - p_2 \frac{\partial q_2}{\partial x} \right) \frac{dx_1}{dE} + \left(p_2 \frac{\partial q_2}{\partial x} - p_x \right) \frac{dE}{dE}.$$

Where the first term is the "own" value of the marginal product of education, the worker effect, the next three terms refer to the gains from allocating the respective factors, education, supplied inputs, and purchased inputs, efficiently between competing uses, and the last term refers to the allocative gain from selecting the "right" quantity of purchased inputs, X. If this were a production function of sales, dX/dE would equal zero and the effects of selecting the input bundle would be lost.

Since returns to education include allocative ability, estimates of the productive value of education should include a provision for these returns. This can be done explicitly by the use of total derivatives or implicitly through profit or value-added functions.[7] Production functions of gross revenue include the worker effect and the effect of allocating factors between competing uses but exclude the effect of selecting the "right" quantities of other inputs. Engineering production functions reveal only the worker effect.

Perhaps this helps reconcile the inconsistency between the estimates of Griliches (1964) and Kislev (1965) of the productive value of education in agriculture. Using similar data, both estimated an agricultural production function of gross revenue for 1959. At the state level of aggregation, Griliches found schooling to be an important source of productivity, whereas Kislev, working with county data, found little or no return to schooling. The level of aggregation may be the key to understanding the difference in their estimates. While both used gross revenue as their measure of output and therefore permit education to capture the gains from allocating resources between competing uses, it is clear that agriculture at the state level is much more diversified, vis-à-vis product, than at the county level. Thus the state aggregate permits more "room" for allocative ability than does the county. It is also clear that to the extent that education affects the choice of which inputs to use, both Griliches and Kislev understated the productive value of education because both held other input quantities (including purchased inputs) constant in estimating marginal productivity.

This also helps interpret a peculiar result of an earlier attempt of my own (Welch 1966) to analyze the determinants of the value of schooling in U.S. agriculture. The dependent variable in my analysis, the return to eight years of schooling, was assumed to be the value of the marginal product (as a partial derivative) of schooling in agriculture. Clearly, when the return to schooling is estimated from wages, it includes gains to allocative ability. The coefficient estimates indicated that the share of labor in agriculture is about three-fourths of total

---

[7]Value added functions become profit functions in the extreme as all inputs are treated as purchased (variable).

output and the share of nonlabor inputs is one-fourth; factor shares more relevant to value-added than to gross sales.[8]

The first clear-cut distinction between worker and allocative effects is provided by Chaudhri (1968). In trying to assess the impact of education on Indian agriculture, he estimates an aggregate production function (at the state level) of gross revenue. Although statistical problems of few observations and large error-variance in coefficients preclude strong statements, Chaudhri fails to demonstrate that education is an important source of productivity. He argues (partly in error) that, in his estimated function, marginal product of education refers to the worker effect alone, and to capture the allocative effect he provides evidence showing in case after case that the composition of the "other" input bundle varies with the incidence of secondary schooling in the farm labor force. His conclusions reinforce the Nelson and Phelps (1966) contention that education enhances innovative ability as he demonstrates that the use of modern, as opposed to conventional, inputs is positively related to education. In this context, innovative ability is one dimension of allocative ability.

THE CASE OF AGRICULTURE

The empirical analysis of factors determining the productivity of schooling is restricted to agriculture in the United States. There are two good reasons for doing so. First, the data are fairly accessible. The effort of others, particularly Griliches in his work on the sources of measured productivity growth (1963a, and 1963b, 1964) shows many relevant considerations; also the work of Evenson (1967, 1968) refines some aspects of the original Griliches measures. The ability to build on this kind of empirical foundation does not exist outside of agriculture. The second reason is that U.S. agriculture is highly dynamic technically. The well-known concept of the farmer on the treadmill places peculiar emphasis upon innovative effort. A rapid rate of "technical change" together with an inelastic aggregate product demand implies that there is continual pressure on some factors, particularly labor, to leave agriculture, and the ability to stay current with respect to productive techniques determines whether a firm will exist in the long run. While these factors favor the selection of agriculture, there is one shortcoming.

[8] I failed to recognize the significance of this result, and although I referred to the underlying production process as one of value added, the measure of non-labor inputs included purchased inputs.

Agriculture is probably atypical inasmuch as a larger share of the productive value of education may refer to allocative ability than in most industries. Farming usually includes a diversified set of activities for which allocative decisions are made continuously as part of the normal routine. In other industries, the jobs of a large portion of the work force do not involve decisions for which prices are relevant. Too, in most industries jobs performed by persons with different education are more sharply differentiated than in agriculture, and, in these cases, the physical productivity of education is more easily understood. In agriculture, differences in job complexity associated with differences in education are less noticeable, and the product of education is more likely to be associated with allocative efficiency. Does education enable one to pick more grapes or do a better job of driving a tractor? Even if it does, these "worker" effects are probably small when compared with the considerable differences revealed in income. Allocative ability plays a key role in determining education's productivity in agriculture and is most relevant in a dynamic setting.

The relevance of dynamical factors is stressed by Schultz (1964) when he suggests that, in economies in which agricultural production is accomplished almost solely by the use of "traditional" factors, there is reason to believe that factors are more efficiently allocated than in "modern" agricultural economies. Schultz's interpretation is that traditional agriculture is close to an economic equilibrium in adjusting to relatively stationary techniques. Because of this, judgments about factors are based upon extensive observation; the stationary technology guarantees ample time to explore the potential of factors being used.

In contrast, in a technically dynamic agriculture, a factor may be obsolete before its productivity can be fully explored! Herein, I think, lies the explanation of education's productivity. If educated persons are more adept at critically evaluating new and reportedly improved input varieties, if they can distinguish more quickly between the systematic and random elements of productivity responses, then in a dynamical context educated persons will be more productive. Furthermore, the *extent* of the productivity differentials between skill levels will be directly related to the rate of flow of new inputs into agriculture.

In the empirical analysis that follows, I concentrate on determinants of relative wages among three skill classes: college graduates, high school graduates, and persons with one to four years of schooling (functional illiterates). As is described in the Appendix, laborers in intermediate classes are treated as linear combinations of persons in these three classes. For example, a person with eight years of schooling is "counted" as 0.46 of a person with one to four years of schooling, 0.53 of a high school graduate, and so on for the schooling classes: 0, 5–7, 9–11, and 13–15 years. Wages refer to males 45–54 years old, and the associated number of persons in each skill class refers to a white male, 45–54 years old, equivalent wage earner. It is assumed that a laborer's wage is his marginal product from an underlying production process of value added by labor and inputs supplied by farms. Nonlabor inputs include a measure of the flow of services from land, machinery, and livestock inventories. Purchased inputs are excluded.

The measure that I use for the rate of flow of new inputs is a weighted average of expenditures per farm for research over the past nine years. As a measure of the availability of information about new inputs, I include an average over the past four years of the number of days spent (per farm) on farms by state and federal extension staff.

The unit of observation is the "state" of which there are forty-nine. The thirty-nine "states" used by Griliches (1964) are included together with a breakdown of ten Southern states[9] into white and nonwhite. The white-nonwhite specification is in recognition of the segregation of the Federal Extension Service prior to 1962. While factor ratios and research are treated as the same level in the white and nonwhite sector of each of the ten states, the extension variable refers to days spent on white and nonwhite farms, respectively.[10]

Table 4 provides estimates of factors affecting relative wages in agriculture. Although coefficients on inputs are reported separately, the equations are estimated using factor ratios so that the sum of the coefficients on the inputs is constrained to equal zero. All variables except research and extension are in logarithms.

In Table 4, regression equations (1) and (2) raise as many questions as they answer. Notice that in each equation the coefficient estimates indicate that the relative productivity of a college graduate is increased by increasing the number of college graduates, although not "significantly" so. There is another peculiarity of these two equations. In

[9] The states include: Alabama, Arkansas, Georgia, Louisiana, Mississippi, North Carolina, South Carolina, Tennessee, Texas, and Virginia.

[10] For an enlightening discussion of the segregation of the Federal Extension Service, see U.S. Commission on Civil Rights (1965).

TABLE 4

Estimates of Factors Affecting the Productivity
of More Relative to Less Schooled Persons
in U.S. Agriculture, 1959*

Independent Variables	Dependent Variables			
	W_{16+}/W_{12} (1)	W_{16+}/W_{1-4} (2)	W_{12}/W_{1-4}	
			(3)	(4)
1. Functional	.054	.442	.388	.359
illiterates	(.037)	(.048)	(.039)	(.038)
2. High school	.034	−.426	−.460	−.359
graduates	(.084)	(.109)	(.089)	(.038)
3. College	.048	.062	.014	
graduates	(.064)	(.083)	(.068)	
4. Non-labor	−.136	−.078	.058	
inputs	(.034)	(.045)	(.036)	
5. Research	.056	.179	.123	
expenditures	(.094)	(.122)	(.100)	
($00) per farm				
6. Days per farm	−.130	−.136	−.006	
by extension	(.078)	(.101)	(.082)	
7. Nonwhite	.138	−.122	−.260	−.281
	(.043)	(.056)	(.045)	(.045)
8. Intercept	1.742	2.008	.266	.744
R^2	.578	.737	.722	.671
Residual sum of s squares	.436	.737	.486	.574
(Degrees of freedom)	(42)	(42)	(42)	(46)

*Subscripts indicate years of school completed. Standard errors of the coefficient estimates are in parentheses. Variables other than research, extension, and nonwhite (a dummy variable) are in logarithms.

Definitions of Variables

1. Wages: Wages refer to total income in 1959, for males with income, age 45–54 years. The estimation procedure is discussed in the appendix.

2. Number of persons: The number of persons in each schooling class is estimated in terms of age constant, white, male equivalent earners. The estimation procedure and the procedure for reducing the schooling distribution to three classes is described in the appendix. The procedure described there results in estimates of number of persons in the rural farm population, not in the farm labor force *per se*. To adjust for this overstatement of numbers of persons, the number in each schooling class was multiplied by the ratio, R, for each state. Where R = number of employed male farmers, farm managers, farm laborers, and foremen in 1960 divided by the number of rural farm males employed in 1960. *1960 Census of Population* Table(s) 121. The national average for this ratio is .965.

3. Non-Labor inputs supplied by farms: A linear aggregate of the estimated flow of

services from land and buildings, machinery, and livestock inventories. The measure includes

(a) 3 percent of the value of farm land and buildings. The land and buildings variable is taken from Griliches (1964). His series adjusts for differences in quality of crop, irrigation, pasture land, etc., using relative prices for 1940. A uniform price index adjustment was used by Griliches to express values in 1949 dollars and I multiplied his values by 1.69 (the ratio of the 1959/1949 price indexes for farm real estate) so that value is in 1959 dollars. The 3 percent refers to an assumed 8 percent competitive rate of return (à la Griliches) and an assumed 5 percent rate of appreciation in farm real estate values.

(b) 15 percent of the value of machinery on farms. A measure of the value of machinery on farms is constructed using price indexes supplied by Kislev (1965) and *Census of Agriculture* estimates of the stock of machines on farms. The 0.15 refers to an assumed average machine life of ten years and an 8 percent rate of interest.

(c) 8 percent of the value of the livestock inventory: *U.S. Census of Agriculture,* 1959 estimates.

4. Research per farm: A weighted average of total research expenditures over the past nine years divided by *Census of Agriculture* number of farms. Research expenditures refer to all Federal and State expenditures (including farm management research). These data are provided by Evenson (1968). The annual weights are: .04, .08, .12, .16, .12, .08, and .04 for the years 1959 to 1951 respectively.

5. Days per farm by Extension personnel: A weighted average over four years of the total days spent by extension personnel in eight selected activities divided by *Census of Agriculture* number of farms. The included activities are: crops, livestock, marketing, soils, planning and management, land, buildings and machinery, and forestry. These data are obtained from unpublished reports of the Federal Extension Service. The annual weights are: 1/3. 1/3, 1/6, 1/6 for the years 1959–1956, respectively. For the Southern states, days per farm is computed from separate statistics for the Negro and white extension services, and number of farms similarly refers to Negro and white farm operators.

In the Southern states, the number of persons in a schooling class refers to the number of whites plus the product of the number of nonwhites and the relative wage of nonwhites. This number is interpreted as "white" equivalent laborers.

---

equation (1) an increase in the number of functional illiterates *reduces* the wage of high school relative to college graduates. In equation (2) an increase in the number of high school graduates *increases* the wage of functional illiterates relative to college graduates. That is, high school graduates enhance the relative productivity of functional illiterates, but functional illiterates detract from the relative productivity of high school graduates. Strictly speaking, these results are not necessarily contradictory because the coefficients refer to the elasticity of the relative wage of two factors with respect to a third and are not transitive. Nevertheless, this result is contrary to the usual interpretation of factor substitutability and questions the form in which equations (1) and (2) are specified.

Before discarding these two equations, consider the remaining results. In each case, nonlabor inputs supplied by farms detract from the *relative* productivity of college graduates. Too, the evidence is that research activity, the rate of flow of new inputs, enhances the relative productivity of college graduates and that extension activity, the flow of information about new inputs, detracts from the relative productivity of college graduates. This is as it should be. If education enhances the ability of a producer to decode information about the productive characteristics of new inputs, then the more rapid the rate of flow of new inputs, the greater will be the productivity differential associated with additional education. Further, if the advantages associated with added education refer to a differential ability to acquire and decode information, then an activity of disseminating information (extension) can short-circuit the gains to education. In a sense, the Extension Service may serve the purpose of overcoming the disadvantages associated with insufficient schooling. Unfortunately, the effect of extension seems more apparent than real, inasmuch as in considering a (hopefully) superior specification of equations (1) and (2), the effect of extension disappears.

Regression equations (3) and (4) provide the most valuable information of Table 4. In fact, equation (3) is implied by equations (1) and (2) and can be calculated simply as equation (2) less (1). Nevertheless, when (3) is compared with (4), the evidence is that the wage of high school graduates relative to functional illiterates depends neither upon the number of college graduates, the quantity of nonlabor inputs, research, nor upon extension activities. Equation (4) is estimated with the constraint that the coefficient on each of these four variables is zero. Deleting these variables reduces R^2 by only .051 (from .722 to .671), indicating that the partial R^2 of these four variables with the relative wage is .16. In testing for the joint significance of these variables, the computed $F_{(4,42)}$ statistic is 1.90, whereas the associated critical value of F at a confidence level of .05 is 2.59.[11] I therefore accept the hypothesis that the marginal rate of substitution (assumed equal to the relative wage) of functional illiterates for high school graduates is a function of the ratio of high school graduates to func-

---

[11] The test that a subset of coefficient in a regression equation is equal to zero is given in Graybill (1961, pp. 133–140).

tional illiterates only. Under this hypothesis the coefficient on the factor ratio, .359, can be interpreted as an estimate of a special kind of elasticity of substitution. It is not the partial elasticity in its most general form, but it is the elasticity of the factor ratio with respect to the marginal rate of substitution. The point estimate of the elasticity of substitution is 2.8 (the reciprocal of .359). The evidence here is that the elasticity of substitution between these classes is significantly different from unity so that the commonly used Cobb-Douglas and linear forms for combining inputs seem inappropriate.

Solow (1956), à la the Leontief separability theorem, has pointed out that, if the marginal rate of substitution between two inputs is independent of other inputs, production can be considered as a multistage process in which the two are first combined into an intermediate good which is then combined with other inputs to form the final product. The evidence here is that functional illiterates and high school graduates can be aggregated into an intermediate good. Call it "conventional labor" in contrast to the "modern" skills acquired in college. If the production process is viewed as a nested C-E-S function of the form suggested by Mundlak and Razin (1967) and if high school graduates and functional illiterates belong in the same subaggregate, then equation (4) is correctly specified, and equations (1) and (2) are not.

Table 5 provides estimates of regressions when high school graduates and persons with one to four years of schooling are aggregated using the C-E-S form into conventional labor, CL, and the wage is estimated as the average cost of CL. The aggregate is:

$$CL = (\delta N_{12}^{-\beta} + (1 - \delta)N_{1-4}^{-\beta})^{-1/\beta}$$

$$1 + \beta = .359$$

$$\log_e\left(\frac{\delta}{1 - \delta}\right) = .744,$$

where N_{12} and N_{1-4} indicate the numbers, respectively, of high school graduates and functional illiterates. The wage of the aggregate is computed as

$$W_{CL} = \frac{W_{12}N_{12} + W_{1-4}N_{1-4}}{CL}.$$

These results appear superior to those provided in equations (1) and (2) of Table 4. The major change in specification is the form of

TABLE 5

Estimates of Factors Determining the Productivity
of College Graduates Relative to Laborers with
Conventional Skill, an Aggregate of Functional
Illiterates and High School Graduates,
in U.S. Agriculture, 1959*

Independent Variables	Dependent Variable, the Relative Wage		
	(1)	(2)	(3)
1. The aggregate of functional illiterates and high school graduates	.699 (.062)	.699 (.061)	.711 (.081)
2. College graduates	−.377 (.084)	−.377 (.084)	−.711 (.081)
3. Non-labor inputs	−.322 (.056)	−.322 (.055)	
4. Research expenditures ($00)/farm	.485 (.163)	.482 (.150)	.663 (.194)
5. Days per farm by extension personnel	−.009 (.148)		
6. Nonwhite	−.637 (.084)	−.637 (.079)	−.540
7. Intercept	1.167	1.157	−2.314
R^2	.803	.803	.648

*Standard Errors are in parentheses. Inputs and wages are in logarithms. The equations are estimated subject to the constraint that the coefficients on inputs (excluding Research and extension) sum to zero. For definitions of variables, see the notes to Table 4.

the labor variables, and coefficients on labor inputs have much smaller standard errors relative to the estimated coefficients than in the earlier equations.

If the average cost of the combined high school graduates and functional illiterates is considered as the marginal product from an underlying production process, then the relations between the wages (marginal products) of high school graduates and functional illiterates are given as:

$$W_{12} = W_{CL} \frac{\partial CL}{\partial N_{12}}$$

and

$$W_{1-4} = W_{CL} \frac{\partial CL}{\partial N_{1-4}}.$$

From this it follows that equations (1) and (2) of Table 4 should be:

$$\frac{W_{16+}}{W_{12}} = \frac{W_{16+}}{W_{CL}} \delta \left(\frac{N_{12}}{CL}\right)^{1+\beta}$$

and

$$\frac{W_{16}}{W_{1-4}} = \frac{W_{16+}}{W_{CL}} (1 - \delta) \left(\frac{N_{1-4}}{CL}\right)^{1+\beta}$$

Since the function W_{16+}/W_{CL} is estimated in Table 5 and $(1 + \beta)$ and δ are estimated in equation (4) of Table 4, estimates of these relative wage equations are easily derived. Too, when viewed this way, the misspecification of equations (1) and (2) of Table 4 is obvious. The variable, conventional labor, is simply left out.

Thus, Table 5 together with equation (4), of Table 4, provides an internally consistent set of estimates of factors determining relative wages in agriculture.

In Table 5, equation (1) indicates that extension activities are not important in determining relative wages, and equation (2) presents the regression estimates when this factor is deleted. It represents my "best" estimate of the equation. The third column also excludes non-labor inputs to provide an estimate of the long-run (since other factors are left free to vary) elasticity of substitution between college graduates and conventional labor. That estimate is 1.41 (the reciprocal of .711).

One important by-product of these estimates is that the marginal rate of substitution between college graduates and other labor appears to be *significantly* related to the quantity of nonlabor inputs. As such, it does not appear that all forms of labor can be aggregated into a single input.

From regression equation (2) of Table 5, the coefficient on research can best be interpreted by asking the question: What would happen to the relative wage of college graduates if the research variable were to become zero? At the sample's geometric mean, the wage of college graduates relative to high school graduates is 1.62, and relative to functional illiterates it is 1.75. The sample mean value of research expenditures per farm is $26.74. If this value were to fall to zero, the estimate here is that the relative wage in each case would fall by about 14 percent or to 1.39 and 1.50, respectively. Thus, about one-third of the productivity differential between college graduates and either high school graduates or functional illiterates is directly attributable

345

to research. In fact, this is probably an understatement of the impact of research. If production were to become technically static, eventually the productive characteristics of all inputs would become fairly well understood. This common information would be passed by word of mouth from one generation of farmers to the next, and under such conditions it is difficult to understand how education could enhance allocative efficiency. In a dynamic setting discretionary abilities may be the key to allocative efficiency. In a static setting these abilities seem unimportant.

That the partial effect of nonlabor inputs supplied by farms is negative (with respect to the relative wage of college graduates) is consistent with many explanations that cannot be distinguished with these data.[12] It is likely that the productive characteristics of land, buildings, machinery, and livestock (the supplied inputs) are more commonly understood than are the characteristics of the purchased inputs, seeds, commercial fertilizers, pesticides, and so forth. If true, we would expect farmers who are adept at assessing the productivity of modern inputs to rely more heavily on them, that is, to allocate a larger share of their input bundles to modern inputs than would farmers less certain of the capacities of modern inputs; and if this is true, a plausible explanation of the negative effect of supplied inputs is that, for college graduates, the productivity gains associated with increments in supplied inputs are less than proportionate to relative wages. Recall that, at the sample mean, the relative wage of college to high school graduates is 1.62. For supplied inputs to be neutral between high school and college graduates, the rate of increase in productivity of college graduates from increments in supplied inputs would have to be 1.62 times the corresponding rate for high school graduates. The evidence here is that, while it is possible that an increment in supplied inputs increases the productivity of college graduates by more in absolute terms than for less schooled persons, the ratio of

[12]One possibility is that given existing factor and product prices and the quantities of labor inputs, there will exist a corresponding combination of nonlabor inputs that is optimal. Call that combination K^*. If we assume that the farm enters the production period with K of these inputs (K denotes the inputs supplied by the farm), then $K^* - K$ remain to be purchased. If more educated persons possess superior allocative ability, the gains to this ability will be positively related to the "room" for selecting inputs, i.e., to $K^* - K$, and will therefore be negatively related to K. This, of course, is true only if K^* is independent of K which seems unlikely, and if the "superior" allocative ability is superior only in the short run. Otherwise, this ability would be reflected in the previous selection of K.

346

the absolute increments is less than the prevailing relative wages. College graduates presumably get the added leverage (that results in relative wages being what they are) through the use of other inputs.

Since the effects of extension activities appear neutral, that is, they do not seem to alter relative wages, a question arises as to whether the nonwhite "states" should be included in the analysis. This is because extension is the only variable other than the dummy for the "level effect" distinguishing the Southern white and nonwhite observations. To "test" for the sensitivity of the coefficient estimates to the nonwhite observations, the regressions presented in Tables 4 and 5 are estimated for the thirty-nine white "states" and are provided in the Appendix in Tables 7 and 8. There is marked agreement in the two sets of estimates.

SUMMARY AND CONCLUSIONS

One of the most important phenomena of our time is that rates of return to investments in schooling have failed to decline under the pressure of rapidly rising average educational levels. Viewing education as a factor of production, for "other things" equal, we would expect returns to decline as the quantity of education rises; so the obvious implication is that "other things" have *not* been equal. This is an analysis of underlying changes that may have resulted in the maintained incentive for investing in education.

Three broad classes of changes which may explain the phenomenon are considered. Roughly, they include the changing composition of industrial activity, non-neutralities in production, and rising quality of schooling. I then focus upon the second: non-neutralities in production.

First, the role of education in production is stressed, showing that, while it can be considered as any other factor in the sense that it may directly contribute to physical product, the effects of allocating other factors must also be recognized. If education enhances allocative ability in the sense of selecting the appropriate input bundles and of efficiently distributing inputs between competing uses, the return to this ability is part of the return to education. The empirical analysis refers to determinants of relative wages in agriculture.

The evidence is that, while factor ratios are important, much of the "leverage" associated with added schooling is drawn from the dynamical implications of changing technology. But this appears to hold only for skills that result from college. Relative wages for persons who have not attended college are determined by labor ratios only.

Thus the empirical evidence says nothing about the stability of the relative wage of high school graduates. One possibility is that production processes have simply become more complicated through time and require increasing skill. This phenomenon cannot be captured in a cross-sectional analysis of the type presented here. On the other hand, the information presented here is important in explaining the growth in demand for college graduates. Consider the effects of research. Research expenditures per farm were $4.30 in 1940 and $28.40 in 1959.[13] Based on coefficient estimates in table 5, if research were to fall from $28.40 to $4.30, holding factor ratios constant, the relative wage of college to high school graduates would fall from 1.62 to 1.43, indicating that about one-third of the wage differential would disappear. Too, purchased inputs have become relatively more important. In 1939, inputs purchased from other industries accounted for 38 percent of agricultural output, and by 1959 the share had increased to 48 percent.[14] This trend should have increased the role of the innovator-allocator.

APPENDIX

The *Census of Population* provides data for persons with 0, 1–4, 5–7, 8, 9–11, 12, 13–15, and 16 or more years of school completed. In this Appendix, I describe the computation technique used to derive wages representative of each schooling class in each state and, correspondingly, the "number" of persons in each class.

Wages. — The wage variable refers to total income for persons in the rural farm population in 1959. Although data for earnings which exclude transfers and income from property not managed directly are preferable, they are not available. The U.S. Census (1963) provides for each state the joint income-schooling (tables 138), age-income (tables 134), and age-schooling (tables 103) distributions for males 25 years old and over. These three distributions are used to compute the cross-products matrix required for a regression of the logarithm of income on two classes of dummy variables, the eight schooling classes and six age classes (25–34, 35–44, 45–54, 55–64,

[13] Constant 1959 dollars, Evenson (1968).

[14] Agricultural output excludes the intermediate goods, feed and livestock, Welch (1969b).

65–74, and 75 and over). Income estimates are interval midpoints for the $1,000 intervals from $0 to $7,000; for the interval $7,000–$9,999, $8,200 is used, and for the open-ended interval $10,000 and over, the mean is estimated from a Pareto distribution. With this cross-products matrix, the regression coefficients are computed using the standard linear regression formula. For each schooling class, the antilog of the predicted log of income for persons 45–54 years old is multiplied by the ratio of the arithmetic to the geometric mean of income for the class. This is so that estimates refer to mean rather than geometric mean values of income. In the joint age-schooling distributions, it is not possible to identify persons without income so that all persons, with and without income, are included in the income predictions. To correct for this error, a regression equation is estimated in which the dependent variable is the proportion of persons in an age or schooling class with income in 1959 and the independent variables are the same age and schooling "dummies." With the estimate of this equation, the probability of having income is computed for each schooling class (conditional on age = 45–54), and that probability is divided into the income estimate. The resulting wage is interpreted

TABLE 6

Estimated Linear Relationships Among Wage Rates (Annual Incomes) of the Eight Schooling Classes for the United States, 1959.
(Subscripts on the wage variables indicated years of school completed.)

Wage Rates Taken as Independent Variables	Wage Rates Taken as Dependent Variables, Their Coefficients and (Standard Errors)				
	W_0	W_{5-7}	W_8	W_{9-11}	W_{13-15}
Regression No.	1c.	2c.	3c.	4c.	5c.
W_{1-4}	1.147	.633	.456	.210	−.084
	(.082)	(.034)	(.045)	(.026)	(.069)
W_{12}	−.170	.322	.529	.758	.588
	(.050)	(.021)	(.027)	(.016)	(.130)
W_{16+}	—	—	—	—	.431
					(.075)
R^2	.991	.984	.980	.995	.981

Source: The basic data are derived as described in the above, except in this case wages refer to the total population instead of rural farm only. There are 58 observations including the 48 states of the conterminous United States with a separation of 10 southern states into 10 white and 10 nonwhite states.

as the wage representative of a schooling class for males 45–54 years old with income in 1959.

Number of persons.—The number of persons in each schooling class is computed in terms of male, 45–54 years old, earning units. This number is calculated as the total income of all persons in a schooling class including females 25 years old and over and young persons ages 14–24, divided by the wage representative of the class. The estimates of total income are derived for persons 25 and over from census tables 138 and for persons 14–24, from census tables 134. The income estimates for the closed intervals are the same as those used in the estimation of wages, but for the open-ended intervals, means are estimated using separate approximations to Pareto distributions.

Following the derivation of the standardized schooling distribution for each state, the number of schooling classes is reduced from the eight census classes to three: 1–4 years, 12, and 4 or more years of college following a procedure described in Welch (1969a). The pro-

TABLE 7

Estimates of Factors Affecting the Productivity of More Relative to Less Schooled Persons in U.S. Agriculture, 1959. 39 "States" Only.*

Independent Variables	Dependent Variables			
	W_{16+}/W_{12} (1)	W_{16+}/W_{1-4} (2)	W_{12}/W_{1-4} (3)	(4)
1. Functional illiterates	.065 (.033)	.456 (.038)	.391 (.040)	.362 (.039)
2. High school graduates	.008 (.082)	−.471 (.098)	−.479 (.101)	−.362 (.039)
3. College graduates	.081 (.064)	.107 (.094)	.026 (.077)	
4. Non-labor inputs	−.154 (.033)	−.092 (.040)	.062 (.041)	
5. Research expenditures ($00)/farm	.045 (.090)	.170 (.107)	.125 (.110)	
6. Days per farm by extension personnel	−.166 (.072)	−.173 (.086)	−.007 (.088)	
7. Intercept	1.992˙	2.250	0.258	0.745
R^2	.517	.844	.760	.701
Residual sum of squares	.264	.369	.389	.482
(Degrees of freedom)	(33)	(33)	(33)	(37)

*Subscripts indicate years of school completed. Standard errors of the coefficient estimates are in parentheses. Notes: See Table 4.

cedure is used in recognition of the fact that 99+ percent of the total wage variation between states and across schooling classes for the five classes, 0, 5–7, 8, 9–11, and 13–15 years of schooling is reflected in the variance of the three remaining classes, 1–4, 12, and 16+ years. Table 6 summarizes results for regressions of wages for the five excluded classes on the remaining three. Let the coefficient falling on the ith row and the jth column of Table 6 be a_{ij}, and let N_i represent the age-adjusted number of persons in each schooling class. Then

$$N_i^* = N_i + \sum_{j=1}^{5} N_j a_{ij}$$

(i = 1–4, 12, and 16+) defines the estimated number of persons for each of the three classes.

TABLE 8

Estimates of Factors Determining the Productivity
of College Graduates Relative to Laborers With
Conventional Skill in U.S. Agriculture,
1959. 39 "States" Only.*

	Dependent Variable, the Relative Wage		
Independent Variables	(1)	(2)	(3)
1. The aggregate of functional illiterates and high school graduates	.743 (.055)	.741 (.056)	.756 (.078)
2. College graduates	−.420 (.079)	−.423 (.078)	−.756 (.078)
3. Non-labor inputs	−.323 (.055)	−.318 (.053)	
4. Research expenditures ($00)/farm	.557 (.138)	.535 (.135)	.720 (.184)
5. Days per farm by extension personnel	−.052 (.138)		
6. Intercept	1.173	1.102	−2.334
R^2	.865	.864	.724

*Standard Errors are in parentheses. Notes: See Table 4.

REFERENCES

Becker, Gary S. "Underinvestment in College Education?" *American Economic Review*, May 1960.

———. *Human Capital*. New York: The National Bureau of Economic Research, 1964.

Investment in Education

Chaudhri, D. P. "Education and Agricultural Productivity in India," Unpublished Ph.D. dissertation, Department of Economics, University of Delhi, Delhi, India, 1968.

Coleman, James S., *et al. Equality of Educational Opportunity.* Washington, D.C.: U.S. Office of Education, 1966.

Evenson, Robert. "The Contribution of Agricultural Research to Production," *Jour. Farm Econ.* (December 1967).

———. "The Contribution of Agricultural Research and Extension to Agricultural Production." Unpublished Ph.D. dissertation, Department of Economics, University of Chicago, 1968.

Graybill, Franklin A., *An Introduction to Linear Statistical Models,* Vol. I, New York, McGraw-Hill Book Company, Inc., 1961.

Griliches, Zvi. "Estimates of the Aggregate Agricultural Production Function from Cross-Sectional Data," *Jour. Farm Econ.,* XLV (May 1963).

———. "Notes on the Role of Education in Production Functions and Growth Accounting." Unpublished paper, 1968.

———. "Research Expenditures, Education, and the Aggregate Agricultural Production Function," *A.E.R.,* LIV (1964), 961.74.

———. "The Sources of Measured Productivity Growth: U.S. Agriculture, 1940-1960," *Jour. Pol. Econ.,* LXXI (August 1963), 331–46(b).

Kislev, Voav. "Estimating a Production Function from U.S. Census of Agriculture Data." Unpublished Ph.D. dissertation, Department of Economics, University of Chicago, 1965.

Klinov-Malul, Ruth. *The Profitability of Investment in Education in Israel.* Jerusalem: The Maurice Falk Institute for Economic Research in Israel, April 1966.

Mundlak, Y. and Razin, A. "On Multistage Production Functions, The Theory of Aggregation and Technical Change," CMSBE Report No. 6716, Chicago, 1967.

Nelson, R. R. and Phelps, E. S. "Investment in Humans, Technological Diffusion, and Economic Growth," *American Economic Review,* May 1966, pp. 69–75.

A Report of the United States Commission on Civil Rights, *Equal Opportunity in Farm Programs,* 1965.

Schultz, T. W. *Transforming Traditional Agriculture.* New Haven: The Yale University Press, 1964.

Solow, R. M. "The Production Function and the Theory of Capital," *Rev. Econ. Studies.* II (1956).

Thomas, J. Alan. "Efficiency in Education: A Study of Mean Test Scores in a Sample of Senior High Schools." Unpublished Ph.D. dissertation, School of Education, Stanford University, 1962.

U.S. Bureau of the Census. *U.S. Census of Population: 1960.* Washington, D.C.: U.S. Government Printing Office, 1963.

Welch, Finis. "Linear Synthesis of Skill Distributions," *Journal of Human Resources,* Summer 1969(a).

———. "Measurement of the Quality of Schooling," *A.E.R.,* LVI (May 1966), 379–92.

———. "Some Aspects of Structural Change and the Distributional Effects of Technical Change and Farm Programs in Agriculture," Unpublished paper, 1969(b).

D. Human Capital and Occupational Choice

18. Human Capital and Occupational Choice — A Theoretical Model*

MAURICE C. BENEWITZ AND ALBERT ZUCKER
The City College, New York

Recent pathbreaking work by Gary Becker has shown the essential similarity between human and physical investment.[1] Given any two alternative human activity sequences (investment programs), Becker has shown how to calculate the incremental investment embodied in the higher investment sequence, and the rate of return to that investment. But while a well integrated theory exists concerning the determinants of the quantities of physical investment in different uses, and the mechanisms bringing about equilibrium among these investments, relatively little attention has been paid to similar questions for human capital.

In this paper we will discuss those investments in human capital associated with occupational choice. By developing a model of occupational choice centered on the preferences of individuals for particular time shapes of their income streams, we will attempt to isolate the underlying role these time-preferences play in determining the distribution of total investment among the various occupations.

A sequence of investment activities undertaken for entry into an occupation can be conceived of as an ordered chain, the links of which are conceptually—if somewhat arbitrarily—separable. Each part of the investment chain will have a rate of return associated with it. This internal rate of return is defined as the rate of discount that equates the present values of the future income streams of two groups of

*Reprinted from "Human Capital and Occupational Choice — A Theoretical Model," *Southern Economic Journal*, XXXIV (January, 1968), 406–409.

[1]G. S. Becker, *Human Capital* (New York: National Bureau of Economic Research, 1964).

individuals identical in all essential respects, but differing in that one group undertakes the increment investment in question and the other group does not. Although an identification of two such groups is an ideal at best imperfectly realized in practice,[2] we proceed for simplicity as though such a separation of groups is always possible.

We now adopt the following model of occupational choice: *an individual chooses that occupation for which the present value of his expected income stream is a maximum.*[3]

The rate at which an individual is assumed to discount an increment to future income is the subjective rate that equates the present worth of that increment with the maximum current income the individual would be willing to forego in exchange for the future gain.[4] We assume these rates of discount are determined for each individual by his "time-preference" function:

$$r_i = f_i(Y_0, Y_t, g, u) \tag{1}$$

where r_i is the rate at which the *ith* individual would discount an increment to future income, Y_t, given his present level of income, Y_0. The variable g stands for the individual's age at time zero, and u represents all other determinants of r_i.

To begin, we adopt the restrictive assumptions that the rate of discount for any given individual is stable over time, independent of the amount of per period investment contemplated or past investments undertaken.[5] However the r_i's vary *among* individuals according to their tastes for present as against future income.

Now consider a closed-end investment chain; that is, one in which no further occupation-oriented investment can take place without at least some previous investment becoming superfluous.[6] An individual who has progressed part way along this chain must decide at each stop whether to stop or to go on — if he stops then he is thought of as entering a lower investment occupation than if he continues.

---

[2] Jacob Mincer discusses some of the difficulties in identifying appropriate comparison groups in his "On-the-Job Training: Costs, Returns, and Some Implications," *Journal of Political Economy*, October 1962 Supplement. See especially p. 53.

[3] Clearly the choice is more complicated than this. Below we discuss this further.

[4] Given the oft-noted imperfections in human capital markets, the rate of interest would not be a meaningful rate for discounting.

[5] The consequences of modifying these assumptions will be examined later.

[6] An example might be a medical specialist who decided to become a nuclear physicist.

Investment in Education

Suppose the individual is up the the *kth* step of the investment sequence. Will he continue? Let the moment of decision be time $t = 0$. Also let

n = the duration of the *kth* lump of investment.

C_m = amount of investment (income foregone) in period m.

r_k = rate of return to all units of the *kth* investment.

Then if V_m is the increase in the present value of the individual's future income stream due to the investment C_m, we have

$$V_m = \frac{-C_m}{(1 + r_i)^{m+1}} + \sum_{j=m+1}^{\infty} \frac{r_i C_m}{(1 + r_i)^{j+1}} \tag{2}$$

The first term on the right represents the present value of the income loss; the second term is the present value of returns assuming infinite working life for convenience. Summing and simplifying, we have

$$V_m = \frac{C_m}{(1 + r_i)^{m+1}} \left[\frac{r_k}{r_i} - 1 \right] \tag{3}$$

For the full n periods of investment, the total addition to present value is

$$\sum_{m=0}^{n-1} V_m = \left[\frac{r_k}{r_i} - 1 \right] \sum_{m=0}^{n-1} \frac{C_m}{(1 + r_i)^{m+1}} \tag{4}$$

Clearly, from equation (4), present value of future income will be augmented by investing if $r_i < r_k$, diminished if $r_i > r_k$, and will remain unchanged if $r_i = r_k$. Thus only those individuals will undertake the additional investment whose rates of time discount are below the objective rate of return on the investment.[7]

From the above an interesting theorem follows: *If X_{k-1} and C_k represent occupations resulting respectively from $k - 1$ and k periods of sequential investment, then in equilibrium $r_{k-1} > r_k$.* Proof: consider any individual with time preference rate $r_i < r_{k-1}$. If $r_{k-1} = r_k$, then not only will the individual invest in occupation X_{k-1}, but he will undergo the additional training necessary for X_k. That is, no one will enter occupation X_{k-1}.

[7] If capital markets were perfect this analysis would not hold. For if the market rate of interest r was below r_k, then for *any* r_i, the individual would realize gain from investing. Funds could be borrowed at rate r, returns received at rate $r_k > r_i$ and the present value of the surplus would be positive at any finite rate of discount. The amounts of investment, both physical and human, would be such that in equilibrium all rates would be the same. But capital markets are not perfect.

If, on the other hand, $r_{k-1} > r_k$, all individuals with time preference rates satisfying $r_{k-1} > r_i \geq r_k$ will enter X_{k-1}, and go no further. Therefore, the decline in rates of return with further investment makes determinate the amount of investment an individual on the investment chain will undertake. Further, the distribution of time-preference rates will determine, together with the rates of return, the total amount of human investment in each occupation.

Declining rates of return are consistent with the available evidence on returns to schooling. Becker estimates that the private rate of return, adjusted for differential ability, for white male college graduates is of the order of 12 percent.[8] For high school graduates he estimates an 18 percent return, *before adjusting for ability.* Since the ability adjustment brought the college rate down some 12%, a similar adjustment for high school would result in roughly a 16 percent rate of return.[9] The return to elementary school education is still higher.

Rates of return on selected apprenticeships, normally begun after the completion of high school, have been estimated by Mincer at about 9–10 percent. This too is consistent with our result. However, he estimates a return to medical specialization of 11.3 percent, although he notes that this return may have been above equilibrium.[10]

An apparent exception to our results is presented in a recent paper by Gary Becker and Barry Chiswick.[11]

By means of a multiple regression model in which the log of earnings is regressed on years of formal schooling, with the regression coefficients representing "adjusted rates of return,"[12] they obtained

---

[8] Becker, *loc. cit.,* p. 82.

[9] Becker argues that adjustment for ability would probably result in a more drastic reduction of the high school rate than for college. "Fully adjusted rates, therefore, might show no diminishing returns . . . to additional years of schooling." (*Ibid.,* p. 127). He bases this conclusion partly on the fact that "the average I.Q. of high school graduates is more than 30 percent higher than that of persons with seven or eight years of schooling." as against a further increase of only 12 percent for college graduates. (*Ibid.,* pp. 124, 125). However, unless it is known how incremental earnings per incremental I.Q. point is related to the I.Q. level, other things held constant, it is not clear what information these percentages convey.

[10] Mincer, *loc. cit.,* p. 65.

[11] Gary S. Becker and Barry R. Chiswick, "The Economics of Education and the Distribution of Earnings," Papers and Proceedings of the Seventy-eighth Annual Meeting of the American Economic Association, published in the *American Economic Review,* May, 1966.

[12] If $\bar{r}_j$ is the mean rate of return of all individuals for the *j*th period of schooling, and $\bar{k}_j$ is the average "cost" of the *j*th period as a fraction of earnings that otherwise would be received, then $\bar{r}_j = \bar{k}_j \cdot \bar{r}_j$ is the adjusted rate.

357

rates for low (0–8 yrs), medium (8–12 yrs), and high (over 12 yrs) education of .05, .06 and .08 respectively for the non-south, and .07, .09 and .09 respectively for the south.

While space precludes a more complete analysis, a few sources of possible bias will be mentioned. In the process of isolating the effects on earnings of the numbers of years of schooling, the error term is made to carry a heavy burden. Included in the error term are such factors as "ability," luck, motivation, initial endowment and number of years invested in other human capital. Becker and Chiswick argue that although a positive correlation between ability and years of schooling would tend to produce an upward bias in the estimated rates of return, random errors in measuring the years of schooling and a possible negative correlation between years of schooling and *years* invested in other human capital would tend to bias the estimates downward. Thus the biases would tend to be offsetting.[13] But the correlation, if negative, between years of schooling and of other human capital may well be quite weak, whereas ability is very clearly positively correlated with schooling. It is quite possible, then, that given the nature of the error term, the rates for earlier units of schooling have been understated both in the South and non-South, relative to the rates for later units.

QUALIFICATIONS

We assumed earlier that equation (1) took on the exceedingly simple form: $r_i = k_i$, where k_i is a constant specific to the *i*th individual. But the traditional assumption that indifference curves for present versus future income are convex to the origin is partly based on the notion of diminishing marginal utility for successive units of income received in a given time period. In our terminology, people would

---

[13] Becker and Chiswick note that although the correlations are somewhat offsetting, "a sizable error probably remains in estimating the adjusted rates. . . ." (*Ibid.*, p. 365). This is also indicated by the fact that the standard errors of the regression coefficients are of the same order of magnitude as the coefficients themselves. Finally, they mention a study of G. Hanoch, "Personal Earnings and Investment in Schooling," (unpublished Ph.D. dissertation, Univ. of Chicago, 1965, Chap. IV) in which the estimates are almost uniformly higher than ours . . . ," suggesting, "if anything, a negative correlation between school years and the years invested in other human capital. This could also explain why Hanoch's rates tend to decline [consistent with our model— M.B. and A.Z.] with increases in years of schooling while ours tend to rise." (Becker and Chiswick, *loc. cit.*, n17, p. 367). But if the impact of ability on earnings should be greater for later units of schooling, a progressive upward bias could be introduced that might explain why Becker's and Chiswick's rates rise.

tend to discount the returns from additional amounts of investment *in the same period* at rising rates. Thus our conclusion that rates of return decline as total investment required increases may need modification in the (exceptional) case where a very *intensive* investment period followed a less intensive one. But if at a certain point in an investment sequence either of two alternative investments may be undertaken, then if they are approximately equal in duration (equally extensive), in equilibrium the rate of return to the more *intensive* investment should be higher, *ceteris paribus*. Again, the apprenticeships mentioned by Mincer have an average duration of about 4½ years. This is comparable in duration to college where the rate of return is somewhat higher.

Our earlier analysis was conducted entirely in monetary terms. Consumption elements in education, tastes for one kind of work as against another, differential ability among individuals — all these will affect the nature of the ultimate equilibrium arrived at. Suffice it to say that if for the population as a whole, increasing non-monetary utility is associated on the average with increasing investment, the monetary rates of returns would decline even more drastically than would otherwise be the case. On the other hand, if those who invest little tend to do so partly out of a distaste for such investments (e.g., low motivation toward schooling), and if time preference rates are uncorrelated with the nonwage aspects of different occupations, our analysis is unaffected.

In the short run shifts in demand will result in non-equilibrium rates of return and in short-run wage distortions. The mechanism of mobility will adjust these disequilibria. In the short run adjustments may occur through withdrawal from, or entry into, the labor force by some individuals. Additional on-the-job training may be undertaken. The ultimate adjustment will be in shifts of the supply of labor provided by new entrants into the labor force and the type of training they have undertaken.

One final qualification may be noted. We assumed above that the rates of time discount were independent of the ages of the investing individuals. But if the cautious conservatism of age extends to investment in oneself, rates of time discount will rise with age. If this rise should begin before the age at which investment in human capital tends to cease, it could not only help to explain that cessation, but reverse the pattern of rates derived above.

19. Hedging in the Labor Market*

CORINDO CIPRIANI
Siena College, New York City

Hedging is a process by which an existing risk is reduced, generally at a cost.[1] Since recent economic literature[2] has invited us to view the worker as an investor—and since, as such, he must face risk—it is perhaps worthwhile to determine whether some approach to hedging is applicable to the labor market.

THE NATURE OF THE WORKER'S RISK

The currently-developing body of thought to which we refer above views the stream of marketable services which the worker offers for sale as flowing from a stock of human capital. The worker must devote resources to the formation of this "capital"; hence the investment.

Like other types of investors, the worker faces risk: there is danger that the demand for his type of service will decline. Note especially that it is this demand—nothing else—that gives value to the worker's human capital. It is meaningless, in the absence of slavery, to speak of demand for the "human-capital stock" itself; for unlike other types of investors, the worker holds "capital" (human wealth) which is *nonnegotiable*. Once resources are thus invested, they cannot be transferred into an alternative income-producing use, even by a worker who uniquely foresees a weakening of the market. In short, the worker cannot "sell out."

---

*Reprinted from "Hedging in the Labor Market," *Southern Economic Journal*, XXXIV (October, 1967), 286–292.

[1] The purchase of insurance can thus be regarded as one type of hedge.

[2] Especially significant are Gary S. Becker's groundbreaking "Investment in Human Capital: A Theoretical Analysis" and articles by Schultz, Mincer and Mushkin in *The Journal of Political Economy,* "Supplement": October, 1962.

Conventional notions of hedging involve an avoidance of the impact of some price change. In the market for agricultural commodities, for example, a trader may assume two opposite positions ("long" and "short") in one commodity by making the appropriate transactions in "futures." Subsequent price movements have little or no effect on him.

Product diversification by a firm may be regarded as a hedging technique. Simon Rottenberg points out that ". . . a buggy-whip maker who is doubtful that the demand for his product will remain high for a long time . . . may also make diapers."[3] The usefulness of such a hedge depends, of course, upon such factors as the assumed life span of the firm, demand elasticities, the ease with which buggy-whip machinery can be adapted to diaper-making, etc. Two features of diversification of this sort are clear, however:

(1) The resources invested by the firm are divided into two (or more) different types of capital goods;

(2) The firm takes like positions (seller) in *more than one market at the same time.*

It is clear that the worker cannot behave as a commodities trader. He cannot sell "short" his services; there is no futures market for them.

We must proceed more slowly with regard to the technique of diversification. A worker *can* divide his investable resources into two (or more) different types of human capital. He may, for example, acquire two skills. Alternatively, in addition to a particular skill, he may invest in a broad education to gain adaptability. As Weisbrod points out:

Education may be viewed as a type of private (and social) hedge against technological displacement of skills. New technology often requires new skills. New technology often requires new skills and knowledge; and those persons having more education are likely to be in a position to adjust more easily than those with less education, and to reap the returns from education which the new technology has made possible.[4,5]

[3] Simon Rottenberg, "Property in Work," *Industrial and Labor Relations Review,* April 1962.

[4] Burton A. Weisbrod, "Education and Investment in Human Capital," *The Journal of Political Economy,* "Supplement," October 1962.

[5] Simon Rottenberg (see note 3) writes:
". . . a worker may acquire skills that are specialized to a narrow occupation or, if he is doubtful about the long-run demand for these skills, he may acquire other skills that

Investment in Education

At first glance, it might appear that the *second* feature of a firm's product diversification—the maintenance of like positions in more than one market at the same time—is also available to a worker. A person who holds two jobs, for example—using a different skill in each—would appear to be in this situation.

But the buggy-whip firm which conducts an *expansion* program into diaper machinery (as a worker would "expand" his stock of human capital by acquiring a second skill) can increase its overall sales *per unit of time*, and thus begin immediately to collect returns from its diaper division.

On the other hand, the keypunch operator at the Last National Bank who learns baby-care "on the side" continues to receive only the same paycheck from Last National *per forty-hour week*.

Thus, while the diaper sales in our two-product firm bring returns to the diaper-machinery investment, a second job for the two-skill worker brings returns largely to the additional "time outlay." Since even a one-skill worker can presumably acquire a second job, investment in a second skill cannot normally be recouped in this way.

HEDGING IN THE LABOR MARKET

It appears, then, that a worker has flexibility only to the extent that he can divide the placement of his available resources. Several decades ago, Douglas and Director, urging the acquisition of more than one form of human capital, wrote: If specialized occupations are taught the young workers, it would be well that they should be taught a supplementary as well as a principal trade so that they might have another string to their bow in case they were displaced.[6]

In this section, we shall try to determine under what circumstances it would be worthwhile for a worker to divide his human-capital investment. We shall regard an investment in a second skill or ability as "worthwhile" if its cost is recovered during the individual's lifetime.

We shall assume that when a skill becomes obsolete, the demand for

---

are more general and transferable among a number of occupations and industries. He may . . . hedge."

To the extent that by "more general," Rottenberg is referring to a broad education, his idea is like that of Weisbrod (above). If he refers to manual skills, however, transferability among industries, etc. cannot protect them from obsolescence if equal access to technology prevails.

[6] Douglas and Director, *The Problem of Unemployment* (The MacMillan Co., 1931).

its services drops instantaneously to zero everywhere. Any worker having only this skill can command, at this point, only the wage U, which is equal to the wage (and marginal product) of an unskilled worker.

Consider now a worker who is employed at the wage W ($W > U$), and who has a (remaining) working life of n periods. Assume that at time $t = 0$ he makes an investment C_2 and acquires a second (spare) skill. The wage which he could earn through the employment of this spare skill is assumed equal to the marginal product in this skill (MP_2) and

$$U < MP_2 < W. \tag{1}$$

Maintenance of the second skill (which is unused) may be assumed to give rise to a cost k in each time period during which it is "idle," where all the k's are equal. (Such a cost might be due, for example, to periodic practice, review-study, or reading to stay abreast of developments in the field.)

If the worker's "primary" skill were not to become obsolete during the ensuing n periods, the investment in the second skill would not be worthwhile or successful. In this case, the worker would suffer a loss equal to the entire expenditure E_2 (discounted at $t = 0$) on the acquisition and maintenance of the spare skill. This amount would be

$$E_2 = C_2 + \sum_{t=0}^{n-1} \frac{k_t}{(1 + i)^{t+1}} \tag{2}$$

where i represents the market rate of interest.

Suppose, however, that the principal skill becomes obsolete at time $t = m$ ($m < n$). If the worker has no spare skill, he can secure employment, at this point, at the wage U (as we have noted). Following this course, the cost which he would incur as a result of the obsolescence, discounted (for convenience) at $t = 0$, would be

$$\sum_{t=m}^{n-1} \frac{W - U}{(1 + i)^{t+1}}. \tag{3}$$

With a spare skill available, however, he may take up employment realizing a wage equal to MP_2. (Assume that when he brings the spare skill into actual use, the maintenance cost is discontinued.) Doing so, he is able to *salvage*

$$\sum_{t=m}^{n-1} \frac{MP_2 - U}{(1 + i)^{t+1}} \tag{4}$$

of the loss which he would have otherwise sustained.[7] The hedge may thus be regarded as successful if

$$\sum_{t=m}^{n-1} \frac{MP_2 - U}{(1 + i)^{t+1}} \geq C_2 + \sum_{t=0}^{m-1} \frac{k_t}{(1 + i)^{t+1}}. \tag{5}$$

It is clear from the above inequality that with a given work-life and second-skill investment (with its accompanying k and MP_2), the likelihood of a successful hedge increases the smaller is m (the sooner the principal skill becomes obsolete).

This being the case, it is difficult to see why a worker would ever choose to follow this procedure, even if he has a reasonably good estimate of m. A safer hedge could be conducted simply by avoiding any second-skill investment until obsolescence of the principal skill actually occurs (if then). Instead, a worker could place the available resources (say C_2 in the first period plus a periodic amount k) in some form of negotiable wealth yielding the market rate of interest.[8] If the principal skill should "expire," he would be in a position to transfer his wealth into a skill; moreover, he could presumably judge better (than at $t = 0$) which (if any) skill to choose.

In an economy characterized by creeping inflation, the worker might anticipate a rising price level (which would increase the future dollar-cost of skill-acquisition) and thus wish to avoid holding fixed-dollar obligations. Under these circumstances, he could make use of an "inflation-hedge," i.e., purchase common stocks or other equities. Admittedly, this course would reduce his liquidity and thus the speed with which he could react to sudden obsolescence. In fact, if he refused to tolerate delay at time m, he might suffer a capital loss in transferring his resources into a skill. But accepting this risk, the worker would be conducting *two* hedges: one against obsolescence and the other against inflation!

This procedure has another important feature:

At time m when the principal skill becomes obsolete, the individual's remaining work-life $(n - m)$ might be too short to provide an internal rate of return at least as great as the market rate of interest on any

---

[7] The "salvaged" amount is measured in absolute terms.

[8] In general, some of these resources would be in the form of man-hours; and this suggestion simply means that the worker might better, for example, work more hours per week than otherwise and place the funds thus earned in (say) government bonds.

skill acquisition.[9] If so, the worker would abandon any plan to acquire another skill, and simply turn to unskilled work at the wage U. As for his stock of negotiable wealth, he might, for example, transform it into some sort of annuity contract (neglecting any concern for the establishment of an estate) and thus realize a return greater than any which he could secure on human capital.

SECOND SKILL ACQUIRED OVER TIME

Assume that the worker whom we treated earlier, while employed at the wage W, begins a part-time training program whose duration is known to be p periods ($p < n$); and that at the end of this interval (p periods) the worker will have a marginal product MP_2 (as before) through the employment of his spare skill. For simplicity, maintenance costs may be assumed not to arise until the training interval has been completed. Assume further that in each period of the training interval the worker incurs a training cost q where all the q's are equal and

$$\sum_{t=0}^{p-1} \frac{q_t}{(1+i)^{t+1}} = C_2 , \tag{6}$$

i.e., the non-maintenance training expenditure, discounted at $t = 0$, is as before.

If the worker's principal skill were "alive" at the end of p periods, the analysis would actually correspond to that of a lump-sum investment except that for any given m, the second term on the right side of (5), expressing (discounted) maintenance costs, would be smaller.[10]

Let us examine, however, the situation wherein the principal skill becomes useless *before* the spare-skill training interval is completed. Again denote by m the time of sudden obsolescence ($m < p$).

It is reasonable to expect that at this point, the worker would decide to continue his periodic training and to seek to employ his second skill *to whatever extent he has acquired it.*

He has some marginal productivity (in the use of the second skill)

---

[9] For a discussion of the concept of an internal rate of return on investment in human capital, see Becker, *op. cit.*

[10] For the same m, the second term on the right side of (5) would be smaller by

$$\sum_{t=m}^{p-1} \frac{k_t}{(1+i)^{t+1}} .$$

$U + s$, where s has arisen out of the training thus far conducted and

$$0 \leqslant s < MP_2 .[11] \tag{7}$$

The obsolescence of the principal skill would have no effect on C_2. The (discounted) value of the earnings salvaged, however, can, in this case, be viewed in two parts. *First,* the gains occurring during the interval from the completion of training to the end of the work-life,

$$\sum_{t=p}^{n-1} \frac{MP_2 - U}{(1 + i)^{t+1}} . \tag{8}$$

Second, the amount salvaged between $t = m$ and $t = p$ which (discounted at $t = 0$) is

$$\sum_{t=m}^{p-1} \frac{s_t + s_t'}{(1 + i)^{t+1}}, \tag{9}$$

where s' is the periodic increment in productivity which the (continuing) training brings about during the interval from $t = m$ to $t = p$.

The success of a hedge consisting of training over time thus depends not only on the length of time $n - m$, but also upon how quickly productivity rises during the training interval.

A LESS RESTRICTIVE VIEW

The analysis becomes less simple, but more interesting, if we drop the assumption that the hedging worker can expect to receive a wage equal to his marginal product in each period. (Gary S. Becker's analysis[12] shows that under certain conditions of training, this assumption is not valid.) We shall simply emphasize instead that the (discounted) differences between the worker's *wages* and U, after the occurrence of m, constitute the "salvage" made possible by the hedge.

Under these circumstances, two major points must be considered:

1. For any worker, the *possible* length of the interval $n - m$ is becoming continuously shorter as long as his principal skill is used; in other words, the "present" is moving ever-closer to n. But under our assumptions, the interval from $t = m$ to $t = n$ (if it occurs) represents the *first $n - m$ periods of a "career" in the second skill.* It follows that second-skill programs which typically have a steep "time-earnings profile" are relatively poor hedges. Committing oneself to low earn-

---

[11] If s were equal to MP_2, the worker would discontinue training.

[12] (See note 2.)

ings during the early periods of a second-skill "career" is clearly unwise if the "early" periods may be the *only* periods during which the skill is employed!

2. On the other hand, *m* may occur *before* training is completed. In this case, a relative disadvantage is introduced by the selection of a hedging program which leads to a license, badge, or other socio-legal achievement-measuring devices; for often, practice of the skill or employment in the field before the acquisition of such license, etc. is prohibited by law, labor-management contracts, or other institutional arrangements.

GENERAL EDUCATION

These reflections cast doubt on the usefulness of general education, *beyond* the basic "3R's" stage, as a hedge;[13] for *such educational programs usually manifest the two "risky" characteristics mentioned above.*

A steep "time-earnings profile" may be expected from a "groundwork" of general education mainly because, as has been found, this background often leads to *subsequent* job- or on-the-job training. Jacob Mincer has presented convincing evidence to this effect.[14] Thus, the role of general education suggested by Mincer's findings and specified by Weisbrod (see page 2) involves sufficient *time* (of which the hedging worker is uncertain) to recoup the investments in both the education and the subsequent process of "adapting."

The occurrence of principal-skill obsolescence *during* a program of general education may cause the worker to receive substantially reduced earnings during the time between *m* and *p* for reasons analogous to those where a license is sought.[15] There is some indication that diplomas and degrees perform an "admission-ticket" function; that they often provide, in fact, the only means of entry to certain types of on-the-job training. Evidence of these features is provided in the find-

---

[13]Admittedly, a knowledge of the "3R's" is critically important in our society. But we are considering a worker who already possesses a skill; it is thus reasonable to continue the discussion with the assumption that he is "functionally literate."

[14]"On-the-Job Training: Costs, Returns, and Some Implications," *The Journal of Political Economy*, "Supplement," October, 1962.

[15]Consider another problem: a worker who is studying part-time, say, for a high school diploma may have to secure employment at the wage *U* if *m* occurs. Unless he and his family can readjust their current expenditures immediately, he may have to divert his unexpended investment resources (his spare time) to producing current income. Interruption or discontinuance of the education program (with its accompanying capital loss) may result.

ings of Miller[16] and Hansen,[17] who report that the rate of return on the "completion period" of an interval of educational pursuit is significantly higher than the return to any of the earlier periods (where the "periods" are typically years). Hansen remarks, "At this point one can only speculate as to the reasons for this phenomenon."

The "reasons" seem to lie, as with licensing, etc. in institutional factors. In *The Status Seekers*, Vance Packard, focusing on the college degree, mentions two factors contributing to its function as an admission device:

> One is the growing use of the blueprint approach to the selection of personnel. . . . It is easier for a personnel department to draw up its job specifications and then "go by the book." Its officials impersonally build their organization and, for each level, assign minimum qualifications. Typically, the minimums become higher in terms of schooling with each step in the hierarchy. It's neater that way.
>
> . . . Patricia Salter West quotes "a big corporation executive" as saying he realizes fully that a college education is no magic way to make "a silk purse out of a sow's ear." But then he adds: "Still, we always pick our junior management from the colleges . . . deciding in advance to pick a college boy gives you a good way to eliminate a lot of candidates right off the bat."[18]

It should be emphasized that we question the usefulness of education only as it affects the safety of a hedge; and it appears to affect this safety because it tends (for whatever reasons) to yield earnings through *time* in a way which does not lend itself well to situations of uncertain time-availability.

The younger a hedging worker is, the more time he has available to recoup any investment he makes; also, the younger he is, the more risky it is for him to invest in a second skill which is to some extent *specialized;* for this, too, could become obsolete. Since *general* education is not characterized by this drawback, our above objections to a broad-education hedge are correspondingly weakened — and Weisbrod's "flexibility" notion is strengthened — as the worker in question is assumed younger.

From this, we would expect to find that relatively older persons have less tendency to undertake general education on a part-time

[16] Herman P. Miller, "Annual and Lifetime Income in Relation to Education: 1939–1959," *American Economic Review*, December 1960.

[17] W. Lee Hansen, "Total and Private Rate of Return to Investment in Schooling," *The Journal of Political Economy*, April 1963.

[18] Vance Packard, *The Status Seekers* (New York: David McKay Co., 1959).

basis. (A part-time scheme can best suggest a hedge of the sort we discuss.) Of course, data involving adult education and training cannot reveal who is hedging and who is not; nor can it separate the consumption from the investment component in these activities. Nevertheless, it is of interest to note the results of two recent investigations into the pattern of adult education and training:

The National Opinion Research Center estimates that one-fifth of the nation's adults (some 25 million persons) follow some plan of education or other form of self-improvement; Professor John W. C. Johnstone of the University of Chicago stresses that the emphasis among such programs is found to be on " . . . the practical rather than the academic, on the applied rather than the theoretical, on skills. . . ."[19]

The Center for the Study of Liberal Education for Adults makes an estimate "over 17 million" in these activities for the period June, 1961 to June, 1962. Of these, it finds that 9 million were engaged in "some form of *independent* self-education," and that approximately 6½ million of these cases were on a part-time basis. The major stress is found to be practical rather than academic; again, "skills" were emphasized rather than "knowledge or values."[20]

One approach through which a self-educating person can minimize the cost of this activity is to devote to it those time periods which have the lowest value in alternative uses. Thus, it is not surprising to learn that correspondence courses, which make this possible, have grown increasingly popular. Edward P. Neilan writes:

These correspondence schools have been eminently successful because correspondent training can be adapted . . . to fit into . . . time schedules and, as a result, its adaptability has provided many avenues for individuals to improve their knowledge and capability without being restricted to regular classroom hours. Correspondence schools have the advantage that they permit the students to complete their instruction in a short time or over a longer period at their own choice. . . .[21]

In short, correspondence schools appear to offer something of which a hedging worker has a critical need: *flexibility.*

[19] *The New York Times,* May 20, 1963, page 31.

[20] *Ibid.,* April 21, 1963, Sec. IV, page 7. Italics are mine.

[21] "Training—One Solution to the Unemployment Problem," *Training Directors Journal,* November, 1963.

Because human wealth is non-negotiable, it is extremely difficult to protect an investment in a skill from the effects of a volatile labor market. Of the various techniques used to protect investments in other markets, only one is available to a worker: the choice of dividing his resources into two (or more) different forms of capital.

Time governs the success of a worker's hedge in several ways. If a "spare skill" can be acquired quickly, it may be safest for a worker to delay its acquisition until it is needed. Skills acquired over time are risky if they do not tend to "pay up" quickly. The older a worker is, the less safe is general education as a hedge relative to a readily-applicable skill.

20. Hedging in the Labor Market: Comment*

ARIE R. MELNIK

Michigan State University

In a recent article in this Journal, Professor Cipriani argued that of the various techniques used to protect investments in other markets, only one is available to the holder of human capital: the choice of dividing his resources into two (or more) different forms of capital.[1] The worker who holds human capital cannot take positions in more than one market at the same time (e.g. he cannot sell "short" his services). The need to diversify the "human capital portfolio" is demonstrated by assuming that there is some positive probability that a skill will become obsolete. When a skill becomes obsolete, the demand for its services drops instantaneously to zero everywhere.[2] To avoid the possible capital loss associated with the complete obsolescence of a skill, a worker will diversify his investment portfolio by acquiring a second skill and by investing in non-human capital.

The purpose of this note is to relax the assumption of sudden obsolescence of skills and to introduce some considerations of skill development and growth. Changing this assumption sheds some more light on the choice of the "human capital portfolio."

I

In a broad sense, we can define investment in human capital as an investment in both formal and informal education and training. Following Professor Cipriani, our analysis takes Becker's study as a point

---

*Reprinted from "Hedging in the Labor Market (Comment)," *Southern Economic Journal*, XXXV (January, 1969), 270–272.
[1] Corindo J. Cipriani. "Hedging in the Labor Market," *The Southern Economic Journal*, October 1967, pp. 286–92.
[2] C. J. Cipriani, *op. cit*, p. 287.

of departure and elaborates on it by borrowing from conventional investment theory.[3]

Following Cipriani we assume that a given profession or job Y, yields a real earning stream $Y_0, Y_1, \cdots, Y_n$. The present value of the occupation is:

$$V = \sum_{t=0}^{n} \frac{Y_t}{(1+i)^{t+1}} \tag{1}$$

where i is the market discount rate and it is assumed to be the same in each period. If we let X be an alternative occupation with income stream X_t, then the gain from choosing Y is:

$$d = \sum_{t=0}^{n} \frac{Y_t - X_t}{(1+i)^{t+1}} \tag{2}$$

Cipriani assumed that X is the wage of an unskilled worker and thus arrived at the conclusion that (2) may be the 'cost' of obsolescence. However, since investment in human capital is made over a long time period, the assumption about X seems to be very strong. A worker who starts an investment in human capital takes into consideration not only possible obsolescence but also the growth potential. This growth potential exists especially in cases where there are different degrees of skill in the same occupation. As one invests in Y continuously, he is upgrading his skill. As a result, his alternative skill changes over time and hence one's alternative costs also change and are not measured by (2). This means that the loss from obsolescence—even if it occurs instantaneously—may not be as great as Cipriani implies. Consequently, the need for a second occupation may not be so great.

II

The need to hedge in the labor market is based on the assumption of instantaneous and drastic obsolescence of skills. The young worker will undoubtedly consider the prospect of obsolescence in his skill. However in most cases the skill will not become obsolete over night and if we also assume that there is some potential for improvement within the chosen occupation we may reach the opposite conclusion; namely, that the best hedge against the uncertain future will be

---

[3]Becker's theoretical analysis is basically an adaptation of investment theory. See Gary S. Becker, "Investment in Human Capital: A Theoretical Analysis," *The Journal of Political Economy*, Supplement, October 1962, pp. 9–49.

further investment in the acquired occupation rather than in a different one.

Let us consider the initial position of an individual who has to consider investment in human capital. The person facing such a decision will presumably evaluate the cost of investment and weigh it against the present value of the expected return. If the training period is not too long, say four years of college, the cost can be estimated with reasonable accuracy. The returns however, are hard to measure. Even if we take the current income of this occupation as a proxy, it is unlikely to remain the same in the future. If the demand for the occupation is growing at a rate slower than supply (the case of obsolescence), the future income stream will decrease. If, on the other hand demand grows faster than supply, the future income stream should increase. To take account of both obsolescence and skill development potential, it should be assumed that increased income involves continuous investment in order to keep up-to-date in the profession. The continuous investment is done not only to avoid obsolescence but also to take advantage of the development potential.

Returning to equation (1) we now observe that a given occupation Y yields an expected earning stream of E_t. If θ is the expected rate of return and we use a continuous form of (1), the value of this occupation is:

$$V' = \int_0^n E_t e^{-\theta t}\, dt. \tag{3}$$

We are concerned here with *expected* future returns from human capital. Expected future income is an estimate that can be derived — conceptually — from known data in the most objective manner. The relation of E_t to Y_t is obtained using the following two assumptions:[4] (a) The worker will consistently invest b percent of his income in improving and up-dating his knowledge. (b) On his additional investment he expects a rate of return of r.[5]

If part of Y_t is invested, then expected net income is:

$$E_t = (1 - b)Y_0. \tag{4}$$

To this we should add that Y_t itself is changing from period to period.

[4] Both the assumptions and the approach are taken from M. J. Gordon and E. Shapiro "Capital Equipment Analysis: The Required Rate of Profit," *Management Science*, October 1956, pp. 103–107.

[5] The magnitude of r is directly related to the growth potential of the skill and inversely related to the obsolescence potential.

Investment in Education

Income at time t is the sum of income received in $(t-1)$ and r percent of the invested portion of that income. Formally we can write:

$$Y_t = Y_{(t-1)} + rbY_{(t-1)}.$$ (5)

This equation represents a periodical growth of Y_t. In the case of a continuous rate of growth $g = rb$ we may write:

$$Y_t = Y_0 e^{gt}.$$ (6)

From equations (4) and (6) we get:

$$E_t = E_0 e^{gt}.$$ (7)

Substituting the expression in (7) for E_t in (3) we get:

$$V_0' = \int_0^n E_0 e^{gt} e^{-\theta t}\, dt = E_0 \int_0^n e^{-(\theta-g)t}\, dt = \frac{E_0}{\theta - g}(1 - e^{-(\theta-g)n}).$$ (8)

This simplified version means that the rate of return which the worker expects from his investment is a function not only of the present value of earnings and costs but also of the rate at which earnings are expected to grow.[6]

III

The "growth model" presented above is not the most elaborated one. We assumed a constant rate of growth which was the product of the fraction of earning reinvested and the rate of return earned on the reinvestment. In reality, different portions of current income may be invested in different periods (i.e., $b \neq$ const.) and the rate of return may not be the same. In spite of this admitted oversimplification, we may argue that as long as $r > 0$, the growth potential is more influential than obsolescence. Furthermore, it seems that growth considerations should also be introduced conceptually to the case of investment in human capital. An investor in human capital should consider the amount of investment needed—in addition to the original investment—to keep up with technological changes (i.e., the investment in updating and upgrading himself). In fact the growth model helps to explain why in many cases even when rapid technological changes are taking place—the worker would choose to invest more in adjusting to those changes rather than invest in another skill.

[6]The condition for solution is $\theta > g$. If we assume a time horizon sufficiently long, then the expression $e^{-(\theta-g)n}$ in (8) becomes very small and for all practical purposes $V_0' = E_0/\theta - g$ or, solving for θ: $\theta = E_0/V_0' + g$.

Our result is not in contrast with Cipriani. He assumed sudden obsolescence which means in terms of our model a negative r. If growth potential is taken into account and if obsolescence is not instantaneous and can be compensated for by investment in adjustments to technological changes, then r is positive (and hence g is positive). In such cases the need to hedge in the labor market is not so strong.

PART IV Investment in Health

Introduction

Health service expenditures which tend either to increase the supply of labor or increase labor's productivity are being treated within the human capital theoretical framework. The presumption is that expenditures which reduce the incidence of death, disability, and debility generally lead to an increase in output—assuming, of course, full employment and a population level which does not exceed its maximum (defined by a zero rate of return on the existing stock of conventional capital).

Part IV of the volume deals with the health service component of human capital. It attempts to treat the investment aspect of health services in much the same manner, albeit in abbreviated form, as education was treated in the preceding part.

In the lead contribution (Reading 21) to this part, Selma J. Mushkin compares health and education as types of investment in people. She then presents a brief summary of measures of capital formation through health programs.

Dr. Mushkin and Francis d'A. Collings in the second article (Reading 22) in this part, discuss the concepts and definitions in the measurement of labor-product loss owing to disease. This is the first step in estimating the increase in the value of output owing to a reduction in deaths, disability, and debility. The second step is to assign a monetary value to the output that such added labor product (man-hours) represents.

The third article (Reading 23) in Part IV is a survey of the current literature, by Herbert E. Klarman, on the subject of investment in health care. He points out many of the problems involved in treating health care expenditures as investment, e.g., the consumption-investment dichotomy, choosing the "proper" rate of discount, calculating output loss, and the desirability of using the human capital concept for an investment criterion.

A more thorough critique of the literature on investment in health care is provided by Jack Wiseman in the fifth reading (Reading 24) in this part. He concludes that although the capital analytical framework as applied to health care may be useful for an investment criterion, it is important to stress that the results of such application, e.g., internal rate of return estimates and benefit-cost ratios, are only minimum criteria upon which to base public policy decisions.

21. Health as an Investment*

SELMA J. MUSHKIN[1]

Advisory Commission on Intergovernmental Relations, Washington, D.C.

A theory of human capital is in the process of formulation. The primary question is "What is the contribution of changes in the quality of people to economic growth?" The academic economists first raised the question after their research showed that production in developed economies had been increasing much faster than could be explained by inputs of physical capital and additions to the labor force.[2] But the wide interest which the question has aroused indicates much more than academic curiosity. It reflects the desires and aspirations of people throughout the world — people anxious to add weight to their demands for action against disease and illiteracy by showing that such action is not only humanitarian, but will make a major contribution to economic growth as well. Though research on the return to investment in people is barely getting started, even the most tentative conclusions have been widely quoted. Preliminary indications that the rate of return on investment in people is high have been seized upon in a growing number of countries as justification for including investment in people in economic development programs.

In 1961 two important international conferences were held on investment in people as a facet of economic development.[3] One of

*Excerpt from "Health as an Investment," *Journal of Political Economy*, Supplement, LXX (October, 1962), 129–138. Copyright by The University of Chicago Press.

[1] This article necessarily was prepared in a short period of time. The views expressed are the author's own and do not necessarily accord with those of the Advisory Commission on Intergovernmental Relations.

[2] S. Fabricant, *Basic Facts on Productivity Change* ("Occasional Papers," No. 63, New York: National Bureau of Economic Research, 1959), and R. M. Solow, "Technical Change and the Aggregate Production Function," *Review of Economics and Statistics*, Vol. XXXIX (August, 1957).

[3] World Health Organization and Pan American Sanitary Bureau, thirteenth meeting of Directing Council, October, 1961, Washington, D.C.; and the OEEC Policy Conference on Economic Growth and Investment in Education, Washington, D.C., October 16–20, 1961.

these discussed health programs, the other education. Given the climate of thought today it seems difficult to imagine that only four years ago authorities writing on economic development, with few exceptions, omitted consideration of investments in people. A footnote in one such volume may be cited as illustrative. In explaining the omission, the authors write, "once one leaves the *terra firma* of material capital and branches out into the upper aether of human capital there is endless difficulty in finding a resting place."[4]

Research leading toward a theory of human capital formation has been largely pioneered by Professor Theodore W. Schultz and supported by the Ford Foundation's Fund for the Advancement of Education. This work centers on investment through education. Basic economic research on investment through health programs is receiving far less attention, and sustained financial support for such research is even at this time uncertain. But out of the work that Schultz has done and the work of others whom he has encouraged has come a better understanding of the economic processes that apply to health programs as well as to education. The far more intensive work on education as an investment suggests that it may be useful to start this paper with a comparison of health and education as types of investment. The first part of this paper, therefore, states briefly some of the similarities between the two programs, as well as characteristic differences between them.

The second part deals with capital formation through health care and returns to investment in health. Some empirical work on specific diseases has been done; work has also been done on the over-all problems of disease. Although I do not review these specific empirical studies, I attempt to summarize the basic assumptions underlying their estimates and to point to examples of the "payoff" on investment in eradication of disease.

Throughout I address myself to the economic effects of health programs—public and private, curative and preventive. Promotion of health patently involves more than health services and the related commodities used in the provision of these services. It includes food, housing, recreation and clothing. Although they contribute importantly to health, the present inquiry is limited to investment in health services and their component commodities. It appears necessary, however, in the present context to include water supplies among the

[4]P. T. Bauer and B. C. Yamey, *The Economics of Underdeveloped Countries* (Cambridge: Cambridge University Press, 1957), p. 27.

investments in health. Environmental health programs, including safe water supplies, are largely responsible for the rate of decline in death rates in the United States between 1900 and 1917. In this period the over-all age-adjusted death rates decreased at 1.074 per year, a higher rate of decrease than took place in the subsequent period 1921–37. Diseases that can be controlled through sanitation and safe water supplies — typhoid, diarrhea, and dysentery — are among the major diseases today in the underdeveloped countries which give a high priority to investment in water supplies and sanitation.

I. EDUCATION AND HEALTH: SIMILARITIES AND DIFFERENCES

The concept of human capital formation through both education and health services rests on the twin notions that people as productive agents are improved by investment in these services and that the outlays made yield a continuing return in the future. Health services, like education, become a part of the individual, a part of his effectiveness in field and factory. The future increase in labor product resulting from education or from health programs can be quantified to an extent useful for programming purposes. While there are apparent limitations to such measures, these limitations can be identified.

COMPLEMENTARY CONTENT OF INVESTMENT

Health and education are joint investments made in the same individual. The individual is more effective in society as a producer and as a consumer because of these investments. And often the return on investment in health is attributed to education.

The interrelations between health and education are many, as suggested by the illustrations which follow. Some types of health programs essentially depend upon education in personal hygiene and sanitation. On education falls responsibility for training of health personnel (both professional and ancillary) to provide the health services. A child's formal schooling is impossible unless he is well enough to attend school and to learn. Loss in days of schooling due to ill health, which in the United States in 1958 averaged 8.4 days per school year, reduces the effectiveness of investment in education. And death of children of school age adds to the cost of education per effective labor-force member. A lengthening of life expectancy through improved health reduces the rate of depreciation of investment in education and increases the return to it. An increase in productive efficiency through improved education, on the other hand, increases the return on a lifesaving investment in health.

It is a fairly simple bit of arithmetic to determine the differences in human capital formation through education, given the mortality experience of the early 1900's and today. Differences in years of work expectancy on the average between two periods will change the value of lifetime income differentials between the high-school and the college graduate, for example. It is also simple arithmetic to compute the value of future earnings, on the average, of a death postponed to old age when the number of years of schooling approximates the norm of the early 1900's and the norm of today. But far more difficult is the problem of assessing the loss to the country from the early death or incapacity of a would-be inventor, scientist, or political leader. What would have been the loss if Einstein had died during the flu epidemic following World War I, or had Keynes' last work been his *Treatise on Money*?

Educational levels determine to a large extent the seeking out of health services and the selection of appropriate kinds of services. A large body of information exists pointing to a high correlation between use of health services and educational status.[5] And one of the major health problems that confronts public health officers is education of groups in the community to use available public services, for example, Salk vaccine. Delays in seeking care, due to ignorance, intensify disease problems and convert cases that could be prevented or controlled into serious disabilities or premature deaths.[6]

Health services are similar to education, too, in that they are partly investment and partly consumption, and the separation of the two elements is difficult. An individual wants to get well so that life for him may be more satisfying. But also when he is well he can perform more effectively as a producer. What part of the expenditure made to cure his illness is a consumption expenditure, and what part is an investment in a producer? The type of issue involved is familiar to those who have been working on investment in education.

As consumer goods, both education and health are extraordinary. They are not sought simply to satisfy human wants but are essential ingredients of human welfare. The distinction I have in mind was

[5] E. L. Koos, *The Health of Regionville: What the People Thought and Did about It* (New York, 1954).

[6] J. W. Bergsten, "Volume of Physician Visits, U.S., July 1957–June 1959," *Statistics from the U.S. National Health Survey* (Ser. B-19, Washington, 1960).

made several years ago by Munoz-Marin, the governor of Puerto Rico, when he proposed an "Operation Serenity" through which society "would use its economic power increasingly for the extension of freedom, of knowledge, and of understanding imagination rather than a rapid multiplication of wants." Levels of education and health are implicit components of a standard of living.[7] When man does not have sufficient vitality to function normally, other consumption loses its significance, and without education the distinctive qualities of the human being are lost.

Return to investment in both health and education accrue in part to the individual who makes the investment and in part to other individuals. Purchase of health services for the prevention of contagious and infectious diseases, such as smallpox, poliomyelitis, and whooping cough, benefits the community as a whole. Curative health services, such as those for the treatment of tuberculosis or syphilis, help prevent the spread of the disease; thus an individual's purchase of services for his own care benefits his neighbors. By his improved health status and by that of his neighbors the productivity of the economy is increased.

Health, like education, is being financed largely out of current consumption funds. Denison has pointed out that whether the individual spending for education thinks of himself as consuming or investing is not so important as whether the resources used for financing the services have come from consumption funds or investment funds.[8] He emphasizes that funds used for education—both public and private—largely reduce consumption and thus make a positive net contribution to economic growth. Educational outlays, assuming this diversion of funds from consumption to investment, increase the total volume of investment even if the rate of return on educational investment is considerably lower than that on investment in physical capital. Denison's observations on the sources of educational funds apply by and large to sources of health funds as well. But here we have the perhaps curious juxtaposition of circumstances that funds, at least in the United States, are withdrawn from alternative invest-

[7] World Health Organization, "Measurement of Levels of Health" (Technical Report No. 137, 1957), and United Nations, International Labour Office, and UNESCO (jointly), "Report on International Definition and Measurements of Standards and Levels of Living" (Committee of Experts E/CN./179, 1954).

[8] E. F. Denison, *The Sources of Economic Growth in the United States and the Alternative before Us* (New York: Committee for Economic Development, 1962).

ments primarily to finance those health-service costs that most clearly could be classified as consumption — costs of major medical incidents that lead to disabling chronic illness and to death.

It must be remembered that health and education services in most countries are financed in part through the public sector of the economy and in part through the private sector. The mixture of public and private varies widely, however, from nation to nation, and the mix may not be the same for health as it is for education within a nation. Expenditures for health in the United States amount to more than $25 billion; expenditures for education also are about $25 billion. But public outlays for health account for less than 25 cents of each $1 spent; and private outlays for the remaining more than 75 cents. In the case of education the proportions are reversed; about 80 cents of each $1 of educational costs is publicly financed and about 20 cents privately financed.

DIFFERENCES BETWEEN HEALTH AND EDUCATION

There are these important similarities between health and education as investments. But the differences between them necessitate different approaches to the problem of measurement of human capital. As I see the differences, they are:

1. Health programs increase the numbers in the working force as well as the quality of labor's product. Education chiefly affects quality of the producers. The people added to the work force through a reduction in number of deaths and in disability provide a direct measure of the units of labor resulting from improvement in health status. By valuing these added workers at the present value of their future earnings, the capital stock in health status can be determined. This is analogous to valuing physical capital, such as real property, on the basis of its rental income. But as indicated below, the health-program content of this health status is difficult to disentangle from other factors affecting health of a population. And valuation of changes in quality of the work force attributable to health programs presents an additional problem.

The number of potential workers that may be added through health programs is especially large in the non-industrial nations. Average life expectancy at birth in many nations of Asia and Africa — nations that include almost two-thirds of the world population — was until recently about thirty years. This may be contrasted with almost

385

seventy years of life expectancy achieved in the United States. Large increases in life expectancy for these non-industrial nations can be brought about quickly and with fairly small direct outlays. Spraying with DDT, immunization with BCG, and treatment with penicillin have yielded dramatic results in reduced mortality from malaria, tuberculosis, syphilis, and yaws. An intensification of programs to control these diseases could reduce death rates rapidly.

2. Units of quality change through human capital formation by health programs cannot be defined as tidily as units of education embodied in the labor force. There is no quality unit comparable to that of the number of years of schooling, devised by Schultz as a measure of educational stock in the labor force.[9] To assess the quality changes resulting from the health-program content embodied in the labor force, a positive measure of health status would be required. The most frequently used indexes of health status, however, are negative — death rates and morbidity rates that reflect changes in numbers rather than quality. There are two other types of indexes in use: first, measures of the relative availability of health facilities, for example, the number of physicians or the number of hospital beds per 1,000 population. Second, the number of services rendered is used, for example, the number of children vaccinated or the number of births in hospitals.

Some indicators of change in health status exist, but they have a limited use; for example, in the United States and Great Britain children in each age group are taller today than their fathers and grandfathers were at the same age. Puberty comes at an earlier age. More recently work has been done on physical fitness, which may have some application in the future to the measurement of work capacity of a population. Physiological tests have been developed of the individual's total ability to perform prolonged physical work. "For all practical purposes, this means the ability of the cardiopulmonary system to take up, transport, and give off oxygen to the muscle tissue for the performance of physical work."[10] Muscle strength, oxygen uptake, and pulse responses have been combined in a series of tests.

[9] T. W. Schultz, "Education and Economic Growth" in *Social Forces Influencing American Education*, ed. N. B. Henry (Chicago, 1961).

[10] T. Hettinger *et al.*, "Assessment of Physical Work Capacity: A Comparison between Different Tests and Maximal Oxygen Intake," *Journal of Applied Physiology*, XVI (1961), 1; see also K. Rodahl *et al.*, "Physical Work Capacity," *Archives of Environmental Health*, II (May, 1961), 23–24.

At present, it is difficult to disentangle the effects on the health status of the population that are attributable to health programs from those attributable to better nutrition, better housing, better working conditions, and higher incomes. Sickness is a cause as well as a consequence of poverty. Tuberculosis, for example, is closely related to housing conditions. "Lung block" in New York City conveyed the image of this association. Indeed, Lowell, after a detailed study of the tuberculosis problem in New York City, wrote: "if optimum benefits are to be realized in mastering tuberculosis progress in medicine and public health, they must be accompanied by comparable and parallel socioeconomic improvements in living conditions."[11] Communicable diseases generally have a higher rate of incidence among the poor than among the rich. Conditions of poverty give rise to the easy transmission of infectious diseases; thus improved living standards contribute importantly to reduction in prevalence and incidence rates. The improvement in health status in the past six decades in the United States is in part the result of health services that brought the infectious and contagious diseases under control. (In part, too, it is the result of the growth in the economy.) For example, of one hundred white males born in 1900–1902, seventy-nine reached age fifteen and thirty-nine will reach sixty-five years of age. In 1958, out of one hundred white males born, ninety-six will reach age fifteen and sixty-six will reach age sixty-five. Isolation of some of the major factors responsible for prolonging life would help to identify the contribution of health programs as well as the contribution of specific aspects of health programs such as sanitary control of the environment, widespread immunization, better medical care, and community health services. But we are a long way from identifying the contribution of health programs.

3. Closely related to the problem of measuring quality changes attributable to health programs is the question of assessing earning differences. In assessing the private return to investment in education, one begins with data on differentials in earnings according to years of schooling. Average differences in lifetime incomes of high-school and college graduates, for example, corrected for differences in ability and other factors, serve as an index of return to higher education. We now have no similar indexes of differences in income associ-

---

[11] A. M. Lowell, *Socio-economic Conditions and Tuberculosis Prevalence in New York City, 1949–51* (New York: New York Tuberculosis and Health Association, 1956).

ated with gradations in health. More particularly, we have no indexes of differences in earnings reflecting such gradations.

The National Health Survey provides information on the time lost from work because of temporary sickness. Bergsten, analyzing the results of this survey, shows an inverse relation between family income and time lost from work. While persons (usually working) in families with income under $2,000 lose an average of 10.3 days a year from work due to illness and injury, those with income of $7,000 or more lose only 5.9 days.[12] Data on differences in sickness rates by income class, however, reflect the interaction of illness and income.

We have some negative measures that indicate the market's evaluation of risk of sickness and death and potential loss in earning due to permanent impairment. Rates under workmen's compensation laws reflect differences in the risk of death and injury in different occupations. If a correction is made for the effects of statutory limits on benefit payments, workmen's compensation rates should reflect the "charge" for the risks of death and disability. Rates levied in the states vary widely for different employers depending upon their industrial accident experience. For certain types of iron and steel erection in the construction industry, for example, rates are in the neighborhood of 20 percent of wages, while in the same state, large retail trade outlets pay premium rates in the neighborhood of only 0.5 percent. If workmen's compensation charges, as adjusted, can be used to measure the risk of death and disability, it may be possible to use premiums paid for extra occupational risks — or "hazard pay" — as an index of the market evaluation of the risk of continuing debility. Hazard pay is paid to persons in occupations such as airplane pilots, undersea divers, and longshoremen handling dangerous cargoes. And injury rates become one of the many factors considered in wage negotiation even when separate hazard premiums are not paid.

4. Educational investment is a developmental process, which ferrets out and encourages native talent. It proceeds step by step from one level to another, transmitting a cultural environment by building on the existing store of knowledge. Health programs seek basically to prevent a hostile environment from killing and crippling. They seek to stay the natural forces of biological selection.

[12] J. W. Bergsten, "Disability Days, U.S., July 1957–June 1958," *Statistics from the U.S. National Health Survey* (Ser. B-10, Washington, 1960).

Peoples throughout history have invested in health; even the most primitive of peoples have invested in a selectivity process whereby those most fit for their environment survived. The survivors developed immunities to the diseases of their environment, but the price of these immunities (the investment in health) was the early deaths of the less fit with the consequent loss of their net productive contribution. In some early cultures an even larger investment was made in the selectivity producing a health status through the killing of the disabled and the weak.

Many underdeveloped countries or regions within these countries have progressed in health programs little beyond sustaining a natural death rate—a rate reflecting the early deaths of those unable to withstand the dangers of a hostile environment. And while modern medicine has been brought into such regions and has lowered death rates, modern civilization in some remote places has destroyed the earlier investment of the people in these places in building immunity to disease. New diseases have been brought in.

In a modern economy biological selection is no longer an acceptable method of investing in health, not only because our humanitarian instincts rebel against it, but because it costs too much. The cost of foregoing the productive contribution of those who would die early is now too great. In our present economy, in the United States and other industrially developed nations, physical strength of the human hand is not often used in the production processes. People with so-called impaired lives can and do make great contributions to our national output. Brain power and other human capabilities and talents are far more important than physical stamina. In replacing the physical energy of people by inanimate power, and crude natural products by synthetic substitutes, mankind has altered the nature of its investment requirements, both human and physical.

The significance of the difference between education and health as an investment lies in the range of choices to be considered in the regions of the world that are in the twilight of a cultural transition from the ancient to the modern. The choice in the case of health is not between some investment and no investment; it is between investment in biological selection and investment in modern public health measures or in other measures that indirectly promote health.

One word of further qualification is needed so that I will not be misunderstood. Biological selection does not necessarily result in a strong and virile and creative people; it results only in the survival of those best able to withstand the rigors of their physical and biological environment.

These then are some important differences between health and education investments. Some of the differences are pertinent only to consideration of health programs in the underdeveloped nations; others to industrialized countries.

II. MEASURING CAPITAL FORMATION THROUGH HEALTH CARE

In its simplest form the economic resources (labor and commodities) devoted to health care represent in some part an investment in health. In some part, that is, the health outlays improve the labor product and continue to yield a return over a period of years. The labor product created by this care and savings in health expenditures in the future, if any, as a consequence of reduction in disease is the yield.

Just as the stock of physical capital may be measured in a number of different ways, so the stock of health capital in people may be variously measured. This human capital formation by health care for a population may be counted, for example, at cost — the cost of environmental and curative health services embodied over their life spans in each of the age cohorts in the present labor force. Cost for this purpose may be set at the cost of acquisition of the health services in the years they were acquired; they may be determined on a replacement cost basis, or at constant prices prevailing in a base year.

At today's prices if we valued the health care received by persons currently in the labor force, for example, we might arrive at a figure of, let us assume, about $250 billion. Is the yield on this $250 billion stock $12 billion, $25 billion, or of what order of magnitude? What, in other words, has been the money value of the annual labor product added as a consequence of the health investments made?

A study of the stock of health-program capital on a cost basis stimulated by the Exploratory Conference on Investment in Human Beings is in progress. This study has not progressed sufficiently to describe fully its scope nor patently to yield findings. Some preliminary and very partial figures may illustrate the possible quantities, however. Medical care costs of child-bearing in 1957–58 averaged $272;[13] the

[13] Health Information Foundation, *Progress in Health Services* (New York), Vol. X (March, 1961) (newsletter).

health costs for an infant and child (at 1957–58 prices) come to about $45 a year. If we include all medical care expenditures for a child up to age eighteen, the average child uses more than $1,000 in health and medical services.[14] To produce a labor force member aged eighteen at today's quantities and quality of health care and at today's prices, accordingly, upward of $1,000 is spent in health resources alone. For the seventy-three million persons in the labor force of 1960 this would mean a $73 billion stock of health care up to age eighteen when valued on replacement costs basis, without adjustment for losses due to early death. At pre-World War I quantities and quality of health care and medical prices prevailing then, the health stock in a labor force of 1960 size (counting costs only up to age eighteen) would have been about $5.5 billion before addition of costs lost through these earlier deaths prior to age eighteen. Data on per capita expenditures for health care are shown in Table 1.

The capital stock of health services may also be measured as the present value of the added labor product acquired through health

TABLE 1

Health-Care Expenditures, Selected Years, 1914 to 1958–59

Year	Amount (In Millions)	Per Capita	As Percentage of Gross National Product
1914*	$ 1,091	$ 11	2.7
1921*	2,024	19	2.7
1927*	3,030	25	3.1
1956*	18,358	109	4.4
1928–29†	3,650	30	3.6
1939–40†	3,915	30	4.1
1949–50†	12,365	83	4.7
1956–57†	21,027	125	4.9
1958–59†	25,196	145	5.4

*Compiled from United States Bureau of Census, *Historical Statistics of the United States, Colonial Times to 1957*. Includes personal consumption expenditures and also public outlays for health programs, federal, state, and local.

†From Ida C. Merriam, "Social Welfare Expenditures, 1958–59," *Social Security Bulletin*, November, 1960, p. 43. Includes industrial-in-plant services and philanthropy as well as personal health expenditures and public outlays for health programs.

---

[14]These figures are approximate and may be revised substantially when additional research is done.

programs, that is, the stock may be valued at the present value of the future earnings generated through the health programs. In some health programs, the labor product added is contingent on the services received by a specific individual, and on his death or retirement the capital value of health services is lost. Accordingly, the future earnings to be valued for the present period are limited by survival and retirement rates.

The present value of future labor product created by health care becomes a second measure of capital value. The question that is being asked in this measurement of investment is: "What is the expected return from the health care which in turn determines its value?"

The cost in terms of health-program expenditures and, in turn, in terms of resources devoted to health care may be greater or less than the capitalized value of the added labor product created through improved health status.

This measure of the capitalized expected income over the productive life span of the new labor product added through a health program takes account of the depreciation on the investment by the loss of labor product through retirement and death. There are types of health programs, however, which yield returns into perpetuity. The asset created in the main does not depreciate. The value of the health services continues beyond the life span of the individuals for whom the services initially are provided. For example, complete eradication of malaria or of typhoid from an area means that individuals of succeeding generations are not subject to these diseases. In instances where there is a return into perpetuity, in effect the labor product added through a health program may be capitalized without allowance for depreciation, that is, for retirements from the labor force and deaths.

As this brief summary of measures of capital formation through health programs suggests, a central problem in assessing yields and investment in health is the measurement of labor product added through health care. . . . [*Editor's note:* The discussion of labor product measurement which follows in the original article appears, with minor exceptions, in the following article (Reading 22); see pp. 404–14.]

22. Economic Costs of Disease and Injury*

SELMA J. MUSHKIN and
FRANCIS d'A. COLLINGS

What is the cost of sickness and the price of health? What are the costs and prices of alternative health activities and how much should be spent for control of a disease as compared with other programs? What can we afford to do, and afford not to do, in meeting disease problems?

Such questions are raised repeatedly about the costs of specific diseases and about comparative amounts spent for prevention and treatment. These are issues which quantification of costs and prices cannot resolve alone; but, as Winslow emphasized, such quantification can provide a most valuable tool to assist in consideration of these issues. [1].

The arithmetic of economic gains and losses brought about by health programs can be an important tool, especially in planning for economic development in parts of Asia, Africa, and South America. For these countries, the real price of health programs often includes not only expenditures for public health programs but also costs occasioned by pressures of population growth. These pressures have been intensified by a marked fall in death rates from the application of modern public health measures and techniques. It has been estimated, for example, that the introduction of modern medical technology into some of the nonindustrial nations has resulted in a decline in mortality and a net increase of 1 to 2 percent in population per year.

While cost-price equations have more urgent application in health programing in nonindustrial nations of the world, they also apply to health programing in the United States. They supply a tool for appraising the adequacy of resources devoted to specific health prob-

*Reprinted from "Economic Costs of Disease and Injury," *Public Health Reports,* LXXIII (September, 1959), 795–809.

lems and the comparative economic returns from public investment in different disease problems. They permit a summary type of comparison between the costs of a specific disease and the price of the health care associated with the disease. With this type of summary in view, the National Health Education Committee collects information on the major killing and crippling diseases in the United States [2].

Review of existing work on costs of specific diseases and health programs, however, suggests a need for clarifying cost concepts in current use, setting forth in a summary way the information now available to estimate costs, and assessing the additional information required. This paper attempts to meet this need by setting forth a tentative classification of costs based on their effects on the use, distribution, and quantity of economic resources, which may help clarify the concept of economic costs of disease. In the context of each of these cost components, the types of information available for measurement are discussed and the additional information required is summarized.

Economic costs, as we are viewing them here, arise out of the impact of disease and injury upon economic resources. The question we must ask is: What is the difference between what actually happens in the economy now and what might happen in the hypothetical situation where sickness from specific causes is eliminated? In other words: What is the impact of a disease upon the use, distribution, and availability of economic resources?

Economic costs may be more sharply defined into three types: The first is actual use of economic resources (manpower and materials) for prevention, diagnosis, treatment, and rehabilitation. This represents the direct price of health programs; it is measured by actual expenditures, both public and private, for health services and their complement of commodities and facilities. In the absence of disease, these expenditures would not be necessary. The second type consists of transfers (of resources or of income) which arise out of mitigating the burdens of sickness. Costs in this category do not, in the first instance, affect the total resources used up by sickness in the economy as a whole, but they do affect the distribution of resources among individuals or families. Many of these transfers are designed to mitigate the impact on family income of losses due to death or disability. The third type, less clearly defined but perhaps more pervasive in effect than either of the other two, is loss of resources occasioned by sickness — human resources lost or impaired as a result of death, disability, and debility caused by sickness.

For convenience, we will call these three categories of cost resource-use, resource-transfer, and resource-loss. Other classifications have been used. Dr. Rashi Fein, in a recent work for the Joint Commission on Mental Illness and Health, used direct and indirect cost to refer to resource-use and resource-loss respectively. He combined the transfer category with direct costs [3].

Each of the major diseases and disabilities requires the use of man-power and material for prevention, treatment, and rehabilitation. If it were not for disease and injury, these resources of men and material could be used to produce other want-satisfying goods and services. The actual use of these resources in the health industry thus constitutes the type of cost of sickness that we have termed resource-use.

Available estimates suggest that the part of the Nation's manpower and of goods and services produced that is devoted to health care has increased in recent years. In 1929, the Committee on the Costs of Medical Care estimated health and medical expenditures at $3.9 billion [4], or 3.8 percent of the gross national product; an estimate by the Social Security Administration for 1957 showed that the health share of the Nation's output had risen to 4.7 percent [5].

The resources directly devoted to the research, prevention, diagnosis, treatment, and rehabilitation in a specific program or disease category are represented by the outlays of public and private health agencies, employers, and individuals and their families. They include expenditures for (a) health services provided by physicians, hospitals, dentists, nurses, and other health personnel; (b) complementary commodities such as drugs, prosthetic appliances, and medical supplies; (c) public health programs, including, for some disease categories, environmental health services; (d) medical research; (e) a part of costs of training health personnel; and (f) a part of capital expenditures for construction of health plant and facilities used in the provision of health services and the production of complementary health goods.

While progress has been made in the development of estimates for global health expenditures which encompass most of these categories of outlays, figures in current use for specific diseases fall far short of even a complete count of expenditures for hospital and physician services, both public and private [2, 3, 6].

Estimates of expenditures by disease category may be approached and combined from available data in several ways. The following summary of methods consists partly of alternative approaches and partly of methods for approximating additive segments.

1. Data on average cost per case of a disease times number of cases give a rough approximation of total cost of a disease.

2. If the average cost per case is not known, average duration of hospital care, times number of cases, times cost per unit of service, plus average drug use times costs of other health services yields a similar approximation.

3. Expenditures (both current and capital) of hospitals and nursing homes specially designed for a specific disease can indicate the costs, as can the allocation of expenditures of general hospitals (or nursing homes) based on hospital use by diagnosis.

4. Expenditures for specific disease-connected commodities complementary to health services, for example, eyeglasses and hearing aids, identify special costs connected with some conditions.

5. Number and income of providers of services whose specialty relates to a disease category, such as psychiatrists and ophthalmologists, are indicators of special costs.

6. Expenditures under public and private agency programs earmarked for services, research, or prevention in a special disease category provide a source of costs.

7. Allocation of "overhead" costs, such as costs of training health personnel and construction of facilities, to a disease category can be based on some index of relative importance like number and use of personnel and facilities.

There are several possible methods of combining these approaches. Expenditures can be classified in terms of who pays the bills, either initially or ultimately. Much of the information now available on aggregate health expenditures in the United States is classified in this way: by expenditures of Federal, State, and local official agencies, insurance carriers, employers, and private persons [5, 7]. Another classification is by the category of services purchased, for example, dental or hospital [8, 9]. A third classification is by age group of patient. Recently, a World Health Organization study suggested still another type of classification based on a rough index of the physical status of the patient, that is, whether the patient is in a hospital, is ambulatory, or is at home on his back [10]. In each of these classifications, preventive services may be distinguished from curative services, and current outlays from capital outlays for plant and physical facilities.

Sources of data for estimating the resources consumed by a specific disease vary by the nature of the disease, the identification of medical specialties and special hospitals with the disease problem, and the extent of identifiable public and private support for the agency program. Some of the source data represent national compilations of statistics on facets of expenditures, but for the most part the materials must be drawn from special regional or community studies. References to such special studies are compiled by the clearinghouse on morbidity projects of the Public Health Service [11] and by the Health Information Foundation [12]. Detailing each source of data for estimates on expenditures for specific disease categories is outside the scope of this paper. The general types of source data, however, are as follows:

Public hospital expenditures. Data on mental hospitals are compiled annually by the National Institute of Mental Health, Public Health Service [13]; expenditures on tuberculosis hospitals and tuberculosis control are compiled by the Bureau of State Services, Public Health Service [14]. In some communities, information has been tabulated on public hospital use by diagnosis, for example, morbidity in New York City's municipal hospitals [15]. Similar material on Federal hospital use by diagnosis is brought together by the Veterans Administration, the Public Health Service, and the Defense Department and is being collected as a byproduct of the administration of the medical care program for dependents of the uniformed services.

Other public expenditures. Data are available on research and related training expenditures for specific disease categories for which separate appropriations are made by the Congress. These amounts are published as part of the U.S. budget and also in the reports of the National Institutes of Health [16].

Household surveys of health service costs per illness case. A number of special household surveys have been made on the nature of illness in population groups, including medical services received and cost of such services. The North Carolina Agricultural Experiment Station, for example, has made such a study from samples of population in Stokes and Montgomery Counties, N.C. [17]. The Research Council for Economic Security has studied the volume of prolonged non-occupational illness among 400,000 employees in private nonagricultural employment, and the types and cost of treatment [18]; a survey in Lyon County, Kans., included data on amount and types of different health services as well as costs of hospitalization and cause of hospital care [19]; and the Kansas City regional health and hospital survey also included information on both health services and conditions reported [20].

Surveys of patients. A number of different types of sample surveys have been made of persons in hospitals or other institutions and of physicians' patient loads which include, along with diagnostic information, data on use of the different classes of health services, or cost of care or treatment. One example is the Dane County, Wis., survey of services and cost of treatment of the aging and long-term patient [21]. A nationwide study of all patients discharged in a week in 1956 by hospital use and diagnostic category as well as of physician services received has been made by the Bureau of Medical Economic Research of the American Medical Association [22]. A nationwide study is reported to have been made of drug therapies and morbidity reported by physicians based on case records kept on patients seen in private practice during a 2-day period.

Prepayment plan and insurance carrier data. Some compilations have been made of the experience under prepayment plans such as Health Insurance Plan of Greater New York and Kaiser-Permanente indicating volumes of selected health services for different conditions or hours of professional work time involved for different procedures [23–26]. Insurance claims data which have been published for special purposes also provide useful materials [27]. Fairly detailed data on costs by diagnosis are becoming available in administration of the Medicare program and provide an important source of cost information for the types of conditions to which the Medicare beneficiary group are subject [28].

Census and trade data. For some types of health commodities, such as hearing aids, eyeglasses, and drugs, data are available from the retail, wholesale, and manufacturing censuses conducted by the U.S. Census Bureau and from trade journals such as *American Druggist* and *Drug Topics* [29–31].

Professional income, fees, and hospital rates. The publication *Medical Economics* has put out information from a sample of physicians on gross and net physician income by specialty [32]. Fee allowances for specific procedures are set up by Blue Shield plans, Medicare, Veterans Administration, and in the course of administration of other health programs. Hospital charges and costs are available from the publications of the American Hospital Association, regional hospital councils [33], and from public medical care programs. However, these hospital data are not generally classified by disease category.

National Health Survey. Perhaps the most important single source of data by nature of condition or diagnostic category is the National Health Survey [34]. From the household surveys, information is being obtained on the condition reported at the time of the interview. In the medical examination survey, information is being obtained on selected conditions for which standard diagnostic procedures have been developed. In both types of surveys, data are being collected on items of medical service use, including hospitalization, physician visits, dental visits, nursing care, and use of specified special aids (hearing aids, artificial limbs, braces, and wheelchairs). Information from the household survey on numbers of days of hospital care and average length of hospital stay have been published for specified hospitalized conditions including malignant neoplasms, heart diseases, arthritis, hernia, fractures and dislocations, and infective and parasitic diseases. Dental visits have been published by type of services received. Other types of services have not been related thus far to the nature of the condition reported.

The various estimates that have been compiled of resources devoted to health services and related commodities on account of specific diseases point up the inadequacies of existing information on which such estimates are based. Additional collection of expenditure data cross-classified by nature of illness is needed.

The problems of collecting information of this type are many. Household surveys are limited by the types of conditions that families are likely to report, and by the undercount of expenditures for terminal cases. Many household surveys omit institutional populations. In addition, with the increase in voluntary health insurance coverage, expenditures for services are paid by the insurance plans and families often have no record of these costs. Other more technical problems include the use of health services and drugs for multiple conditions, the difficulties of obtaining accurate reporting on relatively small expenditure items, and memory biases in reports from households in which detailed expenditure records are not kept.

Small sample studies, moreover, yield an inadequate number of cases on many of the illnesses for which data are sought, such as cerebral palsy cases. The Health Information Foundation in its 1952–53 survey attempted to obtain information from the surveyed families on both expenditures and health conditions but the illness data were not tabulated [35]. A review of the information obtained by the Bureau of Labor Statistics in its 1950 survey of urban families on the illness for which the major part of the family's medical care expenditures were incurred indicated that the information reported was too sparse to permit analysis by disease category [36].

Another step in obtaining materials for estimates of expenditures by specific disease category would be to gather more information as part of the National Health Survey. A tabulation of information on physician visits and on practical and professional nurse services by nature of condition would make a beginning toward approaching expenditures through volume of services. Other health service items and commodities might be incorporated on the questionnaire for special analysis. Information on number of prescriptions, X-ray services, ambulance services, laboratory tests, oxygen, transfusions, and on physical and occupational therapy services and public health services might be obtained. It would probably be desirable to develop a series of questions on health services used for several major disease categories in a supplement to the general questionnaire for surveyed families.

Other approaches might be followed in the collection of information, such as a sampling of hospital and physician records to define the classes and volumes of services used in the diagnosis and treatment of the major diseases, and the independent collection of price data for the defined classes of health services and commodities used. Collation of public expenditure data for specified disease categories would also facilitate the approximation of aggregate expenditures for a disease. The National Institute of Mental Health has worked toward the collection of costs of mental illness not only by assisting in improved financial reporting from State hospitals but also by bringing together other data on public expenditures for mental patients, but these data combining Federal and State mental hospital expenditures are not published.

RESOURCE-TRANSFER

Disease and injury occasion not only a direct use of economic resources for the provision of health services and supporting goods but also transfers of income between the sick and the well. These transfers are costs to the givers, benefits to the receivers; but because they entail a reallocation of resources away from uses which, in the absence of sickness, would be preferred, transfers must be considered in assessing the economic impact of disease.

The size and importance of these transfers in the American economy have increased rapidly in the last two decades. They take two principal forms. One consists of payments made directly to the sick and disabled (or their survivors) and financed from taxes or contributions levied; social security protection under public and private auspices is the principal example. The other is the hidden redistribution of the tax burden that comes about through statutory tax provisions designed to assist families and voluntary agencies in meeting problems arising out of sickness. On both these counts, disease takes resources away from those who are well, and who would otherwise have alternative uses for them, and gives them to those who are sick and to survivors.

CASH PAYMENTS

A wide range of cash payments are made to individuals to mitigate the effects of loss of income due to death and disability. It is difficult to distinguish transfer payments attributable to sickness alone. For example, a part of old-age assistance and of old-age insurance benefits are paid because the aged person became disabled and was forced to retire. Under Federal programs, payments are provided to disabled veterans, to survivors and the disabled under the old-age, survivors, and disability insurance (OASDI) program, under the Civil Service system, and under the railroad retirement program. Compensation benefits for work connected with injuries are paid to Federal employees and sickness benefits to railroad workers. In cooperation with the States, the Federal Government finances payments to the needy blind, disabled, and aged. Under State and local laws sizable cash payments are made to families whose income has been impaired by sickness. These cash payments include workmen's compensation benefits, cash sickness benefits (in four States), benefits under State and local retirement systems, and a part of the general assistance caseload as well.

Figures on these public outlays are available, and give some idea of the magnitude of resource-transfer under public auspices that occurs in our economy as a result of sickness. Disability payments under social insurance and related programs alone total more than $3.5 billion at the present time [37]. Aid to the needy blind and disabled under the assistance program accounts for an additional $340 million per annum [38].

Private health, sickness, and disability plans have reached major proportions, but data in this area are piecemeal and often incomplete. In 1957, employer contributions to private pension and welfare plans totaled $7 billion [9]. Alfred M. Skolnik, of the Social Security Administration, has estimated premiums paid under group cash sickness insurance plans alone at $434.5 million. A survey of 3,100 firms employing 6.8 million persons made by the National Industrial Conference Board found that 85 percent of hourly workers and 75 percent of salaried workers were covered under group accident and sickness insurance [39]; the benefits for slightly under half of these employees were paid for entirely by the employers, and in almost all the remainder the employers contributed substantially.

Current practice in national income accounting does not define employer contributions to disability, cash sickness, and life insurance plans as transfer of income. They are regarded as supplements to wages and salaries, thus as part of the current return for productive services given. These contributions, however, are essentially pooled and go to finance payments to survivors and to those who are sick or disabled. The benefit payments accordingly represent from our point of view not an addition to national output but a shift in the shares of the national output from all workers covered to those whose income is impaired by death and disease. However, if sickness were miraculously eliminated it may be assumed that these employer payments would go instead directly into wages and salary compensation for the services.

Data on total benefits for each of the various types of protection are piecemeal and incomplete. For specific disease categories, they are even less adequate. Under the OASDI program, data are available on the number of beneficiaries by disability group and primary diagnosis, although amounts paid are not tabulated in this way [40]. Benefits paid to disabled veterans, by broad disease categories, are included in the Annual Report of the Administrator of Veterans Affairs [41], but more detailed figures are not published. Benefits paid under State workmen's compensation programs are not recorded on a national basis, but some States publish data by diagnostic

category. Some studies of State temporary disability insurance programs provide information on benefits paid by cause of disability
[42].

The tax structure is increasingly being used to foster redistribution
of income in the interests of specific public program ends. This
amounts to a form of hidden subsidy. Under National, State, and
local statutes there are a wide variety of exclusions, exemptions,
deductions, and allowances made for reducing the costs of operating
health facilities, for stimulating private giving, for reducing the
burden of taxation on families incurring sickness and disability. For
every deduction, or equivalent means of reducing the tax on those
who are sick, there must be a corresponding increase in some other
tax source to maintain a given level of revenue. Tax relief for some
groups, for example those who are sick, means larger tax burdens
for others. The losses in revenue from those who contribute to
health agencies, who take deductions allowed for medical expenses,
or who deduct income received as sick pay must be made up in the
form of higher tax rates or additional tax levies. This shift in tax
burden represents a shift in income after taxes and in the distribution
of funds available for consumption among families.

Estimates of the magnitude of resources transferred in this indirect
way are naturally lacking in precision. Some illustrative magnitudes
may be suggested. Deductions from income on account of medical
expense amounted to $3.5 billion in 1956, the latest year for which
data are available [43]. Sick leave pay and cash sickness benefits
deducted from income amounted to $1.4 billion [43].

A large part of these costs appear again either as resource-use or
resource-loss. The hidden transfers are not generally additive to these
other types of cost because they do not represent a change in the total
cost to the community as a whole; they represent rather a shift in
command over income within the community. Similarly, cash transfer
payments in large part represent payments made to individuals and
families to partially compensate them for a loss in earnings represented more fully in the estimates of loss in labor product due to
deaths and disabilities. Cash transfers included in the resource-loss
estimates are not an additional cost item; where they are added there

is a double counting [3]. However, in the absence of estimates of resource-loss, cash transfer payments as a partial measure of income loss attributable to a disease may be added to resource-use.

The type of sickness cost we have categorized as resource-use relates to the way in which existing economic resources are diverted to the sector of the economy that produces health services. Without sickness and injury, these health services would be unnecessary and the resources would be free for other productive uses. Resource-transfer represents shifts in command over resources between persons or groups, which may be direct costs to one sector of the economy but are of benefit to another. However, sickness and injury also affect the quantity of resources available in the first place. Disease and impairments cause a loss of economic resources, a loss that would cease if disease and injury were to be eliminated. This is also part of the total economic costs of sickness.

The resource lost as a result of sickness is human labor. In order to value the loss in dollars, it is necessary to estimate the output foregone. The question is, if there were no sickness how much would those persons who are now sick have produced?

The effects of sickness upon the amount of human labor available for productive purposes can be summarized under three heads: deaths (loss of workers), disability (loss of working time); and debility (loss of productive capacity while at work).

Essentially, there are two stages in calculating the output foregone: (a) estimating the loss in productive work time, and (b) assigning a money value to the output that this lost work time represents. The result is then a dollar figure which represents the value of the loss in output attributable to deaths, disability, and debility. In other words, it is a rough estimate of the increase in output that would occur if the loss of resources due to sickness were eliminated.

In view of the conceptual difficulty of the idea of resource-loss, we will explain the problems involved in arriving at an estimate at somewhat greater length than we have done for resource-use and resource-transfer.

CONCEPTUAL PROBLEMS

An estimate of work-loss due to a disease involves the assumption that, if it were not for the disease, those persons in the productive age groups stricken by the disease would have been employed. In fact, where there is unemployment or substantial underemployment, improved health may result in more unemployment rather than more output. One obvious reason for using the simplifying assumption of full employment is that unless we do so we cannot arrive at any definite concept of what the resource-loss is. Apart from this, however, the fact that production losses resulting from poor health cannot be realized in an unemployment situation should be attributed to unemployment, not to ill health. Unemployment has its own costs which in effect may cancel out reductions in the costs of sickness, but for analytical purposes it is valuable to distinguish between the two. We, therefore, measure the costs of disease in the assumed absence of costs of unemployment, recognizing, however, that unemployment itself may have an impact on the incidence of illness [44].

There is another assumption implicit in the view that loss in production due to death, disability, and debility can be attributed to a particular disease. This is that the persons who die from or are disabled by the disease would otherwise be in good health. Here again, it is possible that persons saved from one disease may promptly die of another, and their production thus be lost in any case. It seems reasonable enough to disregard this possibility for clearly defined diseases that strike primarily at persons of working age; but it is less reasonable for cases where the disease, or treatment required to overcome it, weakens the patient by making him more prone to other ailments, and for cases when the disease strikes mainly at persons who are constitutionally weak in any case, as with the diseases of old age. In these cases, the loss in production can less clearly be identified with the effects of one disease. The result of disregarding the presence of multiple diseases is an overestimate of the cost of any single disease. At some later stage in refinement of the concept of disease cost, a methodology must be developed to deal with this problem.

Moreover, the assumption that side effects of other diseases may be disregarded in order to measure the direct effects of the disease in question means that the indirect costs of each disease, taken individually, cannot be added together to make a meaningful total for all diseases. Conceptually, such a summation could be made only if all alternatives to every disease were eliminated, in which case there would be nothing to sum. This problem illustrates the difficulty in applying the concept of resource-loss, as we are describing it here, to sickness as a whole.

The time scale of any estimate of resource-loss due to sickness involves further problems. Conceptually, it is possible to view the loss in production as (a) the loss in a given time period (for example, 1 year), (b) the loss over a productive work life.

The first of these seems most relevant to the present discussion because it is most nearly comparable to the types of estimates of resource-use and resource-transfer described earlier. It should be recognized, however, that death and permanent disability this year have a continuing cost in terms of productive resources lost in the years that follow. Cost studies by Weisbrod (cancer, poliomyelitis, and tuberculosis), Malzburg (mental illness), Reynolds (road accidents) and Laitin (cancer) relate their estimates to the second of these concepts, the loss over a productive work life [45–48]; the Fein study on the cost of mental illness developed 1-year estimates as well [3]. The emphasis upon the lifetime estimate is perhaps due to the far-reaching influence of Dublin and Lotka's "Money Value of a Man," which presented an actuarial approach to this problem; but the authors of this work recognized that their method might not be applicable to the economy as a whole; it was intended originally to value a life for indemnity purposes only [49].

The 1-year estimate is conceptually much simpler, involves fewer assumptions, and in addition yields the most conservative estimate of resource-loss; for these reasons, we feel it to be the most appropriate measure in this context. The difference in estimates derived by these alternative approaches will not be so great as might appear at first, because (a) the appropriate disability figure in the case of a single-period estimate is that of disease prevalence, whereas in the case of a lifetime estimate it must be disease incidence, and (b) a rapidly diminishing value is attributed to future output in the process of placing a present value on these future earnings. Different interest rates assumed will affect the rapidity of the decrease as illustrated by the Weisbrod study which used alternatively interest rates of 4 and 10 percent—these being based respectively on the cost of long-term Government borrowing and the rate of return on corporate taxes [45]. Conceptually the two types of estimates—for a single year and over a lifespan—must be regarded, however, as distinctly different.

There has been suggested earlier a threefold classification of resource-loss: losses from death, disability, and debility. In practice, these categories need closer definition, and it may be necessary to subdivide them further to make them correspond to available data.

Death is unambiguous in meaning, but cause of death is sometimes not. In estimates of resource-loss caused by a particular disease, deaths from multiple causes may need to be treated differently from those caused by the disease in question alone. Disability caused by sickness may be partial or total, and it may be short term or long term. Cases of long-term disability, especially when total, may be found primarily in institutions, and thus it may be convenient to subclassify again into institutional and noninstitutional populations and use data available on institutional cases to measure a part of the disability caseload. The division between disability and debility, furthermore, will not be clearcut in many cases.

LOSS OF WORKING TIME

The loss in resources through death, disability, and debility must, for the first stage of the estimate, be stated in terms of units of productive work time lost. The second stage to be dealt with later is to assign a value to these units. In the case of death and long-term disability, these units of work time are lost because of subtractions from the productive work force. With short-term disability, the loss will take the form of periods of lost time from the job and these may be converted into equivalent units of full-time work lost. Debility, defined as reduced productive efficiency per man, too may be converted into full-time equivalents. For convenience, the following discussion will refer to man-years as the units of productive work time.

How the equivalent of the full-time work force is defined operatively is of central importance to the estimate. For purposes of a single-year estimate, for example, a decision must be made on the age limits within which persons who contract disease will be considered as productive workers. In the United States, the age of entry into the work force is usually considered as 14 years. This starting age is largely a historical carryover in definition which has been perpetuated for comparative purposes in spite of the trend toward later entry into the work force. The retirement age varies widely among different groups and in different areas; the average age of retirement for the United States is estimated at present at 68 years of age for men [50].

The consequence of this limitation of work-force participation, for a single-period estimate, is to count the resource-loss from death, disability, and debility of the young and retired aged as zero. This is consistent with the definition, since persons outside the work force are not considered to contribute anything to production in the year in question. For the extended time-scale analysis, however, infant and childhood deaths represent a future loss to society and must be allowed for, although the time interval between death and anticipated entry into the work force may be such that the present value of the future loss of working time is small.

The importance of the retirement-age assumption will vary with different social and economic settings. In some economies, the urgency of production for survival leaves little room for retirement prior to death or total disability; with higher productivity and industrial advances, cessation of work activity becomes feasible before extreme old age is reached. In an industrial community, therefore, it seems reasonable to exclude retired persons who cease to contribute to production, but in others retirement may be disregarded.

Whatever age limitations are set upon the productive work force, further qualification is necessary because not all persons of productive age are actually engaged in production. At full employment, only a certain proportion of the members of each age group will be productively employed, and the loss in man-years attributable to these persons alone should be counted toward the estimate of resource-loss. Here again, this implies that the death or disability of a person not in the active work force occasions no loss of productive resources.

Special problems arise in the case of women working in the home. Such women are not normally included in standard definitions of the work force, and their product, unlike that of paid domestic workers, is not included in the national economic accounts. Thus defined, their death or disability is not an economic cost. However, this is clearly highly anomalous; it implies that the national product is increased if every wife does housework for pay for the family next door, and lowered if every man marries his cook. The only alternative is to impute some value to the services of housewives in the home, thus imputing an indirect cost to their death or disability. Although proposals have been advanced for broadening the concept of production used for national product purposes to include such nonmarket services, no generally agreed way to do so at present exists [51]. To simplify the estimate and to follow an approach consistent with national product accounting it seems desirable at this stage of analysis to omit the valuation of housewife services.

A related problem concerns the method of counting deaths and disabilities among unpaid family workers. In the United States and several other countries, unpaid family work is included in the national product accounts, in effect requiring a prorating of income among the working members of the family enterprise. In this case, there is a basis for allocating a value to the services of such a worker. The importance of this problem obviously varies in different social settings, but in countries where a large proportion of production is carried on on farms and in other family enterprises it would be clearly advisable to count deaths and disabilities among those who work within the family unit without money wages.

In estimates over a lifespan, work life tables developed by the Bureau of Labor Statistics may be applied which identify the remaining years of work life at each age group. Estimates of work life years have been developed for 1940 and 1950 for both men and women; and historical changes in the pattern of work life expectancies have been estimated for 1900 and projected to the year 2000 [52–54].

Further problems arise in connection with part-time workers. The loss of productive work time for a given impact of disease among these persons will be less than that among full-time workers, and this loss will have to be converted to a full-time equivalent for purposes of the estimate. The effect will be to consider the loss of, say, two part-time workers as being equivalent to that of one full-time worker; the exact ratio might be determined with reference to average hours of work or other available criteria.

The most practical solution to these definitional problems may be to use existing concepts of "work force" and "labor force" (converted to full-time equivalents) to distinguish the cases of the disease that result in actual loss of productive work time. In the United States, the basis for classifying persons in or out of the "labor force" is their activity during a specified week. Employed members of the labor force comprise those at work for pay or profit during the survey week, those who worked without pay for more than 15 hours on farms or in family businesses, and those who would have been in these two categories in the work force but for vacation, temporary illness, bad weather, or industrial disputes. Unemployed members of the labor force comprise all those without work who were actively seeking work during the survey week. Data will often be available only within this framework, and this method has the further advantage that it makes the estimate of resource-loss comparable in scope with existing national product estimates. The effect, however, is to exclude almost all the nonmarket costs of death, disability, and debility from our estimate of resource-loss, and this should be clearly recognized as a serious source of understatement of the total.

Our measure of resource-loss is posited on the assumption of full employment. However, it may be felt desirable to make an allowance for frictional unemployment, that is, the essential unemployment that exists even at full-employment levels as when persons change jobs or are temporarily laid off. In the United States, this is usually considered to run at about 3 percent of the labor force at any time; thus 3 percent fewer deaths and disabilities than the total of those from the labor force actually affect production at any time. It is also desirable to allow for absenteeism over-employment, which is normal absenteeism of workers from jobs because of vacations, bad weather, and temporary sickness. These adjustments may be applied to the final estimate of productive work time lost due to the disease as a straight percentage reduction, or in terms of a full-time equivalent number of man-years.

It is apparent even from this brief discussion of the problems of defining lost work time due to disease that many of the factors involved are dynamic. The single-period type of estimate, which sets out to quantify the gain in work time in a given year that would result if a specific disease were eliminated, avoids the problems of estimating future trends in work-force participation. For the lifespan type of estimate, these problems could only be solved by making a large number of assumptions about the future course of such trends, and the uncertainty and complexity of the estimate would be greatly increased.

Loss of output

The previous stage in the computation has resulted in an estimate of the productive man-years lost because of deaths, disability, and debility from sickness. This, in itself, may prove a useful piece of political arithmetic, but in most cases it will be desirable to translate this into dollar cost by assigning a value to the man-years foregone in terms of lost production.

In the available studies on losses from illness, two essentially divergent approaches have been used in assigning a value to each unit of labor work time. The first is to value each unit by an amount equivalent to total product per worker; the other is to use earnings as a measure of labor product per worker.

The first of these assumes, as Fein (3) has indicated, ". . . that all of the national product (income), and therefore any gains in national product, are attributable to labor rather than to some combination of joint factors of production, land, labor, capital, etc. Although it may, indeed, be true that if there were no labor there would be no product, it is equally true that if there were no capital there would be very little product."

The total-product-per-worker approach was used by Reynolds in his study of the cost of road accidents in Great Britain [47] and also in the National Planning Association study on the costs of tuberculosis in the United States [55].

The second alternative — to use earnings as a measure of the output attributable to labor — seems to us to be more appropriate for purposes of estimating resource-loss. Earnings, in this case, must be distinguished from income, which includes returns on property or capital; earnings consist only of wages and salaries (or equivalents for the self-employed). These wages and salaries are paid in direct return for productive services, and, according to economic theory, they correspond to the individual's contribution to production. The estimate of resource-loss put in these terms thus measures the loss of production attributable to labor which this earnings-loss represents.

A choice between these two alternatives arises also in estimates of the costs of unemployment, which are perhaps more familiar than those of the costs of disease. Here, however, gross product per worker seems the more appropriate concept, because it is fair to assume in these circumstances that some capital will be unemployed along with labor. This brings to light another assumption implicit in our concept of resource-loss from a disease: this is that the ratio of investment of capital to labor used remains approximately constant. If this were not so (as, for example, if the investment or capital stock were assumed to be constant and unchanging), the labor released by eliminating the disease might have to work with less capital per capita, and diminishing marginal returns to labor would ensue. A related implicit assumption is that the capital stock is infinitely divisible, so that there is no question of the product of each man being tied to the availability of a machine or implement.

The earnings figure used may be an average for all employed workers. This assumes that the average earnings pattern among those who contract the disease is the same as that of the working population at large. For greater accuracy, it would be preferable to use a series of averages applied to sex-age groups, occupational categories, or other subdivisions and to take account of the findings of studies relating earning levels and disease incidence.

The use of average earnings per full-time employed worker is in fact only an approximation of marginal earnings, which are needed to actually measure the additional labor product that would become available as a result of eliminating the disease. Under the assumptions of full employment of labor and constant labor-capital ratio that we have made, average and marginal earnings will be the same. In practice, however, if elimination of the disease were to throw a relatively large number of workers onto the labor market, it might be found that these assumptions would need to be relaxed for purposes of realistic prediction.

A word must be added about an argument appearing sometimes in the literature [49] that a man's contribution to production should be considered net, exclusive of the essential consumption required to maintain him as a producer, rather than gross as we have taken it here. Quite apart from the virtually insoluble difficulty of defining "essential" consumption, the frame of reference of our problem is to determine the loss in total output caused by disease and thus by definition the gross approach is indicated. The fact that saving a life adds a consumer as well as a producer to the economic process is immaterial to an estimate of change in total output. Calculation of the resulting change in consumption levels per capita is basically a problem of resource-use rather than losses in production.

Average earnings multiplied by the number of man-years lost as a result of the disease yields the dollar estimate of resource-loss caused by a disease. We are now in a position to define the result more closely. It is, essentially, an estimate of the money value of the labor product lost as a result of death, disability, and debility due to a disease.

GAPS IN STATISTICAL DATA

The foregoing summary of concepts and definitions in the measurement of output-loss due to a disease suggests the wide range of assumptions and approximations which must sometimes take the place of factual information in estimating the dollar amounts.

Statistics on employment patterns are applied to data on deaths by cause, age, and sex without taking account of the specific employment history of those who die. The assumption of average work-force participation is made necessary by the absence of specific information on employment status of the deceased. In fact, there will be differences in the importance to productivity of each death: elimination of a key worker in a basic industry, for example, might affect the ultimate output of hundreds of others.

Estimates of average full-time earnings are applied to deaths in the productive age groups without taking into account the differential death rates in different industries and occupations, which may pay different wages. The absence of recent data on deaths by occupational groups and by earnings classes necessitate the use of average figures.

Improvement of the estimates now in current use of the resource-loss due to deaths not only requires agreement on concepts and definitions for measurement, but also additional data on mortality by cause of death, relation of the deceased to the work force in a period preceding death, and occupation and earnings in a period prior to death.

Data on work-loss days for those attached to the work force have become available through the U.S. National Health Survey of the Public Health Service. These data, however, are published only for the following groups of conditions: infectious and parasitic, circulatory, respiratory, digestive, genitourinary, arthritic and rheumatic, injury and impairment due to injuries, other impairments, and all other conditions. Until such data become available for more specific disease categories, information on disease prevalence and on duration of illness will be combined with average work-force participation for age and sex groups to approximate the work-loss days. Moreover, data are needed on usual earnings rates received by persons reporting work loss due to a condition. The existence of multiple conditions yields an inflated count of work loss attributable to each condition and an overcount of the sum of days for more than one condition.

The impact of diseases which cause debility, or loss of working efficiency, is no simple matter to define. In its broadest dimension, a measure of loss of output due to disease debility requires formulation of a standard of output in the absence of the disease, from which shortcomings may be measured. Additional work is required on the concept of measurement, as well as on the collection of data permitting a count of lost product per unit of work time. In highly industrialized countries, machines have taken over much of the physical work of man, and maximum demands are seldom made upon the physical energy of the average worker in the mechanized industries. What, however, are the appropriate counts of maximum output in terms of human capacity in service and nonmechanized employment and of deviations from these maximums? In other economic settings, the energy capacity of a man at work may be of great importance. In subsistence agriculture, reduction in debility from malaria, trachoma, or dysentery can be as important a factor in increasing productivity as a change in tools or technology.

Debility, where relevant, thus represents the least well defined of the three categories through which we examine the resource-loss from disease. However, its influence is so pervasive that some basis for estimating its impact on the economy is badly needed.

CONCLUSIONS

To summarize, the economic costs of disease and injury are of three types: (a) costs which use a share of the Nation's resources of manpower and materials to supply health services and their commodity components; (b) costs represented by the transfer of income and resources from the well to the sick in public and private efforts to mitigate the burdens of illness; (c) costs reflected in a reduced national production of all goods and services. These three types of costs are termed resource-use, resource-transfer, and resource-loss.

The price of control of a disease is the health resources used up in the treatment and control of a disease. In economies characterized by severely limited resources and low food supplies, there must be added the minimum essential consumption of people whose lives are saved by the successful disease control action.

The economic cost of a disease for price-cost comparisons is the loss in labor product, or the amount by which the national output in a year is reduced by death, disability, and debility.

The omissions and limitations of this type of economic arithmetic are many. The scheme fails to take into account the pervasive force for social and economic change released by improvement in mortality rates and changes in expectations of survival. Changes in life expectancy and in health status radically alter attitudes toward work and enterprise. Disease and early death are deeply implanted in the mores of many people of the world. The fears, superstitions, rigid social patterns, and resistance to change are in part cultural adjust-ments to high disease and death rates. While they are not to be changed overnight, one cause of them will be removed when illness is limited and death rates sharply reduced.

Changes in expectation of life, moreover, alter individual attitudes toward sacrifice of some part of today's consumption for tomorrow's. The time perspective of planning and investment for economic development is deeply affected by health levels. A prospect of longer life disposes the individual to support long-run development projects because he sees for himself a better chance of reaping some of their benefits. Changes in life expectancy, especially of infants and children, offer some promise of adjustment, over a period of time, in size of family, fertility rates, and age structure of the population.

The accounting of economic gains and losses as described also omits what is perhaps the simplest and most direct economic effect of all. Health is itself an element in the standard of living. Concentra-tion on health as an investment in economic resources—an interme-diate product of value in that it helps to increase national output—must not obscure its parallel importance as a final product for human welfare.

Objection on ethical grounds has sometimes been raised to con-version of human lives to money terms, to the disregarding of human suffering and to the counting of saved lives of children and other nonproducers as a price rather than gain. The value of human life and relief of suffering obviously cannot be disregarded in health programing. Disease prevention and control measures which yield zero or even negative economic returns can be fully justified in terms of human values. The fact that the economic arithmetic of a disease is only one of a number of tools for evaluation of health programs does not in itself argue against development of cost estimates of disease.

Voluntary and public agencies concerned with specific diseases have developed or used such estimates to further programs of medi-cal research and disease control. They have financed studies of these costs to give them a tool to describe the size of the problem in public discussion. Review of these studies indicates clearly the need for development of a conceptual framework for such estimates, for a clearer formulation of their assumptions and limitations, and for indication of the areas in which relevant data still need to be collected.

415

REFERENCES

1. Winslow, C.-E.A.: The cost of sickness and the price of health. World Health Organization Monogr. Series No. 7. Geneva, 1951, 106 pp.
2. National Health Education Committee: Facts on the major killing and crippling diseases in the United States today. New York, 1957.
3. Fein, R.: Economics of mental illness. A report to the staff director, Jack R. Ewalt, 1958. Joint Commission on Mental Illness and Health Monogr. Series No. 2. New York, Basic Books, Inc., 1958, 164 pp.
4. Falk, I. S., Rorem, C. R., and Ring, M. D.: The costs of medical care. Chicago, University of Chicago Press, 1933, p. 9.
5. Merriam, I. C.: Social welfare expenditures in the United States, 1956–57. Social Security Bull. 21: 27, October 1958.
6. Weisbrod, B. A.: The nature and measurement of the economic benefits of improvements in public health; a proposal for a study. Northfield, Minn., Carlton College, Department of Economics, 1958, 9 pp. (unpublished).
7. Klarman, H. E. (Hospital Council of Greater New York): Changing costs of medical care and voluntary health insurance. Extended version of paper delivered before joint session of American Economic Association and American Association of University Teachers of Insurance, Cleveland, Ohio, December 28, 1956, 67 pp.
8. Brewster, A. W.: Voluntary health insurance and medical care expenditures: A ten year review. Social Security Bull. 21: 8–15, December 1958.
9. U.S. Office of Business Economics: U.S. income and output. Supplement to the Survey of Current Business. Washington, D.C., U.S. Government Printing Office, November 1958, p. 150.
10. Abel-Smith, B., and Mann, K. J.: Medical care in relation to public health; a study on the costs and sources of finance. WHO/OMC/30, rev. 1. Geneva, World Health Organization, October 9, 1958, 43 pp.
11. U.S. Public Health Service: Clearinghouse on current morbidity statistics projects. Sources of morbidity data, listing No. 6. PHS Pub. No. 628. Washington, D.C., U.S. Government Printing Office, 1958, 83 pp.
12. Health Information Foundation: An inventory of social and economic research in health. New York, 1957, 327 pp.
13. U.S. Public Health Service: Patients in mental institutions, 1955. PHS Pub. No. 574, Part 1. National Institute of Mental Health, 1958, 55 pp.
14. U.S. Public Health Service: Tuberculosis chart series, 1957. PHS Pub. No. 534. Bureau of State Services, 1957, 22 pp.
15. Fraenkel, M., and Erhardt, C. L.: Morbidity in the municipal hospitals of the City of New York. Report of an exploratory study in hospital morbidity reporting. New York, Russell Sage Foundation, 1955, 229 pp.
16. U.S. Public Health Service: Research grants and awards, National In-

stitutes of Health, fiscal year 1957 funds. PHS Pub. No 571. Washington, D.C., U.S. Government Printing Office, 1957, 147 pp.
17. North Carolina Agricultural Experiment Station: North Carolina rural health studies. Use of health care services and enrollment in voluntary health insurance in Stokes County, North Carolina, 1956. Use of health care services and enrollment in voluntary health insurance in Montgomery County, North Carolina, 1956. Raleigh, North Carolina State College, 1958, 15 pp. and 12 pp.
18. Research Council for Economic Security: Prolonged illness absenteeism. Summary report. Chicago, 1957, 237 pp.
19. Kansas State Board of Health: Lyon County, Kans., citizen's community health study. Tabulated data gathered by household interviews. Topeka, 1958, 54 pp.
20. U.S. Public Health Service: Clearinghouse on current morbidity statistics projects. Sources of morbidity data, listing No. 5. PHS Pub. No. 565. Washington, D.C., U.S. Government Printing Office, 1957, 81 pp.
21. Beattie, W. M., Jr.: Dane County survey of health needs, services and facilities for the aging and long-term patient. Madison, Wis., Community Welfare Council, July 1956, 106 pp.
22. American Medical Association: Far-reaching study at midpoint. Bureau of Medical Economic Research Pub. No. M-107. Chicago, 1956, 1 p.
23. Health Insurance Plan of Greater New York, Division of Research and Statistics: HIP statistical report for the year 1957. New York, 1957, 21 pp.
24. Weissman, A.: A morbidity study of the Permanente health plan population: A preliminary report. Permanente Found. M. Bull. 9: 1–17, January 1951.
25. Weissman, A.: A morbidity study of the Permanente health plan population. II. Comparison of utilization and morbidity data with experience of other population groups. Permanente Found. M. Bull. 10: 12–25, August 1952.
26. U.S. Public Health Service: Comprehensive dental care in a group practice. A study of service and time requirements. PHS Pub. No. 395. Washington, D.C., U.S. Government Printing Office, 1954, 48 pp.
27. Society of Actuaries: Transactions of the 1956 reports of mortality and morbidity experience. Chicago, 1957, 169 pp.
28. U.S. Department of Defense, Office for Dependents' Medical Care: First annual report: Dependents' medical care program. June 1, 1958, 153 pp.
29. U.S. Bureau of the Census: United States census of business, 1954. Vol. I. Retail trade—summary statistics. Washington, D.C., U.S. Government Printing Office, 1957.
30. U.S. Bureau of the Census: United States census of business. Vol. III.

Wholesale trade—summary statistics. Washington, D.C., U.S. Government Printing Office, 1957.

31. U.S. Bureau of the Census: United States census of manufactures, 1954. Vol. II. Industry statistics. Washington, D.C., U.S. Government Printing Office, 1957.

32. Yardsticks for your practice. How much are physicians earning? Medical Economics 33: 110–29, October 1956.

33. Kansas City Area Hospital Association: Report of patient statistics and financial data, 1957. Kansas City, 1958, 15 pp.

34. U.S. Public Health Service: Health statistics from the U.S. National Health Survey: (a) Selected survey topics, United States, July 1957–June 1958. PHS Pub. No. 584–B5, November 1958, 49 pp.; (b) Origin and program of the U.S. National Health Survey. PHS Pub. No. 584–A1, May 1958, p. 9; (c) Hospitalization: Patients discharged from short-stay hospitals, United States, July 1957–June 1958. PHS Pub. No. 584–B7, December 1958, 40 pp.; (d) Preliminary report on volume of dental care, United States, July–September 1957. PHS Pub. No. 584–B2, March 1958, 22 pp. Washington, D.C., U.S. Government Printing Office.

35. Anderson, O. W., and Feldman, J. J.: Family medical costs and voluntary health insurance; a nationwide survey. New York, McGraw-Hill Book Co., 1956, 251 pp.

36. Mushkin, S.: Age differential in medical spending. Pub. Health Rep. 72: 115–20, February 1957.

37. U.S. Social Security Administration: Table: Beneficiaries and benefits under social insurance and related programs, by risk and program, 1940, 1950–1957. Annual Statistical Supp., Social Security Bull., 1957, p. 14.

38. Social Security Bull. 22: 34, 36, April 1959.

39. National Industrial Conference Board: Personnel practices in factory and office. Ed. 5. Studies in Personnel Policy, No. 145. New York, 1954, 128 pp.

40. U.S. Bureau of Old-Age and Survivors Insurance, Division of Program Analysis: Selected data on operations under the disability provisions of the Old-Age, Survivors, and Disability Insurance Program. Washington, D.C., February 1957, 12 tables.

41. U.S. Veterans Administration: Annual report, administrator of veterans affairs, 1958. Washington, D.C., U.S. Government Printing Office, 1959, 327 pp.

42. State of Rhode Island and Providence Plantations, Department of Employment Security: 22d annual report, 1957. Providence, 1958.

43. U.S. Internal Revenue Service: Statistics of income, 1956. Individual

income tax returns. Pub. No. 79 (11–58). Washington, D.C., U.S. Government Printing Office, 1958, 119 pp.

44. Feldman, J. J.: Barriers to the use of health survey data in demographic analysis. Milbank Mem. Fund Quart. 3: 203–21, July 1958.
45. Weisbrod, B.A.: The nature and measurement of the economic benefits of improvement in public health with particular reference to cancer, tuberculosis and poliomyelitis. St. Louis, Mo., Washington University, 1958, 147 pp.
46. Malzburg, B.: Mental illness and the economic value of a man. Ment. Hyg. 4: 582–91, October 1950.
47. Reynolds, D. J.: The cost of road accidents. J. Roy. Statist. Soc. 119: 393–409 (part 4, 1956).
48. Laitin, H.: The economics of cancer. (Doctoral thesis.) Cambridge, Harvard University, 1956, 335 pp.
49. Dublin, L. I., and Lotka, A. J.: The money value of a man. Rev. ed. New York, Ronald Press, 1946, 214 pp.
50. Myers, R. J.: Some implications of a retirement test in social security systems. Conference of actuaries in public practice. *In* The proceedings, 1957–58, vol. 7, pp. 337–50.
51. Copeland, M. A.: The feasibility of a standard comprehensive system of social accounts. Conference on research in income and wealth. *In* studies in income and wealth. Vol. 20. Problems in the international comparison of economic accounts. Princeton, Princeton University Press, 1957, pp. 19–95.
52. U.S. Bureau of Labor Statistics: Tables of working life; length of working life for men. Bull. No. 1001. Washington, D.C., U.S. Government Printing Office, 1950, 74 pp.
53. U.S. Bureau of Labor Statistics: Tables of working life for women, 1950. Bull. No. 1204. Washington, D.C., U.S. Government Printing Office, 1956, 33 pp.
54. Garfinkle, S.: Changes in the working life of men, 1900–2000. Month. Labor Rev. 78: 297–301, March 1955.
55. National Planning Association: Good health is good business; a summary of a technical study. Planning Pamphlet No. 62. Washington, D.C., 1948, 44 pp.

23. Investment in Health Care*

HERBERT E. KLARMAN

John Hopkins University

Health and medical services may represent an investment in human capital or final consumption [26, p. 283]. (One economist has suggested that health and medical care expenditures should be viewed as neither investment nor consumption, but as repair or maintenance expenditures on the human machine [5, p. 29]. The writer cannot agree: man is not a machine; and why should not other expenditures, including food, be treated similarly?)

The distinction between consumption and investment has serious implications for policy. If health and medical services are consumer goods, the best way to go about getting more of them is, first, to invest in those things that raise the national output and, then, to devote part of the increment to buying additional health services [33, p. 40]. Conversely, if health services are investment goods, it may be practicable to buy more of them directly.

INVESTMENT VERSUS CONSUMPTION

Calculating the difference between economic benefits and costs is an obvious step in justifying expenditures on health and medical services as a form of investment [9, p. 785]. In the past this type of calculation was usually performed by public health officials [9, p. 788]. In recent years economists working on problems of health and medical care have come to regard the estimate of net economic yield as a guide to society's demand for health services [28, p.1; 43, p. 28]. Many economists share the view that health and medical care expenditures are primarily an investment in human beings [14, p. 140; 24, p. 129; 27, p. 15]. Pigou has stated, "The most important in-

*Reprinted from *The Economics of Health* (New York: Columbia University Press, 1965), pp. 162–173 and footnotes.

vestment of all is investment in the health, intelligence and character of the people" [11, p. 138].

Expenditures for medical care to diagnose and treat a disease (or injury) are not its total costs. The costs of a disease comprise at least two components: direct costs and indirect costs. Direct costs are the medical care expenditures associated with a disease. Indirect costs are the loss of output, attributable to the disease, that result from premature death or disability. (Some economists list additional losses, such as those due to debility [38, p. 801] and avoidance costs [43, p. 45]. However, these have not been measured.) It is possible to reduce direct costs by failing to provide services, but indirect costs continue [24, p. 128].

The total costs of a disease per case serve as the measure of benefits derived from preventing that case [43, p. 90]. In a cost-benefit calculation the comparison is between contemplated additional expenditures for health and medical services, on the one hand, and the anticipated reduction in costs (direct plus indirect), on the other hand. This is the essential conceptual framework. (Although Fein states in his study of mental illness that the focus is on costs [24, pp. 3,5], and Weisbrod states in his study of cancer, poliomyelitis, and tuberculosis that it is limited to benefits [43, p. 5], both deal with the same problem in similar fashion.) In practice, difficulties may arise as decisions are made on the methods of handling the several elements of the calculation and, as compromises are struck, by measuring the elements for which data are available rather than those which are indicated by the conceptual framework or theoretical model.

Some economists view medical services, if not public health services, primarily as consumer goods [4, p. 119; 8, p. 29; 17, p. 32]. (Denison states that the great majority of employed persons in this country have access to reasonable medical care, so that there is not much prevailing illness that can be cured [2, p. 52]. The writer is more inclined to agree with the conclusion than with the premise.) The calculation is then reduced to a comparison of expenditures for alternative programs that promise the same degree of health improvement [1, p. 251; 39, p. 215].

One difficulty is that few (if any) health services are pure investment goods or pure consumption goods. It is customary to recognize the consumption benefit of most health and medical care expenditures, to comment on the difficulty of measuring it, and then to dismiss it [40, p. 393; 43, p. 29]. What is measurable may not be necessarily important, but it is recorded and, therefore, cited. The measurable part (the investment component) is not likely, however, to bear a uniform relationship to the consumption component in all health and medical care programs. Attaching a value to the consumption part of the benefit, lest it be totally neglected (or treated as zero), is a challenging task [37, p. 156].

A possible approach is through the device of the analogous disease (one that may be regarded as inflicting equal pain or discomfort [44, p. 139]). Consider a disease, B, for which medical care expenditures are incurred without any prospect of a return in increased output, either because the disease is not disabling or because the patient has retired from the labor force. These expenditures are incurred for consumption purposes only and may be held to indicate the value of the consumption benefit attached to avoiding or curing the disease A that is under study [30, p. 5].

In comparing programs for which both costs and benefits are pertinent, the ratio of benefits to costs is not the proper criterion for choosing among them. This is true in part because a ratio of benefits to costs in excess of one is an insufficient criterion for justifying a program, since other programs may show a higher ratio. The principal reason is that a ratio of annual gross receipts (benefits) to annual expenses is not the correct criterion for evaluation [34, p. 110]. The proper test is that the return on investment or, more precisely, the present worth of the project be maximized [34, p. 76]. (This is also the ultimate criterion for optimum behavior in business when the rate of profit fluctuates through time [126, p. 150].)

THE RATE OF DISCOUNT

To repeat, the calculation of costs and benefits properly compares the present value of proposed costs and of expected benefits. If the time span is longer than one year, the two streams should be discounted to the present by means of an appropriate rate of interest. A given amount of money has different values when it is realized (or spent) at different times. Discounting converts a stream of costs or benefits into its present worth. The higher the rate of interest adopted for discounting, the lower the present value of a given money stream.

Discounting assumes particular importance when the time span is long. Waterworks are a good example of long-lived investments. Another is a syphilis control program, the benefits (prevention of disability and premature death) of which accrue 15 to 30 years after the costs are incurred [30, p. 6].

At what level should the rate of discount be set? Some economists employ the going market rate of interest [24, p. 73; 34, p. 79; 40, p. 398]. It is not clear whether this is always the appropriate rate. In general, the discount rate balances the productivity of an investment and time preference (reluctance to sacrifice current for future consumption) [29, p. 11]. But the sum of individual preferences in the market and the collective estimate of time preference need not agree. It may be necessary to employ a rate that synthesizes the social rate of discount and opportunity cost (investment foregone) in the private sector [25, p. 130; 29, p. 23]. Much work remains to be done in this area.

Pure time preference is likely to vary with the life expectancy of a population [23, p. 457]; it may also vary by socioeconomic class. An individual's discount rate for the distant future is likely to be higher than that of society [15, pp. 91–92], which has the greater regard for later generations.

Some economists see the selection of a discount rate as expressing a judgment on the relative importance of successive generations. Accordingly, they prefer to offer two alternatives—4 percent and 10 percent [28, p. 6; 43, p. 57] or 4 percent and 8 percent [22, Chap. 5, p. 23].

In the writer's opinion, presenting two or more rates is justified when it is accompanied by criteria for selecting one of them as the appropriate rate under specified circumstances. In the absence of such criteria a single rate is preferable. The rate of 4 (or 6) percent has the advantages of being intermediate along the range of available figures, of wide application [21, p. 76; 24, p. 87; 29, p. 11; 40, p. 398], and of immunity from obvious objections.

CALCULATING HEALTH AND MEDICAL CARE EXPENDITURES FOR A DISEASE

The calculation of health and medical expenditures associated with a disease presents fewer conceptual problems than the calculation of output loss attributable to a disease. The statistical task, may, however, be just as formidable.

One requirement is that the total costs of a program be entered, including the value of services rendered by capital in the current period.

It is necessary to deal with the problem of determining the costs of health programs produced together. The arbitrary allocation of overhead in order to determine the average unit cost of several jointly produced services does not contribute to sound decisions [12a, pp. 306–7; 16, pp. 359–60; 34, pp. 44–45].

Data by disease classification are scarce, especially in private medical practice. Moreover, several diseases may be associated in a person at the same time. Yet, the summary page of the medical record of a hospitalized patient may report only his primary diagnosis (the final diagnosis of the condition for which the patient was admitted).

The presence of associated conditions (or multiple diseases) also poses a difficulty in estimating the contemplated effect of proposed expenditures on alternative programs of health services. Even if all multiple diseases were correctly reported, their simultaneous presence implies overstatement of the economic cost of any disease taken singly and, therefore, overstatement of the potential savings to be achieved by reducing the incidence of any one disease [35, p. 9; 38, p.802].

Another, similar difficulty is presented by competing causes of death. This difficulty is manifested in the uncertainties that surround the preparation of a life table from which a given cause of death is removed [43, pp. 34–35]. Moreover, if the effect of a program is to prolong life expectancy, morbidity may also rise [28, p. 12].

Owing to the presence of multiple diseases and of competing causes of death, it is a mistake to add the calculated costs of individual diseases in an attempt to estimate the total cost of disease to a society [38, p. 802].

CALCULATING OUTPUT LOSS

The calculation of the indirect costs of a disease or injury presents several problems. Among them are the treatment of transfer payments, taxes, consumption, the work of housewives, the appropriate measure of output loss, and the choice of assumptions regarding employment as well as the discount rate. About some of these elements of cost students of the economic costs of road accidents, mental illness, cancer, tuberculosis, poliomyelitis, ulcers, alcoholism, and job accidents are approaching a consensus. Differences of opinion and in approach persist regarding others.

Transfer payments. The consensus revolves about the treatment of transfer payments, taxes, and the measure of output loss. When expenditures are incurred without any cost in resources, they constitute transfer payments. Since transfer payments do not entail a change in resource cost to the community, they represent a redistribution of income within the community and a shift in command over resources. Once resource loss is taken into account, there is no reason to bring transfer payments into the calculation [38, p. 801]. If relief checks are replaced by earnings as the source of family support, it is the earnings that measure society's gain in output. To count the reduction in relief grants as well is to count this amount twice. The social desirability of having families live on their own earnings, rather than on relief grants, does not enter into this calculation; it may be entitled to separate recognition.

Taxes. The argument concerning the proper treatment of taxes is similar. It is double counting to include tax receipts by government once earnings have been counted. Although some may disagree [22, p. 131], the amount of taxes and the distribution of the burden of taxes have no proper bearing on decisions made concerning health and medical care programs, unless the beneficiaries are subject to a special tax. It would perhaps be realistic to recognize that the proposed expenditures may fall on one pocketbook while the potential benefits accrue to other pocketbooks or are widely diffused [24, p. 132; 28, p. 4; 41, pp. 12–13].

Earnings. Increasingly regarded as the appropriate measure of output loss are the earnings of employed members of the labor force (wages and salaries and net income from self-employment) [20, p. 18; 24, p. 69; 43, p. 49]. To count total output per employed member of the labor force, as some economists do [40, p. 396], is tantamount to attributing to labor the entire output of the economy [38, p. 805].

Owing to continuing improvement in the economy's productivity, future earnings per worker are almost certain to exceed current earnings (in real terms, that is, apart from a rise in the general price level). If an average (geometric) annual rate of gain in productivity is projected, it can be conveniently applied as a partial offset to the discount rate [30, p. 13; 37, p. 148].

Rate of unemployment. A difference of opinion prevails regarding the rate of unemployment to assume for the beneficiaries of a health program. The current consensus favors the assumption of full employment (4 percent unemployment). The justification is that, if a health program is effective in preventing or curing a disease and makes people available for productive employment, then the program has achieved its objective [38, p. 801].

Yet it seems reasonable to suppose that even in a period of full employment there may be a difference in employment potential between a group of persons in whom a disease has been prevented and one in whom that disease occurs and is cured. Past job history may also be a factor.

The applicability of the full employment assumption to developing countries has been challenged. The economic benefit of preventing premature death depends on whether a survivor is in fact offered productive work [39, p. 211]. The economic value of health reform depends on the rate of economic development; it can be negative in a stagnant system [39, p. 214].

Consumption. Wide differences of opinion obtain regarding the treatment of consumption. Economists agree that in calculating the economic value of a man insurance companies should deduct his consumption [21, pp. 76–82]. Unlike insurance companies or the man's family, however, society as a whole is concerned with total output, of which consumption is a part [38, p. 806]. After all, it is consumption that is the end (goal) of economic activity [39, pp. 19–20]. According to this view, net earnings after consumption are irrelevant to the economist's central concern, and consumption should not be deducted from gross earnings in estimating the gain in output attributable to a health program.

It has been stated that the treatment of consumption depends on one's definition of society, that is, whether the potential survivor is regarded as a member. If he is, consumption should not be deducted from earnings; and conversely [43, pp. 35–36]. Weisbrod does not explicitly choose between the two definitions. However, he develops elaborate and carefully calculated estimates of consumption and employs them in the estimates of economic loss [43, p. 84].

Some economists deduct consumption as a matter of course, without explanation [31, p. 130; 40, p. 396]. In their work the calculation of benefits can result in a negative figure, such as Laitin's finding for cancer among the aged [31, p. 130]. This finding has been erroneously interpreted to mean that killing of the ill may be economically desirable—a repugnant notion [20, p. 18; 25, p. 129].

How to treat consumption is a problem because a health program affects not only a nation's output but also the size of population. It is necessary to distinguish between a program that saves people from death to perform useful labor and one that saves people from death to pursue an unproductive life.

In a poor nation it would seem important to pose a clear-cut choice between programs, in terms of their effect on per capita output. In this country it may not be necessary to pose such a choice. If it is, separate weights might be attached to changes in per capita output and in aggregate output. The relative magnitudes of these weights is a matter for political decision.

The above approach would lend consistency to the position of those economists who consider the deduction of consumption invalid for the United States but deem it necessary to deduct the minimum essential consumption of survivors in a developing country [38, p. 807].

The medical care expenditures in behalf of a survivor in an institution automatically include his ordinary expenditures as a consumer. These should be deducted to the extent that his family makes downward adjustments in its own expenditures [22, Chap. 2, p. 16]. Such adjustments are more likely to be associated with long-term institutional care than with short-term hospitalization.

Services of housewives. Differences of opinion prevail regarding the proper treatment of the services of housewives. Those who would disregard them acknowledge a serious understatement of the costs of some diseases but justify the exclusion on two grounds. It is difficult to measure the value of the services of housewives, since they occur outside the market mechanism. The imputation (attributing the equivalent of a market price where none exists) of economic value raises too many statistical problems [24, pp. 23–24, 143]. To include the services of housewives is also inconsistent with the accepted procedures of national income accounting [38, pp. 803–4].

Others prefer to include the economic contribution of housewives, despite the complexities involved [20, p. 18; 40, p. 396; 43, p. 56]. When the housewife is sick, it costs money to hire a replacement. The housewife's services must be counted in comparing costs among diseases, for the distribution of diseases between the sexes is not uniform. To disregard the services of housewives in calculating output loss is to understate the economic benefits of a health program that serves a preponderantly female population. Moreover, if the costs of several diseases are not additive, there is no occasion to relate the total costs of all diseases to the national output.

One economist measures the value of housewives' services in terms of the cost of a housekeeper replacement who would assume responsibility for running the same size of household [43, p. 70]. From a practical standpoint it is simpler to employ the earnings of a domestic servant. This amount is on the low side, but it offsets the tendency to overvalue a product not sold in the market when it is assigned the price of a counterpart [7, p. 22–23, 432].

APPLICATION OF THE COST-BENEFIT CALCULATION

In his book Weisbrod develops estimates of costs for three diseases — cancer, poliomyelitis, and tuberculosis. For each disease he calculates separately the direct costs of medical care and the loss of net earnings due to premature death and sickness (disability). He then states the general rule for the optimum allocation of funds among disease programs, namely, that the ratios of marginal benefit (the benefit of preventing an additional case of a disease) to marginal cost (the cost of preventing an additional case) should be equal [43, p. 88]. This criterion is tantamount to requiring equal benefits to accrue from spending one additional dollar on each disease [43, p. 63].

It is not possible, however, to eliminate each of the three diseases. A given program in cancer is likely to have only a partial effect on morbidity. It is the benefit of the partial reduction in morbidity that should be measured [29, pp. 129–30], with due cognizance of the continuing costs, if any, of a surveillance program.

For the final calculation of cost and benefit it is necessary to have an estimate of the cost of preventing an additional case of disease. The cost of case finding may be high (both financially and psychologically) even when a highly sensitive test is available, if the prevalence rate of the disease is fairly low. For example, Wallis and Roberts assume an annual incidence of cancer of 5 per 1,000 population (not an unrealistic figure at the middle ages) and a test for detecting cancer that possesses a high degree of reliability, say 95 percent. Under these conditions only 1 in 11 or 12 persons with positive reactions to the test would really have the disease, and the others would be falsely identified as positive [13, pp. 328–29]. Screening tests yield a larger economic benefit to the community when the morbidity rate is higher [19, pp. 358–59].

In considering a new health program, expenditures of effort and money should be related to possible accomplishments. "Diseases of the circulatory system may be the most important cause of death in a community but these conditions are not affected by known preventive measures to the same extent as typhoid fever" [10, p. 232].

It goes without saying that economic arithmetic is only one factor in evaluating programs of health services. Ultimately the preservation of life and the alleviation of pain represent value judgments. It may be that the cost-benefit calculation is useful as an affirmative argument in support of a program and not so useful as an argument against a program that is advocated on humanitarian or other grounds. The question has been raised whether the investment criterion may not be taken as a minimum one, that is, as setting a floor to the size of a proposed health services program [26, p. 283; 40, p. 403; 43, p. 94].

APPLICATIONS TO MEDICAL RESEARCH

It has been proposed that the allocation of research funds among diseases should be similar to the ranking of diseases by economic loss [24, p. 124; 43, p. 87]. This policy was recommended to the federal government shortly after World War II, as follows: "The (medical research) problems under investigation should bear a reasonably close relation to those questions of illness and death which are most common in the population" [36, p. 423].

It is questionable on several grounds whether research funds should be allocated among diseases in relation to the severity of the economic problems they present. This view neglects differences at a given time in the expected difficulty and cost of making comparable improvements in the prevention or treatment of different diseases [36, p. 424]. In evaluating a research proposal the appropriate question is whether, in the present state of knowledge and techniques, it offers a promising lead or chance of further development [25, p. 130]. Nor is it desirable to turn research efforts on and off at will, as the calculated criteria for the allocation of funds change [20, p. 58].

Also to be considered is the large contribution to health advances made by basic research. Ginzberg asserts flatly that most of the outstanding advances in health research have been by-products of basic research in biology, chemistry, physics, and the other sciences [3, p. 735]. Others have noted that basic research is the foundation upon which all other research rests [42, p. 154]; and the uncertainty of discovery is such that it is not possible to buy the specific discoveries one wants [6, p. 71].

Finally, a given health services program may receive dividends from many and unexpected directions. Consider the field of psychiatry. Mental diseases due to nutritional deficiency were eliminated when a vitamin was discovered as a cure and preventive for pellagra. Paresis (a wasting disease of the central nervous system caused by syphilis) is being eliminated by penicillin. The tranquilizing drugs derive from research in diseases of the circulatory system.

The limiting factor in medical research today is not money but scientists [2, p. 53; 4, p. 113; 32, p. 174]. Some believe that there are not enough qualified men available to carry out the work that Congress wishes to pay for with the appropriations it votes [42, p. 156], so that research in one field is performed at the cost of neglecting another. Support and expansion of training [2, p. 52; 6, p. 71; 20, p. 58] are, therefore, prerequisite—both logically and in time—to the effective expansion of research.

NOTES

[1] Jesse Burkhead. *Government Budgeting.* New York, John Wiley, 1956.

[2] Edward F. Denison. *The Sources of Economic Growth in the United States and the Alternatives before Us.* Supplementary Paper No. 13 by Committee for Economic Development. New York, 1962.

[3] Eli Ginzberg. "Health, Medicine, and Economic Welfare," *Journal of the Mount Sinai Hospital,* 19: No. 6 (March–April, 1953), 734–43.

[4] Eli Ginzberg. "What Every Economist Should Know About Health and Medicine," *American Economic Review,* 44: No. 1 (March, 1954), 104–19.

[5] Harry I. Greenfield. *Medical Care in the United States: an Economic Work-up.* Paper delivered at annual meeting of the American Association for the Advancement of Science, Cleveland, Ohio, December 26, 1963.

[6] Alan Gregg. *Challenges to Contemporary Medicine.* New York, Columbia University Press, 1956.

[7] Simon Kuznets. *National Income and Its Composition, 1919–1938.* New York, National Bureau of Economic Research, 1947.

[8] D. S. Lees. *Health through Choice.* London, Institute of Economic Affairs, 1961.

[9] Selma J. Mushkin. "Toward a Definition of Health Economics," *Public Health Reports,* 73: No. 9 (September, 1958), 785–93.

[10] Thomas Parran, Harry S. Mustard, Dean A. Clark, eds., *Selected Papers of Joseph W. Mountin.* Washington, D.C., Joseph W. Mountin Memorial Committee, 1956.

[11] A. C. Pigou. *Socialism vs. Capitalism.* London, Macmillan, 1947.

[12] George J. Stigler. *The Theory of Price.* New York, Macmillan. a. First edition, 1946. b. Revised edition, 1952.

[13] W. Allen Wallis and Harry V. Roberts. *Statistics: A New Approach.* Glencoe, Ill., The Free Press, 1956.

[14] Burton A. Weisbrod. "Anticipating the Health Needs of Americans: Some Economic Projections," *Annals of the American Academy of Political and Social Science*, 337 (September, 1961), 137–45.

[15] William J. Baumol. *Welfare Economics and the Theory of the State.* Cambridge, Mass., Harvard University Press, 1952.

[16] William J. Baumol, and others. "The Role of Cost in the Minimum Pricing of Railroad Services," *Journal of Business*, 35: No. 4 (October, 1962), 357–66.

[17] Kenneth E. Boulding. "An Economist's View of the Manpower Concept," in National Manpower Council, *Proceedings of a Conference on the Utilization of Scientific and Professional Manpower.* New York, Columbia University Press, 1954. Pp. 11–26.

[18] Herbert E. Klarman. "Requirements for Physicians," *American Economic Review, Papers and Proceedings*, 41: No. 2 (May, 1951), 633–45.

[19] Mark S. Blumberg. "Evaluating Health Screening Procedures," *Operations Research*, 5: No. 3 (June, 1957), 351–60.

[20] I. S. Blumenthal. *Research and the Ulcer Problem.* Santa Monica, Calif., The Rand Corporation, 1960.

[21] Earl E. Cheit. *Injury and Recovery in the Course of Employment.* New York, John Wiley, 1961.

[22] Ronald W. Conley. The Economics of Vocational Rehabilitation. Ph.D. Dissertation, Johns Hopkins University, Baltimore, Md., 1964.

[23] Otto Eckstein. "A Survey to the Theory of Public Expenditure Criteria," in National Bureau of Economic Research, *Public Finances: Needs, Sources, and Utilization.* Princeton, N.J., Princeton University Press, 1961. Pp. 439–94.

[24] Rashi Fein. *Economics of Mental Illness.* New York, Basic Books, Inc., 1958.

[25] Martin S. Feldstein. "Review of Weisbrod's *Economics of Public Health*," *Economic Journal*, 73: No. 289 (March, 1963), 129–30.

[26] Richard Goode. Comment on paper by Rashi Fein, "Health Programs and Economic Development," in *The Economics of Health and Medical Care.* Ann Arbor, Mich., Bureau of Public Health Economics and Department of Economics, The University of Michigan Press, 1964. Pp. 282–85.

[27] Seymour E. Harris. *National Health Insurance and Alternative Plans for Financing Health.* New York, League for Industrial Democracy, 1953.

[28] A. G. Holtmann. *Alcoholism, Public Health, and Benefit-Cost Analysis.* Paper delivered before National Institutes of Mental Health Seminar, Bethesda, Md., December 6, 1963.

[29] Maynard M. Hufschmidt, Chairman, Panel of Consultants to Bureau of the Budget. *Standards and Criteria for Formulating and Evaluating Federal Water Resources Developments.* Washington, D.C., Bureau of the Budget, 1961.

[30] Herbert E. Klarman. *Measuring the Benefits of a Health Program — The Control of Syphilis.* Paper delivered at the Brookings Institution Conference on Public Expenditures, Washington, D.C., November 8, 1963.

[31] Howard Laitin. The Economics of Cancer. Ph.D. Dissertation, Harvard University, Cambridge, Mass. 1956.

[32] Louis Lasagna. *The Doctors' Dilemmas.* New York, Harper, 1962.

[33] D. S. Lees. "The Economics of Health Services," *Lloyds Bank Review*, New Series, No. 56 (April, 1960), 26–40.

[34] Ronald McKean. *Efficiency in Government through Systems Analysis.* New York, John Wiley, 1958.

Investment in Health

[35] Leonard W. Martin. *Limitations on the Measurement of Costs of Medical Care.* Paper delivered before the Chicago Chapter of the American Statistical Association, Chicago, Ill., November 22, 1960.

[36] Robert Merrill. "Some Society-wide Research and Development Institutions," in National Bureau of Economic Research, *The Rate and Direction of Inventive Activity: Economic and Social Factors.* Princeton, N. J., Princeton University Press, 1962. pp. 409–34.

[37] Selma J. Mushkin. "Health as an Investment," *Journal of Political Economy,* 70: No. 5, Part 2 (October, 1962, Supplement), 129–57.

[38] Selma J. Mushkin and Francis d'A. Collings. "Economic Costs of Disease and Injury," *Public Health Reports,* 74: No. 9 (September, 1959), 795–809.

[39] Gunnar Myrdal. "Economic Aspects of Health," *Chronicle of the World Health Organization,* 6: No. 7–8 (August, 1952), 203–18.

[40] D. J. Reynolds. "The Cost of Road Accidents," *Journal of the Royal Statistical Society,* 119 (1956, Part 4), 393–408.

[41] Jerome Rothenberg. *Economic Evaluation of Urban Renewal: Conceptual Foundation of Benefit-Cost Analysis.* Washington, D.C., The Brookings Institution, 1963 (manuscript).

[42] John M. Russell, "Medical Research: Choked by Dollars," *Harper's* Special Supplement, The Crisis in American Medicine, 221: No. 1325 (October, 1960), 153–57.

[43] Burton A. Weisbrod. *Economics of Public Health.* Philadelphia, University of Pennsylvania Press, 1961.

[44] Jack Wiseman. "Cost-Benefit Analysis and Health Service Policy," *Scottish Journal of Political Economy,* 10: No. 1 (February, 1963), 128–45.

24. Cost-Benefit Analysis and Health Service Policy*

JACK WISEMAN[1]
University of York

There is growing interest among economists in the development of
a theory of human capital, which would complement the theory of
physical capital, and enable capital theory as a whole to make a more
satisfactory contribution than at present to our understanding of
such questions as the nature and problems of economic growth.
As part of this development, attempts have been and are being made
to estimate the effects on community output of the provision of
such services as health and education, with the purpose of discovering the rate of return to investment of particular kinds in human
beings.

The studies use the general techniques of cost-benefit analysis.
A prime purpose of such analysis is to provide criteria for the identification of 'preferred' public policies. In doing so, the analysis should
provide useful (though not necessarily complete) information as to
the 'efficient' size of the general programmes under review (e.g. the
'right' amount of expenditures on the British National Health Service),
and also give guidance about the associated problems of optimal
allocation of medical resources between different possible uses and
of ensuing 'efficient' utilisation of those resources in the use to which
allotted. The potential importance of such studies in the field of
health needs no emphasis: these are precisely the problems that have
plagued (*inter alia*) those responsible for National Health Service
expenditures since the inception of the Service.

In this paper, I shall provide a brief description of these studies

*Reprinted from "Cost-Benefit Analysis and Health Service Policy," *Scottish Journal
of Political Economy*, (February, 1963), 128–145.

[1] This article was written during a year spent at the University of California, Berkeley.

of investment in health, as a basis for assessing their (actual or potential) contribution to the resolution of the problems described. This is a relatively new field of study, and I shall interest myself in its methodology rather than in specific results so far obtained. For the same reason, the fact that I shall suggest deficiencies in the approach now being developed should not be taken to imply criticism of the writers to whom I refer. The two related questions that concern them, of the characteristics of investment in people and of efficiency in the activities of government, have long been given inadequate attention by economists. The studies thus break new ground, and the fact that they can be criticised is less important than the fact that they should be made.[2]

II. INVESTMENT IN HEALTH

In this section, I shall provide an (inevitably inadequate) summary of the purposes, procedures, and problems of studies of investment in health, in order subsequently to consider the contribution that these studies might make to better decision-taking about the allocation of community resources to the provision of health, and how that contribution might be enhanced.

The broadest approaches to the study of investment in health attempt in some fashion to measure the value of the 'stock' of health

[2] It is of course also true that the studies considered are not identical in approach. But I do not think my generalisations about them are seriously misleading.

The *Journal of Political Economy*, Col. LXX, No. 5, Part 2 (Oct. 62), deals entirely with investment in human beings and in doing so provides a useful survey of the field and the literature. In that Journal, Selma J. Mushkin, 'Health as an Investment' deals with our immediate topic. Relevant recent studies (mostly American) are: B. A. Weisbrod: *Economics of Public Health;* R. Fein: *Economics of Mental Illness,* Joint Commission on Mental Illness and Health, Monograph Series No. 2, New York, Basic Books 1958; I. S. Blumenthal: *Research and the Ulcer Problems,* Rand Corporation Report R-336-RC, 1959; H. Laitin: The Economics of Cancer (unpublished doctoral dissertation, Harvard University, 1956); National Health Education Committee: *Facts on the Major Killing and Crippling Diseases in the United States To-Day* (New York, 1959).

Other studies of interest are B. Abel-Smith and R. M. Titmuss. *The Cost of the National Health Service,* D. J. Reynolds, 'The Cost of Road Accidents', *Journal of the Royal Statistical Society,* CXIX, Part 4, 1956. M. Beesley and D. J. Reynolds, *The London-Birmingham Motorway and Economics,* Road Research Technical Paper No. 46, 1960.

The general study now under way in U.S.A. and discussed in the text is described in Mushkin, *op. cit.;* preliminary findings are published in *Progress in Health Services,* Vol. X, March 1961 (Health Information Foundation Newsletter). Apart from its intrinsic interest, the Mushkin article gives numerous references to earlier material and associated topics.

capital invested in people: 'In its simplest form the economic re-sources (labor and commodities) devoted to health care represent in some part an investment in health. In some part, that is, the health outlays improve the labor product and continue to yield a return over a period of years. The labor product created by this care and savings in health expenditure in the future, if any, as a consequence of reduction in disease is the yield.'[3] The stock of 'health capital' can thus be computed by measuring the cost (actual purchase price, replacement cost, or cost at constant prices) of acquisition of environ-mental and curative health services in the years they were acquired, and relating these costs over their life-spans to age groups in the existing labour force. The measure of the capital stock so obtained can then be related to its yield — that is, to the money value of the annual labour product added as a consequence of the investments. An alternative possibility would be to assess the labour product added by health programmes, and use this to obtain a present value of the relevant (human) capital stock. This in turn can be compared with the cost of the requisite resource-inputs in order to provide a measure of the rate of return to health investment.

This summary description conceals formidable conceptual and computational problems. Since these affect the actual form taken by cost-benefit studies of health, some general explanation is a necessary prerequisite for further comment on the relation of the studies to decisions about public policy. I shall first set out some of the partic-ular economic characteristics of health services, then describe the procedure of the studies and the measurement etc. problems they meet.

III. CHARACTERISTICS OF HEALTH SERVICES

Ideally, we should like to be able to discover the 'resources' that comprise investment in health, and relate these to the increases they generate in community output. But this is difficult if not impossible to do in practice, for a number of reasons. Perhaps the most im-portant are:

(a) Health is affected by many other environmental etc. factors that are not normally thought of as a part of the 'health industry' and that cannot easily be incorporated into cost-benefit studies with-

[3] Mushkin, *op. cit.*, p. 136.

out a tremendous widening of the scope of study. Obvious examples of such other activities and policies influencing health are those concerned with food, housing, road improvement, recreation, smoke abatement, and water supply. There are clearly many others.

(b) The value of 'investment in health', by means of measures directly concerned with the improvement of the health of individuals, is dependent upon the other 'investments in people' that are being made, such as the collateral 'investments' made in education and work-training. There are complementaries here that are peculiarly difficult to sort out. For example, insofar as education increases people's productivity, the 'gain' from investment in health is the greater the higher the level of the associated investment in education. At the same time, health education may itself be a substitute for other forms of investment in health: a general understanding of the importance of personal hygiene reduces the importance (and therefore cost) of particular kinds of infection.

(c) Investment in health may affect both the *numbers* and the (productive) *quality* of the population through time. The consequences of these quality changes are not easy to quantify: how to assess the gain to society from an outstandingly able man being kept healthy or prevented from dying? Even more difficult, how to identify the particular health 'resource inputs' without which this result would not have been obtained?

(d) The returns to the community from investment in health differ from the returns that individuals obtain directly from their expenditures on health services. This means, it is argued, that individual valuations provide an inadequate measure of the social value of health resources. Since the nature of this proposition of 'market failure' is of some importance in our later discussion, I shall set out the essentials of the argument at this point. The suggested deficiencies fall into four broad groups:

(1) There are some kinds of factor-input in the provision of health whose benefits are not capable of being subjected to a principle of exclusion: if the input is made at all, everyone benefits irrespective of whether they have shared in the cost of provision. The spraying of a swamp to clear mosquitoes provides an illustration. If such resource-inputs depend upon individual demand, they will not be made at all, however highly valued by the community, unless some individual believes the resultant benefit *to him* to be greater than the cost.

(2) There may be external effects of the purchase of 'good health' by individuals. Any member of a society who takes steps to protect himself against a communicable disease, for example, must in the process reduce the likelihood that others will catch it, since they now cannot (or are less likely to) catch it from him. Thus, the social benefit from individual purchases of health resources with this characteristic is greater than the individual benefit, and an unadjusted private market would cause 'too little' of such resources to be demanded.

(3) Many health projects 'are supplied and operated under conditions of considerable economies of scale. Sewage disposal, insect control, X-ray detection of diseases are far more expensive to an individual than on a group basis.'[4] This, it is argued, constitutes another way in which 'outsiders' gain when individuals or groups decide to improve their health: the decision brings lower average costs of providing the service for all.

(4) The market functions imperfectly in any case, because of the ignorance or irrationality of the 'consumers'.

This is a formidable enough list to warrant careful examination: we shall find that the argument is less unambiguous than might at first appear, and also that alone it leads to no simple conclusions about such matters as public policy towards the provision of health services. We can begin our examination by suggesting that the first two propositions about 'market failure' are essentially similar in character. An individual cannot exclude any other member of society from the benefits accruing from his own inoculation, any more than he can exclude others from the benefits ensuing from his spraying of a swamp. The difference between the two situations lies solely in the personal nature of the relevant resource-use. In the second case, each individual can decide independently whether to participate or not (e.g. by obtaining an inoculation), while in the first case the decision to commit resources is essentially a single decision, whether taken by an individual or a co-operating group. But the economic significance of this distinction is not established: essentially, the two cases both concern divergences between the social and private benefits stemming from particular resource-using acts, and it is to this matter that I shall now address myself.

It does not follow unambiguously from the existence of exter-

[4]Weisbrod, *op. cit.*, p. 20.

nalities of production or consumption that some particular kind of corrective public policy is required. Thus Weisbrod, who argues strongly for public action on grounds of the inadequacy of the private market in health, accepts that interpersonal subsidisation could take care of many of the externality problems, but maintains that there is no mechanism by which such a subsidisation process can take place. Curiously enough, he cites the 'extra-market' efforts of private foundations or charitable groups in the field of health as evidence for this view.[5] But could not such activities equally plausibly be argued as evidence that individuals conscious of the possibility of benefits from group action including cross-subsidisation will co-operate to obtain them? The importance of this is reinforced when it is appreciated that Weisbrod's interpretation is an oversimplification: recent writing has thrown considerable doubt upon the adequacy of the traditional 'Pigovian' approach to external economies and diseconomies, and in doing so has brought into question the general conclusions that approach invites as to the appropriate 'correctives' for such a situation.[6] There is no space to pursue this question here, interesting though it is. It must suffice to offer a general conclusion that, insofar as the existence of externalities of the type described is accepted, this will call for consideration of whether or not the character of the particular externality under examination requires action of some kind to adjust the outcome of the operations of the market, or whether the necessary adjustments, if any, are or can be achieved without such action. There is no *general* argument for action being needed.[7] Further, it would not seem possible, on the basis of the argument so far, to specify any particular *method* of adjustment as 'ideal' in any given case. The discussion has suggested no means of choosing (e.g.) between legally compulsory vaccination by private doctors, voluntary but free or subsidised vaccination of the same kind,

---

[5] Weisbrod, *op. cit.*, Chapter III.

[6] See, for example: J. M. Buchanan and W. C. Stubblebine: 'Externality', *Economica*, Nov. 1962, and R. H. Coase: 'The Problem of Social Cost', *Journal of Law and Economics*, vol. III, 1960.

Also of relevance is a paper about to be published by J. M. Buchanan and M. Z. Kafoglis: 'More or Less National Health? A Note on Public Goods Supply'. This question whether we can infer from the existence of externalities that public provision of services would increase resource investment in them.

[7] For a similar view, see D. S. Lees, *Health Through Choice*, Institute of Economic Affairs, Hobart Paper No. 14, 1961.

and voluntary or compulsory vaccination through publicly-provided services. This point requires emphasis since, while some of the writers under review recognise the diversity of methods used in the real world to provide medical care, there is nevertheless a general tendency to move directly from the assertion of the existence of social benefits to acceptance of the need for general public provision of health services.[8] This is a *non sequitur:* even where corrective action is required, it need not take the same form in all cases (for it is clear that we are dealing with a diversity of possible externalities), and certainly need not always take the form of public provision. This is a matter to which we shall have to return when discussing the contribution of the cost-benefit studies to policy formation.

The third argument, which is effectively that the market works imperfectly because there are economies of scale, also needs to be treated with caution. In the general form presented, e.g. that X-rays can be provided more cheaply to all consumers if a large number use the relevant equipment, it amounts to no more than a proposition that factors of production are indivisible. This is true in all venues of production; a problem arises for market provision only if the indivisibilities are such that technically efficient production is incompatible with competition. There may be health resources of which this is true, but the case remains to be demonstrated. It is interesting to observe, in this connection, that of the three cases cited in the quotation above, two are instances of externalities of consumption (discussed at (1) above), and one (the X-ray example) clearly does not meet the requirements. X-ray equipment is not large relative to the demand for X-rays, and there is no more reason for a man to have his own X-ray apparatus than there is for him to have his own steel plant.

Finally, the argument that consumers are ignorant or irrational about their health needs also requires careful handling. No convincing evidence has been adduced that individuals cannot (or do not) take as adequate steps to discover their health needs as they do to discover their needs for technical equipment or services of other kinds. Consumers have to rely on other people's experience in respect of the technical properties of a very large range of their purchases, and this is a situation that market forces can ordinarily take care of.

[8]Cf. Weisbrod, *op. cit.*, p. 22. But for a general rebuttal of this position, see Lees, *op. cit.*

More important from our present viewpoint, no clear conclusions for public policy would seem to follow from acceptance of the proposition, save the conclusion that health education would increase the demand for health services. The fact of public or private provision of health services will not *per se* affect the state of ignorance of the potential consumer.[9]

There is one further argument that is commonly adduced about the imperfection of the private market in health services, which needs to be mentioned but which I have distinguished from the rest because it is of a different nature. This is the argument that governments universally intervene in the health market, so that a purely private market does not exist. But if our concern is to provide guidelines for public policy in the field of health, it is surely uncomfortable to begin by citing the fact of public action as a reason for its necessity. Also, it is equally true that the *form and extent* of public intervention varies greatly from one community to another.

IV. MEASURING THE RETURN TO HEALTH SERVICES

The most embracing approach to the evaluation of the costs and benefits of health services is one that attempts to relate the costs of medical resources in general to the increase in national income that results from these costs having been incurred. Another, narrower, approach considers the return to be expected from the elimination or reduction of particular diseases: such studies may attempt to assess the relation between medical outlays and losses of product in the case of some specified disease, or may attempt to rank several diseases according to the (monetary) losses they impose on the community.

Both types of study are still in process of development, but there is now enough information to make methodological comment pointful. At the global level, a study of considerable dimensions is being undertaken in the U.S.A., and is sufficiently advanced for some 'preliminary and very partial' figures to be made available. Studies of particular diseases etc. are available: these either lack comparative information or provide such information only about the relative benefits of some few specified diseases. The two approaches should complement each other, and each type has potential relevance to the decision-taking problems that I earlier suggested to be of interest. Global studies should provide guidance for the determination of the overall size of

[9]Cf. Lees, *op. cit.*

the 'health sector,' while partial studies should help guide the allocation of medical resources to particular uses. They are also similar in general approach and in many of the methodological difficulties they face and the means they use to overcome them. I shall now turn to these matters, treating the two approaches together as far as this is possible.[10]

The studies generally try to surmount or circumvent the difficulties itemised in the last section by attempting to evaluate costs and benefits by direct assessment: they ask, not how much individuals (or a decision taking authority) would value specific kinds of health provision, but rather how specified changes in the incidence of diseases would affect (real) national income or output.[11] This has some important implications:

(a) No satisfactory solution is offered to the difficulty, discussed earlier, of distinguishing the contribution made by health resources from that made by other forms of 'investment in persons.' As a result, 'the estimates considerably overstate the magnitude of capital formation through improved health care.'[12] Also, in the case of studies of particular diseases, there are outstanding problems concerned with the relation between the incidence of particular diseases and the health environment in general. There is a partial-general equilibrium difficulty here, of the kind economists have become familiar with in other fields. 'The assumption that side effects of other diseases may be disregarded in order to measure the direct effects of the disease in question', says Mushkin, 'means that the gains from prevention or cure of each disease, taken individually, cannot be added together to make a meaningful total of gains from prevention or cure of all diseases.'[13]

(b) Although the market is rejected as a general guide for reasons already discussed, studies that concern themselves with costs of provision commonly take existing prices of medical resource-inputs as their basis. Thus, Mushkin quotes preliminary figures from the general study cited above, giving estimates of the cost of medical care

---

[10]References to some of these studies were given at the beginning of the article.

[11]I am aware that the studies are not all formulated in the same fashion. But they are all concerned in some way with the relation between health 'inputs' and product 'outputs', and hence with the size of national income.

[12]Mushkin, *op. cit.*, p. 149.

[13]Mushkin, *op. cit.*, p. 139.

for an American child up to age 18, which seem to be derived directly from available market data.[14]

(c) Returns are measured by some method of estimation of the labour-time (and hence product) added by health resource-inputs which lead to a reduction in deaths and ill-health. This product can then be valued. Some of the conceptual problems of this approach have already been mentioned (e.g. in the partial studies, the assumptions that have to be made about the incidence of other diseases). There are a number of other problems to which solutions have to be found, and some of these are of sufficient importance for the procedures adopted to be of great importance for the conclusions reached. To illustrate, any measure of increase in output through reduction in disease (improvement in health) needs to specify a working life — that is to specify childhood and retirement ages. It is also necessary to distinguish working from non-working population. Apart from such hoary difficulties as the identification of the net product of housewives, the researcher is faced with a fundamental conceptual problem: the 'community' rate of return to health-inputs is going to depend upon who 'consumes' those inputs. I shall be considering this kind of question at greater length when I turn to questions of policy. For the moment, a single illustration must suffice. Consider the data earlier referred to, providing information on health outlays on children up to age 18. The return to this 'input' will be determined by who 'consumes' it (e.g. the average rate of return might be the higher, the greater the proportion of 'consumption' going to the more intelligent and/or better educated), and is also going to be affected by the subsequent size (and interpersonal distribution) of health provision during working life.

Again, the very concept of 'good health' creates problems. In the case of partial studies, these extend to death itself: the fact of death is not too difficult to establish, but cause of death is a much more sophisticated matter, and its identification is clearly a necessary prerequisite for the discovery of the consequences of particular diseases (or freedom therefrom). At the general level, account has to be taken of the fact that death is not the only way in which ill-health reduces output: there are also losses through disablement and debility, and these are peculiarly difficult to quantify. New difficulties arise in turning estimates of returns to health investment in terms of 'labour

[14] Mushkin, *op. cit.*, p. 136.

time' into returns in terms of value. The usual procedure is either to use some measure of earnings (wages and salaries), or to value units of work-time in terms of total product per worker. Neither method is free from ambiguity. The total product measure implicitly attributes all output to labour, while the earnings measure leaves out all contributions to the growth of national income that are not classified as wages and salaries, but that nevertheless inhere in persons and could be lost with their death. How, for example, does such a measure deal with the contribution to output of the Henry Fords?

A final problem arises in reducing the time-streams of outlays and returns to a comparable basis. This requires some method of discounting. But there is continuing disagreement as to what is the 'appropriate' discounting process or interest rate for cost-benefit analyses: a 'social' judgment is involved that cannot be resolved by reference to Pareto-type welfare criteria.[15] The decision reached on this matter may clearly be of great significance for the final results of cost-benefit studies, and the difficulties are especially great in the field of health because there is a considerable variation in the relevant time-horizon for computation of returns to different kinds of health input. Thus, treatment of an ingrowing toe-nail is of relevance only through the lifetime of the patient, while the elimination of a disease by provision of pure water supply will yield returns to infinity. The researcher's only escapes from this problem are either to adopt a particular rate for stated reasons, or to use more than one interest rate, and leave the choice to the policy-maker.[16] How useful this is will depend upon the capacity of the policy-maker to interpret such information in a fashion that helps him take better decisions. This is the general question examined in the next section.

V. THE POLICY PROBLEM

The contribution of cost-benefit analyses generally to the 'efficiency' with which policy decisions are taken must depend to an important extent upon the degree to which the value-system implicit in the analysis is consonant with the value-system of the policy-maker. This is not to say, of course, that such analyses must be useless unless they incorporate all the considerations that are of interest to the

[15] See J. Margolis, 'Water Resource Development', *American Economic Review*, March, 1959, for a survey of the different approaches and their problems.

[16] E. g., Weisbrod, *op. cit.*, uses both 4 and 10 percent.

443

policy-maker. Rather, the studies need to be so formulated that the relation between the valuations that are dealt with and those that are not is capable of reasonably unambiguous explanation and communication, so that the decision-taker can make up his own mind, on the basis of the (cost-benefit) information furnished, as to how he would wish to modify the conclusions of the analysis in deciding policy.

Those who have worked in this field are of course aware of the problem. They have adopted one of two general fashions of dealing with it:[17]

(a) develop the study on the broad general assumption that Pareto's optimal conditions exist elsewhere in the economy, and that the objective of the exercise is to determine how similar conditions might be brought about in the area under examination.

(b) begin from an explicit recognition of the existence of a government as a decision taking entity with unique characteristics, and endeavour to develop analyses that are relevant to the value-system of that entity.

Neither approach is free from difficulty. The first is 'single-objectived', and thus deficient to the extent that aims other than Pareto-type choice are of importance to the policy-maker. There is consequently need for amplification by comment upon the nature and possible importance of other kinds of gains and losses that lie outside the direct scope of the study; in some cases studies are also accompanied by discussion of the *methods* by which services might appropriately be provided (and, arising out of this, of the reasons why the government should participate at all in the kind of economic activity being considered). The second approach is more direct, but faces problems of complexity: practical considerations make it inevitable that such studies be conceived in relation to a context (and criteria) narrower than that implicit in a general equilibrium ideal-allocation approach. This generates problems of interpretation and a need for caution in not losing sight of the alternative methods that may be available for the pursuit of similar ends.

Whichever approach is adopted, and despite the qualifications, cost-benefit analysis is supposed to provide a useful means of providing guidance for policy decisions. If the context is clearly specified,

[17]Relevant discussion will be found in Margolis, *op. cit.,* J. V. Krutilla, 'Welfare Aspects of Benefit-Cost Analysis', *Journal of Political Economy,* June 1961, P. O. Steiner, 'Choosing Among Alternative Public Investments', *American Economic Review,* Dec. 1959, and in papers in *Public Finances: Needs, Sources and Utilization* (ed. J. M. Buchanan).

it is said, and if it is clear what part of the value of a project is incorporated in the analysis, and if information is provided about the *nature* of the ancillary costs and benefits that have not been quantified but that may interest the policy-maker, then cost-benefit analysis provides the decision-taker with improved information, and so must conduce to better decisions. I do not wish to take issue with this general proposition, though I am uncomfortable about the notion that better information about one part of an indefinite whole must always make for a better understanding of that whole: it seems at least possible that it might make for difficulty in taking a balanced view of the relative importance of the things that have been quantified and those that have not (the so-called 'intangibles'). Rather, I shall consider simply how far the kind of studies of health investment that I have been describing can plausibly be fitted into a decision-taking nexus that relates the (actual or potential) results of the analysis to the value-system of the policy-maker. This can be done by considering the studies in relation to the two general approaches just described.

1. THE WELFARE APPROACH

There are two reasons for thinking that the health studies under consideration might be capable of interpretation and evaluation by way of the conceptions and criteria of welfare economics. In the first place, as has already been indicated, the studies are commonly justified, and the need for public policies in the field of health asserted, on grounds of 'market failure'. Thus, they might be expected to bring out the requirements of a policy that would prevent or adjust that failure. In the second place, the relation between health as an investment and the other aspects of demand for (valuation of) health services, insofar as it is discussed at all, is commonly described in the form of the propositions (1) that to the individual good health constitutes 'both investment and consumption'[18] and (2) that there are humanitarian aspects of health service provision that may modify the policies that should be adopted on purely economic grounds. It would seem to follow that the policy-maker's task must be simplified by the availability of measures of the return to health investment: all he has to do is to adjust the results to take account of the individual

---

[18] Investment being the individual desire for good health because it brings a 'pay-off' in output and income; consumption the desires to live, be free from pain, etc. for their own sake.

demand for health as a consumption good, so obtaining an estimate of the 'aggregate demand' of individuals for health services, and then adjust the conclusions to take account of 'humanitarian'[19] considerations in order to arrive at a final policy. But there are some discomforts about this suggested procedure. The most obvious one is that the studies do not measure *individual* valuations of health as an investment, but jump from propositions about market failure to methods of evaluation of the 'community' return to health services that pay no direct attention at all to individual valuations of 'good health.' Thus, there is no way in which the results of these studies can be 'added' to data of private 'consumption' demand to provide a meaningful statement about individual valuations of health services. Further, even if we adopted the very dubious device of assuming that the studies described can tell us what private 'investment demand' for health 'would' be if the market imperfections discussed earlier did not exist, we would still face formidable problems in discovering an appropriate measure of the 'consumption demand' that must be related to this to obtain a 'total private demand' for health services.[20] The distinction between consumption and investment components of individual demand is not a common one, or one that consumers themselves habitually make. My demand for steak has a consumption and an investment component, but this does not weigh with me when I order a chateaubriand, nor do I believe it would were I concerned to study the market demand for steak. Nor is it entirely satisfactory to answer this by pointing out that there is an adequately functioning market for steak, while it is the essence of our problem that the private market in health services functions unsatisfactorily. This invites the rejoinder that, if the proposition is true, it makes the separate valuation of consumption demand for health even more difficult, since we need to know not simply what it is but what it 'would' be did the market imperfections not exist. It is possible to envisage methods of trying to estimate 'consumption' demand (e.g. by trying to estimate the

[19] The 'humanitarian' motives are not usually spelled out in a fashion that permits them easily to be related to the other sources of demand for health. Formally, this could be done, at least in part, by treating them as manifestations of interdependent utility functions. This suggests some interesting lines of thought about the value of the 'welfare' model used in this approach to the policy problem. From our immediate point of view, I do not see that the formalisation helps us simplify or resolve the 'adding-up' problems here being considered, and I shall not pursue it further.

[20] For a somewhat different, but equally negative, discussion of this kind of problem, see Weisbrod, *op. cit.*, Chapter IV.

demand for health of those whose 'investment' demand can reasonably be argued to be zero, and using this information for estimates about others). But the whole procedure bristles with problems, and it is for those who favour a 'welfare' interpretation to suggest how they might be resolved.

2. The direct-evaluation approach

This would treat the end-results of the studies simply as information about one element in the policy-maker's decision-system, to be considered in relation to other available information and to his whole set of policy aims in arriving at an 'optimal' policy decision. In addition to the difficulties that the policy-maker always faces in interpreting any cost-benefit study in such a context (such as the problems posed by the choice of interest rates or the formulation of conclusions in terms of comparable rates of return), the form of the health studies makes for some additional problems: these are in a sense the counterpart of the problems discussed in the last section. There, the problems resulted from the fact that the studies were not formulated by reference to individual demand. Here, they result from the fact that the existing health etc. environment is an element in the calculations.

The essential matter is that the studies do not provide 'pure' information either about the implications of any one policy aim or about any explicitly stated group of aims. Rather, they measure the rate of return to 'investment in health', or some aspect thereof, in relation to an existing environment. Since that environment (e.g. existing size, character and cost of health services, existing 'investment' in such 'co-operating' services as education, and existing productivity of labour) is itself the product of a complex set of policies and aims, the rate of return to 'health investment' can only be satisfactorily interpreted in relation to the constraints imposed by these policies and aims, and particularly in relation to the methods of health provision currently being adopted. The point perhaps requires amplification. It was earlier pointed out that the rate of return to health investment depends upon who 'consumes' the health resources. Consider a community of ten people, nine of whom are over working age. The rate of return to health outlays will be lower if those outlays are distributed over all ten people rather than restricted to the one potentially productive member. But access to health resources must itself be the result of a policy decision. The same point might be made in another way. Insofar as the investment-type studies are designed to throw light on any particular policy aim, it is presumably that of economic growth. Let us therefore consider a situation in which growth is the sole interest of our policy-maker, and ask what an 'ideal' cost-benefit analysis for his purpose would look like.

In the first place, he would need to know the rate of return to investment, not simply in 'health services' considered as some sort of homogeneous whole, but rather to 'health investment' of *particular kinds in particular groups* of people, distinguished by age, earnings, and other characteristics that might affect the return to health investment in them. Armed with this information (we are now assuming away all the problems that would arise in trying to get it), he could then assess how far 'health investment' of particular kinds should be pushed for particular groups, and devise schemes that related ease of access to medical services to that assessment. It is interesting to consider a plausible outcome of such an exercise. The young (with the longest expectancy of working life), the basically fit, and those with the highest expected earnings, would provide the highest rate of return and would therefore be given access to medical resources on the most favourable terms. The old, in contrast, constitute a liability: there would be no point in providing medical services for them unless this is a necessary part of investment in others (e.g. they would be protected against contagious diseases), or because the very nature of the service makes it impossible or too costly to exclude them. Indeed, if growth is the sole aim of our policy-maker, there might be a strong case for providing only one medical service for those who can no longer work: euthanasia. The only argument against such a step, in the given context, would be that family ties are such that the productivity of the young might be adversely affected by the euthanasia of the old. But against this, there might be a very strong incentive for the old themselves to keep on working as long as they can.

Let us consider an even more extreme case. Suppose our concern is with the medical services of a poor country in which malnutrition is a serious health problem. Then, given our policy aim, the 'appropriate' policy might incorporate cannibalism: those with the most favourable cost-benefit ratios would be permitted (required?) to eat those whose contribution to growth was negative—that is, the old and perhaps some of the children.[21]

---

[21]Mr. H. Folk has pointed out to me that such a policy proposal would not be novel, even outside cannibalistic communities. See Dean Swift: 'A Modest Proposal'.

The illustrations are deliberately extreme. While they incidentally throw further light upon the dangers of 'single-objectived' analysis, their prime purpose is to demonstrate the need for a clear understanding of the relation between the apparent aims and the methods of cost-benefit studies. The major difference between the above formulations and actual studies of investment in health is that, while both are concerned with the rate of return to investment, the latter do so on the basis of a set of assumptions about other aims of policy that are never made satisfactorily explicit. This can be expected to result in less startling conclusions than those invited by our imaginary study, but it does not make those conclusions more easily usable for policy purposes: rather the reverse. Thus, a true 'growth' study could fairly readily be modified by the policy-maker, at least in principle, e.g. to take account of humanitarian considerations that make cannibalism or euthanasia unthinkable, and allow for at least minimal access to health resources for all members of the population. It is more difficult to do this with studies that measure rates of return in relation to an existing environment, which means in effect some mixture of market provision of health services, charitable and voluntary action, direct governmental provision, legal control, etc., and so on. It is not enough to say that these are considerations about which the policy-maker must make up his own mind. Since the calculated rate of return to health investment depends upon these things, the results of cost-benefit studies concerned with that return would be altered by changes in them. The researcher thus cannot avoid his obligation to take explicit account of them in his study, at least to the extent of indicating the differences that particular charges might make to his investment data.

VI. CONCLUSIONS AND SUGGESTIONS

It is clear that the studies that have been discussed present major problems of interpretation from the point of view of policy: the relevant methodology has not been worked over to an extent that encourages the belief that we are ready to undertake studies that might serve, e.g., to guide the size and direction of expenditures on Britain's National Health Service. The point is not made in criticism; the approach clearly holds more promise than earlier suggestions for efficient decision-taking about resource use in health; also, the studies are in an early (in the case of general analysis, embryonic) stage of development, and it is a good deal easier to find questions that require answers than it is to suggest how the answers might be found. Further, despite all the limitations to which attention has been drawn, some of the partial studies have produced results striking enough to demand attention.[22] At the same time, it is appropriate to consider the future possibilities of health-investment studies in the light of the accumulating material; as McKean points out in this volume, these studies are themselves resource-using activities, to which cost-benefit concepts may reasonably be applied.

In my view, the earlier discussion invites two inferences that have relevance to the direction of future development. First, while the idea of study of investment in humans is an appealing one, it encourages an approach to the economics of health services that has some important limitations for those whose interest is to help policy-making. It is worth considering the alternative possibilities of an approach of the second kind described above (i.e., concerned directly with the value system of the policy-maker), but taking a fairly narrow view of the range of activities to be considered, that is, the procedure would follow similar lines to that used in recent studies of defence.[23] There are some additional and intractable problems (such as the need to take some kind of account of consumer demand), but none that do not arise in at least as acute a form in the 'investment' approach. On the positive side, such a procedure might find it possible to take over the methodology of existing 'partial' studies, and attempt to overcome the difficulties of aggregation in order to present a more general (though still restricted) survey of the implications of resource-use in the provision of health. This apart, two other possibilities suggest themselves. First, it might be possible to restrict a cost-benefit study to the 'pay-offs' to particular kinds of research activity in the health field. Second, it is worth considering the possibility of distinguishing health resources having 'proplutic' (wealth restoring), anti-plutic (wealth consuming) and neutral effects, for purposes of cost-benefit studies.[24] This might throw light upon the weight being given to 'productivity' and 'humanitarian' considerations respectively, and so provide valuable information if public policy treats both considerations as relevant.

---

[22] See e.g. the examples quoted by Mushkin, *op. cit.,* pp. 156–57.

[23] See C. J. Hitch and R. McKean: *Economics of Defense in a Nuclear Age.*

[24] The terminology is borrowed from F. Roberts: *The Cost of Health.*

The second need is to try to formulate studies in a fashion that gives some indication of the implications of choices between alternatives, not only in the sense of alternative uses of resources but also of alternative methods of provision of health resources. Earlier criticism of the investment studies incorporates the fact that they can throw no light, as formulated, on this second set of choices. Cost-benefit studies in general suffer from a failure to take adequate account of the importance of the institutional arrangements through which the resource-allocation process works. This is a serious deficiency, for several reasons, all particularly relevant to 'social welfare' services such as health. In the first place, if we are to treat the government as a decision-taking organism with aims and means of implementation of its own, then we cannot provide satisfactory advice to the policy-maker without relating that advice to the actual or possible means of implementation. It is clear that in many fields, including health, similar resource-allocation etc. objectives can be pursued by a variety of different means, private and public. But these differ in their specific implications for individual citizens, and neither citizens nor policy-makers can be assumed to be indifferent as between the means available. In other words, alternative methods of resource-allocation must be assumed themselves to have an end-content, and economists who wish their conclusions to guide policy are therefore not entitled to treat the existing institutional environment as an unchangeable constraint. Environmental change may be one of the most important ways of improving an existing situation, but this can never be demonstrated by studies that assume the environment to be given.[25] Again, 'efficiency' problems of the kind we have here been discussing vary in tractability with institutional arrangements, which may or may not facilitate the use (e.g.) of indirect checks.[26]

Once more, the difficulties of setting up and carrying out studies broad enough to meet this requirement are clearly formidable. But the sooner the necessity is appreciated the sooner the problems may begin to be solved.

[25] On all this, cf. Margolis, *op. cit.*, pp. 108–109.
[26] See for example my own proposal to provide an efficiency check for the National Health Service by the introduction of compulsory insurance plus optional (private or public) health treatment. (In *The Finance of the National Health Service:* A Symposium to be published by the Acton Society Trust.)

PART V Investment in Human Migration

Introduction

Perhaps the best way to treat the question of determining the economic benefit from human migration is to treat migration within the theoretical framework of human capital. To do this, migration must be treated as an investment increasing the future productivity of the migrant—an investment which has costs and yields a return. It is important, however, to recognize that complementary investments in the migrant—investments in education and/or health care—are probably as important or, in most cases, more important than migration costs as such in affecting the migrant's future productivity in his new location, a fact which carries us back to the discussion of investment in education and health care.

The first contribution (Reading 25) in Part V is by Larry A. Sjaastad. He discusses both the direct and indirect costs of human migration within the United States. The direct costs consist of any increase in money expenditures incurred by migrating. The indirect costs include earnings foregone while traveling, searching for, and learning a new job. For an individual, the return from migrating consists of a change in his future real earnings stream.

Herbert G. Grubel and Anthony D. Scott, in the second reading (Reading 26) in this part, have applied human capital theory to analyze a muddled current policy issue: the problem of "brain drain." They conclude that the transfer of human capital between countries always reduces the economic and military power of the country that is the net loser of human capital—although the reduction is smaller than is commonly believed.

In the third contribution to this part, Mary Jean Bowman and Robert G. Myers, after briefly surveying the current literature on human investment models applied to migration, conclude that the current methods of calculating human capital gains and losses from migration are inadequate. The reason for this assertion is that re-migration, which they believe to be important quantitatively, has been disregarded. They then develop a series of models that correct this and other deficiencies in current models.

In the final paper (Reading 28) in this part, H.-J. Bodenhöfer integrates labor mobility and the theory of human capital. The inferences for the functioning of labor mobility drawn from the Bodenhöfer model appear to be in accordance with common knowledge about mobility patterns with respect to education, age, and other factors.

25. The Costs and Returns of Human Migration*

LARRY A. SJAASTAD[1]
University of Minnesota

Migration research has dealt mainly with the forces which affect migration and how strongly they have affected it, but little has been done to determine the influence of migration as an equilibrating mechanism in a changing economy. The movements of migrants clearly are in the appropriate direction, but we do not know whether the numbers are sufficient to be efficient in correcting income disparities as they emerge.[2] There is a strong presumption that they are not.

The central purpose of this paper is to develop the concepts and tools with which to attack the latter problem. I propose to identify some of the important costs and returns to migration—both public and private—and, to a limited extent, devise methods for estimating them. This treatment places migration in a resource allocation framework because it treats migration as a means in promoting efficient resource allocation and because migration is an activity which requires

*"The Costs and Returns of Human Migration," *Journal of Political Economy,* Supplement, LXX (October, 1962), 80–93. Copyright 1962 by The University of Chicago Press.

[1] I wish to acknowledge discussion and comments on an earlier draft by Anthony M. Tang and John C. Hause. In addition, I am indebted to T. W. Schultz for extensive comments and aid in revision. Remaining errors and omissions are, of course, my sole responsibility.

[2] A substantial number of highly creditable studies on the nature and strength of the forces affecting human migration have been completed; the earliest of these was published more than seventy-five years ago (see E. G. Ravenstein, "The Laws of Migration," *Journal of the (Royal) Statistical Society,* Vol. XLVIII [June, 1885]). The main concern of economists has been with the response of individuals to economic opportunity at a distance. Harry Jerome's *Migration and Business Cycles* (New York: National Bureau of Economic Research, 1926) leaves little doubt that international migration is influenced by the business cycle, and more recent work indicates a parallel relation for internal migration. Moreover, recent statistical studies have revealed a relationship between internal migration and income differentials as well.

resources. Within this framework, my goal will be to determine the return to investment in migration rather than to relate rates of migration to income differentials.

I. MIGRATION: TOO MUCH OR TOO LITTLE?

Economists and others are generally dissatisfied with the past performance of migration in narrowing geographic income differentials, in spite of the tremendous amount of internal migration taking place in the United States.[3] During the twelve months preceding the 1950 Census of Population, 5.6 percent of the United States population moved to a different county and 2.6 percent to a different state.[4] Accordingly, there were enough interstate migrants to replace the population of Delaware every month and even that of mighty New York within twenty-one months. Nevertheless, Delaware's per capita personal income continues to be two and one-half to three times that of Mississippi. How can these large income differences persist in the face of such massive movements?

Part of the answer lies in the fact that these movements are *gross* rather than *net* migration rates, and that the gross migration rate at the state level is typically several times the net rate. But this fact raises an even more perplexing problem: why is gross migration in one direction the best single indicator of the amount of backflow, as appears to be true? For example, the Census estimates that 62,500 persons migrated from Mississippi in the year preceding the 1950 count; but it also estimates that 51,900 migrated into that state during the same period.[5] If people insist upon migrating into the lowest income state in the union at such a rate, how are economists to rationalize their behavior—much less prescribe the remedy for their alleged sorry earnings? If we take the out-migration of 62,500 persons as evidence that Mississippi is a low earnings area, we must by the same token accept the 51,900 as counter evidence that it is indeed a good place to earn a living. The simple majority favors the out-migrants, but this majority is unimpressively small put alongside the

[3]On this point see George H. Borts, "The Equalization of Returns and Regional Economic Growth," *American Economic Review*, L, No. 3 (June, 1960), 319–47.

[4]United States Bureau of the Census, *1950 Population Census Report*, P–E, No. 4B (Washington: Government Printing Office, 1956), p. 13, Table 1.

[5]United States Bureau of the Census, *op. cit.*, p. 32, Table 8.

income statistics. It is one thing to find lack of mobility the culprit that prevents spatial equalization of incomes; it is quite another to suggest that a lot of mobility in the wrong direction may be the cause!

These remarks, of course, beg the question. Mississippi's per capita income may have risen as much from the 51,900 influx as from the 62,500 outflow. Men are not created equal, nor would they be likely to stay so if they were. A 10 percent in-migration of highly skilled persons (with few children) may improve Mississippi's per capita income more than a larger but less selective outflow. One can conceive of conditions which would cause incomes to rise faster the smaller is net migration.

How may one explain Mississippi's migration pattern (which, incidentally, is typical of that of most states)? The year 1949 was one of recession, which generates an increase in return migration. Moreover, Mississippi is homogeneous neither in occupations nor in industries. The out-migrants may have left declining industries and may not have been qualified for employment in the expanding ones. Or, some or all of the in-migrants may have been disillusioned out-migrants of previous years. There are also retirements. Retired persons may seek places where labor is cheap, whereas employed people are attracted to areas where it is dear; or people who are retiring return to communities in which they were reared and spent the earlier years of their lives.

Whatever may be the best hypothesis for this seemingly paradoxical behavior, three related points become clear: (1) Net migration is not necessarily a useful measure for testing the labor market's ability to remove earnings differentials. (2) Disaggregation of both the migrant and parent population by at least age and occupation may be required to confirm (or deny) the alleged failure of migration to achieve a reasonably equal income distribution over space. (3) The "perverse" behavior of gross migration is consistent with observed income differentials being generated by occupational as well as geographic immobility. Let me add that the somewhat paradoxical relation between gross in- and out-migration may be substantially an aggregation problem, as I have argued elsewhere.[6]

[6]See my "Migration in the Upper Midwest" in "Four Papers on Methodology" (an unpublished manuscript of the Upper Midwest Economic Study, University of Minnesota).

Migration poses two broad and distinct questions for the economist. The first, and the one which has received the major attention, concerns the direction and magnitude of the response of migrants to labor earnings differentials over space. The second question pertains to the connection between migration and those earnings, that is, how effective is migration in equalizing inter-regional earnings of comparable labor? The latter question has received much less attention than the former. It is also the more difficult of the two.

Most studies concerned about the first question have focused upon *net* migration to or from various geographic areas or between pairs of such areas. Most of them have found a relationship between income or earnings and migration, and usually in the expected direction (that is, high earnings are associated with net *in*-migration, low earnings with net *out*-migration). The qualifications, however, are numerous; and the observed relationship is usually quite small and weak. My study of interstate migration, for example, shows that over the 1940–50 decade, an increase in per capita labor earnings of $100 (1947–49 dollars) induces net in-migration or retards net out-migration by only 4 or at most 5 percent of the population aged fifteen to twenty-four years at the end of the decade.[7] The percentage was lower for other ages and hence lower for the total population. This modest response of net migration to earnings differentials implies that per capita earnings must be low indeed for net out-migration to overcome natural increase and effect a local population reduction. My study indicates that during the 1940's the earnings level in a particular state would need to be roughly one-half the national average in order for migration from that state to offset completely the natural increase, thus leaving a static population.

But as was suggested earlier, net migration alone is not the only mechanism for removing earnings differentials; one should also consider gross migration. Presumably, net migration is required only from those industries (or occupations) with locally depressed wage rates. If low earnings characterize all or most industries in a particular area, net out-migration is required; and it should bring about an increase in the wage rate relative to the case without out-migration. If some industries in the area, however, are paying higher

---

[7] Larry A. Sjaastad, "Income and Migration in the United States" (unpublished Ph.D. dissertation, University of Chicago, 1961), p. 38.

wages than elsewhere, and the workers leaving the low-wage industries are unqualified and cannot easily become qualified for employment in the high-wage industries, in-migration should also occur. But this diversification among high- and low-wage industries is almost certain to *weaken* the expected relation between average earnings levels and net migration, although there remains a strong presumption that low average earnings will induce net out-migration.

Occupation composition can account for some, but not all of the differences in earnings among states. The results of Frank Hanna's admirable study show that: (1) the low income states are dominated by occupations with relatively low earnings at the national level, and (2) the earnings within particular occupations in low-income states tend to be lower than the national average.[8] Opposite relationships characterize the high-income states. Hanna's study, together with the observed relation between income and net migration, supports the hypothesis that migration does constitute a response to *spatial* earnings differentials; moreover, this evidence is consistent with the hypothesis that migration is a search for opportunities in *higher-paying occupations*. Both hypotheses are reassuring to the economist.

Although the studies of net migration to date partially reveal the functioning of the labor market, they tell us little more than the fact that net migration is in the "right" direction. The estimated response magnitude of net migration to gaps in earnings is of little value in gauging the effectiveness of migration as an equilibrator. There are, however, several alternative approaches. One simple approach is to compare rates of (gross) migration with changes in earnings over time. Numerous compositional corrections would be necessary, and this approach would still have to answer the difficult question of how much equalization of earnings should be brought about by a given amount of migration. Moreover, it is possible that the impact of migration can be offset by further changes in the economic forces which originally generated the earnings differentials.

A better alternative, at least analytically, is to cast the problem strictly as one of resource allocation. To do this, we treat migration as an *investment increasing the productivity of human resources*, an investment which has costs and which also renders returns.

Treating migration as an investment removes one of the difficulties

---

[8] Frank A. Hanna, *State Income Differentials, 1919–1954*, (Durham, N.C.: Duke University Press, 1959), p. 128.

inherent to the first approach; there exists a ready-made criterion to test the effectiveness of migration in reducing earnings differentials over space. That criterion is, of course, the rate of return on resources allocated to migration. The difficulty of the method is that it is necessary to identify and measure the costs as well as the returns to migration; its credit is the possibility of meaningful comparisons between migration and alternative methods of promoting better resource allocation.[9]

III. THE PRIVATE COSTS OF MIGRATION

The private costs can be broken down into money and non-money costs. The former include the out-of-pocket expenses of movement, while the latter include foregone earnings and the "psychic" costs of changing one's environment. Each of these is treated in turn below.

1. THE MONEY COSTS

There are no data to my knowledge on the expenses incurred by migrants in the course of moving. Although these data could be collected only from the migrants themselves, these costs could, no doubt, be estimated reasonably well for given distances (and number of dependents, if one treats migration of families). Such estimates have been made, but I suspect they are quite conservative.[10] Nevertheless, since the money costs one ought to include are only the *increase* in expenditure for food, lodging, transportation (for both migrants and their belongings), etc., necessitated by migration, the order of magnitude of these costs is surely sufficiently small that it cannot account for the large earnings differentials encountered in the data (even after taking into account foregone earnings). Moreover, the results of my study of internal migration in the United States, 1949–50, suggest that the marginal costs associated with addi-

[9] Obviously, complete or perfect spatial equalization of earnings is ruled out (other than by chance) so long as migration involves costs to the migrant.

[10] James G. Maddox, for example, estimates "that many farm people can travel as far as five hundred miles from their home, take ten days to find non-farm jobs, and wait a week for their first paycheck after they start work with a nest egg of no more than $100 per person" ("Private and Social Costs of Movement of People out of Agriculture," *American Economic Review*, L [May, 1960], p. 393). Note that this is an estimate of capital requirements as opposed to money costs, since Maddox does not take account of what it would cost to live without migrating.

tional distance are considerably higher than could be attributed to the costs considered in Maddox's estimate. The migration variable was defined as the number of (net) migrants going from state i to state j as a fraction of all (net) migrants from state i. Regression coefficients obtained indicate that the attractiveness of a given destination was unaffected by a 10 percent gain in annual per capita labor earnings *and* a simultaneous 16 percent increase in distance.[11] At the mean of the income and distance variables these percentages imply that the typical migrant would be indifferent between two destinations, one of which was 146 miles more distant than the other, if the average annual labor earnings were $106 (1947–49 dollars) higher in the more distant one.[12] Marginal costs per mile of migration would have to be high indeed to reconcile this negative effect of distance with the present value of the earnings differential even at very high discount rates, particularly since the persons involved are already migrants and only their allocation over space is in question. Moreover, this result cannot stem from migrants moving in a series of short jumps. That explanation would be plausible if the allocation of gross migrants were being studied; in the case under question, however, the variable is net migration. One is strongly tempted to appeal to market imperfections such as the lack of information to explain the apparently high distance cost of migration. Unfortunately, no simple way has been devised for testing that hypothesis–although attempts have been made.[13] Even so, the migration-impeding effects of uncertainty remain to be measured.

2. The non-money costs

The non-money considerations involved in migration are surely significant, probably far more so than the money costs. The first non-money costs to consider are opportunity costs — the earnings

---

[11] Sjaastad, "Income and Migration in the United States," p. 63.

[12] These estimates are partial regression coefficients and since an occupational mix variable was also present, it is assumed that the occupational mix is either constant or changes such that average earnings of the labor force remain constant if each member earns the national average within his occupation. The occupational mix correction is that devised by Hanna and called "rate constant earnings" (*op. cit.*, chap. v.).

[13] In particular, see Philip Nelson, "A Study in the Geographic Mobility of Labor" (unpublished Ph.D. dissertation, Columbia University, 1957.)

foregone while traveling, searching for, and learning a new job.[14] Part of these foregone earnings will be a function of the distance of migration. In addition the time required to find a new job is presumably affected by the level of unemployment. Clearly one should be able to estimate these components. The costs of learning a new job (on-the-job training) are treated in detail by Mincer in another paper in this Supplement. As Mincer demonstrates, these costs are subject to measurement. Since they are reflected by reduced earnings, these costs are to be taken into account by choosing the appropriate expected earnings stream (after migration) for comparison with the expected stream had the migrant not moved.[15]

A second form of non-money costs must be considered. Since people are often genuinely reluctant to leave familiar surroundings, family, and friends, migration involves a "psychic" cost. It would be difficult to quantify these costs; moreover, if they were quantified, they should be treated quite differently from the costs previously considered. The costs treated above represent real resource costs; however, the psychic costs do not. Rather they are of the nature of lost consumer (or producer) surplus on the part of the migrant. Given the earnings levels at all other places, there is some minimum earning level at location i which will cause a given individual to be indifferent between migrating and remaining at i. For any higher earnings at i, he collects a surplus in the sense that part of his earnings could be taxed away and that taxation would not cause him to migrate. The maximum amount that could be taken away without inducing migration represents the value of the surplus. By perfect discrimination, it would be possible to take away the full amount of the surplus, but in doing so leave resource allocation unaffected (other than through distributive effects). Hence, the psychic costs of migration involve no resources for the economy and should not be included as part of the investment in migration.

Although the psychic costs involve no resource cost, they do affect

---

[14] One could include in opportunity costs the entire earnings stream the migrant is expected to earn had he not migrated, and then include in returns the expected earnings stream after migration. The alternative followed in this paper is to look only at the increment to costs and earnings associated with migration.

[15] Risk and uncertainty "costs" can be treated in a fashion similar to on-the-job training costs; that is, by an appropriate increase in the rate of discount for the increment to expected future earnings created by migration. Moreover, the adjustment in the discount rate need not be made explicitly if internal rate of return calculations are made.

resource allocation. Very likely, more migration would take place if psychic costs were zero for everyone. In addition, even if knowledge were perfect, psychic costs could explain the existence of earnings differentials larger than those implied by the money and opportunity costs of migration. However, these excessive differentials would not represent resource misallocation. The optimal allocation of resources must take tastes as given, and will differ accordingly if people prefer familiar over strange surroundings. Migration incentive transfers to compensate for these psychic costs would be as inappropriate as transfers to render people indifferent among occupations even though strong preferences may exist. To compensate for psychic costs would result in resources being used for migration to obtain earnings with a lower value than those received before. To draw upon an old example, because the public hangman earns a high income owing to his distasteful job, it does not necessarily follow that welfare would be improved with more hangmen!

Although we should not treat psychic costs as a component of the costs of migration, they pose a problem for the analysis of rate of return. To the extent that some part of existing earnings differentials represents tastes alone, the rate of return to resources allocated to migration is biased. One manner in which this problem can be partially circumvented is to consider only persons for whom the marginal psychic cost is zero. The allocation of actual migrants by distance migrated should be relatively free of the influence of psychic costs, although the percentage of all persons who become migrants is not. Using education as an analogy, this approach is similar to determining the rate of return on the nth year of schooling as compared to the rate on n years.

IV. THE PRIVATE RETURNS TO MIGRATION

For any particular individual, the money returns to migration will consist of a positive or negative increment to his real earnings stream to be obtained by moving to another place. This increment will arise from a change in nominal earnings, a change in costs of employment, a change in prices, or a combination of these three. Money returns so defined are sufficiently general to encompass not only those returns stemming from earnings differentials between places, but also the returns accruing to the migrant in his capacity as a consumer. Both of these returns are net gains; increased efficiency in consumption is logically equivalent to increased efficiency in production. In addition, there will be a non-money component, again positive or negative, reflecting his preference for that place as compared to his former residence.[16] Finally, there is pure consumption. The pure consumption return should be regarded as the satisfaction or dissatisfaction the migrant receives in the course of his actual travel. This is analogous, again in the case of education, to the satisfaction the student experiences merely from being on campus, quite apart from the non-marketable satisfactions he may obtain over his life span as a result of his education.[17] The non-money returns will be examined first.

1. THE NON-MONEY RETURNS

Earlier it was found that we can safely ignore psychic costs of migration since they involve no resource cost; likewise, we should ignore non-money returns arising from locational preferences to the extent that they represent consumption which has a zero cost of production. Some people, for example, may be indifferent between earnings at one level in Minnesota and a lower level in California owing to a preference for the latter's climate. If a large portion of the population showed this preference, California would have a locational advantage, and industry would migrate in that direction to enjoy the resultant lower labor costs. In a world of perfect competition and resource mobility no earnings differentials arising from these preferences would remain in final equilibrium; if discrimination were perfect, the existence of the preferences would be totally reflected in rents earned by factors (land) specific to the climate. Moreover, the pure rents so paid should not be treated as costs of employment since they arise from tastes for location rather than differences in productivity.

[16] Preference for familiar versus strange surroundings are included in psychic cost and are excluded here. Preference at this point refers to such factors as climate, smog, and congestion. It is assumed that the individual's production and consumption occur at the same place; if that were not true, his preferences would be reflected in the amount of cost he is willing to bear to consume at one place and to be employed at another.

[17] The consumption-investment dichotomy I have in mind is based strictly upon the point in time at which the migrant actually receives the satisfactions. An outlay made to increase future productivity is usually called an investment; an outlay for immediate satisfaction is labeled consumption. Moreover, if a person uses some of his resources to increase future satisfactions, it should not matter whether or not the increase is reflected in future market transactions. From this point of view, there is no logical difference between a consumer or producer durable; I choose to call them both an investment.

Even in a world of perfect competition and resource mobility there can be earnings differentials arising from variations in costs of employment (which must be offset by corresponding differentials in productivity). Larger cities typically reveal higher earnings within occupations than smaller cities. Costs of employment are higher in larger cities due to additional transportation, rent, etc., which are compensated by higher earnings. If one includes the former as a return to migration to the larger city, he should deduct the latter as additional cost of employment. Locational preferences pose a problem in estimating the return to migration to the extent that they can give rise to rents not to be counted as costs of employment; but additional costs arising from the superior productivity of a specific location are to be deducted. Although a distinction between those returns to migration which represent higher productivity and those which are merely consumption of zero cost goods is analytically useful for considering the returns to migration arising from increased efficiency, it is of no practical use. Final spatial equilibrium in the real world would permit variations in earnings (within occupations) resulting from non-labor resource immobility (particularly natural resources) and from lack of competition as well as from differentials in cost of employment and labor immobility. Moreover, since discrimination in the land market is not perfect, persons can and do receive windfalls by moving to a place of their preference. Private non-money returns to migration may very well exist and influence behavior; and they cannot be separated from those private returns reflecting higher productivity alone. Even in a world of perfect competition, of resource mobility, and of discrimination according to preference it would not be feasible to classify costs of employment into the two categories outlined above. For practical purposes, the only alternative appears to be the unrealistic assumption that variation in tastes permits a spatial distribution of persons such that no rents arise from differences in amount and composition of natural amenities, and that this distribution does not seriously differ from the "optimal" distribution from the viewpoint of resource allocation.

2. THE MONEY RETURNS

It is obviously not sufficient simply to compare labor earnings over space and assume that any observed differences arise from disequilibrium in the labor market. Hanna's study reveals that occupational composition explains a significant portion of earnings differentials

467

among states.[18] Other variables such as age and sex affect earnings within an occupation.[19] However, assuming occupation, age, and sex to be the more important compositional variables affecting earnings, first estimates of the return to migration is the difference in earnings within occupations, ages, and sexes, and between all places. These estimates would almost surely be underestimates because they fail to take into account possible disequilibrium between as well as within occupations and because a change in occupation may necessitate migration. The more relevant alternatives for migrants may be *among* rather than *within* occupations. While one may be able to show that the Alabama farm laborer can improve his earnings on an Iowa farm, his prospective opportunities may be far more in an urban area and occupation.

If the return to migration can be increased by occupational upgrading, the problem in estimating the return becomes far more complex. In this context it is particularly useful to employ the human capital concept and to view migration, training, and experience as *investments in the human agent*. These investments, specific to the individual, are subject to depreciation and deterioration both in a physical and an economic sense. If market forces reduce the relative wages of a particular occupation, practitioners of that occupation suffer a capital loss and are faced with the alternatives of accepting the lower earnings or making additional investments in themselves to increase their earnings in a more favorable market. If the relative wages in an occupation are adversely affected locally, migration alone is sufficient; if the adverse effect is national, such as the earnings in agriculture, the entire occupational earnings structure is under stress and migration is feasible only if new skills are acquired by the migrant. Whether or not the additional investment is worthwhile depends crucially upon the age of the individual. Young persons will typically have made only a small investment in themselves through training for and experience in a specific occupation and a relatively large one through formal education; whereas a larger portion of the investment in older persons presumably arises from skill and experience

---

[18]*Op. cit.*, p. 121.

[19]The value of leisure is also neglected when comparing earnings. If the individual labor supply function is not backward bending, smaller earnings will necessarily be accompanied by larger amounts of leisure time, which should not be valued at zero. Thus one should look at hours of work as well as earnings. There remains the problem of the value to impute to an hour's leisure. While an imputation probably cannot be accurately made, this omission should be borne in mind.

specific to a particular employment.[20] For the former group, obsolescence is a far smaller threat; moreover, their longer life expectancy increases the present value of the returns to additional investment relative to the older group.

Since the age-income relation within an occupation is at least partially due to the accumulated experience (on-the-job training), older persons entering a given occupation even after minimal training are likely to receive lower earnings than persons of similar age but well experienced in that occupation. Hence, comparisons across occupational groups but within age groups lead to overestimates of the rate of return to migration alone. The return so estimated is to be attributed to *both* the migration investment and the investment in on-the-job training, as well as costs of pre-employment training. Estimates of the return to migration alone must be preceded by an explanation of the age-earnings relation so that earnings representing equal experience are compared.

If it is true that complementary investments are required to make migration feasible, particularly among the older migrants, one must be extremely careful in making broad comparisons of earnings and, upon finding significant differences over space, in concluding that voluntary migration is incapable of efficient allocation of labor resources. It is clearly possible that the migration mechanism could be working extremely well in the sense that the marginal return to additional migration is not "high," but that substantial differentials in earnings may persist. I strongly suspect, for example, that the lack of relevant alternatives for older farmers in non-farm occupations may go a long way in explaining why off-farm migration has not increased relative earnings in agriculture so that "comparable" factors receive comparable returns. The point is that factors are not really comparable, having had different occupational histories.

I have estimated net migration rates from rural areas in the upper Midwest which sharply reveal the age selectivity of net migration from agricultural areas.[21] These are presented in Table 1.[22] Although

[20] In the United States, the difference in this intangible "portfolio" is exaggerated by the secular increase in levels of formal education attained.

[21] The upper Midwest includes the following states and parts of states: Montana, North and South Dakota, Minnesota, northwestern Wisconsin and Upper Michigan. The migration rates are estimated by the census-survival rates developed by the author in connection with his research on the Upper Midwest Economic Study.

[22] Since these migration estimates are from rural areas only, the problem of the difference between net and gross migration is less serious than suggested earlier. The

TABLE 1

1950–60 Net Out-Migration from Rural Areas, Upper Midwest,
as a Percent of 1950 Population, and Gross Migration Rates,
United States, 1949

1950 Age	Upper Midwest Percent Out-Migration Rate	United States Percent Gross Migration*
0–4	13.7	7.0†
5–9	25.1	5.0
10–14	44.5	4.0‡
15–19	30.6	6.9§
20–24	9.1	11.3
25–29	10.4	9.4
30–34	10.7	6.7
35–39	9.8 }	4.7
40–44	8.6 }	
45–49	9.2 }	
50–54	7.5 }	3.0
55–59	9.4 }	
60–64	8.8 }	
65+	1.8	2.6

*Source: Bureau of the Census, *1950 Population Census Report*, P–E, No. 4D, Tables 1 and 2.
† Aged 1–4 in 1950.
‡ Aged 10–13 in 1950.
§ Aged 14–19 in 1950.

nearly half of the persons, aged 10–14 years in 1950, migrated from the rural areas during the 1950–60 decade, less than one in ten of the persons 20 years of age and over in 1950, migrated. Although one might plausibly argue that both money and non-money costs of migration increase with age, it seems doubtful that the increase in these costs as initial age rises from 15–19 to 20–24 can be sufficient to reduce the out-migration rate from over 30 percent to less than 10 percent. If increases in costs reduce rural out-migration as age increases, the same cost increases should be borne by all migrants. Table 1 also presents gross migration in 1949 for the United States as a percent of parent population. The age-migration pattern there is quite different. However, the data are not comparable since the

---

rural areas of a given region are likely to be quite homogeneous, so only a small amount of cross-migration is anticipated.

TABLE 2

Comparison of Rural Out-Migration, Upper Midwest,
with Gross Migration Rates, United States

Age Range	Average of Range	Upper Midwest Percent Out-Migration Rate	United States Percent Gross Migration
0–14	7.5	13.7	5.5*
5–19	12.5	25.1	5.4
10–24	17.5	44.5	7.6
15–29	22.5	30.6	9.1†
20–34	27.5	9.1	9.1
25–44	35.0	10.5	6.5
35–44	40.0	10.0‡	4.7
45–64	55.0	8.4	3.0
65+		1.8	2.6

*Aged 0–13.
†Aged 14–29.
‡Approximate.

age range for 1950–60 upper Midwest migrants differs, for example, 0 to 4 in 1950 is from 0 through 14 over the decade. The data are reorganized in Table 2 for identical age groups, and the pattern is similar. Although the migration rate falls 70 percent in the upper Midwest as one goes from age ranges 15–29 to 20–34, it remains constant for the United States. Although not conclusive, the evidence for the United States strongly suggests that little of the decline in migration rates as age increases can be explained by associated increases in the money or non-money costs of migration.

As age increases, of course, there is a shortening of the time period over which the migrant expects to recapture these costs; but again it seems unlikely that this effect can so sharply reduce the migration rate. If retirement comes at age 65 to 70, the group aged 15 to 19 in 1950 will have about 45 years, on the average over the decade, remaining in the labor force — as compared with 40 years for those initially aged 20 to 24. At a discount rate of 10 percent, the present value of an additional dollar per year for the former group is $9.89; for the latter group it is $9.82, a mere 7 cents less. The dispersion in cost of migration would have to be fantastically small if a reduction in present value of returns by less than 1 percent (owing to the shortening of the amortization period) would reduce the migration rate by 70 percent. Neither increasing costs of migration nor reduction in the amortization period alone can explain the age-migration relation observed in the upper Midwest.[23]

However, if substantial additional costs of retraining for a new occupation must be borne by these rural out-migrants, the age-migration pattern displayed in Table 2 becomes more comprehensible. The majority of the rural out-migrants from the upper Midwest will necessarily be changing occupations. Clearly they come from agricultural occupations but are entering urban occupations. New skills must be acquired. Only a smaller portion of the gross United States migrants, however, need to change occupations; much of this mobility can be merely geographic and not occupational. For the latter group, the total costs to the individual for migration and acquiring new skills can be much smaller than for the former.

The sharp reduction in rural out-migration at relatively early ages and its near constancy thereafter suggests that (a) the investment in skills in rural occupations is concentrated in early years, and (b) consequently, the rural age-earning relation should rise sharply as returns to this investment are realized. Both of these propositions can be tested by the analysis developed in Mincer's paper. Moreover, this hypothesis implies that the degree of disequilibrium may differ among age groups — being largest for the young and less for the older persons. Differences in earnings could, of course, become larger for the older persons; but this is not inconsistent with efficient resource allocation. These older people may have suffered a capital loss, and their remaining lifetime is too short to justify large additional investments in themselves. To the extent that the above characterization is true, such disparities in earnings become a question of social policy rather than one of resource allocation.[24]

---

[23] Suppose that the distribution of costs, as well as the present value, of returns to migration for all potential migrants is normal, mean C and PV, respectively; variance S^2 and zero, respectively, and that costs and returns are independent. For the 15–19 age group, $C = C_1$, $S^2 = S_1^2$, $PV = PV_1$; for 20–24, $C = C_2$, $S^2 = S_2^2$, $PV = PV_2$; assume a discount rate less than 10 percent so that $PV_2 = 0.99PV_1$. For 30.6 percent of the persons aged 15–19, $PV_1 \geq$ cost; for 9.1 percent of those aged 20–24, $PV_2 \geq$ cost. At the margins, $PV_1 = C_1 - .5S_1$; $PV_2 = C_2 - 1.3S_2$. Let $C_1 = C_2 = C$; $S_1 = S_2 = S$; then $S/C = 0.0135$. The implied coefficient of variation is a mere 1.35 percent. More reasonable coefficients of variation for both costs and present values are possible if there exists a strong positive correlation between these two variables. Some positive correlation is expected.

[24] For a bold approach to the social policy question posed by persons "locked-in" their historic occupations, see T. W. Schultz, "A Policy to Redistribute Losses from Economic Progress" (prepared for a labor mobility conference, Iowa State University, November, 1960) (mimeographed). In this paper Schultz argues that since the losses to individuals

If, as I suggest, interoccupational earning differences may be the more relevant ones in dealing with migration, but if there is as yet no way of making sense out of these differences in terms of actual incentives offered migrants of different ages, some alternative approach to estimating the rate of return on migration is necessary. Fruitful lines of attack may be to focus upon migrants only or to make comparisons between migrants and non-migrants of similar age.[25] Conceptually, there is no problem in determining whether and by how much a migrant's earnings are altered by his move. Cross-classified data concerning vital characteristics of migrants such as age, occupation, earnings before and after migration, etc., are a prerequisite to a thorough study of return to migration along these lines. Fortunately, substantial data of this sort will be available in the 1960 *Population Census Special Reports* and will cover a five-year period; the negative transitory effect of migration upon the earnings of migrants should largely disappear. As far as I know there will be no earnings data for migrants before migration, but cross-classification may permit use of earnings of comparable non-migrants as a substitute.[26]

V. PRIVATE VERSUS SOCIAL COSTS AND RETURNS

Does the migrant bear all the costs of migration and receive the total reward for his activity? The obvious answer is probably not. Migration will typically involve costs (and rewards) to non-migrants as well as migrants; the relative prices seen by the migrant are likely to

---

from economic progress are much more narrowly distributed than are the gains, a case can be made for redistributing those losses over a larger group.

[25] By focusing upon migrants only it would be possible to eliminate the effects of differences in psychic costs, as was mentioned above.

[26] If a study of the returns to migration were carried out along these lines, one additional factor must be considered. I have assumed that migration is mainly in response to differences in earnings over space. In the case of off-farm migration, however, rising unemployment in the non-farm sector has been observed to attentuate sharply the outflow from agriculture even though we may assume earnings differentials (for employed persons) to remain relatively stable. If unemployment is high, the probability of the off-farm migrant obtaining a job at a given level of earnings is reduced, perhaps much more than rates of unemployment would indicate, owing to seniority rules and the like. Observed earnings differentials must be further discounted for the risk of unemployment and the appropriate discount rate may be very high, as imperfections in the capital market may prevent potential migrants from assuming this risk during periods of moderate to heavy unemployment. The logical choice in this circumstance is to defer the move until more favorable labor market conditions prevail.

be at variance with transformation rates for the economy as a whole. Divergences between social costs and returns arising from externalities pose knotty analytical problems; those arising from market imperfections and institutional factors are somewhat easier to examine and are my main concern here. The cases considered are illustrative rather than exhaustive; consequently, the omissions may be the more important.[27]

The above discussion of private costs and returns places voluntary migration in the general framework of a competitive economy satisfying the minimal requirements permitting an "optimum" allocation of resources. Among other features, wages must be freely determined and there must be no barriers to the free movement of labor and other inputs among industries or across space.[28] Even if wages are freely determined and equal marginal product, differences in the relation between wages and, for example, retained earnings in different areas will cause private returns to differ from social returns. Consider the case of local differences in the degree of progression in income taxation; migration redistributes resources in a fashion to equate earnings over space *subject to the taxation structure*, a process which may indeed be detrimental to resource allocation.

Divergence between private and social costs of migration can also occur when the charges for services collectively provided (such as schools) are based upon the per capita cost rather than the actual marginal cost of providing those services to migrants. However, capital losses imposed by migrants upon the privately held fixed assets of non-migrants in an area experiencing a population decline generally cannot be admitted as an excess of social over private cost. These losses involve no resource cost; persons presumably will not migrate until their productivity elsewhere is sufficiently high to compensate for rent differentials.

Another source of an excess of social over private returns to migration arises from a failure of migrants to consider the returns to their progeny from the resulting change in the latter's (initial) location. By assuming the current change in market conditions to continue indefinitely into the future, a crude first approximation of this excess is

[27] This section draws heavily upon the comments of Anthony M. Tang on an earlier draft.

[28] We must also require that product prices also be freely determined and barriers to free trade nonexistent.

possible. Suppose the migrant includes as private return the additional earnings obtained by himself and his immediate family but excludes any return to unborn children. The rate of interest, compounded instantaneously, is assumed to be 10 percent per year; and the rate of population increase at 1.5 percent per year. If his first as-yet-unborn child enters the labor market in twenty years, and if earnings differentials are and remain the same for all occupations (since there is no certainty that the migrant's progeny will enter his occupation), each dollar of his (uniform) earnings stream for a forty-five year participation in the labor force has a present value of $9.90. The present value of a permanent income stream of $1.00 beginning in twenty years and growing at the rate of 1.5 percent per year (due to natural population increase) is about $1.62. The first figure is the present value of the return to the migrant aged twenty years of each dollar of earnings differential; the second is the present value of the return to the stream of unborn children he will generate.[29] If the migrant neglects the latter completely, the social return to migration will be 16.4 percent in excess of the private return; if the private rate of return is in fact 10 percent, the additional social rate of return will be 1.164 percent. For older migrants the excess of the social return over the private will approach zero (they are less likely to have more children); and for younger migrants the social rate also approaches the private rate because a longer period will elapse before their children enter the labor

---

[29] The present value of the income stream of the migrant of $1.00 per year is computed as

$$\int_0^{45} e^{-rt} \, dt = 9.90$$

when $r = 0.10$. It is assumed that the migrant's children will realize an equal gain per year, and that the first child will not enter the labor force until twenty years in the future, their number growing continuously at 1.5 percent per year thereafter. The present value of one income stream of $1.00 per year but which grows in number at 1.5 percent per year and which will not begin for twenty years is

$$\int_0^{\infty} \frac{(e^{nt})e^{-rt}}{(e^{20r})} \, dt,$$

which reduces to

$$\left(\frac{1}{e^{20r}}\right) \frac{1}{(n-r)e^{-(r-n)t}} \Big]_0^{\infty}.$$

If r is greater than n, the expression is finite and equal to 1.62 for $r = 0.10$ and $n = 0.015$.

market. For all migrants the excess of the social over the private rate of return is less than the estimate made above.

VI. CONCLUDING COMMENTS

My effort in this paper has been to place human migration in an investment context and in so doing to formulate testable hypotheses germane to observed migration behavior. My main conclusion remains that migration cannot be viewed in isolation; complementary investments in the human agent are probably as important or more important than the migration process itself. As I have indicated, cognizance of, and attention to, these additional investments offer a promising clue to observed immobility in the face of large differentials in *current* earnings. In addition, only the estimation of the direct as well as associated costs of migration together with returns can reveal the extent of resource misallocation created by the frequently alleged barriers to mobility.

Costs and returns to migration have been consistently viewed in a real resource sense. Our tools of analysis are applicable only when costs and returns are so restricted; measures of psychic cost of migration, for example, are hard to come by. As I have suggested at various points, indeed the very need for these measures can often be circumvented.

Although my discussion provides only a sketchy framework for further empirical study of migration, the following additional conclusions are relevant to empirical undertakings. (1) Gross rather than net migration is a more relevant concept for studying the returns to migration as well as the impact of migration upon earnings differentials. (2) Migration rates are not an appropriate measure for estimating the effect of migration. (3) Age is significant as a variable influencing migration and must be considered in interpreting earnings differentials over space and among occupations. (4) The relation between private and social costs of, and returns to, migration at best depends upon market structure, resource mobility in general, and revenue policies of state and local governments.

26. The International Flow of Human Capital*

HERBERT G. GRUBEL, *University of Chicago*
and ANTHONY D. SCOTT, *University of British Columbia*

I

We have been drawn to the subject of this paper by recent strong manifestations of public interest in two major problems in international relations: first, the migration of highly skilled individuals to the U.S.—often referred to as the "brain drain"—and, second, the large-scale program of training foreign students in the U.S. Both of these problems have in common that they involve an international transfer of resources in the form of human capital that goes completely unrecorded in any official balance-of-payments statistics. This common feature clearly defines our field of analysis and excludes problems associated with the transfer of human capital services, such as occur in connection with the Peace Corps, programs of technical assistance through governmental agencies, technical and scientific advice by private corporations, etc.—all of which are reflected in official balance-of-payments statistics.

We have prepared some empirical estimates of the U.S. balance of trade in human capital from foreign student exchange and the immigration of scientists and engineers, which will shortly be published. These studies, while involving interesting conceptual problems of measurement, produced no startling results and suggest that in comparison with the size of the U.S. economy these capital flows are quite small. We present here only a few summary statistics to give an impression of the nature of the empirical results we have obtained. First, it turns out that the total U.S. program of foreign college student exchange, involving 58,000 foreign students in the U.S. and 11,000 American students abroad, resulted in a maximum net U.S.

Reprinted from "The International Flow of Human Capital, the Brain Drain," *American Economic Review, Papers and Proceedings,* LVI (May, 1966), 268–74.

cost of only $17 million in 1962, after appropriate adjustment of the gross cost for the human capital value of students electing to remain in the U.S. Second, the total human capital value of scientists and engineers immigrating to the U.S. during the thirteen-year period from 1949 to 1961 came to $1.0 billion. Third, the role of foreigners in the American economics profession estimated on the basis of the National Science Foundation survey statistics is as follows: 12 percent are foreign born, 9 percent had also foreign high school training, but only 3 percent earned their highest professional degree abroad. Fourth, the shares of annual output of first-degree engineers lost by emigration to the U.S. by some major individual countries were found to differ widely between countries and tended to be surprisingly high in some instances. For example, Norway lost 24.1 percent, Greece 20.9 percent, Germany 9.5 percent, and France 1.2 percent of their annual output of first-degree engineers to the U.S. Finally, scientists and engineers are from six to twelve times as likely to emigrate to the U.S. as people in other professions, judging from the occupational composition of all immigrants and that of the labor force in the migrants' native countries.

While such empirical work sheds light on the quantitative importance of issues which all too often are argued in complete ignorance of any facts, we have found that nearly all discussions of the brain drain and exchange student programs suffer most seriously from the absence of any theoretical framework. The main part of this paper is devoted to a theoretical analysis of issues surrounding the international flow of human capital embodied in highly skilled migrants to the U.S. and in foreign students electing not to return to their native countries.

II

The argument that a country "loses" by the emigration of highly skilled individuals is most nearly always valid when we consider the "country" to be a nation state whose national objective is to maximize its military and economic power. From this point of view, a person's emigration absolutely reduces his country's mobilizable manpower, and its national output is lowered by the amount the emigrant contributed to it.

While this view of national losses is held quite widely, it is sorely outmoded in our age. The identification of military power with the number of a country's inhabitants, even if they are highly skilled, is very vague and precarious. Wealth, science, and technology dominate modern warfare, and it is quite easy for most nations to purchase military equipment on the world market at costs much below those that would have to be incurred in the development of individual national weapons systems. Economic power, in turn, depends not so much on aggregate national output as it does on per capita income, which may or may not be affected by an individual's emigration.

In place of this outmoded nationalist concept of a country, we suggest the use of another one, according to which a country is an association of individuals whose collective welfare its leaders seek to maximize. While the level of individual welfare is determined by many factors, including items of collective consumption such as military might and foreign economic influence, the most important determinant of human welfare in the long run is the standard of living; that is, the quantity of goods and services available for consumption. Therefore, in the following analysis we will focus our attention on the changes in income brought about by the emigration of highly skilled individuals.

If a country wishes to maximize the income available to all its people, then emigration should be welcomed whenever two conditions are met. These are, first, that the emigrant improves his own income and, second, that the migrant's departure does not reduce the income of those remaining behind. The first condition is normally met when emigration is voluntary. Specification of the circumstances under which the second holds true will occupy the rest of this paper.

III

According to the traditional analysis of the migration of labor, the departure of a person normally raises the long-run average income of the people remaining, because it results in an increase in the nation's capital-labor ratio. In the case of the migration of a highly skilled person, however, this conclusion does not hold if the human capital embodied in the emigrant is greater than the country's total per capita endowment of human and physical capital, assuming perfect substitutability of the two forms of capital in the long run. In this case the emigration of a highly skilled person reduces the total income to be distributed among the residents of a country and it follows that in societies where this distribution occurs through planning or other nonmarket means the remaining population suffers a reduction in welfare.

In a market economy where persons are paid their marginal product, however, such a reduction in per capita income is only a statistical phenomenon which has no influence on the welfare of the remaining people: the emigrant removes both his contribution to national output and the income that gives him a claim to this share, so that other incomes remain unchanged. There may be income redistribution effects through changes in the marginal products of the remaining people, but since the brain drain involves rather small numbers of people, these effects are likely to be small enough to be safely considered negligible.

Thus it follows that in a market economy any effects that the emigration of a highly skilled person is likely to have on the welfare of those remaining behind must be sought either in short-run adjustment costs or in market failures.

The short-run costs are due to production losses — specifically those created by the unemployment or inefficient employment of factors of production whose effectiveness depends on cooperation with the skills the departing person takes along. The size of these costs depends on two elements. First, the greater the short-run substitutability of other factors of production or skills for those that have emigrated, the smaller the inefficiencies and loss of output. Second, the more rapidly a replacement for the emigrant can be trained, the smaller the losses. It is difficult to generalize about the characteristics of individual professions or national education systems in regard to these qualities, but it seems reasonable to expect that the emigration of a well-established, experienced professional will cause greater frictional losses than would the emigration of a common laborer or the decision of a student not to return home. Also, we would expect that bursts of heavy emigration alternating with periods of low emigration rates present more difficult adjustment problems than do steady flows, even if the latter represent a greater long-run average than do the former, because of the economy's likely structural adjustments to predictable changes.

Of greater analytical interest than these short-run costs of adjustment to emigration are the long-run effects on welfare associated with failures of the free market to allocate resources efficiently. There are two main sources of such inefficiencies which appear to underlie most of the arguments about losses from the emigration of highly skilled persons.

The first category of losses has to do with genuine externalities, where the market fails properly to compensate the individual for the contributions he makes to society. It is important to note that these externalities must be directly associated with the personal characteristics of the emigrant and not his profession. Thus, if a typical doctor's work contains a large measure of social benefits for which he does not get compensated, these benefits are lost to society only for the length of time required to train another person to take his place as a doctor. It therefore follows that in many of the well-known instances of genuine external effects in consumption or production, emigration imposes only short-run frictional costs to society which disappear in the long run.

While it is difficult enough to find genuine cases of economically significant externalities in the real world, it is even more difficult to find cases which have the added limitation of being associated with a specific person. Examples coming to mind are the external diseconomies from alcoholism or the nonmarket benefits accruing to others from a person's propensity to engage in political or charity work without monetary compensation. The difficulty of finding meaningful examples may legitimately be taken as an indication of the relative unimportance of most externalities given the size of the resources allocated through properly functioning markets.

The second category of losses stems from market failure remedied through activities of the government. It is alleged that the emigration of highly skilled persons affects others most significantly through changes in the cost of providing such government services.

In this connection, it is frequently suggested that public education is a social investment in individuals which emigrants fail to repay, and that therefore the highly trained in particular ought to be forced to repay this investment before they are allowed to leave the country. Such suggestions and the entire idea of a "debt to society" due to publicly-financed education appear to be based on misapprehension.

Society is a continuing organism, and the process of financing education represents an intergeneration transfer of resources under which the currently productive generation taxes itself to educate the young, who in turn upon maturity provide for the next generation of children and so on. What is relevant for our purposes of analysis is that the average burden of financing education falling on the emigrant's generation is not changed by this departure, because he takes along not only his contribution to tax revenue but also his children, on whom this share of revenue would have been spent.

Analogous arguments can be made for the financing of other government services such as defense, police protection, judicial services, etc. However, in all of these instances, including education, the conclusion that no adverse welfare effects result from a person's emigration is valid only if the incidence of taxes is equal to the incidence of benefits from government services.

There is evidence that the enjoyment of the quantitatively most significant services provided by governments is largely proportional to the taxpayers' income, which includes return on human capital. Defense—the largest item in the budget of many nations—benefits more those persons who, as a result of foreign conquests, would lose sizable stock of assets than those who do not. Roads are used more by those who drive cars than those who walk. The amount of education demanded by the offspring of the highly educated is likely to be above that demanded by the children of people with average education. Only relatively few government services, such as public parks and those related directly to the welfare of the poor, contain elements of subsidy by high-income taxpayers. Therefore, the presumption is strong that the government can reduce many of the services it provides by nearly the same proportion by which tax revenues decline when a highly skilled person emigrates, changing the tax burden or income of the remaining people only marginally and certainly by much less than the gross reduction in tax revenues suggests.

It is true that if government services are provided through lumpy investment projects, reductions in government services may not be possible without increases in average cost. However, such increased burdens from reduced population are short run and last only until either a new, optimum-scale plant replaces the old or as population returns to its old level. At any rate, in most countries complaining of the brain drain the problem is not one of possible excess capacity in public projects but rather one of overcrowding.

It is often argued that a country loses because the highly skilled emigrants would have worked on projects of great importance to the development of the country had they stayed at home. This argument is valid either if we take the nationalistic view of the country or if the person's work would have been associated with large external effects. In this case, also, the nationalistic view is to be rejected for the reasons presented earlier. While it is popular to argue that external effects are frequent in market economies, we have been unable to discover economically significant instances where individuals provide social services associated with their person rather than profession for which they are not paid — including in work fostering economic development.

Another frequently heard allegation is that the emigration of the highly educated is equivalent to a Darwinian process of selecting the best, which causes a reduction in the genetic "quality" of the country's human stock and influences national welfare in the long run. This is probably a valid argument in principle but its empirical significance is likely to be quite small, given the small relative size of the migratory flows and the population stocks. It should also be noted that the transmission of human characteristics through the genes is a rather unreliable process, and that the offspring of many intellectually distinguished emigrants never achieve their parents' level of attainment.

IV

While our analysis so far suggests that the emigration of highly skilled persons reduces the welfare of the remaining people only under rather rare circumstances, we can make a good case for the proposition that these types of emigrants in fact tend to increase the welfare of their former countrymen in several important ways.

Historically, emigrants have been known to raise significantly the incomes of their families at home through remittances. In more subtle ways emigrants can influence policies in the country of their new residence towards their native country, and often the emigrants retain an interest in their home countries' affairs, giving counsel and advice, which carry great weight because of the positions of independence and prestige they hold in the foreign country. Furthermore, the very act of emigration may be beneficial to those remaining behind just because of the public attention given to the individual's departure, which can lead to critical reappraisals of institutions and procedures and their ultimate modernization and improvement.

The potentially largest benefit to the people remaining behind, however, may accrue through the pure research of scientists and engineers in the foreign countries, contrary to the often heard allegation that the emigration of people in these fields is the source of greatest material losses. The product of basic research, knowledge, is a free good becoming available to all as it is published. Since most scientists move to countries where conditions of work are better for them, either because the new country is better able to furnish research equipment or because of stimulating colleagues, the probability is great that such moves increase the scientists' overall productivity. As a consequence of such emigration by scientists, the native countries not only obtain the scientific knowledge free, but they are actually likely to get more than they would have had the men stayed at home. Applied research also tends to benefit countries other than the one in which it is first put to use. Reductions in the cost of production or new product developments tend to spread through the world as a result of competition. As far as national prestige from scientific achievements is concerned, the scientists' native countries are perfectly free to claim these men as native sons, which in no way reduces the host-country's right to be proud that the work was done within its borders.

V

We conclude from this analysis that the transfer of human capital occurring when highly skilled people emigrate between countries always reduces the economic and military power of the migrant's native country, though by a smaller amount than it is often alleged. We have argued, however, that such concern with the effects on economic and military power is anachronistic and that a concern with the individual welfare of the population ought to take its place. From this point of view it was seen that the emigration of highly skilled persons is likely to cause economic losses in the short run until replacements for the emigrants can be trained. Long-run losses in a market economy are likely to be small and are primarily associated with externalities and with elements of income redistribution, in the government's tax and expenditure policies. Benefits to the native countries of the emigrants may be sizable, primarily because much of the output of highly skilled persons, especially scientists and engineers, tends to benefit the people of all countries. A good case can therefore be made for a continuation of present policies and the free movement of human capital throughout the world.

27. Schooling, Experience, and Gains and Losses in Human Capital Through Migration*

MARY JEAN BOWMAN and ROBERT G. MYERS

University of Chicago

Application of human capital concepts to migration holds promise, not only for calculating "gains and losses," but also for conceptualizing and analyzing empirically both individual and social investment choices regarding the locus, duration, and sequences of schooling and experiential learning.

In discussing aggregative measures, stress is placed upon the desirability of assessing gross flows, of properly disaggregating migrant populations (including attention to locus of schooling and experience) before attaching human capital values, and of sorting out the substantial remigration component in migration figures. Taking into account the existence of differentiated markets in which people sell their services leads to speculations concerning the role of "package migration" and remigration in diffusion of skills and know-how.

The cost-benefit models presented are human investment models which begin with an individual viewpoint but which are transformed into social decision models as parameters are readjusted to allow for cost and income transfers, as individually expected earnings are replaced by socially expected or realized productive contributions and as probability values are applied to allow for rates of return or non-return of migrants. They are illustrated with respect to choices among training alternatives and choices among policies for importing manpower.

Suggestions are made throughout the article for new census tabulations which would allow more sophisticated application of human capital concepts to migration.

*Reprinted from "Schooling, Experience, and Gains and Losses in Human Capital Through Migration" *American Statistical Association Journal* (September, 1967), 875–98.

Since the revival of the concept of human capital in the 1950's, many areas of economic research, including the economics of migration, have undergone a rethinking. Although neither the idea of human capital nor its application to migration can be termed "new," current estimating procedures and their economic applications are much more sophisticated than earlier ones.[1] In considerable part new approaches and greater sophistication reflect improvements in the quality and availability of data. However, new appreciation of critical problems is always some jumps ahead of the data — and also, we might add, behind them.

We will first sketch briefly several recent treatments of human capital in migration. Some of their methodological implications will become evident in a reexamination of one-way migration that takes into account place and timing of schooling and work experience. We turn then to the more complex analysis required when we include remigration possibilities. Along the way suggestions will be made for useful new tabulations of 1960 census data together with some pleas or hopes of the 1970 census.

In discussing the relation between "Migration and Economic Opportunity," we might emphasize migration as a means of responding to economic opportunity or as a means for creating economic opportunity. Heretofore more attention has been given to the passive view of migration as an allocative mechanism than to the view of migration as playing a dynamic training role. But migrants often move out and return with new skills, and in-migrants bring and transfer know-how. We emphasize these linkages among investments in schooling, experi-

[1] In the 19th Century, estimates of human capital gains and losses were made for the United States, England, and Germany, using both present values and cost replacement methods. Discussions of the estimates and methods may be found in: Richmond Mayo–Smith, *Emigration and Immigration*, New York: Scribner's Sons, 1892, Chapter VI, and in Grace Abbott, ed., *Historical Aspects of the Immigration Problem, Select Documents*, Chicago: The University of Chicago Press, 1926, 370–81. Discussions of "Human Capital" and attempts to measure it in other contexts go back to Wm. Petty if not earlier. For perspectives on this history see E. A. J. Johnson, "The Place of Learning, Science, Vocational Training, and 'Art' in Pre-Smithian Economic Thought," in the *Journal of Economic History*, XXIV (June, 1964), 129–44. Also, Rudolf Blitz, "Education, the Nature of Man, and the Division of Labor," and "Education in the Writings of Malthus, Senior, McCulloch and J. S. Mill" (English language revisions of an article in Spanish), forthcoming in UNESCO, *Readings in Education and Economic Development* (1967), and B. F. Kiker, "The Historical Roots of the Concept of Human Capital," *Journal of Political Economy*, LXXIV, No. 5 (October, 1966), 481–99.

ence, and migration. We present decision models incorporating various migration and remigration sequences and argue their value as tools for analysis of migration behavior, human resource policies, the transfer of know-how, and the diffusion of development.

1. RECENT APPLICATIONS OF HUMAN INVESTMENT MODELS TO MIGRATION

A. MIGRATION AS A PRIVATE INVESTMENT

In a 1962 article, Larry Sjaastad[2] looked at migration primarily as a form of private, rational decision-making—as a private investment that entails costs and engenders increments to lifetime earnings streams. To oversimplify, people discount expected earnings streams to set present values on themselves for alternative courses of action: migration or remaining put. In theory, people will move if they can increase their present value by an amount greater than the cost of moving. This added value might be attained if, by moving, a person finds a better market for his existing skills, upgrading himself within his occupation, or if migration provides an opportunity for him to change occupations, thereby acquiring a new skill and increasing his remuneration. Sjaastad emphasizes occupational change in attempting to analyze rural-urban migration and to account for observed age patterns in such migration.

Costs, according to Sjaastad, include direct costs of moving, earnings foregone while moving, earnings foregone while searching for employment and training for a new position. He gave special emphasis to the training or retraining costs of urban newcomers, which are identified with the initial excess of foregone rural earnings over realized urban wages. Returns (benefits) are the expected income stream at the destination.[3]

Sjaastad's primary concern was with the efficiency of migration as a process of resource allocation. He argued that much of the seemingly non-rational response or lack of response to economic incentives to move is really a matter of measurement methods which look at net migration rather than gross figures. He also criticized failures to disaggregate populations sufficiently before associating them with differential opportunities and earnings. In order to identify statistically

---

[2] Larry Sjaastad, "The Costs and Returns of Human Migration," *The Journal of Political Economy*, LXX, No. 5, Part 2 (October, 1962), 80–93.

[3] In his theoretical formulation, Sjaastad also considers "psychic" costs and benefits.

the potential earnings streams of migrants at places of origin and destination, Sjaastad suggested that comparisons must be made among more homogeneous sub-groupings, specifying in particular use of age-occupational classifications. (Curiously, he said nothing about classifications by schooling.)

Statistical averages of costs and earnings for each population category are used as proxy measures in a decision model that is fundamentally individualistic. Despite his work with the Upper Midwest Project, Sjaastad's interest in spatial resource allocation remains spatially neutral; hence we find neither aggregated human capital measures nor "regionalism." The important thing is the micro-economic allocative process.

B. MIGRATION AND A RATIONALE OF COMMUNITY INVESTMENTS IN EDUCATION

In his treatment of migration, Burton Weisbrod[4] takes a very different tack—even though he starts from the same base in human investment theory as Sjaastad and, like Sjaastad, computes "human capital" in present value terms.

Weisbrod sets up a model in which the community is treated not only as an aggregative entity that receives benefits and incurs costs, but also as a decision-making unit analogous to the individual decision-maker of micro-economic theory. The decision on which he focuses is local community investment in schooling. He is concerned with how migration will affect benefits accruing to the community from investments in education, and hence with how it affects the cost-benefit balances that would determine rational investment decisions. He argues that rational community behavior in this context will lead to under-investment in education on a national scale because of "spill-over" effects—"external benefits" of a community's investments that accrue to other communities. This treatment of the community as a decision unit has been attacked from several sides.[5] However, the empirical part of Weisbrod's work is relevant to aggregative analysis of human capital gains and losses, flights of the imagination quite aside.

A careful study of Weisbrod's method for computing "spill-overs"

---

[4]Burton Weisbrod, *External Benefits of Public Education*, Princeton, N.J.: Industrial Relations Section, Princeton University, 1964.

[5]In particular, see A. G. Holtman's, "A Note on Public Education and Spillovers through Migration," *Journal of Political Economy*, LXXIV, No. 5 (October, 1966), 524–25.

points up the problems involved in assigning values to human capital flows. In working from incremental income[6] streams associated with varying levels of educational attainment through high school graduation, he assumes, for instance, that the relevant income streams for valuing both *in* and *out* migrants of given age, race, and sex are the same. All those who migrate to and from the Clayton, Missouri community are valued at non-South rates, regardless of their origin or the location of their previous education. This is an empirical compromise dictated by data limitations, and is discussed by the author at some length.

C. Cost Valuations of International Migration

Grubel and Scott[7] focus on international migration of "human capital," and on arguments concerning "brain drains." Although they discuss individual decision-making in a framework similar to Sjaastad's, in their published work they emphasize the effects of out-migration on social welfare. There is no community decision unit, such as Weisbrod's; in fact, they discard aggregates and GNP in theoretical presentations. Social welfare they define as the *per capita* incomes of all initial residents, whatever their place of residence after migration.

However, appealing as the welfare measure they suggest may be, it is no accident that in the end Grubel and Scott make no attempt at direct empirical assessments in such a framework; the practical difficulties are manifold. Instead, they go to quite the other extreme of empirical pragmatism. Not only do they forsake their welfare concept for an aggregative type of social assessment, but they also by-pass human capital measurement in present value terms, choosing to use cost assessments instead.[8]

---

[6]Census cross-classifications are by income, not earnings. There are substantial difficulties involved in establishing a "correct" figure for such groups as proprietors. Neither income nor earnings is quite accurate.

[7]See the following three articles of Herbert Grubel and Anthony Scott: (1) "The International Flow of Human Capital, the Brain Drain," *American Economic Review, Papers and Proceedings,* LVI, No. 2 (May 1966), 268–74, (2) "The Immigration of Scientists and Engineers to the United States," *The Journal of Political Economy,* LXXIV, No. 4 (August 1966), and (3) "The Characteristics of Foreigners in the U.S. Economics Profession," *American Economic Review,* forthcoming.

[8]Herbert Grubel, "Non-returning Foreign Students and the Cost of Student Exchange," *International Educational and Cultural Exchange* (a publication of the United States Advisory Commission on International Educational and Cultural Affairs), Spring, 1966.

National gains are measured by the cost-savings realized in acquiring human capital formed elsewhere without paying for its formation. National losses are incurred when a nation pays for the formation of human capital that others then acquire free.

Using figures from an annual census of foreign students in the United States, interesting estimates are derived for United States gains and losses. The value of the gain (saving in costs) to the United States of acquiring "non-returning foreign students" is taken as what it would have cost to "produce" an American equivalent. Against these cost-savings are set the costs incurred by the United States in providing education for all foreign students. Similar human capital estimates are made for scientists and engineers who have migrated to the United States.[9]

Measurement of human capital in cost terms as a way of assessing the resources that have gone into the making of a man is one thing. Using cost valuations in assessing gains and losses through migration is quite another. Serious distortions are apt to occur when reproduction cost estimates exceed present value. Thus a fallacious cost view of human capital can explain many of the complaints that have been so common concerning Southern or Appalachian losses through migration.[10]

D. PRESENT VALUE ESTIMATES OF INTERREGIONAL MIGRATION

Rashi Fein,[11] like Weisbrod, was concerned with the measurement of aggregate human capital gains and losses of spatially defined units—in Fein's case, regions within the United States. Like Weisbrod, Fein used a present value measure of human capital (discounting future income streams at 5 percent). There is no decision theory in Fein's analysis, however, and he draws no inferences for public policy.

Fein's first task, a considerable one, was to lay out the census data in a form that would permit examination of gross 1955–1960 migration streams for males. Male migrant flows are disaggregated by age,

[9] Herbert Grubel and Anthony Scott, "The Immigration of Scientists and Engineers to the United States," *loc. cit.*

[10] This, by the way, is where Grubel and Scott's social welfare view of effects on per capita incomes could prove especially fruitful—and empirically operational up to useful approximations.

[11] Rashi Fein, "Educational Patterns in Southern Migration," *The Southern Economic Journal*, XXXII, No. 1, Part 2 (July 1965), 106–24.

race, and educational attainment. Focusing on the South and its sub-regions, he then computes net in- or outflows for each age-race-education category. To get estimates of social net capital gains or losses associated with migration he first multiplies net flows by average discounted values of Southern income streams associated with each age-race-education category. These sub-aggregates are then summed to give the overall net gain or loss to the region. Present values have, in effect, become weightings for the various statistical categories. Although this procedure preserves the disaggregation by sex, age, race, and schooling, the distinction between characteristics of inflows and outflows is unfortunately lost in the procedure for valuing human capital. We will come back to this later.

2. ALTERNATIVE EARNINGS STREAMS AND ONE-WAY MIGRATION

From the above discussions of recent work, it is evident that analysis of migration in human investment terms has opened up over a wide front. There are at once common elements and sharp distinctions in problem foci, in theoretical frameworks applied, in the kinds of compromises made in using incomplete and sometimes inappropriate sets of data. Back of all this are some fundamental theoretical problems in decision theory on the one hand, some critical issues for public policy on the other. Theory and policy are in fact quite closely related. It is with such basic questions in mind that we ask: Which earnings streams are the relevant ones in *either* private or social assessments of migration? Whichever the viewpoint, identification of the conceptually appropriate future earnings streams is a necessary first step. We start in this section with the simplest case—one-way migration. This in fact is the only case for which earnings streams have been examined in anything we have seen.

A. THE NET FLOW FALLACY AND ESTIMATES OF HUMAN-CAPITAL GAINS AND LOSSES

In estimating human-capital gains and losses in the South, Fein took a short cut. As noted earlier, instead of valuing the gross inflows and outflows he took the net flows for each age-race-schooling category of males, computing the aggregate present values of these net flows on the basis of *Southern* life-income patterns. To the extent that he was dealing with flows among regions within the South he had no alternative; the needed income data are not available for sub-regions. Ideally we would want such figures, and we would want to maintain clear distinctions among parts of the South, for it is a very heterogeneous region. However, when it comes to flows between Southern and other regions the situation is changed; we have data on life-income streams by race, sex, age, and schooling that can differentiate at least on this gross regional dichotomy.

Weisbrod also used a single set of values in his study of gains and losses through migration into and out of the Clayton school district, in Missouri. However, our chief criticism of this aspect of his work is that he did not check for the sensitivity of his results to his valuation procedure. Since he was only incidentally interested in his quantitative results, and was not posing the more substantive and analytical questions concerning migration in which we are most interested, this omission is understandable, even if regrettable.

We assume, with Sjaastad, that an individual will not normally migrate unless his potential discounted earnings stream in the new area is going to be at least as high as that at the area of origin. When the average stream for the area of destination is obviously lower than that in the area of origin, but people move anyway, this would suggest that the rational in-migrant is not typical of the area into which he is moving. When this happens even within particular race-sex-age-schooling categories, the fallacy of using average incomes at the lower income destination for migrants to that area is underlined. Until data that distinguish migrants are available there can be no firm answer as to what is happening, and how. At present we can only hypothesize, meanwhile making some crude estimates as to what alternative hypotheses may imply.

The potential importance of taking market differences into account can be illustrated by making some simple calculations. The distribution of schooling among 1955–60 out-migrants from the South as a whole is very close to the distribution of schooling among 1955–60 migrants into the South. However, except at college levels, incomes of white males with the same years of schooling are higher in the North than in the South. After a bit of rough pencil-and-paper work we picked $40,000 as an average present-value figure for income streams of white male Southerners leaving the South and $50,000 for white male migrants from other regions into the South.

Valuing in-migrants at their place of origin (Table 1, b) rather than at their destination (as Fein did, Table 1, a) results in a substantial increase in the estimated gain, both in relative and in absolute terms. Raising or lowering per-migrant present values or varying the ratio

TABLE 1

Alternative Estimates of Net Human Capital Gains From Migration
for the United States South; 1950–1960

	Number Migrating[12]	Present Value (Per Migrant)	Present Value (Millions)	Net Human Capital Gain (Millions)
Out Migration	554,900	40,000	22,196	——
In Migration:				
a. Valued at destination	579,100	40,000	23,164	968
b. Valued at origin	579,100	50,000	28,955	6759

between non-Southern and Southern present values would change our numbers but not our argument. From the perspective of the South, Fein's method sets a minimum for net gains, while valuing both in- and out-migrants at their origin sets a maximum.

We have not considered what proportion of the in-migrants may have been unsuccessful returning Southerners, or what proportion of the out-migrants were originally from the North. Our estimates are still gross over-simplifications. Until data that distinguish migrants and their associated income streams are available, there can be no firm answer.

Typically applications of human investment models to migration have suffered from insufficient disaggregation of the population of migrants, though industrious scholars in and outside of the Census Bureau are beginning to remedy the most serious gaps. It is obvious by now that within-each-region disaggregation by age, sex, race, educational attainment, and income (preferably earnings) is needed. Both Weisbrod and Fein recognize this and adjust their human capital estimates accordingly. Actually for the 5 percent sample of the 1960 census we have, within South and within North, cross tabulations of all these variables plus 1960 occupations. However, there is no breakdown that would separate out migrants within each of these cells.

A possibility we would very much like to see followed up in 1970 would be refinement of the regional tables on incomes by sex, race, age, and schooling of 1960 residents in order to distinguish the new migrants (1955–60) from others, and each of these groups in turn by

[12] The figures for numbers migrating in and out of the South, exclusive of intra-South migration, are taken from William N. Parker's comment on the Rashi Fein article (see footnote 11), in *The Southern Economic Journal*, XXXII, No. 1, Part 2 (July, 1965), 126, Table I.

place of birth and occupation—ideally both at origin and destination. Obviously this will be possible only if all these items are obtained on the 25 percent sample.

Suppose we had all of this information. What else should we know to distinguish migrants and their earnings in a meaningful way? It is obvious that many other factors affect productivity and earnings streams of any given population of migrants. Ability, attitudes toward work, quality of schooling, environmental experiences as a youth, and job experience differentials will all be reflected in differential earnings streams. Important also are labor market imperfections that may partially segregate migrant from native populations of the same race, sex, age, and reported years of schooling.

Concerning ability and attitudes we will be brief. We can reasonably assume that the ability distribution for a given age, race, sex, education category of the population will not differ much among regions; hence we need not be concerned on this score with places of origin of migrants. However, in these pages we go further to make the more vulnerable assumption that the average ability of migrants is no different from that of non-migrants once disaggregation has established homogeneity of population sub-groups in other critical respects. The saving feature of this assumption is the critical disaggregation presupposed; there can be no presumption that within each population sub-category mobility will be correlated either positively or negatively with ability.[13] Differences in attitudes toward work are a problem that we will simply have to ignore for the present. It should be noted, however, that both ability and attitudes can be objectively assessed, and for special migrant groups this has been done.

Experience and quality of schooling differentials are at the heart of our analysis, and command more careful attention.

B. Schooling and Experience

School-quality differences can be critical in the economics of migration from many points of view, one, but only one, of which is estimation of regional gains or losses in human capital through migration. If the distributions of quality of schooling among men of the same

[13] See, for example, Donald J. Bogue, "International Migration," in Philip M. Hauser and Otis Dudley Duncan (ed.), *The Study of Population*, Chicago: University of Chicago Press, 1959, especially pp. 504–505.

race and age with the same reported schooling were the same in one region as in another (or in urban as in rural areas), we could forget about this problem. However, despite large within-area differences in quality of schools there are also large and significant differences between rural and urban schools and between schools in one region as against another.

To get at effects of differences in average quality of schooling we need to know where the migrant was schooled (ideally for secondary school by sub-region or state and by type of community). Present census data do not permit disaggregation by locus of schooling even on a broad regional basis. However, one could make some assumptions about the location of both schooling and previous job experience by looking at place of birth, place of 1955 residence, and 1960 residence in relation to age at the time of migration.

The first component of experience, a very important one, is the learning that goes on outside of school during school years. There is ample evidence to show that youth from rural communities start at a disadvantage when they come to the city; the extent of the disadvantage varies with the nature of the rural area. This is one among many reasons why data concerning location at the time when a young man attended secondary school (or if he stopped short of that, where he last attended elementary school) would be more valuable than information concerning where he attended college.[14] In fact we strongly urge inclusion in the 1970 census of information concerning the state and type of community in which a man resided at the time when he last attended school below the college level (or alternatively, at, say, age 16).

The importance of what men learn on the job has been reappraised recently and given new theoretical respectability in the economics journals. If we accept Mincer's estimates, over a life-time investments in learning on the job typically exceed investments in schooling

---

[14]The critical importance of community characteristics in determining differences among schools in distributions of achievement has been well documented. See, for example, H. T. James, J. Alan Thomas and Harold J. Dyck, *Wealth, Expenditure and Decision-Making for Education*, in U.S. Department of Health, Education, and Welfare, Cooperative Research Project No. 1241, Stanford (School of Education), 1963, and Charles Benson, et al., "State and Local Fiscal Relationships in Public Education in California," State of California Senate Fact Finding Committee on Revenue and Taxation, *Report*, Sacramento, March, 1965.

in the United States today.[15] In any case, whatever the relative magnitudes, learning through on-the-job training and experience is a major component in the formation of human competencies. Given this fact, we must ask what and how much of such learning has been built into which groups of migrants.

Taking it for granted that we will not be working with full life histories—such data would swamp us in any case—what might we hypothesize as the best statistical clues to sort out categories of migrants (and non-migrants) by experience? Obviously age is part of the picture. So is schooling if we look at the national scene, since over-all there is a positive correlation between schooling and on-the-job training and learning. However, this is much too crude an approximation. How do people of the same age and years of schooling differ in competencies acquired at work? As a first step we would look for two kinds of information: what a man was doing (his occupation) prior to migration, and where he was doing it.

The 1960 census does not provide information on prior occupations, and collection of data on past occupations in both difficult and expensive; however, this possibility has been considered for the 1970 census. If collection of such data proves feasible for a large enough sample, it will open up a range of possibilities for hypothesis testing that must challenge many researchers on both migration and the economics of education.

There can be no doubt that work opportunities and with them opportunities for on-the-job training and learning vary substantially from one place to another. This is glaringly obvious if we look across nations on a world scale. It is sufficiently evident within the United States, and even if we control for age, sex, and prior schooling. There is a strong presumption that knowledge of the location in which men have acquired their work experience will improve statistical predictions of their competencies. How far a migrant's previous experiential learning may be transferable to his new setting is another matter. Undoubtedly there is selectivity in such transferability; he can move into the new environment carrying his experience with him only to the extent that the new environment gives scope for its use.

[15] Jacob Mincer, "On-the-Job Training: Costs, Returns, and Some Implications," *The Journal of Political Economy*, LXX, No. 5, Part 2 (October, 1962), 50–79.

At any given time, however, the aggregate on-the-job training embodied in the labor force will be the lower figure since young people who have completed school have yet to accumulate the learning on-the-job that Mincer measures by opportunity costs.

This may contribute to differentiation of labor markets between natives and in-migrants, especially in the middle and higher occupational brackets. It is a reasonable generalization that unless a man can take enough of his acquired competencies with him to ensure earnings at least as high as those he would receive at home, our "average" migrant will not move—at least not if he already has a substantial investment in such competencies and there is a demand for them at home. For youth who have little or no such investment the problem does not arise. Rather, the question may be, where can I go to get the best learning and long-term income opportunities?

We may systematize these comments concerning effects on potential earnings associated with location of schooling and experience by setting up a rough typology of schooling-work combinations as between two regions, A and B. Within any age, sex, race, educational, and, ideally, prior occupational grouping of migrants who moved from place A to place B, we would distinguish the following (still deferring consideration of temporary migration and return):

1. Those born in A, but who migrated to B for schooling and work.

2. Those born in A and schooled in A, but who migrated to B as soon as their formal schooling was completed and who have worked only in B.

3. Those born in A and schooled in A who remained to work for some time in A, but moved to B before they were 40, continuing to work in B thereafter.

4. Those born in A and schooled in A who worked in A to at least the age of 40, migrating to B after that age.

1. The first category of individuals might be expected to have an age-earnings profile very close to or even the same as comparable life-time B residents of the same race, sex, age, years of schooling—and perhaps prior occupation—because all schooling and work experience is in B.

2. Those in the second category were schooled in A but their entire work experience is in B. We would expect their average earnings profiles to fall somewhere between those of life-time residents of A and of B, but closer to the latter. Deviations from average B earnings streams would be greater the greater the regional differences in average quality of schooling.[16] It will be greater the greater the dif-

---

[16]This makes the further assumption that migrants average the same schooling quality as comparable non-migrants in their area of origin.

ferences between out-of-school environment of the migrant's adolescent years (rural or urban, and where) and the environment into which he is moving. Related to this, though partially independent of it, is also the extent to which migrants from A enter labor markets in B that are distinct from those in which lifetime residents of B sell their services.

3. Migrants in category 3 should also, on the average, have future income streams falling somewhere between those of lifetime residents of A and of B. The older they are at migration and the more experience they bring with them, the closer we should expect them to be to the lifetime residents of their area of origin. Here (as also in case 2), if migrants to B work in branch organizations which have head offices in and are operated by individuals from A, their earnings streams should approximate A-type earnings. This is merely an extreme of differentiated labor markets—islands of A located within the geographic boundaries of B. On the other hand, the younger the migrant the larger the part of his experience he will accumulate in B (segregation of labor markets aside), and the more clearly will his future income stream approach the B pattern.

4. If the movement to region B comes after age 40, it is probable that earnings in B will be similar to those in A where schooling and work experience where obtained. Non-economic locational preferences for B aside, the A income potential should in fact give us a minimum estimate of earning streams in B. We assume that a rational person established in a career in A will not move after age 40 unless he can earn at least as much in his new location virtually from the start. Although there are exceptions, there is sufficient empirical evidence to show that after age 40 most men are recouping investments in themselves rather than making new ones, intuitive reasoning quite aside.

A fifth category which is really a special case of the fourth has quite different implications, however. Suppose an individual born in A, schooled and with his work experience in A, whose skill has become obsolete after age 40 (or somewhat earlier). In this case the migrating individual has suffered a severe "human capital loss." He has little or no learned competence to apply in either A or B, and his expected future earnings stream cannot be measured by an average in either area. Though a special case, this is an important one, which merits the special study that is beginning to be given to it.

Schooling, Experience, and Gains and Losses through Migration

C. Package Migration and the Transfer of Experience

In discussing the locus of schooling and experience as related to likely future income streams of migrants we commented upon the possibilities—in some cases the strong likelihood—that there would be some differentiation of markets in which migrants and non-migrants resident in a given area sell their services. We specified further that this differentiation could and does occur even among men of the same race, age, and years of schooling. Even if we went all the way from regions down to state economic areas in an attempt to assure greater homogeneity we would not necessarily get rid of such labor market differentiation.

Taking the more dramatic in-migrant labor market segments to illustrate the extreme case, there are "Northern firms" in the deep South, firms from the United States in Sao Paulo, French firms in the Ivory coast. Traditionally such "foreign" firms have preferred to import talent from their area of origin rather than to employ locals who lack not only the technical know-how acquired on a job but also, equally important, know-how with respect to how a modern Northern organization operates.[17] (In addition the Northern highschool graduate is likely to be better schooled than the Southern.) Many of the men who have been brought into the South when a Northern firm established a branch there would not otherwise have migrated; there would have been no opportunities for them to work in the South at jobs in which they could use their Northern skills and experience. Transfer of those skills would not have been possible. Conversely, the firm would not have moved into the South had it not been possible to bring Northerners with know-how along. This is what we mean by "package migration."[18]

To the extent that migration is associated with these segmentalized

---

[17]Roy L. Lassiter reports Southern Business preference for Northerners with high school education or more in "The Experience of Selected Manufacturing Firms with the Availability, Skills, and Training of Manufacturing Workers in Florida," Occasional Paper No. 1, Bureau of Economic and Business Research, College of Business Administration, University of Florida, 1961. The reluctance of U.S. firms abroad to employ local management is illustrated by John Shearer in his *High-Level Manpower in Overseas Subsidiaries: Experience in Brazil and Mexico,* Princeton, New Jersey: Industrial Relations Section, Princeton University, 1960, especially Chapter VI.

[18]For some related discussions of transfer of know-how, see Mary Jean Bowman, "From Guilds to Infant Training Industries," in C. A. Anderson and Mary Jean Bowman, eds., *Education and Economic Development,* Chicago: Aldine Publishing Company, 1965, pp. 98–129.

labor market structures, differences in earnings stream between migrants and permanent residents should appear. However, this assumes further that there are not parallel opportunities of a very different kind to which the local population has the readier access. When a traditional elite, experienced in its own culture and perhaps protected by other barriers to entry[19] exists along with a "foreign" class of high-salary professionals and technicians, income data alone will conceal important differences between the new and native populations. How far this pattern characterizes the South is not entirely clear, though the statistics on education, occupation, and income by region do suggest that it exists in some degree and is not uniform. Such a pattern is unstable, however. It fades away with development. Ultimately, we suspect, it is eroded more by the progress of native populations at the middle level than by any direct impact at the top.

As the number of "Northern" firms in the "South" multiplies, and as a few and then a few more Southerners filter into and through these enterprises at the middle levels, the transfer of skill and experience from North to South becomes easier. Migrants now come in greater numbers without any special prior association with the enterprises in which they find jobs. The process of diffusion of development is well under way.

How much validity there may be in this theorizing concerning relations between migration and the process of diffusion of development remains to be seen. Existing evidence is spotty. But there is clearly a challenge to test hypotheses of this kind. To what extent are Southern labor markets differentiated or even sharply segmentalized? For any given race, age, and schooling, how do earnings of Southerners working in Southern-type firms compare with those in Northern-type firms in the South? How do earnings of similar individuals in Northern firms in the North compare with those in Northern firms in the South? Looking at the shapes of income streams and applying Mincer's method of analyzing on-the-job learning, do we find that Northern profiles transfer to the South intact? If there are differences between Northern firms in the South and Southern firms with respect to training and learning opportunities, who is reaping the

---

[19] However, the high incomes of the "traditional" or native elite groups may be largely property income (for instance, Southern farmers with college education) or their salaries may be bureaucratic sinecure (as in many developing areas).

benefits—migrants from the North (temporary or permanent) or locals? Over time are profiles in Southern firms changing—and can we observe this in cross-section by comparing the border South with the deep South? Turning to data on occupations, types of firms quite aside, are occupation and occupation-earnings patterns quite different among migrants into the South and native Southerners of comparable race-sex-age-schooling categories? Are these differences persistent, and repeated over large parts of the South, or are they changing?

Many of these questions concerning segmentalization of labor markets, transferability of experience, the relative role of experience and schooling in shaping productivity, and the processes of diffusing skills might be tested by using human capital models and U.S. census data.[20]

3. MIGRATION AND REMIGRATION

The common tendency to treat migration as though it were a once-and-for-all affair, often combined with a definition of migration that in itself suggests permanency, has many unfortunate results.

One of the more obvious of these may be faulty assessments of "brain drains" and gains (the latter rarely noted). It is evident that once remigration is considered, new difficulties arise in such assessments. Are the migrants college students returning home, prodigal sons, disappointed job-seekers, retrained workers, retiring elders, or former political "outs" who are now "in"?

Further, how does the human capital value of these re-migrants differ from what it was when they first migrated? This question points to a more basis weakness of one-way migration simplifications; they disregard the duration of migration. There is a continuum from brief periods away at school or on a short-term job assignment to

---

[20]In the 1970 census and thereafter, social security numbers may be included, making possible special studies that can be linked into census information for the same individuals. This should allow many kinds of research on migration that have not been feasible previously without incurring prohibitive costs. For example, a special survey might obtain rosters of individuals working in Southern firms and in Northern firms in the South. By matching, these individuals could be located in the census and their age, schooling, and migrant status identified. Such data would permit analysis of the degree of labor market differentiation and of native Southerners and immigrants of comparable age and education employed in establishments with Southern and Northern managers. Many other possibilities, including migration sequences as revealed by social security data, come to mind.

permanent residence at destination. To disregard temporary migration is to disregard the important linkages among private investments, on-the-job learning, and migration which, when coupled with regional differentials in quality and availability of schooling and experiential learning, can provide extremely important channels for the transfer and local acquisition of know-how. A developing country seeking to build up its cohorts of qualified people is faced with important choices as to how this can best be done. How many and which sorts of individuals should be sent for study and/or for work experience "abroad"? How many will return? What about the importing of outside experts on a temporary basis? How can these choices be evaluated from the points of view of the receiving and of the sending nations? What about problems of recruiting such men, of the strategies of inducing higher rates of return among those subsidized for study or training abroad, or in another region of the United States? Human investment decision models that incorporate re-migration sequences can aid in such evaluations. We will develop this theme shortly. First, however, we look briefly into the quantitative importance of remigration as return to the sub-regions (Divisions) of birth within the United States and a few distinctive patterns in these respects.

A. The quantitative importance of remigration in the United States

Although U.S. census publications do not permit breakdowns by earnings, sex, age, schooling, occupations for migrants—let alone re-migrants—they do permit a partial assessment of the extent of remigration. This is made possible by the tabulations of 1960 division of residence against residence in 1955 and according to whether division of birth was or was not the same as that of residence in 1960. We selected three divisions as illustrations and computed for selected age and education groups the proportions of the white male 1955–60 in-migrants who were coming "back home" and of out-migrants who were returning to the division in which they were born. The results are shown in Tables 2 and 3.

The most striking feature of Table 2 is the generally high rates of return to division of origin. The only exception is the migrants into the Pacific Division, only a small proportion of whom were returning to the part of the country in which they were born. This is, of course, to be expected. Almost equally striking in the Pacific ratios is the

TABLE 2

Return Migration Rates Among 1955–60 Migrants Into and Out of the
East South Central, East North Central, and Pacific Divisions:
White Males in Selected Age and Schooling Categories

Schooling	Proportion of 1955–60 in-migrants who were returning to division of birth 1960 Age			Proportion of 1955–60 out-migrants who were returning to division of birth 1960 Age		
	25–29	30–34	35–39	25–29	30–34	35–39
	EAST SOUTH CENTRAL					
Highschool 1–3	.59	.56	.53	.24	.18	.17
Highschool 4	.52	.42	.36	.32	.23	.23
College 1–3	.46	.35	.26	.37	.26	.23
College 4	.32	.32	.28	.30	.30	.27
	EAST NORTH CENTRAL					
Highschool 1–3	.43	.30	.27	.29	.29	.26
Highschool 4	.56	.36	.30	.25	.21	.19
College 1–3	.53	.34	.30	.22	.18	.18
College 4	.40	.34	.30	.18	.21	.20
	PACIFIC					
Highschool 1–3	.09	.06	.05	.60	.46	.47
Highschool 4	.10	.07	.07	.61	.42	.36
College 1–3	.15	.09	.09	.60	.38	.30
College 4	.11	.12	.09	.46	.37	.30

Source: Computed from data in the 1960 U.S. Census of Population, *Lifetime and Recent Migration*, PC (2) 2D, Table 8. Ratios are computed excluding persons for whom residence was not reported.

extremely high proportion of the younger out-migrants who were returning to their home divisions and virtually regardless of educational attainment levels — though the proportion is less extreme for college graduates. As Table 3 shows, the ratio of in to out-migrants among young college men is exceptionally high for the Pacific Division, though in all age and schooling groups that division had net inflows.

At the opposite extreme is the East South Central region, which had net outflows in every case. The differences in the gross in and out movements were small, however. The most interesting thing to us in the East South Central figures is the rising proportion of in-migrants who were returning home as we move down from college graduates

TABLE 3

Number of 1955–60 White Male In-Migrants and Out-Migrants
for Whom Residence Was Reported: The East South Central,
East North Central, and Pacific Divisions

	1955–1960 In-Migrants 1960 Age			1955–1960 Out-Migrants 1960 Age		
	25–29	30–34	35–39	25–29	30–34	35–39
	EAST SOUTH CENTRAL					
Highschool 1–3	7300	5750	4280	9585	6955	5145
Highschool 4	13367	7960	6716	16279	9296	7690
College 1–3	6781	4067	3441	8064	4573	3679
College 4	9752	7485	5372	13743	9577	6303
	EAST NORTH CENTRAL					
Highschool 1–3	18305	10884	7455	15488	15558	13185
Highschool 4	36831	14659	12030	25922	21715	20856
College 1–3	17920	8615	6752	13918	11793	10456
College 4	33906	24707	15326	31472	28233	20950
	PACIFIC					
Highschool 1–3	22146	20800	16556	14764	10011	7453
Highschool 4	36646	27640	26411	31305	14452	13301
College 1–3	22645	14578	12942	16439	7592	7432
College 4	35438	27629	19899	16825	13764	9626

Source: Same as Table 1.

to the highschool drop-outs. This pattern is repeated for every age group. We strongly suspect that had we computed ratios below highschool 1–3 those ratios would have been even higher than for men with one to three years in highschool. Here a very distinctive migration and remigration phenomenon is evident. It should come as no surprise, for this is a manisfestation of "the poverty problem" in one of its most serious and difficult forms—and of the failures of migration to solve problems of Galbraith's "insular poverty" where men have become obsolete or have never been sufficiently equipped to enter into jobs that offer opportunities for new training or learning.

The least predictable of the results, at least to us, were those for youth returning to the East North Central Division. Even though this has not been a growing area, we had expected that lower proportions of inmigrants would be returnees. Even the lowest ratios are around 30 percent. It is interesting that the highest ratios are for young men, and are associated with absolute net inflows, while in the older age categories the East North Central Division was a net loser in each of the age-schooling groups we examined. Such findings invite further speculation, but we resist that temptation in favor of a more generalized (and safer) procedure — the presentation of migration and re-migration decision models with some of their analytical and policy potentials.

B. Decision Models for Migration and Remigration

The interpretation of migration behavior in economic terms and the analysis of potential strategies in social policy require something more than aggregate estimates of gains and losses.

With this in mind, we have developed models that begin with the individual viewpoint but are transformed into social decision models as parameter values are readjusted to allow for cost and income transfers, as individually expected earnings are replaced by socially expected or realized productive contributions, and as probability values are applied to allow for rates of return and non-return of migrants. The models allow choices with respect to locus, duration, and sequences of schooling and experiential learning. Relevant earnings streams are those of an "average individual" within a sex, race, age, and initial educational attainment and occupation category.[21] Our presentation is necessarily summary.[22]

The following notation is used:

a — age at the first decision point relating to migration
b — date of actual or intended out-migration
m — age at return from residence abroad
n — retirement age
R_t — expected earnings in the year t at the place of origin prior to (or in the absence of) any migration

---

[21] The models could of course be generalized to incorporate nonpecuniary benefits and returns or to disaggregate down to the individual decision maker with all his personal and environmental characteristics. However, we have limited the model to include only key economic variables and to keep it potentially operational data-wise.

[22] The models used here are part of a family of such models for analysis of investment in human resources (and before that in business economics). Their relation to Gary Becker's approach is evident. (See his "Investment in Human Capital," *The Journal of Political Economy,* LXX, No. 5, Part 2 (October, 1962) and his *Human Capital,* Columbia University Press, 1964). However, for our purposes, comparison of present values taking an assumed external discount rate is more flexible and is generally more appropriate than the "internal rates of return." Use of the "internal rate of return" method entails unnecessarily restrictive assumptions. (See also footnote 23).

D_t—expected earnings abroad in the year t

Y_t—expected earnings in the year t at the place of origin for migrant returnees $(t > m - a)$

C_t—direct cost in the year t of schooling or training in the area of origin

K_t—direct cost in the year t of schooling or training abroad

Z_t^0—direct cost of out-migration incurred in year t

Z_t^h—direct cost of return migration incurred in year t

r—discount rate

V—present value of future income streams

j—superscript denoting a particular race, age, sex, school attainment, and occupation (if any) at time a

We limit ourselves to the following possible migration sequences:

1. Remain in the area of origin permanently (no migration)

$$V_1^j = \sum_{t=a}^{n} \frac{R_t - C_t}{(1 + r)^{-a}} \tag{1}$$

2. Migrate immediately and remain permanently in the area of destination

$$V_2^j = \sum_{t=a}^{n} \frac{D_t - K_t - Z_t^0}{(1 + r)^{t-a}} \tag{2}$$

3. Migrate immediately, remain temporarily in the area of destination, then return to the area of origin

$$V_3^j = \sum_{t=a}^{m-1} \frac{D_t - K_t - Z_t^0}{(1 + r)^{t-a}} + \sum_{t=m}^{n} \frac{Y_t - Z_t^h}{(1 + r)^{t-a}} \tag{3}$$

4. Remain temporarily in the area of origin, then migrate permanently

$$V_4^j = \sum_{t=a}^{b-1} \frac{R_t - C_t}{(1 + r)^{t-a}} + \sum_{t=b}^{n} \frac{D_t - K_t - Z_t^0}{(1 + r)^{t-a}} \tag{4}$$

5. Remain temporarily in the area of origin, migrate and remain temporarily in the area of destination, then return to the area of origin

$$V_5^j = \sum_{t=a}^{b-1} \frac{R_t - C_t}{(1 + r)^{t-a}} + \sum_{t=b}^{m-1} \frac{D_t - K_t - Z_t^0}{(1 + r)^{t-a}} + \sum_{t=m}^{n} \frac{Y_t - Z_t^h}{(1 + r)^{t-a}} \tag{5}$$

These models could be generalized to admit unlimited numbers of moves (or migration), of learning situations, and of successive cost-benefit relationships. Also, the external interest rates used could be varied to allow for shifts in relevant criterion or reservation rates.[23]

1. Individual Choices

An individual has many alternatives within each of the five sequences. To illustrate the complexity of choice, we begin with sequence one, the simplest case.[24] Think of a high school graduate deciding about his future. He must weigh going to work immediately against spending one, two, five, or more years in school during which his earnings are low or zero. He must weigh schooling now against schooling later. If he is in the United States he is faced with a bewildering array of institutional settings. Each of the above carries implications for cost streams (C_t) and for future earnings (R_t).

Each of the schooling choices can be associated with a set of alternative occupational and job choices with varied amounts of experiential learning. The potential occupation and/or job choice implies visualizing a series of future yearly earnings (R values). These separate streams may differ in their present value and in the amount of associated experiential learning.

A person may choose between positions with higher learning potential which pay little at first but will bring higher pay later and positions with less or negligible potential which pay well at first but

[23] In some cases this could lead to incorrect optimizing solutions even with the present-value, external rate method, but such cases entail very special forms of preference functions. (See Martin J. Bailey, "Formal Criteria for Investment Decisions," *Journal of Political Economy*, LXVII, No. 5 (October, 1959), 476–88.) Over the past decade a number of economists have been pressing these problems on the frontiers of capital theory proper, though spill-over of these analyses to discussions of investments in Human Resource Development have been tardy. Bruce Wilkinson, who builds his argument on Hirshleifer, is an exception. (See Bruce W. Wilkinson, "Present Values of Life-Time Earnings for Different Occupations," *Journal of Political Economy*, LXXIV, No. 6 (December, 1966), 556–72, and J. Hirshleifer, "On the Theory of Optimal Investment Decision," *Journal of Political Economy*, LXVI, No. 4 (August, 1958), 329–52. Valerian Harvey demonstrates the advantages of using both internal rate-of-return and present value schedules in an assessment of *Economic Aspects of Teachers' Salaries* in Quebec (Chicago Ph.D. dissertation, 1967).

[24] Though this complexity is further compounded by various kinds and degrees of uncertainty, we follow here the common practice of abstracting from uncertainty. This simplification is necessary for expositional purposes but should not be taken to imply that effects of uncertainty and ignorance are unimportant either in individual behavior or in social policy making. (See also footnote 25).

promise little or no earnings increase in the future.[25] The relation of experiential learning to earnings stream differences and the place of experiential learning in our models is less observable than that of schooling. Schooling obviously involves foregone earnings: most students do not work or they have earnings far below what they might have if employed full-time. And schooling also carries direct costs — tuition, books, fees — that are only too evident to all who have paid them at one time or another. However, costs to an individual of experiential learning, embedded as they are in the earnings streams and usually involving less contrast in earnings, are less conspicuous even when they are cumulatively substantial.[26]

From the above it is apparent that even within sequence one, there is potentially almost an infinity of schooling and experience mixes from which to choose, each with its earnings stream and associated costs. Within sequence two, the possibilities for mixing schooling and experience are increased as a geographical dimension is introduced; within sequence three, the number of possibilities is further multiplied as the geographical progression becomes more complicated; and so forth.

In theory, one could identify the costs and earnings streams for every conceivable combination within and between each of the five migration sequences and select that one giving the highest present value. However, many combinations can be immediately discarded as unpromising ones. Furthermore, in practice any one individual will be constrained by his native ability, his interests, his financial situation, behavior of acquaintances, etc. The possibilities actually considered are reduced to the most promising and feasible ones,

---

[25] Note that this description of choices, and our use of present value comparisons, requires no assumption with respect to year-to-year choices of alternatives or constancy of internal rates of return to successive self-investments such as Mincer used (*op. cit.*). For some remarks on Mincer's as one of a broader set of models that varies the length of a contract term, see M. J. Bowman, "The Costing of Human Resource Development," in E. A. G. Robinson and J. E. Vaizey, eds., *The Economics of Education* (Proceedings of the 1963 Conference of the International Economics Association), London and New York: Macmillan and Co., 1966. A few aspects of decision-making with respect to human resource formation under uncertainty are also included in that article.

[26] Stress here is on cost *to the individual* because we are speaking of an individual decision. There is no need to assume year-to-year matching of incomes and productivity even in social assessments however, since only the present value enters into our social decision models; more than one income sequence can yield the same present value. Becker's "general" learning will cause no trouble. Some part of what he terms "specific" on-the-job training will escape measurement in the estimations of present values of income streams accruing to individuals.

even to choices among two or three specific combinations for which costs and benefits are weighed and compared.

The most interesting aspect of this exercise for analysis of migration concerns how the locale of schooling and/or experiential learning up to any given age affects subsequent income streams for each work location which might be chosen after that age.

How great are the differences in particular cases? How stable are they? What explains them? How fully do they, in turn, explain migrant behavior? By what processes and how rapidly are they changed in the wake of migration? These questions are key ones for a positive economics that would go beyond traditional resource allocation to merge decision theory into a theory of development dynamics.

2. Social Choices and Migration Probabilities

Now, suppose we shift our viewpoint to a social one, for instance that of a regional or national body which is deciding whether or not to subsidize study outside the area. Social gains and losses may be evaluated by using the same basic models used for individual decisions. However, the costs and returns are now those to the society. For example, all costs of educational services (teacher time, physical facilities, etc.) are real social costs, even though subsidies may reduce or eliminate such costs to the individual. In this section we assume that market prices (wages, etc.) coincide with social shadow prices.[27]

Permanent migration, as in sequences 2 and 4, is commonly regarded as unambiguous loss from a social viewpoint. This position, which assumes that to add to the productivity of an area an individual must be physically present, has been challenged.[28] However, in most

---

[27] Evidently the use of shadow pricing for public cost and benefit assessments will sometimes be required — where there are substantial discrepancies between present values of what men will be paid and what they will produce over ensuing years; this is why, earlier, we spoke of transformations from "individual earnings" to productive contributions. The discussion in this section identifies "social" returns with returns to the entire society, as measured by national product. Often foundations may take similar ultimate goals as a basis for decisions to allocate funds to one or another type of educational project in one or another location. Narrower definitions of "social" that balance flows into and out of one versus another public exchequer are a very different matter.

[28] For a listing and discussion of contributions to the area of origin which might be made from outside the area, see Harry Johnson, "Economics of the 'Brain Drain': The Canadian Case," *Minerva*, III, No. 3 (Spring, 1965), 299–311, and Herbert Grubel and Anthony Scott, "The International Flow of Human Capital, the Brain Drain," *op. cit.* An allowance for such contributions could, in principle, be incorporated in the social present value equations though it poses some elusive measurement problems.

cases policy-makers are concerned with the problem of non-return and regard physical presence as a crucial consideration from the national or regional point of view.

Temporary migration, as in sequences 3, and 5, when viewed socially as a training alternative, requires a major adjustment.[29] Unless a government coerces in some way, it cannot insure that those trained at home will stay at home or that those trained abroad will necessarily return. Therefore it is necessary to allow for the possibility that students trained at home will emigrate and that students trained outside will not return. This is done by including probabilities in the models.

As an example, we focus on comparisons between longer and shorter periods of training abroad. Let α_t^m be the probability that students trained outside the area for $(m - a)$ years will return before age t. To illustrate, sequence three then becomes:

$$V_{3m}^j = \sum_{t=m}^{n} \frac{\alpha_t^m Y_t^m - \alpha_t^m Z_t^h}{(1 + r)^{t-a}} - \sum_{t=a}^{m-1} \frac{K_t + Z_t^0}{(1 + r)^{t-a}} \tag{6}$$

For each value of $(m - a)$ there will be a different set of income variables, Y_t^m, and of probabilities of return, α_t^m. The probability set α_t^m is likely to be a declining function of $(m - a)$; the rate at which α_t^m declines will be one of the critical elements in the comparison of social net returns from longer or shorter periods of training abroad. In this form the equation refers to one individual (or a fraction thereof) but with appropriate identification of Y, K, and Z it is also a marginal social benefit-cost summation. (Any part of costs for training or travel borne by other than the area of origin would of course be deducted from the K and Z figures.)

Another type of comparison involves locus of training for any given training period as, for instance, in a comparison of sequences 1 and 3. A concrete example is the argument over establishing local medical schools (versus training doctors abroad or out-of-state). The answer will depend on rates of migration and retention as well as on the relative cost and quality of the training in each locality. The argument usually given is that probabilities of retention for those trained at home so exceed the probability of return for those trained elsewhere as to outweigh all other considerations. From a "nationalistic" or

[29] One of the authors—Myers—has been developing implications of this approach more fully. Our discussion here is limited by space considerations.

"localistic" point of view, the economic validity of this argument will depend, among other things, upon who bears the costs of training in the alternative locales.

Another practically important issue is whether and how long students sent overseas should be allowed or encouraged to stay beyond formal schooling in order to acquire experience. The solution will depend, in part, on what "wastage" from non-return is associated with the experiential learning. This "wastage" is incorporated into our social decision model by introducing the migration probabilities.

The dependence of social policy upon understanding individual behavior is particularly evident in attempts to decrease wastage by influencing rates of out-migration and remigration. Also, knowledge of how migration probabilities vary with individual characteristics within each schooling-work alternative would provide guidelines for efficient selection of individuals to the training programs, further reducing wastage.

3. Long Versus Short-Term Importations of Highly Qualified Manpower

As a final example of human capital models applied to migration, we turn to decisions in developing nations concerning imported skills. We by-pass comparison of more training of local people against more importing of outside talent to focus on models weighing three alternatives in the purchase of foreign experts' services: a one-man, long-term contract, a sequence of short-term contracts to several people, and a system of two-year rotations between two individuals.

When decisions involve a continuous series of replacements, the succession of short income streams can be regarded as one long one. The equivalence is not complete, however. The sharpest contrasts and associated problems can be most clearly illustrated by looking at human capital migration from the point of view of the developing nations and their needs for highly qualified manpower from the more advanced economies.

There is much discussion today of alternatives and combinations in the flow of high-level manpower for shorter or longer stays in the developing nations. In the terminology of the previous section, should a man be kept abroad for a period $(m - a) = 2$ or for, say, $(m - a) = 5$, or 10, or even 20 years? For that matter, what about double appointments in which two individuals alternate with each other at home and abroad?

In this discussion, present value refers to the value of imported

511

services to the importing country, independent of the supply prices of these services. We will look at how supply conditions may affect optimal choice. Note that previously we used observed incomes as measures of both demand and supply prices in market equilibrium.

Let us designate the present value to the importing country, X, of a single individual for 10 years as V_x^1, that of two individuals who replace each other every two years over a period of 10 years as V_x^2, and that of a sequence of five individuals staying two years each as V_x^5. In the third case, on our assumption that each successive individual is the twin of his predecessor D_t for $t = 1$ will have the same current year value as D_t where $t = 3, 5, 7$, or 9 and D_t where $t = 2$ will have the same value as where $t = 4, 6, 8$, or 10. We make the simplifying assumption that the importing country pays for all travel expenses. Let these travel expenses be represented by:

$$Z^j = \sum_{t=a}^{a+10} \frac{Z_t^0}{(1+r)^{t-a}} + \sum_{t=a}^{a+10} \frac{Z_t^h}{(1+r)^{t-a}}$$

Also, let $D_{1,t}$ represent the earnings of individual 1 in year t, $D_{2,t}$ represent the earnings of individual 2 in year t and so forth.

Then the maximum present values and hence the amounts that the importing country would be justified in paying for the production streams generated by each of these alternatives can be represented as follows:

$$V_x^1 = \sum_{t=a}^{a+10} \frac{D_t^1}{(1+r)^{t-a}} + Z^1 \tag{7}$$

$$
\begin{aligned}
V_x^2 = {} & \frac{D_{1,1}^2}{(1+r)} + \frac{D_{1,2}^2}{(1+r)^2} + \left[\frac{D_{2,3}^2}{(1+r)^3} + \frac{D_{2,4}^2}{(1+r)^4}\right] \\
& + \left[\frac{D_{1,5}^2}{(1+r)^5} + \frac{D_{1,6}^2}{(1+r)^6}\right] + \left[\frac{D_{2,7}^2}{(1+r)^7} + \frac{D_{2,8}^2}{(1+r)^8}\right] \\
& + \left[\frac{D_{1,9}^2}{(1+r)^9} + \frac{D_{1,10}^2}{(1+r)^{10}}\right] + Z^2
\end{aligned}
\tag{8}
$$

$$
\begin{aligned}
V_x^5 = {} & \left[\frac{D_{1,1}^5}{(1+r)} + \frac{D_{1,2}^5}{(1+r)^2}\right] + \left[\frac{D_{2,3}^5}{(1+r)^3} + \frac{D_{2,4}^5}{(1+r)^4}\right] \\
& + \left[\frac{D_{3,5}^5}{(1+r)^5} + \frac{D_{3,6}^5}{(1+r)^6}\right] + \left[\frac{D_{4,7}^5}{(1+r)^7} + \frac{D_{4,8}^5}{(1+r)^8}\right] \\
& + \left[\frac{D_{5,9}^5}{(1+r)^9} + \frac{D_{5,10}^5}{(1+r)^{10}}\right] + Z^5
\end{aligned}
\tag{9}
$$

Assuming successive twins for V_x^5 with $D_{1,1} = D_{2,3} = D_{3,5} = D_{4,7} = D_{5,9}$ and $D_{1,2} = D_{2,4} = D_{3,4} = D_{4,6} = D_{5,10}$ we have:

$$V_x^5 = D_{1,1}\Sigma\left[\frac{1}{(1+r)} + \frac{1}{(1+r)^3} + \frac{1}{(1+r)^5} + \frac{1}{(1+r)^7} + \frac{1}{(1+r)^9}\right]$$

$$+ D_{1,2}\Sigma\left[\frac{1}{(1+r)^2} + \frac{1}{(1+r)^4} + \frac{1}{(1+r)^6} + \frac{1}{(1+r)^8} + \frac{1}{(1+r)^{10}}\right] + Z^5 \quad (10)$$

We can simplify in comparing these alternatives by assuming that the amounts and timing of travel costs paid by the receiving country are the same in all three cases. This is evidently the case as between V_x^2 and V_x^5, and it is consistent enough with common practice respecting travel allowances for vacation at home in the case of expatriates on long-term appointments. Which alternative will yield the highest present value then depends upon the summations of sets of terms incorporating the D's.

If there is any learning on the job at all, the V_x^5 stream will clearly have the lowest present value. In fact, if we had made any allowance for direct outlays on training, this disadvantage of the V_x^5 stream would be still more apparent. There is good reason for the widespread concern over the cutting off of so many technical assistance activities at two years per man, and even stronger reason for the increasingly firm attempts to adhere to a two-year minimum, to permit men to learn about the situation in a strange environment and to attain a reasonably high level of effectiveness in it. Two-year appointments may serve very well when there is a special job that needs to be done by a man with unusual qualifications, after which the requirements of the task are less demanding—in other words, when the calibre of the first man has to be higher than that of his successors. But that is a different sort of situation, and not the "successive twin" case with which we started and by which we defined V_x^5.

Comparison between V_x^1 and V_x^2 must be a bit more subtle. In case V_x^1 there is the advantage of continuity on the job in country X, but offsetting this is loss of contact with dynamic centers of activity in the expert's home country; he tends to fall progressively further behind his colleagues there. Case V_x^2 has the advantage that experiences in the home country and in the importing country may well feed into each other, to enhance a man's effectiveness in both. This is one of the arguments in favor of developing career opportunities in technical assistance by establishing supernumerary university posts (double staffing) in selected fields and locations.

If V_x^5 is so likely to be the inferior choice for value to the importing country, why is this alternative so common in practice? Evidently there are two reasons. First is the political reaction to colonial experience and the desire to avoid entrenchment of foreigners who might build up too much power in the country. In many cases ex-colonial countries have quite deliberately made a trade-off between economic and political ends by their policies with respect to expatriates. However, this phase of the transition is fading, and with this change the economic decision models may have greater potential impact on policies. In strictly economic terms, what can be said for V_x^2? To properly evaluate V_x^1, V_x^2, and V_x^5 we also need to know the supply prices involved. It seems clear that set against the lower present values of a V_x^5 stream are lower recruitment costs; it is easier to get good men for a short than for a long time, and primarily for two reasons: First, the pace of learning in the first year is likely to be especially high, and what is learned over a two-year period may have more transferability to the job market in the expert's home country than the learning that cumulates with longer time abroad. He loses little, if anything, in carrying this learning home with him. Second, he has suffered less loss in getting out of touch and losing contacts with colleagues at home when his stay is not too prolonged. (In addition, a reasonably short term abroad may be enticing for quite non-economic considerations that would pall if the stay were extended.) Thus set over against the lower value of the V_x^5 stream is the greater ease and lower cost of maintaining it.

This brings us back to V_x^1 against V_x^2 once again. Let us take another look at V_x^1. Unless a man becomes a permanent migrant, he is likely to suffer a disadvantage when he returns home after a long stay abroad. He has foregone learning opportunities suited to his home country, and the experience he has accumulated in his years abroad often has limited transferability back into an advanced industrial nation. (In lesser degree this may happen with migration from North to South in the United States, unless the migrant is associated with a Northern or a Northern-type firm.) In order to attract a man for 10 years, it would be necessary to pay him a very high salary to compensate for this accumulation of obsolescence. There is evidently a point at which long-term stays abroad must become permanent ones if they are to prove beneficial both to the receiving country and to the individual involved.

V_x^2 is quite another matter. In this case the learning process continues and contacts at home are maintained. No special bribe need be paid to attract a man into such a career. On balance it looks very much as though V_x^2 might come out as the best alternative in a large proportion of cases. Systematic application of human investment decision models to particular cases will help sort these alternatives out. They just might lead to some important innovations in technical assistance and in relations between universities and the Department of State.

4. IN CONCLUSION

1. *Current methods of calculating human capital gains and losses from migration take a too simplistic view of migration.*

a. Even adhering for the moment to the prevalent treatment of migration as if it were a one-way affair, it is of the greatest importance that gross flows be analyzed: the critical problems and evidence concerning the effects of migration are concealed when net flows only are assessed—even when the latter are broken down into finely disaggregated population categories.

b. Remigration is important quantitatively. Furthermore, disregard of remigration leads to serious misinterpretations of even the gross flows and even when the latter are disaggregated on a number of key variables. The importance of analyzing remigration is underlined where regions differ in quality of schooling and experiential opportunities and where there is rotating migration of obsolescent and undereducated men.

2. *Human investment decision models provide useful conceptual and empirical tools when applied to migration, from both individuals and social perspective.*

a. The models add insight into motivations of migrants. Understanding migrant behavior provides points of leverage for channeling migration to social purposes, and provides a means of determining to what extent the socially rational may coincide or conflict with effects of individual behavior that are rational.

b. Social decisions involving the locus of training may be put in a cost-benefit framework and evaluated. Major decisions such as whether to train elsewhere or at home can be weighed. Losses from non-return and their probabilities can be valued and included in assessing investment alternatives. The potential gains from policies to reduce rates of non-return could also be estimated.

c. Migration, coupled with regional differentials in quality of schooling and experience, can be examined as it relates to the diffusion of know-how among regions or nations. Of particular interest

515

would be application of human capital concepts to understanding "package migration" as an agent of change.

d. Effects of social decisions to import manpower on a short-term continuous replacement basis, an alternating basis, or a long-term basis can be sorted out using human capital investment models. For each situation, individual decision models provide estimates of outlays necessary to attract the talent desired. Costs and benefits can be compared to determine the best alternative.

3. *Availability of census tapes with data for samples large enough to permit refined breakdowns would permit new kinds of research on critical aspects of migration as a human investment.* Potential contributions to both theoretical developments in the social sciences and to public policy formation are substantial.

a. Even if no data other than those collected in 1960 were obtained, larger samples would permit multiple breakdowns that distinguish migrant status by origin, destination, and place of birth for Divisions, within existing categories on age-sex-race-income-education-occupation tables.

b. All too sizeable a list of other items might be suggested, but we will use restraint. A high priority item would be occupation just prior to migration, but we recognize that occupation data are costly. Home residence of college students is presumably being included. We would be interested in dates of migration, together with state and type of community in which a migrant last resided, but we would not want to give up the identification of residence and other traits at a fixed time interval (5 years) before the census. Obviously not all these things can be done.

c. Because of the importance we attach to it, we list separately information concerning residence when last attending high school (or, for those who never entered high school, elementary school). Alternatively, the question could be asked for age 16, though this might be more difficult for some to answer. State of residence and type of community would both be desirable; together they should provide valuable indexes of the combined effects of quality of schooling and experiential learning from adolescent environment. Such information could be extremely useful not only in analysis of migration but in many other aspects of the economics of human resource development and utilization.

28. The Mobility of Labor and the Theory of Human Capital*

HANS-JOACHIM BODENHÖFER
Max-Planck-Institute for Educational Research

I. INTRODUCTION: THE DEVELOPMENT OF HUMAN CAPITAL THEORY

Having left Malthusianism behind, economic theory has in effect excluded problems of population development from its area of study and its range of competence. Population problems have become so-called exogenous factors—comparable, for example, to political institutions and motivation for achievement.[1] In addition to problems of over-all population growth and manpower development, the structural aspects of the labor force—especially the education and training of its members but also the spatial (regional) and sectoral (industrial) distribution of manpower and the mechanisms for their reshaping—have become of only minor importance. Therefore, theorizing on problems of labor mobility has seemed somewhat unsatisfactory, since it has been mainly oriented toward mass migration and refugee problems but has not sufficiently considered the continuous dynamic processes of labor markets in a growing economy and the bearing of qualitative facets of manpower on labor mobility. At least, the functioning of labor mobility as an equalization mechanism among labor markets *seems* unsatisfactory, if its effect in equating existing interregional or interindustrial wage-differentials is compared with the assumptions of marginal productivity theory. However, in connection with recent conclusions concerning growth, we can derive a frame of reference for problems of manpower develop-

*Reprinted from "The Mobility of Labor and the Theory of Human Capital," *Journal of Human Resources*, II (Fall, 1967), 431–48. (Copyright 1967 by the Regents of the University of Wisconsin.)

[1]Cf., for an exception in recent literature, the models of Jürg Niehans, "Economic Growth with Two Endogenous Factors," and Stephen Enke, "Population and Development, a General Model," *Quarterly Journal of Economics*, Vol. 77 (1963).

ment that also appears to offer new explanations for the enigmas of labor mobility.

Labor as a production factor has not received much attention in modern growth theory; it has been generally treated in an aggregative manner and is often considered simply a ceiling of growth—more a subject of interest in studies on employment policy. Evidently this situation has come about because modern growth theories have developed out of Keynesianism; but, conversely, it also reflects the disinterest of economic theorists in population problems. It was empirical research that directed the attention of growth theorists to this neglected aspect of the production capacity of an economy and thus led to a new understanding of the contribution of human resources to production and growth. Empirical investigations of growth processes gave perplexing results concerning the relative share of various production factors (i.e., labor and capital) in the total growth rate.[2]

Since the high percentage of the unexplained factor—technical progress—in total income growth, could no longer be accepted simply as a "measure of our ignorance,"[3] according to these calculations, it became necessary to attempt to isolate and quantify those factors of growth and determinants of rising total productivity which comprised the heterogeneous residuum.[4] Further investigation along this line brought the qualitative aspects of labor-inputs—i.e., education and training—to the forefront of interest and gave rise to a renaissance of the concept of investment in human capital.[5]

[2]Cf. S. Fabricant, *Economic Progress and Economic Change* (New York: NBER, 1954); Moses Abramovitz, "Resource and Output Trends in the United States Since 1870," *American Economic Review*, Vol. 46, No. 2 (Papers and Proceedings, May 1956); Robert M. Solow, "Technical Change and the Aggregate Production Function," *Review of Economics and Statistics*, Vol. 39 (1957); John W. Kendrick, asst. by Maude R. Pech, *Productivity Trends in the United States* (Princeton: NBER, 1961); Olavi Niitamo, "The Development of Productivity in Finnish Industry, 1925–1952," *Economic Studies*, Vol. 20 (Helsinki: Economic Society, 1958); Odd Aukrust and Juul Bjerke, "Real Capital and Economic Growth in Norway, 1900–1956," in Raymond Goldsmith and Christopher Saunders, eds., "The Measurement of National Wealth," *Income and Wealth Series* VIII (London: International Association for Research in Income and Wealth, 1959); Gerhard Gehrig and Karl Christian Kuhlo, "Ökonometrische Analyse des Produktionsprozesses," *IFO-Studien*, Vol. 7 (1961), Nos. 1 and 2.

[3]M. Abramovitz, "Resource and Output Trends . . . ," p. 11.

[4]See especially the pioneering study by Edward F. Denison, *The Sources of Economic Growth in the United States and the Alternatives Before Us* (New York: Committee for Economic Development, 1962).

[5]The tradition of this concept in economic literature reaches back as far as the writings of William Petty, *Political Arithmetick, or a Discourse Concerning the Extent and Value*

Investment in human capital could be defined as the employment of resources for the development of human capacities from which an improvement of individual welfare in the future occurs.[6] Expected improvement of future welfare refers not only to monetary income — according to factor productivity development — but also to the "psychic" income of possible future consumer benefits. Costs incurred for developing human capacities therefore have at least two components: (1) as investment in future higher earnings (producer capacity) and (2) as investment in the type of consumer durables (consumer capacity). Moreover, a third component in total outlay, immediate consumption, should be separated if the on-going investment process by itself improves current welfare, as in the case of education that is immediately enjoyed.[7] The private costs of investment in human capital (real resource costs and income foregone) and private returns expected from it (monetary and "psychic") constitute the variables of our individual decision-model. External costs and external returns are by definition without meaning for the decision-making unit. If, therefore, investment costs and/or returns are not to be fully internalized, inevitably distorting effects on resource allocation and distribution of investment-burdens and benefits will result. Economic policy that aims to approximate optimum conditions of the marginalistic setting accordingly must attempt to counter these effects by compensatory subsidies and interventions.

In can easily be seen that the magnitude and development of investments to improve the future productivity of manpower are determined by a great number of variables and activities. Most important may be the "educational capital" produced by formal education and training processes, which was first investigated. Early research concentrated on problems of measuring human capital items and investment returns — as components of individual earnings and as the

---

of Lands, People, Buildings (London, 1960); Adam Smith, *Inquiry into the Nature and Causes of the Wealth of Nations* (London, 1776); and Johann Heinrich von Thünen, *Der isolierte Staat* (Berlin, 1826), without showing, however, any important development.

[6] And which, one should add, has it purposes in this result. Such an investment-type model of decisions regarding human resource development does not imply, however, the pretension to describe reality adequately, but only the hypothesis that the model could help to explain reality, since its implications are in accordance with empirically observable behavior.

[7] Cf. for example Theodore W. Schultz, "Investment in Human Capital," *American Economic Review*, Vol. 51 (1961).

macro-economic contribution to total income growth.[8] Another quantitatively important determinant is the acquisition of qualifications and skills through informal vocational and on-the-job training. Further, we must consider the variety of organized and informally operating influences from the private and social environment of individuals (including, e.g., family life, mass media, adult education, and training in the army) which are educational in a broad sense.[9] Finally, the concept also embraces the costs of maintaining an optimum state of health in the labor force — which can be compared with the productivity gains, from better health, for the economy as a whole.[10]

These factors demonstrate the variety of heterogeneous, individual facets which comprise the stock of human capital in an economy. The production potential of a given labor force is determined not only by these qualitative aspects of labor or "real" factors of labor productivity, but also by the pattern of allocation of labor inputs. Inputs of production factors can be allocated into a system of economic sectors (e.g., primary, secondary, and tertiary production), branches, and individual industries, as well as into a system of "regional" units (which also may be structured hierarchically). The term "labor mobility" can now be defined according to the processes of change in this twofold allocation pattern of a given labor force and the changes in the qualitative structure of the labor force (i.e., changes of qualifications and skills due to further education or retraining and regrouping of labor force members according to functional or job classification). Labor mobility now includes all the processes of reallocation of manpower with regard to industrial, regional, and qualitative classifications which occur as concomitants of economic growth.

II. THE HUMAN CAPITAL APPROACH TO LABOR MOBILITY

The qualifications of labor which were relevant for more than one period as production input (thus representing a stock of working

[8] An excellent survey of the rapidly developing literature in the economics of education, also covering other implications of the investment-approach and interconnections with other variables of growth, is given by Mark Blaug, *A Selected Annotated Bibliography in the Economics of Education* (London: London University, 1964).

[9] See, for an exhaustive discussion and tentative estimates of costs involved, Fritz Machlup, *The Production and Distribution of Knowledge in the United States* (Princeton: Princeton University Press, 1962).

[10] Cf. Selma J. Mushkin, "Health as an Investment," *Journal of Political Economy*, Vol. 70 (Supplement, October 1962).

capacity) have been defined as human or intangible capital. According to the marginal productivity theory, different additive, constituent parts of individual earnings may be separated according to the productive contribution of different components of total labor product. Our investment approach to human resource development then requires an investment component in total earnings which corresponds to investment returns but, during the period of investing, which must be negative, representing the costs of investment in foregoing earnings possibilities and incurring direct outlays. These effects of human capital investment on labor efficiency and individual life-income cycles are then the basic requisites for identifying and measuring human capital items and investment returns. In the special case of on-the-job training, the life-income curve of the worker who improves his future earning capacity (TT), as contrasted to the income-curve of unqualified manpower (UU) is schematically presented in Figure 1.

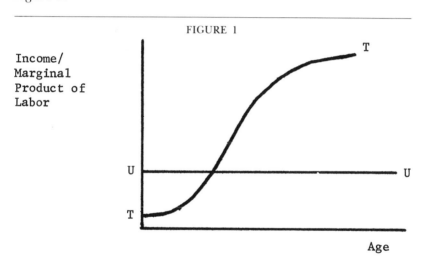

FIGURE 1

Income/ Marginal Product of Labor

Age

Investments in human capital accordingly create a "deepening" of the age-income structure of qualified manpower against non- or less-qualified personnel. If economic resources are required to change the allocation of labor inputs and if this change is undertaken because of expected future returns, we can include labor mobility in this model of human capital investment; if labor mobility is regulated in its economic function by price mechanisms and if we can further assume that factor-price differences represent (or at least indicate) differences in factor productivity, then price-regulated labor mobility causes improvements in labor productivity which may be relevant for more than one future period. If there are costs involved in labor mobility, we have a simple investment framework of costs and future returns. Investment balance would accordingly be determined as the balance of the present values of the relative time series of costs and returns.

The cost of mobility for the individual who moves must be conceived as additional costs which would not otherwise arise, and may also be computed with the same result by a comparison of two alternative real income streams as the (transitory) reduction of welfare through mobility. Total costs comprise a monetary component (costs of transport and earnings foregone) as well as a nonmonetary portion. The main problem in computing the first component of monetary costs—expenditure for transportation, search for lodging, etc.—is that of insufficient or unavailable statistics and estimates; as an impediment to mobility this factor seems to be of minor importance.[11] The bulk of monetary costs consists of opportunity costs which arise as earnings foregone while on the move and during the period of getting acquainted with the new job, and evidently are difficult to estimate. Nonmonetary psychic costs, however—of changing from familiar to strange environments—cannot be regarded as genuine costs from the economist's point of view, although they possibly appear as an important impediment to mobility; they do not require real resources and, theoretically, are rather to be interpreted as a rent of location lost with the decision to move, a rent which could also be removed by perfectly discriminating taxation without affecting resource allocation.[12] However, policy measures undertaken to create compensatory incentives to mobility with regard to these impediments cannot in any event operate as a means of optimum resource allocation policy. Only insofar as individual preferences do not reflect *real* factors such as climate conditions, etc., but rather familiarity with environment which would soon apply also for any new location, could economic rationale justify compensatory support of labor mobility.

---

[11]Cf. Larry A. Sjaastad, "Costs and Returns of Human Migration," *Journal of Political Economy,* Vol. 70 (Supplement, October 1962).

[12]Cf. L. A. Sjaastad, "Costs and Returns . . . ," p. 85.

As with costs, we can differentiate between the monetary and nonmonetary components of private returns to labor mobility. One does not need much discussion of nonmonetary components in this context;[13] they might, for convenience, be conceived as the counterpart of psychic costs or as negative psychic costs. Monetary returns from mobility are defined as the *certis paribus* improvement of real money income—i.e., the individual's income gain due to mobility. The magnitude of this improvement is determined by the change in nominal money earnings, the change in the costs of living, and the change in the costs of job performance. Such a calculation of the returns, which are immediately attributable to mobility, however, meets with a host of difficulties—such as, in the case of worker migration, the derivation of income gain from regional wage differences within a qualification group or special job. Most relevant[14] is the difficulty in isolating the effects of mobility on income from the effects of returns on other investment in human capital which are simultaneously taking place, and which are different components of the total return on manpower reallocation. A discussion of this problem emphasizes the relevance of a general concept of investment in human capital, whereof education, training, health, mobility, etc., constitute interrelated parts.

The structural effects of economic and technical progress which operate through the system of production and employment may have consequences for relative wages and absolute wage differences, given a certain situation of labor supply and flexibility of adaptation. Whereas changes in relative factor prices have a feedback effect on factor demand and supply, changes in absolute price differences are relevant for return on (and rate of return of) investments in human capital. A reduction of the current return on an investment means a reduction of its capital value. If a certain category of labor force members with a certain type of qualifications is affected in this way, these individuals have the alternative of accepting lower earnings or of acquiring additional or new qualifications to change to another labor market that is either favored or unaffected by technical progress. Migration alone may be sufficient to secure, or even improve, the

---

[13] For detailed exposition see L. A. Sjaastad, "Costs and Returns . . . ," pp. 86–87.

[14] For our problem one can ignore all the statistical difficulties in an international (interregional) comparison of real wages and also the difficulties in evaluating legal regulations and restrictions, social security titles, seniority rules, etc. (which perhaps constitute a major impediment to labor mobility).

value of human capital investments if different regional labor markets are affected to a different degree or in different directions by technical progress. If, however, regional labor markets are equally influenced by structural change, an effective reallocation of labor requires the acquisition of new qualifications and skills—i.e., reallocation represents a complex investment in human capital with nonidentifiable components. Thus, regional, industrial, and occupational mobility may represent complementary investments which determine the potentialities and limitations of manpower reallocation in growth.

Because of these correlations, one must consider general qualifications—i.e., the education and training of manpower. The kind and length of formal education as a determinant of labor mobility may not only be relevant as factual or institutional prerequisite for the further acquisition of knowledge and skills but also, perhaps more significantly, indirectly contribute to the readiness of individuals to change, to continue learning, etc.

A second factor influencing mobility is the vocational training, experience, and qualifications acquired on the job. There are two basic types of on-the-job training: (1) general training, increasing labor productivity in many firms at the same time, and (2) specific training, increasing productivity only in the firm providing the training.[15] With qualifications of the first type, acquired by broad, general training, the firm providing this training cannot reap, under conditions of perfect competition, any of the future returns on the investment. Accordingly, the cost of investment (in the case of a profit-maximizing firm) should be fully borne by the individuals trained. In the case of specific training, conversely, the firm is in a position fully to reap the returns of higher labor productivity and therefore should bear the costs of the investment, with individual earnings, as a consequence, becoming independent of investment in human capital.

In reality, on-the-job training represents a mixture of these theoretical types. It comprises both general and specific components, the respective weights of which partially depend on market structures. The above conclusions regarding the distribution of investment costs and returns, accordingly, are valid only in relation to the degree of generality (specificity) of the on-the-job training.

[15]Cf. G. S. Becker, *Human Capital* (New York: Columbia University Press, 1964), p. 11.

These distinctions are relevant to our problem in various ways. First, the willingness of a firm to pay for the specific training of its employees tends to increase as the mobility of these employees decreases—i.e., when the turnover of personnel is low. Labor turnover is an important factor, since the departure of specifically trained manpower implies a capital loss for the firm which paid for the training, there being neither a present nor a future return on the investment cost.[16]

However, since labor mobility is determined by relative wage levels, the firm may achieve both specifically trained personnel and concomitantly a low turnover rate by paying only a portion of the costs of specific training and giving a corresponding share of future returns to employees in higher wages, including a premium for specific training. There is thus a functional correlation between the degree of generality or specificity of on-the-job training and the relative mobility of labor.[17]

General (and specific) on-the-job training has been defined according to the applicability of training in a single *vs.* a multitude of firms. However, the criterion can be given another useful connotation by extending it to regional units, separate groups of firms (industries, branches, sectors), and sectors in the occupational or functional classification of the labor force. For example, national economies may function as regional units in an international framework. On-the-job training is always specific, inasmuch as language, institutions (e.g., the legal system), training, and formal job requirements, etc., differ nationally and are of importance as qualifications for a job. Moreover, vocational training has developed in advanced economies from a limited number of apprenticeships and basic qualification patterns to a wide range of industry-specific training programs and worker-trait requirements. On the other hand, one can differentiate in an international (interregional) and/or interindustrial comparison of worker-trait requirements among various functionally defined occupational groups, for which training may be specific. These types of regionally specific, industry-specific and occupation-specific training correspond, in their effects on labor mobility, to the specific training for a single firm, to the extent that now mobility among regions, industries, and occupational groups (instead of firms) is

[16] *Ibid.*, p. 21.
[17] *Ibid.*, p. 24.

limited.[18] In practice, any kind of training and of occupational activity is associated with elements of specific on-the-job training (e.g., elements of regionally or industry-specific training, experience on a job, knowledge of the firm and its branch of activity, etc.). Therefore, the distinction between general and specific training, together with its implications for labor mobility and the financing of training, seems to offer a valuable instrument for analysis.

Formal education and on-the-job training also have an indirect bearing on labor mobility by influencing potentialities for reshaping the occupational structure and for adapting manpower qualifications to changing requirements. Sufficient flexibility of occupational structures and manpower qualifications must be maintained, however, by arranging the organization and content of education and training to favor motivation for mobility and for additional knowledge and skills, as economic growth proceeds and requires an increased adaptability of labor.[19]

The close correlations between education, on-the-job training, and labor mobility increase the difficulty of isolating the different components of total productivity gained from reallocating manpower. Already the length of schooling and participation in higher education (as well as its future economic efficiency in monetary returns) cannot be evaluated independently of individual capacities, motivation, and other personal and family characteristics. The investment component may even presuppose special personal characteristics, inasmuch as complementaries are involved, such as, to a certain degree, between higher education and IQ's or performance test scores. Higher levels of general education and increased amounts of subsequent on-the-job training appear to be positively correlated.[20] Years spent in general education, according to statistical records (with the exception of highly mobile unqualified manpower), also seem to increase the relative

---

[18] *Ibid.,* p. 28.

[19] The essentially educational consequences of this conclusion may be ignored in our context. It appears that a sequence is evolving, from a single training period at the beginning of the work period to a number of training programs distributed over the years of an individual's economic activity.

[20] Cf. Jacob Mincer, "On-the-Job Training: Costs, Returns, and Some Implications," *Journal of Political Economy,* Vol. 70 (Supplement, October 1962), pp. 59–60; U.S. Department of Labor, Bureau of Employment Security, U.S. Employment Service, "Estimates of Worker Trait Requirements for 4,000 Jobs as Defined in the Dictionary of Occupational Titles" (Washington: GPO, 1956).

mobility of the more educated.[21] The connection between intelligence and mobility was earlier noted by A. Marshall.[22]

It is difficult to identify the bearing of these interdependencies on the functioning of labor mobility and almost impossible to resolve satisfactorily the methodological difficulties implied. One point, however, is revealed in connection with the role of general education, intelligence, etc., that needs discussion in the context of our investment model of mobility: the role of information in the labor market.

As economic theorists suggest, the expected rates of return for an investment opportunity and the incentive to invest are positively correlated. The interest rate for discounting future returns on human capital investments in our decision-model not only covers capital interest but also expresses the risk of the investment, as it is subjectively estimated, and individual liquidity preference. Because of long terms and the nonliquidity of human capital investments, both variables may require high positive premiums.

The risk of an investment increases according to the length of time required to collect the expected returns (whereby the distribution pattern of returns is meaningful, too). Compared with long-term investments in tangible capital, however, one can infer, for investments in oneself, a systematic difference in risk assessment and a lower risk premium from the presumably greater readiness to undergo risk.[23]

In the short-run view, the risk of investment in human capital corresponds to the probability of being affected by cyclical (or seasonal) unemployment. In evaluating this short-run risk, however, one must bear in mind the empirical fact of a decrease of cyclical responsiveness of employment and the respective rate of unemployment

[21]U.S. Bureau of the Census, *U.S. Census of Population: 1950,* Vol. IV, Special Reports, Part 4, "Population Mobility—Characteristics of Migrants" (Washington: GPO, 1957), cited in Burton A. Weisbrod, *External Benefits of Public Education—An Economic Analysis* (Princeton: Princeton University, Industrial Relations Section, 1964), pp. 48–49. For sociological aspects of the considerable increase of empirical incremental migration rates with respect to college education see also F. Musgrove, *The Migratory Elite* (London: Heinemann, 1963).

[22]Alfred Marshall, *Principles of Economics,* London (1890) (New York: Macmillan and Company, 1949), p. 199.

[23]Cf. also M. Friedman and L. J. Savage, "The Utility Analysis of Choices Involving Risks," in G. J. Stigler and K. Boulding, eds., *Readings in Price Theory* (Chicago: American Economic Association, 1952); cited in G. S. Becker, *Human Capital,* p. 55.

with the rising level of manpower qualification.[24] Among other factors (e.g., production techniques and management organization in industry), this observation may also be explained by the effects of specific on-the-job training.[25] Cyclical unemployment, however (as well as depressed cyclical expectations), will reduce the total mobility of labor as an effect of both demand and supply factors in diverse labor markets. Conversely, differences in cyclical development among regions or industries may also favor labor mobility proportionately to relative imbalances of corresponding labor markets.

The inferences to be drawn from the long-term structural changes of an economy undergoing economic and technical progress are analogous. The risks of human capital investments increase according to the rapidness and depth of structural changes, the degree of manpower specialization (i.e., specialization of human capital investments), and the narrowness of the labor market geographically and in numbers, which partially depends on impediments to mobility for different kinds of manpower. Structural changes of labor demand thereby involve a risk not only for the amortization of investments in qualifications and skills but also for the profitability of an individual's decision to relocate or to change industry.

The effect of time on investment decisions has been considered in the context of risk, but there are some additional implications. The empirical fact of a decrease in relative mobility with age, as exemplified by the decline of age-specific migration rates after a peak for lower age brackets, can be partly explained by a variety of psychological and sociological factors. In fact, inferences can be drawn from the investment approach to labor mobility that correspond exactly to the mobility pattern for different age classes.

Total returns on an investment not only are a function of the rate of return but equally depend on the period of time during which returns can be expected. Accordingly, the effect of age—thereby the length of expected economic activity—on the profitability of an investment in human capital is positively correlated with the foreseeable pay-off period of the specific investment opportunity. If this period

[24]See U.S. Department of Labor, Bureau of Labor Statistics, Special Labor Force Reports, No. 1; cited in B. A. Weisbrod, *External Benefits of Public Education*, p. 81.

[25]For an attempt to test this hypothesis empirically see Walter Y. Oi, "Labor as a Quasi-fixed Factor of Production," unpublished Ph.D. dissertation, University of Chicago, 1961; and "Labor as a Quasi-fixed Factor," *Journal of Political Economy*, Vol. 70 (December 1962); cf. also J. Mincer, "On-the-Job Training," pp. 69–72.

is shortened, for example, as a result of quickened technical progress that increases the rate of obsolescence of knowledge and skills, the investment character of an activity is less accentuated. If it pays, in a very short time, to change employment or occupation or to migrate, there exists also, from the purely economic standpoint, an incentive for older employees to invest in higher future earnings.[26] On the other hand, investments will be relatively great at young ages even if investment returns are distributed over a rather long span of time. Empirical data, therefore, clearly show a decrease in investments in on-the-job training with age or time after entry into the labor force respectively.[27]

Relatively short periods of acquired (specific) on-the-job training and job experience at younger ages conversely favor the mobility of these persons. The impact on labor mobility of the remaining length of active life will, furthermore, increase in proportion with volume and pay-off period of complementary investments in human capital that are required as preconditions of reallocation. The mobility-impeding effects of age accordingly increase with the necessity to acquire new and additional qualifications, knowledge, and skills, or to be retrained for a new job. The effects of age may thus prevent the working of mechanisms of reallocation and leveling out of existing income differentials. For laborers in the higher age brackets, the problem of income disparity thus becomes a question more of social policy than of resource allocation.[28]

The impact of the availability of information in the labor market on the functioning and efficiency of reallocation mechanisms is our last point of discussion. Regularly a member of the labor force envisages a large number of potential employers and employment possibilities. The problem of obtaining sufficient information with regard to these alternatives consists of being able to estimate for a relevant period of time (e.g., a time horizon defined as a fixed pay-

[26]Analogous to this is the situation for women in the labor force, normally being economically active for shorter periods of time. Cf. also G. S. Becker, *Human Capital,* p. 51, and J. Mincer, "On-the-Job Training," pp. 67–69.

[27]Cf. J. Mincer, "On-the-Job Training," p. 54 and tables A5–A7, pp. 76–78.

[28]Welfare problems in this case might justify social policy interventions insofar as they attempt to redistribute losses from economic and technical progress, which are far less widespread than the benefits. For the same argument see Theodore W. Schultz, "A Policy to Redistribute Losses from Economic Progress," in *Labor Mobility and Population in Agriculture* (Ames: Iowa State College Press, 1961).

off period) and for all choices possible the prospective earnings developments.[29] Complete knowledge of all alternatives is prevented by the mere fact that additional information has a price and, therefore, in economic rationality, will not be acquired beyond the point of equalization of marginal costs and return.[30] Imperfect knowledge, however, will represent an additional element of wage dispersion. Because of existing wage differentials, the costs incurred for additional information in the labor market (exploration of employment offers by employees and of labor supply by employers) may effectuate returns on the improvement of knowledge accruing for more than one period—perhaps even for the whole period of the employment contract. Costs of information and returns on exploration and inquiries into the labor market—represented by higher wage offers to the employee or lower costs of labor-inputs to a firm—thus can also be treated in an investment-type model.[31]

Making an employment decision concerning the total possible return on improved knowledge *ceteris paribus* increases with the expected length of employment. Accordingly, the actual dispersion of wage rates diminishes as an effect of a more intensive investigation into the market. Given the amount of potential return from search, the economic limitations of improving knowledge depend on the costs of acquiring additional information. Costs may be a function of various factors determining the transparency of different labor markets but are also related to the general educational level of a specific group of employees. From the macro-economic point of view, returns accruing from better information in the labor market are represented in a more efficient allocation of manpower. This implies, however, that labor mobility, in permanently approximating actual marginal products of workers to maximum potential products, simultaneously realizes returns on additional information—a component that cannot be isolated, since it constitutes a complementary concomitant of human resource development.

---

[29] A more realistic view of labor mobility than our price-regulated model could provide, of course, must also take into account information on conditions of work, imponderabilities of a job, etc. Fringe benefits, stability of employment, and related variables, however, would be embraced by the earnings concept.

[30] See George J. Stigler, "The Economics of Information," *Journal of Political Economy*, Vol. 69 (June 1961).

[31] For an elaboration of this approach see George J. Stigler, "Information in the Labor Market," *Journal of Political Economy*, Vol. 70 (Supplement, October 1962).

III. SOME ASPECTS OF LABOR MOBILITY AND POTENTIALS FOR GROWTH

The discussion in our preceding paragraph has demonstrated how the pursuit of qualitative aspects in the labor force has given rise also to a new understanding of the problems of labor mobility. The development of human capital theory offers new or modified hypotheses and explanations for a variety of phenomena and enigmas concerning mobility that have been unsatisfactorily considered in economic theory. Of primary importance are the implications concerning the economic function of labor mobility as an equalization mechanism among labor markets. These new facets of the problem not only are of interest from the explicative-theoretical point of view but also have significant consequences for planning in economic, regional development, labor market, social, and educational policies.

Before we can legitimately draw such far-reaching conclusions from the tentative implications of our approach, it is necessary, however, to develop the hypotheses further and to test their implications by additional theoretical and broad empirical investigations. These studies must primarily attempt to abandon a treatment of labor mobility which is isolated from structural changes of the growing economy and from problems of interregional and international economic exchange. On the contrary, it is necessary to analyze mobility patterns in connection with total growth and regional economic development. On the one hand, manpower movements must be understood as being produced by economic and technical development; on the other hand, the contribution of mobility to (regional) growth achievement must be evaluated via changes in relative (regional) factor potential and factor productivity.

The first of these two approaches emerges from the analysis of historical processes of growth. Were it possible to present the production system of a growing economy by applying a dynamic interregional input-output model (thereby taking into consideration the qualitative differentiation of labor inputs), we could obtain a complete picture of the interrelations we are interested in. Regional, sectoral, and temporal structures of a production system undergoing growth would enable us further to develop a system of regional, sectoral, and qualification-specific (occupational) manpower accounts from which foreseeable and necessary manpower movements are determined. Irrespective of problems of data collection and processing, however, this all-embracing approach has a number of theoretical difficulties especially owing to the assumption of constant technical and regional input coefficients or, alternatively, in establishing reasonable assumptions concerning the changes of input coefficients in growth.[32]

Despite these problems, it does not follow that trustworthy estimates of future manpower shifts and mobility patterns could not be undertaken as a basis for policies for growth. At least for a less ambitious analysis of the problem, corresponding to the more limited scope of actual policy undertakings and concepts, the investigator is in an excellent position to make such estimates. Although his efforts are somewhat hampered by data limitations, the variety of instruments and the stock of experience of regional science, together with the results of theoretical and empirical research on growth problems, enable him to reasonably judge possible future manpower developments.

The second approach mentioned refers to the interrelationship between labor mobility, growth potentials of winning and losing regions (or nations), and the financing of investments in human capital.[33] Movements of manpower among regions or nations which imply a transfer of human capital, in their bearing on growth potentials of attracting and delivering economies, have been discussed mainly with regard to international movements of highly qualified manpower—the so-called "brain-drain."[34] However, the effects on the

---

[32] These difficulties, which cannot be further treated in our context, already arise for the still extensively discussed manpower-requirements approach to educational planning that was also widely used for practical purposes. See the outstanding example of the Mediterranean Regional Project (MRP) of OECD for six member countries. For a mathematical presentation of the simplest setting of the method see Hector Correa and Jan Tinbergen, "Quantitative Adaptation of Education to Accelerated Growth," *Kyklos*, Vol. 15 (1962); and Hector Correa, "The Economics of Human Resources," *Contributions to Economic Analysis*, Vol. 34 (Amsterdam: North Holland Publishing Co., 1963). Fundamental for MRP country-studies was the study by Herbert S. Parnes, Forecasting Educational Needs for Economic and Social Development (Paris: OECD, 1962). For an excellent critical evaluation of the approach see M. R. Hollister, *Technical Evaluation of the First Stage of the Mediterranean Regional Project*, OECD, DAS/MRP/65.6; see also U.S. Department of Labor, Bureau of Labor Statistics, *The Long-Range Demand for Scientific and Technical* Personnel, a Methodological Study, prepared for the National Science Foundation (NSF 61–65).

[33] This latter point also includes aspects of interregional and international public finance relations and development policies which so far seem to have been altogether neglected.

[34] Harry G. Johnson, "The Economics of the 'Brain Drain': The Canadian Case," *Minerva, a Review of Science Learning and Policy*, Vol. III (1965); H. G. Grubel and A. D. Scott, "The International Flow of Human Capital," *American Economic Review*, Vol. 56 (Papers and Proceedings, May 1966); H. G. Grubel and A. D. Scott, "The Immigration

expansion of a net gain or loss of scientists, engineers, etc., are difficult to identify and to evaluate, since presumably the human capital investments represented by this category of manpower in relatively high proportions produce external benefits which are widely distributed and almost unidentifiable.[35] The wide dispersion of external benefits — e.g., in the case of freely available results of fundamental research — on the other hand, may reduce the loss to the economy which is suffering out-migration. Such dispersion of benefits, within and outside a country with unusually superior or unique research facilities, may even create a profitable situation for the countries losing human capital investments by enabling immigrant scientists to produce outstanding results that would otherwise be unobtainable and which become available to other countries as well. However, if an economy experiences a continuing process of out-migration of highly qualified personnel, a cumulative erosion of its basic potential for scientific, technical, and economic progress must necessarily result which is difficult to stop or even reverse. The implications of the U.S.-European migration balance with respect to qualified manpower since the war — especially the "brain drain" in countries most affected by out-migration — still remain an open question, if only because of insufficient knowledge of the empirical side of the problem.

The distribution aspect, concerning the costs and returns which accrue regionally from investments in human capital, is but one facet of the regional transfer of human capital by migration. A second aspect comprises the effects on the allocation of resources to investment in human capital caused by regions experiencing out-migration. If one assumes that the allocation to human capital investments made by the region (e.g., local expenditures or state support for

---

of Scientists and Engineers to the United States, 1949–1961," *Journal of Political Economy*, Vol. 74 (August 1966); Friedrich Edding and H.-J. Bodenhöfer, "Communication on Movements of Intellectuals," Council of Europe, European Population Conference, Strasbourg, 1966, CDE (66)C 33.

[35] This implies that the economic value of the kind of human capital represented, e.g., by the training of a scientist, cannot be adequately determined by capitalizing expected future earnings. Unfortunately this problem also partly applies to other kinds of human capital, according to the existence and relative importance of externalties. Apart from the inadequacies of existing income date, this difficulty may have been a further reason for empirical evaluations of human capital investments to proceed, for the most part, according to the cost-of-production scheme of capital-value determination (the latter, of course, having serious limitations, too).

education in the national framework and national investment outlays in the international setting) depends on the returns expected to accrue internally (as the individual investment decisions are assumed to be determined by expected private returns), the existence of external benefits from investments made by a region will cause suboptimal allocation judged from marginal productivity rules.[36]

A comprehensive discussion of the role of labor mobility for regional growth developments must consider not only both these aspects of the transfer of human capital, but also questions of public finance relationships between school districts and states, problems of institutional structures in financing investments in human capital and in education policy, and finally possibilities to internalize investment returns or, alternatively, to compensate for external benefits. Many of these problems are discussed in the pioneering study of Weisbrod on the external benefits of education in publicly supported schools. This study also discusses the nonmonetary components of investment returns and external benefits. Most important, however, is the attempt to proceed from theoretical considerations to an empirical assessment of the major components of spill-overs in a case study for a certain school district.

IV. CONCLUSIONS

In the second part of this paper the analytical tools of human capital theory have been used to construct a simple model of labor mobility as a constituent part of human resource development. The view adopted is incomplete, however, as it neglects the complex nature of manpower problems—i.e., the sociological and psychological determinants of changing labor markets. Despite this deficiency the inferences to be drawn from the model for the functioning of labor mobility seem to be in accordance with common knowledge about mobility patterns with respect to age, education, etc. Especially important are the implications of the approach for the possible contribution of labor mobility to the equalization of regional income levels and the bearing of factor mobility on relative growth achievement of regions. Empirical data on the development of regional

[36] Even if the total migration balance operates in favor of the region under consideration, the argument will hold true, since effects emanating from other regions are not considered dependent on own investment decisions. Cf. also B. A. Weisbrod, *External Benefits of Public Education*, Ch. 9.

or state income differentials show poor effects, if any, of equalization mechanisms, and differentials of growth rates also seem rather to perpetuate than to diminish. Therefore more interest should be given to the determinants of labor mobility, i.e., the adaptive potential of the existing labor force, in the context of regional income differentials. Furthermore, as was concisely shown in section three of the paper, the effects on regional growth rates of transfers of manpower — representing increments of externally financed human capital for the attracting region — need to be fitted into the larger framework of factor potential and factor productivity developments in spatially defined units of an economy. As our preliminary results seem to suggest, the human capital approach to labor mobility deserves a more complete examination that profitably should combine theoretical analysis and empirical work.

PART VI Miscellaneous

Introduction

In the first contribution (Reading 29) to this part, Finis Welch suggests a new approach for interpreting labor-market discrimination. The essential feature of his analysis is that education is assumed to be an input in production which is distinct from physical labor.

Professor Welch's analysis is followed by an article (Reading 30) by Richard Goode. Dr. Goode argues that a reexamination of the tax treatment of educational expenditures is necessary. Since the income tax discriminates against persons who invest in themselves as compared to those who invest in physical assets, he asserts that human capital formation should be treated as conventional capital investment—that is, amortized over a period of years.

In the final contribution (Reading 31) to the volume, A. G. Holtmann applies the theory of human-capital investment to the phenomenon of migration to the suburbs. He concludes that migration to the suburbs reduces the human capital so vital to the renewal of cities.

29. Labor-Market Discrimination: An Interpretation of Income Differences in the Rural South*

FINIS WELCH

*Southern Methodist University and National
Bureau of Economic Research*

The first-order economic effects of discrimination are easily observed — Negroes simply receive less income than whites. For example, in the rural South, average Negro income is less than one-half average white income. Broadly speaking, all of this difference can be viewed as resulting from discrimination, but not current discrimination alone, since the cumulative effects of fewer opportunities are obviously important. Part of the difference in income is a consequence of the fact that Negroes own less property and have less education. Of course these differences in earning potential may have discriminatory origins. For example, Negroes may own less property because they have had lower income and consequently less saving — and they may have been discriminated against in acquiring property. In addition, they may have less education because of inferior quality of schooling and because of having anticipated discrimination against their education. In principle, all of these effects should be considered before the extent of current discrimination can be determined.

My approach to determine the economic effects of discrimination entails using a model of market discrimination which is based upon factor externalities; this type of discrimination, as I shall show, is generated by a class of inefficiencies which occurs when laborers are required to associate with members of other groups (races). Specifically, I shall concentrate upon differences in quality and quantity of schooling when education is assumed to be a distinct factor of production complementary to physical (unskilled) labor and capital.

*Reprinted from "Labor-Market Discrimination: An Interpretation of the Income Differences in the Rural South," *Journal of Political Economy*, LXXV (June, 1967), 225–40. Copyright by The University of Chicago Press.

Each person is assumed to be a composite factor of production, consisting of one unit of physical labor and a "bundle" of education. My plan is first to consider the theoretical issues and then proceed to an empirical analysis of white–non-white income differentials in ten southern states[1] for rural farm males who were twenty-five years old or over in 1959. The burden of the empirical analysis is to identify the parts of per capita income differentials which are attributable to (1) differences in the ownership of physical property, (2) differences in years of school completed, (3) inferior quality of schooling, and (4) market discrimination against physical labor and education. The most important result is that the market evidently discriminates much more heavily against a Negro's education than against his unskilled labor. Thus, relative to whites with similar schooling, Negro income declines as school completion increases. In addition, inferior-quality schooling is an important source of differential income.

Before formulating the model, I shall consider some of the often asserted origins of market discrimination. According to the definition used here, discrimination is assumed to exist whenever physically equivalent factors receive different wages. Since we are more concerned with discrimination as it affects earnings, I will consider only two types: discrimination against producers and against employees. Discrimination against consumers may affect the psychic evaluation of income as well as the manner in which income is distributed among its alternatives. But this type of discrimination is considered here only as it affects incentives to acquire education.

Discrimination against a producer may lower the price of his product and/or raise the price of his purchased inputs. Producer discrimination therefore refers to product and factor discrimination. For products, two important classes are distinguishable, the first being personalized services which, by definition, are associated with their producer, whereas the second refers to impersonal or standardized products. Presumably, impersonal products do not have unique characteristics which permit producers to be identified. Now, if consumers receive disutility from associating with members of a group which provides personalized services, they will discount the value of these services. If, on the other hand, the product is impersonal, any discount must be attributed to disutility occurring at the time the product is

[1] The states are: Alabama, Arkansas, Georgia, Louisiana, Mississippi, North Carolina, South Carolina, Tennessee, Texas, and Virginia.

purchased, for thereafter the producer of that product is irrelevant. In this case, an individual who receives little or no disutility from purchasing these products would have a comparative advantage as an intermediary.[2] The role of the intermediary would simply be that of absorbing the difference between the subjective discount rate of consumers (or potential intermediaries) and his own discount rate. Thus, to the extent that transaction disutility is an important consideration, we would expect to observe persons who derive relatively little disutility from this association to serve as intermediaries. Furthermore, if there is a relatively large supply of potential intermediaries who possess no disutility for association with persons of different race, price discrimination against impersonal products will not occur.

To test for product discrimination it is necessary to compare prices, but, for reasons that later become obvious, such comparisons should be restricted to impersonal products. Factor externalities may distort the comparison of personalized services.

Factor discrimination is the mirror image of product discrimination, and the analysis is equivalent. If there is discrimination in factor markets, those discriminated against pay higher prices for productive inputs; assuming profit maximization, we would expect these factors to have greater marginal products than if a lower price were charged. Again, if this sort of discrimination exists, an incentive for intermediation will also exist. To test for discrimination against impersonal factors, either prices or marginal productivities must be observed. In the following analysis, it will be assumed that no discrimination exists against products or factors other than labor. To the extent that these forms of discrimination are important, my empirical results will be biased.[3]

The most important distinction between employees and producers is that employees always provide personalized services, whereas producers may provide impersonal products. In the marketplace, a producer's race may not be discernible from his product; but, in the firm, an employee's race is obviously identified. In his pioneering book, *The Economics of Discrimination,* Gary Becker (1957) distinguishes

---

[2] I am indebted to H. G. Lewis for pointing to the possibility of intermediation.

[3] Here, I think that the burden of proof lies with the protagonists. For example, does the price of corn depend upon the race of its producer? If so, is the dependence causal? Prices may depend on information and information upon education. Since education is correlated with race, there may be spurious correlation between race and prices.

two types of market discrimination: (1) discrimination by employers and (2) discrimination by employees. If employers discriminate, they do so by discounting the value of services provided by Negroes. White employees presumably discriminate by discounting the value of wages they earn if these wages are earned in the presence of Negro employees. These effects are achieved operationally by the use of a discount factor which varies with a person's "taste for discrimination" but, according to Becker's assumption, does not vary with the degree of association between discriminators (whites) and discriminatees (Negroes). Becker's analysis indicates that production is segregated if Negroes and whites are substitutes and that it may be integrated if they are complements. If they are substitutes discrimination is unstable in the long run because firms employing Negroes are more efficient. By assumption, these firms purchase equivalent services at lower cost. There is reasonably good evidence indicating market discrimination against Negroes since the time of their emancipation. In view of the rather long history of discrimination, it seems to me that explanations which are stable only in the short run are unsatisfactory.

In the following section I present an operational specification of employee discrimination and consider some of the prerequisites for racially integrated production. One basic presumption is that education and physical labor can be considered as separate factors of production. An implication is that laborers with different "amounts" of education are complements rather than substitutes. Now, complementarity can be demonstrated when differences in education are the *only* features by which laborers are distinguished. If persons with unequal education are also members of different races or if they possess any characteristics that impose either real or psychic externalities on other laborers the mutual complementarity may be impaired. The proposition forwarded here is that in production racial integration does impose external inefficiencies. Thus, complementarity implies that the joint product of two laborers with unequal education is greater than the sum of their individual products. But, if the laborers are of different races, their joint product is assumed to be less than if they are of the same race. It is even possible that the external inefficiencies exceed the complementarities so that the joint product is less than the sum of the individual products; yet, if this were the case, we would not expect to observe integration. To the extent that laborers are income maximizers, we expect to observe integration only if there is "net" complementarity. The essence of the model is the interaction between external effects—the inefficiencies and the complementarities. An advantage of this interpretation is that although integration can lead to discrimination it may nevertheless result in increased wages to both Negroes and whites. Also, this interpretation does not imply, as does the Becker model, that monopoly rents accrue to those who hire only Negroes at a lower wage.

Consider a market composed of two groups of persons, N_1 and N_2, and assume that there is no discrimination in either product or non-labor markets. Production, Y^*, is a function of three inputs. The labor input is assumed to be separable into two components—N, physical labor (the original properties), and E, education (the acquired skill). Each laborer constitutes one unit of physical labor and a bundle of education. The quantity of education varies between persons. The third input, X, represents the class of non-labor inputs. The production process is described by

$$Y^* = f(N, E, X) \tag{1}$$

and is assumed to be homogeneous of the first degree. The price of output is assumed to be unity, and p_x, the price of X, is equated between N_1 and N_2 and is assumed to be constant.[4] The price of each factor is the value of its marginal product.

As is indicated in the Appendix, by imposing the constraint of equilibrium in the non-labor-input market, that is, $p_x = \partial Y^*/\partial X$, labor's product—the return to physical labor plus the return to education—can be written as a function of N and E only, in which p_x appears as a parameter. This function, represented by

$$Y = F(N, E), \tag{2}$$

is also homogeneous of degree 1, that is, it has constant returns to scale.

It should be observed that whatever the physical substitution relationship between N and E may be, by allowing for equilibrium in the non-labor-input market, the "net" effect is that physical labor and education cannot be substitutes, that is, $\partial^2 Y/\partial N \partial E \geq 0$. This result follows directly from the Euler equation for first-degree homogeneity.[5]

---

[4] The restriction of a unity price for output does not affect the degree of generality, but the assumed perfectly elastic supply function of non-labor inputs is slightly restrictive. For example, if the supply function were positively sloped, the function indicating value added by labor would possess diseconomies of scale.

[5] If the functional form $Y = \alpha N + \beta E$ is excluded, as in the remaining parts of this paper, then $\partial^2 Y/\partial N \partial E > 0$.

If it is assumed that units of physical labor in one individual substitute perfectly for units of physical labor in other individuals and similarly for education, then

N = the number of laborers employed, for each is assumed to possess one unit, and

$E = \Sigma_i r_i N_i$, where r_i is the number of units of education possessed by members of the ith labor group and N_i is the number of such laborers.

The wage of a laborer in the ith group will then be

$$W_i = \frac{dY}{dN_i} = \frac{\partial Y}{\partial N} + r_i \frac{\partial Y}{\partial E}. \tag{3}$$

That is, a laborer's wage will be the price of one unit of physical labor plus the unit price of education times the number of units of education the individual possesses. Thus without any form of discrimination, laborers' wages would vary only according to the quantities of education they "own."

If all firms have the same production function, then linear homogeneity implies that firm size and the number of firms are indeterminant, but marginal productivities (factor prices) are determined *as though* there were a single producer who equates marginal cost with product price. When considering a market in which labor is segregated, two firms will be considered, one consisting of N_1 laborers and the other of N_2. For an integrated market, only one firm is considered. Assume that r_1 and r_2 represent the per capita quantities of education of the respective groups. And persons who possess, respectively, r_1 and r_2 units of education are defined as being representative of their group, that is, their income will be the average income of their group.

Now, consider the average wage of each group when production is integrated and no external inefficiencies exist.

$$\overline{W}_1 = \frac{\partial Y}{\partial N} + r_1 \frac{\partial Y}{\partial E}$$

and

$$\overline{W}_2 = \frac{\partial Y}{\partial N} + r_2 \frac{\partial Y}{\partial E}.$$

Since Y is homogeneous of degree 1, it follows that

$$\frac{d\overline{W}_1}{dN_2} = \frac{d\overline{W}_2}{dN_1} \sim (r_1 - r_2)^2 \; \frac{\partial^2 Y}{\partial N \partial E}.$$

Thus, so long as $r_1 \neq r_2$, integration will increase the average wage of each group (recall that $\partial^2 Y / \partial N \partial E > 0$), and, therefore, the individuals in different groups are complementary. In fact, in this world of constant returns to scale, the addition of any given person to the labor force will not affect the wage of those persons having the same quantity of education and will raise the wage of all other laborers. It is this complementarity which, it seems to me, helps to contradict the segregation tendencies implicit in the Becker model. Of course, segregation can still result. Psychic income discounts may exceed gains, and/or external inefficiencies may accompany integration.

Let us now assume a form of discrimination in which laborers of group 1 become less efficient when they work in the presence of laborers of group 2 and, symmetrically, members of group 2 may become less efficient in the presence of members of group 1. This assumption of factor externality is basic to the remainder of the paper and should be explored. Presumably, the efficiency of integrated laborers could decline simply because they have disutility for integration, and, under integrated conditions, some of a laborer's time may be wasted because of his disgruntlement. However, this is undoubtedly an oversimplification. The incentive to integrate is derived from the assumption that laborers with unequal quantities of education are complementary in production. In turn, any resultant complementarity must be derived from an exchange between the laborers which results in specialization of function. (Perhaps, the more educated person assumes a supervisory role.) It is therefore possible that the full amount of the complementarities which would be derived from combining two laborers of the same group is not derived when the laborers of the two groups are integrated. An obvious example of this sort of "friction" occurs when the two groups of laborers speak different languages.

Another example would be a case in which intergroup association results in overspecialization of labor. Combining laborers of the two groups might result in a precise division of tasks such that if a given task were in the domain of group 1 it must always be performed by a member of that group even in circumstances in which a member of group 2 could perform the task with less resource cost. This case would be particularly likely if members of one of the groups considered themselves superior to the other group and consequently believed that certain tasks (perhaps menial) were "beneath" them. Of course, this condition may also exist when members of different trade

unions are associated because of the rigidly defined domain of activities for each trade.

In each of these examples, association has an implicit cost, so that
the increase in production from combining laborers of different
groups is less than it would be if the combination consisted only of
members of a particular group.[6] That is, the full advantages of the
complementarities are not realized with integration. Rather than re-
define the production function to allow for the reduction in complementarities, I have redefined the quantities of labor in terms of segregated equivalent efficiency units.

The impact of the induced inefficiency is expressed *as though* a
portion of a laborer's working time is lost when working under integration. Thus for a firm employing laborers of the two groups, the
apparent quantities of physical labor and education would exceed
their *effective* quantities because of efficiency losses, that is, $N = N_1 +
N_2 -$ type 1 loss and $E = E_1 + E_2 -$ type 2 loss. The losses are assumed
to be a function of association between laborers of the two groups.
However, the incentive to combine laborers must also derive from
association to gain the benefits of complementarity between physical
labor and education. An entrepreneur is therefore faced with a di-
lemma: association of the groups results in both advantages and disadvantages. Presumably, optimal association is determined such that
the marginal efficiency gains resulting from the complementarity between education and physical labor are offset by equal marginal losses
resulting from inefficiencies of association between the groups. For
simplicity, I will assume that the optimal association is achieved by
associating laborers of the two groups in a one-to-one correspondence.
That is, if a laborer of group 1 is hired by a firm in which laborers of
group 2 are preponderant, he will, at each point in time, be associated
with one laborer of group 2. When he is isolated, the complementari-

[6]J. K. Chadwick-Jones (1964) reports a case study in which the effects were similar
to those hypothesized here. Chadwick-Jones tells of the recruitment of unskilled
laborers in Italy who joined skilled British laborers in the steel industry. Since the laborers were to perform complementary functions, the British labor union supported the
recruitment policy. A discussion of the problems arising due to association between the
laborers is provided although there is no empirical support. "It was observed, not only
that the extent of verbal communication possible with the Italian recruits was, naturally,
very limited, but also that their culturally-derived attitudes and expectations were
inappropriate" (p. 194). Although we may question the use of the word "inappropriate," it is evident that the anticipated complementarity was not fully realized.

Miscellaneous

ties are assumed to be lost, and when he associates with more than one member of group 2, there may be additional losses without compensating gains. Assume also that when a member of group 1 associates with a member of group 2, proportion p_1 of the first laborer's effective time is lost and that the corresponding proportion for the second laborer is p_2. In this case the effective quantities of labor are given by

$$N = N_1 + N_2 - \min \{N_1, N_2\}(p_1 + p_2),$$

and

$$E = r_1 N_1 + r_2 N_2 - \min \{N_1 N_2\}(r_1 p_1 + r_2 p_2).$$

The forms of the type 1 and type 2 losses are important since they determine how the cost of the inefficiency is to be distributed between the groups. In general, the form is simply the product of two quantities: (1) the number of associating units and (2) the effective input loss for each associating unit. Let us assume that optimal intergroup association occurs when an associating unit consists of K members of group 1 for each member of group 2. Now the number of associating units is given as $K^{-1} \min \{N_1, KN_2\}$. For physical labor, the loss accompanying each unit is $Kp_1 + p_2$ and for education is $Kr_1 p_1 + r_2 p_2$. If, as I assume, K is independent of the respective numbers of persons in each group, then $\min \{N_1, KN_2\}$ defines an economic minority and majority in a very special sense. As in this paper, let $K = 1$ so that the concepts of the economic majority and minority are consistent with their numerical definitions. Thus, members of the minority group must absorb the full effects of the decline in labor efficiency because the addition of a minority laborer will reduce his effective working time and that of one laborer in the majority group with whom he is associated, whereas the addition of a majority laborer will not increase the amount of association between the groups. In this case a laborer's wage is given by

$$W_i = \frac{dY}{dN_i} = \frac{\partial Y}{\partial N} \cdot \frac{\partial N}{\partial N_i} + \frac{\partial Y}{\partial E} \cdot \frac{\partial E}{\partial N_i}; \tag{4}$$

assuming that N_1 represents the minority group

$$W_1 = (1 - f_1)\frac{\partial Y}{\partial N} + (1 - f_2)r_1 \frac{\partial Y}{\partial E},$$

where the discrimination coefficients f_1 and f_2, are defined as:

548

$$f_1 = p_1 + p_2 \,,$$

$$f_2 = p_1 + p_2 \frac{r_2}{r_1} \,,$$

and

$$W_2 = \frac{\partial Y}{\partial N} + r_2 \frac{\partial Y}{\partial E} \,.$$

W_1 and W_2 indicate the *average* wage of persons in groups 1 and 2, respectively. Thus, to the extent that the above interpretation is descriptive of reality, we would expect discrimination against members of the economic minority. Furthermore, if the majority possessed greater per capita education, we would expect discrimination against education to exceed discrimination against physical labor.

If a laborer derives disutility from associating with persons of other groups, a necessary condition for him to integrate is that doing so increases his wage. Although this condition is necessary, it is not sufficient, since, as in Becker's example of employee discrimination, laborers discount the value of wages earned under integration. For his model, the increase in wages would have to be sufficient to compensate laborers for the psychic costs of integrating.

It is important that the analysis has considered only average wages. Thus, to the extent that there is variation in the quantities of education possessed by laborers in a given group, the implications can be misleading. For example, a highly educated laborer in the economic minority could not increase his wage by integrating since he could select members of his own group such that the ratio of education to physical labor would be the same in either segregated or integrated production. The incentive to integrate is derived solely from the possibility of obtaining factor combinations different from those which exist under segregation. Notice that as the concept is defined here, the incentive to integrate is proportionate to the group differences in per capita education, $(r_1 - r_2)^2$. Thus, if over time, educational differences disappear, the incentive to integrate also disappears. Of course, this result is highly speculative. The inefficiency parameters, p_1 and p_2, are assumed to be constants in this model. Yet they are obviously affected by social and psychological factors, of which one is almost certainly the per capita difference in education. If, through time, the gains from integration diminish because of convergence of educational levels, the costs of integration may decline for the same reason.

A COMPARISON OF WHITE-NON-WHITE INCOME DIFFERENTIALS FOR RURAL FARM MALES IN THE SOUTH AS OF 1959

The empirical implications of the preceding model are straightforward.

1. The quantities of effective labor inputs (physical labor and education) are determined by weighting labor services proportionately to their marginal products (wages).

2. For the group against which there is discrimination, the discrimination coefficient is defined as the proportionate difference in marginal products of seemingly equivalent factors. Thus, the discrimination coefficient against physical labor is $p_1 + p_2$ (as earlier defined), and the discrimination coefficient against education is $p_1 + p_2(r_2/r_1)$.

In this section, I compare incomes of white and non-white rural farm males, twenty-five years old or over, in ten southern states as of 1959. Three distinct types of discrimination are considered: (1) market discrimination in the context of the above model, (2) historic or derived discrimination, and (3) discrimination in publicly provided services. Although there may be several important forms of discrimination in public services, the only one considered here is differential quality of schooling. Thus, I attempt to measure the effects of "separate and unequal" school systems. The quantity of education a person possesses is defined as the product of the quantity and quality of schooling. Quality of schooling is defined as being a function of the inputs into school systems, and the quantity of schooling is a non-linear function of the number of years of school completed.

Market discrimination is a measure of differences in the wages of equivalent factors. Since, for example, Negroes have less education, earnings should be adjusted for differences in education before estimating the extent of *current* discrimination. However, the differences in education may have been generated by *past* market discrimination and by discrimination in the quality of schooling and should be included in a measure of the total. As long as the magnitudes are observable, current and historic discrimination can be separately identified. However, the incidence of past discrimination can take more subtle forms in which the separation of effects is impossible. For example, earlier discrimination against the products and services purchased by non-whites may have generated differences in tastes for market as opposed to non-market sources of income.[7] We can

---

[7] This would be expected if there is discrimination against purchased goods since there can be no discrimination against leisure.

observe only the earning capacity of incremental schooling, without an adjustment for non-pecuniary reward, and would therefore expect the measured productivity of schooling to be lower for persons who place relatively high value on sources of satisfaction that are external to the market.

It is also important to note that the quantity of schooling a person possesses is affected by his *effective learning time,* for which years of attendance may be a rather poor approximation. The number of days in attendance may vary, and it is obvious that time passed in school is not necessarily productive. Idleness is a student's prerogative. During any given period a person can choose between school attendance, work, and leisure. Presumably, he will be idle as long as the marginal value of leisure exceeds the marginal value of present or future income foregone. For a student, the higher the reward for increased effort, the greater will be the effort forthcoming.[8] Thus, market discrimination against the services provided by the education of non-whites can affect their behavior as students. For example, non-white students who anticipate discrimination against their education might be absent a higher proportion of the time, and, while in school, a higher proportion of their time may be devoted to leisure activities. Hence, the effort expended in learning may be less because of the lower value of schooling. This is an instance of derived discrimination in which income differentials would reflect the compounded effects of market discrimination and the *rational* response to this discrimination. Since derived discrimination is observed simultaneously with market discrimination, a problem of identification arises. Of course, the effects of derived discrimination are partially observed since non-whites characteristically attend school for fewer years and for fewer days each year. Nevertheless, the incidence of leisure while attending school is indistinguishable from current discrimination. Thus the estimates of market discrimination against the education of non-whites provided here are biased upward.

For the base population, the average income of the whites is $2,690 and for non-whites $1,045, the ratio being .39. Although a slightly higher proportion of non-whites had no income, an adjustment for those without income increases the relative income of non-whites by less than .01.[9]

In order to adjust income for differences in age and the ownership

[8] Here I assume a positively sloped supply function of labor.
[9] The average income of whites with income was $2,865 and $1,130 for non-whites.

of farm capital, I have estimated an income-generating function for the rural farm population in which the logarithm of income was regressed upon (1) state of residence, (2) years of school completed, (3) age, and (4) farm capital.[10] Table 1 provides estimates of average

TABLE 1

Estimated Average Income for Rural Farm Males by Years of School Completed

	Years of School Completed							
	0	1–4	5–7	8	9–11	12	13–15	16 or more
Whites	$1,320	$1,590	$2,090	$2,340	$3,060	$3,790	$4,700	$6,400
Non-Whites	1,070	1,140	1,300	1,480	1,570	1,840	1,920	3,260

income by years of school completed for whites and non-whites in the ten states, holding the age distribution and the ownership of farm capital constant at their national average levels. Having adjusted for age and farm capital, the relative income ratio of non-whites rises to .48 – an increase of .09. The most striking feature demonstrated in Table 1 is that the increase in income, in both relative and absolute terms, per year of school completed is greater for whites than for non-whites. For example, if the distribution of schooling among the non-white population were the same as the white distribution, the relative income of non-whites would increase to only .56. That an additional year of school is less valuable for a non-white may be interpreted as follows. First, quality of schooling may have been an important source of discrimination. Second, the market may discriminate more heavily against the productive services provided by the education of non-whites than against the physical labor of non-whites. Third, the non-white may not work as hard while in school so that equivalent quality of services offered by the school systems may not provide equivalent education. This is the effect of derived discrimination and cannot be fully identified.

To distinguish between the effects of inferior quality of schooling and market discrimination, it is necessary to specify the income-generating process for rural farm areas and to measure the quantities of productive factors used to generate income.

Let W_{ij} represent the predicted income of a representative indi-

[10]The estimates and the estimation procedure are discussed in detail in my dissertation (Welch, 1966a).

vidual in state $-j$ who has completed i years of school, holding age and the ownership of farm capital constant at their national average levels. An individual's wage is the sum of the marginal product of physical labor, of which he has one unit, and the marginal product of education times the number of units of education he possesses. Assume that the marginal products of physical labor and education are constant *within* states but vary *between* states. Then,

$$W_{ij} = MP(N)_j + e_{ij}MP(E)_j,$$

where $MP(N)_j$ and $MP(E)_j$ denote the marginal products of physical labor and education, respectively, in state $-j$, and e_{ij} represents the quantity of education possessed by a representative individual in state $-j$ who has attended school for i years. Assume, further, that a person who has not attended school has no education so that his wage is the marginal product of physical labor. Thus, the knowledge and skill normally associated with a person who has no formal education is embodied in the physical component of labor. It follows that $W_{ij} - W_{0j} = e_{ij}MP(E)_j$.

Now consider the definition of a person's education as being the quantity times the quality of his schooling. The quality of schooling, Q_j, is assumed constant within states, and the quantity of schooling is determined by the number of school years completed. Let $\beta_i = g(S_i)$ represent the quantity of schooling possessed by a typical individual who has attended school for i years. Under these assumptions, $W_{ij} - W_{0j} = \beta_i Q_j MP(E)_j = \beta_i C_j$, where $C_j = Q_j MP(E)_j$ is the marginal product of schooling in state $-j$. The values of the β's and the C's can be estimated by covariance techniques where the logarithm of the annual return to schooling, $W_{ij} - W_{0j}$, is regressed upon two sets of dummy variables, one denoting years of school completed, i, and the other state of residence, j. The resulting estimate for the profile of time-in-school attendance into schooling and the *average* marginal product of schooling for southern whites and non-whites are provided in Table 2. Since the units in which schooling is measured are arbitrary, the estimate is scaled so that one unit of schooling represents eight years of attendance. The marginal product of schooling, therefore, corresponds to an estimate of the annual increment in income derived from eight years in attendance.

Thus, from Table 1, the discrimination coefficient against non-white physical labor is .19 (1 minus the ratio of the income of non-whites without schooling to whites without schooling). From Table 2,

TABLE 2

Schooling-Attendance Time Profile and (Average) Marginal Product
of Schooling for Southern Whites and Non-Whites

	Years of School Completed							
	0	1–4	5–7	8	9–11	12	13–15	16 or more
Units of schooling ($\beta_0 = 0$ and $\beta_8 = 1$)	0	0.25	0.65	1.00	1.63	2.26	2.64	4.24

Average Return to One Unit of School (Eight Years)	
White: $1,160	Non-White: $320

Note: These estimates were derived from observations of fifty-seven "states" for the eight schooling classes in each state. The states were ten southern white and ten southern non-white plus thirty-seven states in which no separation by color was possible. Alaska, Hawaii, and Rhode Island were omitted. The dependent variable for the regression was log $(W_{ij} - W_{0j})$, and the independent variables were (1) a set of seven dummy variables to indicate years of school completed, the zero attendance class being omitted, and (2) a set of fifty-seven dummy variables to indicate state of residence. $R^2 = .89$.

the discrimination coefficient against non-white schooling is .72. Although the discrimination coefficient against schooling is the composite effect of inferior quality of schooling and market discrimination, it is important to recognize that *a non-white with no schooling will receive 81 percent of the income of a similar white. Yet, for non-whites, school attendance increases income at a rate which is only 28 percent of the corresponding increase for whites.* Thus, school attendance is simply a better investment for whites. In short, the opportunity cost of school attendance, relative to income gains from attendance, is much higher for non-whites.

Although discrimination against schooling is the relevant parameter to consider for analyzing investments in school attendance by non-whites, it is useful to separate this factor into two components: differential quality of schooling and current market discrimination.

Value added by the rural farm population is assumed to be a Cobb-Douglas linear-in-the-logarithms function of three inputs: (1) N, physical labor, (2) E, education, and (3) K, an aggregation of non-labor inputs. By assumption this function is homogeneous of degree 1. The quantity of physical labor is given by the number of persons employed, since each represents one unit, and the quantity of education is the quantity times the quality of schooling, where the quantity of schooling is the summation over the eight schooling classes of the number of persons in each class multiplied by the estimated units of schooling for persons in that class. Units of schooling per person are given by schooling class in Table 2. The quantity of non-labor inputs represents an aggregation (by weights proportional to factor shares) of non-labor inputs used in agriculture, adjusted for the proportion of persons in the rural farm population whose industry is not agriculture.[11] Finally, the quality of schooling is assumed to be a Cobb-Douglas function of inputs into school systems.[12] Observations are for individual states.

In order to estimate the importance of the factors determining the marginal value of schooling, it is necessary to observe school-system inputs which determine the quality of schooling. Since the Supreme Court decision regarding segregated schools in 1954, separate data for white and Negro schools have been unavailable. The last complete enumeration of Negro school-system inputs is for 1945 (U.S. Office of Education, 1950) and is for state aggregates, combining rural and urban school systems. Data for rural school systems are, however, provided only for 1955 (U.S. Office of Education, 1959). By computing input ratios for non-whites in 1945, the 1955 inputs were prorated between whites and non-whites according to the proportions of Negro students enrolled.[13] Estimates of the more important white and non-white school-system inputs are summarized in Table 3.

The determination of factors affecting the quality of schooling is complex; for example, rural schools are faced with special problems because of low population density and the lack of centralized control,

---

[11] The factor-share weights and the definition of non-labor inputs are given by Yoav Kislev (1965).

[12] Thus, according to these assumptions: $C_j = Q_j MP(E)_j = Q_j^{\alpha_2} AN^{\alpha_1}(S)^{\alpha_2-1}K^{\alpha_3}$, $Q_j = BZ_1^{\gamma_1} \ldots Z_n^{\gamma_n}$, and $\alpha_1 + \alpha_2 + \alpha_3 = 1$. (The Z's refer to school system inputs, and S is the quantity of schooling.)

The quantities N and $S = \Sigma\beta_1N_1$ refer to the effective quantities of physical labor and schooling. Non-whites should be weighted by their relative marginal products in determining the effective labor inputs. The basic unit of observation is the state, and for the ten southern states considered here the effective input of physical labor is given by $N_j = N_{wj} + (W_{n0j}/W_{w0j}) N_{nj}$, where the subscript, j, refers to the state and the subscripts n and w denote, respectively, non-whites and whites. Accordingly, the quantity of education is given as $E_j = Q_{wj}(\Sigma\beta_iN_{wi})_j + pQ_{nj}(\Sigma\beta_iN_{ni})_j$, where $p = 1 - [p_1 + p_2(r_2/r_1)]$ is the relative marginal product of non-white education. Omitting the state subscript, j, $C_n/C_w = pQ_n/Q_w$. $E = Q_w[\Sigma\beta_iN_{wi} + (C_n/C_w)\Sigma\beta_iN_{ni}] = pQ_n[(C_w/C_n)\Sigma\beta_iN_{wi} + \Sigma\beta_iN_{ni}]$. Thus $C_n = (pQ_n)^{\alpha_2}AN^{\alpha_1}S_n^{\alpha_2-1}K^{\alpha_3}$ and $C_w = Q_w^{\alpha_2}AN^{\alpha_1}S_w^{\alpha_2-1}K^{\alpha_3}$, where $E = Q_wS_w + pQ_nS_n$, as above, define the effective quantities of white and non-white schooling, S_w and S_n.

[13] The exact procedure used is described in my dissertation (Welch, 1966a).

Miscellaneous

TABLE 3

Average Rural School-System Inputs for Southern
Whites and Non-Whites, 1955–1956

	Total Current Expenditures per Pupil*	Members of Instructional Staff per 100 Pupils*	Average Salary per Member of Instructional Staff	Average Number of Pupils Enrolled per Secondary School
White	$230	4.6	$3,330	230
Non-white	120	4.0	2,310	175

*Per pupil in average daily attendance.

and as a consequence there are apparent scale economies in school size which are probably related to the lack of teacher specialization implicit in small rural schools.[14] I find that two variables, teacher quality—approximated by salary—and size of secondary school, provide as much information as is available concerning quality of schooling. And by using these variables as the quality index, the function determining the value of the marginal product of schooling can be estimated.[15]

The estimates appearing in Table 4 when combined with the average teacher salary and size of secondary school (Table 3) imply that the quality of non-white schooling is inferior to that of whites and that, for equivalent years of school completed, we would expect a non-white to obtain only 73 percent as much *education* as a white. This difference in the quality of schooling is directly attributable to the smaller quantity of inputs offered by the non-white school systems. The estimates also indicate that equivalent education returns only 32 percent as much to a non-white as a white: $a_2\log(p) = -.434$; $\hat{p} =$ antilog $(-.434/.385)$. Thus, the first-order estimate of the market-discrimination coefficient against education is .68, $1 - .32$.[16]

[14]These problems are discussed more fully in my "Measurement of the Quality of Schooling" (Welch, 1966b).

[15]The estimation procedure is least-squares regression upon the logarithms of the variables.

[16]These estimates are marginally inconsistent with the earlier estimate of the discrimination coefficient against schooling, .72. They imply a discrimination coefficient of .76. However, it is likely that the unidentified effects of historic discrimination may have led to an overestimation of the incidence of market discrimination against education. For example, if these estimates are taken literally, they can be used to estimate

The above estimates can be considered as (1) an overestimate of discrimination against education and (2) an underestimate of discriminatory quality of schooling. These biases arise largely because I have not explicitly considered the effects of historic discrimination.[17] For example, average annual days of attendance can be observed, yet for statistical purposes[18] this variable was not included, and the effect of differences in days of attendance is included in the estimated discrimination coefficient for education. In 1945, southern white students who were enrolled in school averaged 149 days in attendance, whereas Negro students averaged 136 days (U.S. Office of Education, 1950). If we assume that the skill acquired per day of attendance is constant, differences in attendance rates imply that Negroes acquire only 91 percent as much schooling per year of enrolment, and, allowing for differences in the quality of the services offered by school systems (relative quality for Negro schools is estimated as .73), the relative quantity of education per year of school enrolment is only .66 for Negroes. This alteration requires an adjustment in the estimated discrimination coefficient for education which reduces it from .68 to .58.[19]

---

p_1 and p_2, the proportionate decline in labor efficiency, respectively, for non-whites and whites. The estimates, together with the distribution of whites and non-whites by years of school completed, imply that the average white person has 2.9 times as much education as the average non-white. If we assume $p_1 + p_2 = .19$ and $p_1 + p_2(r_2/r_1) = .68$, this implies that by associating one white with one non-white the non-white's effort increases by 7 percent and the white's declines by 26 percent. But, when the discrimination coefficients are adjusted for differences in school attendance rates, the estimate of p_1 becomes 0 and of p_2, .20.

[17] There are also statistical reasons for anticipating these biases. The school systems' inputs are observed subject to rather large errors of estimation which bias the quality coefficients downward and understate differences in quality of schooling. Also, the residual variance of the logarithmic estimating equation is likely to be greater for non-whites than for whites, implying that by taking the antilog of the average predicted log, the relative understatement of average values is greater for non-whites than whites.

[18] There is apparently no systematic *within* race relationship between days of attendance and the value of schooling. The only significant variation occurs between whites and non-whites. Thus annual days in attendance is highly collinear with the white-non-white dummy variable which identifies the market discrimination coefficient for education. The separate effects of these variables could not be observed, and the estimated discrimination coefficient for education contains the effects of differences in attendance rates.

[19] This adjustment alters the implicit estimates of p_1 and p_2 (see n. 16) to $p_1 = 0$; $p_2 = .2$.

TABLE 4

Estimated Coefficients of Variables Determining the Value of the Marginal Product of Schooling*

	Non-White	Quantity of Schooling $\Sigma\beta_i N_i$	Variable Quantity of Physical Labor, N	Non-Labor Inputs, K	Average Salary of Instructional Staff, Z_1	Enrolment per Secondary School, Z_2
Coefficient	$\alpha_2 \log(j)$	$\alpha_2 - 1$	α_1	α_3	$\alpha_2\gamma_1$	$\alpha_2\gamma_2$
Estimate	−.434	−.615	.374	.241	.268	.087
S. E.†	(.326)	(.276)	(.228)	(.126)	(.188)	(.069)

*The dependent variable is the estimated marginal product of one unit of schooling derived from the regressions summarized in Table 2. The observations were for forty-five "states," ten southern white and ten southern non-white states plus twenty-five other states. Of the fifty-seven "states" described in Table 2, twelve were omitted due to insufficient school-systems data.
†Standard errors are given in parentheses.
$R^2 = .914$.

My approach to the explanation of market discrimination entails using a model in which the integration of laborers generates external effects which move in opposite directions. First, integration increases the productivity of laborers as a consequence of complementarity between workers of different education. Second, it generates a class of external inefficiencies in which the productivity of a laborer may decline if he is required to work alongside a laborer of a different race. The advantage of this interpretation is that it does not rely upon the imperfections in capital markets and product differentiation by consumers or upon an assumption of specialized factors such as "entrepreneurship." It is not that these considerations are irrelevant; rather, it is suggested that labor externalities should also be considered in a complete specification of discrimination. Discrimination and segregation should be distinguished, since, as the analysis indicates, discrimination does not necessarily result in segregation. Other advantages are that the model provides for measurement of the direct social cost of discrimination in terms of product foregone and that the model is operational since it provides an aggregation criterion for combining labor inputs for persons of different races. The most critical features are: (1) the assumed constancy of the inefficiency parameters, p_1 and p_2, and (2) the assumption that the optimal ratio for association between workers of different groups is constant. More generality would be beneficial. In particular, if the inefficiency parameters are allowed to vary so that they can be estimated for a wide array of market settings, the determinants of their variation can be analyzed to provide a better understanding of the underlying sources, social, psychological, and economic, of market discrimination.

To illustrate the essential characteristics of the model, I have provided estimates for males in the rural South. These estimates are best summarized by considering the impact on earnings of both inferior quality of schooling and market discrimination for persons who have completed five to seven and eight years of school since these schooling classes are representative of rural areas. One feature of the findings which is of particular importance is that as a non-white increases his investment in schooling, the impact of inferior quality of schooling and market discrimination against education increases. To elucidate this point I have also included the estimates corresponding to twelve years of school completed. These results appear in Table 5.

559

TABLE 5

Estimated Impact on Non-White Income of Market Discrimination
and Inferior Quality of Schooling

	Years of Schooling Completed		
	5–7	8	12
Income:			
White	$2,090	$2,340	$3,790
Non-white	1,300	1,480	1,840
Difference	790	860	1,950
1. Impact of market discrimination against physical labor	250	250	250
2. Impact of discrimination against schooling*	540	610	1,700
a) Inferior quality of schooling	200	230	630
b) Market discrimination against education	340	380	1,070

*The adjustment for interaction between quality of schooling and market discrimination against education is prorated according to the proportion of the total (difference in the return to schooling) accounted for by each. Actually, interaction represents 14 percent of the total discrimination against schooling.

The policy and social implications of these findings raise difficult, unsettled questions. Discrimination against schooling obviously discourages its acquisition for non-whites. Furthermore, the estimates of differences in quality of schooling, although substantial, account for only 37 percent of the discrimination against schooling—implying that market discrimination against education is a more important source of income differentials. It would seem that discriminatory quality of schooling is more easily eliminated than market discrimination, because legislative authorities have relatively little control over such markets. In fact, to the extent that market discrimination is determined largely by sociological phenomena, we cannot expect these factors to be eliminated either quickly or easily. Nevertheless, the elimination of discrimination in quality of schooling may be an inportant vehicle for removing income differences; for an improvement in the quality of schooling will: (1) reduce the observed discrimination against schooling, (2) induce an increased investment in schooling, and (3) induce greater effort while in school, which will increase the quantity of education per unit of attendance time. In addition, the reduction of differences in education may reduce associational friction, which then reduces discrimination.

Given that $Y^* = f(N, E, X)$ is homogeneous of the first degree, according to Euler's theorem,

$$Y^* = NF_n + EF_e + XF_x. \tag{1}$$

Also

$$F_x = g\left(\frac{N}{X}, \frac{E}{X}\right). \tag{2}$$

By imposing,

$$P_x = F_x,$$

we have

$$X = h(N, E, \mid P_x), \tag{3}$$

which is also homogeneous of degree 1 in N and E. Let labor's product be represented by

$$Y = Y^* - P_x X = Y^* - P_x h(N, E \mid P_x). \tag{4}$$

Thus it is obvious that Y is a function of N and E, given P_x, and it is also homogeneous of the first degree. If N and E are varied equiproportionately, X, according to (3), must vary by the same proportion. Thus, total product will vary equiproportionately with N and E, but since X does also and its marginal product is given, the return to X, $P_x X$, will vary by the same proportion, and labor's product will vary equiproportionately with N and E.

REFERENCES

Becker, Gary S. *The Economics of Discrimination.* Chicago: Univ. of Chicago Press, 1957.

Chadwick-Jones, J. K. "Italian Workers in a British Factory: A Study of Informal Selection and Training," *Race, J. Institute Race Relations* (July, 1964).

Kislev, Yoav. "Estimating a Production Function from 1959 to U.S. Census of Agriculture Data." Unpublished Ph.D. dissertation, Dept. of Econ., Univ. of Chicago, 1965.

U.S. Office of Education. *Biennial Survey of Education, 1944–46.* Washington: U.S. Government Printing Office, 1950.

561

Miscellaneous

———. *Biennial Survey of Education, 1954–56.* Washington: U.S. Government Printing Office, 1959.

Welch, F. "Determinants of the Return to Schooling in Rural Farm Areas, 1959." Unpublished Ph.D. dissertation, Dept. of Econ., Univ. of Chicago 1966 (*a*).

———. "Measurement of the Quality of Schooling," *A.E.R.,* LVI, No. 2 (May, 1966), 379–92. (*b*)

30. Educational Expenditures and the Income Tax*

RICHARD GOODE

Brookings Institution

A tax on net income should provide for tax-free recovery of the expenditures entailed in earning income, including investment outlays. Although this principle is generally applied in the Federal income tax, it is not applied consistently with respect to the costs of acquiring an income through personal services. Among these costs are educational expenditures that increase earning capacity or that are made for that purpose. In computing taxable income, no allowance is made for the costs of general education or of basic professional or vocational education, and only limited deductions are allowed for other educational expenses.

The present tax treatment of educational costs gives rise to inequities and is especially questionable at a time when the need for highly trained persons is growing. The income tax discriminates against persons whose earned income represents in part return of capital previously invested in education compared with persons who have invested little in preparation for their occupations. There is also discrimination against persons who invest in themselves compared with those who invest in physical assets. For example, a person who attends engineering school is usually not allowed to deduct his educational expenditures from his earnings, whereas a taxpayer who buys a truck can recover the cost through depreciation allowances. A physician who takes graduate courses to qualify himself for a new specialty cannot write off the cost against taxable income, though he can amortize outlays for office equipment, laboratory facilities, or waiting room furniture. When income tax rates are high, discrimination against investment in education may discourage entry into occupations re-

*Reprinted from "Educational Expenditures and the Income Tax," *Economics of Higher Education*, ed. Selma J. Mushkin (Washington: Department of Health, Education, and Welfare, 1962), 281–304.

quiring expensive training, and may discourage persons already at work from preparing themselves for more skilled and responsible jobs.[1]

Two factors greatly mitigate the discrimination against education. First, tuition and fees are not charged in public elementary and secondary schools; and in colleges and universities the charges are usually much lower than the costs of instruction, with the difference being made up by State and local government funds, gifts, and endowment income. Secondly, a large part of students' investment in education consists of opportunity costs in the form of foregone earnings. These costs are already free of income tax.

Many proposals have been advanced in recent years for deductions or credits under the income tax law for certain educational expenditures. Most of these proposals are intended to grant tax relief to parents of college students. There has been little systematic discussion of broad questions of tax policy respecting educational expenses or technical problems that would be involved in development of new income tax provisions relating to education.

This paper reviews the present treatment of educational expenditures under the Federal income tax and considers the possibility of permitting certain educational expenditures to be charged against taxable income through current deductions or amortization allowances.[2] Attention is given to the technical difficulties of devising a feasible plan for this purpose and to the probable effects of such a plan on Government revenues, on enrollments and tuition charges, on the amount of educational expenditures, and on occupational choice. Proposals for deductions or tax credits allowed to parents of college students are briefly compared with the more general approach to the problem.

I. PRESENT TREATMENT OF EDUCATIONAL EXPENDITURES

The Federal income tax makes no provision for current or future deductions for expenditures incurred for education or training

---

[1] Richard Goode. The Income Tax and the Supply of Labor. *Journal of Political Economy*, 57: 428–37, October 1949. Reprinted in American Economic Association, *Readings in the Economics of Taxation*, Richard A. Musgrave and Carl S. Shoup, eds., Homewood, Ill., Richard D. Irwin, 1959. p. 456–69.

[2] "Amortization" is a procedure by which the cost of an asset is charged against income over a period of time through annual allowances or charges. The word is often used as a synonym of "depreciation," but is more commonly applied to intangibles than to tangible property.

undertaken to prepare oneself for a vocation or profession or to meet the minimum qualifications for any employment. Deductions are allowed for expenditures for certain kinds of supplementary, continuation, or refresher courses. Official regulations adopted in 1958 provide that—

Expenditures made by a taxpayer for his education are deductible if they are for education (including research activities) undertaken primarily for the purpose of:
(1) Maintaining or improving skills required by the taxpayer in his employment or other trade or business, or
(2) Meeting the express requirements of a taxpayer's employer, or the requirements of applicable law or regulations, imposed as a condition to the retention by the taxpayer of his salary, status, or employment.[3]

The regulations state that deductions will ordinarily be allowed for the cost of education for the purpose of maintaining or improving skills "if it is customary for other established members of the taxpayer's trade or business to undertake such education." Deductions for required education are restricted to expenditures "for the minimum education required by the taxpayer's employer, or by applicable law or regulations, as a condition to the retention of the taxpayer's salary, status, or employment."

On the other hand, the regulations provide:

Expenditures made by a taxpayer for his education are not deductible if they are for education undertaken primarily for the purpose of obtaining a new position or substantial advancement in position, or primarily for the purpose of fulfilling the general educational aspirations or other personal purposes of the taxpayer. The fact that the education undertaken meets express requirements for the new position or substantial advancement in position will be an important factor indicating that the education is undertaken primarily for the purpose of obtaining such position or advancement, unless such education is required as a condition to the retention by the taxpayer of his present employment. In any event, if education is required of the taxpayer in order to meet the minimum requirements for qualification or establishment in his intended trade or business or specialty therein, the expense of such education is personal in nature and therefore is not deductible.[4]

Illustrating the meaning of these rules, the authors of the regula-

---

[3] Regulations, 1.162-5 (T.D. 6201, *Internal Revenue Bulletin,* Cumulative Bulletin, 1958–1, p. 67).
[4] *Ibid.*

tions mention the case of A, who is employed by an accounting firm and who takes courses to enable him to qualify as a certified public accountant. Expenditures for these courses are not deductible, as they were made before A became qualified as a CPA. B, a general practitioner of medicine, takes graduate courses in order to become a specialist in pediatrics and is allowed no deductions for his expenses. C, a less ambitious general practitioner, takes "a 2-week course reviewing developments in several specialized fields, including pediatrics, for the purpose of carrying on his general practice" and is entitled to deductions for his expenses. D is a schoolteacher who is required by his employer or by law "either to read a list of books or to take certain courses" in order to hold his job. After completing the prescribed courses, he receives a master's degree and is given an automatic salary increase. D can deduct his educational expenses. G, a graduate student at a university, aspires to become a professor and must obtain an advanced degree to do so. While working toward the degree, G is a part-time teacher at the university. His educational expenses are not deductible since he has not completed the education required to become qualified as a regular faculty member.

In attempting to limit deductions to educational expenditures that are clearly related to the taxpayer's income from his current employment, the authors of the regulations have excluded educational outlays that contribute to future earning capacity and which for this reason have great economic significance for the individual and for society. If a similar attitude were taken toward physical capital, deductions from taxable income presumably would be allowed for maintenance expenditures and capital replacement costs, but would be denied for depreciation on capital outlays intended to establish new firms, to enlarge existing enterprises, or to introduce new products. The regulations concerning educational expenditures discriminate against the new man and the ambitious, compared with the established and the timeserver. Unsatisfactory as the present rules may seem, readers may wish to suspend judgment on the regulations until they consider the difficulties that would be involved in formulating more liberal rules without opening loopholes. These problems are examined in a later section of this chapter.

Two other features of the income tax that relate to educational expenditures are the provision excluding scholarship and fellowship aid from taxable income[5] and the provision allowing parents to

[5] Internal Revenue Code, sec. 117.

claim a $600 exemption for a son or daughter over 19 years of age who is a student and who receives more than half his support from his parents, even though he would otherwise not qualify as a dependent because his gross income exceeds $600.[6]

II. POSSIBLE PLAN FOR DEDUCTION OR AMORTIZATION OF EDUCATIONAL EXPENDITURES

The logic of the net income tax seems to imply that persons who make expenditures for education that increases their earning power, or that is intended to do so, should be permitted to capitalize these outlays and write them off against taxable income through depreciation or amortization allowances. Income-producing educational expenditures are investments with a limited life and, if it is feasible, they should be given the same tax treatment as other investments. Failure to allow tax-free recovery of educational outlays means that the income tax falls in part on the return of capital rather than on net income.

Though they may suffer discrimination under the income tax, persons who obtain much formal education benefit from the fact that tuition charges are generally far lower than the costs of instruction. On balance, those who attend a college or university no doubt receive favorable treatment from society. The present income tax treatment, however, does not reflect a conscious recognition of the subsidy received by students. The income tax discrimination is most severe against those who receive the smallest subsidy in the form of below-cost tuition charges. Low average tuition charges do not wipe out inequities that are due to failure to allow educational expenses to be written off against taxable income, but the lowness of tuition charges does reduce the possible adverse effect of the income tax on private investment in education and on occupational choice.

Although an allowance for income-increasing educational expenditures is consistent with the theory of net income taxation and might be highly desirable from the point of view of social policy, great practical difficulties would be encountered in devising and administering an acceptable plan to put the principle into effect. These difficulties are attributable to the mixed nature of educational expenditures, which include consumption as well as investment elements, the lack of legal and accounting conventions formalizing the economic aspects of education, and other complications. In order to

---

[6] Internal Revenue Code, secs. 151, 152.

bring out some of the more significant issues, I shall attempt to give the broad outlines of a plan that might prove acceptable. My suggestions are highly tentative, and on some points I have not been able to make definite recommendations. I recognize the need for further debate and technical work on the subject.

ALLOWANCE TO WHOM?

The general principle is that costs incurred to acquire a taxable income should be charged against taxable income. Applied to education, the principle indicates that the personal costs[7] of that education which increases earning capacity should be written off against the taxable income attributable to the education. This means that the writeoff should be available to the person receiving the education and the income.

Students might properly be allowed current or deferred deductions for their own educational expenditures and for outlays on their behalf by their parents, relatives, or friends. Expenditures by parents or other persons could be considered as equivalent to gifts to the student. He would be allowed to recover free of income tax the value of these gifts just as he can now write off against income the cost of a depreciable asset acquired as a gift or through the expenditure of money received as a gift.[8] As a rule, no gift-tax problem would be involved because the amounts advanced by parents and others for amortizable expenditures would ordinarily fall within the $3,000 annual exemption under the gift tax. (Logically, this approach would imply that eligible educational expenditures should not be considered "support" in determining whether a student is a dependent.) The privilege of writing off against taxable income the value of gifts in the form of education probably should not extend to the value of scholarships and other aid received from educational institutions, governmental units, corporations, or other organized bodies. These awards are presumably intended to promote the general welfare rather than the economic interests of the recipient.

Most past discussions of the relation between the income tax and educational expenditures have centered on the question of who pays

[7]The phrase "personal costs" is intended to mean costs met by students or by parents or other individuals on behalf of students, as distinguished from costs met by publicly or privately controlled educational institutions, governmental bodies, foundations, or other organizations.

[8]Internal Revenue Code, secs. 167, 1011, 1015.

the personal costs rather than who receives the return. This approach has led to proposals for income tax deductions or tax credits to parents or others who finance education. Deductions or credits allowed to parents, however, cannot be justified on the basis of a general definition of income; they must be regarded as a means of subsidizing and encouraging family support of students. Proposals of this nature are briefly examined in a later section.

ELIGIBLE ITEMS

If an allowance is to be made for educational costs, decisions will have to be made concerning the kinds of education that will be eligible and the components of total educational expenditures that will be charged against income. General income tax principles suggest that deductions should be granted, either currently or through amortization allowances, for education that is undertaken for the purpose of adding to earning power. The emphasis on the purpose of the expenditures, rather than on their results, is in accord with established practice. "Ordinary and necessary" business and professional expenses are deductible without a showing that any gross income is directly attributable to the particular items of expense. In doubtful cases and in respect of nontrade or nonbusiness expenses for the production or collection of income, the intent of the taxpayer is highly important in determining deductibility, although not always controlling. Usually some reasonably objective evidence can be adduced to corroborate or refute a claim that an expenditure was made in order to obtain income.[9]

In determining whether expenditures for a class of education should be considered costs of earning income, primary reliance might be placed on the intent of the taxpayer. The apparent influence of the education on earning capacity would constitute an important secondary criterion that might be decisive when motivation was uncertain. A precise measure of earning capacity would not be required, but merely an indication whether a significant influence could reasonably be expected on the basis of the experience of other persons who have acquired similar education, or other evidence.

[9] Internal Revenue Code, secs. 162 (a), 212; Regulations 1.162-1, 1.212 (1). The intent of the taxpayer is highly significant in indicating whether an activity is a business or a hobby and in determining whether deductions will be allowed for expenditures for items such as professional association or club dues, specialized books and journals, attendance at conventions, travel, entertainment, and rental of safe deposit boxes.

Miscellaneous

Basic professional, technical, and vocational education may be presumed to be motivated primarily by economic considerations, and the same may be said of a refresher course and supplementary training relating directly to the occupation of the person taking it. The connection between such education and earning capacity is fairly clear, and current deduction or amortization could properly be allowed so long as the amounts were reasonable. On the other hand, elementary education seems to have little economic motivation and to have no claim for consideration as an investment for income tax purposes. It is much more difficult to classify college liberal arts education and high-school education. General college education increases earning capacity and is surely motivated in part by this consideration even when pursued primarily for its cultural and civic values. An attempt to distinguish clearly between general education and vocational or professional education in colleges and universities, furthermore, would encounter serious difficulties. Undergraduate students in business administration, teacher-training, engineering, and other professional fields take general courses as well as specialized courses, and many courses are hard to classify. General education, moreover, is less subject to obsolescence than highly specialized training and may often constitute a better investment from the strictly economic standpoint. The high-school curriculum also combines general education with vocational training, but economic considerations seem less important in high-school than in college. Rising standards of living and compulsory attendance laws, together with the development of public high schools, have greatly extended secondary education and reduced its personal costs. Although high-school attendance is still not universal, children can go to high school in their home communities at little direct monetary cost to their parents.[10]

[10] Theodore W. Schultz outlines a somewhat similar ranking of attitudes toward different kinds of education, but places more emphasis on the investment aspect of high school attendance ("Education and Economic Growth," in National Society for the Study of Education, 60th yearbook, Nelson B. Henry, ed., *Social Forces Influencing American Education*, 1961, Part 2, Chicago, University of Chicago Press, p. 52–53). In his 1960 presidential address to the American Economic Association and in private correspondence, Schultz suggests that educational expenditures be classified as investment or consumption by reference to their influence on earnings rather than by the purpose of the outlay. See his "Investment in Human Capital," *American Economic Review*, 51: 1–17, March 1961. I hesitate to recommend this approach for tax purposes for fear that it would discriminate against education, particularly new and unusual kinds of education, and because most existing measures of educational yield are very crude. Some estimates indicate higher rates of return on elementary education than on high-school and college education (Schultz, "Education and Economic Growth," *op. cit.* p. 81); this finding seems implausible and of doubtful relevance for tax policy.

Perhaps the best plan would be to allow the deduction or amortization of educational expenditures relating to: (1) any program of study leading toward a degree from an accredited college or university; (2) vocational training at a recognized trade school, business college, or similar institution; and (3) a supplementary, continuation, or refresher course of a predominantly professional or vocational nature taken at a recognized or accredited institution. Presumably the new treatment should apply only to expenditures made after its authorization. "Degree-credit students" at colleges and universities, in the terminology of the Office of Education, would qualify regardless of whether they obtained degrees or not. Part-time studies and correspondence courses as well as full-time resident study should be eligible. Expenditures for ordinary high-school studies would be classified as personal expenses rather than costs of earning income.

As regards college and university studies, this plan would err on the side of liberality. The allowance for all kinds of college and university courses would cover some educational expenditures that are in the nature of consumption, as judged by presumed motivation or apparent influence on income. At the present time, however, most college and university education seems to add to earning capacity, and it is difficult to rule out the possibility of economic motivation in connection with any part of it. The rate of private monetary return on total private costs of college education appears to be high—about 12.5 percent net of income tax in 1940 and 10 percent in 1950, according to Becker's estimates.[11] If a large fraction of college costs were classified as consumption expenditures, the calculated rate of return on the remaining outlays would be high indeed. The imperfection due to a liberal allowance for college costs seems less objectionable, from the point of view of income theory and broad public policy, than that due to the present practice of permitting virtually none of these expenditures to be charged against taxable income.

The diversity of trade schools, business colleges, and similar institutions and the absence of a comprehensive accrediting system for them would complicate the application of administrative checks to assure that the expenses of study at these institutions were legitimate educational expenditures. Under the veterans' educational program

---

[11] Gary S. Becker, Underinvestment in College Education? *American Economic Review*, Papers and Proceedings of the American Economic Association, 50: 346–54, May 1960. Becker's estimates are for urban white males. His figures on costs include foregone earnings, and returns are adjusted for differential ability. The decline in the rate of return between 1940 and 1950 is due almost entirely to higher income tax rates.

after World War II, difficulties and abuses were reported with respect to many of these institutions, particularly proprietary schools below college level. Standards were tightened in 1948 and again in the legislation providing benefits for Korean war veterans.[12] The need for controls of quality would presumably be less acute under a tax deduction or amortization plan than under the veterans' program inasmuch as the Government's share of the cost would be much smaller under the tax scheme.

The principal difficulty in connection with supplementary training and continuation or refresher courses, which are often undertaken on a part-time basis, would be to distinguish vocational courses from other courses. Many extension courses, evening classes, and correspondence courses are almost entirely consumption, dealing with subjects such as hobbies, arts and crafts, current events, and music appreciation. Courses cannot always be distinguished on the basis of their content. A music course, for example, may be vocational training for one person but avocational for another. It seems that the best rule would be to allow current deductions or amortization charges only for expenses relating to education which the taxpayer represents as being primarily vocational or professional and which the authorities consider reasonably related to his occupation or occupational plans. The difficulties in applying this standard would be greater than those arising under the present rule, but they seem little if any more serious than the problems associated with deductions for items such as entertainment, travel expenses, and club memberships. The amounts involved may be smaller and many may feel that it is better public policy to be liberal with respect to educational expenses than with respect to some of the items now deductible.

The suggestion that no income tax allowance be made for ordinary high-school education is debatable. There is considerable overlap between high-school courses and the training offered by trade schools and business colleges, on the one hand, and by liberal arts colleges, on the other. For pupils in public high schools, however, the amount that could be written off would be small even if the plan were extended to

---

[12] U.S. President's Commission on Veterans' Pensions, *Readjustment Benefits: Education and Training, and Employment and Unemployment*, Staff Report IX, part A, House of Representatives Committee on Veterans' Affairs, House Committee Print No. 291, 84th Cong., 2d sess., 1956.

them. Since most young people now go to high school, the principal effect of an income tax allowance for the personal costs of secondary education would be to encourage attendance at private schools.[13]

An alternative plan would be to treat as investment varying proportions of the personal costs of different kinds of education with the objective of reflecting differences in normal contribution to future earnings. For example, the proportions to be capitalized might range as follows: 100 percent for professional schools, postgraduate courses, and vocational training; 75 percent for general college and university studies; and 25 percent for high-school courses.[14] This approach has the merit of recognizing the mixed nature of educational expenditures. Any set of percentages chosen for the schedule, however, would be almost as arbitrary as the all-or-none rule previously suggested. The difficulty of distinguishing between professional or vocational studies and general studies would remain.

Current or deferred deductions might be allowed for expenditures for tuition and fees, books and equipment, and necessary travel relating to eligible education. No deduction should be granted for normal living expenses since these expenses would be incurred in any event. Although additional living expenses necessary to the educational purpose should in principle be deductible, the difficulty of distinguishing necessary additional expenses from normal or optional expenses would be great, and it seems advisable to deny deductions for living expenses. Alternatively, a small, fixed allowance for additional living expenses might be deductible for students while they are away from home.

Although foregone earnings of students are a large part of the real cost of education, it would not be necessary to allow this item to be written off against taxable income. This part of educational costs is already free of income tax. Students and others who directly invest their time and energy in the creation of an income-yielding asset, in effect, enjoy an immediate writeoff of investment costs. Because of time discount and uncertainty, an immediate writeoff is more valuable than a series of charges. Furthermore, the income tax does not directly reduce the capacity of a student to invest his time in his educa-

[13] In 1959, 10.9 percent of high-school pupils were enrolled in private schools (*Statistical Abstract of the United States*, 1960. p. 107).

[14] I am indebted to Prof. Theodore W. Schultz for this suggestion.

tion. In contrast, a person who works for wages must pay an income tax, which leaves him less to invest.[15]

A strict rule would be to allow educational expenses to be charged only against income earned in the occupation for which the education prepared the taxpayer. This degree of refinement does not seem feasible or desirable in view of the great difficulty of establishing a clear connection between different kinds of education and activities. Professional education, for example, may be adaptable to the requirements of work in fields that are only loosely related to the specialty. A striking illustration is legal education, which has often been the route to leadership in business and politics. If a specific linkage between the kind of education and the source of earnings is not required, interruption of professional or vocational studies before completion of the course or failure to pursue the occupation for which one prepared should not disqualify one for the allowance for educational expenditures.

It would seem reasonable to limit the deductions or amortization charges to earned income. Although education may make one a better investor, the relation between property income and amount of education is rather tenuous. If educational expenditures could be written off against property income, this might give an undue advantage to persons with inherited wealth. Even with the earned-income limitation, the applicable marginal tax rate and hence the value of the deduction would be influenced by the amount of property income received.

A politically sensitive problem would be presented by the case of housewives who do not work outside the home. It is suggested that no amortization allowance be granted for a housewife during any period in which she has no taxable earned income. Although the housewife's services have economic value and her contribution to the family's economic welfare is enhanced by her education, the value of her services does not enter into taxable income. Hence denial of a writeoff for educational costs that qualify the housewife to perform her services more effectively cannot be regarded as discriminatory in

---

[15] The student's advantage is reduced if, as is likely, the marginal tax rate that would have applied to his earnings while he is a student is lower than the rate that applies to his later earnings.

the same way as failure to take account of costs of earning a taxable income.

By analogy with the treatment of the cost of physical assets, educational expenditures should be capitalized and written off against taxable income over the period in which they contribute to earnings. Ordinarily this period would be the whole normal working life of the person. This approach, however, might be cumbersome for major expenditures and ridiculous for small items.

It is tempting to suggest that the taxpayer be allowed to write off expenditures at any rate he chooses. This would leave him complete freedom in selecting the beginning date for amortization and would permit him to deduct his expenditures currently if that were most beneficial. Most students do not have enough income to be liable for tax, and in professions such as medicine and law, earnings are often small in the first few years of practice. Usually therefore students would wish to postpone the beginning of amortization until they left school or perhaps a few years later. On the other hand, students who earn enough to be subject to income tax would find it especially helpful to deduct educational expenditures currently. If the deductions were taken currently, much of the recordkeeping that would be involved in amortization over a long period of time would be avoided. Complete freedom to the taxpayer in timing the amortization of educational expenditures, however, may be considered too liberal so long as similar treatment is not accorded to those who invest in physical assets. Because of time discount, an immediate writeoff of the cost of a capital investment may be much more advantageous than a writeoff extending over a long period of time. At a compound interest rate of 5 percent, for example, the present value of a series of annual deductions of equal size extending over 20 years in the future is only 62 percent of the face amount of the deductions. A precedent for liberality respecting the timing of deductions exists in the treatment of research and experimental expenses of a trade or business. These expenses may be currently deducted, or capitalized and written off over a period of 5 years or more, at the option of the taxpayer.[16]

A possible compromise would be to allow persons incurring major

[16] Internal Revenue Code, sec. 174.

educational expenses to capitalize their outlays and amortize them over a fixed period of say 20 years, or the period ending when the taxpayer reaches age 65 if that is shorter. The taxpayer could appropriately be given some leeway as to the date at which amortization would begin. Taxpayers incurring minor educational expenses might be given the option of capitalizing their outlays or deducting them currently. Major and minor expenses could be defined in terms of percentages of current income. Outlays by full-time students would nearly always be major expenses. Most expenditures for supplementary training or refresher courses would qualify as minor expenses and thus would be currently deducted or capitalized at the taxpayer's option.

Persons who die before the end of the amortization period would not have completed the writeoff of their educational expenses. In such cases it would seem reasonable to allow the unamortized balance to be deducted in the last taxable year.[17] If this deduction reduced the income below zero, a carryback of net loss might be allowed and a refund of taxes for prior years granted. Similar treatment could be justified for a person who becomes totally and permanently disabled. It might be urged for women who marry and withdraw from the labor force, but the termination of the amortization period would not be clearly appropriate in these cases since many married women leave their jobs but later resume employment outside the home.

III. EFFECTS OF REVISED TREATMENT OF EDUCATIONAL EXPENDITURES

The effects of allowing educational expenditures to be charged against taxable income may be considered from the standpoint of Government revenues, college and university tuition charges and enrollments, and occupational choice.

REVENUES

Government revenues would be reduced unless offsetting increases in tax rates were adopted. Under a plan allowing current deduction of minor educational expenses and amortization of major outlays for education, the full impact would be felt only after a period of years roughly equal to the amortization period. Over the transi-

---

[17]Under present law, when depreciable property (tangible or intangible) suddenly loses its usefulness and is discarded, the difference between its depreciated cost and salvage value if any, may be deducted from income (Income Tax Regulations 1.167 (a)-8).

tion period the annual charges would build up year by year. They would increase thereafter to reflect the growth of population and of educational expenditures.

The available data permit rough estimates of expenditures for education in colleges and universities, but not for trade schools, correspondence schools, and other educational institutions. Reliable statistics are available for tuition and fees paid to colleges and universities, including tuition and fees for extension courses, adult education, and instruction by mail, radio, and television. There are data on which estimates of other expenditures of students at colleges and universities can be based. Some of the relevant information is summarized in Table 1. The estimates given in the table for books and supplies and for travel may be somewhat too high. Mean expenditures of full-time students were used in developing the estimates, but were applied to enrollment figures that include part-time students as well.

In estimating the revenue loss, an allowance has to be made for the expenditures of women who marry and withdraw from the labor force before completing the amortization of their educational outlays and for the expenditures of those who die before completing the amortization period. In March 1957 one-half of the women in the age group 25 to 64 who had one or more years of college education were in the labor force.[18] Rates of participation in the labor force were higher among younger women who had attended college but who were not currently enrolled, and were also higher among women with 4 or more years of college attendance than among those with briefer attendance. Many college women who were not in the labor force in 1957 had previously been employed or would be employed in the future. On the other hand, some of those who were employed would work only a short time. I assume that one-fourth of eligible expenditures of women students at colleges and universities could not be amortized under a general plan because of lack of earned income against which to claim the deductions. In recent years women students accounted for about one-third of college and university enrollment.[19] On the assumption that average expenditures of women students are equal to those of men students, it follows that the

[18] U.S. Bureau of the Census, *Current Population Reports*, Series P-20, No. 77, Population Characteristics (December 27, 1957), and Series P-50, No. 78, Labor Force, November 1957.

[19] U.S. Department of Commerce, Bureau of the Census, *Statistical Abstract of the United States 1959*, p. 106.

Miscellaneous

"wastage" of amortization deductions of women students would amount to about 8 percent of total outlays for eligible items by college and university students. Even with a final-year adjustment, as sug-

TABLE 1

Estimated Expenditures of Students for Selected Items:
Colleges and Universities, United States, 1953–54; 1955–56;
1957–58; and Projected, 1969–70

(In millions)

Item	Expenditures by Year			
	1953–54	1955–56	1957–58	1969–70
Total	$827	$1,038	$1,324	$3,101
Tuition and fees[1]	508	667	873	2,209
Books and supplies[2]	129	152	184	367
Travel[2,3]	190	219	267	525

[1]Estimated from U.S. Department of Health, Education, and Welfare, Office of Education, Biennial Survey of Education in the United States 1952–54, *Statistics of Higher Education: Receipts, Expenditures and Property, 1953–54*, and similar statistics for 1955–56; and from unpublished data compiled by the Office of Education for the 1957–58 edition. The figures represent tuition and fees from students for instruction and for plant expansion or debt retirement, minus the amount of tuition and fees covered by fellowships, scholarships, and prizes administered by colleges and universities (estimated at two-thirds of the institutions' expenditure for these awards). *See* John F. Meck, testimony on behalf of American Council on Education, House Ways and Means Committee, *Hearings on General Revenue Revision*, 85th Cong. 2d sess. (1958), pt. I, p. 1065. The total includes college and university tuition receipts from extension courses and instruction by mail, radio, and television.

The 1969–70 figure is based on the estimate of $2,427 million for total tuition and fees projected by Robert D. Calkins ("Government Support of High Education" in *Financing High Education, 1969–70*, Dexter M. Keezer, *ed.* New York, McGraw-Hill Co., 1959, p. 197), reduced by estimated sums from scholarships, fellowships, and prizes which are assumed to amount to 9 percent of total tuition and fees (the 1957–58 percentage).

[2]Derived by multiplying the number of students enrolled by the amount of estimated mean expenditures for the item. Enrollment figures are from the U.S. Office of Education academic year enrollment series reported in the Biennial Survey of Education 1953–54; and by Seymour E. Harris in *Financing Higher Education, 1969–70, op. cit.*, p. 74. Mean expenditures are estimated from survey data for 1952–53 (adjusted for price changes) by Ernest V. Hollis and associates. *Costs of Attending College* (U.S. Department of Health, Education, and Welfare, Office of Education, Bulletin 1957, No. 9.) p. 40.

For books and supplies, the price index used is the "Reading and recreation" component of the Bureau of Labor Statistics Consumer Price Index; for travel, the "Transpotation" component. The 1969–70 figure is based on mean expenditures computed at 1959–60 price levels.

[3]Travel between home and college or university; excludes travel between college address and campus and "other" travel.

gested above, death or disability would prevent some men and women from completing the amortization of their investment.[20] An allowance for unemployment should perhaps be added, but this should not be large if prosperity is fairly well maintained inasmuch as short-term unemployment would usually not prevent amortization. All told, the wastage of amortization deductions might be about 10 percent.

It seems safe to assume that, so long as income tax exemptions remain at approximately their present level in relation to average income, nearly all former college students will have incomes large enough to be subject to tax when they are employed. Selection of an appropriate marginal rate of income tax is more difficult. The average income of persons who have attended college is considerably higher than the average income of others, but apparently not high enough to raise a large proportion of them into upper tax brackets. In 1958, 23 percent of male college graduates with money income received more than $10,000; only 1.5 percent of women graduates with money income were in this class.[21] I assume that, with present rate schedules, the weighted average marginal rate of income tax applicable to former college students is about 25 percent. (Under present law the marginal rate for a married couple with two dependent children rises from 22 percent to 26 percent at an income of approximately $12,000.)

These estimates and assumptions indicate an ultimate revenue loss of roughly $300 million if amortization or deduction had been allowed for 1957–58 expenditures of college and university students for tuition and fees, books and supplies, and travel (see Table 1). The total revenue loss would be associated with 1 year's expenditures, but would occur only over a period of 20 years if the suggestions made above concerning amortization were adopted. After introduction of the plan, the annual revenue loss would increase year by year as successive groups began to claim deductions or amortization allowances for expenditures made in later years. If students' expenditures remained constant at the 1957–58 level, the annual revenue

[20] On the basis of 1956 mortality rates for white males (*Statistical Abstract of the United States 1959*, p. 60), it may be calculated that, of a group aged 25, about 4 percent would die before reaching age 45, and that on the average about 98 percent would be living during the 20-year period. I have not found comparable statistics of disability.

[21] U.S. Department of Commerce, Bureau of the Census, *Current Population Reports*, Series P-60, No. 33, Consumer Income, January 15, 1960, p. 38.

579

loss would stabilize at approximately $300 million after 20 years. Educational expenditures, however, can be expected to increase rapidly with the growth of enrollment and with probable increases in tuition charges. On the basis of projected increases in enrollment and tuition charges, but assuming no change in prices of other items, amortizable or deductible expenditures made in 1969–70 may be placed at $3.1 billion or more. On the assumption of a 25-percent marginal tax rate and 10 percent "wastage" of deductions, the ultimate revenue loss with respect to that year would amount to $0.7 billion, spread over two decades. These estimates make no allowance for an increase in taxable income due to a stimulus to education provided by tax revision.

INFLUENCE ON TUITION CHARGES AND ENROLLMENTS

The adoption of a plan allowing educational expenditures to be written off against taxable income would probably encourage colleges and universities to raise their tuition charges and fees. Tuition charges are well below instructional costs at most institutions, and the institutions face financial problems. The extent of the increase in charges cannot be forecast with confidence, but informed observers have generally agreed that tax relief for parents of students would lessen the reluctance of colleges and universities to raise charges. Amortization for students is less closely related to the ability of parents or students to meet increased charges, but the adoption of an amortization plan would no doubt increase to some degree capacity and willingness to pay tuition charges.

The amortization plan would complement an arrangement providing higher tuition charges and long-term credit facilities to enable needy students to pay the charges. That system would formalize the resemblance between educational expenditures and investment in physical assets. If liberal credit and tax amortization were available, much could be said for a policy of raising tuition charges high enough to cover the full marginal costs of instruction in courses that are predominantly vocational or professional in nature.[22] The argument for higher tuition charges would be especially persuasive in regard to professional fields such as medicine, where educational costs and

[22] Milton Friedman. "The Role of Government in Education," in *Economics and the Public Interest,* Robert A. Solo, ed. New Brunswick, N.J., Rutgers University Press, 1955. p. 123–44.

earnings are much above the average. Students in these fields now pay only a small fraction of the costs of their education.

Any action that reduces the net cost of tuition payments or facilitates borrowing to cover educational expenses should induce some students who would otherwise have attended public institutions to apply for admission to private colleges and universities. Adoption of an amortization plan would result in tax savings ultimately amounting to perhaps one-fourth of expenditures for tuition and fees and other eligible items. As already noted, however, the fact that the tax savings would be realized in installments over a period of years would considerably reduce their significance. Although it seems clear that the plan would stimulate enrollment in private institutions compared with that in public ones, the probable extent of this influence is hard to appraise.

INFLUENCE ON EDUCATIONAL EXPENDITURES AND OCCUPATIONAL CHOICE

In present circumstances, it seems unlikely that adoption of a plan for amortization of educational expenditures would have a great influence on the total investment in education and on the choice between occupations requiring different amounts of such investment. The role of economic calculations in educational and occupational choices is uncertain, and the tax benefits of an amortization plan would equal only a small proportion of the total personal costs of college and university education. Foregone earnings of college and university students, which are a part of personal costs but which would not be amortizable, are much larger in the aggregate than expenditures for items which might properly be subject to amortization (tuition and fees, books and supplies, and travel). In academic years 1955–56 and 1957–58, the amortizable items accounted for only about 15 to 17 percent of estimated total personal costs of college and university education, exclusive of any additional living expenses of students; the remaining 83 to 85 percent of personal costs consisted of foregone earnings.[23]

---

[23] See estimates of expenditures for tuition and fees, books and supplies, and travel, Table 1. Theodore W. Schultz estimates foregone earnings of college and university students at $5,821 million in 1955–56. See "Capital Formation by Education," *Journal of Political Economy*, 68: 580, December 1960. Applying Schultz's method, I estimate foregone earnings in 1957–1958 at $6,570 million. My estimate, however, relies on the Department of Labor figure for unemployment rather than on the series compiled by Clarence D. Long, which Schultz uses for 1955–56.

On the assumption of a 25-percent marginal tax rate, it appears that the tax saving attributable to amortization of educational expenditures would have equaled only about 4 percent of total personal costs of college and university education under conditions prevailing recently. This figure should be discounted because of the distribution of the tax saving over a period of years. An item as small as this can hardly be a strong influence on the amount of educational expenditures or on occupational choice.

The tax benefits from amortization would not represent a major fraction of personal costs of even the most expensive kinds of education. Although students' outlays for tuition and fees and other expenses at certain prestige colleges and at professional schools of private universities are much larger than average expenditures for all colleges and university students, foregone earnings are still the largest item of personal education costs. For example, I estimate that, at approximately 1959–60 prices and wage rates, the total personal cost of a medical education at private institutions, including a 4-year premedical course at an "Ivy League" college, 4 years at a private medical school, and a 1-year internship, averaged roughly $45,500. (Many physicians also serve residencies in order to qualify as specialists.) Of the $45,500, about $33,500 represented foregone earnings and $12,000 tuition and fees, books and supplies and equipment, and travel (see Table 2). Under an amortization plan, $12,000 could be written off against taxable income at a rate of, say $600 a year. Although this sum is not insignificant, the tax saving, assuming a 30-percent marginal tax rate, would amount to only 8 percent of the personal investment in the physician's education.[24]

If tuition and fees were increased to cover a much larger fraction of total educational costs, the amortization plan would become more significant; nevertheless, amortizable expenses would still represent only a minor part of total costs, owing to the importance of foregone earnings. If, for example, in 1955–56 and 1957–58 tuition and fees had covered all educational costs of colleges and universities, amortizable expenses of students would have equaled only about 40 to

---

[24] Unpublished estimates by Roy E. Moor for the U.S. Public Health Service indicate that physicians (M.D.'s) in the United States received an average net income of $16,500 from medical practice in 1958. A married person with this income would be subject to a 30-percent marginal rate of Federal income tax.

44 percent of total costs.[25] In fields such as medicine and dentistry, where instructional costs are high, the fraction might be somewhat greater but probably not strikingly so, inasmuch as foregone earnings are larger for students in professional schools than for the average student.

It could be argued that, in appraising the influence of amortization of educational expenses, students' benefits from the tax provision should be related to their money outlays for education rather than to total personal costs, including foregone earnings. One basis for this approach might be the hypothesis that, in decisions relating to education and occupational choice, opportunity costs are given much less weight than money expenditures. Granted that many students and parents may not carefully calculate foregone earnings, I do not believe that we should assume that opportunity costs have no influence. Opportunity costs are taken into account partly in the form of students' living expenses, which are included in most published material on educational costs, but not in the estimates presented in this paper. The calculation of opportunity costs requires less sophistication and foresight than the evaluation of the tax benefits due to amortization of educational expenses, and those who ignore opportunity costs might also overlook the more remote advantages of amortization.

A more persuasive reason for concentrating on money outlays, including living expenses but not all foregone earnings, is the possibility that these costs will be financed by borrowing. The availability of tax amortization might increase the willingness of students to borrow and might cause creditors to regard these loans as better risks.

IV. DEDUCTIONS OR TAX CREDITS ALLOWED TO PARENTS OF STUDENTS

In recent years there has been considerable discussion of the possibility of allowing income tax deductions or credits for certain educational expenditures. In 1953 the House Ways and Means Committee

[25] Based on estimated total costs of $9,692 million in 1955–56 and $11,681 million in 1957–1958. These totals include my estimates of students' expenditures on books and supplies and travel (Table 1); Schultz's estimates of foregone earnings and institutional costs in 1955–56 ("Capital Formation by Education," *op. cit.*, p. 579–80); and, for 1957–1958, my estimates of foregone earnings ($6,570 million) and institutional costs ($4,660 million) made by Schultz's method. The figures for institutional costs include all college and university operating costs (except costs of auxiliary enterprises) and implicit interest and depreciation on physical property, thus covering costs of research and administration as well as costs by instruction.

TABLE 2

Estimated Personal Cost of Medical Education

(at 1959–60 Prices and Wages)

Cost Item	1 Year	Total
Premedical course:		
Tuition and fees[1]	$1,380	$5,520
Books and supplies[2]	57	228
Travel[2]	109	436
Subtotal	1,546	6,184
Foregone earnings[3]	2,146	8,584
Total, premedical course	3,692	14,768
Medical school:		
Tuition and fees[4]	1,110	4,440
Books and supplies[4]	150	600
Microscope[5]	350	350
Travel[2]	109	436
Subtotal	1,719	5,826
Foregone earnings[6]	5,441	21,764
Total, medical school	7,160	27,590
Internship: Foregone earnings[7]	3,093	3,093
Total, all items		45,451

[1] Mean for 8 "Ivy League" colleges (Brown, Columbia, Cornell, Dartmouth, Harvard, Pennsylvania, Princeton, and Yale), 1959–60, *American Universities and Colleges,* Mary Irwin, *ed.* Washington, D.C., American Council on Education, 8th edition, 1960.

[2] Mean expenditures of undergraduates in private colleges in 1952–53, adjusted for price changes. For derivation, see Table 1, footnotes 2 and 3.

[3] Average for all college and university students, 1960, derived by the method used by Theodore W. Schultz in "Capital Formation in Education," *Journal of Political Economy,* 68: 575, December 1960. Adjustment for unemployment based on a Department of Labor estimate of the unemployment rate as a percentage of the civilian labor force (*Economic Indicators March 1961* prepared for the Joint Economic Committee by the Council of Economic Advisers, U.S. 87th Cong., 1st sess., House of Representatives).

[4] Median minimum expenses of first-year medical students in 45 private medical schools, 1960–61, from American Medical Association. Council on Medical Education and Hospitals, *Medical Education in the United States and Canada,* reprint from *Journal of the American Medical Association,* 174, 1423–76, Nov. 12, 1960.

[5] Median, 1956–57, from U.S. Congress, *Medical School Inquiry,* Staff Report to House Committee on Interstate and Foreign Commerce, 85th Cong., 1st sess., House of Representatives, 1957 Committee print. p. 388

[6] Median starting salary of $5,880 for inexperienced male graduates in chemistry with a B.S. degree, 1959–60, from American Chemical Society, "1960 Starting Salary Survey," *Chemical and Engineering News,* 38: 107, October 31, 1960, reduced by $439, the estimated earnings of the student during the year. The student's current earnings were estimated by increasing the estimated average for dental students in 1953–54 (American Dental Association, *How Students Finance Their Dental Education,* 1956, p. 49) by an index of average gross weekly earnings in manufacturing (derived from U.S.,

Economic Report of the President, transmitted to the Congress January 20, 1960, p. 184; and *Economic Indicators March 1961,* op. cit.). The total for this item is 4 times the 1-year figure.

[7] Difference between: (a) entrance salary (General Services, grade 9, $6,285 a year) under the Federal civil service for one who has successfully completed graduate study in biochemistry equivalent to the requirements for a doctor's degree, including the thesis (U.S. Civil Service Commission Announcement No. 163B, issued July 22, 1958, supplemented May 2, 1960); and (b) estimated annual compensation of interns in university-affiliated hospitals in 1959–60. The average salary of interns in hospitals affiliated with medical schools was $166 a month. $1,992 for 12 months, as reported in Graduate Medical Education in the United States, *Journal of the American Medical Association,* 174: 575, October 8, 1960. Many interns also receive room, board, and other maintenance, and these items were valued at $1,200 for 12 months. The median cost of room and board at private medical schools in 1959–60 was $900, presumably for 9 months (*Medical Education in the United States and Canada, op. cit.*). Total compensation is therefore estimated at $3,192 and foregone earnings at $3,093.

---

selected college and educational expenses as one of 40 topics for study in preparation for a revision of the Internal Revenue Code.[26] The President's Committee on Education Beyond the High School recommended in 1957 that

. . . the Federal revenue laws be revised, with appropriate safeguards, in ways which will permit deductions or credits on income tax returns by students, their parents or others, who contribute to meeting the expenditures necessarily incurred in obtaining formal education beyond high school; and, further, that provisions be included which will grant proportionately greater tax benefit to those least able to afford those expenditures.[27]

The 1960 platform of one of the major political parties favored "consideration of means through tax laws to help offset tuition costs" without specifying the form of the assistance.[28]

A large number of bills relating to expenses of attending college or university have been introduced in Congress in recent years. Although the bills commonly provide a deduction or tax credit for a person incurring expenditures for himself or for a dependent, the following comments relate solely to the tax relief that would be offered to parents of college students. The analysis, although incomplete, deals with the more important aspect of the bills. Parents, on

[26] U.S., 83d Congress, 1st session, part I, *General Revenue Revision.* Hearings before the Committee on Ways and Means, House of Representatives, 1953. p. 177–201.

[27] U.S., The President's Committee on Education Beyond the High School, *Second Report to the President,* July 1957. p. 11.

[28] *Platforms of the Democratic Party and the Republican Party,* 1960 (Ralph R. Roberts, Clerk, U.S. House of Representatives, September 1960). p. 68.

the average, pay a larger fraction of the money costs of college education than students do and parents also have higher taxable incomes.[29]

Proposals for the deduction from taxable income of educational expenditures have been criticized on the grounds that they would grant proportionately more relief to high-income families than to those with low incomes. The tax saving attributable to any deduction varies directly with the marginal tax rate, and in the graduated schedules employed in the United States, marginal rates rise to high levels for large incomes. Critics have pointed out that a deduction for college expenses would give the largest benefits to families with the least need for financial assistance, and they have expressed the fear that such a plan would accentuate the tendency for college enrollment to be drawn from families with incomes much above the national average.

These objections have prompted the suggestion that parents or others be allowed a tax credit equal to a stated percentage of certain expenditures rather than a deduction for these expenditures. A credit is subtracted from the tax liability otherwise due rather than from taxable income. To illustrate, a 30-percent credit would give a $300 tax reduction to parents who incur $1,000 of eligible expenses for a son or daughter in college. For persons whose tax liability would exceed the amount of the credit, a uniform credit offers benefits equal to the same fraction of eligible expenditures regardless of income level and marginal tax rate. Parents whose incomes are so low that they pay no income tax would receive no assistance, and those whose tax liability is less than the amount of the credit would not be able to take full advantage of it. It appears, however, that only a small minority of parents of college students would be subject to these limitations under most of the tax credit proposals. A considerably greater part of the total tax reduction would accrue to low-income and middle-income families under a tax credit than under a deduction plan costing the Government the same amount of revenue.[30] The

[29] U.S. Department of Health, Education, and Welfare, Office of Education, *Costs of Attending College*, Ernest V. Hollis and associates, OOE Bull. 1957, No. 9. p. 48; John B. Lansing, Thomas Lorimer, and Chikashi Moriguchi, *How People Pay for College*, Ann Arbor, Mich., Survey Research Center, Institute for Social Research, University of Michigan, 1960; American Dental Association, *How Students Finance Their Dental Education*, 1956., p. 49; U.S. Department of Health, Education, and Welfare, Public Health Service, *Physicians for a Growing America*, Report of the Surgeon General's Consultant Group on Medical Education, PHS Pub. No. 709, 1959, p. 20.

[30] For a statistical comparison, see *Stimulating Voluntary Giving to Higher Education and Other Programs*, prepared for the American Association for the Advancement of Science, Washington, Surveys and Research Corporation, 1958, p. 109–30.

credit approach has been endorsed by the American Council on Education[31] and has been embodied in several bills introduced by members of Congress.

The proposed tax credits or deductions allowed to parents of college students would provide immediate tax relief. Government revenues would therefore be reduced more quickly than by an amortization plan covering the same expenditures. In the long run, however, the revenue effects of current deductions and amortization allowances would be much the same, provided the same items were charged against income. A tax credit for particular items would bring about more or less of a revenue loss than a deduction of the same items, depending on whether the credit rate was higher or lower than the weighted marginal rate of income tax. The two approaches would have qualitatively similar influences on the amount of educational expenditures, enrollment at public and private educational institutions, tuition charges, and occupational choice. But in all these respects an immediate deduction or credit allowed to parents would doubtless be more powerful than amortization allowances for students that would bring about the same loss of revenue over a period of years.

As already asserted, tax credits or deductions for parents or others who meet the expenses of students cannot be regarded as an improvement of the definition of taxable income. Granted that certain educational expenditures should be considered an income-producing investment, general income tax principles indicate that the costs should be charged against the yield over the life of the investment. Credits or deductions to parents are inconsistent with these principles because they apply to the tax liability or income of the parents rather than to the investment yield in the form of students' earnings. Neither the Internal Revenue Code nor popular opinion treats parents and their adult sons and daughters as a single economic unit. A second criticism of credits or deductions to parents is that the tax relief would accrue before the receipt of the investment income. A less fundamental objection is that nearly all of the proposals that have received public attention have been limited to college and university expenses and

[31] The council's proposal called for a 30-percent credit for college tuition and fees, subject to a limit of $450 of credit per student year. See U.S., 85th Congress, 2d session, pt. I, *General Revenue Revision,* hearings before the Committee on Ways and Means, House of Representatives, 1958, p. 1061–68; and John F. Meck, "The Tax-Credit Proposal," in *Higher Education in the United States: the Economic Problems,* Seymour E. Harris, ed., supplement to *Review of Economics and Statistics,* Cambridge, Mass., Harvard University Press, 1960, 42: 93–95, August 1960.

would therefore discriminate against other kinds of training. This defect could be eliminated by broadening the credit or deduction.

The proposals for credits or deductions to parents are intended to subsidize and encourage socially meritorious activity. For this reason, questions about the efficacy of the plans in stimulating additional expenditures, the distribution of benefits among income classes, and the needs of beneficiaries are more pertinent to these plans than to the proposals for refining the definition of income by allowing students to write off certain educational expenditures.[32] A deduction or tax credit granted to parents can be justified only on the grounds that educational expenditures are more meritorious or more burdensome than other socially desirable expenditures that do not receive special tax treatment. It is also necessary to argue that tax relief is more efficient or otherwise more acceptable than additional Government expenditures as a means of encouraging education. Some such considerations seem to underlie the approval of deductions for charitable contributions, and several personal deductions have been attacked for failure to conform to similar standards. Deductions that are recognized as necessary for the computation of net income, on the other hand, are not usually expected to meet such exacting requirements.

The difference between a current deduction or credit to parents and a deferred deduction to students may not seem important to most of those who are eager to do something to help education. Although the general public can hardly be expected to be as concerned as tax experts are with refinements of income concepts, the public should recognize that there are important advantages in adhering to the general principles of the income tax. These principles set up a desirable bulwark against erosion of the tax base. Many of our difficulties and discontent with the income tax can be attributed to the lack of adherence to a logical and consistent definition of income. Modification of the income tax for the purpose of subsidizing a desirable activity invites proposals for more questionable tax subsidies.

No great difficulties of administration or compliance would be involved in the tax credit or deduction plans if they were restricted, as is usually suggested, to tuition and fees and perhaps a few other designated expenditures of full-time students at recognized colleges and universities. If an effort were made to extend the plans to ex-

[32] C. Harry Kahn. Personal Deductions in the Federal Income Tax. Princeton, N.J., Princeton University Press, 1960. p. 15–16.

penditures for part-time studies and for courses at trade schools and other institutions, many of the same difficulties would be encountered as under the amortization and deduction plans discussed in a preceding section of this chapter. The same marginal distinctions between eligible and ineligible expenditures would have to be made. Any plan providing current deductions or credits would have one administrative advantage over the amortization plans: it would not require the maintenance of accounts for individual taxpayers over a long period of years. This advantage may become less significant with the installation of automatic data-processing systems by the Internal Revenue Service.

V. CONCLUSION

More liberal deductions and amortization allowances for educational expenditures can be supported as a refinement of the income tax and as a means of encouraging investment in education and entry into occupations requiring expensive education. Current and deferred deductions for students pursuing education that increases their earning capacity are consistent with income tax principles, whereas deductions or tax credits for parents of students must be regarded as a special subsidy or incentive device. The design and administration of an acceptable scheme of current deduction and long-term amortization of educational costs would be difficult but does not seem impossible. The case for modification of the income tax would become stronger if tuition charges were raised to cover a larger fraction of college and university instructional costs. Even in those circumstances, foregone earnings, an item which could not properly be amortized, would be the major component of the costs of education beyond the high-school level. It seems unlikely that the adoption of a tax amortization plan would greatly influence educational expenditures. Nevertheless, the recognition for tax purposes that certain educational expenditures are investments would help establish an important principle that is often overlooked. Further study and public discussion of the subject are desirable.

31. Migration to the Suburbs, Human Capital, and City Income Tax Losses: A Case Study*

A. G. HOLTMANN
Florida State University

Americans have shown a taste for suburban living that has increased unabated for at least the last twenty years. While this movement away from the country's cities no doubt increases the welfare of the migrants, it often leaves those that are left behind worse off. The losses to the central city take several forms. First, there is the loss of revenue through the erosion of the city's tax base. If the city has an income tax that either doesn't apply to nonresidents or which taxes nonresidents at a lower rate, then, the city's revenues are cut directly. On the other hand, losses in sales taxes, as stores follow the population, and losses of property taxes, as property values fall, are more subtle. Second, the migrants may force the city to increase expenditures on certain services. For example, more traffic police may be necessary to handle the movement of traffic leaving and entering the city. Third, there may be external effects which will tend to reduce the welfare of the residents of the city. The undesirable effects of air pollution from the increased auto traffic would be a case in point.

Not only does migration to the suburbs have these undesirable effects, but, as Professor William Baumol has suggested, there may be a dynamic process involved that causes the city's per capita income relative to the suburban area's per capita income to continue to deteriorate.[1] In fact, the deterioration may even increase at an increasing rate. The logic concerning such a process is clear. Individuals move to the suburbs, which causes per capita income in the suburbs to exceed per capita income in the city. The higher incomes in the sub-

---

*Reprinted from "Migration to the Suburbs, Human Capital, and City Income Tax Losses: A Case Study," *National Tax Journal*, XXI, 326–31.

[1]See: William Baumol, "Urban Services: Interaction of Public and Private Decision," *Public Expenditure Decisions in the Urban Community*, Howard Schaller, editor (Washington, D.C.: Resources for the Future, Inc., 1963), pp. 1–18.

urbs permits a higher level of public services in the suburban areas than in the city. More services in the suburbs lure more high-income individuals into the suburbs. At the same time, the tax base of the city is being eroded. This process may continue until the quality of services provided in the city is so poor relative to the quality of services provided elsewhere that outside aid or consolidation is necessary.

The nature of the process of dynamic deterioration can be formally stated quite simply. Assume the rate of increase in migration to the suburbs per period of time is proportional to the amount that per capita income in the suburbs exceeds per capita income in the city.

$$\frac{dM(t)}{dt} = w(Y_s - Y_c) \tag{1}$$

for $Y_s > Y_c$. In this case, Y_s is per capita income in the suburbs; Y_c is per capita income in the city; w is a constant; and $dM(t)/dt$ is the rate of change of migration. Also, assume that per capita income in the city at time t is a linear decreasing function of the amount of migration at time t, and assume that per capita income in the suburbs is an increasing function of the amount of migration at time t. Then,

$$Y_c = b - gM \tag{2}$$

and

$$Y_s = a + kM \tag{3}$$

where a, b, g, and k are constants.

Now subtracting (2) from (3) and writing $Y_s - Y_c$ as Y^* gives

$$Y^* = a - b + (k + g)M. \tag{4}$$

Then, differentiating (4) with respect to time and substituting from (1), results in

$$\frac{dY^*}{dt} = w(k + g)Y^*. \tag{5}$$

Writing $w(k + g)$ as z, we can write (5) as

$$\int \frac{dY^*}{Y^*} = z \int dt \tag{6}$$

or

$$Y^* = e^v e^{zt} \tag{7}$$

where v is a constant.

591

This implies that the difference between per capita income in the city and per capita income in the suburbs will increase with time. And, all other things remaining the same, the difference will increase faster, the greater the responsiveness of per capita income in each area to migration. Naturally, if the quality of public services is directly related to per capita income, differences in the quality of services in the two areas will, also, increase.

Although the model of cumulative deterioration is a simplification of the dynamic process affecting United States cities, there are several important aspects that the model emphasizes. First, if the theoretical model conforms to the actual situation, it is possible to estimate the difference in per capita income between the city and the suburbs at any future time by knowing the difference at two other points in time. For, we know

$$Y*(0) = e^v$$

Therefore, at any other time, say t equal 2, we have

$$Y*(2) = Y(0)e^{2z}$$

Hence, if we define any initial period as t equal zero and if we know the $Y*$ for another t, we can determine all the constants in the system. Secondly, the model may be a close enough approximation to reality to suggest that the financial problems of the city will increase at an increasing rate. Neglect of our cities' problems today, then, means that the problems will be much worse in the future.

ESTIMATING THE LOSS FROM MIGRATION

The previous analysis implicitly suggests that the city's welfare is closely related to per capita income of the residents. Of course, it is quite common to use per capita income as an indication of the welfare of an area. In that per capita income is a measure of the resources available for the provision of both private and public goods, the measure has some justification. There are a number of well known limitations to such a measure of welfare, but they will not be considered here. However, for the purposes of this paper, the total and per capita present value of future income is a superior measure of the decrease in welfare attributable to migration to the suburbs.[2] While this mea-

[2] For a complete discussion of the limitations of both per capita income and per capita present value of future income see: Burton Weisbrod, "An Expected Income Measure of Economic Welfare," *Journal of Political Economy* (August, 1962), pp. 355–67.

sure contains some of the limitations of the ordinary measure of per capita income, it does incorporate expected future income which should be considered when measuring the loss from migration. Therefore, while the present value of future income lost through migration does not actually represent the dynamic loss discussed earlier in the paper, this measure does indicate the value of future losses that are associated with present migration. For example, the present value of future income will indicate the value of the future loss associated with a migrant that is presently too young to be in the labor force. To this extent, we capture, in a static sense, the future losses associated with migration. When better time series data are available, perhaps it will be possible to measure completely the dynamic losses to the city.

At any given date, the present value of future income of individuals that have earlier migrated from the city is a measure of the human capital that the city would gain if it could induce these individuals to return from the suburbs. The present value of future income of an individual of any given age can be estimated from the following formula:

$$V_a = \sum_{n=a}^{79} \frac{P_a^n Y^n}{(1 + r)^{n-a}}$$

where V_a is the present value of future income of a man age a; P_a^n is the probability that a man age a will live to age n; Y^n is a man's expected income at age n; and r is the discount rate.

THE CASE OF DETROIT

As an example of the magnitude of the loss of human capital through migration to the suburbs, estimates of these losses have been made for the city of Detroit. Detroit was selected as an example for several reasons. First, it is a major industrial city that has endured an increasing amount of migration to the suburban areas. Secondly, the recent riots may, in part, be attributable to the inability of the city to provide adequate public services from its own resources. Thirdly, Detroit has an income tax that taxes nonresidents at one half the rate at which it taxes residents. This third attribute means that there is an economic incentive to live in the suburbs, and that there is a direct measurable loss to the city from migration.

The present value of future income by age, sex, and race was estimated from census data for the Detroit metropolitan area. Median incomes for those people with income was adjusted by the percentage of people with income to determine the average income of a resident of a given age, sex, and race. While it would have been better if mean income figures had been given by educational attainment, such data are not available. Therefore, the available cross-section income estimates were used to represent the lifetime income profile for a person of any given age. Of course, we know that lifetime income is underestimated when cross-section data are used to measure future incomes, but there is no adequate means for adjusting the data for this. The cross-section data were used, then, with the knowledge that the human capital losses through migration would be underestimated. These income estimates were then used with the estimated probability of living to a future age to determine the capital value of individuals in the metropolitan area.[3] These data are shown in Table 1, for discount rates of five and ten percent. Two interest rates were used to give a reasonable range for the present value estimates. While it is generally agreed that future income should be discounted, there is no unique discount rate for such purposes.[4]

Ignoring the fact that some migrants to the suburbs will return to the city, the present value of future income figures can be used to estimate the total loss in 1960 of the human capital that had to that time migrated to the suburbs. Using a five percent rate of discount, the present value figures for each age, sex, and race were weighted by the number of people in each category to gain the total human capital losses from migration. Per capita values were derived from these total loss estimates. These estimates are shown in Table 2. In addition, the per capita capital value of residents of the city and of migrants from the suburbs to the city are shown. It is clear from these data that the migration of white males and females tends to reduce the per capita value of human capital in the city, and that these groups represent a large loss of human capital to the city. While white migrants into the city tend to raise the city's per capita value of human capital, this gain is dwarfed by the movement of whites to the suburbs. Conversely, the movement of nonwhites into the city

---

[3] U.S. Department of Health, Education, and Welfare, *Vital Statistics of the United States, 1960 — Life Tables,* (Washington, D.C.: U.S. Government Printing Office, 1960), pp. 2–9.

[4] While there is no unique rate for discounting the lower rate of 5 percent has been suggested by Otto Eckstein. See Otto Eckstein, *Water-Resource Development: The Economics of Project Evaluation* (Cambridge: Harvard University Press, 1958), p. 99.

TABLE 1

Present Value of Future Income for Detroit SMSA by Age, Sex, and Race for 1960, Using Discount Rates of 5 and 10 percent

Age	White				Nonwhite			
	Male		Female		Male		Female	
	.05	.10	.05	.10	.05	.10	.05	.10
Under 5	$42,299	$10,556	$10,468	$ 3,038	$24,285	$ 5,952	$ 6,843	$1,880
5–9	51,565	15,500	12,750	4,457	29,644	8,751	8,348	2,763
10–14	64,947	25,016	16,299	7,189	37,952	14,138	10,681	4,460
15–19	83,441	39,284	19,958	10,630	48,173	22,312	13,267	6,761
20–24	99,074	54,769	21,382	12,571	58,550	32,390	15,250	8,987
25–29	105,608	63,912	19,825	11,480	63,011	38,471	15,340	9,692
30–34	101,799	64,331	19,625	11,875	60,906	38,784	14,337	9,455
35–44	89,514	60,968	18,379	12,104	57,501	38,441	11,712	8,218
45–54	65,630	49,108	14,094	10,306	45,351	33,126	7,706	5,589
55–64	36,571	30,352	8,199	6,380	29,273	23,644	5,135	3,835
65–over	12,398	10,993	3,970	3,396	8,892	7,720	3,513	2,990

Sources: The present value of future income was calculated from the formula given in the text and from income data given for the Detroit SMSA in U.S. Bureau of the Census, *U.S. Census of Population: 1960, Detailed Characteristics Michigan, Final Report* PC(1)–24D (Washington, D.C.: U.S. Government Printing Office, 1962), p. 639. Estimates were taken at the midpoint of the age classification. For the ten-year classifications, estimates were taken at the beginning of the decade. Income was taken at age 70 for those over 65 and, through a minor clerical error, at age 3, rather than 2, for those under 5 years of age. The latter error was so small that recomputation of results was not justified.

TABLE 2

Total and Per Capita Value of Human Capital by Race, Sex, Area and Migration Status

Race and Sex	Central City		Ring to City		Ring		City to Ring	
	Total (millions)	Per Capita	Total (millions)	Per Capita	Total (millions)	Per Capita	Total (millions)	Per Capita
White Male	$36,544	$62,916	$1,491	$71,334	$67,713	$67,513	$10,779	$71,742
White Female	8,543	14,115	362	15,519	15,245	15,200	2,404	15,785
Nonwhite Male	9,792	38,242	256	42,276	1,633	41,330	195	42,161
Nonwhite Female	2,554	10,140	64	10,738	413	10,126	46	10,522

Sources: Values were calculated from data given in Table 1 using a 5 percent rate of discount and from data in the U.S. Bureau of the Census, *U.S. Census of Population: 1960, Subject Reports, Mobility for Metropolitan Areas, Final Report PC(2)–2c* (Washington, D.C.: U.S. Government Printing Office, 1963), p. 100. The population by area and migration status were not reported for those under 5 years of age. This category was estimated by assuming that ratio of those under 5 to those 5 to 9 for each sex and race were the same by area and migration status as they were for the total SMSA.

more than offsets the movement of nonwhites to the suburbs, and this results in a net gain in human capital for the city. Of course, movements of nonwhites and other low income groups into the city from other regions contributes to the problems of the city, but it is clear that migration to the suburbs is a substantial factor in reducing the city's ability to provide needed services. For example, the white males that have migrated to the suburbs represent approximately thirty percent of the human capital of white males presently residing in the city. A return of this amount of capital would surely contribute greatly to reducing the financial problems of the city.

DIRECT TAX LOSSES

Migration of human capital, as suggested earlier, generally erodes the city's tax base. From the estimates given in Table 2, it is possible to estimate the income tax loss to the city of Detroit due to migration. Under the Michigan uniform city tax law, residents of the city are taxed on total income at a rate of one percent and nonresidents are taxed at a rate of one-half of one percent on income obtained in the city.[5] While the Michigan uniform city income tax law did not become effective until 1965, we will use the value of human capital in 1960 as the best estimate of the value of a migrants' future income stream in 1965. If the city could induce individuals who formerly lived in the city, but now reside in the suburbs to return, it would gain either one percent or one-half of one percent of these individuals' taxable income. If the individual presently worked in the city, there would be a gain of one-half of one percent of the individuals' taxable income. However, if the individual worked in a tax free suburb, the city would gain one percent of the individual's taxable income should he return to the city. If he worked in a suburb that taxed income, he would get a one-half of one percent tax credit upon returning to the city, and the city would only gain one-half of one percent of the man's taxable income. Information concerning those that had moved to the suburbs of the city was not detailed enough to determine the relative gain in taxes from the return of individuals in different suburban areas and with different places of work. Hence, it was assumed that the city was losing one-half of one percent of taxable income for each person that had migrated from the city.

Taxable income was determined by taking 70 percent of an in-

[5] *City Income Taxes*, (New York: Tax Foundation, Inc., 1967), p. 23.

Miscellaneous

dividual's actual expected income. This adjustment was based on an estimate in 1962 that the $600 exemption in Detroit for taxpayers and dependents reduced revenue collected by 30 percent.[6] The reliability of this estimate is supported by the fact that in 1962 exemptions amounted to a 28 percent reduction in the Federal income tax base. Given this adjustment, assuming a gain of one-half of one percent of taxable income, and ignoring the probability of a migrant returning, the present value of lifetime tax losses in 1965 due to previous migration from the city are given in Table 3. Table 3 also shows the gain in tax receipts attributable to individuals moving from the ring of the city into the city. Here again, it was assumed that the city gained one-half of one percent of taxable income.

TABLE 3

Present Value of
Future City Income Tax Loss
From Migration to Suburbia

Race and Sex	Central City to Ring (1) (000)	Ring to Central City (2) (000)	Net Loss or Gain (1) − (2) (000)
White Male	$377,261	$52,196	$325,065
White Female	84,123	12,682	71,441
Nonwhite Male	6,819	8,952	−2,133
Nonwhite Female	1,611	2,271	−660
		(Net Total Loss)	$393,713

Sources: Estimated from data given in Table 2.

The net lifetime tax losses, after taking account of the gain from in-migrants, are approximately $394 million. The meaning of this sizable loss of tax income is more evident when one considers that general expenditures, including education, of the city of Detroit were $388 million in 1962.[7] Therefore, the loss to the city of Detroit from all previous migration to the suburbs had a value in 1965 that approximated the total value of public services that the city provides

[6]Leonard D. Bronder, "Michigan's First Local Income Tax," National Tax Journal, (December, 1962), p. 424.

[7]U.S. Bureau of the Census, Census of Governments: 1962; Finances of Municipalities and Township Governments, Vol. IV, No. 3 (Washington D.C.: U.S. Government Printing Office, 1964), p. 205 and U.S. Bureau of the Census, Census of Governments: 1962, Finances of School Districts, Vol. IV, No. 1 (Washington, D.C.: U.S. Government Printing Office, 1964), pp. 42.

in one year. Of course, it could be maintained that the tax loss to the city is equal to the value of the public services that the city would have to provide for those that migrate to the suburbs. Without a detailed statistical study this question cannot be settled unequivocally. There are, however, several reasons for believing that this is not the case. First, the high income groups that are migrating to the suburbs surely supported public services that were primarily for others. Second, many public services are such that consumption by one individual does not reduce the amount available for others. Third, suburban residents continue to consume most of the services of the city when returning to the city for work or for recreational activities. Therefore, considering the tax loss as a pure loss to the city is reasonably accurate.[8] In any case, the magnitude of the tax loss is an index of the size of the problem, if not a complete estimate of the loss in a social accounting sense.

CONCLUSIONS

Clearly, migration to the suburbs of the nations' cities reduces the human capital so vital to the renewal of the cities. While city income taxation is not the major source of income for the cities, it is growing in importance, and, as of 1967, some 171 cities had such a tax. In the majority of these cities, nonresidents paid lower taxes than residents. Even though loss of income taxes is not the whole loss to the city, it is an index of what is happening to the city's tax base due to migration.

The other major feature of the analysis is that it suggests a situation of cumulative deterioration in the nation's cities, and not some type of equilibrium situation. That is, there is no mechanism which will stop the migration to the suburbs or induce people to return to the city. If the process is left to run its course, cities will become geographical areas devoid of the amenities of life. While certain factors, such as increased traffic, may tend to encourage people to return to the city, it is felt that these forces take too long to meaningfully change the predictions based on the model of cumulative deterioration.

[8] Actually, due to the federal income tax credit that the migrants lose when they move to the suburbs and due to the federal expenditures in the city, the loss to the city is somewhat less than stated in this paper. However, the overstatement of loss is quite small.

Miscellaneous

TABLE 4*
Present Value of Future City Income Tax Loss from Migration to Suburbia

Race and Sex	Central City to Ring (1) (000)	Ring to Central City (2) (000)	Net Loss or Gain (1) − (2) (000)
White Male	$37,726	$5,220	$32,506
White Female	8,412	1,268	7,144
Nonwhite Male	682	895	−213
Nonwhite Female	161	227	−66
		(Net Total Loss)	$39,371

*Corrected values for Table III of A. G. Holtmann, "Migration to the Suburbs, Human Capital, and City Income Tax Losses: A Case Study," *The National Tax Journal,* (September, 1968), p. 331. The text should be interpreted according to the corrected values.

Sources: Estimated from data given in Table 2.

Table 4 contains corrected values of the income tax loss estimated. Net lifetime tax losses, after taking account of the gain from in-migrants, are approximately $39.4 million, rather than $394 million as reported in the original article. While this loss of tax income is not as large as suggested earlier, it is greater than any general expenditure item for Detroit in 1962. In that year, the largest expense was $33.0 million for police protection.[9] Surely a loss of this magnitude is a major detriment to municipal finance.

In general, then, the revised estimates still support the conclusions of the original paper: that the income tax loss from migration to the suburbs has important implications for municipal finance, and that this is one index of the possible cummulative deterioration of cities.[10]

[9]U.S. Bureau of the Census, *Census of Governments: 1962; Finances of Municipalities and Township Governments,* Vol. IV, No. 3 (Washington, D.C.: U.S. Government Printing Office, 1964), p. 205. This excludes educational expenditures made by the metropolitan school district. These were well in excess of the tax loss.

[10]I would like to thank Professor William Neenan of the University of Michigan for bringing this error to my attention.

Subject Index

Index

Name Index

Index